STUDENT SOLUTIONS MANUAL

Calculus and Its Applications
Brief Calculus and Its Applications

STUDENT SOLUTIONS MANUAL

Christopher J. Pladdy
Nicholls State University

Calculus and Its Applications, *Second Edition*
Brief Calculus and Its Applications, *Second Edition*

Daniel D. Benice
Montgomery College

HOUGHTON MIFFLIN COMPANY   BOSTON   NEW YORK

Senior Sponsoring Editor: Maureen O'Connor
Associate Editor: Dawn Nuttall
Editorial Assistant: Jennifer Mattson
Senior Manufacturing Coordinator: Priscilla J. Bailey
Marketing Manager: Charles Cavaliere

Printed in the U.S.A.

ISBN: 0-395-83451-1

2 3 4 5 6 7 8 9 - VG - 01 00 99 98 97

CONTENTS

CORRELATION CHART

Brief Calculus and Its Applications	Calculus and Its Applications
Chapter 1	Chapter 1
Chapter 2	Chapter 2
Chapter 3	Chapter 3
Chapter 4	Chapter 4
Chapter 5	Chapter 5
Chapter 6	Chapter 6
Chapter 7	
Sections 7.1–7.5	Sections 7.1–7.5

Section 7.6
  Exercises 1–30
  Exercises 31–39
  Exercise 40
  Exercises 41–42
  Exercises 43–48
  Exercises 49–60
  Exercise 61
  Exercise 62
  Exercise 63
  Exercise 64
  Exercises 65–66
  Technology Exercises
	Sections 9.1 and 9.2
	  Exercises 1–30 (**9.1**)
	  Exercises 1–9 (**9.2**)
	  Exercise 15 (**9.2**)
	  Exercises 11–12 (**9.2**)
	  Exercises 31–36 (**9.1**)
	  Exercises 31–42 (**9.2**)
	  Exercise 39 (**9.1**)
	  Exercise 48 (**9.2**)
	  Exercise 41 (**9.1**)
	  Exercise 50 (**9.2**)
	  Exercises 37–38 (**9.1**)
	  Technology Exercises (**9.1**)

Section 7.7	Section 8.1

Review Exercises
  Exercises 1–48
  Exercises 49–54
  Exercise 55
  Exercise 56
  Exercise 57
  Exercise 58
  Exercise 59
  Exercise 60
  Exercise 61
  Exercise 62
	Review Exercises for Ch. 7, 8, 9
	  Exercises 1–48 (**Ch. 7**)
	  Exercises 3–8 (**Ch. 9**)
	  Exercise 15 (**Ch. 9**)
	  Exercise 17 (**Ch. 9**)
	  Exercise 3 (**Ch. 8**)
	  Exercise 2 (**Ch. 8**)
	  Exercise 5 (**Ch. 8**)
	  Exercise 7 (**Ch. 8**)
	  Exercise 29 (**Ch. 8**)
	  Exercise 30 (**Ch. 8**)

Chapter 8	Chapter 10
Chapter 9	Chapter 11

STUDENT SOLUTIONS MANUAL

Calculus and Its Applications
Brief Calculus and Its Applications

SECTION 1.1 pages 10–12

1. $[5, 9]$

3. $[6, \infty)$

5. $(-\infty, 0)$

7. $(-2, \infty)$

9. $(-\infty, \pi)$

11. $x \geq 0$

13. $1 \leq x \leq 75$

15. $x < -2$

17. $x > -5$

19. $\pi \leq x < 7$

21.   Given $5x - 1 \leq 29$

Then $(5x - 1) + 1 \leq 29 + 1$
$$5x \leq 30$$
$$\frac{1}{5}(5x) \leq \frac{1}{5}(30)$$
$$x \leq 6$$

23.   Given $3x \geq 0$

Then $\frac{1}{3}(3x) \geq \frac{1}{3}(0)$
$$x \geq 0$$

25.   Given $1 - 8x \leq 0$

Then $-1 + (1 - 8x) \leq 0 - 1$
$$-8x \leq -1$$
$$\left(-\frac{1}{8}\right)(-8x) \geq \left(-\frac{1}{8}\right)(-1)$$
$$x \geq \frac{1}{8}$$

27.   Given $5(y + 1) < 13$

Then $\frac{1}{5}[5(y + 1)] < \frac{1}{5}(13)$
$$y + 1 < \frac{13}{5}$$
$$(y + 1) - 1 < \frac{13}{5} - 1$$
$$y < \frac{8}{5}$$

29.   The notation $(3, \infty]$ would refer to a half-open interval containing the endpoint ∞. However, ∞ is not a number and so cannot be included.

31. $x^{12} \cdot x^5 = x^{12+5} = x^{17}$

33. $(b^7)^3 = b^{7 \cdot 3} = b^{21}$

35. $\dfrac{x^{14}}{x^8} = x^{14} \cdot x^{-8} = x^{14-8} = x^6$

37. $2 \cdot x^0 = 2 \cdot 1 = 2$ (recall that $a^0 = 1$)

39. $x^{-3} = \dfrac{1}{x^3}$

41. $\dfrac{7}{x^{-2}} = 7x^2$

43. $3^{-2} = \dfrac{1}{3^2} = \dfrac{1}{9}$

45. $49^{1/2} = \sqrt{49} = 7$

47. $27^{1/3} = \sqrt[3]{27} = 3$

49. $16^{-1/2} = \dfrac{1}{16^{1/2}} = \dfrac{1}{\sqrt{16}} = \dfrac{1}{4}$

51. $4^{3/2} = (4^{1/2})^3 = (\sqrt{4})^3 = 2^3 = 8$

53. $27^{2/3} = (27^{1/3})^2 = (\sqrt[3]{27})^2 = 3^2 = 9$

55. $9^{-3/2} = \dfrac{1}{9^{3/2}} = \dfrac{1}{(9^{1/2})^3} = \dfrac{1}{(\sqrt{9})^3} = \dfrac{1}{3^3} = \dfrac{1}{27}$

57. $2^{3.5} = 11.3137$

59. $15^{2.6} = 1142.4502$

61. $4.3^{0.04} = 1.0601$

63. $\dfrac{4}{\sqrt{3}} = \dfrac{4(\sqrt{3})}{\sqrt{3}(\sqrt{3})} = \dfrac{4\sqrt{3}}{3}$

65. $\dfrac{2}{\sqrt{5}} = \dfrac{2(\sqrt{5})}{\sqrt{5}(\sqrt{5})} = \dfrac{2\sqrt{5}}{5}$

67. $\dfrac{6}{\sqrt{3}} = \dfrac{6(\sqrt{3})}{\sqrt{3}(\sqrt{3})} = \dfrac{6\sqrt{3}}{3} = 2\sqrt{3}$

69. Given $x^2 - 64 = 0$

Then $(x - 8)(x + 8) = 0$

$x - 8 = 0 \quad x + 8 = 0$
$x = 8 \qquad x = -8$

71. Given $x^2 - 9x = 0$

Then $x(x - 9) = 0$

$x = 0 \quad x - 9 = 0$
$\qquad\quad x = 9$

73. Given $y^2 + 9y + 14 = 0$

Then $y^2 + 9y + 14 = (y + 7)(y + 2) = 0$

$y + 7 = 0 \qquad y + 2 = 0$
$y = -7 \qquad\quad y = -2$

75. Given $x^2 - 2x - 8 = 0$

Then $x^2 - 2x - 8 = (x - 4)(x + 2) = 0$

$x - 4 = 0 \quad x + 2 = 0$
$x = 4 \qquad x = -2$

77. Given $2t^2 - 6t - 20 = 0$

Then $2t^2 - 6t - 20 = (2t - 10)(t + 2) = 0$

$2t - 10 = 0 \qquad t + 2 = 0$
$2t = 10 \qquad\quad t = -2$
$t = 5$

79. Given $3x^2 - 10x - 8 = 0$

Then $3x^2 - 10x - 8 = (3x + 2)(x - 4) = 0$

$3x + 2 = 0 \qquad\quad x - 4 = 0$
$3x = -2 \qquad\qquad x = 4$
$x = -2/3$

81. Given $2x^2 + x = 6$

Then $2x^2 + x - 6 = 0$
and $2x^2 + x - 6 = (2x - 3)(x + 2) = 0$

$2x - 3 = 0 \qquad x + 2 = 0$
$2x = 3 \qquad\quad x = -2$
$x = 3/2$

83. Given $x^2 + 3x + 1 = 0$

Then $x = \dfrac{-3 \pm \sqrt{3^2 - 4(1)(1)}}{2(1)} = \dfrac{-3 \pm \sqrt{9 - 4}}{2}$

$\qquad = \dfrac{-3 \pm \sqrt{5}}{2}$

85. Given $t^2 - 2t - 4 = 0$

Then $t = \dfrac{-(-2) \pm \sqrt{(-2)^2 - 4(1)(-4)}}{2(1)} = \dfrac{2 \pm \sqrt{4 + 16}}{2} = \dfrac{2 \pm \sqrt{20}}{2} = \dfrac{2 \pm 2\sqrt{5}}{2}$

$\qquad = 1 \pm \sqrt{5}$

87. Given $x^2 - 4x - 2 = 0$

Then $x = -\dfrac{(-4) \pm \sqrt{(-4)^2 - 4(1)(-2)}}{2(1)} = \dfrac{4 \pm \sqrt{16 + 8}}{2} = \dfrac{4 \pm \sqrt{24}}{2} = \dfrac{4 \pm 2\sqrt{6}}{2}$

$\qquad = 2 \pm \sqrt{6}$

89. Given $4y^2 + 10y - 5 = 0$

Then $y = \dfrac{-10 \pm \sqrt{10^2 - 4(4)(-5)}}{2(4)} = \dfrac{-10 \pm \sqrt{100 + 80}}{8} = \dfrac{-10 \pm \sqrt{180}}{8} = \dfrac{-10 \pm 6\sqrt{5}}{8} = \dfrac{2(-5 \pm 3\sqrt{5})}{8}$

$\qquad = \dfrac{-5 \pm 3\sqrt{5}}{4}$

91. Given $2x^2 + 6x = 3$

Then $2x^2 + 6x - 3 = 0$

and $x = \dfrac{-6 \pm \sqrt{6^2 - 4(2)(-3)}}{2(2)} = \dfrac{-6 \pm \sqrt{36 + 24}}{4} = \dfrac{-6 \pm \sqrt{60}}{4} = \dfrac{-6 \pm 2\sqrt{15}}{4} = \dfrac{2(-3 \pm \sqrt{15})}{4}$

$\qquad = \dfrac{-3 \pm \sqrt{15}}{2}$

93. $\dfrac{x^2 - 9}{x + 3} = \dfrac{(x - 3)(x + 3)}{x + 3} = x - 3 \qquad x \neq -3$

95. $\dfrac{x^2 - 4x}{x^2 - 16} = \dfrac{x(x - 4)}{(x + 4)(x - 4)} = \dfrac{x}{x + 4} \qquad x \neq 4$

97. $\dfrac{2x - 10}{3x - 15} = \dfrac{2(x - 5)}{3(x - 5)} = 2/3 \qquad x \neq 5$

99. $\dfrac{x}{x^2 + 5x} = \dfrac{x}{x(x + 5)} = \dfrac{1}{x + 5} \qquad x \neq 0$

101. $\dfrac{2}{x} + \dfrac{5}{3x} = \dfrac{3 \cdot 2}{3x} + \dfrac{5}{3x} = \dfrac{6 + 5}{3x} = \dfrac{11}{3x}$

103. $\dfrac{7}{x - 1} + \dfrac{1}{x} = \dfrac{7x}{x(x - 1)} + \dfrac{x - 1}{x(x - 1)} = \dfrac{7x + x - 1}{x(x - 1)} = \dfrac{8x - 1}{x(x - 1)}$

105. $\dfrac{3}{2x} - \dfrac{5}{x + 2} = \dfrac{3(x + 2)}{2x(x + 2)} - \dfrac{5(2x)}{2x(x + 2)} = \dfrac{3x + 6 - 10x}{2x(x + 2)} = \dfrac{6 - 7x}{2x(x + 2)}$

107. $\dfrac{x + 1}{2x + 2} \cdot \dfrac{2x}{x - 1} = \dfrac{x + 1}{2(x + 1)} \cdot \dfrac{2x}{x - 1} = \dfrac{x}{x - 1} \qquad x \neq -1$

109. $\dfrac{x}{x - 4} \div \dfrac{2}{5x - 20} = \dfrac{x}{x - 4} \cdot \dfrac{5(x - 4)}{2} = \dfrac{5x}{2} \qquad x \neq 4$

111. $\dfrac{3x - 12}{3x} \cdot \dfrac{5x}{x^2 - 16} = \dfrac{3(x - 4)(5x)}{3x(x - 4)(x + 4)} = \dfrac{5}{x + 4} \qquad x \neq 0, \; -4$

113. $\dfrac{x^2 + x}{2} \div \dfrac{x^2 - 1}{8x} = \dfrac{x(x + 1)}{2} \cdot \dfrac{\overset{4}{8x}}{(x - 1)(x + 1)} = \dfrac{4x^2}{x - 1} \qquad x \neq 1$

115. $\dfrac{\frac{x}{2} + x}{1 - \frac{x}{2}} = \dfrac{\frac{x}{2} + \frac{2x}{2}}{\frac{2}{2} - \frac{x}{2}} = \dfrac{\frac{3x}{2}}{\frac{2 - x}{2}} = \dfrac{3x}{2} \cdot \dfrac{2}{2 - x} = \dfrac{3x}{2 - x}$

117. $\dfrac{\frac{3}{x} + h}{x + \frac{1}{h}} = \dfrac{\frac{3}{x} + \frac{hx}{x}}{\frac{hx}{h} + \frac{1}{h}} = \dfrac{\frac{3 + hx}{x}}{\frac{1 + hx}{h}} = \dfrac{3 + hx}{x} \cdot \dfrac{h}{1 + hx} = \dfrac{h(3 + hx)}{x(1 + hx)}$

119. Given $\frac{x + 1}{3} + \frac{x}{2} = 7$

Then multiply both sides by 6:

$$2(x + 1) + 3x = 42$$
$$2x + 2 + 3x = 42$$
$$5x + 2 = 42$$
$$5x = 40$$
$$x = 8$$

121. Given $2 - \frac{1}{x} = \frac{x + 2}{x}$

Then multiply both sides by x, *but* check the solution, since $x \neq 0$.

$$2x - 1 = x + 2$$
$$2x - x = 2 + 1$$
$$x = 3 \qquad \text{Solution o.k., } x \neq 0.$$

123. a. If $a = 0$ in the expression $ax^2 + bx + c = 0$, then the form reduces to $bx + c = 0$, which is a linear form and is no longer a quadratic.

b. The quadratic formula $x = \dfrac{-b \pm \sqrt{b^2 - 4ac}}{2a}$ is not defined for $a = 0$, since division by zero would occur.

SECTION 1.2 pages 16–18

1. If $f(x) = 5x + 7$, then

$$f(0) = 5(0) + 7 = 7$$
$$f(1) = 5(1) + 7 = 12$$
$$f(2) = 5(2) + 7 = 17$$
$$f(-1) = 5(-1) + 7 = 2$$

3. If $f(x) = x^2 + 3x + 1$, then

$$f(0) = 0^2 + 3(0) + 1 = 1$$
$$f(1) = 1^2 + 3(1) + 1 = 5$$
$$f(2) = 2^2 + 3(2) + 1 = 11$$
$$f(-1) = (-1)^2 + 3(-1) + 1 = -1$$

5. If $f(x) = -x^2 + 5$, then

$$f(0) = -0^2 + 5 = 5$$
$$f(1) = -(1)^2 + 5 = 4$$
$$f(2) = -(2)^2 + 5 = 1$$
$$f(-1) = -(-1)^2 + 5 = 4$$

7. If $f(x) = 6$, then

$$f(0) = 6$$
$$f(1) = 6$$
$$f(2) = 6$$
$$f(-1) = 6$$

9. If $f(x) = \sqrt{x + 1}$, then

$$f(0) = \sqrt{0 + 1} = 1$$
$$f(1) = \sqrt{1 + 1} = \sqrt{2}$$
$$f(2) = \sqrt{2 + 1} = \sqrt{3}$$
$$f(-1) = \sqrt{-1 + 1} = 0$$

11. If $f(x) = x^2 - 3x + 7$, then

$$f(x + 2) = (x + 2)^2 - 3(x + 2) + 7 = x^2 + 4x + 4 - 3x - 6 + 7$$
$$= x^2 + x + 5$$

$$f(x - 3) = (x - 3)^2 - 3(x - 3) + 7 = x^2 - 6x + 9 - 3x + 9 + 7$$
$$= x^2 - 9x + 25$$

13. If $f(x) = 4x^2 + 9x$, then

$$f(x + 2) = 4(x + 2)^2 + 9(x + 2) = 4(x^2 + 4x + 4) + 9x + 18$$
$$= 4x^2 + 16x + 16 + 9x + 18$$
$$= 4x^2 + 25x + 34$$

$$f(x - 3) = 4(x - 3)^2 + 9(x - 3) = 4(x^2 - 6x + 9) + 9x - 27$$
$$= 4x^2 - 24x + 36 + 9x - 27$$
$$= 4x^2 - 15x + 9$$

15. If $f(x) = \frac{x + 5}{x - 7}$, then

$$f(x + 2) = \frac{(x + 2) + 5}{(x + 2) - 7} = \frac{x + 7}{x - 5}$$
$$f(x - 3) = \frac{(x - 3) + 5}{(x - 3) - 7} = \frac{x + 2}{x - 10}$$

17. If $f(x) = 3x - 4$, then

$$f(x + h) = 3(x + h) - 4 = 3x + 3h - 4$$

$$f(x + h) - f(x) = 3x + 3h - 4 - (3x - 4)$$
$$= 3\!\!\!/x + 3h - 4\!\!\!/ - 3\!\!\!/x + 4\!\!\!/$$
$$= 3h$$

19. If $f(x) = -9x + 2$, then

$$f(x + h) = -9(x + h) + 2 = -9x - 9h + 2$$

$$f(x + h) - f(x) = -9x - 9h + 2 - (-9x + 2)$$
$$= -9\!\!\!/x - 9h + 2\!\!\!/ + 9\!\!\!/x - 2\!\!\!/$$
$$= -9h$$

21. If $f(x) = 1.75x - 4.1x^3$, then

$$f(0.4) = 1.75(0.4) - 4.1(0.4)^3 = 0.4376$$
$$f(0.25) = 1.75(0.25) - 4.1(0.25)^3 \cong 0.3734$$
$$f(-1.8) = 1.75(-1.8) - 4.1(-1.8)^3 = 20.7612$$

23. If $c(x) = 32x$, then

$$c(8) = 32(8) = \$256$$

25. If $T(x) = -2x^2 + 64x + 65$, then
   a. $T(10) = -2(10)^2 + 64(10) + 65$
   $$= -200 + 640 + 65$$
   $$= 505°\text{F}$$
   b. $T(0) = -2(0)^2 + 64(0) + 65$
   $$= 65°\text{F}$$

27. If $P(x) = 0.01x^2 + 60x - 500$, then

$$P(1000) = 0.01(1000)^2 + 60(1000) - 500$$
$$= 10{,}000 + 60{,}000 - 500$$
$$= \$69{,}500$$

29. If $n(t) = 1000 + 20t + t^2$, then
   a. $n(1) = 1000 + 20(1) + 1^2$
   $$= 1021$$
   b. $n(10) = 1000 + 20(10) + 10^2$
   $$= 1300$$

31. Let $D(c) = \frac{c+1}{24} \cdot a$, then

   a. If $a = 400$ milligrams, $D(c) = \frac{(c+1)(400)}{24} = \frac{50}{3}(c+1)$

   b. $D(8) = \frac{50}{3}(8+1) = \frac{50 \cdot 9}{3} = 150$ milligrams

   c. $D(8) = 150$ milligrams is the dosage of medicine for an eight-year-old child if the adult dosage is 400 milligrams.

33. If $f(x) = x^2 + 5$, then the domain is all real numbers;

   Dom $f = (-\infty, \infty)$

35. If $f(x) = \sqrt{x - 2}$, then, since the square root is defined only for $x - 2 \geq 0$, the domain of f is $x \geq 2$. In interval notation, $[2, \infty)$.

37. If $f(x) = \frac{1}{x+3}$, then, since $x + 3 = 0$ would cause division by zero, the domain of f is $x \neq -3$.

39. If $g(x) = \frac{1}{x(x-1)}$, then, since $x(x - 1) = 0$ would cause division by zero, the domain of g is $x \neq 0, x \neq 1$.

41. If $f(x) = \sqrt{3x - 2}$, then, since the square root is defined only for $3x - 2 \geq 0$, the domain of f is $x \geq 2/3$ or $[2/3, \infty)$.

43. If $g(x) = (x + 1)^{1/2} = \sqrt{x + 1}$, then, since the square root is defined only for $x + 1 \geq 0$, the domain of g is $x \geq -1$ or $[-1, \infty)$.

45. If $g(x) = \frac{x}{x^2}$, then, since $x = 0$ would cause division by zero, the domain of g is $x \neq 0$.

47. If $f(x) = 2x + 6 = 0$, then

$$2x = -6$$
$$x = -3$$

49. If $f(x) = x^2 - 9 = 0$, then

$$(x - 3)(x + 3) = 0$$
$$x = 3, \quad x = -3$$

51. If $f(x) = x^2 - 9x + 20 = 0$, then

$$(x - 5)(x - 4) = 0$$
$$x = 5, \quad x = 4$$

53. If $f(x) = x^2 + 5x - 2 = 0$, then, using the quadratic formula,

$$x = \frac{-5 \pm \sqrt{5^2 - 4(1)(-2)}}{2(1)}$$
$$= \frac{-5 \pm \sqrt{25 + 8}}{2}$$
$$= \frac{-5 \pm \sqrt{33}}{2}$$

55. If $f(x) = 3x + 1$ and $g(x) = 7x$, then

$$
\begin{aligned}
(f \circ g)(x) &= f(g(x)) \\
&= f(7x) \\
&= 3(7x) + 1 \\
&= 21x + 1
\end{aligned}
$$

$$
\begin{aligned}
(g \circ f)(x) &= g(f(x)) \\
&= g(3x + 1) \\
&= 7(3x + 1) \\
&= 21x + 7
\end{aligned}
$$

57. If $f(x) = x^2 + 2x$ and $g(x) = x - 1$, then

$$
\begin{aligned}
(f \circ g)(x) &= f(g(x)) \\
&= f(x - 1) \\
&= (x - 1)^2 + 2(x - 1) \\
&= x^2 - 2x + 1 + 2x - 2 \\
&= x^2 - 1
\end{aligned}
$$

$$
\begin{aligned}
(g \circ f)(x) &= g(f(x)) \\
&= g(x^2 + 2x) \\
&= (x^2 + 2x) - 1 \\
&= x^2 + 2x - 1
\end{aligned}
$$

59. If $f(x) = \frac{1}{x}$ and $g(x) = 3x$, then

$$
\begin{aligned}
(f \circ g)(x) &= f(g(x)) \\
&= f(3x) \\
&= \frac{1}{3x}
\end{aligned}
$$

$$
\begin{aligned}
(g \circ f)(x) &= g(f(x)) \\
&= g\left(\frac{1}{x}\right) \\
&= 3\left(\frac{1}{x}\right) \\
&= \frac{3}{x}
\end{aligned}
$$

61. f and $f(x)$ do not mean the same thing. f is the *name* of the correspondence that assigns the values to the independent variable x. $f(x)$ is the value assigned to x; it is the y value when $y = f(x)$.

SECTION 1.3 pages 25–27

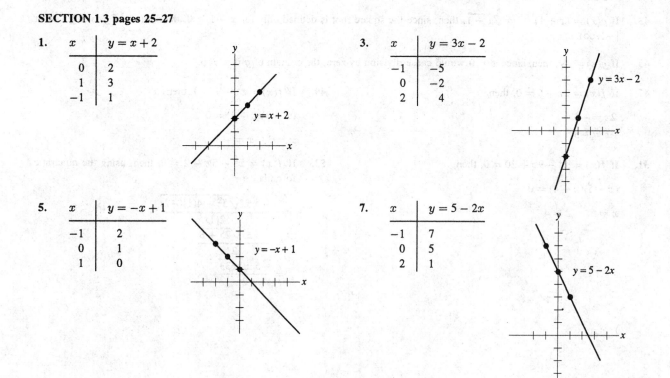

1.

x	$y = x + 2$
0	2
1	3
−1	1

3.

x	$y = 3x - 2$
−1	−5
0	−2
2	4

5.

x	$y = -x + 1$
−1	2
0	1
1	0

7.

x	$y = 5 - 2x$
−1	7
0	5
2	1

9. Given the points (2, 4) and (6, 16), then

$$m = \frac{16 - 4}{6 - 2} = \frac{12}{4} = 3$$

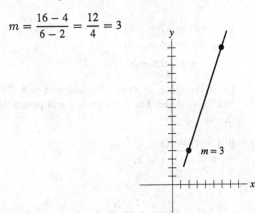

11. Given the points (1, 5) and (3, 1), then

$$m = \frac{1 - 5}{3 - 1} = \frac{-4}{2} = -2$$

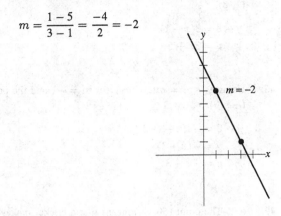

13. Given the points (4, 9) and (7, 9), then

$$m = \frac{9 - 9}{7 - 4} = \frac{0}{3} = 0$$

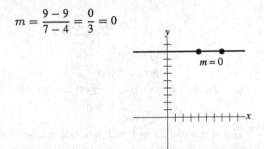

15. Given the points (−2, 1) and (3, 5), then

$$m = \frac{5 - 1}{3 - (-2)} = \frac{4}{5}$$

17. Two points that can be read from the graph are (0, 1) and (1, −1). This gives

$$m = \frac{-1 - 1}{1 - 0} = \frac{-2}{1} = -2$$

19. Given the points (2.71, 8.64) and (1.85, 10.32), then

$$m = \frac{10.32 - 8.64}{1.85 - 2.71} \cong -1.9535$$

21. If $y = 5x + 3$, then

Slope $m = 5$

y intercept (0, 3)

23. If $y = x - 9$, then

Slope $m = 1$

y intercept (0, −9)

25. If $y = 1 - 7x$, then

Slope $m = -7$

y intercept (0, 1)

27. If $y = 3$, then

Slope $m = 0$

y intercept (0, 3)

29. If $y - 8x = 6$ then $y = 8x + 6$ and

Slope $m = 8$

y intercept (0, 6)

31. Using $y = mx + b$, for $m = -2$ and $b = 4$,

$y = -2x + 4$

33. Using $y = mx + b$, for $m = 5$ and $b = -3$,

$y = 5x - 3$

35. Using $y = mx + b$ for $m = 0$ and $b = -1$,

$y = 0(x) - 1 = -1$

37. Using $y = mx + b$, for $m = \frac{2}{3}$ and $b = \frac{1}{2}$,

$y = \frac{2}{3}x + \frac{1}{2}$

39. Using $y = mx + b$, for $m = 1.8$ and $b = 2.4$,

$y = 1.8x + 2.4$

41. Using $y - y_1 = m(x - x_1)$, for $m = 3$ and the point $(1, 8)$,

$$y - 8 = 3(x - 1)$$
$$y = 3x + 5$$

43. Using $y - y_1 = m(x - x_1)$, for $m = -2$ and the point $(5, -3)$,

$$y - (-3) = -2(x - 5)$$
$$y + 3 = -2(x - 5)$$
$$y = -2x + 7$$

45. Using $y - y_1 = m(x - x_1)$, for $m = -1$ and the point $(-3, 0)$,

$$y - 0 = -1[x - (-3)]$$
$$y = -(x + 3)$$
$$y = -x - 3$$

47. The given line $y = 3x + 5$ has slope $m = 3$. The line parallel to it also has slope $m = 3$ and passes through $(2, -4)$.

$$y - (-4) = 3(x - 2)$$
$$y + 4 = 3(x - 2)$$
$$y = 3x - 10$$

49. **a.** The point $(60, 80)$ means that a cricket makes 80 chirps per minute at 60 degrees Fahrenheit.

   b. $m = \dfrac{80 - 0}{60 - 40} = \dfrac{80}{20} = 4$

   $$y - 0 = 4(x - 40)$$
   $$y = 4x - 160$$

51. **a.** Let $y = C - \dfrac{C - S}{n}t$ where

   $$C = 3400$$
   $$S = 400$$
   $$n = 15$$

   Then $y = 3400 - \dfrac{(3400 - 400)}{15}t$

   $$= 3400 - 200t$$
   $$= -200t + 3400$$

   b. For $t = 8$, $\quad y = -200(8) + 3400$
   $$= \$1800$$

53. **a.** m represents the slope of the line, which in this example is the rate of appreciation per year; $m = 100$.

   y represents the appreciated value after x years.

   b. $y = 100x + 2000$

   c. After 7 years ($x = 7$),

   $$y = 100(7) + 2000$$
   $$= \$2700$$

   d. The appreciated value will be \$3200 when

   $$3200 = 100x + 2000$$
   $$100x = 1200$$
   $$x = 12 \text{ years}$$

55. The expression $2x + 1$ defines a real number for any choice of real number x, since multiplication and addition of any two real numbers results in a real number. Thus the domain of the function defined by $f(x) = 2x + 1$ is any real number.

57. The utility function u is more nearly linear. The changes from year 0 to year 1 and year 1 to year 2 for u are 0.7 and 0.8, respectively, compared with 1.65 and 1.15 for g. The changes are closer for u.

SECTION 1.4 pages 37–40

1. **a.** $y = 8$
   b. $f(0) = 6$
   c. $f(x) = 0$ when $x = -4$
   d. $f(11) = 2$
   e. $f(x) = 8$ when $x = 2$ and $x = 6$

3. **a.** $s(60) = 30$
   b. $s(10) = 5$
   c. $s(t) = 20$ when $t = 40$ minutes
   d. From the graph, $s(0) = 0 = m(0) + b$
   $$b = 0$$
   From the graph, $s(10) = 5 = m(10)$
   $$m = \tfrac{1}{2}$$
   e. Domain of s is $0 \le t \le 60$ or $[0, 60]$

5. **a.** $N(t) = S(t)$ when $t = 0$

      b. $N(t) > S(t)$ for $t > 0$.

      c. At every point in time in the 2-week period after memorization, more nonsense words were forgotten than words of a song.

7. **a.** The northeastern U.S. city.

      b. Yes, because at $t = 15$, the graph of w lies above the graph of n.

      c. No, because at $t = 5$, the graph of n lies above the graph of w.

9. Yes, the graph of a function.

11. No, not the graph of a function.

13. Yes, the graph of a function.

15. Given $f(x) = x^2 - 4x + 5$, then

    y intercept $(0, 5)$

    vertex $(2, 1)$

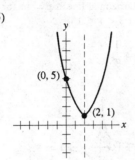

17. Given $f(x) = x^2 + 6x + 6$, then

    y intercept $(0, 6)$

    vertex $(-3, -3)$

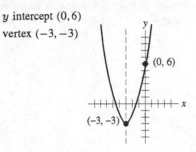

19. Given $y = -x^2 + 2x$, then

    y intercept $(0, 0)$

    vertex $(1, 1)$

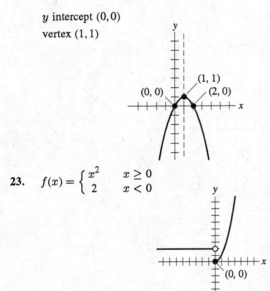

21. Given $y = 2x^2 - 8x + 5$, then

    y intercept $(0, 5)$

    vertex $(2, -3)$

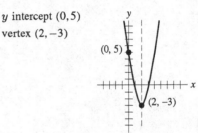

23. $f(x) = \begin{cases} x^2 & x \geq 0 \\ 2 & x < 0 \end{cases}$

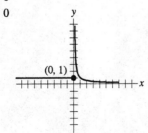

25. $f(x) = \begin{cases} \sqrt{x} & x \geq 0 \\ x & x < 0 \end{cases}$

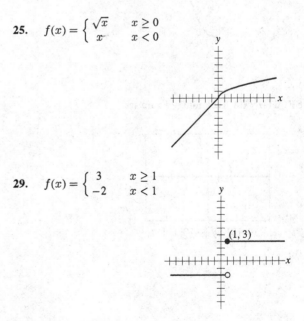

27. $f(x) \begin{cases} \frac{1}{x} & x > 0 \\ 1 & x \leq 0 \end{cases}$

29. $f(x) = \begin{cases} 3 & x \geq 1 \\ -2 & x < 1 \end{cases}$

31. Let x be the number of hours worked. Then $W(x) = \begin{cases} 5x & 0 \le x \le 40 \\ 200 + 7.5(x - 40) & x > 40 \end{cases}$

or, when simplified,

$$W(x) = \begin{cases} 5x & 0 \le x \le 40 \\ 7.5x - 100 & x > 40 \end{cases}$$

33. When x is chosen to be 2, then the y value associated with $x = 2$ must be 8.

35. $P(6) - P(0)$ represents the change in the insect population over a 6-month period starting now.

37. **a.** The graph would be a horizontal line for $0 \le t \le 15$.
  b. Assuming the student is originally taking m courses, the graph would be a horizontal line at $y = m$ for $0 \le t \le 4$ and a horizontal line at $y = m - 1$ for $4 < t \le 15$.
  c. Assuming the student is originally taking m courses, the graph is a horizontal line at $y = m$ for $0 \le t \le 1$, a horizontal line at $y = m + 1$ for $1 < t \le 3$, and a horizontal line at $y = m$ for $3 < t \le 15$.

39. $y = \sqrt{x} + 2$

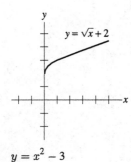

41. $y = -\dfrac{1}{x}$

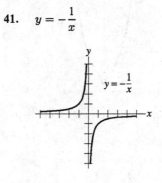

43. $y = x^2 - 3$

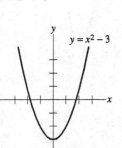

45. $y = -|x|$

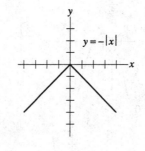

SECTION 1.4 Technology Exercises

1.

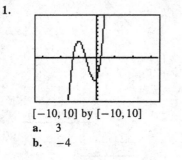

$[-10, 10]$ by $[-10, 10]$
  a. 3
  b. -4

3. **a.** None

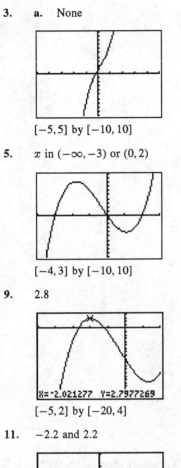

$[-5, 5]$ by $[-10, 10]$

b. -0.2

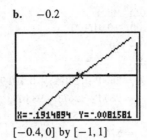

$[-0.4, 0]$ by $[-1, 1]$

5. x in $(-\infty, -3)$ or $(0, 2)$

$[-4, 3]$ by $[-10, 10]$

7. 5.5

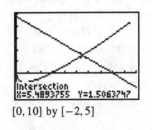

$[0, 10]$ by $[-2, 5]$

9. 2.8

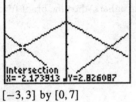

$[-5, 2]$ by $[-20, 4]$

11. -2.2 and 2.2

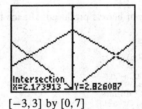

$[-3, 3]$ by $[0, 7]$

$[-3, 3]$ by $[0, 7]$

SECTION 1.5 pages 50–52

1. If $C(x) = 0.1x^2 + 5x + 210$, then
    a. $C(25) = 0.1(25)^2 + 5(25) + 210 = 62.5 + 125 + 210$
        $= 397.50$
    b. $C(25) - C(24) = 397.50 - [0.1(24)^2 + 5(24) + 210]$
               $= 397.50 - (57.6 + 120 + 210)$
               $= 397.50 - 387.6$
               $= 9.90$
    c. $C(0) = 0.1(0)^2 + 5(0) + 210$
        $= 210$

3. If $C(x) = 35x + 195$, then the condition states that

$$C(x) = 35x + 195 = 1000$$
$$35x = 805$$
$$x = 23$$

5. If $R(x) = 27x - 0.01x^2$, then
    a. $R(100) = 27(100) - 0.01(100)^2$
    $$= 2700 - 100$$
    $$= \$2600$$
    b. $R(100) - R(99) = 2600 - [27(99) - 0.01(99)^2]$
    $$= 2600 - (2673 - 98.01)$$
    $$= 2600 - 2574.99$$
    $$= \$25.01$$

7. If $R(x) = 280x$ and $C(x) = 0.1x^2 + 150x + 1000$, then the profit is
    a. $P(x) = R(x) - C(x)$
    $$= 280x - (0.1x^2 + 150x + 1000)$$
    $$= 280x - 0.1x^2 - 150x - 1000$$
    $$= -0.1x^2 + 130x - 1000 \text{ dollars}$$
    b. $P(50) = -0.1(50)^2 + 130(50) - 1000$
    $$= -250 + 6500 - 1000$$
    $$= \$5250$$

9. Let x be the number of tires produced and $29 + 0.02x$ the cost per tire; then
    a. $C(x) = x(29 + 0.02x)$
    $$= 0.02x^2 + 29x \text{ dollars}$$

    b. $R(x) = 54x$ dollars

    c. $P(x) = R(x) - C(x)$
    $$= 54x - (0.02x^2 + 29x)$$
    $$= 54x - 0.02x^2 - 29x$$
    $$= 25x - 0.02x^2 \text{ dollars}$$

11. Let x be the number of barrels produced. If each barrel cost \$6 and is sold for $15 - 0.02x$ dollars, then the profit function is

    $P(x) = R(x) - C(x)$
    $$= x(15 - 0.02x) - 6x$$
    $$= 15x - 0.02x^2 - 6x$$
    $$= 9x - 0.02x^2 \text{ dollars}$$

13. If $P(x) = 0.1x - 410$, then
    a. $P(5800) = 0.1(5800) - 410$
    $$= 580 - 410$$
    $$= \$170$$

    b. $P(2000) = 0.1(2000) - 410$
    $$= 200 - 410$$
    $$= -210 \text{ or a loss of } \$210$$

    c. Solve $P(x) = 0$.

    $0.1x - 410 = 0$
    $$0.1x = 410$$
    $$x = 4100$$

15. The profit from the sale of the 75th unit would be the difference between the revenue from and the cost for the sale of the 75th unit.

17. a. No. The cost is greater than the revenue at $x = x_1$.
    b. $P(x_4)$ because the distance between the revenue and cost curves is the greatest and the revenue curve is above the cost curve.
    c. $P(x_1)$ because the revenue curve is below the cost curve.

19. Solving $p = 90 - 0.02x = 52$ for x yields

$$-0.02x = -38$$
$$x = 1900$$

21. $R(x) = xp = x(50 - 0.1x)$
$$= 50x - 0.1x^2 \text{ dollars}$$

$$R(40) = 50(40) - 0.1(40)^2$$
$$= 2000 - 160$$
$$= 1840$$

23. Solving $p = 0.3x + 17 = 65$ for x yields

$$0.3x = 48$$
$$x = 160$$

25. **a.** $C(x) = xp = x(24 + 0.4x)$
$$= 24x + 0.4x^2$$

b. $C(20) = 24(20) + 0.4(20)^2$
$$= 480 + 160$$
$$= \$640$$

c. $C(10) - C(9) = [24(10) + 0.4(10)^2] - [24(9) + 0.4(9)^2]$
$$= (240 + 40) - (216 + 32.4)$$
$$= 280 - 248.4$$
$$= \$31.60$$

27. Given demand as $p = 20 - 0.3x$ and supply as $p = 0.1x + 8$, then

a. $20 - 0.3x = 0.1x + 8$
$$12 = 0.4x$$
$$x = 30 \text{ equilibrium quantity}$$

b. $p(20) = 20 - 0.3(30)$
$$= 20 - 9$$
$$= \$11 \text{ equilibrium price}$$

c. $(30, 11)$ equilibrium point

29. Given demand as $p = 100 - 0.1x$ and supply as $p = 52$, then

a. $100 - 0.1x = 52$
$$-0.1x = -48$$
$$x = 480 \text{ equilibrium quantity}$$

b. $p(480) = \$52$ equilibrium price

c. $(480, 52)$ equilibrium point

31. Given demand as $p = 47 - 0.2x$ and supply as $p = 1 + 0.03x$, then

a. $47 - 0.2x = 1 + 0.03x$
$$46 = 0.23x$$
$$x = 200 \text{ equilibrium quantity}$$

b. $p(200) = 47 - 0.2(200)$
$$= 7 \text{ equilibrium price}$$

c. $(200, 7)$ equilibrium point

33. Given $S(x) = 2x + 43$ and $D(x) = 160 - x$, then solving $S(x) = D(x)$ yields

$$2x + 43 = 160 - x$$
$$3x = 117$$
$$x = 39$$
$$D(39) = 160 - 39 = 121$$

equilibrium quantity is 39

equilibrium price is \$121

35. Given $S(x) = 5 + 0.3x$ and $D(x) = 29$, then solving $S(x) = D(x)$ yields

$$5 + 0.3x = 29$$
$$0.3x = 24$$
$$x = 80$$

$D(80) = 29$

equilibrium quantity is 80

equilibrium price is \$29

37. At the equilibrium quantity x, the condition $S(x) = D(x)$ must hold; hence, either equation can be used to determine the equilibrium price.

39. $C_3(x)$. $C_3(0)$ is greater than either $C_1(0)$ or $C_2(0)$.

SECTION 1.5 Technology Exercises

1.   17

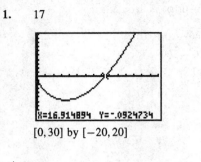

X=16.914894   Y=-.0924734

$[0, 30]$ by $[-20, 20]$

3.

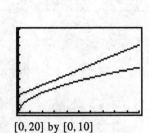

$[0, 20]$ by $[0, 10]$
There is no break-even point. Cost is always greater than revenue. Recommend that this product not be manufactured.

5. $(14, 42)$

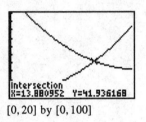

Intersection
X=13.880952   Y=41.936168

$[0, 20]$ by $[0, 100]$

REVIEW EXERCISES FOR CHAPTER 1 pages 53–55

1. $[1, 7)$

3.   Given $4(x - 2) \le 3$, then

$$x - 2 \le \frac{3}{4}$$
$$x \le 2 + \frac{3}{4}$$
$$x \le \frac{11}{4}$$

$(-\infty, \frac{11}{4}]$

5.   Given $2x^2 - x - 3 = 0$, then

$$2x^2 - x - 3 = (2x - 3)(x + 1) = 0$$
$$2x - 3 = 0 \qquad x + 1 = 0$$
$$2x = 3 \qquad\qquad x = -1$$
$$x = \frac{3}{2}$$

7.   Given $x^2 - 5x + 2 = 0$, then

$$x = \frac{5 \pm \sqrt{(-5)^2 - 4(2)(1)}}{2(1)} = \frac{5 \pm \sqrt{25 - 8}}{2}$$
$$= \frac{5 \pm \sqrt{17}}{2}$$

9.   If $f(x) = \frac{3x^2}{1+x}$, then

$$f(0) = \frac{3(0)^2}{1 + 0} = \frac{0}{1} = 0$$
$$f(2) = \frac{3(2)^2}{1 + 2} = \frac{12}{3} = 4$$
$$f(-2) = \frac{3(-2)^2}{1 - 2} = \frac{12}{-1} = -12$$

11.   If $f(x) = 2\sqrt{x - 3}$, then

$$f(4) = 2\sqrt{4 - 3} = 2\sqrt{1} = 2$$
$$f(7) = 2\sqrt{7 - 3} = 2\sqrt{4} = 2 \cdot 2 = 4$$
$$f(8) = 2\sqrt{8 - 3} = 2\sqrt{5}$$

13. If $f(x) = 3x^2$, then

$$f(x+1) = 3(x+1)^2 = 3(x^2 + 2x + 1)$$
$$= 3x^2 + 6x + 3$$

$$f(x+h) = 3(x+h)^2 = 3(x^2 + 2xh + h^2)$$
$$= 3x^2 + 6xh + 3h^2$$

15. If $f(x) = x^2$, then

$$f(x+h) - f(x) = (x+h)^2 - x^2$$
$$= x^2 + 2xh + h^2 - x^2$$
$$= 2xh + h^2$$

17. If $f(x) = \frac{x}{2x-1}$, then the function is not defined when $2x - 1 = 0$. Solving $2x - 1 = 0$ yields

$$2x = 1$$
$$x = \frac{1}{2}$$

Domain of f is $x \neq \frac{1}{2}$

19. If $g(x) = \sqrt{x+9}$, then the function is not defined for $x + 9 < 0$. Solving $x + 9 \geq 0$ yields

$$x \geq -9$$

Domain of f is $x \geq -9$ or $[-9, \infty)$

21. Solving $f(x) = 3x^2 - 27 = 0$ yields

$$3x^2 = 27$$
$$x^2 = 9$$

$$x = 3, -3$$

23. Given $f(x) = x^2 - 3$ and $g(x) = x + 1$, then

$$(f \circ g)(x) = f(g(x))$$
$$= f(x+1)$$
$$= (x+1)^2 - 3$$
$$= x^2 + 2x + 1 - 3$$
$$= x^2 + 2x - 2$$

25. Slope $m = \frac{5-2}{1-(-1)} = \frac{3}{2}$

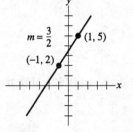

27. Given $y = 5x - 1$,

slope $m = 5$

y intercept $(0, -1)$

29. Given $m = 6$ and point $(2, -7)$, then

$$y - (-7) = 6(x - 2)$$
$$y + 7 = 6(x - 2)$$
$$y = 6x - 19$$

31. The two given points are $(0, 6)$ and $(2, 0)$.

$$m = \frac{0 - 6}{2 - 0} = -\frac{6}{2} = -3$$

$$y = -3x + 6$$

33. $f(x) = x^2 - 2x + 7$

y intercept $(0, 7)$

vertex $(1, 6)$

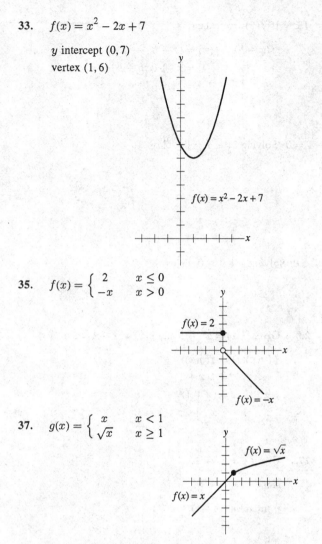

35. $f(x) = \begin{cases} 2 & x \le 0 \\ -x & x > 0 \end{cases}$

37. $g(x) = \begin{cases} x & x < 1 \\ \sqrt{x} & x \ge 1 \end{cases}$

39.   No. There are two values for y when $x = 3$.

41.   Let x be the number of miles driven. If the cost is 30¢ per mile ($0.3) and the cost of the rental is $26, then the cost function is

$y = 0.3x + 26$ dollars

43.   Let $n(t) = 300 + 12t + t^2$ be the number of bacteria present in a lab culture after t hours; then
   a.   At $t = 0$, $n(0) = 300$
   b.   For $t = 5$, $n(5) = 300 + 12(5) + 5^2$
$$= 385$$

After 5 hours, the culture has grown to 385 bacteria

45.   **a.** $R(x) = 300x$

       b. $P(x) = R(x) - C(x)$

$$= 300x - (0.1x^2 + 170x + 900)$$
$$= 300x - 0.1x^2 - 170x - 900$$
$$= -0.1x^2 + 130x - 900$$

       c. $P(5) = -0.1(5)^2 + 130(5) - 900$

$$= -2.5 + 650 - 900$$
$$= -252.50$$

Selling 5 stereo units results in a loss of $252.50.

       d. $C(10) = 0.1(10)^2 + 170(10) + 900$

$$= 10 + 1700 + 900$$
$$= 2610$$

       e. $C(10) - C(9) = 2610 - [0.1(9)^2 + 170(9) + 900]$

$$= 2610 - (8.1 + 1530 + 900)$$
$$= 2610 - 2438.1$$
$$= 171.90$$

47.   Let the demand be $p = 25 - 0.1x$ and the supply be $p = 1 + 0.02x$. Solving $25 - 0.1x = 1 + 0.02x$ yields

$$24 = 0.12x$$
$$x = 200$$

$$p(200) = 25 - 0.1(200)$$
$$= \$5$$

equilibrium point (200, 5)

49.   **a.**   At $t = 0$, $y = 30{,}000$. At $t = 2$, $y = 35{,}000$. Using the two points (0, 30000) and (2, 35000),

$$m = \frac{35000 - 30000}{2 - 0} = 2500$$

Using $y - y_1 = m(t - x_1)$,

$$y - 30000 = 2500(t - 0) \qquad \text{or} \qquad y = 2500t + 30000$$

       b.   Solving

$$47500 = 2500t + 30000$$
$$17500 = 2500t$$
$$t = \frac{17500}{2500} = 7 \text{ years}$$

51. As can be seen from the graphs, productivity growth during the period 1982–1995 is nearly linear.

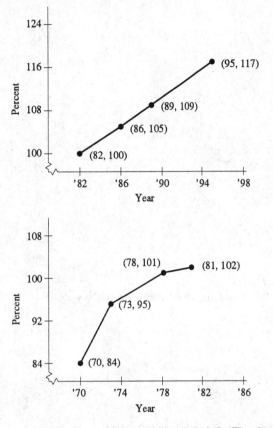

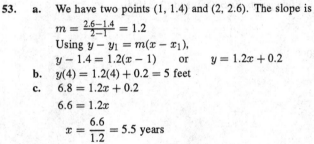

53. **a.** We have two points $(1, 1.4)$ and $(2, 2.6)$. The slope is
$m = \frac{2.6 - 1.4}{2 - 1} = 1.2$
Using $y - y_1 = m(x - x_1)$,
$y - 1.4 = 1.2(x - 1)$ or $y = 1.2x + 0.2$
b. $y(4) = 1.2(4) + 0.2 = 5$ feet
c. $6.8 = 1.2x + 0.2$
$6.6 = 1.2x$
$x = \frac{6.6}{1.2} = 5.5$ years

SECTION 2.1 pages 63–65

1. $\lim\limits_{x\to 0}(-6)=-6$

3. $\lim\limits_{x\to 4}5x=\lim\limits_{x\to 4}5\cdot\lim\limits_{x\to 4}x$
$=5\cdot 4$
$=20$

5. $\lim\limits_{x\to 5}(4x-1)=\lim\limits_{x\to 5}4\cdot\lim\limits_{x\to 5}x-\lim\limits_{x\to 5}1$
$=4\cdot 5-1$
$=19$

7. $\lim\limits_{t\to -3}t^2=\left(\lim\limits_{t\to -3}t\right)^2$
$=(-3)^2$
$=9$

9. $\lim\limits_{x\to 0}\dfrac{x+2}{9}=\dfrac{\lim\limits_{x\to 0}(x+2)}{\lim\limits_{x\to 0}9}$
$=\dfrac{\lim\limits_{x\to 0}x+\lim\limits_{x\to 0}2}{\lim\limits_{x\to 0}9}$
$=\dfrac{0+2}{9}$
$=\dfrac{2}{9}$

11. $\lim\limits_{x\to 8}\sqrt{x+1}=\sqrt{\lim\limits_{x\to 8}x+\lim\limits_{x\to 8}1}$
$=\sqrt{8+1}$
$=\sqrt{9}$
$=3$

13. $\lim\limits_{x\to -1}(x^3+x)=\left(\lim\limits_{x\to -1}x\right)^3+\lim\limits_{x\to -1}x$
$=(-1)^3+(-1)$
$=-1-1$
$=-2$

15. The values appear to approach 7.5 from both the left and the right, so
$\lim\limits_{x\to 4}f(x)=7.5$

17. $\lim\limits_{x\to 2}\dfrac{x^2-4}{x-2}$ cannot determine by substitution

x	$\dfrac{x^2-4}{x-2}$
1.9	3.9
1.99	3.99
2.1	4.1
2.01	4.01

$\lim\limits_{x\to 2}\dfrac{x^2-4}{x-2}=4$

19. $\lim\limits_{x\to 0}\dfrac{x}{3}=\dfrac{0}{3}=0$

21. $\lim\limits_{t\to 2}\dfrac{t^2-7t+10}{t-2}$ cannot determine by substitution

t	$\dfrac{t^2-7t+10}{t-2}$
1.9	-3.1
1.99	-3.01
2.1	-2.9
2.01	-2.99

$\lim\limits_{t\to 2}\dfrac{t^2-7t+10}{t-2}=-3$

23. $\lim\limits_{t\to 3}\dfrac{t^2-9}{t^2+9}=\dfrac{9-9}{9+9}$
$=\dfrac{0}{18}$
$=0$

25. **a.** $p(x)=50$ cents
b. $\lim\limits_{x\to 2000}p(x)=\lim\limits_{x\to 2000}50$
$=50$

27. $\lim\limits_{t\to 25}N=0$ will indicate that the species will be extinct after 25 years.

29. If $C(x) = 4x - 160$ is the number of chirps per minute, then

$$\lim_{x \to 40} C(x) = \lim_{x \to 40} (4x - 160) = 4(40) - 160$$
$$= 160 - 160$$
$$= 0$$

31. **a.** $\lim_{t \to 4} S(t) = A$

     b. $\lim_{t \to 7} S(t) = B$

SECTION 2.1 Technology Exercises

1. 2

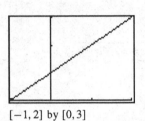

$[-1, 2]$ by $[0, 3]$

3. 0.4

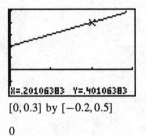

$[0, 0.3]$ by $[-0.2, 0.5]$

5. 2.7

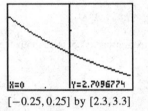

$[-0.25, 0.25]$ by $[2.3, 3.3]$

7. 0

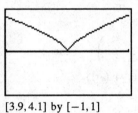

$[3.9, 4.1]$ by $[-1, 1]$

SECTION 2.2 pages 72–74

1. $\lim_{x \to 10} (3x - 2) = 3(10) - 2 = 28$

3. $\lim_{x \to -3} (1 - 9x + x^2) = 1 - 9(-3) + (-3)^2$
$$= 1 + 27 + 9$$
$$= 37$$

5. $\lim_{x \to 5} \dfrac{x - 3}{x + 2} = \dfrac{5 - 3}{5 + 2} = \dfrac{2}{7}$

7. $\lim_{x \to 2} \dfrac{1 - x}{x^2 + 1} = \dfrac{1 - 2}{2^2 + 1} = \dfrac{-1}{4 + 1} = -\dfrac{1}{5}$

9. $\lim_{x \to -4} \sqrt{x^2 + 9} = \sqrt{(-4)^2 + 9} = \sqrt{16 + 9} = \sqrt{25} = 5$

11. $\lim_{x \to 4} \dfrac{x^2 - x - 12}{x - 4} = \dfrac{4^2 - 4 - 12}{4 - 4} = \dfrac{0}{0}$

     $\lim_{x \to 4} \dfrac{(x - 4)(x + 3)}{x - 4} = 4 + 3 = 7$

13. $\lim_{x \to 0} \dfrac{x^2}{x} = \dfrac{0}{0}$

     $\lim_{x \to 0} \dfrac{x \cdot x}{x} = 0$

15. $\lim_{x \to 2} \dfrac{x - 2}{x + 3} = \dfrac{2 - 2}{2 + 3} = \dfrac{0}{5} = 0$

17. $\lim_{x \to 1} \dfrac{3x - 3}{x^2 - 1} = \dfrac{3(1) - 3}{1^2 - 1} = \dfrac{0}{0}$

     $\lim_{x \to 1} \dfrac{3(x - 1)}{(x - 1)(x + 1)} = \dfrac{3}{1 + 1} = \dfrac{3}{2}$

19. $f(x) = \dfrac{x^2 - x - 12}{x - 4} = x + 3 \qquad x \neq 4$

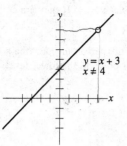

$y = x + 3$
$x \neq 4$

21. $f(x) = \dfrac{3x}{x} = 3 \qquad x \neq 0$

$y = 3$
$x \neq 0$

23. If $f(x) = \sqrt{x - 4}$, then

$f(3) = \sqrt{3 - 4} = \sqrt{-1}$ does not exist, since the square root of a negative number is not defined to be a real number.

25. If $f(x) = \dfrac{x - 1}{x + 1}$, then

$f(-1) = \dfrac{-1 - 1}{-1 + 1} = \dfrac{-2}{0}$ does not exist, since division by zero is not defined.

27. Discontinuous at $x = 3$

29. Discontinuous at $x = 4$

31. **a.** Discontinuities occur at 1/95 and 1/96.
  b. The discontinuities occur at the beginning of each year because, as new cases are assigned on January 1, the number of workload hours jumps by a discrete amount.

33. Discontinuities at 50, 100, and 200.

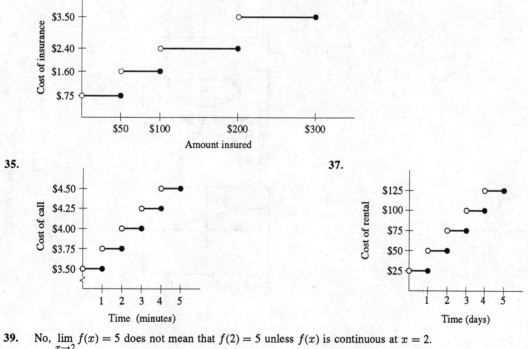

35.

37.

39. No, $\lim\limits_{x \to 2} f(x) = 5$ does not mean that $f(2) = 5$ unless $f(x)$ is continuous at $x = 2$.

For example, let $f(x) = \begin{cases} \dfrac{x^2 + x - 6}{x - 2} & x \neq 2 \\ 7 & x = 2 \end{cases}$

Then $\lim\limits_{x \to 2} \dfrac{(x+3)(x-2)}{x-2} = 5$, but $f(2) = 7$.

41.   **1.**   Compute $f(4)$; if it does not exist, then the function is not continuous at $x = 4$.

   2.   Compute $\lim\limits_{x \to 4} f(x)$; if it does not exist, then the function is not continuous at $x = 4$.

   3.   Compare $f(4)$ and $\lim\limits_{x \to 4} f(x)$; if they are not equal, then the function is not continuous at $x = 4$. If they are equal, the function is continuous at $x = 4$.

43.   Usually the level of sound is very low, and the graph appears as a horizontal line. When the person hiccups, the sound is immediately louder for a moment. Thus the graph jumps up to a higher level and then falls down to the lower level. There is a discontinuity each time the person hiccups.

45. $f(x) = x^2 + 8x + 1$ is continuous on $(-\infty, \infty)$ **47.** $f(x) = \dfrac{1}{x^2}$ is discontinuous at $x = 0$

49. $f(x) = \sqrt{x}$ is discontinuous on $(-\infty, 0)$

51. $\lim\limits_{x \to 1} \dfrac{\sqrt{x} - 1}{x - 1} = \dfrac{\sqrt{1} - 1}{1 - 1} = \dfrac{0}{0}$

$\lim\limits_{x \to 1} \dfrac{(\sqrt{x} - 1)(\sqrt{x} + 1)}{(x - 1)(\sqrt{x} + 1)} = \lim\limits_{x \to 1} \dfrac{\cancel{(x - 1)}}{\cancel{(x - 1)}(\sqrt{x} + 1)} = \dfrac{1}{\sqrt{1} + 1} = \dfrac{1}{2}$

53. $\lim\limits_{x \to 3} \dfrac{\frac{1}{x} - \frac{1}{3}}{x - 3} = \dfrac{\frac{1}{3} - \frac{1}{3}}{3 - 3} = \dfrac{0}{0}$

$\lim\limits_{x \to 3} \dfrac{\frac{3 - x}{3x}}{x - 3} = \lim\limits_{x \to 3} -\dfrac{\cancel{(x - 3)}}{3x} \cdot \dfrac{1}{\cancel{x - 3}} = -\dfrac{1}{3(3)} = -\dfrac{1}{9}$

SECTION 2.2 Technology Exercises

1.   0.7, 4.3

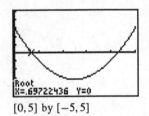   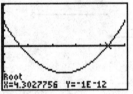

[0, 5] by [−5, 5]   [0, 5] by [−5, 5]

3.   1.8   **5.** $(5, \infty)$

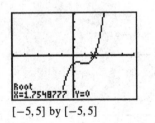   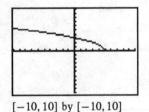

[−5, 5] by [−5, 5]   [−10, 10] by [−10, 10]

7. $(-\infty, 0)$

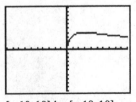

[−10, 10] by [−10, 10]

SECTION 2.3 pages 79–82

1. **a.** $\lim\limits_{x\to 2^-} f(x) = 2$
    b. $\lim\limits_{x\to 2^+} f(x) = 1$

3. **a.** $\lim\limits_{x\to 1^-} h(x)$ does not exist
    b. $\lim\limits_{x\to 1^+} h(x) = 2$

5. **a.** $\lim\limits_{x\to 5^-} m(x) = -1$
    b. $\lim\limits_{x\to 5^+} m(x) = -1$

7. $\lim\limits_{x\to 0^-} \sqrt{2x}$ does not exist because $\sqrt{2x}$ is not defined for $x < 0$.

9. $\lim\limits_{x\to 1^+} \sqrt{1-x}$ does not exist because $\sqrt{1-x}$ is not defined for $x > 1$.

11. $\lim\limits_{x\to 0} \sqrt{3x}$ does not exist because $\lim\limits_{x\to 0^-} \sqrt{3x}$ does not exist, since $\sqrt{3x}$ is not defined for $x < 0$.

13. **a.** $\lim\limits_{x\to 0^-} f(x) = 2$
     b. $\lim\limits_{x\to 0^+} f(x) = -1$

15. **a.** $\lim\limits_{x\to 2^-} h(x) = -1$
     b. $\lim\limits_{x\to 2^+} h(x) = -1$

17. $\lim\limits_{x\to 0} f(x)$ does not exist

19. $\lim\limits_{x\to 2} h(x) = -1$

21. **a.** $M(120) = \$2.40$
     b. $M(100) = \$1.60$
     c. $\lim\limits_{x\to 50^+} M(x) = \$1.60$
     d. $\lim\limits_{x\to 50^-} M(x) = \$0.75$
     e. $\lim\limits_{x\to 50} M(x)$ does not exist, since $\lim\limits_{x\to 50^-} M(x) \neq \lim\limits_{x\to 50^+} M(x)$.
     f. M is *not* continuous at 50.
     g. Yes, M is continuous at 120, since $\lim\limits_{x\to 120} M(x) = 2.40 = M(120)$.

23. **a.** $H(60) = 10$
     b. $H(100) = 10.5$
     c. No, H is not discontinuous at 30.
     d. $\lim\limits_{t\to 60^-} H(t) = 9.5$
     e. $\lim\limits_{t\to 60^+} H(t) = 10$
     f. No, H is *not* continuous at 60, since $\lim\limits_{t\to 60^-} H(t) \neq \lim\limits_{t\to 60^+} H(t)$.

25. **a.** $\lim\limits_{t\to 3^-} A(t) = 300$
     b. $\lim\limits_{t\to 3^+} A(t) = 500$
     c. At 3 hours, the patient receives 200 more milligrams of medicine, so there is a difference of approximately 200 milligrams just before and just after 3 hours.

27. $\left.\begin{array}{l} \lim\limits_{x\to 3^-} f(x) = 11 \\ \lim\limits_{x\to 3^+} f(x) = 11 \end{array}\right\} \lim\limits_{x\to 3} f(x) = 11$

     $f(3) = 11$

     f is continuous at 3, since $\lim\limits_{x\to 3} f(x) = f(3) = 11$.

29. $\lim\limits_{x\to 2} f(x) = 5$

     $f(2) = 5$

     f is continuous at 2, since $\lim\limits_{x\to 2} f(x) = f(2) = 5$.

31. $\lim\limits_{x\to 2^-} f(x) = 11$

     $\lim\limits_{x\to 2^+} f(x) = 16$

     Since $\lim\limits_{x\to 2^-} f(x) \neq \lim\limits_{x\to 2^+} f(x)$, then $\lim\limits_{x\to 2} f(x)$ does not exist and f is not continuous at 2.

33. $\lim\limits_{x\to 4^-} f(x) = 14$

     $\lim\limits_{x\to 4^+} f(x) = 13$

     Since $\lim\limits_{x\to 4^-} f(x) \neq \lim\limits_{x\to 4^+} f(x)$, then $\lim\limits_{x\to 4} f(x)$ does not exist and f is not continuous at 4.

35. No. If $\lim\limits_{x\to 3} f(x) = 5$, then by the statement on page 83, $\lim\limits_{x\to 3^-} f(x) = \lim\limits_{x\to 3^+} f(x) = 5$.

SECTION 2.3 Technology Exercises

1.

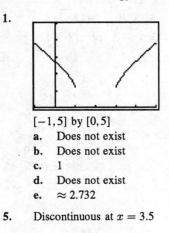

$[-1, 5]$ by $[0, 5]$
a.   Does not exist
b.   Does not exist
c.   1
d.   Does not exist
e. ≈ 2.732

3.   1

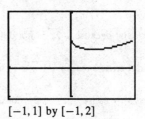

$[-1, 1]$ by $[-1, 2]$

5.   Discontinuous at $x = 3.5$

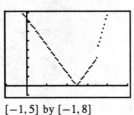

$[-1, 5]$ by $[-1, 8]$

7.   Continuous

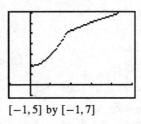

$[-1, 5]$ by $[-1, 7]$

SECTION 2.4 pages 88–90

1.

x	$\dfrac{x+1}{x}$
100	1.01
1000	1.001
10,000	1.0001
100,000	1.000001

$$\lim_{x \to \infty} \frac{x+1}{x} = 1$$

3.

x	$\dfrac{1+3x}{2x}$
-100	1.495
-1000	1.4995
$-10,000$	1.49995
$-1,000,000$	1.4999995

$$\lim_{x \to -\infty} \frac{1+3x}{2x} = 1.5$$

5. $\displaystyle\lim_{x \to \infty} \frac{1}{x} = 0$

7. $\displaystyle\lim_{x \to \infty} = \frac{-20}{x^4} = 0$

9. $\displaystyle\lim_{x \to \infty} \frac{1000}{x^2} = 0$

11. $\displaystyle\lim_{x \to -\infty} \left(-\frac{1}{x^4} \right) = 0$

13. $\displaystyle\lim_{x \to \infty} \frac{3x+2}{5x-4} = \lim_{x \to \infty} \frac{3 + \frac{2}{x}}{5 - \frac{4}{x}} = \frac{3+0}{5-0} = \frac{3}{5}$

15. $\displaystyle\lim_{x \to \infty} \frac{2x^2 + 8x + 6}{x^2 - 3x + 1} = \lim_{x \to \infty} \frac{2 + \frac{8}{x} + \frac{6}{x^2}}{1 - \frac{3}{x} + \frac{1}{x^2}} = \frac{2+0+0}{1-0+0} = 2$

17. $\displaystyle\lim_{x \to \infty} \frac{x^3 - 15}{2x^3 + x^2 - 3x + 1} = \lim_{x \to \infty} \frac{1 - \frac{15}{x^3}}{2 + \frac{1}{x} - \frac{3}{x^2} + \frac{1}{x^3}} = \frac{1}{2}$

19. $\displaystyle\lim_{x \to \infty} \frac{1-x}{1+2x} = \lim_{x \to \infty} \frac{\frac{1}{x} - 1}{\frac{1}{x} + 2} = -\frac{1}{2}$

21. $\displaystyle\lim_{x \to \infty} \frac{1+3x}{x^2 - 5x + 2} = \lim_{x \to \infty} \frac{\frac{1}{x^2} + \frac{3}{x}}{1 - \frac{5}{x} + \frac{2}{x^2}} = \frac{0}{1} = 0$

23. $\lim\limits_{x\to\infty}\dfrac{2x+1}{x-4}=\dfrac{2+\frac{1}{x}}{1-\frac{4}{x}}=2$

horizontal asymptote: $y=2$

25. $\lim\limits_{x\to\infty}\dfrac{x}{1-x}=\lim\limits_{x\to\infty}\dfrac{1}{\frac{1}{x}-1}=-1$

horizontal asymptote: $y=-1$

27. $\lim\limits_{x\to\infty}\dfrac{x^2+3}{x^3-1}=\lim\limits_{x\to\infty}\dfrac{\frac{1}{x}+\frac{3}{x^3}}{1-\frac{1}{x^3}}=\dfrac{0}{1}=0$

horizontal aymptote: $y=0$

29. $\lim\limits_{x\to\infty}\dfrac{x^2-8x+2}{3x^2+6x-5}=\lim\limits_{x\to\infty}\dfrac{1-\frac{8}{x}+\frac{2}{x^2}}{3+\frac{6}{x}-\frac{5}{x^2}}=\dfrac{1}{3}$

horizontal asymptote: $y=\frac{1}{3}$

31. a. $\lim\limits_{x\to\infty}\dfrac{8}{x^2+4}=\lim\limits_{x\to\infty}\dfrac{\frac{8}{x^2}}{1+\frac{4}{x^2}}=\dfrac{0}{1}=0$

b. horizontal asymptote: $y=0$

33. Given the average cost function $\overline{C}(x)=\frac{1500+12x}{x}$, then

$$\lim\limits_{x\to\infty}\dfrac{1500+12x}{x}=\lim\limits_{x\to\infty}\dfrac{\frac{1500}{x}+12}{1}=12$$

$$\lim\limits_{x\to\infty}\overline{C}(x)=\$12$$

35. Given the height function $h(t)=\dfrac{5t-2}{t}$, then $\lim\limits_{t\to\infty}h(t)=\lim\limits_{t\to\infty}\dfrac{5t-2}{t}=\lim\limits_{t\to\infty}5-\dfrac{2}{t}=5$

$$\lim\limits_{t\to\infty}h(t)=5\text{ ft}$$

37. Given the function $f(t)=\dfrac{0.15t}{1+t^2}$, then

a. $\lim\limits_{t\to\infty}f(t)=\lim\limits_{t\to\infty}\dfrac{0.15t}{1+t^2}=\lim\limits_{t\to\infty}\dfrac{\frac{0.15}{t}}{\frac{1}{t^2}+1}=\dfrac{0}{1}=0$

$$\lim\limits_{t\to\infty}f(t)=0$$

b. As time passes, the amount of a drug that remains in a person's bloodstream after it has been injected disappears.

39. Given the intensity of an electric current defined by
$I(t)=\frac{a}{t}+b$, then

$$\lim\limits_{t\to\infty}I(t)=\lim\limits_{t\to\infty}\left(\dfrac{a}{t}+b\right)=0+b=\;b$$

41. $\lim\limits_{x\to\infty}f(x)$ resembles a one-sided limit because the computation takes place for values of x that are increasing only. That is, x increases without bound in one direction only, much like x approaching b from below in the expression $\lim\limits_{x\to b^-}f(x)$.

SECTION 2.4 Technology Exercises

1.

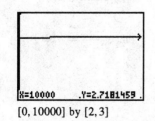

$[0,10000]$ by $[2,3]$

3.   **a.**   1

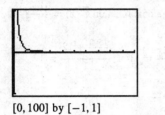

[0, 10000] by [0, 2]

b.   1

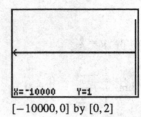

[−10000, 0] by [0, 2]

5. $y = 0$

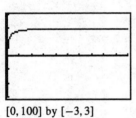

[0, 100] by [−1, 1]

7. $y = 2, y = -2$

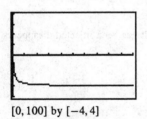

[0, 100] by [−3, 3]

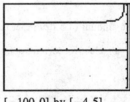

[−100, 0] by [−3, 3]

9. $y = -3, y = 3$

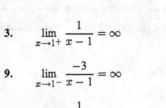

[0, 100] by [−4, 4]

[−100, 0] by [−4, 5]

SECTION 2.5 pages 96–97

1. $\displaystyle\lim_{x \to 0} \frac{2}{x^2} = \infty$

3. $\displaystyle\lim_{x \to 1^+} \frac{1}{x - 1} = \infty$

5. $\displaystyle\lim_{x \to 3^+} \frac{-6}{x - 3} = -\infty$

7. $\displaystyle\lim_{x \to 4^-} \frac{11}{x - 4} = -\infty$

9. $\displaystyle\lim_{x \to 1^-} \frac{-3}{x - 1} = \infty$

11. $\displaystyle\lim_{x \to 2^+} \frac{5}{2 - x} = -\infty$

13. $\displaystyle\lim_{x \to 1^+} \frac{-9}{1 - x} = \infty$

15. $\displaystyle\lim_{x \to 4^-} \frac{1}{4 - x} = \infty$

17. $\displaystyle\lim_{x \to 2^-} \frac{-3}{2 - x} = -\infty$

19. a.

Percent removed	Cost
10	10,000
25	12,000
50	18,000
80	45,000
90	90,000
95	180,000
98	450,000

The more pollutant removed, the higher is the cost.

b. No, it is not possible to remove all the pollutant.

$$\lim_{x\to100^-} C(x) = \lim_{x\to100^-} \frac{900,000}{100-x} = \infty$$

so it would take an infinite amount of money to remove all the pollutant.

21. $\lim\limits_{x\to5^+} \dfrac{4}{x-5} = \infty$

vertical asymptote: $x=5$

23. $\lim\limits_{x\to0} \dfrac{2}{x^2} = \infty$

vertical asymptote: $x=0$

25. $\lim\limits_{x\to-2^+} \dfrac{1}{x+2} = \infty$

vertical asymptote: $x=-2$

27. $\lim\limits_{x\to1} \dfrac{-3}{(x-1)^2} = -\infty$

vertical asymptote: $x=1$

29. $\lim\limits_{x\to\infty} (3x^2) = \infty$

31. $\lim\limits_{x\to\infty} \dfrac{x^3-6x^2+3}{5x^2+x-1} = \lim\limits_{x\to\infty} \dfrac{x-6+\frac{3}{x^2}}{5+\frac{1}{x}-\frac{1}{x^2}} = \dfrac{\infty}{5} = \infty$

33. $\lim\limits_{x\to\infty} \dfrac{5x-2}{7x+1} = \lim\limits_{x\to\infty} \dfrac{5-\frac{2}{x}}{7+\frac{1}{x}} = \dfrac{5}{7}$

35. a. In 6 innings there are $(6)(3)=18$ outs. The ERA is given by

$$A = \frac{27r}{t} = \frac{27\cdot3}{18} = 4.5$$

b. Having given up 3 runs means $r=3$. If no one was out, then $t=0$, so we would use

$$\lim_{t\to0^+} \frac{27\cdot3}{t} = \lim_{t\to0^+} \frac{81}{t}$$

c. $\lim\limits_{t\to0^+} \dfrac{81}{t} = \infty$

SECTION 2.5 Technology Exercises

1.

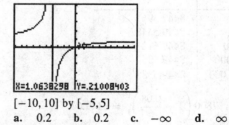

$[0,2]$ by $[-100,100]$
a. $-\infty$ **b.** ∞

3.

$[-10,10]$ by $[-5,5]$
a. 0.2   **b.** 0.2   **c.** $-\infty$ **d.** ∞

5. $x = 4$

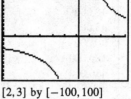

[3,5] by [−5,5]

7. $x = 2.6$

[2,3] by [−100,100]

REVIEW EXERCISES FOR CHAPTER 2 pages 98–101

1. $\displaystyle\lim_{x\to 4} x^{-3} = 4^{-3} = \frac{1}{64}$

3. $\displaystyle\lim_{x\to 6} \frac{\sqrt{37 - 2x}}{x + 7} = \frac{\sqrt{37 - 2(6)}}{6 + 7} = \frac{\sqrt{25}}{13} = \frac{5}{13}$

5. $\displaystyle\lim_{x\to 5} \frac{x^2 - 25}{2x - 10} = \frac{5^2 - 25}{2(5) - 10} = \frac{0}{0}$

$\displaystyle\lim_{x\to 5} \frac{x^2 - 25}{2x - 10} = \lim_{x\to 5} \frac{(x - 5)(x + 5)}{2(x - 5)} = \frac{5 + 5}{2} = 5$

7. $\displaystyle\lim_{x\to 7} \frac{14 - 2x}{7x} = \frac{14 - 2(7)}{7(7)} = \frac{0}{49} = 0$

9. $\displaystyle\lim_{x\to 1^-} f(x) = 4$

11. $\displaystyle\lim_{x\to 0^-} g(x) = 0$

13. $\displaystyle\lim_{x\to\infty} \frac{5x - 19}{7x + 2} = \lim_{x\to\infty} \frac{5 - \frac{19}{x}}{7 + \frac{2}{x}} = \frac{5 - 0}{7 + 0} = \frac{5}{7}$

15. $\displaystyle\lim_{x\to\infty} \frac{3x^2}{x^3 - x^2 + x} = \lim_{x\to\infty} \frac{\frac{3}{x}}{1 - \frac{1}{x} + \frac{1}{x^2}} = \frac{0}{1} = 0$

17. $\displaystyle\lim_{x\to 5^-} \frac{2}{x - 5} = -\infty$

19. $\displaystyle\lim_{x\to 0^+} \frac{3}{2x^5} = \infty$

21. $\displaystyle\lim_{x\to 2} f(x) = 6$

23. $\displaystyle\lim_{x\to 2} g(x)$ does not exist

25.
a.   No
b.   Yes
c.   Yes
d.   No
e.   No
f.   No
g.   Yes
h.   Yes

27.   Given the function $T(n) = 4 + \frac{6}{n}$, then

$$\lim_{n\to\infty} T(n) = \lim_{n\to\infty} \left(4 + \frac{6}{n}\right) = 4 \text{ minutes}$$

29.

n	$\$7800\left(1 + \frac{0.08}{n}\right)^n$
12	8447.3961
365	8449.5648
1000	8449.6121
10,000	8449.6364
100,000	8449.6388

$$\lim_{n\to\infty} 7800\left(1 + \frac{0.08}{n}\right)^n = 8449.64$$

31.
a. $C(x) = 2300 + 7x$

b. $\overline{C}(x) = \dfrac{C(x)}{x} = \dfrac{2300 + 7x}{x} = \dfrac{2300}{x} + 7$

c. $\displaystyle\lim_{x\to\infty} \overline{C}(x) = \lim_{x\to\infty}\left(\frac{2300}{x} + 7\right) = \lim_{x\to\infty}\frac{2300}{x} + \lim_{x\to\infty} 7 = 0 + 7 = 7$

33.   **a.** $\lim\limits_{x \to 50^+} y = 4.50$

       b. $\lim\limits_{x \to 100^-} y = 4.50$

       c. $\lim\limits_{x \to 200} y$ does not exist because $\lim\limits_{x \to 200^-} y = 5.50$

         and $\lim\limits_{x \to 200^+} y = 6.50$.

35.   **a.** $B(1) = 103.7 - \dfrac{5.1(1) - 4.5}{1} = 103.1$

          $B(3) = 103.7 - \dfrac{5.1(3) - 4.5}{3} = 100.1$

          $B(10) = 103.7 - \dfrac{5.1(10) - 4.5}{10} = 99.05$

       b. $\lim\limits_{t \to \infty} \left(103.7 - \dfrac{5.1t - 4.5}{t} \right) = \lim\limits_{t \to \infty} 103.7 - \lim\limits_{t \to \infty} 5.1 + \lim\limits_{t \to \infty} \dfrac{4.5}{t}$

                                   $= 103.7 - 5.1 + 0 = 98.6$

37.   No, the function will not appear continuous at $x = 1$, even though $\lim\limits_{x \to 1} f(x) = 9$ because $f(x)$ is not defined at $x = 1$.

39.   Yes, if the limit did not exist, the function could not be continuous.

CHAPTER 3   Derivatives

SECTION 3.1 pages 112–113

1. If $f(x) = 5x + 1$, then

$$f'(x) = \lim_{\Delta x \to 0} \frac{f(x + \Delta x) - f(x)}{\Delta x}$$
$$= \lim_{\Delta x \to 0} \frac{5(x + \Delta x) + 1 - (5x + 1)}{\Delta x}$$
$$= \lim_{\Delta x \to 0} \frac{5x + 5(\Delta x) + 1 - 5x - 1}{\Delta x}$$
$$= \lim_{\Delta x \to 0} 5$$
$$= 5$$

5. If $f(x) = x^2 - 4x + 2$, then

$$f'(x) = \lim_{\Delta x \to 0} \frac{f(x + \Delta x) - f(x)}{\Delta x}$$
$$= \lim_{\Delta x \to 0} \frac{(x + \Delta x)^2 - 4(x + \Delta x) + 2 - (x^2 - 4x + 2)}{\Delta x}$$
$$= \lim_{\Delta x \to 0} \frac{x^2 + 2x(\Delta x) + (\Delta x)^2 - 4x - 4(\Delta x) + 2 - x^2 + 4x - 2}{\Delta x}$$
$$= \lim_{\Delta x \to 0} \frac{(2x - 4 + \Delta x)\Delta x}{\Delta x}$$
$$= 2x - 4$$

7. If $f(x) = 3x^2 + 7x$, then

$$f'(x) = \lim_{\Delta x \to 0} \frac{f(x + \Delta x) - f(x)}{\Delta x}$$
$$= \lim_{\Delta x \to 0} \frac{3(x + \Delta x)^2 + 7(x + \Delta x) - (3x^2 + 7x)}{\Delta x}$$
$$= \lim_{\Delta x \to 0} \frac{3[x^2 + 2x(\Delta x) + (\Delta x)^2] + 7x + 7(\Delta x) - 3x^2 - 7x}{\Delta x}$$
$$= \lim_{\Delta x \to 0} \frac{3x^2 + 6x(\Delta x) + 3(\Delta x)^2 + 7x + 7(\Delta x) - 3x^2 - 7x}{\Delta x}$$
$$= \lim_{\Delta x \to 0} \frac{[6x + 7 + 3(\Delta x)]\Delta x}{\Delta x}$$
$$= 6x + 7$$

3. If $f(x) = x^2 + 3$, then

$$f'(x) = \lim_{\Delta x \to 0} \frac{f(x + \Delta x) - f(x)}{\Delta x}$$
$$= \lim_{\Delta x \to 0} \frac{(x + \Delta x)^2 + 3 - (x^2 + 3)}{\Delta x}$$
$$= \lim_{\Delta x \to 0} \frac{x^2 + 2x(\Delta x) + (\Delta x)^2 + 3 - x^2 - 3}{\Delta x}$$
$$= \lim_{\Delta x \to 0} 2x + \Delta x$$
$$= 2x$$

9. If $f(x) = 6$, then

$$f'(x) = \lim_{\Delta x \to 0} \frac{f(x + \Delta x) - f(x)}{\Delta x}$$
$$= \lim_{\Delta x \to 0} \frac{6 - 6}{\Delta x}$$
$$= \lim_{\Delta x \to 0} 0$$
$$= 0$$

11. If $f(x) = x^3 + 2$, then

$$f'(x) = \lim_{\Delta x \to 0} \frac{f(x + \Delta x) - f(x)}{\Delta x}$$

$$= \lim_{\Delta x \to 0} \frac{(x + \Delta x)^3 + 2 - (x^3 + 2)}{\Delta x}$$

$$= \lim_{\Delta x \to 0} \frac{x^3 + 3x^2(\Delta x) + 3x(\Delta x)^2 + (\Delta x)^3 + 2 - x^3 - 2}{\Delta x}$$

$$= \lim_{\Delta x \to 0} \frac{[3x^2 + 3x(\Delta x) + (\Delta x)^2]\Delta x}{\Delta x}$$

$$= 3x^2$$

13. If $f(x) = x^3 + x^2 + x$, then

$$f'(x) = \lim_{\Delta x \to 0} \frac{f(x + \Delta x) - f(x)}{\Delta x}$$

$$= \lim_{\Delta x \to 0} \frac{(x + \Delta x)^3 + (x + \Delta x)^2 + (x + \Delta x) - (x^3 + x^2 + x)}{\Delta x}$$

$$= \lim_{\Delta x \to 0} \frac{x^3 + 3x^2(\Delta x) + 3x(\Delta x)^2 + (\Delta x)^3 + x^2 + 2x(\Delta x) + (\Delta x)^2 + x + \Delta x - x^3 - x^2 - x}{\Delta x}$$

$$= \lim_{\Delta x \to 0} \frac{[3x^2 + 3x(\Delta x) + (\Delta x)^2 + 2x + \Delta x + 1]\Delta x}{\Delta x}$$

$$= 3x^2 + 2x + 1$$

15. If $f(x) = \dfrac{2}{x}$, then

$$f'(x) = \lim_{\Delta x \to 0} \frac{f(x + \Delta x) - f(x)}{\Delta x}$$

$$= \lim_{\Delta x \to 0} \left(\frac{\frac{2}{x + \Delta x} - \frac{2}{x}}{\Delta x} \right)$$

$$= \lim_{\Delta x \to 0} \frac{2x - 2(x + \Delta x)}{x(\Delta x)(x + \Delta x)}$$

$$= \lim_{\Delta x \to 0} \frac{2x - 2x - 2\Delta x}{x(\Delta x)(x + \Delta x)}$$

$$= \frac{2}{x^2}$$

17. If $f(x) = x^4$, then

$$f'(x) = \lim_{\Delta x \to 0} \frac{f(x + \Delta x) - f(x)}{\Delta x}$$

$$= \lim_{\Delta x \to 0} \frac{(x + \Delta x)^4 - x^4}{\Delta x}$$

$$= \lim_{\Delta x \to 0} \frac{x^4 + 4x^3(\Delta x) + 6x^2(\Delta x)^2 + 4x(\Delta x)^3 + (\Delta x)^4 - x^4}{\Delta x}$$

$$= \lim_{\Delta x \to 0} \frac{[4x^3 + 6x^2(\Delta x) + 4x(\Delta x)^2 + (\Delta x)^3]\Delta x}{\Delta x}$$

$$= 4x^3$$

19. Given $f(x) = x^2 + 6x$ and the point (2, 16), then

$$2x + 6$$

$$
\begin{aligned}
m_{\tan} &= \lim_{\Delta x \to 0} \frac{f(x + \Delta x) - f(x)}{\Delta x} \\
&= \lim_{\Delta x \to 0} \frac{(x + \Delta x)^2 + 6(x + \Delta x) - (x^2 + 6x)}{\Delta x} \\
&= \lim_{\Delta x \to 0} \frac{x^2 + 2x(\Delta x) + (\Delta x)^2 + 6x + 6(\Delta x) - x^2 - 6x}{\Delta x} \\
&= \lim_{\Delta x \to 0} \frac{(2x + \Delta x + 6)\Delta x}{\Delta x} \\
&= 2x + 6
\end{aligned}
$$

$$\frac{f(x+h) - f(x)}{h} \qquad \frac{f(x+h) - f(x^2 + 6x)}{h}$$

At point (2, 16), $m_{\tan} = 10$

21. Given $f(x) = x^3 - 9$ and the point (4, 55), then

$$
\begin{aligned}
m_{\tan} &= \lim_{\Delta x \to 0} \frac{f(x + \Delta x) - f(x)}{\Delta x} \\
&= \lim_{\Delta x \to 0} \frac{(x + \Delta x)^3 - 9 - (x^3 - 9)}{\Delta x} \\
&= \lim_{\Delta x \to 0} \frac{x^3 + 3x^2(\Delta x) + 3x(\Delta x)^2 + (\Delta x)^3 - 9 - x^3 + 9}{\Delta x} \\
&= \lim_{\Delta x \to 0} \frac{(3x^2 + 3x(\Delta x) + (\Delta x)^2)\Delta x}{\Delta x} \\
&= 3x^2
\end{aligned}
$$

At point (4, 55), $m_{\tan} = 48$

23. $m_{\tan} = 10$ at point (2, 16)

Tangent line: $\begin{aligned} y - 16 &= 10(x - 2) \\ y &= 10x - 4 \end{aligned}$

25. Since the expression $\displaystyle \lim_{\Delta x \to 0} \frac{\Delta x(2x + \Delta x)}{\Delta x}$ is a limit as Δx approaches zero but never actually needs to *equal* zero, the cancellation of Δx is not divison by zero. That is, for all $\Delta x \neq 0$, $\frac{\Delta x(2x + \Delta x)}{\Delta x} = 2x + \Delta x$.

27. **a.** The smallest value of $f'(x)$ is at $x = b$.
  b. The slope of the tangent line is smallest there, and the derivative represents the slope of the tangent line.

29. The graph of g is the graph of f translated vertically upward one unit.

SECTION 3.1 Technology Exercises

1.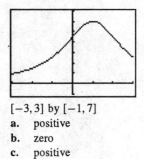

$[-3, 3]$ by $[-1, 7]$
  a. positive
  b. zero
  c. positive
  d. negative

3. No, the line is not tangent.

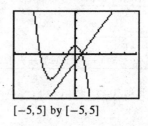

$[-5, 5]$ by $[-5, 5]$

5. 0 and 2

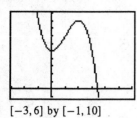

$[-3, 6]$ by $[-1, 10]$

7. $f(x) = -x^2 + 10x - 17$ has the larger derivative at $x = 3$.

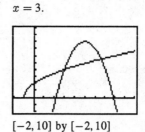

$[-2, 10]$ by $[-2, 10]$

9. $f'(x) = 2x + 4$

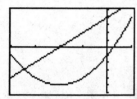

$[-4, 1]$ by $[-6, 5]$

a. The slope of $f(x)$ is negative to the left of $x = -2$.
b. $f'(x)$ is negative to the left of $x = -2$.
c. The slope of $f(x)$ is equal to $f'(x)$.
d. $f'(x)$ and the slope of $f(x)$ are both positive to the right of $x = -2$.

SECTION 3.2 pages 119–121

1. Let $f(x) = x^4$; then

$$f'(x) = 4x^3$$

3. Let $f(x) = x^{-2}$; then

$$f'(x) = -2x^{-3} = -\frac{2}{x^3}$$

5. Let $g(x) = 16$; then

$$g'(x) = 0$$

7. Let $y = x^{3/2}$; then

$$\frac{dy}{dx} = \frac{3}{2}x^{1/2}$$

9. Let $y = x^{-2/3}$; then

$$\frac{dy}{dx} = -\frac{2}{3}x^{-5/3} = -\frac{2}{3x^{5/3}}$$

11. Let $f(x) = \frac{1}{x^5} = x^{-5}$; then

$$f'(x) = -5x^{-6} = -\frac{5}{x^6}$$

13. Let $y = \sqrt[3]{x} = x^{1/3}$; then

$$\frac{dy}{dx} = \frac{1}{3}x^{-2/3} = \frac{1}{3x^{2/3}}$$

15. Let $f(x) = 30\sqrt{x} = 30x^{1/2}$; then

$$f'(x) = 15x^{-1/2} = \frac{15}{x^{1/2}}$$

17. Let $y = \frac{x^4}{4}$; then

$$\frac{dy}{dx} = x^3$$

19. Let $y = \frac{10}{\sqrt{t}} = 10t^{-1/2}$; then

$$\frac{dy}{dx} = -5t^{-3/2} = -\frac{5}{t^{3/2}}$$

21. $D_x(1 - x^3) = -3x^2$

23. $\dfrac{d}{dx}\left(\dfrac{1}{x} + \sqrt{2}\right) = -\dfrac{1}{x^2}$

25. $D_x(\sqrt{x} - 2) = \dfrac{1}{2}x^{-1/2} = \dfrac{1}{2x^{1/2}}$

27. Let $y = x^2 - 5x + 19$; then

$$\frac{dy}{dx} = 2x - 5$$

29. Let $y = x^{3/2} + 4x^2$; then

$$\frac{dy}{dx} = \frac{3}{2}x^{1/2} + 8x$$

31. Let $y = \frac{2}{\sqrt{x}} - 3 + \pi^2 = 2x^{-1/2} - 3 + \pi^2$; then

$$\frac{dy}{dx} = -x^{-3/2} = -\frac{1}{x^{3/2}}$$

33. Let $y = 1 - x^4 + 3x^6$; then

$$D_x y = -4x^3 + 18x^5$$

35. Let $y = 1 - x^{-5}$; then

$$D_x y = 5x^{-6} = \frac{5}{x^6}$$

37. Let $f(x) = x^3 - 6x^2 + 4x - 1$; then

$$f'(x) = 3x^2 - 12x + 4$$

39. Let $f(x) = 8x^{7/4} + 6x^{5/3} - 9$; then

$$f'(x) = 14x^{3/4} + 10x^{2/3}$$

41. Let $f(x) = 3\sqrt{x} + 5x^2 = 3x^{1/2} + 5x^2$; then

$$f'(x) = \frac{3}{2}x^{-1/2} + 10x = \frac{3}{2x^{1/2}} + 10x$$

43. Given $f(x) = x^2 + 8x + 4$ and $x = 3$, then

$$f'(x) = 2x + 8$$
$$\text{and } f'(3) = 2(3) + 8 = 14$$

45. Given $f(x) = 4x^3 - 7x^2 + 8x - 12$ and $x = -1$, then

$$f'(x) = 12x^2 - 14x + 8$$
$$\text{and } f'(-1) = 12(-1)^2 - 14(-1) + 8 = 34$$

47. Given $f(x) = 1 + \sqrt{x} = 1 + x^{1/2}$ and $x = 9$, then

$$f'(x) = \frac{1}{2}x^{-1/2} = \frac{1}{2x^{1/2}}$$
$$\text{and } f'(9) = \frac{1}{2(9)^{1/2}} = \frac{1}{2 \cdot 3} = \frac{1}{6}$$

49. Given $y = x^2 + 3x + 4$ and the point $(-1, 2)$, then

$$\frac{dy}{dx} = 2x + 3 \qquad \frac{dy}{dx}\bigg|_{x=-1} = 2(-1) + 3 = 1$$

$$m_{\tan} = 1$$

51. Given $y = 1 - x^3$ and the point $(-2, 9)$, then

$$\frac{dy}{dx} = -3x^2 \qquad \frac{dy}{dx}\bigg|_{x=-2} = -3(-2)^2 = -12$$

$$m_{\tan} = -12$$

53. Given $y = 8\sqrt{x} = 8x^{1/2}$ and the point $(4, 16)$, then

$$\frac{dy}{dx} = 4x^{-1/2} = \frac{4}{x^{1/2}} \qquad \frac{dy}{dx}\bigg|_{x=4} = \frac{4}{\sqrt{4}} = 2$$

$$m_{\tan} = 2$$

55. Using $y - y_1 = m(x - x_1)$ with $m = -32$ and the point $(-2, 16)$ yields

$$y - 16 = -32(x + 2)$$
$$y = -32x - 48$$

57. If $f(x) = c$, then

$$f'(x) = \lim_{\Delta x \to 0} \frac{f(x + \Delta x) - f(x)}{\Delta x}$$
$$= \lim_{\Delta x \to 0} \frac{c - c}{\Delta x}$$
$$= \lim_{\Delta x \to 0} \frac{0}{\Delta x}$$
$$= 0$$

59. If $f(x) = \frac{1}{x}$, then $f'(0) = \lim_{\Delta x \to 0} \frac{f(0+\Delta x) - f(0)}{\Delta x}$.

Since $f(0)$ does not exist, the limit, and consequently $f'(0)$, does not exist.

61. If the substitution took place before the differentiation, then, since $f(3)$ is a constant, the derivative formulas would always give an answer of zero.

63. **a.** $f'(x_1) > g'(x_1)$

b. $g'(x_2) > f'(x_2)$

c. $f'(x_3) > g'(x_3)$

65. The limit is $2x$ because the expression is the definition of the derivative for the function $x^2 + 7$.

SECTION 3.2 Technology Exercises

1. $f'(3) > f'(2)$

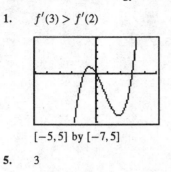

$[-5, 5]$ by $[-7, 5]$

3. $f'(5) > g'(-2)$

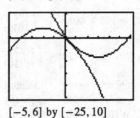

$[-5, 6]$ by $[-25, 10]$

5.   3

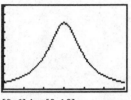

$[0, 6]$ by $[0, 10]$

7.

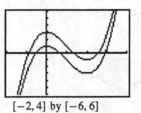

$[-2, 4]$ by $[-6, 6]$

a. The slopes are the same.

b. $f'(x) = 3x^2 - 6x$; $g'(x) = 3x^2 - 6x$.
The derivatives are the same.

c. Since $f'(x) = g'(x)$ and the derivative is the slope
of the tangent line, the slopes of the tangent lines
for $f(x)$ and $g(x)$ are the same, point for point.

SECTION 3.3 pages 127–130

1.   Average rate of increase $= \dfrac{18}{12}$

$\qquad\qquad\qquad\qquad = 1.5\%$ per month

3.   Average rate of change in population $= \dfrac{328{,}000 - 355{,}000}{1990 - 1980}$

$\qquad\qquad\qquad\qquad\qquad\qquad = -2700$ people per year

5.   Average rate of increase $= \dfrac{162}{3}$

$\qquad\qquad\qquad\qquad = 54$ points per day

7.   Average velocity $= \dfrac{s(4) - s(0)}{4 - 0}$

$\qquad\qquad\qquad = \dfrac{-16(4)^2 + 400 - (0 + 400)}{4}$

$\qquad\qquad\qquad = -64$ feet per second

9.   Given $y = x^2 - 6x + 2$ and $x = 4$, then

$$\frac{dy}{dx} = 2x - 6$$

$$\left.\frac{dy}{dx}\right|_{x=4} = 2(4) - 6 = 2$$

11.   Given $f(t) = 4.2\sqrt{t} - 3 = 4.2t^{1/2} - 3$ and $t = 15$, then

$$f'(t) = 2.1t^{-1/2} = \frac{2.1}{\sqrt{t}}$$

$$f'(15) = \frac{2.1}{\sqrt{15}} = 0.54$$

13.   If the distance function is $s(t) = 150 - 16t^2$, then, for
$t = 3$,

$$s'(t) = -32t$$
$$s'(3) = -96 \text{ feet per second}$$

15. $n = 1000 + 100t + 20t^2$ (inhibitor A used)

$n = 1000 + 200t - 10t^2$ (inhibitor B used)

Inhibitor A used $n'(t) = 100 + 40t - \begin{cases} n'(5) = 100 + 40(5) = 300 \\ n'(10) = 100 + 40(10) = 500 \end{cases}$

Inhibitor B used $n'(t) = 200 - 20t - \begin{cases} n'(5) = 200 - 20(5) = 100 \\ n'(10) = 200 - 20(10) = 0 \end{cases}$

	Inhibitor A used	Inhibitor B used
after 5 hours	$n'(5) = 300$	$n'(5) = 100$
after 10 hours	$n'(10) = 500$	$n'(10) = 0$

17. If the number of people who have the flu is $n(t) = 100t^2 - 2t^3$, then

a. $n(20) = 100(20)^2 - 2(20)^3$
   $= 24,000$

b. $n'(t) = 200t - 6t^2$
   $n'(20) = 200(20) - 6(20)^2$
   $= 1600$

19. If the intensity of light is $I(r) = kr^2$, then

$I'(r) = 2kr$

21. If the factory produces $s(t) = 48t - t^2$ tires in t hours, then $s'(t) = 48 - 2t$
a. $s'(4) = 48 - 2(4) = 40$
b. $s'(t) = 48 - 2t = 36$
   $12 = 2t$
   $t = 6$ hours

after 6 hours

23. If the area of a circle is $A(r) = \pi r^2$, then

$A'(r) = 2\pi r$

25. If the distance traveled is $s(t) = t^2 + t + 4$, then

$s'(t) = 2t + 1$ and

a. $s'(1) = 3$ feet per second
   $s'(5) = 11$ feet per second

b. Solve

   $s(t) = 24$
   $t^2 + t + 4 = 24$
   $t^2 + t - 20 = 0$
   $(t - 4)(t + 5) = 0$

   $t = 4, \quad t = -5$

   after 4 seconds

c. $s'(4) = 9$ feet per second

d. $2t + 1 = 23$
   $2t = 22$
   $t = 11$

   after 11 seconds

27. · **a.** Although the function value $g_2(T_1)$ is greater than the function value $g_1(T_1)$ (i.e. $g_2(T_1) > g_1(T_1)$), the slope of the tangent line to g_1 at T_1 is greater than the slope of the tangent line to g_2 at T_1. (The tangent line is steeper.) Thus, the derivative $g_1'(T_1) > g_2'(T_1)$ and function g_1 shows the greater rate of increase of GNP.

   b. Similarly, the function values $g_1(T_2) = g_2(T_2)$ but the slope of the tangent line to g_1 at T_2 is again greater than the slope of the tangent line to g_2 at T_2. Thus, the derivative $g_1'(T_2) > g_2'(T_2)$ and function g_1 shows the greater rate of increase of GNP. The rates of increase are *not* the same for both g_1 and g_2.

29. **a.** The boy stopped after 6 minutes and remained there for 2 minutes.
   b. The boy is going the fastest just before 2 minutes.
   c. His speed is constant between 2 and 4 minutes (the graph is a straight line there). His speed is also constant (since he is not moving) between 6 and 8 minutes.
   d. He turned around after 4 minutes.

31. **a.** In 6 hours 14 inches of snow will fall.
   b. The expression $s(4) - s(3)$ represents the amount of snow that falls between the third and fourth hours.
   c. After 2 hours snow is falling at a rate of 3 inches per hour.
   d. The snow is falling faster at 4 hours than at 3 hours.

33. Let $f(x) = 10x + 25$. The average rate of change of f for *any* x_1 and x_2 is

$$\frac{\Delta f}{\Delta x} = \frac{f(x_1) - f(x_2)}{x_1 - x_2} = \frac{10x_1 + 25 - (10x_2 + 25)}{x_1 - x_2}$$
$$= \frac{10(x_1 - x_2)}{x_1 - x_2}$$
$$= 10$$

Also, $f'(x) = 10$.

Therefore $\frac{\Delta f}{\Delta x} = 10 = f'(x)$

SECTION 3.3 Technology Exercises

1.
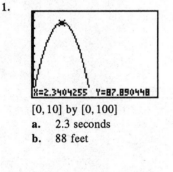
X=2.3404255 Y=87.890448

[0, 10] by [0, 100]
   a. 2.3 seconds
   b. 88 feet

3.
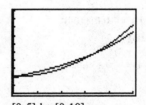

[0, 5] by [0, 10]
   a. $y = 2(1.3)^x$
   b. $y = 0.25x^2 + 2$

SECTION 3.4 pages 136–138

1. If $C(x) = 50 - 0.1x^2$, then

   $MC(x) = C'(x) = -0.2x$

3. If $C(x) = 1000 + 150x - x^2$, then

   $MC(x) = C'(x) = 150 - 2x$

5. If $C(x) = 90x + 0.02x^2$, then

   $MC(x) = C'(x) = 90 + 0.04x$

7. Given the cost function $C(x) = 150 + 40x - x^2$, then

$MC(x) = C'(x) = 40 - 2x$ and

a. $MC(10) = 40 - 2(10) = 20$

b. $C(11) - C(10) = 150 + 40(11) - (11)^2 - [150 + 40(10) - (10)^2]$

$= 469 - 450$

$= \$19$

c. $MC(10)$ is the approximate cost of producting the 11th unit.

9. Given the cost function $C(x) = \frac{1}{2}x^2 + 50x + 90$, then

$MC(x) = C'(x) = x + 50$

Solving $MC(x) = 70$ yields

$x + 50 = 70$

$x = 20$

11. Given the cost function $C(x) = x^2 + 3x + 75$, then

$MC(x) = C'(x) = 2x + 3$

Solving $MC(x) = 31$ yields

$2x + 3 = 31$

$2x = 28$

$x = 14$

13. Given the revenue function $R(x) = 50x + 0.2x^2$, then

$MR(x) = R'(x) = 50 + 0.4x$

15. Given the revenue function $R(x) = 0.001x^2 + 0.7x$, then

$MR(x) = R'(x) = 0.002x + 0.7$

17. If the revenue function is $R(x) = 400x - 0.01x^2$, then

a. $R(1) = 400(1) - 0.01(1)^2$

$= \$399.99$

$R(10) = 400(10) - 0.01(10)^2$

$= \$3999$

$R(100) = 400(100) - 0.01(100)^2$

$= \$39\,900$

b. $MR(x) = R'(x) = 400 - 0.02x$

c. $MR(1000) = 380$

$MR(1000)$ is the approximate increase in revenue from the sale of the 1001st compact disc player.

19. Given the profit function $P(x) = 0.02x^2 + 9x - 72$, then

$MP(x) = P'(x) = 0.04x + 9$

21. Given the profit function $P(x) = 40x - 0.01x^2$, then

$MP(x) = P'(x) = 40 - 0.02x$

23. If the profit function is $P(x) = 0.0005x^2 + x - 160$, then

a. $P(200) = 0.0005(200)^2 + 200 - 160$

$= \$60$

b. $P(50) = 0.0005(50)^2 + 50 - 160$

$= -108.75$

Lose $108.75

c. $MP(x) = P'(x) = 0.001x + 1$

25. Given $R(x) = 95x - 0.01x^2$ and $C(x) = 140 + 10x - 0.02x^2$, then

$$P(x) = R(x) - C(x)$$
$$= 95x - 0.01x^2 - 140 - 10x + 0.02x^2$$
$$= 0.01x^2 + 85x - 140$$

$$MP(x) = P'(x) = 0.02x + 85$$

27. Given $R(x) = 80x + 0.001x^2$ and $C(x) = 210 + 70x + 0.001x^2$, then

$$P(x) = R(x) - C(x)$$
$$= 80x + 0.001x^2 - 210 - 70x - 0.001x^2$$
$$= 10x - 210$$

$$MP(x) = P'(x) = 10$$

29. Given $R(x) = 300x - 0.02x^2$ and $C(x) = 100x$, then

$$R'(x) = 300 - 0.04x$$
$$C'(x) = 100$$

Solving $R'(x) = C'(x)$ yields

$$300 - 0.04x = 100$$
$$200 = 0.04x$$
$$x = 5000$$

31. Given $R(x) = 150x + 0.01x^2$ and $C(x) = 120x + 0.03x^2$, then

$$R'(x) = 150 + 0.02x$$
$$C'(x) = 120 + 0.06x$$

Solving $R'(x) = C'(x)$ yields

$$150 + 0.02x = 120 + 0.06x$$
$$30 = 0.04x$$
$$x = 750$$

33. Given $R(x) = 80x - 0.01x^2$ and $C(x) = 130 + 90x - 0.02x^2$, then

$$R'(x) = 80 - 0.02x$$
$$C'(x) = 90 - 0.04x$$

Solving $P'(x) = R'(x) - C'(x) = 0$ yields

$$80 - 0.02x - 90 + 0.04x = 0$$
$$0.02x - 10 = 0$$
$$0.02x = 10$$
$$x = 500$$

35. Given $R(x) = 7x + 0.001x^2$ and $C(x) = 5x + 0.003x^2$, then

$$R'(x) = 7 + 0.002x$$
$$C'(x) = 5 + 0.006x$$

Solving $P'(x) = R'(x) - C'(x) = 0$ yields

$$7 + 0.002x - 5 - 0.006x = 0$$
$$-0.004x + 2 = 0$$
$$0.004x = 2$$
$$x = 500$$

37. Given $R(x) = 90x - 0.03x^2$ and $C(x) = 240 + 64x - 0.02x^2$, then

a.
$$\begin{aligned}
P'(x) &= R'(x) - C'(x) \\
&= 90 - 0.06x - (64 - 0.04x) \\
&= 90 - 0.06x - 64 + 0.04x \\
&= 26 - 0.02x
\end{aligned}$$

b. Solving $P'(x) = 0$ yields

$$\begin{aligned}
26 - 0.02x &= 0 \\
0.02x &= 26 \\
x &= 1300
\end{aligned}$$

39. If $p = 140 - 0.02x$ is the price per bicycle and x is the number of bicycles, then

$$\begin{aligned}
R(x) &= xp = x(140 - 0.02x) \\
&= 140x - 0.02x^2
\end{aligned}$$

Given $C(x) = 900 + 80x - 0.01x^2$, then

$$\begin{aligned}
R'(x) &= 140 - 0.04x \\
C'(x) &= 80 - 0.02x \\
P'(x) &= R'(x) - C'(x) \\
&= 140 - 0.04x - 80 + 0.02x \\
&= 60 - 0.02x \\
P'(20) &= 60 - 0.02(20) \\
&= 60 - 0.4 \\
&= 59.6
\end{aligned}$$

41. Let x be the number of stereos sold. If the cost per unit is $600 - 0.02x$ dollars and the selling price per unit is $p = 1000 - 0.04x$, then

a.
$$\begin{aligned}
R(x) &= xp = x(1000 - 0.04x) \\
&= 1000x - 0.04x^2
\end{aligned}$$

$$MR(x) = R'(x) = 1000 - 0.08x$$

b.
$$\begin{aligned}
C(x) &= x(600 - 0.02x) \\
&= 600x - 0.02x^2 \\
C'(x) &= 600 - 0.04x
\end{aligned}$$

$$\begin{aligned}
MP(x) = P'(x) &= R'(x) - C'(x) \\
&= 1000 - 0.08x - 600 + 0.04x \\
&= 400 - 0.04x
\end{aligned}$$

$$P'(150) = 400 - 0.04(150)$$

$$MP(150) = P'(150) = \$394$$

c.
$$\begin{aligned}
P(x) &= R(x) - C(x) \\
&= 1000x - 0.04x^2 - 600x + 0.02x^2 \\
&= 400x - 0.02x^2 \\
P(151) &= 400(151) - 0.02(151)^2 = 59{,}943.98 \\
P(150) &= 400(150) - 0.02(150)^2 = 59{,}550.00
\end{aligned}$$

Exact profit on the 151st stereo unit $= 59{,}943.98 - 59{,}550.00$
$$= \$393.98$$

43. The tax due function is defined by:

$$T(x) = \begin{cases} 0 & 0 \le x < 8000 \\ 0.16x & 8000 \le x < 20{,}000 \\ 3200 + 0.26(x - 20{,}000) & x \ge 20{,}000 \end{cases}$$

The marginal value of the function T is

$$T'(x) = \begin{cases} 0 & 0 \le x < 8000 \\ 0.16 & 8000 \le x < 20{,}000 \\ 0.26 & x \ge 20{,}000 \end{cases}$$

This derivative shows why 16% (0.16) and 26% (0.26) are called "marginal" rates.

45. The marginal cost is greater at $x = x_1$ than at $x = x_2$ because the slope of the tangent line is greater there.

SECTION 3.4 Technology Exercises

1. 26 units

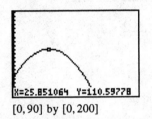

X=25.851064 Y=110.59778

[0, 90] by [0, 200]

3.

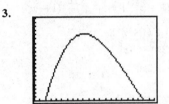

[0, 22] by [0, 2000]
a. $P'(6) > 0$, so marginal profit is positive.
b. $P'(14) < 0$, so marginal profit is negative.

5.

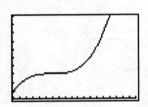

[1, 20] by [0, 50]
The marginal revenue is greater at $x = 14$ because the slope of the tangent line to the graph of $R(x)$ is greater.

SECTION 3.5 pages 144–145

1. Given $y = (x + 1)(x - 2)$, then

$$\begin{aligned} \frac{dy}{dx} &= (x + 1)\frac{d}{dx}(x - 2) + (x - 2)\frac{d}{dx}(x + 1) \\ &= (x + 1)(1) + (x - 2)(1) \\ &= 2x - 1 \end{aligned}$$

3. Given $f(x) = (5x - 3)(2x + 1)$, then

$$\begin{aligned} f'(x) &= (5x - 3)\frac{d}{dx}(2x + 1) + (2x + 1)\frac{d}{dx}(5x - 3) \\ &= (5x - 3)(2) + (2x + 1)(5) \\ &= 10x - 6 + 10x + 5 \\ &= 20x - 1 \end{aligned}$$

5. Given $y = (t^2 + 6)(1 + t^2)$, then

$$\begin{aligned} \frac{dy}{dt} &= (t^2 + 6)\frac{d}{dt}(1 + t^2) + (1 + t^2)\frac{d}{dt}(t^2 + 6) \\ &= (t^2 + 6)(2t) + (1 + t^2)(2t) \\ &= 2t^3 + 12t + 2t + 2t^3 \\ &= 4t^3 + 14t \end{aligned}$$

7. Given $f(x) = (4x - 3)x^3$, then

$$\begin{aligned} f'(x) &= (4x - 3)\frac{d}{dx}(x^3) + x^3\frac{d}{dx}(4x - 3) \\ &= (4x - 3)(3x^2) + x^3(4) \\ &= 12x^3 - 9x^2 + 4x^3 \\ &= 16x^3 - 9x^2 \end{aligned}$$

9. Given $g(x) = (4x + 1)(1 + \frac{1}{x})$, then

$$g'(x) = (4x + 1)\frac{d}{dx}(1 + \frac{1}{x}) + (1 + \frac{1}{x})\frac{d}{dx}(4x + 1)$$

$$= (4x + 1)(-x^{-2}) + (1 + \frac{1}{x})(4)$$

$$= -\left(\frac{4x + 1}{x^2}\right) + \frac{4x^2 + 4x}{x^2}$$

$$= \frac{-4x - 1 + 4x^2 + 4x}{x^2}$$

$$= \frac{4x^2 - 1}{x^2}$$

11. Given $y = (x^3 + 2)(1 - x)$, then

$$\frac{dy}{dx} = (x^3 + 2)\frac{d}{dx}(1 - x) + (1 - x)\frac{d}{dx}(x^3 + 2)$$

$$= (x^3 + 2)(-1) + (1 - x)(3x^2)$$

$$= -x^3 - 2 + 3x^2 - 3x^3$$

$$= -4x^3 + 3x^2 - 2$$

13. Given $y = (1 - x^3)(1 + x^2)$, then

$$\frac{dy}{dx} = (1 - x^3)\frac{d}{dx}(1 + x^2) + (1 + x^2)\frac{d}{dx}(1 - x^3)$$

$$= (1 - x^3)(2x) + (1 + x^2)(-3x^2)$$

$$= 2x - 2x^4 - 3x^2 - 3x^4$$

$$= -5x^4 - 3x^2 + 2x$$

15. Given $y = \frac{x}{1+x}$, then

$$\frac{dy}{dx} = \frac{(1 + x)\frac{d}{dx}(x) - x\frac{d}{dx}(1 + x)}{(1 + x)^2}$$

$$= \frac{(1 + x)(1) - x(1)}{(1 + x)^2}$$

$$= \frac{1}{(1 + x)^2}$$

17. Given $f(x) = \frac{2x}{3x+1}$, then

$$f'(x) = \frac{(3x + 1)\frac{d}{dx}(2x) - 2x\frac{d}{dx}(3x + 1)}{(3x + 1)^2}$$

$$= \frac{(3x + 1)(2) - 2x(3)}{(3x + 1)^2}$$

$$= \frac{6x + 2 - 6x}{(3x + 1)^2}$$

$$= \frac{2}{(3x + 1)^2}$$

19. Given $f(t) = \frac{1-t}{t-1}$, then

$$f'(t) = \frac{(t - 1)\frac{d}{dt}(1 - t) - (1 - t)\frac{d}{dt}(t - 1)}{(t - 1)^2}$$

$$= \frac{(t - 1)(-1) - (1 - t)(1)}{(t - 1)^2}$$

$$= \frac{-t + 1 - 1 + t}{(t - 1)^2}$$

$$= 0$$

21. Given $s(t) = \frac{4t^2+t}{1+3t}$, then

$$s'(t) = \frac{(1 + 3t)\frac{d}{dt}(4t^2 + t) - (4t^2 + t)\frac{d}{dt}(1 + 3t)}{(1 + 3t)^2}$$

$$= \frac{(1 + 3t)(8t + 1) - (4t^2 + t)(3)}{(1 + 3t)^2}$$

$$= \frac{1 + 11t + 24t^2 - 12t^2 - 3t}{(1 + 3t)^2}$$

$$= \frac{12t^2 + 8t + 1}{(1 + 3t)^2}$$

$$= \frac{(2t + 1)(6t + 1)}{(1 + 3t)^2}$$

23.   Given $y = \frac{x^2+5x-3}{x+4}$, then

$$\frac{dy}{dx} = \frac{(x+4)\frac{d}{dx}(x^2+5x-3) - (x^2+5x-3)\frac{d}{dx}(x+4)}{(x+4)^2}$$

$$= \frac{(x+4)(2x+5) - (x^2+5x-3)(1)}{(x+4)^2}$$

$$= \frac{2x^2+13x+20-x^2-5x+3}{(x+4)^2}$$

$$= \frac{x^2+8x+23}{(x+4)^2}$$

25.   Given $y = \frac{4+2x}{x^{3/2}}$, then

$$\frac{dy}{dx} = \frac{x^{3/2}\frac{d}{dx}(4+2x) - (4+2x)\frac{d}{dx}(x^{3/2})}{(x^{3/2})^2}$$

$$= \frac{x^{3/2}(2) - (4+2x)\left(\frac{3}{2}x^{1/2}\right)}{x^3}$$

$$= \frac{2x^{3/2} - 6x^{1/2} - 3x^{3/2}}{x^3}$$

$$= \frac{-x^{3/2} - 6x^{1/2}}{x^3}$$

$$= \frac{-x^{1/2}(x+6)}{x^3}$$

$$= \frac{-(x+6)}{x^{5/2}}$$

27.   Given $y = 1 - x - \frac{1}{x^3} = 1 - x - x^{-3}$, then

$$\frac{dy}{dx} = -1 + 3x^{-4}$$

29.   Given $f(x) = \frac{1}{x} + 7x - \frac{x^2}{3} = x^{-1} + 7x - \frac{x^2}{3}$, then

$$f'(x) = -\frac{1}{x^2} + 7 - \frac{2}{3}x$$

31.   Given $f(t) = (t^2-8)(t^3+1)$, then

$$f'(t) = (t^2-8)\frac{d}{dt}(t^3+1) + (t^3+1)\frac{d}{dt}(t^2-8) \qquad \text{product rule}$$

$$= (t^2-8)(3t^2) + (t^3+1)(2t)$$

$$= 3t^4 - 24t^2 + 2t^4 + 2t$$

$$= 5t^4 - 24t^2 + 2t$$

33. Given $s = \frac{t^2+3t+5}{1-t}$, then

$$\frac{ds}{dt} = \frac{(1-t)\frac{d}{dt}(t^2+3t+5) - (t^2+3t+5)\frac{d}{dt}(1-t)}{(1-t)^2} \qquad \text{quotient rule}$$

$$= \frac{(1-t)(2t+3) - (t^2+3t+5)(-1)}{(1-t)^2}$$

$$= \frac{-2t^2 - t + 3 + t^2 + 3t + 5}{(1-t)^2}$$

$$= \frac{-t^2 + 2t + 8}{(1-t)^2}$$

$$= \frac{-(t^2 - 2t - 8)}{(1-t)^2}$$

$$= \frac{-(t-4)(t+2)}{(1-t)^2}$$

35. Given $f(x) = (x^2 - 4)(1 + 2x)$ and the point $(-1, 3)$, then

$$f'(x) = (x^2 - 4)(2) + (2x)(1 + 2x)$$

and $f'(-1) = [(-1)^2 - 4](2) + [2(-1)][1 + 2(-1)] = (-3)(2) + (-2)(-1) = -4$

$m_{\tan} = -4$

37. Given $y = \frac{x^2-4}{x+8}$ and the point $(4, 1)$, then

$$\frac{dy}{dx} = \frac{(x+8)(2x) - (x^2 - 4)(1)}{(x+8)^2}$$

and $\left.\frac{dy}{dx}\right|_{x=4} = \frac{(4+8)(2)(4) - [(4)^2 - 4]}{(4+8)^2}$

$$= \frac{96 - 12}{(12)^2}$$

$$m_{\tan} = \frac{7}{12}$$

39. Given $y = \frac{x^2+3}{x+1}$ and $x = 1$, then

$$\frac{dy}{dx} = \frac{(x+1)(2x) - (x^2+3)(1)}{(x+1)^2}$$

and $\left.\frac{dy}{dx}\right|_{x=1} = \frac{(1+1)(2) - (1+3)}{(1+1)^2}$

$$= \frac{4-4}{4}$$

$$= 0$$

41. Given $y = (1-x)(1-x^2)$ and $x = 2$, then

$$\frac{dy}{dx} = (1-x)(-2x) + (1-x^2)(-1)$$

and $\left.\frac{dy}{dx}\right|_{x=2} = (1-2)(-2)(2) + (1-2^2)(-1)$

$$= 4 + 3$$

$$= 7$$

43. If the distance function is $s = \frac{4t^2+6}{t+1}$, then the velocity is

$$\frac{ds}{dt} = \frac{(t+1)(8t) - (4t^2+6)(1)}{(t+1)^2}$$

and $\left.\frac{ds}{dt}\right|_{t=9} = \frac{(9+1)(8)(9) - [4(9)^2 + 6]}{(9+1)^2}$

$$= \frac{720 - 330}{100}$$

$$= \frac{390}{100}$$

$$= 3.9 \text{ inches per second}$$

45. If the profit function is $P(x) = \frac{10x^2 - 50x}{x+1}$, then

a. $P(1) = \frac{10(1)^2 - 50(1)}{1+1}$

$= \frac{10 - 50}{2}$

$= -20$ The company loses \$20 if it sells only one VCR.

b. $P(5) = \frac{10(5)^2 - 50(5)}{5+1}$

$= \frac{250 - 250}{6}$

$= 0$

c. $P(10) = \frac{10(10)^2 - 50(10)}{10+1}$

$= \frac{1000 - 500}{11}$

$= 45.45$

d. $P'(x) = \frac{(x+1)(20x - 50) - (10x^2 - 50x)(1)}{(x+1)^2}$

$= \frac{20x^2 - 50x + 20x - 50 - 10x^2 + 50x}{(x+1)^2}$

$MP(x) = \frac{10x^2 + 20x - 50}{(x+1)^2}$

47. **a.** $A(0) = 110 - \frac{90(0)}{0+1} = 110$ pounds

$A(2) = 110 - \frac{90(2)}{2+1} = 50$ pounds

$A(5) = 110 - \frac{90(5)}{5+1} = 35$ pounds

b. $A'(t) = \frac{(t+1)(-90) - (-90t)(1)}{(t+1)^2} = \frac{-90t - 90 + 90t}{(t+1)^2} = \frac{-90}{(t+1)^2}$

$A'(2) = \frac{-90}{(2+1)^2} = -10$ pounds per year

c. The fact that the rate of change is negative means that the amount of pollutants is decreasing.

49. Using the quotient rule on $y = \frac{x^2}{9}$ results in the following:

$\frac{dy}{dx} = \frac{9(2x) - x^2(0)}{9^2}$

$= \frac{18x - 0}{9^2}$

$= \frac{18}{81}x$

$= \frac{2}{9}x$

51. It is easier to differentiate $\frac{1}{x^2}$ in the form x^{-2} than as a quotient because x^{-2} is a simple x^n form whose derivative is nx^{n-1}. The quotient rule applied to $\frac{1}{x^2}$ results in a more complicated form, part of which is zero when the derivative of 1 is computed.

SECTION 3.5 Technology Exercises

1.

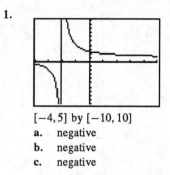

$[-4, 5]$ by $[-10, 10]$
a. negative
b. negative
c. negative

3. $f'(x) = 2x(2x) + (x^2 - 1)(2) = 6x^2 - 2$
$f'(1) = 4$

$[-3.5, 5.5]$ by $[-1, 5]$

SECTION 3.6 pages 151–152

1. Given $y = (x^2 + 3)^5$, then

$$\frac{dy}{dx} = 5(x^2 + 3)^4(2x)$$
$$= 10x(x^2 + 3)^4$$

3. Given $y = (3x)^5$, then

$$\frac{dy}{dx} = 5(3x)^4(3)$$
$$= 15(3x)^4$$

5. Given $y = (3x + 4)^{1/3}$, then

$$\frac{dy}{dx} = \frac{1}{3}(3x + 4)^{-2/3}(3)$$
$$= (3x + 4)^{-2/3}$$
$$= \frac{1}{(3x + 4)^{2/3}}$$

7. Given $s = (1 - t^4)^{-6}$, then

$$\frac{ds}{dt} = -6(1 - t^4)^{-7}(-4t^3)$$
$$= \frac{24t^3}{(1 - t^4)^7}$$

9. Given $y = \sqrt{4x + 1} = (4x + 1)^{1/2}$, then

$$\frac{dy}{dx} = \frac{1}{2}(4x + 1)^{-1/2}(4)$$
$$= \frac{2}{(4x + 1)^{1/2}}$$

11. Given $f(x) = (x^4 + x^2 + 1)^4$, then

$$f'(x) = 4(x^4 + x^2 + 1)^3(4x^3 + 2x)$$
$$= 8x(2x^2 + 1)(x^4 + x^2 + 1)^3$$

13. Given $f(t) = \frac{1}{(t^2+1)^6} = (t^2 + 1)^{-6}$, then

$$f'(t) = -6(t^2 + 1)^{-7}(2t)$$
$$= -\frac{12t}{(t^2 + 1)^7}$$

15. Given $y = \frac{1}{\sqrt{6x+5}} = (6x + 5)^{-1/2}$, then

$$\frac{dy}{dx} = -\frac{1}{2}(6x + 5)^{-3/2}(6)$$
$$= -\frac{3}{(6x + 5)^{3/2}}$$

17. Given $y = x^2(5x - 2)^4$, then

$$\frac{dy}{dx} = x^2[4(5x - 2)^3(5)] + (5x - 2)^4(2x) \quad \text{product rule}$$
$$= 2x(5x - 2)^3(10x + 5x - 2)$$
$$= 2x(5x - 2)^3(15x - 2)$$

19. Given $y = (x + 3)(2x + 1)^3$, then

$$\frac{dy}{dx} = (x + 3)[3(2x + 1)^2(2)] + (2x + 1)^3(1) \quad \text{product rule}$$
$$= (2x + 1)^2(6x + 18 + 2x + 1)$$
$$= (2x + 1)^2(8x + 19)$$

21. Given $y = (x^2 + 1)^4(x - 2)$, then

$$\frac{dy}{dx} = (x^2 + 1)^4(1) + (x - 2)4(x^2 + 1)^3(2x) \qquad \text{product rule}$$
$$= (x^2 + 1)^3(x^2 + 1 + 8x^2 - 16x)$$
$$= x^2 + 1)^3(9x^2 - 16x + 1)$$

23. Given $y = (5x - 2)^2(x^2 + 7)^3$, then

$$\frac{dy}{dx} = (5x - 2)^2(3)(x^2 + 7)^2(2x) + (x^2 + 7)^3(2)(5x - 2)(5) \qquad \text{product rule}$$
$$= 2(5x - 2)(x^2 + 7)^2[3x(5x - 2) + 5x^2 + 35]$$
$$= 2(5x - 2)(x^2 + 7)^2(20x^2 - 6x + 35)$$

25. Given $y = (2t + 3)^4(t - 7)^3$, then

$$\frac{dy}{dt} = (2t + 3)^4(3)(t - 7)^2(1) + (t - 7)^3(4)(2t + 3)^3(2) \qquad \text{product rule}$$
$$= (2t + 3)^3(t - 7)^2(6t + 9 + 8t - 56)$$
$$= (2t + 3)^3(t - 7)^2(14t - 47)$$

27. Given $y = \frac{(x+4)^3}{x+1}$, then

$$\frac{dy}{dx} = \frac{(x + 1)(3)(x + 4)^2(1) - (x + 4)^3(1)}{(x + 1)^2} \qquad \text{quotient rule}$$
$$= \frac{(x + 4)^2(3x + 3 - x - 4)}{(x + 1)^2}$$
$$= \frac{(x + 4)^2(2x - 1)}{(x + 1)^2}$$

29. Given $y = \frac{(2t+3)^4}{t-2}$, then

$$\frac{dy}{dt} = \frac{(t - 2)(4)(2t + 3)^3(2) - (2t + 3)^4(1)}{(t - 2)^2} \qquad \text{quotient rule}$$
$$= \frac{(2t + 3)^3(8t - 16 - 2t - 3)}{(t - 2)^2}$$
$$= \frac{(2t + 3)^3(6t - 19)}{(t - 2)^2}$$

31. Given $y = (2x - 5)(2x + 1)^{3/2}$, then

$$\frac{dy}{dx} = (2x - 5)\left(\frac{3}{2}\right)(2x + 1)^{1/2}(2) + (2x + 1)^{3/2}(2) \qquad \text{product rule}$$
$$= (2x + 1)^{1/2}(6x - 15 + 4x + 2)$$
$$= (2x + 1)^{1/2}(10x - 13)$$

33. Given $y = 2x\sqrt{2x + 1} = 2x(2x + 1)^{1/2}$, then

$$\frac{dy}{dx} = 2x\left(\frac{1}{2}\right)(2x + 1)^{-1/2}(2) + (2x + 1)^{1/2}(2) \qquad \text{product rule}$$
$$= 2(2x + 1)^{-1/2}(x + 2x + 1)$$
$$= \frac{2(3x + 1)}{(2x + 1)^{1/2}}$$

35.   Given $y = \left(\dfrac{x-1}{x+1}\right)^4$, then

$$\frac{dy}{dx} = 4\left(\frac{x-1}{x+1}\right)^3 \left[\frac{(x+1)(1)-(x-1)(1)}{(x+1)^2}\right]$$

$$= 4\left(\frac{x-1}{x+1}\right)^3 \left[\frac{\cancel{x}+1-\cancel{x}+1}{(x+1)^2}\right]$$

$$= \frac{4(x-1)^3}{(x+1)^3}\left[\frac{2}{(x+1)^2}\right]$$

$$= \frac{8(x-1)^3}{(x+1)^5}$$

37.   Given $y = \sqrt{\dfrac{2x+1}{x-1}} = \left(\dfrac{2x+1}{x-1}\right)^{1/2}$, then

$$\frac{dy}{dx} = \frac{1}{2}\left(\frac{2x+1}{x-1}\right)^{-1/2}\left[\frac{(x-1)(2)-(2x+1)(1)}{(x-1)^2}\right]$$

$$= \frac{1}{2}\left(\frac{2x+1}{x-1}\right)^{-1/2}\left[\frac{\cancel{2x}-2-\cancel{2x}-1}{(x-1)^2}\right]$$

$$= \frac{1}{2}\left(\frac{2x+1}{x-1}\right)^{-1/2}\left[\frac{-3}{(x-1)^2}\right]$$

$$= \frac{-3}{2(2x+1)^{1/2}(x-1)^{3/2}}$$

39.   Given $f(x) = (x^2 - 3x + 1)^4$ and the point $(2, 1)$, then

$$f'(x) = 4(x^2 - 3x + 1)^3(2x - 3)$$

and $f'(2) = 4(4 - 6 + 1)^3(4 - 3)$

$$= 4(-1)^3(1)$$

$$m_{\tan} = -4$$

41.   Given $y = \sqrt{4x + 1} = (4x + 1)^{1/2}$ and the point $(2, 3)$, then

$$\frac{dy}{dx} = \frac{1}{2}(4x+1)^{-1/2}(4)$$

$$= \frac{2}{\sqrt{4x+1}}$$

and $\left.\dfrac{dy}{dx}\right|_{x=2} = \dfrac{2}{\sqrt{8+1}}$

$$= \frac{2}{\sqrt{9}}$$

$$m_{\tan} = \frac{2}{3}$$

43.   Given $y = \sqrt[3]{6x - 4} = (6x - 4)^{1/3}$ and $x = 2$, then

$$\frac{dy}{dx} = \frac{1}{3}(6x-4)^{-2/3}(6)$$

$$= \frac{2}{(6x-4)^{2/3}}$$

and $\left.\dfrac{dy}{dx}\right|_{x=2} = \dfrac{2}{(12-4)^{2/3}}$

$$= \frac{2}{8^{2/3}}$$

$$= \frac{2}{4}$$

$$= \frac{1}{2}$$

45.   If the profit function is $P(x) = 100(x^2 - 1)^{1/2}$, then marginal profit is

$$P'(x) = \frac{100}{\cancel{2}}(x^2 - 1)^{-1/2}\cancel{(2x)}$$

$$MP(x) = \frac{100x}{(x^2-1)^{1/2}}$$

47. Given the percent of relative concentration $p = (10{,}000 - x^3)^{1/2}$, then

a.
$$p(0) = 100$$
$$p(10) = \sqrt{10{,}000 - 1000}$$
$$= \sqrt{9000}$$
$$\approx 94.87$$
$$p(20) = \sqrt{10{,}000 - 8000}$$
$$= \sqrt{2000}$$
$$\approx 44.72$$

b.
$$p'(x) = \frac{1}{2}(10{,}000 - x^3)^{-1/2}(-3x^2)$$
$$= \frac{-3x^2}{2\sqrt{10{,}000 - x^3}}$$
$$p'(0) = 0$$
$$p'(10) = \frac{-3(10)^2}{2\sqrt{9000}}$$
$$= \frac{-150}{\sqrt{9000}}$$
$$\approx -1.58$$
$$p'(20) = \frac{-3(20)^2}{2\sqrt{2000}}$$
$$= \frac{-600}{\sqrt{2000}}$$
$$\approx -13.42$$

49. The derivative of a function $y = f(x)$ is the rate of change of y with respect to x. The chain rule is needed for the composite function because y will not depend directly on x; hence, y's rate of change is not directly connected to the change in x. For example, $y = f(x) = (x^2 + 1)^3$ is the composite of the two functions $u = x^2 + 1$ and $y = u^3$. The value of y changes directly with respect to u: $\frac{dy}{du}$ = rate of change of y with respect to u; but the value of u changes directly with respect to x: $\frac{du}{dx}$ = rate of change of u with respect to x. Thus, the derivative of y with respect to x, $\frac{dy}{dx}$, must be the result of the change in y with respect to u, $\frac{dy}{du}$, and the change in u with respect to x, $\frac{du}{dx}$.

Specifically, $\frac{dy}{du} = 3u^2$ and $\frac{du}{dx} = 2x$. If $x = 1$, then $u = 2$ and $\left.\frac{dy}{du}\right|_{u=2} = 12$ and $\left.\frac{du}{dx}\right|_{x=1} = 2$. Thus, at $x = 1$, a 1-unit change in x causes a 2-unit change in u. Also, at $u = 2$, a 1-unit change in u causes a 12-unit change in y. Therefore, at $x = 1$, the 2-unit change in u causes an approximate 24-unit change in y, i.e.,

$$\frac{dy}{dx} = \frac{dy}{du}\frac{du}{dx} = (12)(2) = 24$$

51. Given $y = (x + 1)^2(2x - 3)^5(x^2 + 1)^8$, then, using a repeated product rule,

$$\frac{dy}{dx} = (x + 1)^2(2x - 3)^5 8(x^2 + 1)^7(2x) + (x + 1)^2(5)(2x - 3)^4(2)(x^2 + 1)^8 + 2(x + 1)(1)(2x - 3)^5(x^2 + 1)^8$$
$$= 2(x + 1)(2x - 3)^4(x^2 + 1)^7\left[8x(x + 1)(2x - 3) + 5(x + 1)(x^2 + 1) + (2x - 3)(x^2 + 1)\right]$$
$$= 2(x + 1)(2x - 3)^4(x^2 + 1)^7(8x^3 - 8x^2 - 24x + 5x^3 + 5x^2 + 5x + 5 + 2x^3 - 3x^2 + 2x - 3)$$
$$= 2(x + 1)(2x - 3)^4(x^2 + 1)^7(23x^3 - 6x^2 - 17x + 2)$$

53. Given $y = \dfrac{(x^2+3)^5(x+1)^2}{2x+7}$, then using the quotient rule yields

$$\frac{dy}{dx} = \frac{(2x+7)\left[(x^2+3)^5(2)(x+1)(1) + (x+1)^2(5)(x^2+3)^4(2x)\right] - (x^2+3)^5(x+1)^2(2)}{(2x+7)^2}$$

$$= \frac{(x^2+3)^4(x+1)\left[2(2x+7)(x^2+3) + 10x(x+1)(2x+7) - 2(x^2+3)(x+1)\right]}{(2x+7)^2}$$

$$= \frac{(x^2+3)^4(x+1)(4x^3+14x^2+12x+42+20x^3+90x^2+70x-2x^3-2x^2-6x-6)}{(2x+7)^2}$$

$$= \frac{(x^2+3)^4(x+1)(22x^3+102x^2+76x+36)}{(2x+7)^2}$$

$$= \frac{2(x^2+3)^4(x+1)(11x^3+51x^2+38x+18)}{(2x+7)^2}$$

SECTION 3.6 Technology Exercises

1. positive

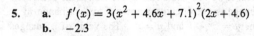

[0, 25] by [0, 300]

3.

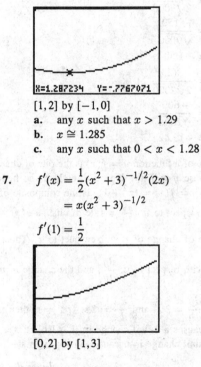

X=1.287234　Y=-.7767071

[1, 2] by [−1, 0]

a. any x such that $x > 1.29$

b. $x \cong 1.285$

c. any x such that $0 < x < 1.28$

5.　**a.**　$f'(x) = 3(x^2+4.6x+7.1)^2(2x+4.6)$

b.　-2.3

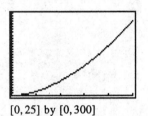

Root
X=-2.3　　Y=0

[−5, 0] by [−10, 10]

7.　$f'(x) = \dfrac{1}{2}(x^2+3)^{-1/2}(2x)$

$\qquad = x(x^2+3)^{-1/2}$

$f'(1) = \dfrac{1}{2}$

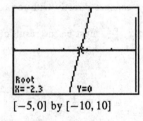

[0, 2] by [1, 3]

SECTION 3.7 pages 157–158

1.　If $f(x) = x^4 - 10x^2$, then

$f'(x) = 4x^3 - 20x$

$f''(x) = 12x^2 - 20$

3.　If $y = x^3 - 7x^2 + 100x + 1$, then

$y' = 3x^2 - 14x + 100$

$y'' = 6x - 14$

$y''' = 6$

5.　If $f(x) = x^4$, then

$f'(x) = 4x^3$

$f''(x) = 12x^2$

$f'''(x) = 24x$

$f^4(x) = 24$

7.　If $y = x^{5/3}$, then

$D_x y = \dfrac{5}{3}x^{2/3}$

$D_x^2 y = \dfrac{10}{9}x^{-1/3}$

$D_x^3 y = -\dfrac{10}{27}x^{-4/3}$

9. If $y = 9x$, then

$$y' = 9$$
$$y'' = 0$$

11. If $y = \frac{x}{1+x}$, then

$$y' = \frac{(1+x)(1) - x(1)}{(1+x)^2} = \frac{1 + \cancel{x} - \cancel{x}}{(1+x)^2} = (1+x)^{-2}$$
$$y'' = \frac{-2}{(1+x)^3}$$

13. If $y = (3x-1)^5$, then

$$\frac{dy}{dx} = 5(3x-1)^4(3) = 15(3x-1)^4$$
$$\frac{d^2y}{dx^2} = 60(3x-1)^3(3)$$
$$= 180(3x-1)^3$$

15. If $s = -16t^2 + 96t + 108$, then

$$\frac{ds}{dt} = -32t + 96$$
$$\frac{d^2s}{dt^2} = -32$$

17. If $y = \frac{10}{t^4} = 10t^{-4}$, then

$$\frac{dy}{dt} = -40t^{-5}$$
$$\frac{d^2y}{dt^2} = 200t^{-6}$$
$$= \frac{200}{t^6}$$

19. If $f(x) = x^3 - 5x^2 + x - 3$, then

$$f'(x) = 3x^2 - 10x + 1$$
$$f''(x) = 6x - 10$$
$$\text{and } f''(4) = 24 - 10$$
$$= 14$$

21. If $f(x) = \frac{1}{x} = x^{-1}$, then

$$f'(x) = -x^{-2}$$
$$f''(x) = 2x^{-3} = \frac{2}{x^3}$$
$$\text{and } f''(4) = \frac{2}{4^3} = \frac{2}{64}$$
$$= \frac{1}{32}$$

23. If $f(x) = 10\sqrt{x} = 10x^{1/2}$, then

$$f'(x) = 5x^{-1/2}$$
$$f''(x) = -\frac{5}{2}x^{-3/2} = -\frac{5}{2x^{3/2}}$$
$$\text{and } f''(4) = -\frac{5}{2\left(4^{3/2}\right)} = -\frac{5}{2(8)}$$
$$= -\frac{5}{16}$$

25. If $f(x) = x^3 - 7x^2$, then

$$f'(x) = 3x^2 - 14x$$
$$f''(x) = 6x - 14$$

27. If $f(t) = \sqrt{8t} = (8t)^{1/2} = \sqrt{8}t^{1/2}$, then

$$f'(t) = \frac{\sqrt{8}}{2}t^{-1/2}$$
$$f''(t) = -\frac{\sqrt{8}}{4}t^{-3/2}$$
$$f''(2) = -\frac{\sqrt{8}}{4} \cdot \frac{1}{2^{3/2}} = -\frac{\sqrt{8}}{4}\frac{1}{\sqrt{8}}$$
$$= -\frac{1}{4}$$

$t = 2$

29. If the cost function is $C(x) = 300 + 40x - 0.06x^2$, then marginal cost is

$$C'(x) = 40 - 0.12x$$
$$\text{and } C''(x) = -0.12$$
$$C''(10) = -0.12$$

31. Given the revenue function $R(x) = 20x - \frac{20}{x} = 20x - 20x^{-1}$, then marginal revenue is

$$R'(x) = 20 + 20x^{-2}$$
$$\text{and } R''(x) = -40x^{-3} = -\frac{40}{x^3}$$
$$R''(20) = -\frac{40}{(20)^3} = -\frac{40}{8000}$$
$$= -\frac{1}{200}$$

33. Given the distance function $s = -16t^2 + 80t$, then the speed is $\frac{ds}{dt} = -32t + 80$

and the acceleration is

$$a = \frac{d^2s}{dt^2} = -32$$

35. If the distance function is $s = t^2 - 2t + \frac{4}{t}$, then

a. $v = \frac{ds}{dt} = 2t - 2 - \frac{4}{t^2}$

b. $a = \frac{d^2s}{dt^2} = 2 + \frac{8}{t^3}$

c. $a(1) = 2 + \frac{8}{1^3}$
$$= 10$$

d. $a(2) = 2 + \frac{8}{2^3}$
$$= 3$$

37. Given $f(x) = \frac{x^3+1}{x^2+1}$, then

$$f'(x) = \frac{(x^2+1)(3x^2) - (x^3+1)(2x)}{(x^2+1)^2},$$
$$= \frac{3x^4 + 3x^2 - 2x^4 - 2x}{(x^2+1)^2}$$
$$= \frac{x^4 + 3x^2 - 2x}{(x^2+1)^2}$$

$$\text{and } f''(x) = \frac{(x^2+1)^2(4x^3+6x-2) - (x^4+3x^2-2x)(2)(x^2+1)(2x)}{(x^2+1)^4}$$
$$= \frac{2(x^2+1)\left[(x^2+1)(2x^3+3x-1) - (x^4+3x^2-2x)(2x)\right]}{(x^2+1)^4}$$
$$= \frac{2(2x^5 + 3x^3 - x^2 + 2x^3 + 3x - 1 - 2x^5 - 6x^3 + 4x^2)}{(x^2+1)^3}$$
$$= \frac{2(-x^3 + 3x^2 + 3x - 1)}{(x^2+1)^3}$$

39. Given $y = 5x\sqrt{1 + x^2} = 5x(1 + x^2)^{1/2}$, then

$$\frac{dy}{dx} = 5x\left(\frac{1}{2}\right)(1 + x^2)^{-1/2}(2x) + 5(1 + x^2)^{1/2}$$
$$= 5(1 + x^2)^{-1/2}(x^2 + 1 + x^2)$$
$$= 5(1 + x^2)^{-1/2}(2x^2 + 1)$$

and $\frac{d^2y}{dx^2} = 5\left[(1 + x^2)^{-1/2}(4x) + (2x^2 + 1)(-\frac{1}{2})(1 + x^2)^{-3/2}(2x)\right]$

$$= 5(1 + x^2)^{-3/2}\left[(1 + x^2)(4x) - x(2x^2 + 1)\right]$$
$$= 5(1 + x^2)^{-3/2}(4x + 4x^3 - 2x^3 - x)$$
$$= \frac{5(2x^3 + 3x)}{(1 + x^2)^{3/2}}$$
$$= \frac{5x(2x^2 + 3)}{(1 + x^2)^{3/2}}$$

41. Given the distance function $s = -2.65t^2 + 106t$, then

   a. $\frac{ds}{dt} = -5.3t + 106$

   b. $a = \frac{d^2s}{dt^2} = -5.3$ feet per second per second

   c. Yes, since acceleration is the rate of change of velocity, the velocity is decreasing more slowly at -5.3 feet per second per second than the velocity on earth, which would be -32 feet per second per second.

   d. Solve for $s = 0$

   $-2.65t^2 + 106t = 0$
   $t(-2.65t + 106) = 0$

   $t = 0 \qquad t = \frac{106}{2.65} = 40$

   leaving   arriving back on the ground $t = 40$ seconds

43. $P''(x)$ is the rate of change of the marginal profit.

45. It is the derivative of $f'(x)$, namely $f''(x)$.

47. The second derivative of $g(x)$ is more difficult to determine because in differentiating the first derivative, the product rule must be used.

SECTION 3.7 Technology Exercises

1.

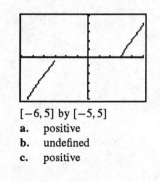

[−6, 5] by [−5, 5]
   a. positive
   b. undefined
   c. positive

3. **a.** $f'(x) = 18x^2 + 80x + 81$
      $f''(x) = 36x + 80$
   b. $x > -2.22$

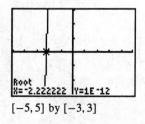

[−5, 5] by [−3, 3]

SECTION 3.8 pages 163–165

1. Given $x^2 + y^2 = 3$, then

$$2x + 2y\frac{dy}{dx} = 0$$

and solving for $\frac{dy}{dx}$ yields

$$\frac{dy}{dx} = -\frac{x}{y}$$

3. Given $y^3 - x^2 = 6x$, then

$$3y^2\frac{dy}{dx} - 2x = 6$$

and solving for $\frac{dy}{dx}$ yields

$$\frac{dy}{dx} = \frac{2x + 6}{3y^2}$$

5. Given $x^3 + y^3 = 9$, then

$$3x^2 + 3y^2\frac{dy}{dx} = 0$$

and solving for $\frac{dy}{dx}$ yields

$$\frac{dy}{dx} = -\frac{x^2}{y^2}$$

7. Given $y^2 = x^2 + 7x - 4$, then

$$2y\frac{dy}{dx} = 2x + 7$$

and solving for $\frac{dy}{dx}$ yields

$$\frac{dy}{dx} = \frac{2x + 7}{2y}$$

9. Given $x^2 + y^2 - y^3 - x = 0$, then

$$2x + 2y\frac{dy}{dx} - 3y^2\frac{dy}{dx} - 1 = 0$$

and solving for $\frac{dy}{dx}$ yields

$$(2y - 3y^2)\frac{dy}{dx} = 1 - 2x$$
$$\frac{dy}{dx} = \frac{1 - 2x}{2y - 3y^2}$$

11. Given $2x^{3/2} + 2y^{3/2} = 15$, then

$$3x^{1/2} + 3y^{1/2}\frac{dy}{dx} = 0$$

and solving for $\frac{dy}{dx}$ yields

$$\frac{dy}{dx} = -\frac{x^{1/2}}{y^{1/2}}$$
$$\frac{dy}{dx} = -\left(\frac{x}{y}\right)^{1/2}$$

13. Given $x^2y^2 - x - 3y = 0$, then

$$x^2\left(2y\frac{dy}{dx}\right) + y^2(2x) - 1 - 3\frac{dy}{dx} = 0$$

and solving for $\frac{dy}{dx}$ yields

$$(2x^2y - 3)\frac{dy}{dx} = 1 - 2xy^2$$
$$\frac{dy}{dx} = \frac{1 - 2xy^2}{2x^2y - 3}$$

15. Given $xy^3 + 5y = 3x$, then

$$x\left(3y^2\frac{dy}{dx}\right) + y^3(1) + 5\frac{dy}{dx} = 3$$

and solving for $\frac{dy}{dx}$ yields

$$(3xy^2 + 5)\frac{dy}{dx} = 3 - y^3$$
$$\frac{dy}{dx} = \frac{3 - y^3}{3xy^2 + 5}$$

17. Given $8xy + x = 9$, then

$$8\left[x\frac{dy}{dx} + y(1)\right] + 1 = 0$$

and solving for $\frac{dy}{dx}$ yields

$$x\frac{dy}{dx} + y = -\frac{1}{8}$$

$$\frac{dy}{dx} = \frac{-\frac{1}{8} - y}{x}$$

$$= \frac{-(1 + 8y)}{8x}$$

19. Given $x^2 + y^3 - y = 7$ and the point $(1, 2)$, then

$$2x + 3y^2\frac{dy}{dx} - \frac{dy}{dx} = 0$$

$$(3y^2 - 1)\frac{dy}{dx} = -2x$$

$$\frac{dy}{dx} = \frac{-2x}{3y^2 - 1}$$

$$= \frac{2x}{1 - 3y^2}$$

and $\left.\dfrac{dy}{dx}\right|_{\substack{x=1 \\ y=2}} = \dfrac{2(1)}{1 - 3(2)^2}$

$$= -\frac{2}{11}$$

21. Given $10xy + x + 45 = 0$ and the point $(5, -1)$, then

$$10x\frac{dy}{dx} + 10y(1) + 1 + 0 = 0$$

$$\frac{dy}{dx} = -\frac{10y + 1}{10x}$$

and $\left.\dfrac{dy}{dx}\right|_{\substack{x=5 \\ y=-1}} = \dfrac{-[10(-1) + 1]}{10(5)}$

$$= \frac{-(-9)}{50}$$

$$= \frac{9}{50}$$

23. Given $x^2 + y^2 = 25$ and the point $(3, 4)$, then

$$2x + 2y\frac{dy}{dx} = 0$$

$$\frac{dy}{dx} = -\frac{x}{y}$$

and $\left.\dfrac{dy}{dx}\right|_{\substack{x=3 \\ y=4}} = -\dfrac{3}{4}$

Thus, the equation of the tangent line is $y - 4 = -\dfrac{3}{4}(x - 3)$

or $3x + 4y - 25 = 0$

25. **a.** Given $9y^2 = 6x^3 - x^4$, then

$$18y\frac{dy}{dx} = 18x^2 - 4x^3$$

and solving for $\frac{dy}{dx}$ yields

$$\frac{dy}{dx} = \frac{18x^2 - 4x^3}{18y}$$

b. $\dfrac{dy}{dx} = 0 = \dfrac{18x^2 - 4x^3}{18y}$

$$18x^2 - 4x^3 = 0$$

$$x^2(18 - 4x) = 0$$

$$x = 0 \qquad x = \frac{18}{4} = \frac{9}{2}$$

27. Given $x^{2/3} + y^{2/3} = 5$,

a. $8^{2/3} + 1^{2/3} = (2)^2 + 1 = 5$, so $(8, 1)$ is on the graph.

$(-1)^{2/3} + 8^{2/3} = 1 + (2)^2 = 5$, so $(-1, 8)$ is on the graph.

b. $\frac{2}{3}x^{-1/3} + \frac{2}{3}y^{-1/3}\frac{dy}{dx} = 0$, and solving for $\frac{dy}{dx}$ yields

$$\frac{2}{3}y^{-1/3}\frac{dy}{dx} = -\frac{2}{3}x^{-1/3}$$

$$\frac{dy}{dx} = \frac{-\frac{2}{3}x^{-1/3}}{\frac{2}{3}y^{-1/3}} = -\frac{y^{1/3}}{x^{1/3}}$$

c. $\left.\dfrac{dy}{dx}\right|_{\substack{x=8 \\ y=1}} = -\dfrac{1^{1/3}}{8^{1/3}} = -\dfrac{1}{2}$

d. $\left.\dfrac{dy}{dx}\right|_{\substack{x=-1 \\ y=8}} = -\dfrac{8^{1/3}}{(-1)^{1/3}} = -\dfrac{2}{-1} = 2$

29. Given $(y-3)^3 = (x+5)^2$, then

$$3(y-3)^2 \frac{dy}{dx} = 2(x+5)$$

and solving for $\frac{dy}{dx}$ yields

$$\frac{dy}{dx} = \frac{2(x+5)}{3(y-3)^2}$$

31. Given $x^2(y^2-1) = x+y$, then

$$x^2\left(2y\frac{dy}{dx}\right) + 2x(y^2-1) = 1 + \frac{dy}{dx}$$

Solving for $\frac{dy}{dx}$ yields

$$2x^2y\frac{dy}{dx} - \frac{dy}{dx} = 1 - 2x(y^2-1)$$

$$\frac{dy}{dx} = \frac{1 - 2x(y^2-1)}{2x^2y - 1}$$

33. **a.** No

   b. Yes

   c. Yes

   d. No

35. Implicit differentiation is *not needed* because y is explicitly stated in terms of x; that is, $y = f(x) = x^2 - 9x$ and no y variable appears on the right-hand side of the equation.

SECTION 3.8 Technology Exercises

1.
$$\frac{d}{dx}(x^2 + y^2) = 25$$

$$2x + 2y\frac{dy}{dx} = 0$$

$$\frac{dy}{dx} = -\frac{x}{y}$$

at $(-3, 4)$, $\dfrac{dy}{dx} = \dfrac{3}{4}$

$$y - 4 = \frac{3}{4}(x+3)$$

$$y = \frac{3}{4}x + \frac{25}{4}$$

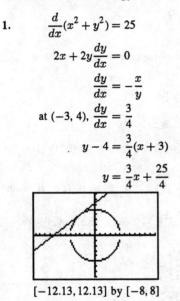

$[-12.13, 12.13]$ by $[-8, 8]$

3.

$[-5, 5]$ by $[-10, 10]$

SECTION 3.9 pages 171–174

1.

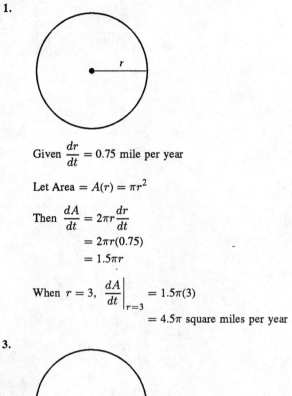

Given $\dfrac{dr}{dt} = 0.75$ mile per year

Let Area $= A(r) = \pi r^2$

Then $\dfrac{dA}{dt} = 2\pi r \dfrac{dr}{dt}$

$\qquad = 2\pi r(0.75)$

$\qquad = 1.5\pi r$

When $r = 3$, $\dfrac{dA}{dt}\bigg|_{r=3} = 1.5\pi(3)$

$\qquad\qquad\qquad\quad = 4.5\pi$ square miles per year

3.

Given $\dfrac{dA}{dt} = 100$ square meters per hour

Let Area $= A(r) = \pi r^2$

Then $\dfrac{dA}{dt} = 2\pi r \dfrac{dr}{dt}$

Solve for $\dfrac{dr}{dt}$: $\dfrac{dr}{dt} = \dfrac{1}{2\pi r}\dfrac{dA}{dt}$

$\qquad\qquad\qquad = \dfrac{1}{2\pi r}(100)$

$\qquad\qquad\qquad = \dfrac{50}{\pi r}$

When $r = 200$, $\dfrac{dr}{dt}\bigg|_{r=200} = \dfrac{50}{200\pi}$

$\qquad\qquad\qquad\qquad\quad = \dfrac{1}{4\pi}$ meters per hour

5.

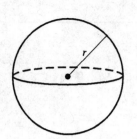

Given $\dfrac{dr}{dt} = 1.25$ millimeters per month

Let Volume $= V(r) = \frac{4}{3}\pi r^3$

Then $\dfrac{dV}{dt} = 4\pi r^2 \dfrac{dr}{dt}$

$\qquad\qquad = 4\pi r^2(1.25)$

$\qquad\qquad = 5\pi r^2$

When $r = 10$, $\ \dfrac{dV}{dt}\bigg|_{r=10} = 5\pi(10)^2$

$\qquad\qquad\qquad\qquad\quad = 500\pi$ cubic millimeters per month

7.

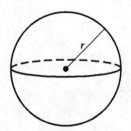

Given $\dfrac{dV}{dt} = 4$ cubic feet per minute

Let Volume $= V(r) = \frac{4}{3}\pi r^3$

Then $\dfrac{dV}{dt} = 4\pi r^2 \dfrac{dr}{dt}$

Solve for $\dfrac{dr}{dt}$: $\ \dfrac{dr}{dt} = \dfrac{1}{4\pi r^2}\dfrac{dV}{dt}$

$\qquad\qquad\qquad\quad = \dfrac{1}{4\pi r^2}(4)$

$\qquad\qquad\qquad\quad = \dfrac{1}{\pi(r)^2}$

When $r = 2$, $\ \dfrac{dr}{dt}\bigg|_{r=2} = \dfrac{1}{\pi(2)^2}$

$\qquad\qquad\qquad\qquad\quad = \dfrac{1}{4\pi}$ feet per minute

9.

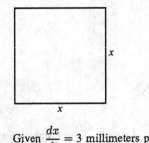

Given $\dfrac{dx}{dt} = 3$ millimeters per second

Let Area $= A(x) = x^2$

Then $\dfrac{dA}{dt} = 2x\dfrac{dx}{dt}$

$\qquad\quad = 2x(3)$

$\qquad\quad = 6x$

When $x = 24$, $\left.\dfrac{dA}{dt}\right|_{x=24} = 6(24)$

$\qquad\qquad\qquad\qquad\quad = 144$ square millimeters per second

11. If x is the number of bats produced, then to increase production at the rate of 50 bats per day means $\dfrac{dx}{dt} = 50$. Given the total cost function $C(x) = 8x + 350$, then

$\dfrac{dC}{dt} = 8\dfrac{dx}{dt} = 8(50) = \$400$ per day

13. $\dfrac{dy}{dt} = -2\dfrac{dx}{dt}$

15. If x is the number of bottles produced and sold, then $\dfrac{dx}{dt} = 250$ bottles per week.

Given the selling price $p = 12 - 0.00015x$ cents, then

a. Revenue $= R(x) = (12 - 0.00015x)x$

$\qquad\qquad\qquad = 12x - 0.00015x^2$

b. $\dfrac{dR}{dt} = (12 - 0.00030x)\dfrac{dx}{dt}$

$\qquad\quad = (12 - 0.0003x)(250)$

When $x = 10,000$, $\left.\dfrac{dR}{dt}\right|_{x=10,000} = [12 - 0.0003(10,000)](250)$

$\qquad\qquad\qquad\qquad\qquad\qquad = 2250$ cents per week

$\qquad\qquad\qquad\qquad\qquad\qquad = \$22.50$ per week

17.

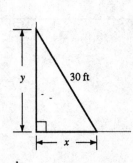

$$\frac{dx}{dt} = 2 \text{ feet per second}$$

The Pythagorean theorem implies that $x^2 + y^2 = 30^2$ at any time t. Thus, $x = \sqrt{900 - y^2}$.

Compute $\frac{dy}{dt}$ when $y = 24$ feet and $\frac{dx}{dt} = 2$ feet per second.

Using $x^2 + y^2 = 900$,

$$2x\frac{dx}{dt} + 2y\frac{dy}{dt} = 0$$

$$\frac{dy}{dt} = -\frac{x}{y}\frac{dx}{dt}$$

$$= -\frac{\sqrt{900 - y^2}}{y}\frac{dx}{dt}$$

$$= -\frac{\sqrt{900 - 24^2}}{24}(2)$$

$$= -\frac{18}{12}$$

$$= -\frac{3}{2} \text{ feet per second}$$

19.

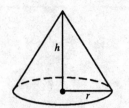

Let Volume $= V = \frac{1}{3}\pi r^2 h$; $\frac{dV}{dt} = 8$ cubic feet per minute

a. If $h = r$ at any time t, then $V = \frac{1}{3}\pi r^2(r) = \frac{1}{3}\pi r^3$

b. $\frac{dV}{dt} = \pi r^2 \frac{dr}{dt}$

Solve for $\frac{dr}{dt}$:

$$\frac{dr}{dt} = \frac{1}{\pi r^2}\frac{dV}{dt}$$

$$= \frac{1}{\pi r^2}(8) = \frac{8}{\pi r^2}$$

When $h = r = 10$, then

$$\frac{dr}{dt} = \frac{8}{\pi(10)^2}$$

$$= \frac{8}{100\pi}$$

$$= \frac{2}{25\pi} \text{ feet per minute}$$

21. Using the relationship given, $y = \sqrt{x^3 + 17}$,

$$\frac{dy}{dt} = \frac{1}{2}(x^3 + 17)^{-\frac{1}{2}}(3x^2)\frac{dx}{dt}$$

At coordinates (2, 5) when $\frac{dx}{dt} = 10$ units per second,

$$\frac{dy}{dt} = \frac{1}{2}(2^3 + 17)^{-\frac{1}{2}}3(2)^2(10)$$
$$= 12 \text{ units per second}$$

23.

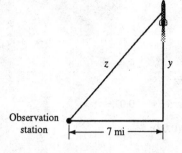

Observation station   ← 7 mi →

Given $\frac{dy}{dt} = 2000$ miles per hour

Using the Pythagorean theorem, $7^2 + y^2 = z^2$; then $z = \sqrt{49 + y^2}$ and

$$2y\frac{dy}{dt} = 2z\frac{dz}{dt}$$
$$\frac{dz}{dt} = \frac{y}{z}\frac{dy}{dt}$$
$$= \frac{y}{\sqrt{49 + y^2}}\frac{dy}{dt}$$

When $y = 24$ and $\frac{dy}{dt} = 2000$, $\frac{dz}{dt} = \frac{24}{\sqrt{49 + 24^2}}(2000)$
$$= 1920 \text{ miles per hour}$$

25. **a.** The related rates in symbols are $\frac{dA}{dt}$ and $\frac{dr}{dt}$.

b. The related rates in words are $\frac{dA}{dt}$ = the change in the area with respect to time, in square miles per year.

$\frac{dr}{dt}$ = the change in the radius with respect to time, in miles per year.

c. $A = \pi r^2$
$$\frac{dA}{dt} = 2\pi r\frac{dr}{dt}$$

SECTION 3.10 pages 177–179

1. Given $y = x^3$, then
$$\frac{dy}{dx} = 3x^2$$
and $dy = 3x^2\, dx$

3. Given $y = x^2 + 5x - 1$, then
$$\frac{dy}{dx} = 2x + 5$$
and $dy = (2x + 5)\, dx$

5. Given $y = (x^2 - 3)^5$, then
$$\frac{dy}{dx} = 5(x^2 - 3)^4(2x)$$
$$= 10x(x^2 - 3)^4$$
and $dy = 10x(x^2 - 3)^4\, dx$

7. Given $y = (1 - 9x)^4$, then
$$\frac{dy}{dx} = 4(1 - 9x)^3(-9)$$
$$= -36(1 - 9x)^3$$
and $dy = -36(1 - 9x)^3\, dx$

9.   Given $y = f(x) = 5x^2$, then

$$\frac{dy}{dx} = 10x$$

and

$$dy = 10x \, dx$$

For $x = 4$ and $dx = 0.02$,

$$dy = 10(4)(0.02)$$
$$= 0.8$$

11.   Given $y = f(x) = (x^2 + 9)^{1/2}$, then

$$\frac{dy}{dx} = \frac{1}{2}(x^2 + 9)^{-1/2}(2x)$$

and

$$dy = x(x^2 + 9)^{-1/2} \, dx = \frac{x}{\sqrt{x^2 + 9}} \, dx$$

For $x = 4$ and $dx = 0.01$,

$$dy = \frac{4}{\sqrt{4^2 + 9}}(0.01)$$
$$= \frac{4}{\sqrt{25}}(0.01)$$
$$= \frac{4}{5}(0.01)$$
$$= 0.008$$

13.   Given $y = f(x) = \dfrac{2x}{x + 1}$, then

$$\frac{dy}{dx} = \frac{(x + 1)(2) - 2x(1)}{(x + 1)^2} = \frac{2x + 2 - 2x}{(x + 1)^2} = \frac{2}{(x + 1)^2}$$

and

$$dy = \frac{2 \, dx}{(x + 1)^2}$$

For $x = 3$ and $dx = 0.001$,

$$dy = \frac{2}{(3 + 1)^2}(0.001)$$
$$= \frac{1}{8}(0.001)$$
$$= 0.000125$$

15.   Given $y = f(x) = 3x^2 + 1$, then the approximate change in f is dy.

Differentiating y gives $\dfrac{dy}{dx} = 6x$; then $dy = 6x \, dx$.

The change in x is $dx = 5.01 - 5 = 0.01$.

Thus, for $x = 5$ and $dx = 0.01$,

$$dy = 6(5)(0.01)$$
$$= 0.3$$

17.   Given $y = f(x) = 2x - 5x^{1/2}$, then the approximate change in f is dy. The change in x is $dx = 9.015 - 9 = 0.015$.

Differentiating y gives $\dfrac{dy}{dx} = 2 - \dfrac{5}{2}x^{-1/2}$ and $dy = \left(2 - \dfrac{5}{2\sqrt{x}}\right) dx$.

For $x = 9$ and $dx = 0.015$,

$$dy = \left(2 - \frac{5}{2\sqrt{9}}\right)(0.015)$$
$$= 0.0175$$

19. Given $y = f(x) = x - \dfrac{20}{x}$, then the approximate change in f is dy. The change in x is $dx = 3.98 - 4 = -0.02$.

Differentiating y gives $\dfrac{dy}{dx} = 1 + \dfrac{20}{x^2}$ and $dy = \left(1 + \dfrac{20}{x^2}\right) dx$

For $x = 4$ and $dx = -0.02$,

$$dy = \left(1 + \dfrac{20}{4^2}\right)(-0.02)$$
$$= -0.045$$

21. From Example 4, the revenue function is $R(x) = -0.25x^2 + 20x + 100$ and $dR = (-0.5x + 20)\,dx$.

If the current amount spent on advertising is \$2300 ($x = 23$) and the planned increase is \$150 ($dx = 1.5$), then the approximate change in revenue is

$$dR = [-0.5(23) + 20](1.5)$$
$$= \$12.75$$

The approximate increase is \$12,750.

23. The revenue function in Example 4 is $R(x) = -0.25x^2 + 20x + 100$.

The exact change in revenue as x increases from 15 to 16 (an increase of 1) is computed by $R(16) - R(15)$. Using a calculator, one computes

$$R(16) = -0.25(16)^2 + 20(16) + 100$$
$$= 356.00$$

and

$$R(15) = -0.25(15)^2 + 20(15) + 100$$
$$= 343.75$$

Thus, $R(16) - R(15) = 356.00 - 343.75$
$$= 12.25$$

The exact increase is \$12,250.

25. Given the demand equation $p = 20 - 0.4x^{1/2}$, the approximate change in price is dp when the change in quantity x is $dx = 101 - 100 = 1$.

Differentiating p gives

$$\frac{dp}{dx} = -0.2x^{-1/2} \quad \text{and} \quad dp = \frac{-0.2}{\sqrt{x}}\,dx$$

For $x = 100$ and $dx = 1$,

$$dp = \frac{-0.2}{\sqrt{100}}(1)$$
$$= -0.02$$

27. Given $n(t) = 6t^2 + 200$ as the function for the number of bacteria in a culture, the approximate change in the number is dn when the change in time t is $dt = 5.05 - 5.00 = 0.05$. (*Note:* 3 minutes = 0.05 hour.)

Differentiating n gives

$$\frac{dn}{dt} = 12t \quad \text{and} \quad dn = 12t\,dt$$

For $t = 5$ and $dt = 0.05$,

$$dn = 12(5)(0.05)$$
$$= 3$$

29. Given $V(h) = 2.25\pi h$ as the volume of the cup to any height h, the approximate decrease in volume is dV when the change in height h is $dh = 7.5 - 8 = -0.5$.

Differentiating V gives

$$\frac{dV}{dh} = 2.25\pi \quad \text{and} \quad dV = 2.25\pi \, dh$$

For $h = 8$ and $dh = -0.5$,

$$dV = 2.25\pi(-0.5)$$
$$= -1.125\pi$$
$$\approx 3.53 \text{ cubic inches}$$

The approximate savings on each serving is 3.53 cubic inches.

31. No, the exact change Δy can be calculated, but dy offers a good, fast approximation.

REVIEW EXERCISES FOR CHAPTER 3 pages 179–182

1. If $f(x) = 2\pi$, then

$$f'(x) = 0$$

3. If $f(x) = \dfrac{x^7}{7}$, then

$$f'(x) = x^6$$

5. If $f(t) = \dfrac{1}{4\sqrt{t}} = \dfrac{1}{4}t^{-1/2}$, then

$$f'(t) = -\frac{1}{8}t^{-3/2}$$

7. If $y = 6x^{2/3} - 14x$, then

$$\frac{dy}{dx} = 4x^{-1/3} - 14$$

9. If $y = 1 + x^{-1}$, then

$$\frac{dy}{dx} = -x^{-2}$$

11. If $y = \dfrac{1}{x} - \dfrac{x^9}{7} = x^{-1} - \dfrac{1}{7}x^9$, then

$$\frac{dy}{dx} = -x^{-2} - \frac{9}{7}x^8$$

13. If $y = \dfrac{3}{\sqrt[3]{x}} = 3x^{-1/3}$, then

$$D_x y = -x^{-4/3}$$

15. If $f(x) = x^{5/3} + 14$, then

$$f'(x) = \frac{5}{3}x^{2/3}$$

17. If $y = (8x)^{1/2} = \sqrt{8}x^{1/2}$, then

$$\frac{dy}{dx} = \frac{\sqrt{8}}{2}x^{-1/2} = \sqrt{2}x^{-1/2}$$

19. If $f(t) = \sqrt[3]{1 + t^2} = (1 + t^2)^{1/3}$, then

$$f'(t) = \frac{1}{3}(1 + t^2)^{-2/3}(2t)$$
$$= \frac{2t}{3}(1 + t^2)^{-2/3}$$

21. If $y = \dfrac{1}{\sqrt[3]{1 + x^3}} = (1 + x^3)^{-1/3}$, then

$$\frac{dy}{dx} = -\frac{1}{3}(1 + x^3)^{-4/3}(3x^2)$$
$$= -x^2(1 + x^3)^{-4/3}$$

23. If $y = \dfrac{(2x - 1)^4}{x^2 + 4}$, then, using the quotient rule,

$$\frac{dy}{dx} = \frac{(x^2 + 4)\left[4(2x - 1)^3(2)\right] - (2x - 1)^4(2x)}{(x^2 + 4)^2}$$
$$= \frac{2(2x - 1)^3\left[4(x^2 + 4) - x(2x - 1)\right]}{(x^2 + 4)^2}$$
$$= \frac{2(2x - 1)^3(4x^2 + 16 - 2x^2 + x)}{(x^2 + 4)^2}$$
$$= \frac{2(2x - 1)^3(2x^2 + x + 16)}{(x^2 + 4)^2}$$

25. If $y = (x^2 + 7)^3(x - 5)^4$, then, using the product rule,

$$\frac{dy}{dx} = (x^2 + 7)^3(4)(x - 5)^3(1) + (x - 5)^4(3)(x^2 + 7)^2(2x)$$

$$= 2(x^2 + 7)^2(x - 5)^3 \left[2(x^2 + 7) + 3x(x - 5) \right]$$

$$= 2(x^2 + 7)^2(x - 5)^3(2x^2 + 14 + 3x^2 - 15x)$$

$$= 2(x^2 + 7)^2(x - 5)^3(5x^2 - 15x + 14)$$

27. Given $y = \sqrt{1 + 3x^2} = (1 + 3x^2)^{1/2}$ and the point (1, 2), then

$$\frac{dy}{dx} = \frac{1}{2}(1 + 3x^2)^{-1/2}(6x)$$

$$\left. \frac{dy}{dx} \right|_{x=1} = \frac{1}{2}[1 + 3(1)^2]^{-1/2}(6)(1) = \frac{6}{(2)(4)^{1/2}} = \frac{3}{2}$$

$$m_{\tan} = \frac{3}{2}$$

29. If $y = \dfrac{2x}{x + 3}$, then

$$y' = \frac{(x + 3)(2) - 2x(1)}{(x + 3)^2}$$

$$= \frac{2x + 6 - 2x}{(x + 3)^2}$$

$$= \frac{6}{(x + 3)^2}$$

$$= 6(x + 3)^{-2}$$

and $y'' = -12(x + 3)^{-3}(1)$

$$= \frac{-12}{(x + 3)^3}$$

31. Given $xy^4 + x^2 - y = 1$, then

$$\frac{d}{dx}(xy^4) + \frac{d}{dx}(x^2) - \frac{dy}{dx} = 0$$

$$x(4)(y^3)\frac{dy}{dx} + y^4(1) + 2x - \frac{dy}{dx} = 0$$

and solving for $\frac{dy}{dx}$ yields

$$y^4 + 2x = \frac{dy}{dx} - 4xy^3\frac{dy}{dx}$$

$$2x + y^4 = (1 - 4xy^3)\frac{dy}{dx}$$

$$\frac{dy}{dx} = \frac{2x + y^4}{1 - 4xy^3}$$

33. Given $y = x + 7\sqrt{x}$, compute the differential $dy = \dfrac{dy}{dx}dx$ for $x = 4$ and $dx = 4.01 - 4.00 = 0.01$.

If $y = f(x) = x + 7x^{1/2}$, then

$$\frac{dy}{dx} = 1 + \frac{7}{2}x^{-1/2}$$

and

$$dy = \left(1 + \frac{7}{2\sqrt{x}} \right) dx$$

For $x = 4$ and $dx = 0.01$,

$$dy = \left(1 + \frac{7}{2\sqrt{4}} \right)(0.01)$$

$$= 0.0275$$

35. If $f(t) = (t^2 + 5)^3$, then

$$f'(t) = 3(t^2 + 5)^2(2t)$$

$$= 6t(t^2 + 5)^2$$

At $t = 2$, $f'(2) = 6(2)(2^2 + 5)^2$

$$= 972$$

37.   The rate of change of temperature at 3 seconds is determined by computing $\frac{dT}{dx}$ at $x = 3$. Given $T = -2x^2 + 60x + 70$, then

$$\frac{dT}{dx} = -4x + 60$$

$$\left.\frac{dT}{dx}\right|_{x=3} = -4(3) + 60 = 48 \text{ degrees per second}$$

39.   The cost function is $C(x) = 400 + 35x - 0.01x^2$.

    a.   The marginal cost is $C'(x) = 35 - 0.02x$

    At $x = 10$,

$$C'(10) = 35 - 0.02(10)$$
$$= 34.8$$

    b.   The exact cost of the 11th unit is $C(11) - C(10)$.

$$C(11) = 400 + 35(11) - 0.01(11)^2$$
$$= 783.79$$

$$C(10) = 400 + 35(10) - 0.01(10)^2$$
$$= 749$$

$$C(11) - C(10) = 783.79 - 749$$
$$= 34.79$$

    c.   The rate of change of the marginal cost is $C''(x)$

$$C'(x) = 35 - 0.02x$$
$$C''(x) = -0.02$$

41.   The marginal profit function is $MP(x) = MR(x) - MC(x)$.

Given $R(x) = 6x + 0.002x^2$ and $C(x) = 150 + 10x + 0.001x^2$, then $MR(x) = R'(x) = 6 + 0.004x$, $MC(x) = C'(x) = 10 + 0.002x$, and

$$MP(x) = MR(x) - MC(x)$$
$$= 6 + 0.004x - (10 + 0.002x)$$
$$= 0.002x - 4$$

43.   The production level at which the marginal cost equals \$150 is found by solving the equation $C'(x) = 150$.

Given $C(x) = x^2 + 80x + 150$, then $C'(x) = 2x + 80$.

Solve $2x + 80 = 150$
$$2x = 70$$
$$x = 35$$

45.   Given $(x^2 + y^2)^2 - 4xy = 0$
    a. $[(-1)^2 + (-1)^2]^2 - 4(-1)(-1) = 2^2 - 4 = 0$, so $(-1, -1)$ is a point on the curve.
    b. $2(x^2 + y^2)(2x + 2y\frac{dy}{dx}) - 4x\frac{dy}{dx} - 4y = 0$

$$[4y(x^2 + y^2) - 4x]\frac{dy}{dx} = 4y - 4x(x^2 + y^2)$$

$$\frac{dy}{dx} = \frac{y - x(x^2 + y^2)}{y(x^2 + y^2) - x}$$

    c. $\left.\frac{dy}{dx}\right|_{\substack{x=-1 \\ y=-1}} = \frac{(-1) - (-1)[(-1)^2 + (-1)^2]}{-1[(-1)^2 + (-1)^2] - (-1)} = \frac{-1 + 2}{-2 + 1} = \frac{1}{-1} = -1$

$$m_{\tan} = -1$$

47. Given $V = \frac{4}{3}\pi r^3$ as the volume of the tumor, the approximate change is dV when the change in radius r is $dr = 1.1 - 1.0 = 0.1$ centimeters. Differentiating V gives

$$\frac{dV}{dr} = 4\pi r^2$$

and $dV = 4\pi r^2 dr$

For $r = 1$ and $dr = 0.1$,

$dV = 4\pi(1)^2(0.1) = 0.4\pi \cong 1.2566$ cubic centimeters.

49. **a.** $630 - 16t^2 = 0$

$$630 = 16t^2$$

$$t^2 = \frac{630}{16} = 39.375$$

$$t = 6.2749 \text{ seconds}$$

b. $s'(t) = -32t$

$$s'(6.2749) = -32(6.2749)$$

$$= -200.7968 \text{ feet per second}$$

51. Let h be the height of the helicopter and s be the distance from the helicopter to the marker. Given $\frac{dh}{dt} = 10$ feet per second. Using the Pythagorean theorem, $s^2 = h^2 + 80^2$, then

$$s = \sqrt{h^2 + 80^2} \quad \text{and} \quad 2s\frac{ds}{dt} = 2h\frac{dh}{dt}$$

$$\frac{ds}{dt} = \frac{h}{s}\frac{dh}{dt} = \frac{h}{\sqrt{h^2 + 6400}}\frac{dh}{dt}$$

When $h = 192$ and $\frac{dh}{dt} = 10$,

$$\frac{ds}{dt} = \frac{192}{\sqrt{192^2 + 6400}}(10) = \frac{192}{208}(10) = 9.2308$$

53. Given $\frac{dr}{dt} = -1$ centimeter per hour and $V = \frac{4}{3}\pi r^3$, then

$$\frac{dV}{dt} = 4\pi r^2 \frac{dr}{dt}$$

When $r = 3$ centimeters,

$$\frac{dV}{dt} = 4\pi(3)^2(-1) = -36\pi \cong -113.0973 \text{ cubic centimeters per hour}$$

55. Given $y = 4.3x^2$,

$$\frac{dy}{dt} = 8.6x\frac{dx}{dt}$$

When $x = 12.8$ and $\frac{dx}{dt} = 5.7$, then

$$\frac{dy}{dt} = (8.6)(12.8)(5.7) = 627.456$$

SECTION 4.1 pages 193–197

1. **a.** f is increasing on the interval $(-2, 3)$.

    b. f is decreasing on the intervals $(-5, -2) \cup (3, 7)$.

3. **a.** f is increasing on the interval $(-3, 2)$.

    b. f is decreasing on the interval $(-5, -3)$.

5. **a.** f is never increasing.

    b. f is decreasing on the intervals $(-6, 0) \cup (0, 6)$.

7. $f(x) = x^2 - 6x + 19$ is increasing when $f'(x) > 0$.

$$f'(x) = 2x - 6 > 0$$
$$2x > 6$$
$$x > 3$$

f is increasing for $x > 3$.

$f(x)$ is decreasing when $f'(x) < 0$.

$$f'(x) = 2x - 6 < 0$$
$$2x < 6$$
$$x < 3$$

f is decreasing for $x < 3$.

9. $f(x) = 1 - 4x^2$ is increasing when $f'(x) > 0$.

$$f'(x) = -8x > 0$$
$$x < 0$$

f is increasing for $x < 0$.

$f(x)$ is decreasing when $f'(x) < 0$.

$$f'(x) = -8x < 0$$
$$x > 0$$

f is decreasing for $x > 0$.

11. $m(x) = 10x - x^2$ is increasing when $m'(x) > 0$.

$$m'(x) = 10 - 2x > 0$$
$$-2x > -10$$
$$x < 5$$

m is increasing for $x < 5$.

$m(x)$ is decreasing when $m'(x) < 0$.

$$m'(x) = 10 - 2x < 0$$
$$-2x < -10$$
$$x > 5$$

m is decreasing for $x > 5$.

13. $f(x) = 50 + 6x - 0.02x^2$ is increasing when $f'(x) > 0$.

$$f'(x) = 6 - 0.04x > 0$$
$$-0.04x > -6$$
$$x < 150$$

f is increasing for $x < 150$.

$f(x)$ is decreasing when $f'(x) < 0$.

$$f'(x) = 6 - 0.04x < 0$$
$$-0.04x < -6$$
$$x > 150$$

f is decreasing for $x > 150$.

15. $f(x) = \frac{1}{x}$ is increasing when $f'(x) > 0$.

$$f'(x) = -\frac{1}{x^2}$$

Since $x^2 > 0$ for all x, then $f'(x)$ is never positive.

f is never increasing.

$f(x)$ is decreasing when $f'(x) < 0$.

$$f'(x) = -\frac{1}{x^2} < 0 \text{ for all } x \qquad x \neq 0$$

f is decreasing for all x, $x \neq 0$.

17. $f(x) = x^{3/2}$ is increasing when $f'(x) > 0$.

$$f'(x) = \frac{3}{2}x^{1/2} > 0$$
$$x^{1/2} > 0$$

Since $x^{1/2} > 0$ for all $x > 0$, then $f'(x) > 0$ for $x > 0$.

f is increasing for $x > 0$.

$f(x)$ is decreasing when $f'(x) < 0$.

Since $f'(x) = \frac{3}{2}x^{1/2}$ is never negative, then $f(x)$ is never decreasing.

Note: The domain of f is $x \geq 0$.

19. $f(x) = \sqrt{x} = x^{1/2}$ is increasing when $f'(x) > 0$.

$$f'(x) = \frac{1}{2}x^{-1/2} = \frac{1}{2x^{1/2}} > 0 \text{ for all } x > 0, \text{ since } \sqrt{x} > 0.$$

f is increasing for $x > 0$.

$f(x)$ is decreasing when $f'(x) < 0$.

$f'(x) = \frac{1}{2x^{1/2}}$ is never negative, since $\sqrt{x} > 0$ for $x > 0$.

f is never decreasing.

Note: The domain of f is $x \geq 0$.

21. $f(x) = \frac{x+1}{x}$ is increasing when $f'(x) > 0$.

$$f'(x) = \frac{x(1) - (x+1)(1)}{x^2}$$
$$= \frac{\cancel{x} - \cancel{x} - 1}{x^2} = -\frac{1}{x^2}$$

$f'(x) = -\frac{1}{x^2} < 0$ for all x, $x \neq 0$, since $x^2 > 0$ for all x, $x \neq 0$.

Thus, f is decreasing when $x < 0$ and $x > 0$.

23. The metal is cooling when the temperature function $T(x)$ is decreasing, that is, when $T'(x) < 0$.
Given $T(x) = -2x^2 + 64x + 65$, then $T'(x) = -4x + 64$; hence, the metal is cooling when

$$-4x + 64 < 0$$
$$-4x < -64$$
$$x > 16 \text{ seconds}$$

25.   **a.**   The rocket is rising when $s'(t) > 0$. Given $s(t) = -16t^2 + 800t$, then $s'(t) = -32t + 800 > 0$ when $-32t > -800$

$$t < 25$$

The rocket is rising for $0 < t < 25$.

b.   Solve

$$s(t) = -16t^2 + 800t = 0$$
$$16t(-t + 50) = 0$$

$$t = 0, \qquad t = 50$$

Since $t = 0$ occurs when the rocket leaves the ground, it must hit the ground after 50 seconds.

c.   The rocket is falling when $s'(t) < 0$.

From part a, $s'(t) = -32t + 800 < 0$ when $t > 25$.

Thus, the rocket is falling for $25 < t < 50$.

27.   The total cost is increasing when $C'(x) > 0$. Given $C(x) = 36x - 0.02x^2$, then

$C'(x) = 36 - 0.04x > 0$
which yields
$$-0.04x > -36$$
$$x < 900$$

Thus, the total cost is increasing for $0 < x < 900$.

29.   Given $f(x) = x^2 - 7x + 50$ and the point $(1, 44)$, then compute $f'(x)$ at $x = 1$.

$f'(x) = 2x - 7$

$f'(1) = 2 - 7 = -5 < 0$

Thus, f is decreasing at $x = 1$.

31.   Given $f(x) = 10 - \frac{1}{x} = 10 - x^{-1}$ and the point $(-1, 11)$, then compute $f'(x)$ at $x = -1$.

$$f'(x) = \frac{1}{x^2}$$

$$f(-1) = \frac{1}{(-1)^2} = 1 > 0$$

f is increasing at $x = -1$.

33.   **a.**   Average cost function $\overline{C}(x) = \dfrac{36x - 0.02x^2}{x}$
$$= 36 - 0.02x$$

b. $\overline{C}(x)$ is decreasing when $\overline{C}'(x) < 0$.

$\overline{C}'(x) = -0.02 < 0 \qquad$ for all $x, 0 < x \le 1200$

Thus, $\overline{C}(x)$ is always decreasing, $0 < x \le 1200$.

35.   Given the revenue function $R(x) = 80x - 0.01x^2$, then compute $R'(x)$ at $x = 600$.

$R'(x) = 80 - 0.02x$
$R'(600) = 80 - 0.02(600) = 68 > 0$

Revenue is increasing at $x = 600$.

37. **a.** $B(t)$ is *not* greater than $C(t)$ on $[0, 6]$, since the graph of $B(t)$ lies below the graph of $C(t)$ on $[0, 6]$.

   b. $B'(t)$ is *not* greater than $C'(t)$ on $[0, 6]$, since $C(t)$ increases more rapidly than $B(t)$, especially on the interval $[0, 4]$.

   c. Although crash dieting appears to cause greater weight loss more rapidly than behavior modification, in the long run, after about 10 months, behavior modification sustains a greater weight loss and the weight loss is more stable, i.e., it doesn't rise and fall.

39. **a.** Inflation is the function graphed. It (i) increases from A to B, (ii) stays the same from B to C, (iii) and decreases from C to D.

   b. The derivative of the price (inflation) is always positive, so the price is increasing in all three intervals.

41. Given $f(x) = x^2 - 16x$, then compute $f'(x)$ and solve

$$f'(x) = 2x - 16 = 0$$
which yields
$$x = 8$$

Critical number: $x = 8$

43. Given $f(x) = 5x^2 + 3x - 2$, then compute $f'(x)$ and solve

$$f'(x) = 10x + 3 = 0$$
which yields
$$x = -\frac{3}{10}$$

Critical number: $x = -\frac{3}{10}$

45. Given $f(x) = x^3 - 2$, then compute $f'(x)$ and solve

$$f'(x) = 3x^2 = 0$$
which yields
$$x = 0$$

Critical number: $x = 0$

47. Given $f(x) = x^3 + x^2 - 5x$, then compute $f'(x)$ and solve

$$f'(x) = 3x^2 + 2x - 5 = 0$$
which yields
$$(3x + 5)(x - 1) = 0$$

$3x + 5 = 0$ or $x - 1 = 0$
$x = -\frac{5}{3}$ $x = 1$

Critical numbers: $x = -\frac{5}{3}$ and $x = 1$

49. Given $f(x) = x^3 - 6x + 1$, then compute $f'(x)$ and solve

$$f'(x) = 3x^2 - 6 = 0$$
which yields
$$3(x^2 - 2) = 0$$
$$x^2 = 2$$
$$x = \pm\sqrt{2}$$

Critical numbers: $x = \sqrt{2}$ and $x = -\sqrt{2}$

51. Given $f(x) = x^3 + 6x^2 + 3x + 1$, then compute $f'(x)$ and solve

$$f'(x) = 3x^2 + 12x + 3 = 0$$

which yields

$$3(x^2 + 4x + 1) = 0$$
$$x^2 + 4x + 1 = 0$$

Using the quadratic formula, $x = \dfrac{-4 \pm \sqrt{4^2 - 4(1)(1)}}{2(1)}$

$$= \frac{-4 \pm \sqrt{12}}{2} = \frac{-4 \pm 2\sqrt{3}}{2}$$

$$= -2 \pm \sqrt{3}$$

Critical numbers: $x = -2 + \sqrt{3}$ and $x = -2 - \sqrt{3}$

53. Given $f(x) = x^{1/3} + 6$, then compute $f'(x)$.

Since $f'(x) = \frac{1}{3}x^{-2/3} = \frac{1}{3x^{2/3}} \neq 0$ for any x, the only critical number is at $x = 0$, where $f'(x)$ is undefined.

55. Given $f(x) = \frac{1}{\sqrt{x}} = x^{-1/2}$, then compute $f'(x)$. Since $f'(x) = -\frac{1}{2}x^{-3/2} = -\frac{1}{2x^{3/2}} \neq 0$ for any x, then the only possible critical number is $x = 0$, where $f'(x)$ is undefined. However, $f(x) = \frac{1}{\sqrt{x}}$ is also undefined at $x = 0$. Therefore, $x = 0$ is *not* a critical number.

There are no critical numbers.

57. Given $f(x) = x^3 + 3x^2 - 15x - 9$, then compute $f'(x)$ and solve

$$f'(x) = 3x^2 + 6x - 15 = 0$$

which yields

$$3(x^2 + 2x - 5) = 0$$
$$x^2 + 2x - 5 = 0$$

Using the quadratic formula,

$$x = \frac{-2 \pm \sqrt{2^2 - 4(1)(-5)}}{2(1)}$$

$$= \frac{-2 \pm \sqrt{24}}{2}$$

$$= -1 \pm \sqrt{6}$$

Critical numbers: $x = -1 + \sqrt{6}$ and $x = -1 - \sqrt{6}$

59. Given $f(x) = \frac{1}{x} = x^{-1}$, then compute $f'(x)$.

Since $f'(x) = -\frac{1}{x^2} \neq 0$ for any x, then the only possible critical number is $x = 0$, where $f'(x)$ is undefined. However, $f(x)$ is also undefined at $x = 0$; thus, $x = 0$ is *not* a critical number.

There are no critical numbers.

61. Given $f(x) = \frac{x^2}{x-1}$, then computing $f'(x)$ yields

$$f'(x) = \frac{(x-1)(2x) - x^2(1)}{(x-1)^2}$$
$$= \frac{2x^2 - 2x - x^2}{(x-1)^2}$$
$$= \frac{x^2 - 2x}{(x-1)^2}$$

Solving $f'(x) = 0$, one gets

$$x^2 - 2x = 0$$
$$x(x-2) = 0$$
$$x = 0, \qquad x = 2$$

Also, $f'(x)$ is undefined at $x = 1$; however, $f(x)$ is also undefined at $x = 1$. Thus, $x = 1$ is not a critical number.

Critical numbers: $x = 0$ and $x = 2$

63. Given $f(x) = (3x-1)(2x+3)^5$, then computing $f'(x)$ yields

$$f'(x) = (3x-1)(5)(2x+3)^4(2) + (2x+3)^5(3)$$
$$= (2x+3)^4[10(3x-1) + 3(2x+3)]$$
$$= (2x+3)^4(30x - 10 + 6x + 9)$$
$$= (2x+3)^4(36x - 1)$$

Solving $f'(x) = 0$, one gets

$$(2x+3)^4(36x-1) = 0$$

$$\begin{array}{cc} (2x+3)^4 = 0 & 36x - 1 = 0 \\ 2x + 3 = 0 & x = \frac{1}{36} \\ x = -\frac{3}{2} & \end{array}$$

Since $f'(x)$ is defined for all x, the critical numbers are $x = -\frac{3}{2}$ and $x = \frac{1}{36}$.

65. Given $f(x) = \sqrt{x^2 + 5} = (x^2 + 5)^{1/2}$, then

$$f'(x) = \frac{1}{2}(x^2 + 5)^{-1/2}(2x) = \frac{x}{\sqrt{x^2 + 5}}$$

Since $x^2 + 5 > 0$ for all x, then $\sqrt{x^2 + 5} > 0$ for all x and $f'(x)$ is defined for all x. Also, $f'(x) > 0$ for $x > 0$ and $f'(x) < 0$ for $x < 0$.

Thus, $f(x)$ is increasing for $x > 0$ and decreasing for $x < 0$.

67.   Given $f(x) = x^4 + 4x^3 - 7$, then

$$f'(x) = 4x^3 + 12x^2$$
$$= 4x^2(x + 3)$$

Solving $x^2(x + 3) = 0$ and using a sign graph to solve the inequalities $f'(x) > 0$ and $f'(x) < 0$, one gets that $f'(x) = 0$ for $x = 0$, $x = -3$ and

Sign of $f'(x)$	$-$	$+$	$+$

x -3 0

Thus, $f'(x) < 0$ for $x < -3$ and $f'(x) > 0$ for $x > -3$, $x \neq 0$.

Therefore, $f(x)$ is decreasing for $x < -3$ and increasing for $x > -3$, $x \neq 0$.

69.   Given $f(x) = x^4 + 8x^3 + 4x^2 + 15$, then compute $f'(x)$ and solve

$$f'(x) = 4x^3 + 24x^2 + 8x = 0$$

which yields

$$4x(x^2 + 6x + 2) = 0$$
$$x = 0, \qquad x^2 + 6x + 2 = 0$$

Using the quadratic formula on $x^2 + 6x + 2 = 0$, one gets

$$x = \frac{-6 \pm \sqrt{36 - 4(1)(2)}}{2}$$
$$= \frac{-6 \pm \sqrt{28}}{2}$$
$$= -3 \pm \sqrt{7}$$

The critical numbers are $x = 0$, $x = -3 + \sqrt{7}$, and $x = -3 - \sqrt{7}$.

71.   **a.**   For $x < 3$, the function is $f(x) = 2x - 3$, which is a straight line. The slope of the tangent line is $f'(x) = 2$.

       b.   For $x > 3$, the function is $f(x) = 6 - x$, which is also a straight line. The slope of the tangent line is $f'(x) = -1$.

       c.   There is no tangent line at $x = 3$; hence there is no slope (no derivative) of the tangent line at $x = 3$.

73.

Point	Continuous	Differentiable
a	Yes	Yes
b	Yes	No
c	Yes	Yes
d	No	No
e	No	No

75.   Yes; if $f'(3) = 0$, then $f(3)$ must be defined, and by definition 3 is a critical number of f.

77.   Use the following steps to find the critical numbers of a function g.

     1.   Compute the derivative $g'(x)$.

     2.   Solve the equation $g'(x) = 0$. Any values of x such that $g'(x) = 0$ will be critical numbers.

     3.   Determine if there are any values of x for which $g'(x)$ is undefined but $g(x)$ is defined. Usually this occurs when division by zero exists, although it may occur in piecewise functions at the points at which the description of the function changes.

79. Suppose $x = c$ is not a critical number but $f(c)$ exists. Then $f'(c) > 0$ or $f'(c) < 0$. Suppose $f'(c) > 0$; then f is increasing at $x = c$ and it would seem, intuitively, that for x_1 and x_2 near c such that $x_1 < c < x_2$, then $f(x_1) < f(c) < f(x_2)$. This would imply that $f(c)$ is neither a relative maximum nor a relative minimum.

This can be proved rigorously if one considers the limit definition of the derivative.

A similar argument can be made if $f'(c) < 0$.

81. The derivative of a difference is the difference of the derivatives.

SECTION 4.1 Technology Exercises

1. increasing on $(-\infty, 0)$, decreasing on $(0, \infty)$

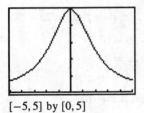

$[-5, 5]$ by $[0, 5]$

3. increasing on $(0, 2)$, decreasing on $(-\infty, 0)$ and $(2, \infty)$

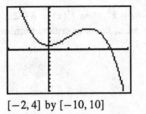

$[-2, 4]$ by $[-10, 10]$

5. $f'(x) = -4x^{-1/3}$

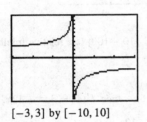

$[-3, 3]$ by $[-10, 10]$

increasing on $(-\infty, 0)$, decreasing on $(0, \infty)$

7. $f'(x) = 3x^2 - 16x + 6$; critical numbers are 0.4 and 4.9.

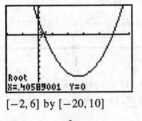

Root
X=.40589001 Y=0

$[-2, 6]$ by $[-20, 10]$

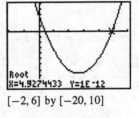

Root
X=4.9274433 Y=1E-12

$[-2, 6]$ by $[-20, 10]$

9. $f'(x) = 0.6x^2 - 0.2x - 1.8$; critical numbers are -1.6 and 1.9.

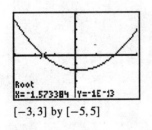

Root
X=-1.573384 Y=-1E-13

$[-3, 3]$ by $[-5, 5]$

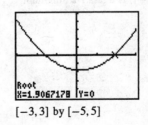

Root
X=1.9067178 Y=0

$[-3, 3]$ by $[-5, 5]$

11. **a.** $f'(x) = \dfrac{4}{3}x^{-1/3}$

$= \dfrac{4}{3x^{1/3}}$

$f'(0) = \dfrac{4}{0}$, which is not defined.

b.

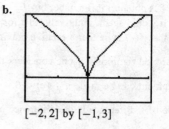

$[-2, 2]$ by $[-1, 3]$

The tangent line is vertical at $x = 0$.

SECTION 4.2 pages 204–206

1. Given $f(x) = 15 + 6x - x^2$, then $f'(x) = 6 - 2x$. Since $f'(x)$ is defined for all x, the only critical numbers will be for $f'(x) = 0$.

Solve $6 - 2x = 0$

$-2x = -6$

$x = 3$

The only critical number is $x = 3$.

$$
\begin{array}{ccc}
f'(2) = 2 & & f'(4) = -2 \\
+ + + + + & | & - - - - - \\
\hline
x = 2 & x = 3 & x = 4
\end{array}
$$

Thus, $(3, f(3)) = (3, 24)$ is a relative maximum.

3. Given $f(x) = x^2 - 20x$, then $f'(x) = 2x - 20$.

Solve $f'(x) = 2x - 20 = 0$

$2x = 20$

$x = 10$

The only critical point is $x = 10$.

$$
\begin{array}{cc}
f'(9) = -2 & f'(11) = 2 \\
- - - - - & + + + + + + \\
\hline
& 10
\end{array}
$$

Thus, $(10, f(10)) = (10, -100)$ is a relative minimum.

5. Given $f(x) = x^3 - 3x - 2$, then $f'(x) = 3x^2 - 3$.

Solve $f'(x) = 3x^2 - 3 = 0$

$3(x^2 - 1) = 0$

$x^2 - 1 = 0$

Factoring, $(x - 1)(x + 1) = 0$

$x = 1, x = -1$

There are two critical numbers, $x = 1$ and $x = -1$.

$$
\begin{array}{ccc}
f^{-1}(-2) = 9 & f'(0) = -3 & f'(2) = 9 \\
+ + + + + + & - - - - - - & + + + + \\
\hline
-1 & & 1
\end{array}
$$

Thus, $(-1, f(-1)) = (-1, 0)$ is a relative maximum, and $(1, f(1)) = (1, -4)$ is a relative minimum.

7. Given $f(x) = x^3 - 6x^2$, then $f'(x) = 3x^2 - 12x$.

Solve $f'(x) = 3x^2 - 12x = 0$

Factoring, $3x(x - 4) = 0$

$x = 0, \quad x = 4$

The only critical numbers are $x = 0$ and $x = 4$.

$$
\begin{array}{ccc}
f'(-1) = 15 & f'(1) = -9 & f'(5) = 15 \\
+ + + + + & - - - - & + + + + \\
\hline
0 & & 4
\end{array}
$$

Thus, $(0, f(0)) = (0, 0)$ is a relative maximum and $(4, f(4)) = (4, -32)$ is a relative minimum.

9. Given $f(x) = 2x^3 + 3x^2 - 36x + 5$, then
$f'(x) = 6x^2 + 6x - 36$.

Solve $f'(x) = 6x^2 + 6x - 36 = 0$

Factoring, $6(x^2 + x - 6) = 6(x + 3)(x - 2) = 0$
$$x = -3, x = 2$$

The only critical numbers are $x = -3$ and $x = 2$.

$$
\begin{array}{ccc}
f'(-4) = 36 & f'(0) = -36 & f'(3) = 36 \\
+ + + + + & - - - - & + + + + \\
\end{array}
$$

$\quad\quad\quad\quad x = -3 \quad\quad x = 2$

Thus, $(-3, f(-3)) = (-3, 86)$ is a relative maximum
and $(2, f(2)) = (2, -39)$ is a relative minimum.

11. Find the critical numbers for $f(x) = x^2 - 8x + 9$ and determine the relative extreme points by solving $f'(x) = 0$ and showing where $f'(x) > 0$ and $f'(x) < 0$.

$$f'(x) = 2x - 8 = 0$$
$$x = 4$$

$$
\begin{array}{cc}
f'(3) = -2 & f'(5) = 2 \\
- - - - & + + + + \\
\end{array}
$$

$\quad\quad\quad 4$

$(4, f(4)) = (4, -7)$ is a relative minimum.

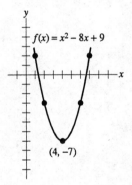

13.   Find the critical numbers for $f(x) = -2x^2 + 4x - 1$ and determine the relative extreme points by solving $f'(x) = 0$ and showing where $f'(x) > 0$ and $f'(x) < 0$.

$$f'(x) = -4x + 4 = 0$$
$$x = 1$$

$f'(0) = 4 \qquad f'(2) = -4$
$+\,+\,+\,+ \qquad -\,-\,-\,-$

1

$(1, f(1)) = (1, 1)$ is a relative maximum.

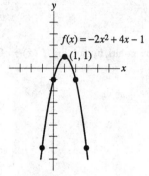

15.   Find the critical numbers for $f(x) = x^3 - 3x + 5$ and determine the relative extreme points by solving $f'(x) = 0$ and showing where $f'(x) > 0$ and $f'(x) < 0$.

$$f'(x) = 3x^2 - 3 = 3(x^2 - 1) = 3(x - 1)(x + 1) = 0$$
$$x = 1, x = -1$$

$f'(-2) = 9 \qquad f'(0) = -3 \qquad f'(2) = 9$
$+\,+\,+\,+ \qquad -\,-\,-\,- \qquad +\,+\,+\,+$

$-1 \qquad\qquad 1$

$(-1, f(-1)) = (-1, 7)$ is a relative maximum. $(1, f(1)) = (1, 3)$ is a relative minimum.

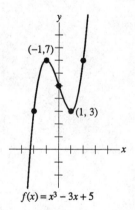

17. Find the critical numbers for $f(x) = -x^3 - 3x^2 + 7$ and determine the extreme points by solving $f'(x) = 0$ and showing where $f'(x) > 0$ and $f'(x) < 0$.

$$f'(x) = -3x^2 - 6x = -3x(x+2) = 0$$
$$x = 0, x = -2$$

$$f'(-3) = -9 \qquad f'(-1) = 3 \qquad f'(1) = -9$$
$$\begin{array}{ccc} ----- & ++++ & ---- \end{array}$$
$$\begin{array}{ccc} -2 & 0 \end{array}$$

$(-2, f(-2)) = (-2, 3)$ is a relative minimum. $(0, f(0)) = (0, 7)$ is a relative maximum.

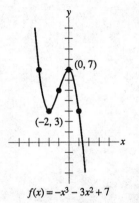

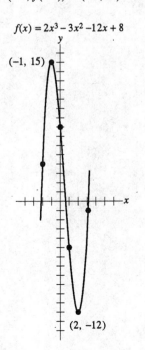

$(0, 7)$

$(-2, 3)$

$f(x) = -x^3 - 3x^2 + 7$

19. Find the critical numbers for $f(x) = 2x^3 - 3x^2 - 12x + 8$ and determine the extreme points by solving $f'(x) = 0$ and showing where $f'(x) > 0$ and $f'(x) < 0$.

$$f'(x) = 6x^2 - 6x - 12 = 6(x^2 - x - 2) = 6(x-2)(x+1) = 0$$
$$x = 2, x = -1$$

$$f'(-2) = 24 \qquad f'(0) = -12 \qquad f'(3) = 24$$
$$\begin{array}{ccc} +++++ & ---- & ++++ \end{array}$$
$$\begin{array}{ccc} -1 & 2 \end{array}$$

$(-1, f(-1)) = (-1, 15)$ is a relative maximum. $(2, f(2)) = (2, -12)$ is a relative minimum.

$f(x) = 2x^3 - 3x^2 - 12x + 8$

$(-1, 15)$

$(2, -12)$

21. Find the critical numbers for $f(x) = 6x^{2/3}$ and determine the extreme points by locating where $f'(x)$ is undefined and showing where $f'(x) > 0$ and $f'(x) < 0$.

$$f'(x) = 6\left(\frac{2}{3}\right)x^{-1/3} = 4x^{-1/3} = \frac{4}{x^{1/3}} \text{ is undefined at } x = 0.$$

$$\begin{array}{cc} f'(-1) = -4 & f'(1) = 4 \\ ----- & ++++ \end{array}$$

0

$(0, f(0)) = (0,0)$ is a relative minimum.

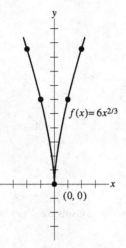

23. Find the critical numbers for $f(x) = 1 - 3x^{2/3}$ and determine the extreme points by locating where $f'(x)$ is undefined and showing where $f'(x) > 0$ and $f'(x) < 0$.

$$f'(x) = -3\left(\frac{2}{3}\right)x^{-1/3} = -2x^{-1/3} = -\frac{2}{x^{1/3}} \text{ is undefined at } x = 0.$$

$$\begin{array}{cc} f'(-1) = 2 & f'(1) = -2 \\ ++++ & ---- \end{array}$$

0

$(0, f(0)) = (0, 1)$ is a relative maximum.

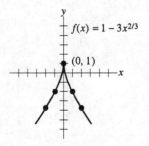

25. Find the critical numbers for $f(x) = (x - 3)^{2/3}$ and determine the extreme points by locating where $f'(x)$ is undefined and showing where $f'(x) > 0$ and $f'(x) < 0$.

$f'(x) = 2/3(x - 3)^{-1/3} = \dfrac{2}{3(x - 3)^{1/3}}$ is undefined at $x = 3$.

$$f'(2) = -2/3 \qquad f'(4) = 2/3$$

$\underset{\displaystyle 3}{\underbrace{-----\,\Big|\,++++}}$

$(3, f(3)) = (3, 0)$ is a relative minimum.

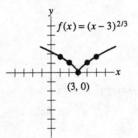

27. Given $f(x) = x^3 + 6x - 19$, then $f'(x) = 3x^2 + 6$.

Solving $f'(x) = 3x^2 + 6 = 0$
yields $3(x^2 + 2) = 0$
$x^2 + 2 = 0$

Since $x^2 + 2 \neq 0$ for any x and $f'(x)$ is defined for all x, *there are no relative extreme points.*

29. Given $f(x) = 10 - 3x^{2/3}$, then

$$f'(x) = -2x^{-1/3} = -\dfrac{2}{x^{1/3}}$$

Now $f'(x) = 0$ has no solution, but $f'(x)$ does not exist for $x = 0$. Since $f(x)$ does exist at $x = 0$, then $x = 0$ is a critical number. The sign of $f'(x)$ is given by

$$f'(-1) = 2 \qquad f'(1) = -2$$

$\underset{\displaystyle 0}{\underbrace{++++\,\Big|\,----}}$

Thus, $(0, f(0)) = (0, 10)$ is a relative maximum.

31. Given $f(x) = x^3$, then $f'(x) = 3x^2$.

Solving $f'(x) = 3x^2 = 0$
yields $x = 0$

Since $f'(x)$ is defined for all x, the only critical number is $x = 0$. The sign of $f'(x)$ is given by

$$f'(-1) = 3 \qquad f'(1) = 3$$

$\underset{\displaystyle 0}{\underbrace{++++\,\Big|\,++++}}$

Since $f'(x)$ does not change sign, there is no relative extreme point at $x = 0$.

33. Given $f(x) = \frac{1}{x} = x^{-1}$, then $f'(x) = -\frac{1}{x^2}$.

Since $f'(x) \neq 0$ for any x and since $f(x)$ and $f'(x)$ are both not defined at $x = 0$, there are no extreme points.

35.   Given $f(x) = (2x + 1)(x + 3)^4$, then

$$\begin{aligned} f'(x) &= (2x + 1)(4)(x + 3)^3 + (x + 3)^4(2) \\ &= 2(x + 3)^3[2(2x + 1) + x + 3] \\ &= 2(x + 3)^3(5x + 5) \\ &= 10(x + 3)^3(x + 1) \end{aligned}$$

Solving $f'(x) = 10(x + 3)^3(x + 1) = 0$
yields

$x = -3, \ x = -1$

The sign of $f'(x)$ is given by

$$\begin{array}{ccc} f'(-4) = 30 & f'(-2) = -10 & f'(0) = 270 \\ +\,+\,+\,+\,+ & -\,-\,-\,-\,- & +\,+\,+\,+ \\ \hline \qquad\quad -3 & \qquad\quad -1 & \end{array}$$

Thus, $(-3, f(-3)) = (-3, 0)$ is a relative maximum and $(-1, f(-1)) = (-1, -16)$ is a relative minimum.

37.   Given $f(x) = 3x^{4/3}$, then $f'(x) = 4x^{1/3}$.

Solving $f'(x) = 4x^{1/3} = 0$
yields $x = 0$

Since $f'(x)$ is defined for all x, the only critical number is $x = 0$. The sign of $f'(x)$ is given by

$$\begin{array}{cc} f'(-1) = -4 & f'(1) = 4 \\ -\,-\,-\,-\,- & +\,+\,+\,+ \\ \hline \\ -\,-\,-\,-\,- & +\,+\,+\,+ \\ \hline \qquad\quad 0 & \end{array}$$

Thus, $(0, 0)$ is a relative minimum.

39.   Given $f(x) = 3x^4 + 4x^3 - 36x^2 + 19$, then $f'(x) = 12x^3 + 12x^2 - 72x$.

$$\begin{aligned} \text{Solving } f'(x) = 12x^3 + 12x^2 - 72x &= 0 \\ \text{yields} \qquad 12x(x^2 + x - 6) &= 0 \\ x = 0 \ \text{ or } \ x^2 + x - 6 &= 0 \\ (x + 3)(x - 2) &= 0 \\ x = -3 \ \text{ or } \ x &= 2 \end{aligned}$$

The critical numbers are $x = -3$, 0, and 2. The sign of $f'(x)$ is given by

$$\begin{array}{cccc} f'(-4) = -288 & f'(-1) = 72 & f'(1) = -48 & f'(3) = 213 \\ -\,-\,-\,-\,- & +\,+\,+\,+\,+\,+ & -\,-\,-\,- & +\,+\,+\,+ \\ \hline \qquad\quad -3 & \qquad\quad 0 & \qquad\quad 2 & \end{array}$$

Thus, $(-3, f(-3)) = (-3, -170)$ is a relative minimum, $(0, f(0)) = (0, 19)$ is a relative maximum, and $(2, f(2)) = (2, -45)$ is a relative minimum.

41.   Given $C(x) = x^3 - 6x^2 + 12x + 1$, then

$$C'(x) = 3x^2 - 12x + 12$$

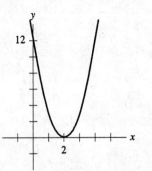

43.   At x_1 the tangent line has slope zero; thus $f'(x_1) = 0$.

At x_2 the function is decreasing; thus $f'(x_2) < 0$.

At x_3 the tangent line has slope zero; thus $f'(x_3) = 0$.

At x_4 the function has a sharp, pointed minimum; thus $f'(x_4)$ is undefined.

45.   Given $f(x) = 4x^2 - 8x^4$, find the critical numbers where $f'(x) = 0$ and where $f'(x)$ is undefined. Using the critical numbers, determine where $f'(x) > 0$ and $f'(x) < 0$.

$$f'(x) = 8x - 32x^3 = 8x(1 - 4x^2) = 8x(1 - 2x)(1 + 2x)$$

$f'(x)$ is defined for all x; $f'(x) = 0$ for $x = 0, x = \frac{1}{2}$, and $x = -\frac{1}{2}$.

$f' > 0$ for $x < -\frac{1}{2}$, $0 < x < \frac{1}{2}$ $f' < 0$ for $-\frac{1}{2} < x < 0$, $x > \frac{1}{2}$

$\left(-\frac{1}{2}, \frac{1}{2}\right)$ is a relative maximum.

$(0, 0)$ is a relative minimum.

$\left(\frac{1}{2}, \frac{1}{2}\right)$ is a relative maximum.

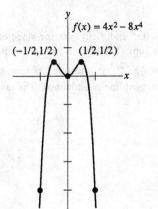

47. Given $f(x) = 3x^{2/3} - x$, find the critical numbers where $f'(x) = 0$ and where $f'(x)$ is undefined. Using the critical numbers, determine where $f'(x) > 0$ and $f'(x) < 0$.

$f'(x) = 2x^{-1/3} - 1 = \frac{2}{x^{1/3}} - 1 = \frac{2 - x^{1/3}}{x^{1/3}}$

$f'(x)$ is undefined for $x = 0$,

and $f'(x) = 0$ for $x^{1/3} = 2$

$\qquad\qquad\qquad\quad x = 8$

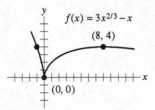

$(0, 0)$ is a relative minimum.

$(8, 4)$ is a relative maximum.

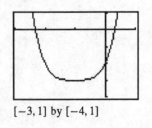

49. **a.** The dog changed direction after 2 minutes.
  b. The dog stopped after 3 minutes for 1 minute.
  c. The dog attained a maximum speed of 6 miles per hour.
  d. Between minutes 5 and 7 the dog is heading north at a constant velocity of 3 miles per hour.

51. A relative maximum function value is the value of the function $f(c)$ at the critical number $x = c$.

A relative maximum point is the point $(c, f(c))$ on the graph of the function at the critical number $x = c$.

53. The point $(2, f(2))$ is a critical point because $f'(2) = 0$. Since $f' > 0$ for $x < 2$ and $f' < 0$ for $x > 2$, $(2, f(2))$ must be a relative maximum.

55. **a.** Since $f'(x) = 3x^2$ and $f'(0) = 0$, the slope of the tangent line is zero. The tangent line is *horizontal*.
  b. Since $f'(x) = \frac{1}{3}x^{-2/3}$ is undefined at $x = 0$, the slope of the tangent line is undefined. The tangent line is *vertical*.

SECTION 4.2 Technology Exercises

1. relative minimum at $(-1, -3)$

$[-3, 1]$ by $[-4, 1]$

3.   relative minimum at $(3.4, -2.7)$; relative maximum at $(0.6, 8.7)$

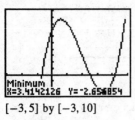

[−3, 5] by [−3, 10]

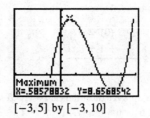

[−3, 5] by [−3, 10]

5.   relative maximum at $x = -1$;
relative minimum at $x = 3$

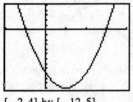

[−2, 4] by [−12, 5]

7. $f'(x) = 2x - 4$

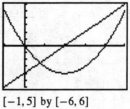

[−1, 5] by [−6, 6]

a. $x = 2$

b.   It isn't just luck; the values for which $f'(x) = 0$ are the critical numbers of $f(x)$.

9. $f'(x) = 2x - 8$

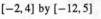
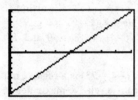

[0, 8] by [−8, 8]

a. $c = 4$

b. $f'(x)$ is negative.

c. $f'(x)$ is positive.

d. $(4, f(4))$ is a relative minimum.

11. $f'(x) = \dfrac{5 - 10x^2}{(2x^2 + 1)^2}$; relative minimum at $x = -0.7$; relative maximum at $x = 0.7$ (by symmetry)

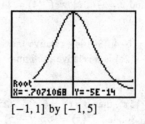

[−1, 1] by [−1, 5]

SECTION 4.3 pages 216–220

1.   The graph is concave up over the interval $(0, 3)$.

The graph is concave down over the interval $(-4, 0)$.

3.   The graph is concave up over the interval $(-\infty, 0) \cup (0, \infty)$.

The graph is never concave down.

5.   Given $f(x) = x^2 - 20x + 13$, then $f'(x) = 2x - 20$ and $f''(x) = 2$.

Since $f''(x) = 2 > 0$ for all x, then f is concave up for all x, $(-\infty, \infty)$.

7.   Given $f(x) = x^3$, then $f'(x) = 3x^2$ and $f''(x) = 6x$. $f''(x) = 6x = 0$ when $x = 0$, $f''(x) < 0$ for $x < 0$, and $f''(x) > 0$ for $x > 0$.

Thus, f is concave up over the interval $(0, \infty)$ and concave down over the interval $(-\infty, 0)$.

9. Given $f(x) = x^3 + 3x^2 + 3x + 1$, then $f'(x) = 3x^2 + 6x + 3$ and $f''(x) = 6x + 6$. Solving $f''(x) = 6(x+1) = 0$ gives $x = -1$.

$$f''(-2) = -6 \qquad f''(0) = 6$$

```
  - - - - -    |    + + +
  _____
            x = -1
```

Thus, f is concave up over the interval $(-1, \infty)$ and concave down over the interval $(-\infty, -1)$.

11. Given $f(x) = -2x^3 + 3x^2 + 12x - 11$, then $f'(x) = -6x^2 + 6x + 12$ and $f''(x) = -12x + 6$. Solving $f''(x) = -6(2x - 1) = 0$ gives $x = 1/2$.

$$f''(0) = 6 \qquad f''(1) = -6$$

```
  + + +    |    - - - -
  _____
          x = 1/2
```

Thus, f is concave up over the interval $\left(-\infty, \frac{1}{2}\right)$ and concave down over the interval $\left(\frac{1}{2}, \infty\right)$.

13. Given $f(x) = \frac{x+1}{x}$, then $f'(x) = \frac{x(1) - (x+1)(1)}{x^2} = -\frac{1}{x^2} = -x^{-2}$ and $f''(x) = 2x^{-3} = \frac{2}{x^3}$. $f''(x)$ is never zero, but $f''x$ is undefined at $x = 0$.

$$f''(-1) = -2 \qquad f''(1) = 2$$

```
  - - - - -    |    + + + +
  _____
            x = 0
```

Thus, f is concave up over the interval $(0, \infty)$ and concave down over the interval $(-\infty, 0)$.

15. Given $f(x) = x^3 + 3x^2 + 5$, then $f'(x) = 3x^2 + 6x$ and $f''(x) = 6x + 6$. Solving $f'(x) = 3x(x + 2) = 0$ gives $x = 0$ and $x = -2$. Now $f''(0) = 6 > 0$ and $f''(-2) = -6 < 0$.

Thus, $(0, f(0)) = (0, 5)$ is a relative minimum and $(-2, f(-2)) = (-2, 9)$ is a relative maximum.

17. Given $f(x) = x^3 - 48x + 2$, then $f'(x) = 3x^2 - 48$ and $f''(x) = 6x$. Solving $f'(x) = 3(x^2 - 16) = 3(x - 4)(x + 4) = 0$ gives $x = 4$ and $x = -4$. Now $f''(4) = 24 > 0$ and $f''(-4) = -24 < 0$.

Thus, $(-4, f(-4)) = (-4, 130)$ is a relative maximum and $(4, f(4)) = (4, -126)$ is a relative minimum.

19. Given $f(x) = -x^3 - 3x^2 + 24x + 7$, then $f'(x) = -3x^2 - 6x + 24$ and $f''(x) = -6x - 6$. Solving $f'(x) = -3(x^2 + 2x - 8) = -3(x + 4)(x - 2) = 0$ gives $x = -4$ and $x = 2$. Now $f''(-4) = 18 > 0$ and $f''(2) = -18 < 0$.

Thus, $(-4, f(-4)) = (-4, -73)$ is a relative minimum and $(2, f(2)) = (2, 35)$ is a relative maximum.

21. Given $f(x) = 2x^3 - 15x^2$, then $f'(x) = 6x^2 - 30x$ and $f''(x) = 12x - 30$. Solving $f'(x) = 6x(x - 5) = 0$ gives $x = 0$ and $x = 5$. Now $f''(0) = -30 < 0$ and $f''(5) = 30 > 0$.

Thus, $(0, f(0)) = (0, 0)$ is a relative maximum and $(5, f(5)) = (5, -125)$ is a relative mimimum.

23. Given $f(x) = x^{1/3}$, then $f'(x) = \frac{1}{3}x^{-2/3}$ and $f''(x) = -\frac{2}{9}x^{-5/3}$. $f'(x)$ is never zero, but $f'(x)$ is undefined at $x = 0$. Since $f''(x)$ is also undefined at $x = 0$, the second derivative test cannot be used. Using the first derivative test gives

$$f'(-1) = \frac{1}{3} \qquad f'(1) = \frac{1}{3}$$

```
  + + + +    |    + + +
  _____
            x = 0
```

Since $f'(x)$ does not change sign at the critical number $x = 0$, there is no relative maximum or minimum.

25. Given $f(x) = 2x^4 + 5$, then $f'(x) = 8x^3$ and $f''(x) = 24x^2$. Now $f'(x) = 8x^3 = 0$ when $x = 0$ and $f''(0) = 0$, which results in no test. Using the first derivative test yields

$$f'(-1) = -8 < 0 \qquad f'(1) = 8 > 0$$

$$\begin{array}{ccc} ------- & & +++++ \\ \hline & \bullet & \\ & x = 0 & \end{array}$$

Thus, $(0, f(0)) = (0, 5)$ is a relative minimum.

27. Given $f(x) = 3x^4 - 2x^3 - 3x^2 + 5$, then $f'(x) = 12x^3 - 6x^2 - 6x$ and $f''(x) = 36x^2 - 12x - 6$. Now

$$\begin{aligned} f'(x) = 12x^3 - 6x^2 - 6x &= 0 \\ 6x(2x^2 - x - 1) &= 0 \\ 6x(2x + 1)(x - 1) &= 0 \end{aligned}$$

so critical values are $x = 0$, $x = -\frac{1}{2}$, and $x = 1$. $f''(0) = -6 < 0$, so $(0, f(0)) = (0, 5)$ is a relative maximum. $f''(1) = 18 > 0$, so $(1, f(1)) = (1, 3)$ is a relative minimum. $f''\left(-\frac{1}{2}\right) = f''(-0.5) = 9 > 0$, so $(-0.5, f(-0.5)) = (-0.5, 4.6875)$ is a relative minimum.

29. Given $f(x) = x^3 - 4$, then $f'(x) = 3x^2$ and $f''(x) = 6x$. Solving $f''(x) = 6x = 0$ gives $x = 0$.

$$f''(-1) = -6 \qquad f''(1) = 6$$

$$\begin{array}{ccc} ----- & & ++++ \\ \hline & \bullet & \\ & x = 0 & \end{array}$$

Thus, $(0, f(0)) = (0, -4)$ is a point of inflection.

31. Given $f(x) = x^3 + 6x^2 + 12x + 12$, then $f'(x) = 3x^2 + 12x + 12$ and $f''(x) = 6x + 12$. Solving $f''(x) = 6(x + 2) = 0$ gives $x = -2$.

$$f''(-3) = -6 \qquad f''(0) = 12$$

$$\begin{array}{ccc} ----- & & ++++ \\ \hline & \bullet & \\ & x = -2 & \end{array}$$

Thus, $(-2, f(-2)) = (-2, 4)$ is a point of inflection.

33. Given $f(x) = x^3 - 3x^2 + 4$, then $f'(x) = 3x^2 - 6x$ and $f''(x) = 6x - 6$. Solving $f''(x) = 6(x - 1) = 0$, gives $x = 1$.

$$f''(0) = -6 \qquad f''(2) = 6$$

$$\begin{array}{ccc} ---- & & ++++ \\ \hline & \bullet & \\ & x = 1 & \end{array}$$

Thus, $(1, f(1)) = (1, 2)$ is a point of inflection.

35. Given $f(x) = 2x^3 - 3x^2 + 12x - 2$, then $f'(x) = 6x^2 - 6x + 12$ and $f''(x) = 12x - 6$. Solving $f''(x) = 6(2x - 1) = 0$ gives $x = \frac{1}{2}$.

$$f''(0) = -6 \qquad f''(1) = 6$$

$$\begin{array}{ccc} ---- & & ++++ \\ \hline & \bullet & \\ & x = \frac{1}{2} & \end{array}$$

Thus, $\left(\frac{1}{2}, f\left(\frac{1}{2}\right)\right) = \left(\frac{1}{2}, \frac{7}{2}\right)$ is a point of inflection.

37. Given $f(x) = x^3 - 3x^2 + 5$, then $f'(x) = 3x^2 - 6x$ and $f''(x) = 6x - 6$. Solving $f'(x) = 3x(x - 2) = 0$ gives the critical numbers $x = 0$ and $x = 2$. Using the second derivative test, $f''(0) = -6 < 0$ and $f''(2) = 6 > 0$. Also, solving $f''(x) = 6(x - 1) = 0$ gives $x = 1$.

$$f''(0) = -6 \qquad f''(2) = 6$$
$$\underset{x = 1}{\underline{\quad - - - - \qquad + + + + \quad}}$$

Thus,

Relative maximum point: $(0, 5)$

Relative minimum point: $(2, 1)$

Point of inflection: $(1, 3)$

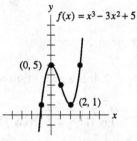

Point of inflection $(1, 3)$

39. Given $f(x) = x^3 - 3x^2 + 3x - 1$, then $f'(x) = 3x^2 - 6x + 3$ and $f''(x) = 6x - 6$. Solving $f'(x) = 3(x^2 - 2x + 1) = 3(x - 1)(x - 1)$ gives the critical number $x = 1$. The second derivative test fails, since $f''(1) = 0$. The first derivative test shows

$$f'(0) = 3 \qquad f'(2) = 3$$
$$\underset{x = 1}{\underline{\quad + + + + \qquad + + + + \quad}}$$

Also, solving $f''(x) = 6(x - 1) = 0$ gives $x = 1$.

$$f''(0) = -6 \qquad f''(2) = 6$$
$$\underset{x = 1}{\underline{\quad - - - - \qquad + + + + \quad}}$$

Thus,

No relative extreme points.

Point of inflection: $(1, 0)$

y intercept: $(0, -1)$

$f(x) = x^3 - 3x^2 + 3x - 1$

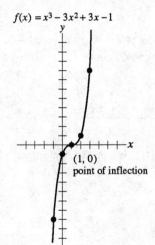

$(1, 0)$
point of inflection

41. Given $f(x) = 1 - 3x^2 - x^3$, then $f'(x) = -6x - 3x^2$ and $f''(x) = -6 - 6x$. Solving $f'(x) = -3x(2+x) = 0$ gives the critical numbers $x = 0$ and $x = -2$. Using the second derivative test, $f''(0) = -6 < 0$ and $f''(-2) = 6 > 0$. Also, solving $f''(x) = -6(1 + x) = 0$ gives $x = -1$.

$$f''(-2) = 6 \qquad f''(0) = -6$$
$$\underline{\;++++\;\;\;\;\bullet\;\;\;\;----\;}$$
$$x = -1$$

Thus,

Relative maximum point: $(0, 1)$

Relative minimum point: $(-2, -3)$

Point of inflection: $(-1, -1)$

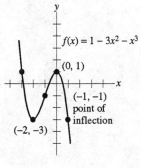

43. Given $f(x) = -x^3 + 3x^2 + 5$, then $f'(x) = -3x^2 + 6x$ and $f''(x) = -6x + 6$. Solving $f'(x) = -3x(x-2) = 0$ gives the critical numbers $x = 0$ and $x = 2$. Using the second derivative test, $f''(0) = 6 > 0$ and $f''(2) = -6 < 0$. Also, solving $f''(x) = -6(x - 1) = 0$ yields $x = 1$.

$$f''(0) = 6 \qquad f''(2) = -6$$
$$\underline{\;++++\;\;\;\;\bullet\;\;\;\;----\;}$$
$$x = 1$$

Thus,

Relative maximum point: $(2, 9)$

Relative minimum point: $(0, 5)$

Point of inflection: $(1, 7)$

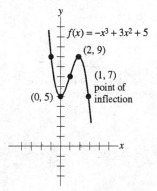

45. Given $f(x) = x^{1/3} + 1$, then $f'(x) = \frac{1}{3}x^{-2/3}$ and $f''(x) = -\frac{2}{9}x^{-5/3}$. Now, $f'(x)$ is never zero, but $f'(x)$ is undefined at $x = 0$. Since $f''(x)$ is not defined at the critical number $x = 0$, the second derivative test cannot be used.

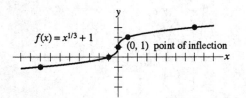

$$f'(-1) = 1/3 \qquad f'(1) = 1/3$$
$$+\!+\!+\!+\!+ \qquad\qquad +\!+\!+\!+$$
$$x = 0$$

$$f''(-1) = 2/9 \qquad f''(1) = -2/9$$
$$+\!+\!+\!+\!+ \qquad\qquad -\!-\!-\!-\!-$$
$$x = 0$$

Thus,

No relative extreme points

Point of inflection: $(0, 1)$

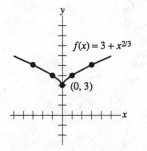

$f(x) = x^{1/3} + 1$

$(0, 1)$ point of inflection

47. Given $f(x) = 3 + x^{2/3}$, then $f'(x) = 2/3x^{-1/3}$ and $f''(x) = -\frac{2}{9}x^{-4/3}$. Now, $f'(x)$ is never zero, but $f'(x)$ is undefined at $x = 0$. Since $f''(x)$ is also undefined at $x = 0$, the second derivative test cannot be used.

$$f'(-1) = -\frac{2}{3} \qquad f'(1) = \frac{2}{3}$$
$$-\!-\!-\!-\!- \qquad\qquad +\!+\!+\!+$$
$$x = 0$$

$$f''(-1) = -\frac{2}{9} \qquad f''(1) = -\frac{2}{9}$$
$$-\!-\!-\!-\!- \qquad\qquad -\!-\!-\!-$$
$$x = 0$$

Thus,

Relative minimum point: $(0, 3)$

No relative maximum point

No point of inflection

$f(x) = 3 + x^{2/3}$

$(0, 3)$

49. Given $f(x) = 2x - 3x^{2/3}$, then $f'(x) = 2 - 2x^{-1/3}$ and $f''(x) = \frac{2}{3}x^{-4/3}$. Solving $f'(x) = \frac{2(x^{1/3}-1)}{x^{1/3}} = 0$ gives $x = 1$. Also, $f'(x)$ is undefined at $x = 0$. The two critical numbers are $x = 1$ and $x = 0$. Using the second derivative test, $f''(1) = \frac{2}{3} > 0$. $f''(x)$ is undefined at $x = 0$.

$$f'(-1) = 4 \qquad f'\left(\tfrac{1}{8}\right) = -2 \qquad f'(8) = 1$$

$$+ + + + \qquad\qquad - - - - - \qquad\qquad + + + +$$

$$x = 0 \qquad\qquad x = 1$$

$$f''(-1) = 2/3 \qquad f''(1) = 2/3$$

$$+ + + + + \qquad\qquad + + + +$$

$$x = 0$$

Thus,

Relative maximum point: $(0, 0)$

Relative minimum point: $(1, -1)$

No point of inflection

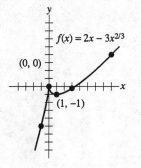

$f(x) = 2x - 3x^{2/3}$
$(0, 0)$
$(1, -1)$

51. Given $f(x) = 3x^{4/3}$, then $f'(x) = 4x^{1/3}$ and $f''(x) = \frac{4}{3}x^{-2/3}$. Solving $f'(x) = 4x^{1/3} = 0$ gives the critical number $x = 0$. Now, $f''(x)$ is undefined at $x = 0$, so the second derivative test cannot be used.

$$f'(-1) = -4 \qquad f'(1) = 4$$

$$- - - - - \qquad + + + +$$

$$x = 0$$

$$f''(-1) = 4/3 \qquad f''(1) = 4/3$$

$$+ + + + + \qquad + + + +$$

$$x = 0$$

Thus,

Relative minimum point: $(0, 0)$

No relative maximum point

No point of inflection

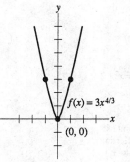

$f(x) = 3x^{4/3}$
$(0, 0)$

53. Given $f(x) = x^3 + 2$, then $f'(x) = 3x^2$ and $f''(x) = 6x$. Solving $f'(x) = 3x^2 = 0$ gives the critical number $x = 0$. Since $f''(0) = 0$, the second derivative test fails. Using the first derivative test gives

$$f'(-1) = 3 \qquad f'(1) = 3$$

$$\begin{array}{c|c} + + + + & + + + + \\ \hline & \\ & x = 0 \end{array}$$

$$f''(-1) = -6 \qquad f''(1) = 6$$

$$\begin{array}{c|c} - - - - - & + + + + \\ \hline \end{array}$$

$$\begin{array}{c|c} - - - - - & + + + + \\ \hline & \\ & x = 0 \end{array}$$

Thus,

No relative extreme points

Point of inflection: $(0, 2)$

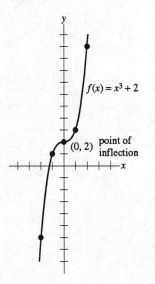

$f(x) = x^3 + 2$

$(0, 2)$ point of inflection

55. Given $f(x) = 3 - x^4$, then $f'(x) = -4x^3$ and $f''(x) = -12x^2$. Solving $f'(x) = -4x^3 = 0$ gives the only critical number, $x = 0$. Since $f''(0) = 0$, the second derivative test fails. Using the first derivative test gives

$$f'(-1) = 4 \qquad f'(1) = -4$$

$$\begin{array}{c|c} + + + + & - - - - \\ \hline & \\ & x = 0 \end{array}$$

$$f''(-1) = -12 \qquad f''(1) = -12$$

$$\begin{array}{c|c} - - - - - & - - - - - \\ \hline & \\ & x = 0 \end{array}$$

Thus,

Relative maximum point: $(0, 3)$

No relative minimum point

No point of inflection

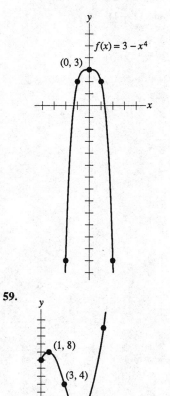

$f(x) = 3 - x^4$

$(0, 3)$

57.

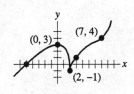

$(0, 3)$

$(7, 4)$

$(2, -1)$

59.

$(1, 8)$

$(3, 4)$

$(5, 0)$

61.

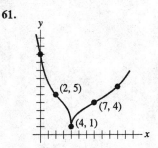

$(2, 5)$

$(7, 4)$

$(4, 1)$

63. Given $f(x) = x^{2/3} + 1$, then $f'(x) = \frac{2}{3}x^{-1/3}$ and $f''(x) = -\frac{2}{9}x^{-4/3}$. By the algebra of exponents, $f''(x) = -\frac{2}{9x^{4/3}}$ and $f''(x)$ is defined for all x except $x = 0$. The expression $x^{4/3} = (x^{1/3})^4 > 0$ for all x; hence $f''(x) = -\frac{2}{9x^{4/3}} < 0$ for all x, $x \neq 0$. Thus $f(x)$ is concave down everywhere.

65. The points $(a, f(a))$ and $(b, g(b))$ in the graphs shown are unusual because they are *both* relative extreme points *and* points of inflection. Usually a point is *either* an extreme point *or* a point of inflection.

67.
  a. Zero; horizontal tangent
  b. Zero; horizontal tangent
  c. Negative; function is decreasing
  d. Negative; function is concave down
  e. Negative; function is decreasing
  f. Positive; function is concave up
  g. Positive; function is increasing
  h. Negative; function is concave down

69. No, it is *not* safe to assume that a graph has a point of inflection wherever $f''(x) = 0$. The condition $f''(x) = 0$ means only that the rate of change of the function $f'(x)$ is zero. Any function of the form $f(x) = x^{2(n+1)}$, n a positive integer, satisfies the condition that $f''(0) = 0$, but $x = 0$ is *not* a point of inflection.

71. The function $f(x) = \frac{x+1}{x}$ does not have a point of inflection at $x = 0$, since $f(0)$ is not defined.

73. f' is increasing. Since f is concave up, $f'' > 0$, so the function f' has a positive derivative and is increasing.

75.
  a. The graph of n is concave up.
  b. $n''(t)$ is positive.

77. Since the population P has been rising (increasing) at an increasing rate, the derivative $P'(t)$ has positive values *and* $P'(t)$ is an increasing function. Thus, $P''(t) > 0$, and the graph of $y = P(t)$ is concave up.

79. Since marginal revenue is the derivative $R'(x)$, marginal revenue is a decreasing function when $[R'(x)]' = R''(x) < 0$.

Thus, $R_1(x)$ is the revenue function for which marginal revenue is a decreasing function, since $R_1(x)$ is concave down.

81. $f'(x) = 0$ for $x = 1$ and $x = -1$.

$$f''(1) = \frac{2(-2)}{2^3} = -\frac{1}{2} < 0$$

$$f''(-1) = \frac{-2(-2)}{2^3} = \frac{1}{2} > 0$$

Thus $x = -1$ is the value of x for which $f(x)$ has a minimum.

83. Given $f(x) = \frac{12}{x^2+3} = 12(x^2 + 3)^{-1}$, then $f'(x) = -\frac{24x}{(x^2+3)^2}$ and $f''(x) = \frac{72(x^2-1)}{(x^2+3)^3}$. Since $x^2 + 3 \neq 0$, $f(x)$, $f'(x)$, and $f''(x)$ are defined for all x. Solving $f'(x) = 0$ gives the only critical number, $x = 0$. Also, $f''(x) = 0$ for $x = 1$ and $x = -1$. The signs of $f''(x)$ are given by

$$
\begin{array}{ccc}
f''(-2) > 0 & f''(0) < 0 & f''(2) > 0 \\
+\,+\,+\,+ & -\;-\;-\;-\;- & +\,+\,+\,+ \\
\hline
\quad\quad x=-1 & \quad\quad x=1 &
\end{array}
$$

Note: $f'(0) < 0$

Thus, $(0, 4)$ is a relative maximum point, and $(-1, 3)$ and $(1, 3)$ are points of inflection. Finally, $\lim\limits_{x \to \infty} \frac{12}{x^2+3} = 0$, so $y = 0$ is a horizontal asymptote.

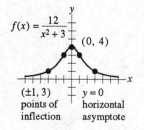

$f(x) = \dfrac{12}{x^2 + 3}$

$(0, 4)$

$(\pm 1, 3)$ points of inflection

$y = 0$ horizontal asymptote

85. Given $f(x) = \frac{2x^2}{x^2+1}$, then using the quotient rule, $f'(x) = \frac{4x}{(x^2+1)^2}$ and $f''(x) = -\frac{4(3x^2-1)}{(x^2+1)^3}$. Since $x^2 + 1 \neq 0$, $f(x)$, $f'(x)$, and $f''(x)$ are defined for all x. Solving $f'(x) = 0$ gives the only critical number, $x = 0$. Also, $f''(x) = 0$ for $x = \sqrt{\frac{1}{3}}$ and $x = -\sqrt{\frac{1}{3}}$. Now $f''(0) = 4 > 0$, and the other signs of $f''(x)$ are given by

$$f''(-1) < 0 \qquad f''(0) > 0 \qquad f''(1) < 0$$

$$- - - - - \qquad + + + + \qquad - - - - -$$

$$x = -\sqrt{\frac{1}{3}} \qquad x = \sqrt{\frac{1}{3}}$$

Thus, $(0,0)$ is a relative minimum point, and $\left(-\sqrt{\frac{1}{3}}, \frac{1}{2}\right)$ and $\left(\sqrt{\frac{1}{3}}, \frac{1}{2}\right)$ are points of inflection. Finally, $\lim\limits_{x\to\infty} \frac{2x^2}{x^2+1} = 2$, so $y = 2$ is a horizontal asymptote.

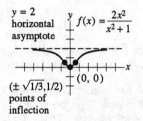

$y = 2$ horizontal asymptote

$f(x) = \dfrac{2x^2}{x^2+1}$

$(0, 0)$

$(\pm \sqrt{1/3}, 1/2)$ points of inflection

87. Given $f(x) = \frac{x+1}{x} = 1 + \frac{1}{x}$, then $f'(x) = -\frac{1}{x^2}$ and $f''(x) = \frac{2}{x^3}$. Now $f'(x)$ and $f''(x)$ are never zero and, although $f'(x)$ and $f''(x)$ are both undefined at $x = 0$, the value $x = 0$ is not in the domain of f. Thus, there are no critical numbers. The signs of $f'(x)$ and $f''(x)$ are given by

$$f'(-1) = -1 \qquad f'(1) = -1$$

$$- - - - - \qquad - - - -$$

$$x = 0$$

$$f''(-1) = -2 \qquad f''(1) = 2$$

$$- - - - - \qquad + + + +$$

$$x = 0$$

Finally, $\lim\limits_{x\to\infty} 1 + \frac{1}{x} = 1$, so $y = 1$ is a horizontal asymptote, and $\lim\limits_{x\to 0} 1 + \frac{1}{x} = \infty$, so $x = 0$ is a vertical asymptote.

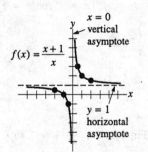

$x = 0$ vertical asymptote

$f(x) = \dfrac{x+1}{x}$

$y = 1$ horizontal asymptote

89. Given $f(x) = \frac{x^2}{x^2-9}$, then using the quotient rule, $f'(x) = -\frac{18x}{(x^2-9)^2}$ and $f''(x) = \frac{54(x^2+3)}{(x^2-9)^3}$. Now $f'(x) = 0$ at $x = 0$, but $f''(x)$ is never zero. At $x = 3$ and $x = -3$, the function f is undefined, as are $f'(x)$ and $f''(x)$. The only critical number is $x = 0$; and since $f''(0) = -\frac{2}{9} < 0$, then $(0,0)$ is a relative maximum point. The signs of $f'(x)$ and $f''(x)$ are given by

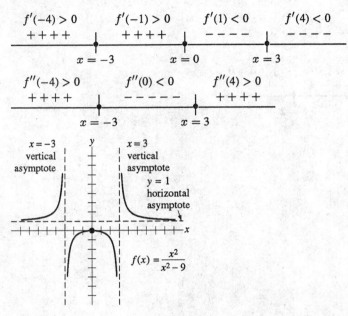

Finally, $\lim_{x\to\infty} \frac{x^2}{x^2-9} = 1$, so $y = 1$ is a horizontal asymptote; and $\lim_{x\to 3+} \frac{x^2}{x^2-9} = \infty$, $\lim_{x\to 3-} \frac{x^2}{x^2-9} = -\infty$, $\lim_{x\to -3+} \frac{x^2}{x^2-9} = -\infty$, and $\lim_{x\to -3-} \frac{x^2}{x^2-9} = \infty$, so $x = 3$ and $x = -3$ are vertical asymptotes.

91. Given $f(x) = \frac{x}{x^2-4}$, then using the quotient rule, $f'(x) = -\frac{x^2+4}{(x^2-4)^2}$ and $f''(x) = \frac{2x(x^2+12)}{(x^2-4)^3}$. Since $x^2 + 4 \neq 0$, then $f'(x)$ is never zero. However, $f''(x) = 0$ at $x = 0$. At $x = 2$ and $x = -2$, the function $f(x)$ is undefined, as are $f'(x)$ and $f''(x)$. There are no critical numbers, but there is a possible point of inflection at $x = 0$. The signs of $f'(x)$ and $f''(x)$ are given by

$$f'(-3) < 0 \qquad f'(0) < 0 \qquad f'(3) < 0$$

$$---- \quad | \quad ---- \quad | \quad ----$$
$$x = -2 \qquad x = 2$$

$$f''(-3) < 0 \qquad f''(-1) > 0 \qquad f''(1) < 0 \qquad f''(3) > 0$$

$$----- \quad | \quad ++++ \quad | \quad ----- \quad | \quad ++++$$
$$x = -2 \qquad x = 0 \qquad x = 2$$

Then $(0, 0)$ is a point of inflection

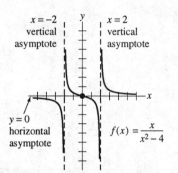

Finally, $\lim\limits_{x \to \infty} \frac{x}{x^2-4} = 0$, so $y = 0$ is a horizontal asymptote; and $\lim\limits_{x \to 2^+} \frac{x}{x^2-4} = \infty$, $\lim\limits_{x \to 2^-} \frac{x}{x^2-4} = -\infty$, $\lim\limits_{x \to -2^+} \frac{x}{x^2-4} = \infty$,

and $\lim\limits_{x \to -2^-} \frac{x}{x^2-4} = -\infty$, so $x = 2$ and $x = -2$ are vertical asymptotes.

93. Choice (ii) because prices rise if there is *any* associated inflation.

SECTION 4.3 Technology Exercises

1. concave down on $(-\infty, -3)$; concave up on $(-3, \infty)$

3. $x \cong 1.7$ (actual value is $\frac{5}{3}$)

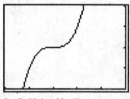

[−5, 0] by [0, 4]

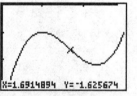

X=1.6914894   Y=-1.625674

[0, 3] by [−3, 0]

5. one

7. two

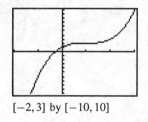

[−2, 3] by [−10, 10]

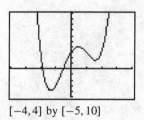

[−4, 4] by [−5, 10]

9.

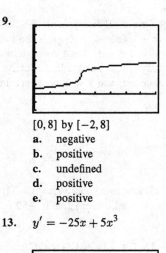

[0, 8] by [−2, 8]

a. negative
b. positive
c. undefined
d. positive
e. positive

13. $y' = -25x + 5x^3$

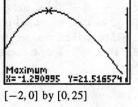

[−2, 0] by [0, 25]

relative maximum at −1.3

11. $f'(x) = 3x^2 - 18x + 10$; $f''(x) = 6x - 18$

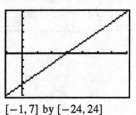

[−1, 7] by [−24, 24]

concave down on $(-\infty, 3)$; concave up on $(3, \infty)$; inflection point at $x = 3$

SECTION 4.4 pages 222–223

1. Relative maximum value is 3 at $x = 1$.

Relative minimum value is 1 at $x = 3$.

Absolute maximum value is 5 at $x = 5$.

Absolute minimum value is 1 at $x = 3$.

3. Relative maximum value is 5 at $x = 2.5$.

No relative minimum.

Absolute maximum value is 5 at $x = 2.5$.

Absolute minimum value is 1 at $x = 5$.

5. Relative maximum value is 6 at $x = 5$.

Relative minimum value is 5 at $x = 2\frac{1}{2}$.

Absolute maximum value is 7 at $x = 0$.

Absolute minimum value is 2 at $x = 8$.

7. Given $f(x) = x^2 + 5$, then $f'(x) = 2x$. Solving $f'(x) = 2x = 0$ gives the only critical number, $x = 0$. Using the endpoints, $x = -1$ and $x = 8$, construct the table:

x	$f(x)$
−1	6
0	5
8	69

From the table, the absolute maximum value is 69 at $x = 8$, and the absolute minimum value is 5 at $x = 0$.

9. Given $f(x) = -2x^2 + 8x - 17$, then $f'(x) = -4x + 8$. Solving $f'(x) = -4(x - 2) = 0$ gives the only critical number, $x = 2$. Using the endpoints, construct the table:

x	$f(x)$
0	−17
2	−9
6	−41

From the table, the absolute maximum value is −9 at $x = 2$, and the absolute minimum value is −41 at $x = 6$.

11. Given $f(x) = x^3 - 6x^2$, then $f'(x) = 3x^2 - 12x$. Solving $f'(x) = 3x(x - 4) = 0$ gives the two critical numbers $x = 0$ and $x = 4$. Using the endpoints, construct the table:

x	$f(x)$
−1	−7
0	0
4	−32
10	400

From the table, the absolute maximum value is 400 at $x = 10$, and the absolute minimum value is −32 at $x = 4$.

13. Given $f(x) = 2x^3 - 3x^2 - 36x + 4$, then $f'(x) = 6x^2 - 6x - 36$. Solving $f'(x) = 6(x^2 - x - 6) = 6(x + 2)(x - 3) = 0$ gives the two critical numbers $x = -2$ and $x = 3$. Using the endpoints, construct the table:

x	$f(x)$
-5	-141
-2	48
3	-77
10	1344

From the table, the absolute maximum value is 1344 at $x = 10$, and the absolute minimum value is -141 at $x = -5$.

15. Given $f(x) = -x^3 + 6x^2 - 50$, then $f'(x) = -3x^2 + 12x$. Solving $f'(x) = -3x(x - 4) = 0$ gives the two critical numbers $x = 0$ and $x = 4$. Since the given interval is $[-1, 2]$, the only critical number in the interval is $x = 0$. Using the endpoints and $x = 0$, construct the table:

x	$f(x)$
-1	-43
0	-50
2	-34

From the table, the absolute maximum value is -34 at $x = 2$, and the absolute minimum value is -50 at $x = 0$.

17. Given $f(x) = x^3 + 3x^2 + 5$, then $f'(x) = 3x^2 + 6x$. Solving $f'(x) = 3x(x + 2) = 0$ gives the two critical numbers $x = 0$ and $x = -2$. Now, $x = 0$ is the only critical number in the given interval, $[0, 5]$. Using the endpoints and $x = 0$, construct the table:

x	$f(x)$
0	5
5	205

From the table, the absolute maximum value is 205 at $x = 5$, and the absolute minimum value is 5 at $x = 0$.

19. Given $f(x) = x^3 - 15x^2 + 72x + 1$, then $f'(x) = 3x^2 - 30x + 72$. Solving $f'(x) = 3(x^2 - 10x + 24) = 3(x - 4)(x - 6) = 0$ gives the two critical numbers $x = 4$ and $x = 6$. Neither critical number is in the given interval, $[-4, 3]$. Thus, using only the endpoints, construct the table:

x	$f(x)$
-4	-591
3	109

From the table, the absolute maximum value is 109 at $x = 3$, and the absolute minimum value is -591 at $x = -4$.

21. There is *only one* absolute maximum value and *only one* absolute minimum value for a function defined on a closed interval. [Note: the absolute maximum (or minimum) value may occur at different values for x. See Exercise 12.] Since the absolute extreme can occur only at an endpoint or at a critical number, it is only necessary to compare function values at these points and choose the largest and smallest value, respectively. It is not necessary to know which values, if any, are relative extrema when only the largest and smallest function value are needed.

SECTION 4.4 Technology Exercises

1. 9.5

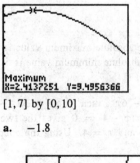

$[1, 7]$ by $[0, 10]$

3. **a.** -1.8

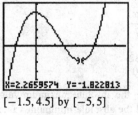

$[-1.5, 4.5]$ by $[-5, 5]$

b. -7.0

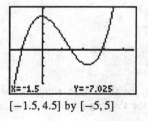

$[-1.5, 4.5]$ by $[-5, 5]$

5. a. The function is defined when $16 - x^2 \geq 0$ or when x is in $[-4, 4]$.

b. $(2.8, 8.0)$

c. $(-2.8, -8.0)$

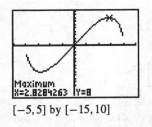

$[-5, 5]$ by $[-15, 10]$

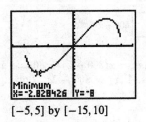

$[-5, 5]$ by $[-15, 10]$

SECTION 4.5 pages 231–236

1. Given the temperature function $T(x) = -3x^2 + 60x + 70$, then $T'(x) = -6x + 60$. Solving $T'(x) = -6(x - 10) = 0$ gives the only critical number, $x = 10$. Since $T''(x) = -6 < 0$, then the maximum temperature occurs at $x = 10$.

The hottest temperature is $T(10) = 370° F$.

3. Given the distance function $s(t) = -16t^2 + 96t + 7$, then $s'(t) = -32t + 96$. Solving $s'(t) = -32(t - 3) = 0$ gives the only critical number, $t = 3$. Since $s''(t) = -32 < 0$, then $t = 3$ will result in a relative maximum.

Thus, the maximum height the ball will travel is $s(3) = 151$ feet.

5. Given the profit function $P(x) = 1300x - x^2$, then $P'(x) = 1300 - 2x$. Solving $P'(x) = 1300 - 2x = 0$ gives the only critical number, $x = 650$. Since $P''(x) = -2 < 0$, then $x = 650$ will give a maximum value.

a. Manufacture 650 items to maximize profit.
b. The maximum profit is $P(650) = \$422,500$.

7. Given the price function $p(x) = 4x^2 - 200x + 2850$, then $p'(x) = 8x - 200$. Solving $p'(x) = 8(x - 25) = 0$ gives the only critical number, $x = 25$. Since $p''(x) = 8 > 0$, the critical number $x = 25$ will result in a minimum value.

Thus, order 25 items to minimize the price.

9. The highest concentration occurs at the absolute maximum of $K(t) = \frac{0.03t}{1+t^2}$.

$$K'(t) = \frac{(1 + t^2)(0.03) - 0.03t(2t)}{(1 + t^2)^2} = \frac{-0.03(t^2 - 1)}{(1 + t^2)^2}$$

$K'(t)$ is zero only when $t^2 - 1 = (t - 1)(t + 1) = 0$. The only critical number in the interval $[0, \infty)$ is $t = 1$. (Note: $K'(t)$ is defined for all t, since $1 + t^2 \neq 0$.) Now, $K'(0) > 0$ and $K'(2) < 0$; thus, $t = 1$ will result in a maximum value.

The highest concentration occurs at $t = 1$ hour.

11. Let x be one number; then $100 - x$ is the other number $[x + (100 - x) = 100]$. The product of the numbers is $P(x) = x(100 - x) = 100x - x^2$.

Differentiating gives $P'(x) = 100 - 2x$, and solving $P'(x) = 2(50 - x) = 0$ gives the only critical number, $x = 50$. Since $P''(x) = -2 < 0$, the critical number will result in a maximum value.

For a maximum product, both numbers should be 50.

13. Let x be the length of the rectangular pen; then $\frac{1600-2x}{2} = 800 - x$ is the width of the pen.

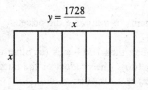

The area is $A(x) = x(800 - x) = 800x - x^2$. Differentiating yields $A'(x) = 800 - 2x$. Solving $A'(x) = 2(400 - x) = 0$ gives the critical number $x = 400$. Since $A''(x) = -2 < 0$, the critical number $x = 400$ will result in a maximum value.

For maximum area, the width is 400 feet and the length is 400 feet.

15. Let x be the length of the rectangle; then the width y must be such that $xy = 900$ or $y = \frac{900}{x}$. Thus, from the figure below, the amount of fencing needed is

$$L(x) = 2x + 2y = 2x + 2\left(\frac{900}{x}\right)$$

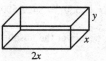

Differentiating yields $L'(x) = 2 - \frac{1800}{x^2}$. Solving $L'(x) = \frac{2x^2 - 1800}{x^2} = 0$ gives

$$2(x^2 - 900) = 2(x - 30)(x + 30) = 0$$

or critical numbers $x = 30$ and $x = -30$. The only possible critical number is $x = 30$. Since $L''(x) = \frac{3600}{x^3}$, then $L''(30) = \frac{2}{15} > 0$, and $x = 30$ produces a minimum value.

The smallest amount of fencing needed to enclose a rectangular area of 900 square feet is $L(30) = 120$ feet.

17. Refer to the figure below.

$$y = \frac{1728}{x}$$

Let y be the length; then $xy = 1728$ or $y = \frac{1728}{x}$. The amount of material needed is $M(x) = 2y + 6x = \frac{3456}{x} + 6x$. Differentiating yields

$$M'(x) = \frac{6x^2 - 3456}{x^2}. \text{ Solving}$$

$$M'(x) = \frac{6x^2 - 3456}{x^2} = \frac{6(x^2 - 576)}{x^2}$$

$$= \frac{6(x - 24)(x + 24)}{x^2} = 0$$

gives the critical numbers $x = 24$ and $x = -24$. Only $x = 24$ is an acceptable critical number, and $M''(24) = \frac{6912}{(24)^3} > 0$ implies that it will result in a minimum value.

For the least amount of material for the walls, the width is $x = 24$ feet and the length is $y = 72$ feet.

19. Let x be the width of the open box; then $2x$ is the length.

If y is the height of the box, then the volume is $x(2x)(y) = 2x^2y = 36,000$, which yields $y = \frac{18,000}{x^2}$. The amount of material required is the surface area of the bottom, $2x^2$, plus the surface area of the sides, $2(xy) + 2(2xy)$. Thus, the total surface area is $2x^2 + 6xy$ or

$$S(x) = 2x^2 + 6x\left(\frac{18,000}{x^2}\right) = 2x^2 + \frac{108,000}{x}$$

Differentiating yields $S'(x) = 4x - \frac{108,000}{x^2}$. Solving

$$S'(x) = \frac{4(x^3 - 27,000)}{x^2} = 0$$

gives $x^3 - 27,000 = 0$, which means that $x = 30$ is the only critical number. $S''(x) = 4 + \frac{216,000}{x^3}$ and $S''(30) > 0$; thus, the critical number $x = 30$ will give a minumum value.

For the least amount of material, the dimensions should be width = 30 inches, length = 60 inches, and height = 20 inches.

21. Refer to the text figure to see that the constructed box has a square base of dimension $40 - 2x$ and height x. The volume of the box is

$$V(x) = (40 - 2x)^2 x = 4x(20 - x)^2$$

Differentiating, using the product rule, yields

$$V'(x) = 4\left[x(2)(20 - x)(-1) + (20 - x)^2(1)\right]$$
$$= 4(20 - x)(-2x + 20 - x)$$
$$= 4(20 - x)(20 - 3x)$$

Solving $V'(x) = 4(20 - x)(20 - 3x) = 0$ gives two critical numbers, $x = 20$ and $x = \frac{20}{3}$. The critical number $x = 20$ does not make sense, since the dimension of the base would become zero. $V''(x) = 4(-80 + 6x)$ and $V''\left(\frac{20}{3}\right) = -160 < 0$, so the critical number $x = \frac{20}{3}$ will result in a maximum value.

For the greatest volume, $x = \frac{20}{3}$ centimeters.

23. Refer to the following figure, using x as the height of the fold.

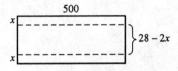

The volume of water in the gutter will be

$$V(x) = 500(28 - 2x)x = 500(28x - 2x^2)$$

Differentiating yields

$$V'(x) = 500(28 - 4x)$$

Solving $V'(x) = 500(28 - 4x) = 0$ gives the only critical number, $x = 7$. Since $V''(x) = -2000 < 0$, the critical number results in a maximum value.

For a maximum volume of water, $x = 7$ centimeters.

25. Given $s(t) = 35t + 9t^2 - t^3$, then $s'(t) = 35 + 18t - 3t^2$ is the velocity.

$$s''(t) = 18 - 6t = 0$$
$$6(3 - t) = 0$$
$$t = 3$$
$$s'''(t) = -6 < 0$$

Thus the maximum velocity is $s'(3) = 35 + 18(3) - 3(3)^2 = 62$ meters per second.

27.   Refer to the figure below.

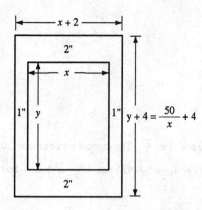

The area of the printed material is $xy = 50$; solving for y yields $y = \frac{50}{x}$.

The area of the sheet of paper is

$$A(x) = (x + 2)(\frac{50}{x} + 4)$$

$$= 4x + \frac{100}{x} + 58$$

Differentiating yields

$$A'(x) = 4 - \frac{100}{x^2} = \frac{4(x^2 - 25)}{x^2}$$

Solving

$$A'(x) = \frac{4}{x^2}(x^2 - 25) = \frac{4}{x^2}(x - 5)(x + 5) = 0$$

gives the two critical numbers $x = 5$ and $x = -5$. Clearly $x = -5$ is not a possible value, and since $A''(5) = \frac{200}{5^3} = \frac{8}{5} > 0$, then $x = 5$ results in a minimum value.

The smallest size piece of paper satisfying the given conditions is 7 inches wide and 14 inches long.

29.   Let $x =$ the number of trees planted
$x - 20 =$ the number of trees in excess of 20
$1(x - 20) =$ the number of bushels less per tree
$24 - (x - 20) = 44 - x =$ the number of bushels per tree

The total yield is

$$Y(x) = x(44 - x) = 44x - x^2$$

Differentiating gives

$$Y'(x) = 44 - 2x = 2(22 - x)$$

Solving $Y'(x) = 2(22 - x) = 0$ gives the only critical number, $x = 22$. Since $Y''(x) = -2 < 0$, then $x = 22$ will result in a maximum value.

For a maximum yield of fruit, plant 22 trees.

31. Using the figure below, if x is the width, then, for an area of 1728, the length is $\frac{1728}{x}$.

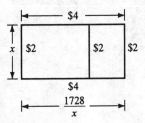

The total cost is

$$C(x) = 2x + 2x + 2x + 4\left(\frac{1728}{x}\right) + 4\left(\frac{1728}{x}\right)$$

$$= 6x + \frac{13{,}824}{x}$$

Differentiating yields

$$C'(x) = 6 - \frac{13{,}824}{x^2} = \frac{6}{x^2}(x^2 - 2304)$$

Solving $C'(x) = \frac{6}{x^2}(x^2 - 2304) = 0$ gives $x^2 - 2304 = 0$, and hence $x = 48$ and $x = -48$. Clearly $x = -48$ is not acceptable, and, since $C''(48) = \frac{27{,}648}{(48)^3} > 0$, $x = 48$ will result in a minimum value.

For a minimum cost, the width $= 48$ feet and the length $= 36$ feet.

33. Use the following figure and note that the width of the window is $2x$.

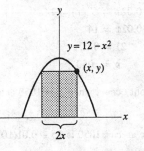

The area of the rectangular window is $2xy$, where $y = 12 - x^2$. Thus,

$$A(x) = 2x(12 - x^2) = 24x - 2x^3$$

Differentiating yields

$$A'(x) = 24 - 6x^2 = -6(x^2 - 4)$$

Solving

$$A'(x) = -6(x^2 - 4) = -6(x - 2)(x + 2) = 0$$

gives the two critical numbers $x = 2$ and $x = -2$. From the diagram, the only critical number that is acceptable is $x = 2$. (Actually, $x = -2$ is the symmetrically located point across the y axis.)

Since $A''(x) = -12x$, then $A''(2) = -24 < 0$ and $x = 2$ will result in a maximum value.

For the rectangular window of largest area, the dimensions of the window are 4 feet wide and 8 feet high.

35. a. Given $R(x) = 80x - 0.02x^2$ and $C(x) = 130 + 74x - 0.01x^2$, then $R'(x) = 80 - 0.04x$ and $C'(x) = 74 - 0.02x$. Solve $R'(x) = C'(x)$:

$$80 - 0.04x = 74 - 0.02x$$

$$0.02x = 6$$

$$x = 300$$

Maximum profit at $x = 300$

b. Given $R(x) = 7x + 0.001x^2$ and $C(x) = 5x + 0.003x^2$, then $R'(x) = 7 + 0.002x$ and $C'(x) = 5 + 0.006x$. Solve $R'(x) = C'(x)$:

$$7 + 0.002x = 5 + 0.006x$$

$$2 = 0.004x$$

$$x = 500$$

Maximum profit at $x = 500$.

37. The revenue function is $R(x) = x(35 - 0.01x) = 35x - 0.01x^2$. The cost function is $C(x) = 14x + 10,000$.

a. The maximum profit occurs when $R'(x) = C'(x)$. Solve

$$R'(x) = 35 - 0.02x = C'(x) = 14$$
$$35 - 0.02x = 14$$
$$21 = 0.02x$$
$$x = 1050$$

Maximum profit occurs when $x = 1050$ calculators are sold.

b. The price at $x = 1050$ is $35 - 0.01(1050) = \$24.50$.

39. Given $C(x) = 192 + 7x + 0.03x^2$, then the average cost per item is

$$\overline{C}(x) = \frac{C(x)}{x} = \frac{192 + 7x + 0.03x^2}{x}$$
$$= \frac{192}{x} + 7 + 0.03x$$

Differentiating yields

$$\overline{C}'(x) = -\frac{192}{x^2} + 0.03$$
$$= \frac{0.03x^2 - 192}{x^2}$$

Solving $\overline{C}'(x) = \frac{0.03x^2 - 192}{x^2} = 0$, gives $0.03x^2 - 192 = 0$ or $x^2 - 6400 = 0$. The solution to this equation gives the two critical numbers $x = 80$ and $x = -80$. The critical number $x = -80$ is unacceptable, and, since $\overline{C}''(80) > 0$, then $x = 80$ results in a minimum value.

Minimum average cost per item for $x = 80$ units.

41. The maximum profit occurs at $x = d$, since the tangent line to the cost function at $x = d$ is parallel to the straight-line revenue function.

43. If the price is $140 - x$, then $100 + 2x$ tickets are sold. The revenue is

$$R(x) = (140 - x)(100 + 2x) = 14000 + 180x - 2x^2$$
$$R'(x) = 180 - 4x$$

Solving

$$R'(x) = 180 - 4x = 0$$
$$x = 45$$
$$R''(x) = -4 < 0$$

so $x = 45$ maximizes the revenue.
a. The price should be $140 - 45 = \$95$.
b. The number of tickets sold will be $100 + 2(45) = 190$.
c. The maximum revenue is $(140 - 45)[100 + 2(45)] = (95)(190) = \$18,050$.

45. Given $A = k(br^4 - r^5)$, then

$$\frac{dA}{dr} = k(4br^3 - 5r^4)$$

Solving

$$k(4br^3 - 5r^4) = 0$$
$$kr^3(4b - 5r) = 0$$
$$r = 0 \quad \text{or} \quad r = \frac{4b}{5}$$

$$\frac{d^2A}{dr^2} = k(12br^2 - 20r^3)$$

$$\frac{d^2A}{dr^2}\left(r = \frac{4b}{5}\right) = k\left[12b\left(\frac{4b}{5}\right)^2 - 20\left(\frac{4b}{5}\right)^3\right]$$
$$= kb^3\left[12\left(\frac{16}{25}\right) - 20\left(\frac{64}{125}\right)\right]$$
$$= -2.56kb^3 < 0$$

Thus $r = \frac{4b}{5}$ gives the maximum flow rate because $r = 0$ and $r = b$ (the endpoints) both give $A = 0$.

47. The perimeter of the square is x, so the area of the square is $\left(\frac{x}{4}\right)^2$. The circumference of the circle is $50 - x$, so the area of the circle is $\pi\left(\frac{50-x}{2\pi}\right)^2 = \frac{(50-x)^2}{4\pi}$. The total area is

$$A = \frac{x^2}{16} + \frac{(50-x)^2}{4\pi}$$

$$A' = \frac{x}{8} + \frac{(50-x)}{2\pi}(-1) = \frac{(2\pi+8)x}{16\pi} - \frac{50}{2\pi}$$

$$A'' = \frac{2\pi+8}{16\pi} > 0 \qquad \text{for all } x$$

Solving

$$A' = \frac{2\pi+8}{16\pi}x - \frac{50}{2\pi} = 0$$

$$x = \left(\frac{50}{2\pi}\right)\left(\frac{16\pi}{2\pi+8}\right) = \frac{(50)(8)}{2\pi+8}$$

$$= \frac{200}{\pi+4}$$

SECTION 4.5 Technology Exercises

1. **a.** $487°\text{F}$

b. at 7 minutes and at 26 minutes

c. between 7 minutes and 26 minutes

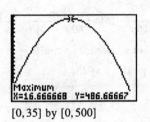

[0, 35] by [0, 500]

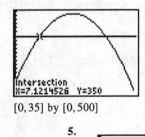

[0, 35] by [0, 500]

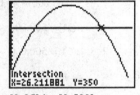

[0, 35] by [0, 500]

3. 20,300 cc

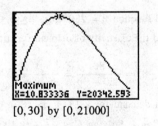

[0, 30] by [0, 21000]

5.

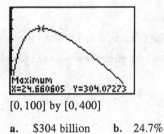

[0, 100] by [0, 400]

a. $304 billion   **b.** 24.7%

SECTION 4.6 pages 241–242

1. Given the demand equation $x = 50 - 3p$, then $\frac{dx}{dp} = -3$. The elasticity of demand function is

$$E = -\frac{p}{x}\frac{dx}{dp} = -\frac{p}{50-3p}(-3) = \frac{3p}{50-3p}.$$

At $p = 10$,
$E = \frac{3(10)}{50-3(10)} = \frac{30}{20} = \frac{3}{2} > 1$
and the demand is elastic.

3.   Given the demand function $x = \sqrt{200 - p} = (200 - P)^{1/2}$, then

$$\frac{dx}{dp} = \frac{1}{2}(200 - p)^{-1/2}(-1) = -\frac{1}{2(200 - P)^{1/2}}$$

The elasticity of demand function is

$$E = -\frac{p}{x}\frac{dx}{dp} = -\frac{p}{(200 - p)^{1/2}}\left[-\frac{1}{2(200 - p)^{1/2}}\right] = \frac{p}{2(200 - p)}$$

At $p = 40$,
$$E = \frac{40}{2(200 - 40)} = \frac{20}{160} = \frac{1}{8} < 1$$
and the demand is inelastic.

5.   Given the demand function $x = 321 - p^2$, then $\frac{dx}{dp} = -2p$. The elasticity of demand function is

$$E = -\frac{p}{x}\frac{dx}{dp} = -\frac{p}{321 - p^2}(-2p) = \frac{2p^2}{321 - p^2}$$

7.   Given the demand function $x = \frac{200}{p} = 200p^{-1}$, then

$$\frac{dx}{dp} = -200p^{-2} = -\frac{200}{p^2}$$

The elasticity of demand function is

$$E = -\frac{p}{x}\frac{dx}{dp} = -\frac{p}{\frac{200}{p}}\left(-\frac{200}{p^2}\right) = -\frac{p^2}{200}\left(-\frac{200}{p^2}\right) = 1$$

9.   Given the demand function $x = 500,000 - 40,000p^2$, $1 \le p \le 3$, then $\frac{dx}{dp} = -80,000p$ and the elasticity of demand function is

$$E = -\frac{p}{500,000 - 40,000p^2}(-80,000p) = \frac{2p^2}{12.5 - p^2}$$

a. $x(1) = 500,000 - 40,000(1)^2 = 460,000$ tickets

b. $x(3) = 500,000 - 40,000(3)^2 = 140,000$ tickets

c.   At $p = 2$

$$E = \frac{2(2)^2}{12.5 - 2^2} = \frac{8}{8.5} \approx 0.94 < 1$$

The demand is inelastic.

11.   Given the demand function $x = 800 - 16p$, $0 \le p \le 50$, then $\frac{dx}{dp} = -16$ and the elasticity of demand function is

$$E = -\frac{p}{800 - 16p}(-16) = \frac{16p}{800 - 16p} = \frac{p}{50 - p}$$

The demand has unit elasticity when $E = 1$; thus, solving $\frac{p}{50 - p} = 1$ yields $p = 25$.

13.   Given the demand function $x = 112 - 8p$, $0 \le p \le 14$, then $\frac{dx}{dp} = -8$ and the elasticity of demand function is

$$E = -\frac{p}{112 - 8p}(-8) = \frac{8p}{112 - 8p} = \frac{p}{14 - p}$$

At $p = 3$,

$$E = \frac{3}{14 - 3} = \frac{3}{11} \approx 0.27$$

which means that a 1% increase in price will result in a 0.273% decrease in demand.

Thus, a 2% increase in price will result in a 0.54% decrease in demand.

15.   Given the demand function $x = 280 - 8p$, $0 \le p \le 35$, then $\frac{dx}{dp} = -8$ and the elasticity of demand function is

$$E = -\frac{p}{280 - 8p}(-8) = \frac{8p}{280 - 8p} = \frac{p}{35 - p^2}$$

A 4% decrease in demand for a 1% increase in price will occur when $E = 4$. Solving $E = \frac{p}{35 - p} = 4$ yields

$$p = 140 - 4p$$
$$5p = 140$$
$$p = 28$$

At $p = \$28$, a 1% increase in price will result in a 4% decrease in demand.

17. Given the demand function $x = 10,000 - 80p$,

$0 \leq p \leq 125$, then $\frac{dx}{dp} = -80$ and the elasticity of demand function is

$$E = -\frac{p}{10,000 - 80p}(-80) = \frac{80p}{10,000 - 80p} = \frac{p}{125 - p}$$

At $p = 30$,

$$E = \frac{30}{125 - 30} = \frac{30}{95} = 0.32 < 1$$

Thus, the demand is inelastic at $p = 30$.

Since the demand is inelastic at $p = 30$, then raising the price to $p = \$35$ will *increase* revenue.

Note: $E = 1$ at $p = 62.5$, so a maximum revenue is reached at $p = 62.5$.

19. Given the demand function $x = 10,000 - 80p$,

$0 \leq p \leq 125$, then $\frac{dx}{dp} = -80$ and the elasticity of demand function is

$$E = -\frac{p}{10,000 - 80p}(-80) = \frac{80p}{10,000 - 80p} = \frac{p}{125 - p}$$

At $p = 90$,

$$E = \frac{90}{125 - 90} = \frac{90}{35} = 2.57 > 1$$

Since $E > 1$, the demand is elastic, and the wholesaler should *decrease* his price to *increase* revenue.

21. Given the demand function $x = 1200 - 20p^{1/2}, 0 \leq p \leq 3600$, then

$$\frac{dx}{dp} = -10p^{-1/2} = -\frac{10}{p^{1/2}}$$

and the elasticity of demand function is

$$E = \left(-\frac{p}{1200 - 20p^{1/2}}\right)\left(-\frac{10}{p^{1/2}}\right)$$

$$= \frac{10\sqrt{p}}{1200 - 20\sqrt{p}}$$

$$= \frac{\sqrt{p}}{120 - 2\sqrt{p}}$$

The maximum revenue occurs when $E = 1$. Solving

$$E = \frac{\sqrt{p}}{120 - 2\sqrt{p}} = 1$$

yields

$$\sqrt{p} = 120 - 2\sqrt{p}$$
$$3\sqrt{p} = 120$$
$$\sqrt{p} = 40$$
$$p = 1600$$

The maximum revenue occurs at $p = \$1600$.

23. Given the demand function $x = 1000 - 2p^3$, then $\frac{dx}{dp} = -6p^2$ and the elasticity of demand function is

$$E = -\frac{p}{1000 - 2p^3}(-6p^2) = \frac{6p^3}{1000 - 2p^3} = \frac{3p^3}{500 - p^3}$$

The maximum revenue will occur when $E = 1$. Solving

$$E = \frac{3p^3}{500 - p^3} = 1$$

yields

$$3p^3 = 500 - p^3$$
$$4p^3 = 500$$
$$p^3 = 125$$
$$p = 5$$

The maximum revenue will occur at $p = \$5$ per wash.

SECTION 4.6 Technology Exercises

1. **a.** 61,859   **b.** $1.80

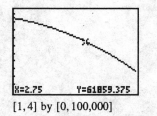

[1, 4] by [0, 100,000]

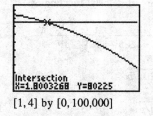

[1, 4] by [0, 100,000]

REVIEW EXERCISES FOR CHAPTER 4 pages 243–246

1. Given $f(x) = -2x^2$, then $f'(x) = -4x$. Solving $f'(x) = -4x = 0$ gives $x = 0$ and results in the sign graph

$$f'(-1) = 4 \qquad f'(1) = -4$$

$$\underset{x = 0}{\underline{\quad ++++ \quad \bullet \quad ---- \quad}}$$

f is increasing on $(-\infty, 0)$.
f is decreasing on $(0, \infty)$.

3. Given $g(x) = \frac{2x}{x-1}$, then

$$g'(x) = \frac{(x-1)(2) - 2x(1)}{(x-1)^2} = -\frac{2}{(x-1)^2}$$

The derivative $g'(x)$ is never zero, but it is undefined at $x = 1$. The sign graph is

$$g'(0) = -2 \qquad g'(2) = -2$$

$$\underset{x = 1}{\underline{\quad ---- \quad \bullet \quad ---- \quad}}$$

g is decreasing on $(-\infty, 1) \cup (1, \infty)$.

5. Given $f(x) = x^3 - 6x^2 - 36x + 5$, then $f'(x) = 3x^2 - 12x - 36$. Solving $f'(x) = 3(x^2 - 4x - 12) = 3(x - 6)(x + 2) = 0$ gives the

critical numbers $x = 6$ and $x = -2$.

7. Given $f(x) = 8\sqrt{x} = 8x^{1/2}$, then $f'(x) = 4x^{-1/2} = \frac{4}{\sqrt{x}}$. $f'(x)$ is never zero, but $f'(x)$ is undefined at $x = 0$. Since $f(x)$ is defined at $x = 0$,

the only critical number is $x = 0$.

9. Given $f(x) = \frac{x}{x^2+1}$, then

$$f'(x) = \frac{(x^2+1)(1) - x(2x)}{(x^2+1)^2} = \frac{1-x^2}{(x^2+1)^2}$$

$f'(x)$ is defined for all x, and $f'(x) = 0$ when $1 - x^2 = 0$. Solving $1 - x^2 = (1-x)(1+x) = 0$ gives the

two critical numbers $x = 1$ and $x = -1$.

11. Given $f(x) = x^3 - 3x^2 + 5$, then $f'(x) = 3x^2 - 6x = 3x(x-2)$. Solving $f'(x) = 3x(x-2) = 0$ gives the critical numbers $x = 0$ and $x = 2$. $f''(x) = 6x - 6$, which gives $f''(0) = -6 < 0$ and $f''(2) = 6 > 0$.

Using the second derivative test, $(0,5)$ is a relative maximum and $(2,1)$ is a relative minimum.

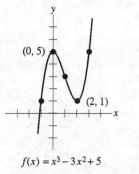

$$f(x) = x^3 - 3x^2 + 5$$

13. Given $f(x) = 1 - x^{2/3}$, then $f'(x) = -\frac{2}{3}x^{-1/3} = -\frac{2}{3x^{1/3}}$. $f'(x)$ is never zero, but $f'(x)$ is undefined at $x = 0$. Since $f(x)$ is defined at $x = 0$, the only critical number is $x = 0$. The signs of $f'(x)$ are

$$f'(-1) = 2/3 \qquad f'(1) = -2/3$$
$$+\!+\!+\!+\!+ \qquad\qquad -\,-\,-\,-\,-$$
$$\text{———————} \vert \text{———————}$$
$$x = 0$$

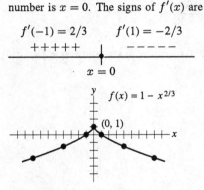

15. Given $f(x) = x^4 - 8x^3 + 17$, then $f'(x) = 4x^3 - 24x^2 = 4x^2(x-6)$. Solving $f'(x) = 4x^2(x-6) = 0$ gives the critical numbers $x = 0$ and $x = 6$. The signs of $f'(x)$ are given by

$$f'(-1) = -28 \qquad f'(1) = -20 \qquad f'(7) = 196$$
$$-\,-\,-\,-\,- \qquad\quad -\,-\,-\,- \qquad\qquad +\!+\!+\!+$$
$$\text{—————}\vert\text{—————}\vert\text{—————}$$
$$\quad\; x = 0 \qquad\qquad x = 6$$

Thus, $(0, 17)$ is not an extreme point, but $(6, -415)$ is a relative minimum.

17. Given $g(x) = 6x^{1/3} - 20$, then $g'(x) = 2x^{-2/3} = \frac{2}{x^{2/3}}$. $g'(x)$ is never zero, but $g'(x)$ is undefined at $x = 0$. Since $g(x)$ is defined at $x = 0$, then $x = 0$ is a critical number. The sign of $g'(x)$ is given by

$$g'(-1) = 2 \qquad g'(1) = 2$$
$$+\!+\!+\!+ \qquad\quad +\!+\!+\!+$$
$$\text{————————}\vert\text{————————}$$
$$x = 0$$

Thus, there are no extreme points.

19. Given $f(x) = 4x^3 - 11x + 1$, then $f'(x) = 12x^2 - 11$ and $f''(x) = 24x$. Solving $f''(x) = 24x = 0$ gives $x = 0$. The signs of $f''(x)$ are given by

$$f''(-1) = -24 \qquad f''(1) = 24$$
$$-\,-\,-\,-\,-\,- \qquad\quad +\!+\!+\!+$$
$$\text{————————}\vert\text{————————}$$
$$x = 0$$

f is concave up on $(0, \infty)$.
f is concave down on $(-\infty, 0)$.

21. Given $f(x) = x^3 - 12x^2 + 17x - 4$, then $f'(x) = 3x^2 - 24x + 17$ and $f''(x) = 6x - 24 = 6(x-4)$. Solving $f''(x) = 6(x-4) = 0$ gives $x = 4$. The signs of $f''(x)$ are given by

$$f''(3) = -6 \qquad f''(5) = 6$$
$$-\,-\,-\,-\,- \qquad\quad +\!+\!+\!+$$
$$\text{————————}\vert\text{————————}$$
$$x = 4$$

Thus, $(4, -64)$ is a point of inflection.

23.
a.	negative	g.	negative
b.	positive	h.	negative
c.	negative	i.	positive
d.	positive	j.	zero
e.	negative	k.	positive
f.	negative	l.	positive

25. Given $f(x) = x^3 + 3x^2 - 105x + 20$, then $f'(x) = 3x^2 + 6x - 105$. Solving $f'(x) = 3(x^2 + 2x - 35) = 3(x-5)(x+7) = 0$ yields the critical numbers $x = 5$ and $x = -7$. Using the critical numbers and the endpoints of the interval gives

x	$f(x)$
-8	540
-7	559
5	-305
8	-116

The absolute maximum is at $(-7, 559)$, and the absolute minimum is at $(5, -305)$.

27. Given the cost function $C(x) = x^3 - 42x^2 - 180x + 500$, then the marginal cost function is $C'(x) = 3x^2 - 84x - 180$. The marginal cost function is minimum at a critical point of $C'(x)$, that is, when $C''(x) = 0$. Solving $C''(x) = 6x - 84 = 6(x - 14) = 0$ yields $x = 14$. Since $C'''(x) = 6 > 0$, then $x = 14$ will result in a minimum value.

At $x = 14$, the marginal cost function is a minimum value.

29. Consider the figure:

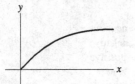

$y = 120 - x$

Let $x =$ the length.
$y =$ the width.

Then $2x + 2y = 240$
$\qquad\qquad y = 120 - x$

The area function is $A(x) = x(120 - x) = 120x - x^2$

Differentiating, $A'(x) = 120 - 2x$, and solving $A'(x) = 0$ yields

$120 - 2x = 0$
$\qquad x = 60$

Since $A''(x) = -2 < 0$, the critical number $x = 60$ will result in a maximum value.

The maximum area will occur for length $= 60$ feet and width $= 60$ feet.

31. Given the demand function $x = 200 - 4p$, then $\frac{dx}{dp} = -4$ and the elasticity of demand function is

$$E = -\frac{p}{x}\frac{dx}{dp} = \left(-\frac{p}{200 - 4p}\right)(-4)$$
$$= \frac{4p}{200 - 4p} = \frac{p}{50 - p}$$

At $p = 10$,

$$E = \frac{10}{50 - 10} = \frac{10}{40} = \frac{1}{4} < 1$$

$E = \frac{1}{4}$; the demand is inelastic at $p = 10$.

33. **a.** $\frac{dn}{dt}$ is negative because the function is decreasing.

b. $\frac{d^2n}{dt^2}$ is positive because the function is concave up.

35. *Yes*; if the function $y = f(x)$ is increasing on the interval $[a, b]$ but is concave downward on $[a, b]$, then $\frac{d^2y}{dt^2} < 0$, which means $\frac{dy}{dt}$ is decreasing. The following graph illustrates a function y that is increasing when $\frac{dy}{dt}$ is decreasing.

37. Given $f(x) = 2x^4 + 3$, then $f'(x) = 8x^3$ and $f''(x) = 24x^2$. Since $f''(x) > 0$ for all x, there cannot be a point of inflection.

39. Since $f''(x) = 12(x-5)^2 > 0$ for all x, $f(x)$ is concave up for all x.

41. Given $f(x) = x^3(x-7)^4$, then

$$f'(x) = 3x^2(x-7)^4 + x^3(x-7)^3(4)$$
$$= x^2(x-7)^3[3(x-7) + 4x]$$
$$= x^2(x-7)^3(7x-21)$$

Solving $f'(x) = x^2(x-7)^3(7x-21) = 0$ gives $x = 0$ or $x = 7$ or $x = 3$, so $x = 3$ is the third critical number.

45. The second derivative is positive from 1986 to 1990; however, it is negative from 1983 to 1986. The rate of increase of CPI decreased from 1983 to 1986 and then increased from 1986 to 1990.

49. If the width is x, the length is $\frac{486}{x}$. The material used for the walls will be $f(x) = 3x + 2\left(\frac{486}{x}\right) = 3x + \frac{972}{x}$.

$$f'(x) = 3 - \frac{972}{x^2}$$

Solving $f'(x) = 3 - \frac{972}{x^2} = 0$

$$x^2 = \frac{972}{3} = 324$$
$$x = 18$$

43. Extension c is correct because it is the only one that is concave down and the curve is concave up to the left of x_1.

47. Given $S = \frac{a}{W+b} - c = a(W+b)^{-1} - c$, then

$$\frac{dS}{dW} = -a(W+b)^{-2} = \frac{-a}{(W+b)^2}$$

Since $a > 0$, $\frac{dS}{dW} < 0$, and so S is a decreasing function.

51. Let y represent the length of the rectangular portion of the track. We know that the total length of the track is $2y + 2\pi x = 1$. The area enclosed will be given by

$$A = 2xy + \pi x^2$$

Using $y = \frac{1}{2} - \pi x$, this becomes

$$A(x) = x(1 - 2\pi x) + \pi x^2$$
$$= x - 2\pi x^2 + \pi x^2 = x - \pi x^2$$
$$A'(x) = 1 - 2\pi x$$

Solving $A'(x) = 1 - 2\pi x = 0$ gives $x = \frac{1}{2\pi}$.

SECTION 5.1 pages 258–260

1. $f(x) = 2^x$

3. $f(x) = 2^{-x}$

5. $y = 0.4^x$

7. $y = 3 \cdot 2^x$

9. $f(x) = e^x$

11. $f(x) = e^{x+1}$

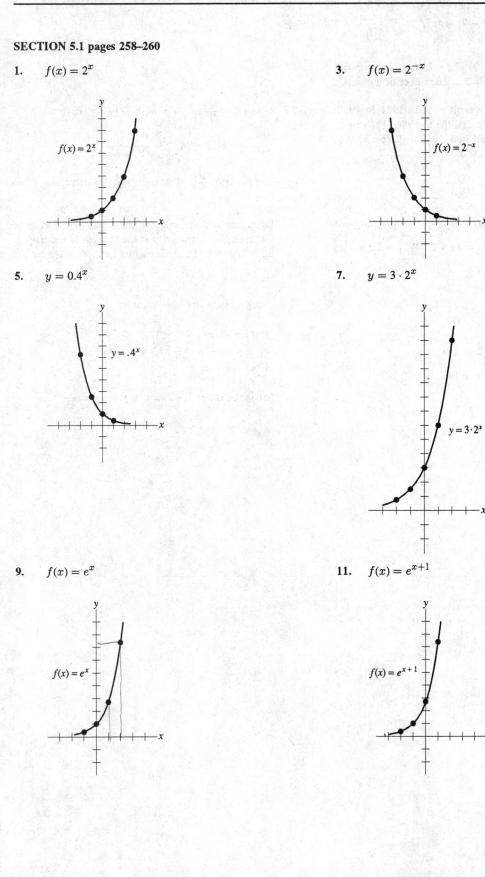

13. $f(x) = 1 + e^x$

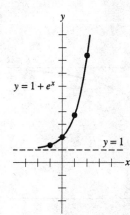

$y = 1 + e^x$

$y = 1$

15. $y = e^x - 2$

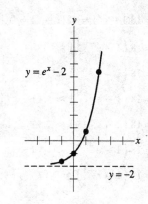

$y = e^x - 2$

$y = -2$

17. $4e^0 = 4(1) = 4$

19. $2 - 7e^0 = 2 - 7(1) = -5$

21. $\dfrac{e^{2x}}{e} = e^{2x}e^{-1} = e^{2x-1}$

23. $e^{3x}e = e^{3x}e^1 = e^{3x+1}$

25. $(e^{2x})^3 = e^{(2x)\cdot 3} = e^{6x}$

27.   Using $A = Pe^{rt}$ and $P = \$1000$

$$r = 8\% = 0.08$$
$$t = 5 \text{ years}$$

Then $A = 1000e^{(0.08)(5)} = 1000e^{0.4}$
$$\approx \$1491.82$$

29.   Using $A = Pe^{rt}$ and $A = \$30,000$

$$r = 9\% = 0.09$$
$$t = 14 \text{ years}$$

Then $30,000 = Pe^{(0.09)(14)} = Pe^{1.26}$
$$P = 30,000e^{-1.26}$$
$$\approx \$8509.62$$

31.   Using $A = Pe^{rt}$ and $P = \$10,000$

$$r = 12\% = 0.12$$
$$t = 9 \text{ years}$$

Then $A = 10,000e^{(0.12)(9)} = 10,000e^{1.08}$
$$A \approx \$29,446.80$$

33.   Given $y = \dfrac{1500}{1 + 29e^{-0.4t}}$

a.   At $t = 0$, $y = \dfrac{1500}{1 + 29e^0} = 50$

b.   At $t = 5$, $y = \dfrac{1500}{1 + 29e^{(-0.4)(5)}} \approx 305$

c.   Maximum number of fish occurs as $t \to \infty$.

$$\lim_{t \to \infty} \frac{1500}{1 + 29e^{-0.4t}} = \frac{1500}{1 + 0} = 1500$$

Note: $\lim\limits_{t \to \infty} e^{-0.4t} = 0$

35.   Given $y = \dfrac{50}{1 + 24e^{-0.36t}}$

a.   At $t = 10$, $y = \dfrac{50}{1 + 24e^{-0.36(10)}} \approx 30$ mm

b. $\lim\limits_{t \to \infty} y = \lim\limits_{t \to \infty} \dfrac{50}{1 + 24e^{-0.36t}} = 50$ mm

c.   Unrestricted exponential growth of fruit is unreasonable. Exponential growth and then the growth rate leveling off is reasonable to model fruit growth (i.e., logistic growth).

37. Given $y = 18\left(1 - e^{-0.3t}\right)$

    a. At $t = 0$, $y = 18(1 - e^0) = 18(1 - 1) = 0$

    b. At $t = 1$, $y = 18\left(1 - e^{-0.3}\right) \approx 5$

         At $t = 2$, $y = 18\left(1 - e^{-0.6}\right) \approx 8$

         At $t = 3$, $y = 18\left(1 - e^{-0.9}\right) \approx 11$

         At $t = 4$, $y = 18\left(1 - e^{-1.2}\right) \approx 13$

         At $t = 5$, $y = 18\left(1 - e^{-1.5}\right) \approx 14$

         At $t = 10$, $y = 18\left(1 - e^{-3}\right) \approx 17$

c. $\displaystyle \lim_{t \to \infty} y = \lim_{t \to \infty} 18\left(1 - e^{-0.3t}\right) = 18$

d.

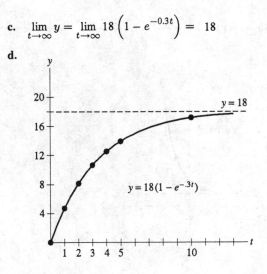

39. **a.** Cost function = (cost per unit) · (number of units)

        Thus, $C(x) = \left(30e^{-0.02x}\right)(x)$

                 $= 30xe^{-0.02x}$

    b. $C(5) = 30(5)\left(e^{-0.1}\right)$

             $\approx \$135.73$

41. The years 1983 to 1985 represent linear growth. The years 1985 to 1987 represent exponential growth, since the increase from 1986 to 1987 is more than double the increase from 1985 to 1986. In fact, for the years 1983 to 1985 we have the model $P(t) = 140 + 20t$, where $P(t)$ are the points and t is the time in years; $t = 0$ corresponds to 1983. For the years 1985 to 1987 we have (with $t = 0$ corresponding to 1985) $P(t) = 180e^{q(t)}$ for $q(t)$ a polynomial of degree 2 satisfying

$q(0) = 0$

$q(1) = \ln \dfrac{11}{9} \cong 0.20$

$q(2) = \ln \dfrac{31}{18} \cong 0.54$

Note: There is a unique polynomial of degree 2 that passes through these three points.

43. If $b = 1$, then $f(x) = b^x = 1^x$, and for any choice of x, $1^x = 1$. Thus, $f(x) = 1^x = 1$ is the constant one function.

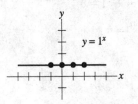

45. **a.**

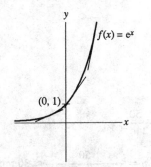

    The tangent lines to $f(x) = e^x$ all have positive slopes, and the slopes get larger and larger in magnitude as $x \to \infty$. Thus, $f(x) = e^x$ is a function that is always increasing.

    b. Since the tangent lines are getting steeper and steeper, the derivative of $f(x) = e^x$ is an increasing function, and the graph is concave up for all x.

47. **a.** For $f(x) = 3^x$, $y = 0$ is the horizontal asymptote. For $f(x) = 0.5^x$, $y = 0$ is the horizontal asymptote.

b. $\lim\limits_{x \to -\infty} 3^x = 0$

$\lim\limits_{x \to \infty} 0.5^x = 0$

49.

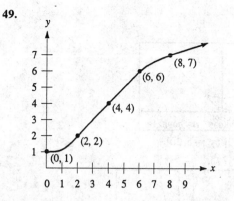

A logistic curve may be fitted through the points.

51.

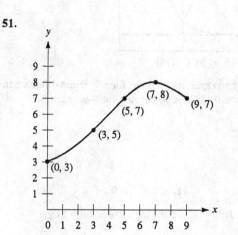

Neither a learning nor a logistic nor an exponential curve may be fitted through the points.

SECTION 5.1 Technology Exercises

1. **a.** about 8 fruit flies

b. about 22 days

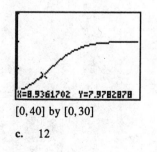

[0, 40] by [0, 30]

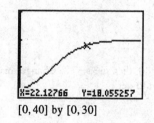

[0, 40] by [0, 30]

c. 12

d. $y = 20$

3.   1.8

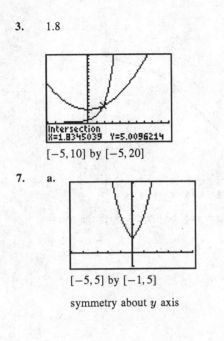

[−5, 10] by [−5, 20]

5.

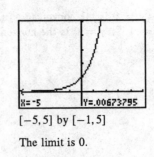

[−5, 5] by [−1, 5]

The limit is 0.

7. a.

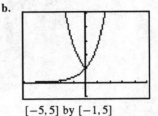

[−5, 5] by [−1, 5]

symmetry about y axis

b.

[−5, 5] by [−1, 5]

The graphs are the same for $x \geq 0$ and differ when $x < 0$. This is so because for $-x$, $|x| = -x$.

SECTION 5.2 pages 272–277

1. $\log_2 32 = 5$

3. $\log_{10} 100 = \log 100 = 2$

5. $\log_e 1 = \ln 1 = 0$

7. $3^2 = 9$

9. $10^2 = 100$

11. $10^{-1} = 0.1$

13. $e^1 = e$

15.   Given $10^x = 2$, use the logarithmic form to get

$$x = \log 2$$

17.   Given $e^{3x} = 2$, use the logarithmic form to get

$$3x = \ln 2$$
$$x = \frac{\ln 2}{3}$$

19.   Given $3e^{5x} = 42$, then $e^{5x} = 14$ and, using the logarithmic form,

$$5x = \ln 14$$
$$x = \frac{\ln 14}{5}$$

21.   Given $\ln x = -2$, change to the exponential form to get $x = e^{-2} = \dfrac{1}{e^2}$

23.   Given $\ln 4x = 30$, change to the exponential form to get

$$4x = e^{30}$$
$$x = \frac{e^{30}}{4}$$

25.   Given $\ln 3x = 0$, change to the exponential form to get

$$3x = e^0 = 1$$
$$x = \frac{1}{3}$$

27.   Given $5 \ln 3x = 40$, then $\ln 3x = 8$. Change this to the exponential form to get

$$3x = e^8$$
$$x = \frac{e^8}{3}$$

29. $\ln e^4 = 4$

31. $5 \ln e^2 = 5 \cdot 2 = 10$

33. $e \ln 1 = e \cdot 0 = 0$

35. $1 + 2e^{\ln 3} = 1 + 2(3) = 7$

37. $\ln \sqrt{e} = \ln e^{1/2} = \frac{1}{2}$

39. $\ln xy = \ln x + \ln y$

41. $\ln ex = \ln e + \ln x$
$$= 1 + \ln x$$

43. $\ln \sqrt{x} = \ln x^{1/2} = \frac{1}{2} \ln x$ **45.** $\ln x + \ln 2 = \ln 2x$ **47.** $\ln 4 - \ln x = \ln \frac{4}{x}$

49. $3 \ln x = \ln x^3$ **51.** $\ln 5 + 2 \ln x = \ln 5 + \ln x^2$

$$= \ln 5x^2$$

53. Using $A = Pe^{rt}$, then the given constants imply $8000 = 4000e^{0.07t}$ or $e^{0.07t} = 2$. Changing to the logarithmic form yields

$0.07t = \ln 2$

$t = \dfrac{\ln 2}{0.07} \approx 9.9$ years

The original investment will double in approximately 9.9 years.

55. Using $A = Pe^{rt}$ and replacing A with $3P$, the formula becomes $3P = Pe^{r(12)}$ or $3 = e^{12r}$. Changing to the logarithmic form yields

$12r = \ln 3$

$r = \dfrac{\ln 3}{12} \approx 0.092$

Money will triple in 12 years at an annual interest rate of approximately 9.2%.

57. **a.** Assuming exponential growth and using the initial population $C = 335{,}000$ ($t = 0$ corresponds to 1995), the exponential growth formula becomes $A = 335{,}000e^{kt}$. When $t = 5$, $A = 450{,}000$; thus $450{,}000 = 335{,}000e^{k(5)}$ or $e^{5k} = \frac{90}{67}$. Changing to the logarithmic form $5k = \ln\left(\frac{90}{67}\right)$, $k = \frac{1}{5} \ln\left(\frac{90}{67}\right) \approx 0.06$. The growth formula is $A = 335{,}000e^{0.06t}$.

  b. Here the k value of 0.06 means that the Fort Myers population is growing at the rate of 6% a year.

59. Assuming exponential growth and using the initial population $C = 2500$, the exponential growth formula becomes $A = 2500e^{kt}$. When $t = 1$, $A = 5000$; thus $5000 = 2500e^{k(1)}$ or $e^k = 2$. Changing to the logarithmic form $k = \ln 2 \approx 0.6931$, the growth formula is $A = 2500e^{0.6931t}$. Let $A = 1{,}000{,}000$ and solve for t by dividing by 2500 and changing to the logarithmic form.

$1{,}000{,}000 = 2500e^{0.6931t}$

$e^{0.6931t} = 400$

$0.6931t = \ln 400$

$t = \dfrac{\ln 400}{0.6931} \approx 8.64$

The bacteria population will grow to 1,000,000 in approximately 8.64 hours.

61. **a.** Assuming exponential growth (continuous compounding) with initial value $C = 20,000$ and a value of 54,000 for $t = 5$, then the exponential growth formula becomes $A = 20,000e^{kt}$ and $54,000 = 20,000e^{5k}$. Divide by 20,000 and change to the logarithmic form to get k.

$$54,000 = 20,000e^{5k}$$
$$2.7 = e^{5k}$$
$$5k = \ln 2.7$$
$$k = \frac{\ln 2.7}{5} \approx 0.199$$

The annual rate of growth is approximately 19.9%.

b. Let $A = 80,000$ and solve for t.

$$80,000 = 20,000e^{0.199t}$$
$$4 = e^{0.199t}$$
$$0.199t = \ln 4$$
$$t = \frac{\ln 4}{0.199} \approx 6.97$$

The land will appreciate to $80,000 in 1998.

63. **a.** $S(6) = 200,000e^{-0.12(6)} \approx 97,350$
b. To find when sales will be reduced to 50,300 units per month, solve for t.

$$50,300 = 200,000e^{-0.12t}$$
$$\frac{503}{2000} = e^{-0.12t}$$
$$\ln\left(\frac{503}{2000}\right) = -0.12t$$
$$t = \frac{1}{-0.12}\ln\left(\frac{503}{2000}\right) \approx 11.5026$$

Since $t = 6$ is now, in approximately $5\frac{1}{2}$ months sales will have fallen to 50,300 units per month, triggering the distress sale.

65. Assuming exponential decay with initial amount $C = 90$ and a half-life of 14 years, then the exponential decay formula yields $45 = 90e^{14k}$. Divide by 90 and change to the logarithmic form to get k.

$$45 = 90e^{14k}$$
$$0.5 = e^{14k}$$
$$14k = \ln 0.5$$
$$k = \frac{\ln 0.5}{14} \approx -0.0495$$

Thus, the exponential decay formula is $A = 90e^{-0.0495t}$. For $t = 100$, $A = 90e^{(-0.0495)(100)} \approx 0.638$ grams.

67. From Question 66 we know that the exponential decay equation for carbon-14 is $A = Ce^{-0.00012t}$. From this equation with $A = 0.91C$, we have

$$0.91C = Ce^{-0.00012t}$$
$$0.91 = e^{-0.00012t}$$
$$\ln(0.91) = -0.00012t$$
$$t = \frac{\ln(0.91)}{-0.00012} \approx 785.9223$$

To the nearest hundred years, the girl died 800 years ago.

69. a. Assuming exponential decay with a half-life of 28 years, the exponential decay formula yields $0.5C = Ce^{28k}$. Divide both sides by C and change to the logarithmic form to solve for k.

$$0.5C = Ce^{28k}$$
$$0.5 = e^{28k}$$
$$28k = \ln 0.5$$
$$k = \frac{\ln 0.5}{28} \approx -0.0248$$

The decay constant for strontium-90 is approximately -0.0248.

b. Let the amount of strontium-90 present in 1963 be some value C. Solve $0.10C = Ce^{-0.0248t}$ for t to determine in what year the amount will be reduced to 10%.

$$0.10C = Ce^{-0.0248t}$$
$$0.1 = e^{-0.0248t}$$
$$-0.0248t = \ln 0.1$$
$$t = \frac{\ln 0.1}{-0.0248} \approx 92.8$$

The strontium-90 will be reduced to 10% of the 1963 level in the year 2056.

71. a. Assuming exponential decay with a half-life of 8.6 days, the exponential decay formula yields $0.5C = Ce^{8.6k}$. Divide both sides by C and change to the logarithmic form to solve for k.

$$0.5C = Ce^{8.6k}$$
$$0.5 = e^{8.6k}$$
$$8.6k = \ln 0.5$$
$$k = \frac{\ln 0.5}{8.6} \approx -0.081$$

The decay constant for iodine-131 is approximately -0.081.

b. Let C be the amount of iodine-131 initially used as a tracer. In 5 weeks ($t = 35$ days), $A = Ce^{(-0.081)(35)} \approx 0.059C$.

Thus, the amount present after 5 weeks is approximately 5.9% of the original amount.

73. Assuming exponential decay with initial value $C = 50$ and decay constant $k = -0.04$, then the exponential decay formula becomes $A = 50e^{-0.04t}$.

a. For $t = 30$, $A = 50e^{(-0.04)(30)} \approx 15.06$ units per volume.

b. For $t = 120$, $A = 50e^{(-0.04)(120)} \approx 0.411$ unit per volume.

c. To eliminate 90% means $A = (0.10)(50) = 5$. Solve for t in the formula

$$5 = 50e^{-0.04t}$$
$$0.1 = e^{-0.04t}$$
$$-0.04t = \ln 0.1$$
$$t = \frac{\ln 0.1}{-0.04} \approx 57.56$$

90% of the drug is eliminated in approximately 58 minutes.

75. a. Revenue $=$ (number of units) $\cdot$ (price per unit)
$$R(x) = (x)\left[\frac{50}{\ln(x+3)}\right] = \frac{50x}{\ln(x+3)}$$

b. $R(30)\dfrac{(50)(30)}{\ln(30+3)} = \dfrac{1500}{\ln(33)} \approx \$429$

77. a. Given $\log D = a - b \log T$, then using the log properties,

$$\log D + b \log T = a$$
$$\log D + \log T^b = a$$
$$\log DT^b = a$$

Changing to the exponential form, $DT^b = 10^a$, and solving for D yields $D = 10^a T^{-b}$.

b. Solving $DT^b = 10^a$ for T yields

$$T^b = \frac{10^a}{D}$$
$$T = \sqrt[b]{\frac{10^a}{D}}$$

79. a. Using $A = 2P = Pe^{rt}$, divide both sides by P and change to the logarithmic form to solve for r.

$$2P = Pe^{rt}$$
$$2 = e^{rt}$$
$$rt = \ln 2$$
$$r = \frac{\ln 2}{t} \approx \frac{0.69315}{t} \quad \text{Note: as a percent, } r = \frac{100\ln 2}{t}$$

b.

t	5	6	7	8	9	10	11	12	(years to double)
r	13.9%	11.6%	9.9%	8.7%	7.7%	6.9%	6.3%	5.8%	(interest rate)

81. The effective rate is given as $e^r - 1$, where r is the interest rate and interest is compounded continuously (nominal rate). Thus, the effective rate is $e^{0.063} - 1 \approx 0.0650268$. The effective rate is approximately 6.50%.

83. Using the formula of Question 81, we have

$$0.0612 = e^r - 1$$
$$e^r = 1.0612$$
$$r = \ln(1.0612) \approx 0.0594003$$

The nominal rate is approximately 5.94%.

85. a. increases
  b. D' is positive.
  c. D'' is positive.
  d. "The function D is increasing at an increasing rate."

87. a. Logistic growth
  b. Learning curve
  c. Exponential decay
  d. Logistic growth
  e. Exponential growth
  f. Logistic growth
  g. Logistic growth
  h. Logistic growth
  i. Learning curve

89. Use the formula $y = S - Ce^{kt}$ where the given conditions state:

$S = 375$

at $t = 0$, $y = 60$

at $t = 45$, $y = 120$

a. To determine C, use $y = 375 - Ce^{kt}$ and let $t = 0$, $y = 60$.

$60 = 375 - Ce^0 = 375 - C$

$C = 375 - 60$

$C = 315$

b. If $y = 120$ when $t = 45$, then, using $C = 315$ from part a, $120 = 375 - 315e^{45k}$. Solve for e^{45k} and change to the logarithmic form to solve for k. Thus, $e^{45k} \approx 0.81$ and

$45k = \ln 0.81$

$k = \dfrac{\ln 0.81}{45} \approx -0.0047$

c. Using the results of parts a and b, $y = 375 - 315e^{-0.0047t}$. Let $y = 160$ and solve for t. $160 = 375 - 315e^{-0.0047t}$ becomes $e^{-0.0047t} = 0.683$.

Using the logarithmic form,

$-0.0047t = \ln 0.683$

$t = \dfrac{\ln 0.683}{-0.0047} \approx 81.1$

Thus, the roast will be cooked ($160°$) in approximately 81 minutes.

91. Given $A = Ce^{kt}$, let $t = 0$; then $A = Ce^0 = C$, since $e^0 = 1$.

93. The expression $\log_b a = c$ is by definition equivalent to the exponential expression $a = b^c$. It is clear that c is an exponent.

95. **a.** The tangent lines all have a positive slope, which indicates that the function is always increasing.

b. From part a, although the tangent lines all have a positive slope, the slope of each tangent line, for increasing values of x, is getting smaller in magnitude. Thus, the logarithmic function, $f(x) = \ln x$, is increasing, but at a decreasing rate. It is, therefore, concave down for all x.

97. For the logarithm to be defined, we require that $x - 2 > 0$. Hence $x > 2$.

SECTION 5.2 Technology Exercises

1. 5 days

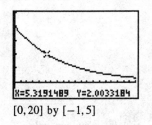

X=5.3191489   Y=2.0033184

$[0, 20]$ by $[-1, 5]$

3. a. 1.6

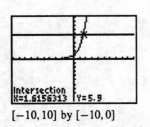

[−10, 10] by [−10, 0]

b. 1.6, the same result as part (a).

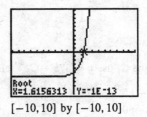

[−10, 10] by [−10, 10]

5. 2.5

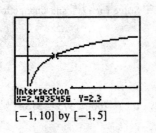

[−1, 10] by [−1, 5]

7. a. 16 years

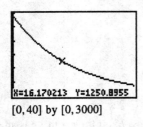

[0, 40] by [0, 3000]

b. \$1800

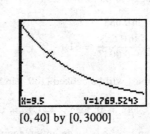

[0, 40] by [0, 3000]

9. a. 6.4%

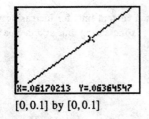

[0, 0.1] by [0, 0.1]

b. 5.5%

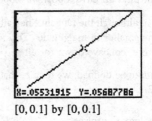

[0, 0.1] by [0, 0.1]

SECTION 5.3 pages 284–286

1. If $y = x^2 e^x$, then

$$\frac{dy}{dx} = x^2 e^x + 2x e^x \qquad \text{product rule}$$
$$= x(x + 2)e^x$$

3. If $y = 5e^x$, then

$$\frac{dy}{dx} = 5e^x$$

5. If $f(x) = (e^x + 2)^4$, then

$$f'(x) = 4(e^x + 2)^3 e^x \qquad \text{general power rule}$$

7. If $y = \frac{e^x + 1}{x}$, then

$$\frac{dy}{dx} = \frac{x(e^x) - (e^x + 1)(1)}{x^2} \qquad \text{quotient rule}$$
$$= \frac{xe^x - e^x - 1}{x^2}$$

9. If $f(x) = \frac{1}{(e^x + x)^3} = (e^x + x)^{-3}$, then

$$f'(x) = -3(e^x + x)^{-4}(e^x + 1) \qquad \text{general power rule}$$
$$= \frac{-3(e^x + 1)}{(e^x + x)^4}$$

11. If $f(x) = \frac{e^x}{e^x + 1}$, then

$$f'(x) = \frac{(e^x + 1)e^x - e^x(e^x)}{(e^x + 1)^2} \qquad \text{quotient rule}$$
$$= \frac{e^x}{(e^x + 1)^2}$$

13. If $f(x) = e^{6x-1}$, then

$$f'(x) = e^{6x-1} \frac{d}{dx}(6x - 1)$$
$$= 6e^{6x-1}$$

15. If $f(x) = e^{-x^2}$, then

$$f'(x) = e^{-x^2} \frac{d}{dx}(-x^2)$$
$$= -2xe^{-x^2}$$

17. If $f(x) = e^{\sqrt{x}} = e^{x^{1/2}}$, then

$$f'(x) = e^{x^{1/2}} \frac{d}{dx}(x^{1/2})$$
$$= e^{x^{1/2}} \left(\frac{1}{2} x^{-1/2} \right)$$
$$= \frac{e^{\sqrt{x}}}{2\sqrt{x}}$$

19. If $y = 0.4e^{-5x^2}$, then

$$\frac{dy}{dx} = 0.4e^{-5x^2} \frac{d}{dx}(-5x^2)$$
$$= 0.4e^{-5x^2}(-10x)$$
$$= -4xe^{-5x^2}$$

21. If $y = xe^{-x}$, then

$$\frac{dy}{dx} = x \left(e^{-x} \frac{d}{dx}(-x) \right) + e^{-x}(1) \qquad \text{product rule}$$
$$= -xe^{-x} + e^{-x}$$
$$= (1 - x)e^{-x}$$

23. If $f(x) = \frac{e^{3x}}{x+1}$, then

$$f'(x) = \frac{(x+1)(e^{3x})(3) - e^{3x}(1)}{(x+1)^2} \qquad \text{quotient rule}$$
$$= \frac{(3x + 3 - 1)e^{3x}}{(x+1)^2}$$
$$= \frac{(3x + 2)e^{3x}}{(x+1)^2}$$

25. If $y = \frac{e^x + e^{-x}}{2} = \frac{1}{2}(e^x + e^{-x})$, then

$$\frac{dy}{dx} = \frac{1}{2}(e^x - e^{-x})$$
$$= \frac{e^x - e^{-x}}{2}$$

27. If $f(x) = \frac{5x}{e^x} = 5xe^{-x}$, then

$$f'(x) = 5 \left[xe^{-x}(-1) + e^{-x}(1) \right] \qquad \text{product rule}$$
$$= 5(1 - x)e^{-x}$$
$$= \frac{5(1 - x)}{e^x}$$

29. If $y = (1 + e^{5x})^{10}$, then

$$\frac{dy}{dx} = 10(1 + e^{5x})^9 \frac{d}{dx}(1 + e^{5x}) \qquad \text{general power rule}$$
$$= 10(1 + e^{5x})^9 [e^{5x}(5)]$$
$$= 50(1 + e^{5x})^9 e^{5x}$$

31. If $f(x) = e^{3x}$, then

$$f'(x) = e^{3x}(3) = 3e^{3x}$$
$$\text{and } f''(x) = 3[e^{3x}(3)]$$
$$= 9e^{3x}$$

33. If $f(x) = xe^x$, then

$$f'(x) = x(e^x) + e^x(1) = (x + 1)e^x$$
$$\text{and } f''(x) = (x + 1)(e^x) + e^x(1)$$
$$= (x + 2)e^x$$

35. Given $f(x) = 3e^{5x}$, then $f'(x) = 15e^{3x}$. Since $e^{3x} > 0$ for all x, then $f'(x) = 15e^{3x} > 0$ for all x.

Thus, $f(x)$ is always increasing.

37. Given $f(x) = 1 + e^{-2x}$, then $f'(x) = -2e^{-2x}$. Since $e^{-2x} > 0$ for all x, then $f'(x) = -2e^{-2x} < 0$ for all x.

Thus, $f(x)$ is always decreasing.

41. Given $f(x) = e^{x^2}$, then $f'(x) = e^{x^2}(2x) = 2xe^{x^2}$. Solving $f'(x) = 2xe^{x^2} = 0$ yields $x = 0$. Since $e^{x^2} > 0$ for all x, the sign of $f'(x)$ depends on x.

$$\underset{\substack{f \text{ decreasing}}}{f'(-1) = -2e}\quad\underset{\substack{f \text{ increasing}}}{f'(1) = 2e}$$

$$\underbrace{\quad-----\quad}_{}\bullet\underbrace{\quad++++\quad}_{}$$
$$x = 0$$

Thus, $f(x)$ is increasing on the interval $(0, \infty)$ and decreasing on the interval $(-\infty, 0)$.

39. Given $f(x) = 1 + xe^x$, then $f'(x) = x(e^x) + e^x(1) = (x+1)e^x$. Solving $f'(x) = (x+1)e^x = 0$ gives $x = -1$. Since $e^x > 0$ for all x, the sign of $f'(x)$ depends on $x + 1$.

$$f'(-2) = -e^{-2}\qquad f'(0) = e^0 = 1$$
$$-----\quad\bullet\quad++++++$$
$$x = -1$$
$$f \text{ decreasing}\qquad f \text{ increasing}$$

Thus, f is increasing on the interval $(-1, \infty)$ and decreasing on the interval $(-\infty, -1)$.

43. Given $y = x^2 e^x$, then

$$\frac{dy}{dx} = x^2 e^x + e^x(2x) = (x^2 + 2x)e^x$$

and

$$\frac{d^2y}{dx^2} = (x^2 + 2x)e^x + e^x(2x + 2) = (x^2 + 4x + 2)e^x$$

Solving

$$\frac{dy}{dx} = (x^2 + 2x)e^x = 0$$

yields

$$x^2 + 2x = x(x + 2) = 0$$

which gives $x = 0$ and $x = -2$.

a. The critical numbers are $x = 0$ and $x = -2$.

b. Evaluating $\frac{d^2y}{dx^2}$ at $x = 0$ yields $\frac{d^2y}{dx^2}\Big|_{x=0} = 2e^0 = 2 > 0$, and at $x = -2$, $\frac{d^2y}{dx^2}\Big|_{x=-2} = (4 - 8 + 2)e^{-2} = -2e^{-2} < 0$

Thus, by the second derivative test,

$(0, 0)$ is a relative minimum and $(-2, 4e^{-2}) = (-2, 0.54)$ is a relative maximum.

45. Given $y = xe^{x/2}$, then

$$\frac{dy}{dx} = xe^{x/2}\left(\frac{1}{2}\right) + e^{x/2}(1) = \left(\frac{x}{2} + 1\right)e^{x/2}$$

and

$$\frac{d^2y}{dx^2} = \left(\frac{x}{2} + 1\right)(e^{x/2})\left(\frac{1}{2}\right) + e^{x/2}\left(\frac{1}{2}\right) = \left(\frac{x}{4} + 1\right)e^{x/2}$$

Solving

$$\frac{dy}{dx} = \left(\frac{x}{2} + 1\right)e^{x/2} = 0$$

yields

$$\frac{x}{2} + 1 = 0$$

which gives $x = -2$.

a. The only critical number is $x = -2$.

b. Evaluating $\frac{d^2y}{dx^2}$ at $x = -2$ yields $\left.\frac{d^2y}{dx^2}\right|_{x=-2} = \frac{1}{2}e^{-1} > 0$.

Thus, by the second derivative test, $\left(-2, -2e^{-1}\right)$ is a relative minimum.

47. Given $y = x^2 e^{-x}$, then

$$\frac{dy}{dx} = x^2 e^{-x}(-1) + e^{-x}(2x) = (2x - x^2)e^{-x}$$

and

$$\frac{d^2y}{dx^2} = (2x - x^2)(e^{-x})(-1) + e^{-x}(2 - 2x) = (x^2 - 4x + 2)e^{-x}$$

Solving

$$\frac{dy}{dx} = x(2 - x)e^{-x} = 0$$

yields

$$x(2 - x) = 0$$

which gives $x = 0$ and $x = 2$.

a. The critical numbers are $x = 0$ and $x = 2$.

b. Evaluating $\frac{d^2y}{dx^2}$ at $x = 0$ yields $\left.\frac{d^2y}{dx^2}\right|_{x=0} = 2e^0 = 2 > 0$, and at $x = 2$, $\left.\frac{d^2y}{dx^2}\right|_{x=2} = (4 - 8 + 2)e^{-2} = -2e^{-2} < 0$.

Thus, by the second derivative test,

$(0, 0)$ is a relative minimum and $(2, 4e^{-2})$ is a relative maximum.

49. Given $y = (1 + x)e^{3x}$, then

$$\frac{dy}{dx} = (1 + x)(e^{3x})(3) + e^{3x}(1) = (3x + 4)e^{3x}$$

and

$$\frac{d^2y}{dx^2} = (3x + 4)(e^{3x})(3) + e^{3x}(3) = 3(3x + 5)e^{3x}$$

Solving

$$\frac{dy}{dx} = (3x + 4)e^{3x} = 0$$

yields

$$3x + 4 = 0$$

which gives $x = -\frac{4}{3}$.

a. The only critical number is $x = -\frac{4}{3}$.

b. Evaluating $\frac{d^2y}{dx^2}$ at $x = -\frac{4}{3}$ yields $\frac{d^2y}{dx^2}\Big|_{x=-\frac{4}{3}} = 3e^{-4} > 0$.

Thus, by the second derivative test,

$\left(-\frac{4}{3}, -\frac{1}{3}e^{-4}\right)$ is a relative minimum.

51. Given $f(x) = e^x$, then $f'(x) = e^x$. Since $e^x > 0$ for all x and is defined for all x, there are no critical numbers; hence, there are no relative extrema.

53. To graph $y = f(x) = x - e^x$, use the graphing techniques of chapter 4, Sections 4.2 and 4.3. Differentiating $f'(x) = 1 - e^x$ and solving $f'(x) = 1 - e^x = 0$ yields the critical number $x = 0$.

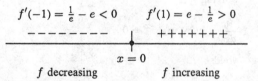

$$f'(-1) = 1 - \frac{1}{e} > 0 \qquad f'(1) = 1 - e < 0$$

f increasing $\qquad$ f decreasing

Thus, $(0, -1)$ is a relative maximum.

$f''(x) = -e^x < 0$ for all x; therefore $f(x)$ is always concave down.

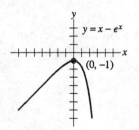

55. To graph $y = f(x) = e^x + e^{-x}$, use the techniques of Chapter 4, Sections 4.2 and 4.3. Differentiating $f'(x) = e^x - e^{-x}$ and solving $f'(x) = e^x - e^{-x} = 0$ yields $e^{2x} - 1 = 0$. Thus, $e^{2x} = 1$ or $x = 0$ is the only critical number.

$$f'(-1) = \frac{1}{e} - e < 0 \qquad f'(1) = e - \frac{1}{e} > 0$$

f decreasing $\qquad$ f increasing

Thus, $(0, 2)$ is a relative minimum. Also $f''(x) = e^x + e^{-x} > 0$ for all x; hence $f(x)$ is always concave up.

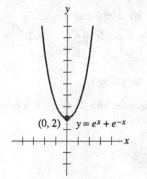

57. **a.** Total cost = (number of units) · (cost per unit)

$$C(x) = 50xe^{-0.04x}$$

b. Marginal cost = $C'(x) = 50\left(xe^{-0.04x}(-0.04) + e^{-0.04x}(1)\right)$

$$MC = (50 - 2x)e^{-0.04x}$$

c. $C(10) = \$335.16$

$C'(10) = \$20.11$

d. Solve $C'(x) = (50 - 2x)e^{-0.04x} = 0$. Since $e^{-0.04x} \neq 0$, this results in $50 - 2x = 0$ or $x = 25$.

59. Profit = Revenue - Cost

$$P(x) = R(x) - C(x) = 40xe^{0.03x} - 40xe^{-0.02x}$$

$$= 40x\left(e^{0.03x} - e^{-0.02x}\right)$$

Marginal profit = $P'(x) = 40x\left(0.03e^{0.03x} + 0.02e^{-0.02x}\right) + 40\left(e^{0.03x} - e^{-0.02x}\right)$

$$= 1.2xe^{0.03x} + 0.8xe^{-0.02x} + 40e^{0.03x} - 40e^{-0.02x}$$

$$= (1.2x + 40)e^{0.03x} + (0.8x - 40)e^{-0.02x}$$

61. Profit is a maximum when $C'(x) = R'(x)$. Differentiating yields

$$C'(x) = 30\left[xe^{-x/10}\left(-\frac{1}{10}\right) + e^{-x/10}(1)\right]$$

$$= (30 - 3x)e^{-x/10}$$

and

$$R'(x) = 50\left[xe^{-x/10}\left(-\frac{1}{10}\right) + e^{-x/10}(1)\right) = (50 - 5x)e^{-x/10}$$

Solving $C'(x) = R'(x)$ results in

$$(30 - 3x)e^{-x/10} = (50 - 5x)e^{-x/10}$$

$$30 - 3x = 50 - 5x$$

$$2x = 20$$

$$x = 10$$

Maximum profit at $x = 10$.

63. Given $c(x) = 0.001e^{-2x}$.

a. At the source $x = 0$ and one mile downstream $x = 1$; thus

$$c(0) = 0.001e^0 = 0.001$$

$$c(1) = 0.001e^{-2} \approx 0.0001$$

b. $c'(x) = -0.002e^{-2x}$

65. If $y = 1 + e^{4x}$, then $\frac{dy}{dx} = 4e^{4x}$. The slope of the tangent line at $(0, 2)$ is given by $\frac{dy}{dx}\Big|_{x=0} = 4e^0 = 4$.

Slope = 4

67. If $y = e^x$, then $\frac{dy}{dx} = e^x$. At the point where the slope of the tangent line is e, $\frac{dy}{dx} = e^x = e$ and $x = 1$. Thus, the tangent line passes through the point $(1, e)$ with slope e. The equation of the tangent line is $y - e = e(x - 1)$ or $y = ex$.

69. Using implicit differentiation on $x + y + xe^y = 10$ yields

$$1 + \frac{dy}{dx} + \left[xe^y\frac{dy}{dx} + e^y(1)\right] = 0.$$

Solve this expression for $\frac{dy}{dx}$.

$$\frac{dy}{dx} + xe^y\frac{dy}{dx} = -1 - e^y$$

$$\left(1 + xe^y\right)\frac{dy}{dx} = -1 - e^y$$

$$\frac{dy}{dx} = \frac{-1 - e^y}{1 + xe^y}$$

71. Using implicit differentiation on $xe^y - ye^x = y$ yields

$$\left(xe^y \frac{dy}{dx} + e^y(1) \right) - \left(ye^x + e^x \frac{dy}{dx} \right) = \frac{dy}{dx}$$

Solve this expression for $\frac{dy}{dx}$.

$$xe^y \frac{dy}{dx} - e^x \frac{dy}{dx} - \frac{dy}{dx} = ye^x - e^y$$

$$(xe^y - e^x - 1)\frac{dy}{dx} = ye^x - e^y$$

$$\frac{dy}{dx} = \frac{ye^x - e^y}{xe^y - e^x - 1}$$

73. Using implicit differentiation on $e^{x+y} + x^2 + y^2 = 0$ yields

$$e^{x+y}\left(1 + \frac{dy}{dx} \right) + 2x + 2y\frac{dy}{dx} = 0$$

Solve this expression for $\frac{dy}{dx}$.

$$e^{x+y} + e^{x+y}\frac{dy}{dx} + 2x + 2y\frac{dy}{dx} = 0$$

$$\left(e^{x+y} + 2y \right)\frac{dy}{dx} = -2x - e^{x+y}$$

$$\frac{dy}{dx} = \frac{-2x - e^{x+y}}{e^{x+y} + 2y}$$

75. Using implicit differentiation on $e^{xy} - 2x = y+3$ yields

$$e^{xy}\left(x\frac{dy}{dx} + y(1) \right) - 2 = \frac{dy}{dx}$$

Solve this expression for $\frac{dy}{dx}$.

$$xe^{xy}\frac{dy}{dx} - \frac{dy}{dx} = 2 - ye^{xy}$$

$$(xe^{xy} - 1)\frac{dy}{dx} = 2 - ye^{xy}$$

$$\frac{dy}{dx} = \frac{2 - ye^{xy}}{xe^{xy} - 1}$$

77. Using implicit differentiation on $xe^{y^2} + x^2e^y = y$ yields

$$x\left[e^{y^2}\left(2y\frac{dy}{dx} \right) \right] + e^{y^2}(1) + \left[x^2e^y\frac{dy}{dx} + e^y(2x) \right] = \frac{dy}{dx}$$

Solve this expression for $\frac{dy}{dx}$.

$$2xye^{y^2}\frac{dy}{dx} + x^2e^y\frac{dy}{dx} - \frac{dy}{dx} = -e^{y^2} - 2xe^y$$

$$\left(2xye^{y^2} + x^2e^y - 1 \right)\frac{dy}{dx} = -e^{y^2} - 2xe^y$$

$$\frac{dy}{dx} = \frac{-e^{y^2} - 2xe^y}{2xye^{y^2} + x^2e^y - 1}$$

79. If $y = 2^x$, then $\frac{dy}{dx} = 2^x \ln 2$.

81. If $y = 7^{4x}$, then

$$\frac{dy}{dx} = 7^{4x}\frac{d}{dx}(4x)(\ln 7)$$

$$= 4(7^{4x})(\ln 7)$$

83. If $f(x) = 3^{-x^2}$, then

$$f'(x) = 3^{-x^2}\frac{d}{dx}(-x^2)(\ln 3)$$

$$= -2x\left(3^{-x^2} \right)(\ln 3)$$

85. If $f(x) = 2 \cdot 9^{1+x^2}$, then

$$f'(x) = 2\left[9^{1+x^2}\frac{d}{dx}(1+x^2) \right](\ln 9)$$

$$= 2\left[9^{1+x^2}(2x) \right](\ln 9)$$

$$= 4x \cdot 9^{1+x^2}(\ln 9)$$

87. If $y = x \cdot 2^{3x}$, then

$$\frac{dy}{dx} = x\left[2^{3x}(3)\ln 2\right] + 2^{3x}(1) \qquad \text{product rule}$$
$$= 3x \cdot 2^{3x}\ln 2 + 2^{3x}$$
$$= (3x\ln 2 + 1)(2^{3x})$$

89. If $y = \frac{3^x}{2x}$, then

$$\frac{dy}{dx} = \frac{1}{2}\left[\frac{x 3^x \ln 3 - 3^x(1)}{x^2}\right] \qquad \text{quotient rule}$$
$$= \left(\frac{x\ln 3 - 1}{2x^2}\right)(3^x)$$

91. If $f(x) = \frac{1 - 10^{2x}}{3x}$, then

$$f'(x) = \frac{1}{3}\left[\frac{x(-10^{2x})(2)\ln 10 - \left(1 - 10^{2x}\right)(1)}{x^2}\right] \qquad \text{quotient rule}$$
$$= -\frac{(2x \cdot 10^{2x}\ln 10 + 1 - 10^{2x})}{3x^2}$$

93. If $y = e^3 + 1$, then

$$\frac{dy}{dx} = 0 \qquad \text{constant function}$$

95. If $y = e^2 x$, then

$$\frac{dy}{dx} = e^2(1) = e^2$$

97. If $y = \frac{x}{1+e}$, then

$$\frac{dy}{dx} = \frac{1}{1+e}(1) = \frac{1}{1+e}$$

99. Differentiating $f(x) = 2^{-x^2}$ yields $f'(x) = 2^{-x^2}(-2x)$ $\ln 2$. Let $f'(x) = -2x \cdot 2^{-x^2}\ln 2 = 0$; then, since $2^{-x^2}\ln 2 > 0$ for all x, $x = 0$ is the only critical number.

$$f''(x) = -2\ln 2\left[x \cdot 2^{-x^2}(-2x)\ln 2 + 2^{-x^2}(1)\right]$$
$$= -2\ln 2\left(-2x^2\ln 2 + 1\right)(2^{-x^2})$$

Using the second derivative test for the only critical number $x = 0$, $f''(0) = -2\ln 2(0+1)2^0 = -2\ln 2 < 0$.

Thus, $(0, 1)$ is a relative maximum.

101. Given $y = 5e^{2x}$, it is unnecessary to use the product rule to find $\frac{dy}{dx}$ because 5 is constant, independent of x. In fact,

$$\frac{dy}{dx} = \frac{d}{dx}(5e^{2x})$$
$$= 5\frac{d}{dx}(e^{2x})$$
$$= 5 \cdot 2e^{2x}$$
$$= 10e^{2x}$$

103. The growth rate is greatest at the point on the graph where the tangent lines to the graph are steepest. From the graph, this can be seen to occur at the point of inflection marked.

SECTION 5.3 Technology Exercises

1.

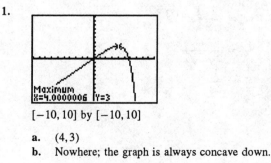

$[-10, 10]$ by $[-10, 10]$

a. $(4, 3)$
b. Nowhere; the graph is always concave down.

3.

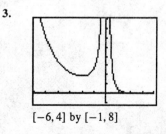

$[-6, 4]$ by $[-1, 8]$

a. negative, since f is decreasing at $x = 1$
b. positive, since f is concave up at $x = -4$
c. $y = 0$ is the only horizontal asymptote.

5. $f'(x) = 2x(3e^{3x}) + 2e^{3x} - 1$
$= 6xe^{3x} + 2e^{3x} - 1$

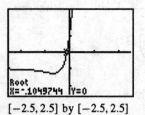

[−2.5, 2.5] by [−2.5, 2.5]

Critical number is $x = -0.105$.

SECTION 5.4 pages 295–297

1.   Given $y = \ln x$, $\frac{dy}{dx} = \frac{1}{x}$

3.   Given $y = x \ln x$,

$$\frac{dy}{dx} = x \left(\frac{1}{x} \right) + \ln x (1)$$
$$= 1 + \ln x$$

5.   Given $y = \frac{\ln x}{x}$,

$$\frac{dy}{dx} = \frac{x \left(\frac{1}{x} \right) - \ln x (1)}{x^2}$$
$$= \frac{1 - \ln x}{x^2}$$

7.   Given $y = \frac{x+1}{\ln x}$,

$$\frac{dy}{dx} = \frac{(\ln x)(1) - (x+1)\frac{1}{x}}{(\ln x)^2}$$
$$= \frac{\ln x - \frac{1}{x} - 1}{(\ln x)^2}$$
$$= \frac{x \ln x - x - 1}{x(\ln x)^2}$$

9.   Given $f(x) = \sqrt{\ln x} = (\ln x)^{1/2}$

$$f'(x) = \frac{1}{2}(\ln x)^{-1/2} \left(\frac{1}{x} \right)$$
$$= \frac{1}{2x\sqrt{\ln x}}$$

11.   Given $f(x) = \frac{x}{1+\ln x}$,

$$f'(x) = \frac{(1+\ln x)(1) - x \left(\frac{1}{x} \right)}{(1+\ln x)^2}$$
$$= \frac{\ln x}{(1+\ln x)^2}$$

13.   Given $y = \ln(x^2 + 7)$,

$$\frac{dy}{dx} = \frac{1}{x^2 + 7}(2x) = \frac{2x}{x^2 + 7}$$

15.   By the properties of logarithms, $y = \ln (2x + 1)^3 = 3 \ln (2x + 1)$; thus

$$\frac{dy}{dx} = 3 \left(\frac{1}{2x + 1} \right) (2) = \frac{6}{2x + 1}$$

17.   By the properties of logarithms, $y = \ln \frac{1}{x} = \ln 1 - \ln x = -\ln x$; thus

$$f'(x) = -\frac{1}{x}$$

19.   Given $f(x) = \ln \sqrt{x}$

$$f'(x) = \frac{1}{\sqrt{x}} \frac{1}{2} x^{-1/2}$$
$$= \frac{1}{2\sqrt{x}\sqrt{x}}$$
$$= \frac{1}{2x}$$

21. By the properties of logarithms, $f(x) = \ln \frac{x}{x+1} = \ln x - \ln(x+1)$; thus

$$f'(x) = \frac{1}{x} - \frac{1}{x+1} = \frac{x+1-x}{x(x+1)}$$
$$= \frac{1}{x(x+1)}$$

23. By the properties of logarithms, $y = \ln(xe^x) = \ln x + \ln e^x = \ln x + x$; thus

$$\frac{dy}{dx} = \frac{1}{x} + 1$$
$$= \frac{x+1}{x}$$

25. If $f(x) = 3\ln x$, then $f'(x) = \frac{3}{x}$ and $f'(1) = 3$. Thus, the slope of the tangent line is 3, and it passes through the point $(1,0)$. The equation of the tangent line is

$$y = 3(x-1)$$
$$= 3x - 3$$

27. Given $f(x) = x\ln x$,

$$f'(x) = x\left(\frac{1}{x}\right) + (\ln x)(1) = 1 + \ln x$$

and

$$f''(x) = \frac{1}{x}$$

29. Given $f(x) = (\ln x)^2$, then

$$f'(x) = 2(\ln x)\left(\frac{1}{x}\right) = \frac{2\ln x}{x}$$

and $f''(x) = \dfrac{2\left[x\left(\frac{1}{x}\right) - (\ln x)(1)\right]}{x^2}$

$$= \frac{2(1 - \ln x)}{x^2}$$

31. Given $f(x) = \frac{\ln x}{x}$, then

$$f'(x) = \frac{x\left(\frac{1}{x}\right) - (\ln x)(1)}{x^2} = \frac{1 - \ln x}{x^2}$$

and $f''(x) = \dfrac{x^2\left(-\frac{1}{x}\right) - (1 - \ln x)(2x)}{x^4}$

$$= \frac{-x[1 + 2(1 - \ln x)]}{x^4}$$
$$= -\frac{3 - 2\ln x}{x^3}$$

33. Given the revenue function $R(x) = 70x + 100\ln x$,
    a. Marginal revenue $= R'(x) = 70 + \frac{100}{x}$
    b. $R'(20) = 70 + \frac{100}{20} = 75$

35. Given the supply equation $p = 3\ln(x+1)$, then
    a. $C(x) = xp = 3x\ln(x+1)$
    b. Marginal cost $= C'(x) = 3\left[x\left(\frac{1}{x+1}\right) + \ln(x+1)(1)\right]$
    $$= \frac{3[x + (x+1)\ln(x+1)]}{x+1}$$

37. $C(t) = 11.9 + 0.1t + \ln(t+1)$ is an increasing function for $0 \le t \le 7$ if $C'(t) > 0$ for $0 \le t \le 7$. $C'(t) = 0.1 + \frac{1}{t+1} \ge 0.1 + \frac{1}{8} = \frac{9}{40} > 0$ for $0 \le t \le 7$. Hence $C(t)$ is an increasing function for $0 \le t \le 7$.

39. Given $f(x) = \ln x^2 = 2\ln x$, then $f'(x) = \frac{2}{x}$. Since $f'(1) = 2 > 0$, $f(x)$ is increasing at $(1,0)$.

41. Given $f(x) = \frac{\ln x}{x}$, then $f'(x) = \dfrac{x\left(\frac{1}{x}\right) - (\ln x)(1)}{x^2} = \dfrac{1 - \ln x}{x^2}$.

Since $f'(1) = \frac{1-0}{1} = 1 > 0$, then $f(x)$ is increasing at $(1,0)$.

43. Given $f(x) = \frac{x+1}{\ln x}$, then

$$f'(x) = \frac{(\ln x)(1) - (x+1)\left(\frac{1}{x}\right)}{(\ln x)^2} = \frac{\ln x - 1 - \frac{1}{x}}{(\ln x)^2}$$

Since $f'(e) = \frac{\ln e - 1 - \frac{1}{e}}{(\ln e)^2} = \frac{1 - 1 - \frac{1}{e}}{1^2} = -\frac{1}{e} < 0$

then $f(x)$ is decreasing at $(e, e+1)$.

47. Given $f(x) = \frac{\ln x^2}{x} = \frac{2 \ln x}{x}$, then

$$f'(x) = 2 \frac{\left[x\left(\frac{1}{x}\right) - (\ln x)(1)\right]}{x^2} = \frac{2(1 - \ln x)}{x^2}$$

and

$$f''(x) = \frac{2\left[x^2\left(-\frac{1}{x}\right) - (1 - \ln x)(2x)\right]}{(x^2)^2}$$

$$= -\frac{2(3 - 2 \ln x)}{x^3}$$

Solving $f'(x) = \frac{2(1 - \ln x)}{x^2} = 0$ yields $1 - \ln x = 0$ or $\ln x = 1$. In exponential form, $x = e' = e$. The only critical number is $x = e$. Since

$f''(e) = -\frac{2[3 - 2(1)]}{e^3} = -\frac{2}{e^3} < 0$, the second derivative test implies that $\left(e, \frac{2}{e}\right)$ is a relative maximum.

49. Given $f(x) = x^2 \ln x$, then $f'(x) = x^2\left(\frac{1}{x}\right) + (\ln x)(2x) = x(1 + 2 \ln x)$ and $f''(x) = x\left(\frac{2}{x}\right) + (1 + 2 \ln x)(1) = 3 + 2 \ln x$. Solving $f'(x) = x(1 + 2 \ln x) = 0$ yields $x = 0$ and $1 + 2 \ln x = 0$. The equation $1 + 2 \ln x = 0$ has solution $\ln x = -1/2$ or, in exponential form, $x = e^{-1/2} = \frac{1}{\sqrt{e}}$.

Since $f(0)$ is not defined, then $x = 0$ is not a critical number. The only critical number is $x = \frac{1}{\sqrt{e}}$.

Since $f''\left(\frac{1}{\sqrt{e}}\right) = 3 + 2\left(-\frac{1}{2}\right) = 2 > 0$, the second derivative test implies that $\left(\frac{1}{\sqrt{e}}, -\frac{1}{2e}\right)$ is a relative minimum.

45. Given $f(x) = 2x - 6 \ln x$, then $f'(x) = 2 - \frac{6}{x}$ and $f''(x) = \frac{6}{x^2}$. Solving $\frac{2x-6}{x} = 0$ yields $2x - 6 = 0$ or $x = 3$. The only critical number is $x = 3$. (*Note:* $x = 0$ is not a critical number because $f(x)$ is not defined at $x = 0$.) Since $f''(3) = \frac{6}{3^2} = \frac{2}{3} > 0$, the second derivative test implies that 3 is a relative minimum.

51. Given $f(x) = \ln(2x - x^2)$, then

$$f'(x) = \frac{2 - 2x}{2x - x^2} = \frac{2(1 - x)}{x(2 - x)}$$

and $f''(x) = \frac{(2x - x^2)(-2) - (2 - 2x)(2 - 2x)}{(2x - x^2)^2} = -\frac{2(x^2 - 2x + 2)}{x^2(2 - x)^2}$

Solving

$$f'(x) = \frac{2(1 - x)}{x(2 - x)} = 0$$

yields $2(1 - x) = 0$ or $x = 1$.

The only critical number is $x = 1$.

Since

$$f''(1) = \frac{-2(1 - 2 + 2)}{1^2(2 - 1)^2} = -2 < 0$$

The second derivative test implies that $(1, 0)$ is a relative maximum.

53. Use the techniques of Chapter 4, Sections 4.2 and 4.3, to graph $y = f(x) = x - \ln x$. $f'(x) = 1 - \frac{1}{x} = \frac{x-1}{x}$ and $f''(x) = \frac{1}{x^2}$. Solving $f'(x) = \frac{x-1}{x} = 0$ yields the only critical number, $x = 1$.

$$\begin{array}{ccc}
f'(1/2) = -1 & \quad & f'(2) = 1/2 \\
- - - - - & \bullet & + + + + \\
 & x = 1 & \\
f \text{ decreasing} & & f \text{ increasing}
\end{array}$$

Thus, $(1, 1)$ is a relative minimum. Also, $f''(x) = \frac{1}{x^2} > 0$; hence $f(x)$ is always concave up. Finally, the domain of $f(x)$ is $(0, \infty)$ since $\ln x$ is undefined for $x \leq 0$.

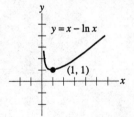

55. Use the techniques of Chapter 4, Sections 4.2 and 4.3, to graph $y = f(x) = \ln(x^2 + 1)$. $f'(x) = \frac{2x}{x^2+1}$ and $f''(x) =$

$$\frac{(x^2+1)(2)-2x(2x)}{(x^2+1)^2} = \frac{2(1-x^2)}{(x^2+1)^2}$$

Solving $f'(x) = \frac{2x}{x^2+1} = 0$ yields the only critical number, $x = 0$.

$$f'(-1) = -1 \qquad f'(1) = 1$$

$$\underset{\substack{\\ x = 0}}{\underline{\quad - - - - - \quad | \quad + + + + \quad}}$$

$$f \text{ decreasing} \qquad f \text{ increasing}$$

Thus $(0, 0)$ is a relative minimum.

Solving $f''(x) = \frac{2(1-x)(1+x)}{(x^2+1)^2} = 0$ yields $x = 1$ and $x = -1$.

$$f''(-2) = -\frac{6}{25} \qquad f''(0) = 2 \qquad f''(2) = -\frac{6}{25}$$

$$\underline{\quad - - - - - \quad | \quad + + + \quad | \quad - - - - - \quad}$$

$$x = -1 \qquad\quad x = 1$$

Thus, $(-1, \ln 2)$ and $(1, \ln 2)$ are points of inflection. Finally, $f(x)$ is defined for all x and $f(x)$ is symmetric with respect to the y axis.

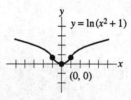

points of inflection $(\pm 1, \ln 2)$

57. Using implicit differentiation on the expression $3 \ln x + xy + y = 1$ yields

$$3\left(\frac{1}{x}\right) + \left[x\frac{dy}{dx} + y(1)\right] + \frac{dy}{dx} = 0$$

Solve this expression for $\frac{dy}{dx}$.

$$(x+1)\frac{dy}{dx} = -\left(\frac{3}{x} - y\right)$$

$$= -\frac{(3+xy)}{x}$$

$$\frac{dy}{dx} = -\frac{3+xy}{x(x+1)}$$

59. First, using the logarithm properties, change the given expression to $x^2 + 2y + \ln x + \ln y = 0$. Using implicit differentiation yields

$$2x + 2\frac{dy}{dx} + \frac{1}{x} + \frac{1}{y} - \frac{dy}{dx} = 0$$

Solve this expression for $\frac{dy}{dx}$.

$$\left(2 + \frac{1}{y}\right)\frac{dy}{dx} = -2x - \frac{1}{x}$$

$$\left(\frac{2y+1}{y}\right)\frac{dy}{dx} = -\frac{(2x^2+1)}{x}$$

$$\frac{dy}{dx} = -\frac{y(2x^2+1)}{x(2y+1)}$$

61. Using implicit differentiation on the expression $x \ln y - y \ln x = 8$ yields

$$\left[x\left(\frac{1}{y}\frac{dy}{dx} \right) + (\ln y)(1) \right] - \left[y\left(\frac{1}{x} \right) + (\ln x)\left(\frac{dy}{dx} \right) \right] = 0$$

Solve this expression for $\frac{dy}{dx}$.

$$\left(\frac{x}{y} - \ln x \right)\frac{dy}{dx} = \frac{y}{x} - \ln y$$

$$\left(\frac{x - y\ln x}{y} \right)\frac{dy}{dx} = \frac{y - x\ln y}{x}$$

$$\frac{dy}{dx} = \frac{y(y - x\ln y)}{x(x - y\ln x)}$$

63. Using implicit differentiation on the expression $e^x \ln y - 3xy + x = 10$ yields

$$\left[e^x\left(\frac{1}{y}\frac{dy}{dx} \right) + (\ln y)(e^x) \right] - \left[3x\frac{dy}{dx} + 3y(1) \right] + 1 = 0$$

Solve this expression for $\frac{dy}{dx}$.

$$\left(\frac{e^x}{y} - 3x \right)\frac{dy}{dx} = 3y - e^x \ln y - 1$$

$$\left(\frac{e^x - 3xy}{y} \right)\frac{dy}{dx} = 3y - e^x \ln y - 1$$

$$\frac{dy}{dx} = \frac{y(3y - e^x \ln y - 1)}{e^x - 3xy}$$

65. If $y = \log_{10} x$, then

$$\frac{dy}{dx} = \frac{1}{x}\frac{1}{\ln 10}$$

67. Using the logarithm properties, change $y = \log_2 9x$ to $y = \log_2 9 + \log_2 x$; then

$$\frac{dy}{dx} = \frac{1}{x} \cdot \frac{1}{\ln 2} \qquad (\log_2 9 \text{ is a constant.})$$

69. If $y = x \log_{10}(1 - 3x)$, then

$$\frac{dy}{dx} = x\left[\frac{1}{1 - 3x}\frac{d}{dx}(1 - 3x) \cdot \frac{1}{\ln 10} \right] + \log_{10}(1 - 3x)(1) \qquad \text{product rule}$$

$$= -\frac{3x}{1 - 3x} \cdot \frac{1}{\ln 10} + \log_{10}(1 - 3x)$$

71. If $y = \frac{\log_{10} x}{x}$, then

$$\frac{dy}{dx} = \frac{x\left(\frac{1}{x} \cdot \frac{1}{\ln 10} \right) - (\log_{10} x)(1)}{x^2} \qquad \text{quotient rule}$$

$$= \frac{\frac{1}{\ln 10} - \log_{10} x}{x^2}$$

$$= \frac{1 - (\ln 10)(\log_{10} x)}{x^2 \ln 10}$$

73. Given $y = x^{2x}$, apply the natural log to both sides to get

$$\ln y = \ln x^{2x} = 2x \ln x$$

then $\dfrac{d}{dx}(\ln y) = \dfrac{d}{dx}(2x \ln x)$

$$\frac{1}{y}\frac{dy}{dx} = 2\left[x\left(\frac{1}{x}\right) + (\ln x)(1)\right]$$

$$= 2(1 + \ln x)$$

$$\frac{dy}{dx} = 2y(1 + \ln x)$$

$$= 2x^{2x}(1 + \ln x)$$

75. Given $y = (x + 1)^x$, apply the natural log to both sides, to get

$$\ln y = \ln (x + 1)^x = x \ln (x + 1)$$

then $\dfrac{d}{dx}(\ln y) = \dfrac{d}{dx}(x \ln (x + 1))$

$$\frac{1}{y}\frac{dy}{dx} = x\left(\frac{1}{x+1}\right) + [\ln (x + 1)](1)$$

$$= y\left[\frac{x}{x+1} + \ln (x + 1)\right]$$

$$= (x + 1)^x\left[\frac{x}{x+1} + \ln (x + 1)\right]$$

$$= x(x + 1)^{x-1} + (x + 1)^x \ln (x + 1)$$

77. Given $y = x^{1/x}$, take natural logarithms of both sides to obtain

$$\ln y = \ln x^{1/2} = \frac{1}{x} \ln x$$

then

$$\frac{d}{dx}(\ln y) = \frac{d}{dx}\left(\frac{1}{x} \ln x\right)$$

$$\frac{1}{y}\frac{dy}{dx} = \frac{1}{x}\left(\frac{1}{x}\right) + (\ln x)\left(\frac{-1}{x^2}\right)$$

$$= \frac{1 - \ln x}{x^2}$$

$$\frac{dy}{dx} = \frac{x^{1/x}(1 - \ln x)}{x^2}$$

$$= x^{\left(\frac{1}{x}-2\right)}(1 - \ln x)$$

79. Given $y = (3x)^{x+1}$, apply the natural log to both sides to get

$$\ln y = \ln (3x)^{x+1} = (x + 1)\ln (3x)$$

then $\dfrac{d}{dx}(\ln y) = \dfrac{d}{dx}[(x + 1)\ln 3x]$

$$\frac{1}{y}\frac{dy}{dx} = (x + 1)\left[\frac{1}{3x}(3)\right] + (\ln 3x)(1)$$

$$\frac{dy}{dx} = y\left(\frac{x + 1}{x} + \ln 3x\right)$$

$$= (3x)^{x+1}\left(\frac{x + 1}{x} + \ln 3x\right)$$

81. **a.** $y = 3^x$. Take natural logs of both sides of the equation to obtain

$$\ln y = \ln(3^x)$$
$$= x \ln 3$$

Then

$$\frac{1}{y}\frac{dy}{dx} = \ln 3$$
$$\frac{dy}{dx} = 3^x \ln 3$$

b. $y = 2^x$. Take natural logarithms of both sides of the equation to obtain

$$\ln y = \ln(2^x) = x \ln 2$$

Then,

$$\frac{1}{y}\frac{dy}{dx} = \ln 2$$
$$\frac{dy}{dx} = 2^x \ln 2$$

c. $y = 5^{3x}$. Take natural logarithms of both sides of this equation to obtain

$$\ln y = \ln 5^{3x} = 3x \ln 5$$

Then

$$\frac{1}{y}\frac{dy}{dx} = 3 \ln 5$$
$$\frac{dy}{dx} = 5^{3x} \cdot 3 \ln 5$$

d. $y = 4^{x^2}$. Take natural logarithms of both sides of the equation to obtain

$$\ln y = \ln(4^{x^2}) = x^2 \ln 4$$

Then,

$$\frac{d}{dx}(\ln y) = \frac{d}{dx}(x^2 \ln 4)$$
$$\frac{1}{y}\frac{dy}{dx} = 2x \ln 4$$
$$\frac{dy}{dx} = 4^{x^2} \cdot 2x \ln 4$$

83. To investigate, with a calculator, the limit $\lim\limits_{x \to \infty} \frac{\ln x}{x}$, consider the following table.

x	$\frac{\ln x}{x}$ (approximate values)
10	0.23
100	0.05
1000	0.007
10,000	0.0009
100,000	
1,000,000	0.00001
10,000,000	0.0000016

It appears that $\lim\limits_{x \to \infty} \frac{\ln x}{x} = 0$.

Chapter 5/Exponential and Logarithmic Functions

85. Given $y = \frac{\ln x}{2}$, it is unnecessary to use the quotient rule

to compute $\frac{dy}{dx}$ because the denominator, 2, is constant.
In fact,

$$\frac{dy}{dx} = \frac{d}{dx}\left(\frac{\ln x}{2}\right)$$

$$= \frac{1}{2}\frac{d}{dx}(\ln x)$$

$$= \frac{1}{2}\frac{1}{x}$$

87. Using implicit differentiation on the expression $y - x + y \ln x = 1 - e$ yields

$$\frac{dy}{dx} - 1 + \left[y\left(\frac{1}{x}\right) + (\ln x)\frac{dy}{dx}\right] = 0$$

Solve this expression for $\frac{dy}{dx}$.

$$(1 + \ln x)\frac{dy}{dx} = 1 - \frac{y}{x}$$

$$\frac{dy}{dx} = \frac{x - y}{x(1 + \ln x)}$$

At the point $\left(e, \frac{1}{2}\right)$, $\frac{dy}{dx}\Big|_{(e, \frac{1}{2})} = \frac{e - \frac{1}{2}}{e(1 + \ln e)} = \frac{e - \frac{1}{2}}{2e} > 0$

Thus, the graph of $y - x + y \ln x = 1 - e$ is increasing at $\left(e, \frac{1}{2}\right)$.

89. Given $f(x) = \ln x$, then $f'(x) = \frac{1}{x}, x > 0$. The expression $\frac{1}{x}$ is never zero and is defined for all $x, x > 0$. Thus, there are no critical numbers, and hence, there are no relative extrema.

91. Given $y = \ln x$, then the slope of the tangent line, for any $x > 0$, is $\frac{dy}{dx} = \frac{1}{x}$.

At $x = 1$, $\frac{dy}{dx} = 1$.

At $x = 10$, $\frac{dy}{dx} = \frac{1}{10}$.

At $x = 100$, $\frac{dy}{dx} = \frac{1}{100}$.

At $x = 1000$, $\frac{dy}{dx} = \frac{1}{1000}$.

The slope of the tangent line will never be zero, since $\frac{1}{x}$ is never zero. However, the slope of the tangent line can be made arbitrarily small because $\lim_{x \to \infty} \frac{1}{x} = 0$. That is, by choosing x very large, we can make $\frac{1}{x}$ as close to zero as desired.

93. Let $f(x) = \ln x$, then

$$f'(x) = \frac{1}{x} = x^{-1}$$
$$f''(x) = -x^{-2}$$
$$f'''(x) = 2x^{-3}$$
$$f^{(4)}(x) = -(2)(3)x^{-4}$$
$$f^{(5)}(x) = (2)(3)(4)x^{-5}$$

The pattern appears to be $f^{(n)}(x) = (-1)^{n+1} 1 \cdot 2 \cdot 3 \cdot 4 \cdots (n-1)x^{-n}$, $n \geq 2$ (check the formula for the cases above). If the factorial notation $k! = 1 \cdot 2 \cdots k$ is used where $0! = 1$, then $f^{(n)}(x) = (-1)^{n+1}(n-1)!x^{-n}$. Thus, $f^{(40)}(x) = (-1)^{41}(40-1)!x^{-40} = -\frac{39!}{x^{40}}$.

SECTION 5.4 Technology Exercises

1.

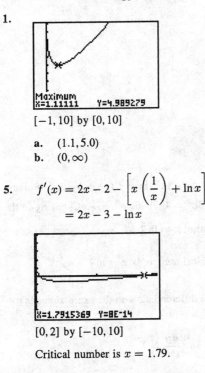

Maximum
X=1.11111   Y=4.989279

$[-1, 10]$ by $[0, 10]$

a. $(1.1, 5.0)$
b. $(0, \infty)$

5. $f'(x) = 2x - 2 - \left[x\left(\frac{1}{x}\right) + \ln x \right]$
$\quad = 2x - 3 - \ln x$

X=1.7915369   Y=8E-14

$[0, 2]$ by $[-10, 10]$

Critical number is $x = 1.79$.

3.

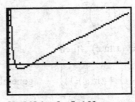

$[0, 20]$ by $[-5, 10]$

a. positive
b. positive

REVIEW EXERCISES FOR CHAPTER 5 pages 299–301

1. Given $5e^{7x} = 30$, then $e^{7x} = 6$ and changing to the logarithmic form,

$$7x = \ln 6$$
$$x = \frac{\ln 6}{7} \approx 0.256$$

3. Given $3\ln 4x = 18$, then $\ln 4x = 6$ and changing to the exponential form,

$$4x = e^6$$
$$x = \frac{1}{4}e^6 \approx 100.86$$

5. Given $4e^{0.03x} = 2$, then $e^{0.03x} = 0.5$ and changing to the logarithmic form,

$$0.03x = \ln 0.5$$
$$x = \frac{\ln 0.5}{0.03} \approx -23.10$$

7. Given $5 - \ln x = 0$, then $\ln x = 5$, and changing to the exponential form, $x = e^5 \approx 148.41$

9. $-e^{\ln 7} = -7 \qquad (e^{\ln x} = x)$

11. $\ln \frac{1}{e^2} = \ln e^{-2} = -2 \qquad (\ln e^x = x)$

13. Given $y = x^4 e^4 = e^4(x^4)$ e^4 is a constant

$$\frac{dy}{dx} = e^4(4x^3) = 4e^4 x^3$$

15. Given $f(x) = (3 - e^x)^7$,

$$f'(x) = 7(3 - e^x)^6(-e^x) \quad \text{general power rule}$$
$$= -7(3 - e^x)^6 e^x$$

17. Given $f(x) = x^3 e^{-3x}$, then

$$f'(x) = x^3 \left[e^{-3x}(-3) \right] + e^{-3x}(3x^2) \quad \text{product rule}$$
$$= 3x^2(1 - x)(e^{-3x})$$

19. Given $f(x) = e^{3x} \ln x$, then

$$f'(x) = e^{3x} \left(\frac{1}{x} \right) + (\ln x) \left[e^{3x}(3) \right] \quad \text{product rule}$$
$$= \left(\frac{1}{x} + 3 \ln x \right) (e^{3x})$$
$$= \left(\frac{1 + 3x \ln x}{x} \right) (e^{3x})$$

21. Given $y = x^2 (\ln x)^2 = (x \ln x)^2$, then

$$\frac{dy}{dx} = 2(x \ln x) \left[x \left(\frac{1}{x} \right) + (\ln x)(1) \right] \quad \text{general power rule}$$
$$= (2x \ln x)(1 + \ln x)$$

23. Given $f(x) = \ln \frac{1}{x^2} = \ln x^{-2} = -2 \ln x$, then $f'(x) = -\frac{2}{x}$

25. Given $y = x \ln x - x$, then

$$\frac{dy}{dx} = \left[x \left(\frac{1}{x} \right) + (\ln x)(1) \right] - 1$$
$$= \ln x$$

27. Given $f(x) = 4x - 3e^x$, then $f'(x) = 4 - 3e^x$. Solving $f'(x) = 4 - 3e^x = 0$ yields $e^x = \frac{4}{3}$. Changing to the logarithmic form, $x = \ln \frac{4}{3}$.

The only critical number is $x = \ln \frac{4}{3}$.

29. Given $y = \ln(x - 3) - \frac{x}{7}$, $\frac{dy}{dx} = \frac{1}{x-3} - \frac{1}{7}$. Solving

$$\frac{dy}{dx} = \frac{1}{x - 3} - \frac{1}{7} = \frac{7 - (x - 3)}{7(x - 3)} = \frac{10 - x}{7(x - 3)} = 0$$

yields $10 - x = 0$ or $x = 10$.

The only critical number is $x = 10$.

Note: $x = 3$ is not a critical number since $f(3)$ is undefined.

31. Using implicit differentiation on the expression $5 \ln y + e^{3y} = 2x$ yields

$$5 \left(\frac{1}{y} \frac{dy}{dx} \right) + 3e^{3y} \frac{dy}{dx} = 2$$

Solve this expression for $\frac{dy}{dx}$.

$$\left(\frac{5}{y} + 3e^{3y} \right) \frac{dy}{dx} = 2$$
$$\left(\frac{5 + 3ye^{3y}}{y} \right) \frac{dy}{dx} = 2$$
$$\frac{dy}{dx} = \frac{2y}{5 + 3ye^{3y}}$$

33. Use the present value formula $P = Ae^{-rt}$ with $A = 10,000$, $t = 4$, and $r = 7.5\% = 0.075$.

$$P = 10,000e^{-(0.075)(4)} = \$7408.18$$

35. If the fungus doubles in size every 7 hours, then, using the exponential growth formula, $2C = Ce^{7k}$ or $e^{7k} = 2$. Changing to the logarithmic form,

$$7k = \ln 2$$
$$k = \frac{\ln 2}{7} \approx 0.099$$

For $t = 32$, $A = Ce^{(0.099)(32)} = 23.76C$, where C is the initial amount.

Thus, in 32 hours, the fungus will be 23.76 times its present size.

37. An initial population of 5000 leads to an exponential growth formula $A = 5000e^{kt}$. If $A = 8400$ when $t = 4$, then $8400 = 5000e^{4k}$ or $e^{4k} = 1.68$. Changing to the logarithmic form,

$$4k = \ln 1.68$$
$$k = \frac{\ln 1.68}{4} \approx 0.13$$

For $t = 8$, $A = 5000e^{(0.13)(8)} = 14,146$

Thus, the population in 8 years will be approximately 14,146 people. Note that answers may vary depending on how many decimal places k is rounded to.

39. a. The exponential growth model is $A = Ce^{kt}$, where $C = \$160$ billion, $k = 0.10$, t is the time in years, with $t = 0$ corresponding to 1994, and A is the projected cost of the Medicare program t years after 1994. The cost of Medicare in 2002 is

$$A = 160e^{(0.1)(8)} \text{ billion dollars}$$
$$= 160e^{0.8}$$
$$\cong 356 \text{ billion dollars}$$

b. Under the Republican plan, the growth rate would be 6.4% per year. The exponential growth model would be $A = Ce^{kt}$, where k is 0.064. In 2002 the cost of Medicare would be

$$A = 160e^{(0.064)(8)} \text{ billion dollars}$$
$$= 160e^{0.512}$$
$$\approx 267 \text{ billion dollars}$$

41. We have $\frac{1}{2}M = Me^{k(5730)}$, where M is the initial mass of carbon-14. Hence,

$$5730k = \ln\left(\frac{1}{2}\right)$$
$$k = \frac{\ln\left(\frac{1}{2}\right)}{5730} \approx -0.00012$$

If the skeleton was dated to be 8000 years old, then the percentage of the original carbon-14 remaining is given by solving

$$pM = Me^{-0.00012(8000)}$$
$$p = e^{(-0.00012)(8000)} \approx 0.3799389$$

There was approximately 38% of the original carbon-14 found in the skeleton.

43. Given the logistic growth function $y = \frac{200,000}{1+1999e^{-0.8t}}$,

a. $y(0) = \frac{200,000}{1 + 1999e^0} = \frac{200,000}{2000} = 100$

b. $y(5) = \frac{200,000}{1 + 1999e^{-(0.8)(5)}} \approx 5317$

c. $\lim_{t\to\infty} y(t) = 200,000$ since $e^{-0.8t} \to 0$ as $t \to \infty$

45. Given $\log P = a - b\log A$

  a. To solve for P, use the logarithm properties to combine $\log P$ and $\log A$.

$$\log P = a - \log A^b$$
$$\log P + \log A^b = a$$
$$\log PA^b = a$$

  Change to the exponential form $PA^b = 10^a$ and solve for P:

$$P = 10^a A^{-b}$$

  b. To solve for A, start with the exponential form $PA^b = 10^a$ and get $A^b = 10^a P^{-1}$. Changing the exponent

  yields $A = \sqrt[b]{10^a P^{-1}}$.

47. $y = 4000e^{-0.02t}$ may be used to describe a decrease in the demand y for food stamps. None of the other functions may be used to describe a decrease in demand because they are all increasing functions.

49. An error message appears in the display if $\ln 0$ or $\ln(-1)$ is attempted on a calculator. This occurs because $\ln x$ is not defined mathematically for $x \le 0$.

51.

x	$\frac{\ln x}{\sqrt{x}}$
10	0.73
100	0.46
1000	0.22
10,000	0.092
100,000	0.036
1,000,000	0.014
10,000,000	0.0051

As x approaches infinity, the value of $\frac{\ln x}{\sqrt{x}}$ is approaching zero (slowly).

53. In Example 7 of Section 5.4 we have $f(x) = 2x - \ln 2x$ and $f''(x) = \frac{1}{x^2}$. Thus, $f''(x) > 0$ for all x in the domain of f. This means that the slopes of the tangent vectors to the graph of f are increasing. Thus, the graph of f is concave up.

55. **a.** $y = 25e^{x/50} + 25e^{-x/50}$

$y(0) = 25e^0 + 25e^0$

$\quad\quad = 50$

The height of the telephone line at its lowest point is 50 feet.

b. The height of the telephone line at its highest point is (using either $x = -25$ or $x = 25$)

$y(25) = 25e^{1/2} + 25e^{-1/2}$

$\quad\quad \approx 41.218 + 15.163$

$\quad\quad = 56.381$ feet

c. Sag$= 56.381 - 50 = 6.381$ feet

d. $\dfrac{dy}{dx} = \dfrac{25}{50}e^{x/50} - \dfrac{25}{50}e^{-x/50} = \dfrac{1}{2}\left(e^{x/50} - e^{-x/50}\right)$

$\dfrac{dy}{dx} = 0$ when $e^{x/50} - e^{-x/50} = 0$; that is, when

$e^{x/50} = e^{-x/50}$

$\ln(e^{x/50}) = \ln(e^{-x/50})$

$\dfrac{x}{50} = \dfrac{-x}{50}$

$x = -x$

$2x = 0$

$x = 0$

$\dfrac{d^2y}{dx^2} = \dfrac{1}{2}\left(\dfrac{1}{50}e^{x/50} + \dfrac{1}{50}e^{-x/50}\right)$

When $x = 0$, $\dfrac{d^2y}{dx^2} = \dfrac{1}{100}(e^0 + e^{-0}) = \dfrac{1}{50} > 0$

Hence $x = 0$ is, in fact, a minimum, by the second derivative test.

SECTION 6.1 pages 310–312

1. $\int 8x\,dx = 8\int x\,dx = \frac{8x^2}{2} + C = 4x^2 + C$

3. $\int 6x^2\,dx = 6\int x^2\,dx = \frac{6x^3}{3} + C = 2x^3 + C$

5. $\int t^3\,dt = \frac{t^4}{4} + C$

7. $\int 10x^5\,dx = 10\int x^5\,dx = \frac{10x^6}{6} + C = \frac{5}{3}x^6 + C$

9. $\int x^{-2}\,dx = \frac{x^{-1}}{-1} + C = -x^{-1} + C$

11. $\int 3x^{-4}\,dx = 3\int x^{-4}\,dx = \frac{3x^{-3}}{-3} + C = -x^{-3} + C$

13. $\int \frac{1}{x^5}\,dx = \int x^{-5}\,dx = -\frac{1}{4}x^{-4} + C$

15. $\int \frac{20}{z^6}\,dz = 20\int z^{-6}\,dz = dz\frac{20}{-5}z^{-5} + C$
$$= -4z^{-5} + C$$

17. $\int \sqrt{x}\,dx = \int x^{1/2}\,dx = \frac{x^{3/2}}{3/2} + C = \frac{2}{3}x^{3/2} + C$

19. $\int x^{3/4}\,dx = \frac{x^{7/4}}{7/4} + C = \frac{4}{7}x^{7/4} + C$

21. $\int x^{-2/3}\,dx = \frac{x^{1/3}}{1/3} + C = 3x^{1/3} + C$

23. $\int 3\,dx = 3x + C$

25. $\int (x^2 + 6x)\,dx = \int x^2\,dx + 6\int x\,dx$
$$= \frac{x^3}{3} + \frac{6x^2}{2} + C$$
$$= \frac{x^3}{3} + 3x^2 + C$$

27. $\int \left(\sqrt{x} - 3x^2\right)\,dx = \int x^{1/2}\,dx - 3\int x^2\,dx$
$$= \frac{x^{3/2}}{3/2} - \frac{3x^3}{3} + C$$
$$= \frac{2}{3}x^{3/2} - x^3 + C$$

29. $\int (x^{-1/2} + 9)\,dx = \int x^{-1/2}\,dx + \int 9\,dx = \frac{x^{1/2}}{\frac{1}{2}} + 9x + C$
$$= 2x^{1/2} + 9x + C$$

31. $\int (t^2 - 8t + 1)\,dt = \int t^2\,dt - 8\int t\,dt + \int dt$
$$= \frac{t^3}{3} - \frac{8t^2}{2} + t + C$$
$$= \frac{1}{3}t^3 - 4t^2 + t + C$$

33. $\int e^x\,dx = e^x + C$

35. $\int (2x - e^x)\,dx = 2\int x\,dx - \int e^x\,dx = \frac{2x^2}{2} - e^x + C$
$$= x^2 - e^x + C$$

37. $\int (e^x + 1)\,dx = \int e^x\,dx + \int dx = e^x + x + C$

39. $\int \frac{1}{z}\,dz = \ln|z| + C$

41. $\int \left(\frac{4}{x} + 6x\right)\,dx = 4\int \frac{1}{x}\,dx + 6\int x\,dx$
$$= 4\ln|x| + \frac{6x^2}{2} + C$$
$$= 4\ln|x| + 3x^2 + C$$

43. $\int \frac{1}{5x}\,dx = \frac{1}{5}\int \frac{1}{x}\,dx = \frac{1}{5}\ln|x| + C$

45. $\int (3 + x^{-1})\,dx = \int 3\,dx + \int \frac{1}{x}\,dx = 3x + \ln|x| + C$

47. $\int e^{7x}\,dx = \frac{1}{7}e^{7x} + C$

49. $\int 5e^x\,dx = 5e^x + C$

51. $\int (e^{0.05t} + 1)\,dt = \int e^{0.05t}\,dt + \int dt$

$$= \frac{1}{0.05}e^{0.05t} + t + C$$

$$= 20e^{0.05t} + t + C$$

53. $\int e^{-6x}\,dx = -\frac{1}{6}e^{-6x} + C$

55. $\int e^{-0.01x}\,dx = -\frac{1}{0.01}e^{-0.01x} + C = -100e^{-0.01x} + C$

57. $\int \dfrac{1 + 2x^2}{x}\,dx = \int \left(\dfrac{1}{x} + 2x\right)dx$

$$= \int \frac{1}{x} + 2\int x\,dx$$

$$= \ln|x| + \frac{2x^2}{2} + C$$

$$= \ln|x| + x^2 + C$$

59. $\int \dfrac{t+1}{t^{1/2}}\,dt = \int \left(t^{1/2} + t^{-1/2}\right)dt$

$$= \frac{t^{3/2}}{\frac{3}{2}} + \frac{t^{1/2}}{\frac{1}{2}} + C$$

$$= \frac{2}{3}t^{3/2} + 2t^{1/2} + C$$

61. $\int \dfrac{x^2 + x}{\sqrt{x}}\,dx = \int \dfrac{x^2 + x}{x^{1/2}}\,dx = \int \left(x^{3/2} + x^{1/2}\right)dx$

$$= \int x^{3/2}\,dx + \int x^{1/2}\,dx$$

$$= \frac{x^{5/2}}{\frac{5}{2}} + \frac{x^{3/2}}{\frac{3}{2}} + C$$

$$= \frac{2}{5}x^{5/2} + \frac{2}{3}x^{3/2} + C$$

63. $\int \dfrac{e^x + 1}{e^x}\,dx = \int \left(1 + e^{-x}\right)dx = \int dx + \int e^x\,dx$

$$= x - e^{-x} + C$$

65. $\int x^2(1 + x)\,dx = \int (x^2 + x^3)\,dx$

$$= \int x^2\,dx + \int x^3\,dx$$

$$= \frac{1}{3}x^3 + \frac{1}{4}x^4 + C$$

67. To decide on the answer, we differentiate expressions (i) through (iv). The correct answer is the one which, when differentiated, gives xe^x.

i. $\dfrac{d}{dx}(xe^x + e^x + x + C) = \dfrac{d}{dx}(xe^x) + \dfrac{d}{dx}(e^x) + \dfrac{d}{dx}(x) + \dfrac{d}{dx}(C)$

$$= xe^x + e^x + e^x + 1 + 0$$

$$= xe^x + 2e^x + 1$$

ii. $\dfrac{d}{dx}(xe^x - e^x + C) = xe^x + e^x - e^x + 0$

$$= xe^x$$

iii. $\dfrac{d}{dx}(e^x - xe^x - x + C) = e^x - xe^x - e^x - 1 + 0$

$$= -xe^x - 1$$

iv. $\dfrac{d}{dx}(xe^x - x + C) = xe^x + e^x - 1 + 0$

$$= xe^x + e^x - 1$$

We see that the answer is (ii). In other words,

$$\int xe^x\,dx = xe^x - e^x + C$$

69.   As in questions 67 and 68, we differentiate expressions (i) through (iv).

    i. $\dfrac{d}{dx}\left(\dfrac{1}{x}+C\right)=\dfrac{-1}{x^2}$

    ii. $\dfrac{d}{dx}(x+\ln x+C)=1+\dfrac{1}{x}$

    iii. $\dfrac{d}{dx}(x+x\ln x+C)=1+x\left(\dfrac{1}{x}\right)+\ln x=2+\ln x$

    iv. $\dfrac{d}{dx}(x\ln x-x+C)=x\left(\dfrac{1}{x}\right)+\ln x-1=\ln x$

Hence, the answer is (iv):

$\int \ln x\,dx=x\ln x-x+C$

71. **a.** yes; $\frac{d}{dx}\left[\int f(x)\,dx\right]=f(x)$

    b. Not necessarily. The antiderivative is a family of functions whose derivatives are the same, but the functions in the family may differ by a constant. For example, let $f(x)=x^2+5$. Then $f'(x)=2x$. The antiderivative of $2x$ is $\int 2x\,dx=x^2+C$, where C is an arbitrary constant that *may* be 5.

73. We can integrate x^n for all real values of n. There are two cases:

    1. $\int x^n\,dx=\frac{x^{n+1}}{n+1}+C$ for all real n, except $n=-1$, and this is by the power rule of Section 6.1.

    2. $\int x^{-1}\,dx=\int \frac{1}{x}\,dx=\ln|x|+C$ using the formula of Example 11 in Section 5.4.

75. If G is another antiderivative of f with $G(3)=2$, then the graph of G is just the graph of F moved up by 2 units.

SECTION 6.1 Technology Exercises

1.

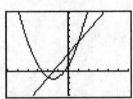

$[-6,6]$ by $[-4,10]$

    a. The graph of f crosses the x axis (a critical number) where F has a relative minimum.

    b. f is below the x axis (and F is decreasing) to the left of the relative minimum; f is above the x axis (and F is increasing) to the right.

3.

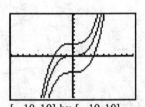

$[-10,10]$ by $[-10,10]$

    a. The slopes are the same.

    b. The derivatives are the same, $f(-2)$ in each case.

SECTION 6.2 pages 317–320

1. If $f'(x)=3x^2-2x+5$ and $f(1)=8$, then

$$f(x)=\int (3x^2-2x+5)\,dx=x^3-x^2+5x+C$$

and $f(1)=1-1+5+C=8$

$$C=8-5$$
$$C=3$$

$$f(x)=x^3-x^2+5x+3$$

3. If $f'(x)=-3x^{-4}$ and $f(1)=3$, then

$$f(x)=\int -3x^{-4}\,dx=x^{-3}+C$$

and $f(1)=1^{-3}+C=3$

$$1+C=3$$
$$C=2$$

$$f(x)=x^{-3}+2$$

5. If $f'(x) = 1 + 3\sqrt{x}$ and $f(4) = 16$, then

$$f(x) = \int (1 + 3\sqrt{x})\,dx = \int \left(1 + 3x^{1/2}\right)\,dx = x + 2x^{3/2} + C$$

and $f(4) = 4 + 2 \cdot 4^{3/2} + C = 16$
$$4 + 16 + C = 16$$
$$C = -4$$

$$f(x) = x + 2x^{3/2} - 4$$

7. If $f'(x) = \frac{1}{x}$ and $f(1) = 5$, then

$$f(x) = \int \frac{1}{x}\,dx = \ln|x| + C$$

and $f(1) = \ln|1| + C = 5$
$$0 + C = 5$$
$$C = 5$$

$$f(x) = \ln|x| + 5$$

9. If $f'(x) = e^{2x} + 8x$ and $f(0) = 2$, then

$$f(x) = \int (e^{2x} + 8x)\,dx = \frac{1}{2}e^{2x} + 4x^2 + C$$

and $f(0) = \frac{1}{2}e^0 + 4 \cdot 0 + C = 2$
$$\frac{1}{2} + C = 2$$
$$C = \frac{3}{2}$$

$$f(x) = \tfrac{1}{2}e^{2x} + 4x^2 + \tfrac{3}{2}$$

11. The given conditions imply $f'(x) = 2x$ and $f(3) = 14$. Thus, $f(x) = \int 2x\,dx = x^2 + C$

and $f(3) = 9 + C = 14$
$$C = 5$$

$$f(x) = x^2 + 5$$

13. The given conditions imply $f'(x) = \sqrt{x} = x^{1/2}$ and $f(9) = 19$. Thus, $f(x) = \int x^{1/2}\,dx = \frac{2}{3}x^{3/2} + C$

and $f(9) = \frac{2}{3} \cdot 9^{3/2} + C = 19$
$$18 + C = 19$$
$$C = 1$$

$$f(x) = \tfrac{2}{3}x^{3/2} + 1$$

15. The given conditions imply $f'(x) = e^x$ and $f(0) = 1$. Thus, $f(x) = \int e^x\,dx = e^x + C$

and $f(0) = e^0 + C = 1$
$$1 + C = 1$$
$$C = 0$$

$$f(x) = e^x$$

17. The given conditions imply $C'(x) = 40 - 0.06x$ and $C(0) = 200$. Thus, $C(x) = \int (40 - 0.06x)\,dx = 40x - 0.03x^2 + K$ and

$$C(0) = 0 - 0 + K = 200$$
$$K = 200$$

$$C(x) = 40x - 0.03x^2 + 200$$

19. The given conditions imply that $C'(x) = \frac{10}{\sqrt{x}} = 10x^{-1/2}$ and $C(0) = 50$. Thus, $C(x) = \int 10x^{-1/2}\,dx = 20x^{1/2} + K$ and

$$C(0) = 0 + K = 50$$
$$K = 50$$

$$C(x) = 20\sqrt{x} + 50$$

21. The given conditions imply that $C'(x) = 100 - 0.50x$ and $C(0) = 40$. Thus, $C(x) = \int (100 - 0.50x)\,dx = 100x - 0.25x^2 + K$

and $C(0) = 0 - 0 + k = 40$
$$k = 40$$

$$C(x) = 100x - 0.25x^2 + 40$$
$$C(10) = 100(10) - 0.25(10)^2 + 40$$
$$= 1000 - 25 + 40$$
$$= 1015$$

The cost of producing 10 units is $1015.

23. The given conditions imply $R'(x) = 50 - 0.4x$ and $R(0) = 0$. Thus, $R(x) = \int (50 - 0.4x)\,dx = 50x - 0.2x^2 + C$ and

$$R(0) = 0 - 0 + C = 0$$
$$C = 0$$

$$R(x) = 50x - 0.2x^2$$

25. The given conditions imply that $R'(x) = 10 - e^{0.05x}$ and $R(0) = 0$. Thus, $R(x) = \int \left(10 - e^{0.05x}\right) dx = 10x - \frac{1}{0.05} e^{0.05x} + C$ and

$$R(0) = 0 - \frac{1}{0.05} e^0 + C = 0$$
$$-20 + C = 0$$
$$C = 20$$

$$R(x) = 10x - 20e^{0.05x} + 20$$

27. The given conditions imply that $P'(x) = 100 + 0.4x - 0.06x^2$ and $P(0) = 0$. Thus, $P(x) = \int (100 + 0.4x - 0.06x^2)\,dx = 100x + 0.2x^2 - 0.02x^3 + C$ and

$$P(0) = 0 + 0 - 0 + C = 0$$
$$C = 0$$

$$P(x) = 100x + 0.2x^2 - 0.02x^3$$

29. The given conditions imply that $P'(x) = 70 - e^{0.01x}$ and $P(0) = -30$. Thus, $P(x) = \int (70 - e^{0.01x})\,dx = 70x - \frac{1}{0.01} e^{0.01x} + C = 70x - 100e^{0.01x} + C$

and $P(0) = 0 - 100e^0 + C = -30$
$$-100 + C = -30$$
$$C = 70$$

$$P(x) = 70x - 100e^{0.01x} + 70$$

31. The given conditions imply that $\frac{dv}{dt} = -32, v(0) = 0$, and $s(0) = 576$. Thus,

a. $v(t) = \int -32\,dt = -32t + C$ and $v(0) = 0 + C = 0$
$$C = 0$$

$$v(t) = -32t$$

b. Since $\frac{ds}{dt} = v(t) = -32t$, then $s(t) = \int -32t\,dt = -16t^2 + C$ and $s(0) = 0 + C = 576$
$$C = 576$$

$$s(t) = -16t^2 + 576$$

c. At $t = 4$, $v(4) = -32(4) = -128$ feet per second

d. The camera will hit the water when $s = 0$; thus, solving $s(t) = -16t^2 + 576 = 0$ yields $t^2 = 36$, or $t = 6$. (Note: $t = -6$ has no physical meaning for this problem.)

The camera will hit the water in 6 seconds.

33. The given conditions imply $\frac{dv}{dt} = -5.3$, $v(0) = 120$, and $s(0) = 0$. Thus,

a. $v(t) = \int -5.3\,dt = -5.3t + C$ and $v(0) = 0 + C = 120$

$$C = 120$$

$$v(t) = -5.3t + 120$$

b. Since $\frac{ds}{dt} = v(t) = -5.3t + 120$, then

$$s(t) = \int (-5.3t + 120)\,dt$$
$$= -2.65t^2 + 120t + C$$

$$s(0) = 0 + 0 + C = 0$$
$$C = 0$$

$$s(t) = -2.65t^2 + 120t$$

35. If the flu virus is spreading at the *rate* of $5t^{2/3} + 22$ people per day, then

a. $\frac{dn}{dt} = 5t^{2/3} + 22$ where n is the number of people who have the flu.

b. Given $n(0) = 50$, then $n(t) = \int (5t^{2/3} + 22)\,dt = 3t^{5/3} + 22t + C$

and $n(0) = 0 + 0 + C = 50$
$$C = 50$$

$$n(t) = 3t^{5/3} + 22t + 50$$

c. At $t = 8, n(8) = 3(8)^{5/3} + 22(8) + 50$
$$= 3 \cdot 32 + 22(8) + 50$$
$$= 322 \text{ people}$$

37. Given $\frac{dn}{dt} = 30 + 2t$ and $n(0) = 2000$, then

a. $n(t) = \int (30 + 2t)\,dt = 30t + t^2 + C$ and $n(0) = 0 + 0 + C = 2000$

$$C = 2000$$

$$n(t) = t^2 + 30t + 2000$$

b. At $t = 3, n(3) = 3^2 + 30(3) + 2000$
$$= 2099$$

39. Given $\frac{dw}{dt} = e^{0.2t}$ and $w(0) = 70$, then

$$w(t) = \int e^{0.2t}\,dt = \frac{1}{0.2}e^{0.2t} + C = 5e^{0.2t} + C \text{ and}$$

$$w(0) = 5e^0 + C = 5 + C = 70$$
$$C = 65$$

Thus, $w(t) = 5e^{0.2t} + 65$

At $t = 10, w(10) = 5e^{0.2(10)} + 65$

$$w(10) \approx 101.95 \text{ milligrams}$$

41. If $\frac{dd}{dt} = -0.03e^{-0.001t}$ and $d(0) = 0.4$ centimeters, then

    a. $d(t) = \int (-0.03e^{-0.001t}) \, dt$

$$= \frac{-0.03}{-0.001} e^{-0.001t} + C$$

$$= 30e^{-0.001t} + C$$

$d(0) = 0.4$ implies that $30 + C = 0.4$

$$C = -29.6$$

$$d(t) = 30e^{-0.001t} - 29.6$$

    b. $d(10) = 30e^{-0.001(10)} - 29.6$

$$\approx 0.1015 \text{ centimeters}$$

43. Given $\frac{dP}{dx} = -3.087e^{-0.21x}$ and $P(0) = 14.7$, then

$$P(x) = \int -3.087e^{-0.21x} \, dx = \frac{-3.087}{-0.21} e^{-0.21x} + C = 14.7e^{-0.21x} + C$$

$$P(0) = 14.7e^0 + C = 14.7 + C = 14.7$$

$$C = 0$$

$$P(x) = 14.7e^{-0.21x}$$

45. Given $\frac{dv}{dr} = 4\pi r^2$ and $V(0) = 0$, then

$$V(r) = \int 4\pi r^2 \, dr = \frac{4\pi r^3}{3} + C \text{ and } V(0) = 0 + C = 0$$

$$C = 0$$

$$V(r) = \frac{4\pi r^3}{3}$$

At $r = 6$, $V(6) = \dfrac{4\pi(6)^3}{3}$

$$= 288\pi$$

47.   **a.** $P(0)$ is the profit when 0 units are sold.

    b. $P(0)$ being negative means that there are costs involved in selling zero units. That is, there are start-up costs for the business.

49. Given $f'(x)$, the specific information needed to determine a particular antiderivative $f(x)$ is one point that lies on the graph of f. (The process of antidifferentiation, which determines f from f', introduces an arbitrary constant whose value can be fixed by knowledge of one point on the graph of f.)

SECTION 6.2 Technology Exercises

1.   **a.** $y = 0.75x^2 + 2$

    b.

3. $C(x) = -0.02x^2 + 110x + 850$

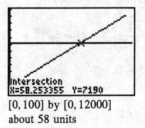

[−5, 5] by [0, 10]

        $y = -3x - 1$ is tangent to the curve at $x = -2$;

        $y = 1.5x + 1.25$ is tangent to the curve at $x = 1$.

    c. -3; this is also the slope of $y = -3x - 1$.

    d. 1.5; this is also the slope of $y = 1.5x + 1.25$.

[0, 100] by [0, 12000]

about 58 units

SECTION 6.3 pages 327–328

1.
$$\sum_{i=1}^{5} i^2 = 1^2 + 2^2 + 3^2 + 4^2 + 5^2$$
$$= 1 + 4 + 9 + 16 + 25$$
$$= 55$$

3.
$$\sum_{k=1}^{6} (2k+1) = (2\cdot 1 + 1) + (2\cdot 2 + 1) + (2\cdot 3 + 1) + (2\cdot 4 + 1) + (2\cdot 5 + 1) + (2\cdot 6 + 1)$$
$$= 3 + 5 + 7 + 9 + 11 + 13$$
$$= 48$$

5.
$$\sum_{j=0}^{5} j(j+3) = 0(0+3) + 1(1+3) + 2(2+3) + 3(3+3) + 4(4+3) + 5(5+3)$$
$$= 0 + 4 + 10 + 18 + 28 + 40$$
$$= 100$$

7.
$$\sum_{n=1}^{3} \frac{n+1}{2n} = \frac{1+1}{2\cdot 1} + \frac{2+1}{2\cdot 2} + \frac{3+1}{2\cdot 3}$$
$$= \frac{2}{2} + \frac{3}{4} + \frac{4}{6}$$
$$= \frac{12}{12} + \frac{9}{12} + \frac{8}{12}$$
$$= \frac{29}{12}$$

9.
$$1 + 2 + 3 + 4 + 5 + \cdots + 9 = \sum_{i=1}^{9} i$$

11.
$$4 + 5 + 6 + \cdots + n = \sum_{k=4}^{n} k$$

13.
$$\frac{1}{2} + \frac{2}{3} + \frac{3}{4} + \frac{4}{5} + \cdots + \frac{49}{50} = \sum_{n=1}^{49} \frac{n}{n+1}$$

15.
$$a_1 x_1 + a_2 x_2 + a_3 x_3 + \cdots + a_{10} x_{10} = \sum_{i=1}^{10} a_i x_i$$

17.
$$f(x_0) + f(x_1) + f(x_2) + \cdots + f(x_n) = \sum_{k=0}^{n} f(x_k)$$

19. If $f(x) = x^3$ and $x_1 = 0, x_2 = 1, x_3 = 2,$ and $x_4 = 3,$ then
$$\sum_{i=1}^{4} f(x_i) = \sum_{i=1}^{4} x_i^3 = x_1^3 + x_2^3 + x_3^3 + x_4^3$$
$$= 0^3 + 1^3 + 2^3 + 3^3$$
$$= 36$$

21. If $f(x) = x^2$ and $x_1 = 1, x_2 = 3, x_3 = 5,$ and $\Delta x = 2,$ then
$$\sum_{i=1}^{3} f(x_i)\Delta x = \sum_{i=1}^{3} x_i^2 \Delta x = \Delta x \sum_{i=1}^{3} x_i^2$$
$$= 2\left(x_1^2 + x_2^2 + x_3^2\right)$$
$$= 2(1^2 + 3^2 + 5^2)$$
$$= 70$$

23.

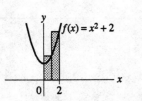

If $n = 2$, then $\Delta x = \frac{2-0}{2} = 1$ and $x_1 = 1, x_2 = 2$

$$\begin{aligned}
\text{Area} &\approx f(x_1)\Delta x + f(x_2)\Delta x \\
&= f(1) \cdot 1 + f(2) \cdot 1 \\
&= (1^2 + 2) \cdot 1 + (2^2 + 2) \cdot 1 \\
&= 3 + 6 \\
&= 9
\end{aligned}$$

25.

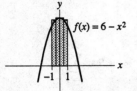

If $n = 4$, then $\Delta x = \frac{1-(-1)}{4} = \frac{2}{4} = 0.5$ and $x_1 = -0.5, x_2 = 0, x_3 = 0.5$ and $x_4 = 1$

$$\begin{aligned}
\text{Area} &\approx f(x_1)\Delta x + f(x_2)\Delta x + f(x_3)\Delta x + f(x_4)\Delta x \\
&= [6 - (-0.5)^2](0.5) + (6 - 0^2)(0.5) + [6 - (0.5)^2](0.5) + (6 - 1^2)(0.5) \\
&= [(6 - 0.25) + (6 - 0) + (6 - 0.25) + (6 - 1)](0.5) \\
&= 11.25
\end{aligned}$$

27.

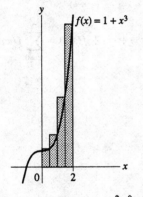

If $n = 4$, then $\Delta x = \frac{2-0}{4} = \frac{1}{2} = 0.5$ and $x_1 = 0.5, x_2 = 1, x_3 = 1.5$, and $x_1 = 2$.

$$\begin{aligned}
\text{Area} &\approx f(x_1)\Delta x + f(x_2)\Delta x + f(x_3)\Delta x + f(x_4)\Delta x \\
&= [1 + (0.5)^3](0.5) + (1 + 1^3)(0.5) + [1 + (1.5)^3](0.5) + (1 + 2^3)(0.5) \\
&= [(1 + 0.125) + (1 + 1) + (1 + 3.375) + (1 + 8)](0.5) \\
&= 8.25
\end{aligned}$$

29.

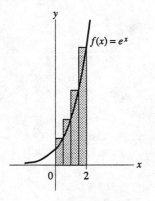

If $n = 4$, then $\Delta x = \frac{2-0}{4} = \frac{2}{4} = 0.5$ and $x_1 = 0.5, x_2 = 1, x_3 = 1.5,$ and $x_4 = 2$.

$$\begin{aligned}
\text{Area} &\approx f(x_1)\Delta x + f(x_2)\Delta x + f(x_3)\Delta x + f(x_4)\Delta x \\
&= e^{0.5}(0.5) + e^{1}(0.5) + e^{1.5}(0.5) + e^{2}(0.5) \\
&= (1.649 + 2.718 + 4.482 + 7.389)(0.5) \\
&= 8.12
\end{aligned}$$

31.   The relationship between n and Δx is that $n(\Delta x) = $ length of the interval; in other words, $\Delta x = \dfrac{\text{length of interval}}{n}$.

33. $f(x) \geq 0$ matters because when $f(x) < 0$, the definition using the limit of the area of approximating rectangular regions will assign a negative value to regions where $f(x) < 0$. We will obtain a "signed area" where regions where $f(x) > 0$ will be assigned a positive area and regions where $f(x) < 0$ will be assigned a negative area. For the illustration shown, the approximating area is given as $f(x_1)\Delta x$, and it is negative, since $\Delta x > 0$ and $f(x_1) < 0$.

SECTION 6.3 Technology Exercises

1.

n	Area
2	9
4	7.75
10	7.08
50	6.7472
100	6.7068
500	6.674672

3.

n	Area
10	18.16359544
25	17.62622098
50	17.44718718

SECTION 6.4 pages 335–337

1.   The area under the marginal revenue curve is *the total revenue.*

3.   The area under the curve that gives the rate at which gasoline was used is *the total consumption of gasoline from 1964 to 1976.*

5.   The area under the curve that gives the interest rates paid by a bank on its money market account is *the total interest paid by the bank on this account from 1984 to 1992.*

7.   The area under the curve that gives the rate at which a yeast culture is growing is *the total amount of yeast in the culture this week.*

9. $\displaystyle\int_0^3 8x\,dx = \left[4x^2\right]_0^3 = 4(3)^2 - 0 = \boxed{36}$

11. $\displaystyle\int_1^4 x^2\,dx = \left[\tfrac{1}{3}x^3\right]_1^4 = \tfrac{1}{3}\left(4^3 - 1^3\right) = \tfrac{1}{3}(64 - 1) = \boxed{21}$

13. $\displaystyle\int_0^2 (1 + x^3)\,dx = \left[x + \frac{x^4}{4}\right]_0^2 = \left(2 + \frac{2^4}{4}\right) - (0 + 0)$
$$= 6$$

15. $\displaystyle\int_1^6 (5t - t^2)\,dt = \left[\frac{5t^2}{2} - \frac{t^3}{3}\right]_1^6 = \left[\frac{5}{2}(6)^2 - \frac{6^3}{3}\right] - \left[\frac{5}{2}(1)^2 - \frac{1^3}{3}\right]$

$$= (90 - 72) - \left(\frac{5}{2} - \frac{1}{3}\right)$$

$$= 18 - \frac{13}{6}$$

$$= \frac{95}{6}$$

17. $\displaystyle\int_0^3 (x^2 + 2x - 5)\,dx = \left[\frac{x^3}{3} + x^2 - 5x\right]_0^3 = \left[\frac{3^3}{3} + 3^2 - 5(3)\right] - [0 + 0 - 0]$

$$= 9 + 9 - 15$$

$$= 3$$

19. $\displaystyle\int_0^1 (e^x - 2x)\,dx = \left[e^x - x^2\right]_0^1 = (e^1 - 1^2) - (e^0 - 0)$

$$= e^1 - 1 - 1$$

$$= e - 2$$

21. $\displaystyle\int_2^5 \frac{1}{t^2}\,dt = \int_2^5 t^{-2}\,dt = \left[-t^{-1}\right]_2^5 = -\left(5^{-1} - 2^{-1}\right)$

$$= -\left(\frac{1}{5} - \frac{1}{2}\right)$$

$$= -\left(-\frac{3}{10}\right)$$

$$= \frac{3}{10}$$

23. $\displaystyle\int_4^9 6\sqrt{x}\,dx = \int_4^9 6x^{1/2}\,dx = \left[4x^{3/2}\right]_4^9 = 4\left(9^{3/2} - 4^{3/2}\right)$

$$= 4(27 - 8)$$

$$= 76$$

25. $\displaystyle\int_1^3 \frac{1}{x}\,dx = \left[\ln|x|\right]_1^3 = \ln 3 - \ln 1 = \ln 3$

27. $\displaystyle\int_0^{100} 0e^{0.05x}\,dx = \left[\frac{1}{0.05}e^{0.05x}\right]_0^{100} = 20\left[e^{0.05(100)} - e^0\right]$

$$= 20(e^5 - 1)$$

29. $\displaystyle\int_1^2 \frac{3x^2 + 4}{x}\,dx = \int_1^2 \left(3x + \frac{4}{x}\right)dx = \left[\frac{3x^2}{2} + 4\ln|x|\right]_1^2$

$$= \left[\frac{3(2)^2}{2} + 4\ln 2\right] - \left[\frac{3(1)^2}{2} + 4\ln 1\right]$$

$$= 6 + 4\ln 2 - \left(\frac{3}{2} + 0\right)$$

$$= \frac{9}{2} + 4\ln 2$$

31. $\displaystyle\int_e^4 \frac{t + 1}{t^2}\,dt = \int_e^4 \left(\frac{1}{t} + t^{-2}\right)dt = \left[\ln|t| - t^{-1}\right]_e^4$

$$= (\ln 4 - 4^{-1}) - (\ln e - e^{-1})$$

$$= \ln 4 - \frac{1}{4} - 1 + \frac{1}{e}$$

$$= \frac{1}{e} - \frac{5}{4} + \ln 4$$

33. $\displaystyle\int_1^9 \frac{1+x}{\sqrt{x}}\,dx = \int_1^9 \frac{1+x}{x^{1/2}}\,dx = \int_1^9 \left(x^{-1/2} + x^{1/2}\right)\,dx$

$$= \left[2x^{1/2} + \frac{2}{3}x^{3/2}\right]_1^9$$

$$= \left[2(9)^{1/2} + \frac{2}{3}(9)^{3/2}\right] - \left[2(1)^{1/2} - \frac{2}{3}(1)^{3/2}\right]$$

$$= (6 + 18) - (2 + \frac{2}{3})$$

$$= 24 - 2 - \frac{2}{3}$$

$$= \frac{64}{3}$$

35.   The area is pictured by

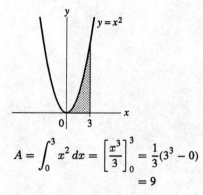

$$A = \int_0^3 x^2\,dx = \left[\frac{x^3}{3}\right]_0^3 = \frac{1}{3}(3^3 - 0)$$
$$= 9$$

37.   The area is pictured by

$y = 9 - x^2$

$$A = \int_1^2 (9 - x^2)\,dx = \left[9x - \frac{1}{3}x^3\right]_1^2$$

$$= \left[9(2) - \frac{1}{3}(2)^3\right] - \left[9(1) - \frac{1}{3}(1)^3\right]$$

$$= \left(18 - \frac{8}{3}\right) - \left(9 - \frac{1}{3}\right)$$

$$= 9 - \frac{7}{3}$$

$$= \frac{20}{3}$$

39. The area is pictured by

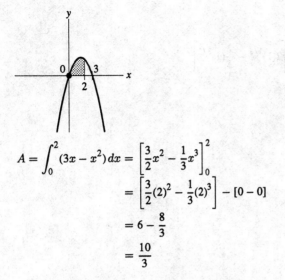

$$A = \int_0^2 (3x - x^2)\, dx = \left[\frac{3}{2}x^2 - \frac{1}{3}x^3 \right]_0^2$$
$$= \left[\frac{3}{2}(2)^2 - \frac{1}{3}(2)^3 \right] - [0 - 0]$$
$$= 6 - \frac{8}{3}$$
$$= \frac{10}{3}$$

41. The area is pictured by

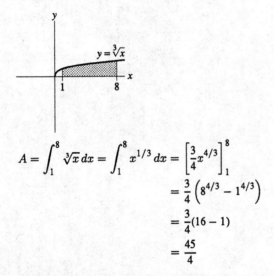

$$A = \int_1^8 \sqrt[3]{x}\, dx = \int_1^8 x^{1/3}\, dx = \left[\frac{3}{4}x^{4/3} \right]_1^8$$
$$= \frac{3}{4}\left(8^{4/3} - 1^{4/3} \right)$$
$$= \frac{3}{4}(16 - 1)$$
$$= \frac{45}{4}$$

43. The area is pictured by

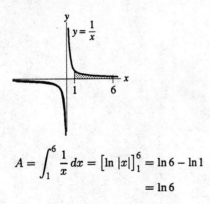

$$A = \int_1^6 \frac{1}{x}\, dx = \left[\ln |x| \right]_1^6 = \ln 6 - \ln 1$$
$$= \ln 6$$

45. The area is pictured by

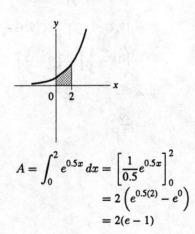

$$A = \int_0^2 e^{0.5x}\, dx = \left[\frac{1}{0.5} e^{0.5x} \right]_0^2$$
$$= 2\left(e^{0.5(2)} - e^0 \right)$$
$$= 2(e - 1)$$

47. Area $= \int_1^3 (x+1)\, dx = \left[\dfrac{x^2}{2} + x\right]_1^3 = \left(\dfrac{3^2}{2} + 3\right) - \left(\dfrac{1^2}{2} + 1\right)$

$$= \left(\dfrac{9}{2} + 3\right) - \left(\dfrac{1}{2} + 1\right)$$

$$= \dfrac{9}{2} - \dfrac{1}{2} + 3 - 1$$

$$= \dfrac{8}{2} + 2$$

$$= 6$$

49. Area $= \int_0^2 (4 - x^2)\, dx = \left[4x - \dfrac{x^3}{3}\right]_0^2 = \left[4(2) - \dfrac{2^3}{3}\right] - (0 - 0)$

$$= \left(8 - \dfrac{8}{3}\right)$$

$$= \dfrac{24}{3} - \dfrac{8}{3}$$

$$= \dfrac{16}{3}$$

51. $\int_2^2 6x\, dx = \left[3x^2\right]_2^2 = 3(2^2 - 2^2) = 3(0) = 0$

$\int_1^1 x^2\, dx = \left[\dfrac{x^3}{3}\right]_1^1 = \dfrac{1}{3}\left(1^3 - 1^3\right) = \dfrac{1}{3}(0) = 0$

$\int_{-2}^{-2} (x^3 + 1)\, dx = \left[\dfrac{x^4}{4} + x\right]_{-2}^{-2} = \left[\dfrac{(-2)^4}{4} - 2\right] - \left[\dfrac{(-2)^4}{4} - 2\right]$

$$= (4 - 2) - (4 - 2)$$

$$= 2 - 2$$

$$= 0$$

53. If the geometric interpretation of $\int_a^b f(x)\, dx$ is the area under the curve, $f(x)$, from a to b, then the area from a to a is the dimensionless area of the line segment $x = a$, which would be zero.

55. $\int_{-1}^0 \dfrac{e^x - 1}{e^x}\, dx = \int_{-1}^0 \left(1 - e^{-x}\right) dx = \left[x + e^{-x}\right]_{-1}^0$

$$= (0 + e^0) - (-1 + e^{-1})$$

$$= 1 + 1 - e^1$$

$$= 2 - e$$

57. $\int_0^3 |x|\, dx = \int_0^3 x\, dx \quad$ since $|x| = x$ on $0 \le x \le 3$

$$= \left[\dfrac{x^2}{2}\right]_0^3$$

$$= \dfrac{9}{2} - 0$$

$$= \dfrac{9}{2}$$

59.
$$\int_0^2 \frac{x^2 - 9}{x - 3}\, dx = \int_0^2 \frac{(x-3)(x+3)}{x-3}\, dx$$

$$= \int_0^2 (x+3)\, dx \qquad \text{since } \frac{(x-3)(x+3)}{x-3} = x + 3 \text{ for } x \neq 3, \text{ and } 3 \text{ is not in the interval } 0 \leq x \leq 2$$

$$= \left[\frac{x^2}{2} + 3x \right]_0^2$$

$$= \left[\frac{2^2}{2} + 3(2) \right] - [0 + 0]$$

$$= 8$$

61. The fundamental theorem of calculus states that if f is continuous on $[a, b]$, then

$$\int_a^b f(x)\, dx = F(b) - F(a)$$

where F is any antiderivative of f. The function graphed has a discontinuity at $x = 3$ (in fact, it is not even defined at $x = 3$). Therefore, the theorem cannot be used in this case to evaluate $\int_1^5 f(x)\, dx$.

SECTION 6.4 Technology Exercises

1. crosses the x axis at 0 and 9

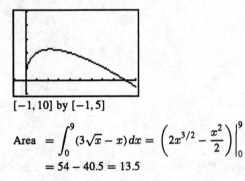

$[-1, 10]$ by $[-1, 5]$

$$\text{Area} = \int_0^9 (3\sqrt{x} - x)\, dx = \left(2x^{3/2} - \frac{x^2}{2} \right)\Big|_0^9$$

$$= 54 - 40.5 = 13.5$$

3. crosses the x axis at -3.3 and 0.3

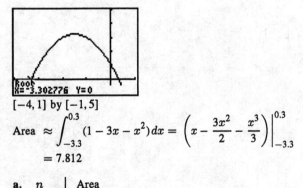

$[-4, 1]$ by $[-1, 5]$

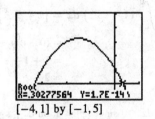

$[-4, 1]$ by $[-1, 5]$

$$\text{Area} \approx \int_{-3.3}^{0.3} (1 - 3x - x^2)\, dx = \left(x - \frac{3x^2}{2} - \frac{x^3}{3} \right)\Big|_{-3.3}^{0.3}$$

$$= 7.812$$

5. a.

n	Area
10	80.115
50	85.6446
100	86.32365

b.
$$\text{Area} = \int_1^4 (50 - 3x^2)\, dx = (50x - x^3)\Big|_1^4$$

$$= 200 - 64 - 50 + 1 = 87$$

SECTION 6.5 pages 346–348

1. If the marginal cost is $C'(x) = 40 - 0.06x$, then the cost is determined by $\int_5^{10}(40 - 0.06x)\,dx$.

$$\text{Cost} = \int_5^{10}(40 - 0.06x)\,dx = \left[40x - 0.03x^2\right]_5^{10} = \left[40(10) - 0.03(10^2)\right] - \left[40(5) - 0.03(5^2)\right]$$
$$= \$197.75$$

3. If the rate of corporation sales is $\frac{ds}{dt} = 1800 - 200e^{0.01t}$, then the

$$\text{total sales} = \int_0^{100}\left(1800 - 200e^{0.01t}\right)dt = \left[1800t - \frac{200}{0.01}e^{0.01t}\right]_0^{100}$$
$$= \left[(1800)(100) - 20{,}000e^{0.01(100)}\right] - \left[0 - 20{,}000e^0\right]$$
$$= (180{,}000 - 54{,}365.64) + 20{,}000$$
$$\approx \$145{,}634.36$$

5. If the marginal profit function is $P'(x) = 300 - 0.2x$, then the total profit gained or lost by increasing x from 1400 to 1700 is determined by $\int_{1400}^{1700}(300 - 0.2x)\,dx$.

$$\int_{1400}^{1700}(300 - 0.2x)\,dx = \left[300x - 0.1x^2\right]_{1400}^{1700}$$
$$= \left[300(1700) - 0.1(1700)^2\right] - \left[300(1400) - 0.1(1400)^2\right]$$
$$= -3000$$

Since the total profit change is a loss of \$3000, the computer manufacturer should *not* raise the production level to 1700 computers.

7. If the velocity function is $v = 5.3t$, then the

$$\text{distance traveled} = \int_0^3 5.3t\,dt = \left[\tfrac{5.3}{2}t^2\right]_0^3 = 23.85 \text{ feet}$$

9. If the flu virus spreads at a rate $\frac{dn}{dt} = 5 + 3\sqrt{t}$, then the number of people to get the flu between the ninth and sixteenth days is determined by

$$\int_9^{16}(5 + 3\sqrt{t})\,dt = \int_9^{16}\left(5 + 3t^{1/2}\right)dt = \left[5t + 2t^{3/2}\right]_9^{16}$$
$$= \left[5(16) + 2(16)^{3/2}\right] - \left[5(9) + 2(9)^{3/2}\right]$$
$$= (80 + 128) - (45 + 54)$$
$$= 109 \text{ people}$$

11. If the rate of pollution change is $\frac{dp}{dt} = 3000 - 10t$, then the

$$\text{total volume} = \int_0^{180}(3000 - 10t)\,dt = \left[3000t - 5t^2\right]_0^{180}$$
$$= \left[3000(180) - 5(180)^2\right] - [0 - 0]$$
$$= 378{,}000 \text{ cubic meters}$$

13. If the rate at which petroleum was consumed is $C'(t) = 21t + 281$ million barrels per year from 1983 ($t = 0$) to 1987 ($t = 4$), then the

total amount of petroleum consumed from 1983 to 1987 $= \displaystyle\int_0^4 (21t + 281)\, dt$

$$= \left[\frac{21t^2}{2} + 281t \right]_0^4$$

$$= \left[\frac{21(4)^2}{2} + 281(4) \right] - (0 + 0)$$

$$= 168 + 1124$$

$$= 1292 \text{ million barrels}$$

15. If water is used at a rate of $\frac{dw}{dt} = 36t - 3t^2$, then the total number of gallons used $= \displaystyle\int_2^{10} (36t - 3t^2)\, dt$

$$= \left[18t^2 - t^3 \right]_2^{10}$$

$$= \left[18(10)^2 - 10^3 \right] - \left[18(2)^2 - 2^3 \right]$$

$$= 736 \text{ gallons}$$

17. Average value $= \frac{1}{1-0} \displaystyle\int_0^1 (x^2 + 4)\, dx = \left[\frac{x^3}{3} + 4x \right]_0^1 = \frac{13}{3}$

19. Average value $= \frac{1}{3 - 0} \displaystyle\int_0^3 (x^2 + 6x - 2)\, dx = \frac{1}{3} \left[\frac{1}{3}x^3 + 3x^2 - 2x \right]_0^3$

$$= \frac{1}{3}(9 + 27 - 6)$$

$$= 10$$

21. Average value $= \frac{1}{16 - 9} \displaystyle\int_9^{16} \frac{1}{\sqrt{x}}\, dx = \frac{1}{7} \displaystyle\int_9^{16} x^{-1/2}\, dx = \frac{1}{7} \left[2x^{1/2} \right]_9^{16}$

$$= \frac{2}{7}(4 - 3)$$

$$= \frac{2}{7}$$

23. Average value $= \frac{1}{100 - 0} \displaystyle\int_0^{100} e^{0.01x}\, dx = \frac{1}{100} \left[\frac{1}{0.01} e^{0.01x} \right]_0^{100}$

$$= e^{0.01(100)} - e^0$$

$$= e - 1$$

25. Average value $= \frac{1}{0.25 - 0} \displaystyle\int_0^{0.25} (63 - 960x^2)\, dx$

$$= 4 \left[63x - 320x^3 \right]_0^{0.25}$$

$$= 4 \left[63(0.25) - 320(0.25)^3 - (0 - 0) \right]$$

$$= 43 \text{ centimeters per second}$$

27. Average velocity $= \frac{1}{5 - 0} \displaystyle\int_0^5 32t\, dt = \frac{1}{5} \left[16t^2 \right]_0^5$

$$= \frac{1}{5} [16(25) - 0]$$

$$= 80 \text{ feet per second}$$

29. Average height $= \dfrac{1}{9-4} \displaystyle\int_4^9 (1.4t + 0.6\sqrt{t} + 7)\,dt$

$$= \dfrac{1}{5} \int_4^9 (1.4t + 0.6t^{1/2} + 7)\,dt$$

$$= \dfrac{1}{5} \left[0.7t^2 + 0.4t^{3/2} + 7t \right]_4^9$$

$$= \dfrac{1}{5} \left\{ \left[0.7(9^2) + 0.4\left(9^{3/2}\right) + 7(9) \right] - \left[0.7(4)^2 + 0.4(4)^{3/2} + 7(4) \right] \right\}$$

$$= \dfrac{1}{5}(130.5 - 42.4)$$

$$\approx 17.6 \text{ feet}$$

31. Using the exponential growth function for the accumulation of $3000 at 8% interest per year yields the function

$$A = 3000e^{0.08t}$$

The average amount of money over the ten-year period is determined by

$$\dfrac{1}{10-0} \int_0^{10} 3000e^{0.08t}\,dt = \dfrac{3000}{10} \left[\dfrac{1}{0.08} e^{0.08t} \right]_0^{10}$$

$$= 3750 \left(e^{0.08(10)} - e^0 \right)$$

$$= \$4595.78$$

33. Average value $= \dfrac{1}{8-1} \displaystyle\int_1^8 5\,dx = \dfrac{1}{7}[5x]_1^8$

$$= \dfrac{1}{7}[5(8) - 5(1)]$$

$$= \dfrac{35}{7}$$

$$= 5$$

This example suggests that the average value of a constant function is that constant value. This is not surprising, since the function value is the same at any point; hence the average should be that same value.

In fact, consider $f(x) = c$ on $[a, b]$; then

average value $= \frac{1}{b-a} \int_a^b c\,dx = \frac{1}{b-a}[cx]_a^b = \frac{1}{b-a}[c(b-a)] = c$

35.

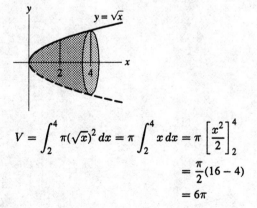

$$V = \int_2^4 \pi(\sqrt{x})^2\,dx = \pi \int_2^4 x\,dx = \pi \left[\dfrac{x^2}{2} \right]_2^4$$

$$= \dfrac{\pi}{2}(16 - 4)$$

$$= 6\pi$$

37.

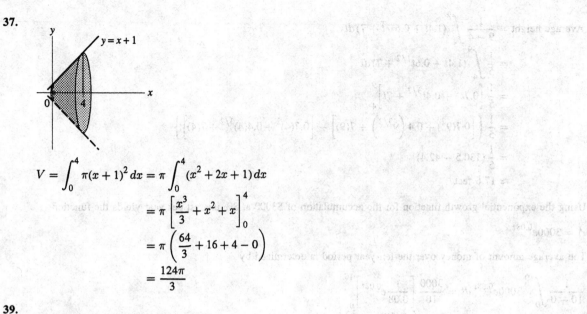

$$V = \int_0^4 \pi(x+1)^2\,dx = \pi \int_0^4 (x^2 + 2x + 1)\,dx$$
$$= \pi \left[\frac{x^3}{3} + x^2 + x \right]_0^4$$
$$= \pi \left(\frac{64}{3} + 16 + 4 - 0 \right)$$
$$= \frac{124\pi}{3}$$

39.

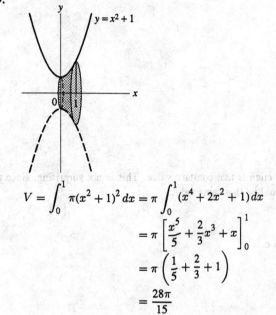

$$V = \int_0^1 \pi(x^2+1)^2\,dx = \pi \int_0^1 (x^4 + 2x^2 + 1)\,dx$$
$$= \pi \left[\frac{x^5}{5} + \frac{2}{3}x^3 + x \right]_0^1$$
$$= \pi \left(\frac{1}{5} + \frac{2}{3} + 1 \right)$$
$$= \frac{28\pi}{15}$$

41.

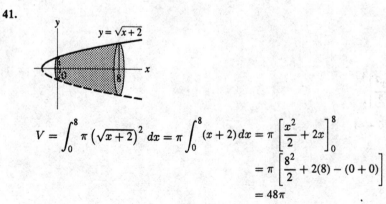

$$V = \int_0^8 \pi \left(\sqrt{x+2} \right)^2\,dx = \pi \int_0^8 (x+2)\,dx = \pi \left[\frac{x^2}{2} + 2x \right]_0^8$$
$$= \pi \left[\frac{8^2}{2} + 2(8) - (0+0) \right]$$
$$= 48\pi$$

43.

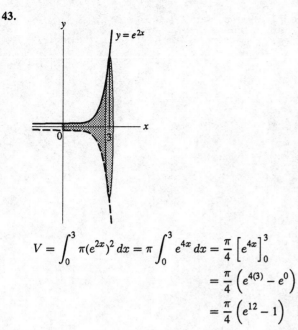

$$V = \int_0^3 \pi (e^{2x})^2 \, dx = \pi \int_0^3 e^{4x} \, dx = \frac{\pi}{4} \left[e^{4x} \right]_0^3$$
$$= \frac{\pi}{4} \left(e^{4(3)} - e^0 \right)$$
$$= \frac{\pi}{4} \left(e^{12} - 1 \right)$$

45.

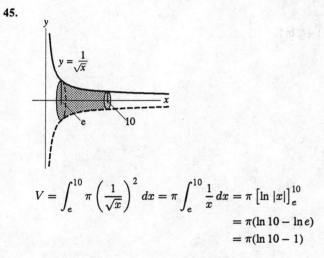

$$V = \int_e^{10} \pi \left(\frac{1}{\sqrt{x}} \right)^2 \, dx = \pi \int_e^{10} \frac{1}{x} \, dx = \pi \left[\ln |x| \right]_e^{10}$$
$$= \pi (\ln 10 - \ln e)$$
$$= \pi (\ln 10 - 1)$$

47.

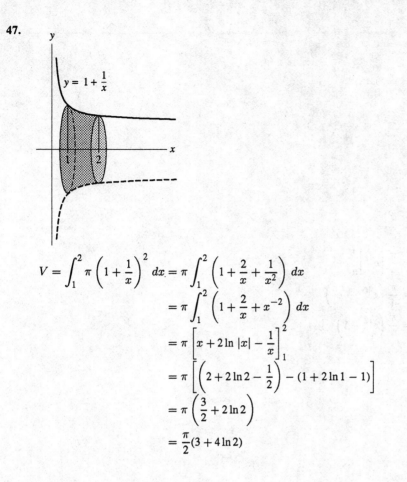

$$V = \int_1^2 \pi \left(1 + \frac{1}{x}\right)^2 dx = \pi \int_1^2 \left(1 + \frac{2}{x} + \frac{1}{x^2}\right) dx$$

$$= \pi \int_1^2 \left(1 + \frac{2}{x} + x^{-2}\right) dx$$

$$= \pi \left[x + 2\ln |x| - \frac{1}{x}\right]_1^2$$

$$= \pi \left[\left(2 + 2\ln 2 - \frac{1}{2}\right) - (1 + 2\ln 1 - 1)\right]$$

$$= \pi \left(\frac{3}{2} + 2\ln 2\right)$$

$$= \frac{\pi}{2}(3 + 4\ln 2)$$

49.

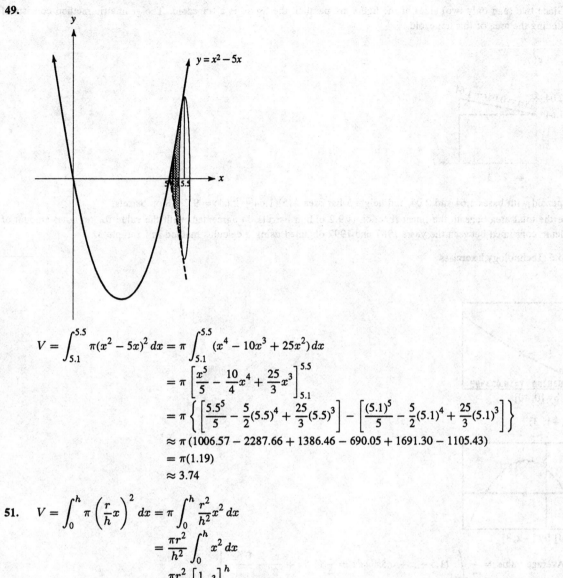

$$V = \int_{5.1}^{5.5} \pi(x^2 - 5x)^2 \, dx = \pi \int_{5.1}^{5.5} (x^4 - 10x^3 + 25x^2) \, dx$$

$$= \pi \left[\frac{x^5}{5} - \frac{10}{4}x^4 + \frac{25}{3}x^3 \right]_{5.1}^{5.5}$$

$$= \pi \left\{ \left[\frac{5.5^5}{5} - \frac{5}{2}(5.5)^4 + \frac{25}{3}(5.5)^3 \right] - \left[\frac{(5.1)^5}{5} - \frac{5}{2}(5.1)^4 + \frac{25}{3}(5.1)^3 \right] \right\}$$

$$\approx \pi(1006.57 - 2287.66 + 1386.46 - 690.05 + 1691.30 - 1105.43)$$

$$= \pi(1.19)$$

$$\approx 3.74$$

51. $$V = \int_0^h \pi \left(\frac{r}{h}x \right)^2 dx = \pi \int_0^h \frac{r^2}{h^2}x^2 \, dx$$

$$= \frac{\pi r^2}{h^2} \int_0^h x^2 \, dx$$

$$= \frac{\pi r^2}{h^2} \left[\frac{1}{3}x^3 \right]_0^h$$

$$= \frac{\pi r^2}{3h^2} \left(h^3 - 0 \right)$$

$$= \frac{1}{3}\pi r^2 h$$

53. a. Since two (and only two) sides of the figure are parallel, the figure is a trapezoid. The geometric method consists of finding the area of this trapezoid.

b.

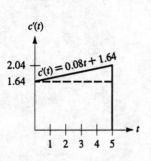

A trapezoid with bases 1.64 and 2.04, and height 5 has area $\frac{1}{2}(5)(1.64 + 2.04) = 9.2$ billion barrels.

Hence the total area beneath the linear function is 9.2 billion barrels, in agreement with the value for the total amount of petroleum consumed between the years 1987 and 1992 obtained using a calculus method in Example 3.

SECTION 6.5 Technology Exercises

1. Yes

[1,3] by [0,40]

3. a. (−1, 3)

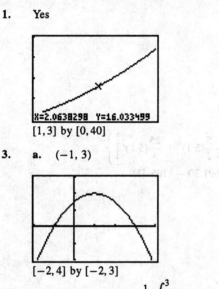

[−2, 4] by [−2, 3]

b. Average value $= \dfrac{1}{4}\displaystyle\int_{-1}^{3}(1.5 + x - 0.5x^2)\,dx = \dfrac{1}{4}\left(1.5x + \dfrac{x^2}{2} - \dfrac{0.5x^3}{3}\right)\Big|_{-1}^{3}$

$$= \frac{1}{4}\left(4.5 + 4.5 - \frac{13.5}{3} + 1.5 - 0.5 - \frac{0.5}{3}\right)$$

$$= \frac{4}{3}$$

SECTION 6.6 pages 352–353

1.   **a.**   Solve $S(x) = D(x)$

$$2x + 7 = 40 - x$$
$$3x = 33$$
$$x = 11 \qquad S(11) = 2(11) + 7 = 29$$

Equilibrium point: $(11, 29)$

b.   Consumer's surplus $= \displaystyle\int_0^{11} (40 - x)\, dx - 11(29)$

$$= \left[40x - \frac{x^2}{2} \right]_0^{11} - 11(29)$$

$$= \left[40(11) - \frac{11^2}{2} \right] - (0 - 0) - 11(29)$$

$$= \$60.50$$

c.   Producer's surplus $= 11(29) - \displaystyle\int_0^{11} (2x + 7)\, dx$

$$= 11(29) - \left[x^2 + 7x \right]_0^{11}$$

$$= 11(29) - \left[11^2 + 7(11) - (0 + 0) \right]$$

$$= \$121$$

3.   **a.**   Solve $S(x) = D(x)$

$$\frac{3}{2}x + 4 = 30 - \frac{1}{2}x$$
$$2x = 26$$
$$x = 13 \qquad D(x) = 30 - \frac{1}{2}(13) = 23.5$$

Equilibrium point: $(13, 23.5)$

b.   Consumer's surplus $= \displaystyle\int_0^{13} \left(30 - \frac{1}{2}x\right) dx - 13(23.5)$

$$= \left[30x - \frac{1}{4}x^2 \right]_0^{13} - 13(23.5)$$

$$= \left[30(13) - \frac{1}{4}(13)^2 \right] - (0 - 0) - 13(23.5)$$

$$= \$42.25$$

c.   Producer's surplus $= 13(23.5) - \displaystyle\int_0^{13} \left(\frac{3}{2}x + 4\right) dx$

$$= 13(23.5) - \left[\frac{3}{4}x^2 + 4x \right]_0^{13}$$

$$= 13(23.5) - \left[\frac{3}{4}(13)^2 + 4(13) - (0 - 0) \right]$$

$$= \$126.75$$

5.   **a.**   Solve $S(x) = D(x)$

$$0.25x + 1 = 15 - 0.25x$$
$$0.5x = 14$$
$$x = 28 \qquad S(28) = 0.25(28) + 1 = 8$$

Equilibrium point: (28, 8)

b.   Consumer's surplus $= \displaystyle\int_0^{28} (15 - 0.25x)\, dx - 28(8)$

$$= \left[15x - 0.125x^2 \right]_0^{28} - 28(8)$$
$$= 15(28) - 0.125(28)^2 - (0 - 0) - 28(8)$$
$$= \$98$$

c.   Producer's surplus $= 28(8) - \displaystyle\int_0^{28} (0.25x + 1)\, dx$

$$= 28(8) - \left[0.125x^2 + x \right]_0^{28}$$
$$= 28(8) - \left[0.125(28)^2 + 28 - (0 + 0) \right]$$
$$= \$98$$

7.   **a.**   Solve $S(x) = D(x)$

$$\frac{1}{10}x^2 + 1 = 11 - \frac{3}{10}x^2$$
$$\frac{4}{10}x^2 = 10$$
$$x^2 = \frac{100}{4} = 25$$
$$x = 5 \qquad S(5) = \frac{1}{10}(5)^2 + 1 = 2.5 + 1 = 3.5$$

Equilibrium point: (5, 3.5)

b.   Consumer's surplus $= \displaystyle\int_0^5 \left(11 - \frac{3}{10}x^2 \right) dx - 5(3.5)$

$$= \left[11x - \frac{1}{10}x^3 \right]_0^5 - 5(3.5)$$
$$= 11(5) - \frac{1}{10}(5)^3 - (0 - 0) - 5(3.5)$$
$$= \$25$$

c.   Producer's surplus $= 5(3.5) - \displaystyle\int_0^5 \left(\frac{1}{10}x^2 + 1 \right) dx$

$$= 5(3.5) - \left[\frac{1}{30}x^3 + x \right]_0^5$$
$$= 5(3.5) - \left[\frac{1}{30}(5)^3 + 5 - (0 + 0) \right]$$
$$= \$8.33$$

9.   **a.**   Solve $S(x) = D(x)$

$$2\sqrt{x} + 1 = 13 - \sqrt{x}$$
$$3\sqrt{x} = 12$$
$$\sqrt{x} = 4$$
$$x = 16 \qquad S(16) = 2\sqrt{16} + 1 = 2(4) + 1 = 9$$

Equilibrium point: $(16, 9)$

b.   Consumer's surplus $= \displaystyle\int_0^{16} (13 - \sqrt{x})\, dx - 16(9)$

$$= \int_0^{16} (13 - x^{1/2})\, dx - 16(9)$$

$$= \left[13x - \frac{2}{3} x^{3/2} \right]_0^{16} - 16(9)$$

$$= 13(16) - \frac{2}{3} \left(16^{3/2} \right) - (0 - 0) - 16(9)$$

$$= \$21.33$$

c.   Producer's surplus $= 16(9) - \displaystyle\int_0^{16} (2\sqrt{x} + 1)\, dx$

$$= 16(9) - \int_0^{16} (2x^{1/2} + 1)\, dx$$

$$= 16(9) - \left[\frac{4}{3} x^{3/2} + x \right]_0^{16}$$

$$= 16(9) - \left[\frac{4}{3} (16)^{3/2} + 16 - (0 + 0) \right]$$

$$= \$42.67$$

11.   **a.**   Solve $S(x) = D(x)$

$$x^2 + 1 = 13 - x$$
$$x^2 + x - 12 = 0$$
$$(x + 4)(x - 3) = 0$$
$$x = -4, x = 3 \qquad \text{Note: } x = -4 \text{ is not a possible solution}$$
$$\text{for this application.}$$

$D(3) = 13 - 3 = 10$

Equilibrium point: $(3, 10)$

b.   Consumer's surplus $= \displaystyle\int_0^3 (13 - x)\, dx - 3(10)$

$$= \left[13x - \frac{x^2}{2} \right]_0^3 - 3(10)$$

$$= 13(3) - \frac{3^2}{2} - (0 - 0) - 3(10)$$

$$= \$4.50$$

c.   Producer's surplus $= 3(10) - \displaystyle\int_0^3 (x^2 + 1)\, dx$

$$= 3(10) - \left[\frac{x^3}{3} + x \right]_0^3$$

$$= 3(10) - \left[\frac{3^3}{3} + 3 - (0 + 0) \right]$$

$$= \$18$$

13.   The consumer's surplus is represented by the area between the p axis and the line $x = x_e$ and beneath the curve $p = D(x)$ yet above the horizontal line $p = p_e$.

SECTION 6.6 Technology Exercises

1.   (6.0, 5.5)

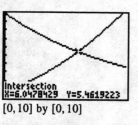

[0, 10] by [0, 10]

3.   **a.**   (5, 6)

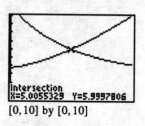

[0, 10] by [0, 10]

b.   consumer's surplus

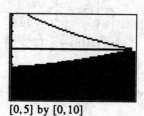

[0, 5] by [0, 10]

SECTION 6.7 pages 360–361

1.   Sketch the graphs of $y = x^2 + 2$ and $y = x$ and shade the area from $x = 0$ to $x = 6$.

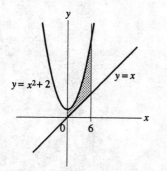

Since $y = x^2 + 2$ lies above $y = x$ on the interval $0 \leq x \leq 6$, then

$$A = \int_0^6 \left[(x^2 + 2) - (x) \right] dx = \int_0^6 (x^2 - x + 2) \, dx$$

$$= \left[\frac{x^3}{3} - \frac{x^2}{2} + 2x \right]_0^6$$

$$= \frac{6^3}{3} - \frac{6^2}{2} + 2(6) - 0$$

$$= 66$$

3.   Sketch the graphs of $y = x + 5$ and $y = \sqrt{x}$ and shade the area from $x = 0$ to $x = 4$.

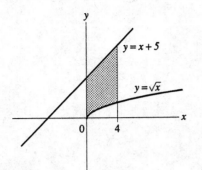

Since $y = x + 5$ lies above $y = \sqrt{x}$ in the interval $0 \leq x \leq 4$, then

$$A = \int_0^4 \left[(x + 5) - (\sqrt{x}) \right] dx = \int_0^4 (x - x^{1/2} + 5)\, dx$$

$$= \left[\frac{x^2}{2} - \frac{2}{3}x^{3/2} + 5x \right]_0^4$$

$$= \frac{4^2}{2} - \frac{2}{3}\left(4^{3/2}\right) + 5(4) - 0$$

$$= \frac{68}{3}$$

5.   Sketch the graphs of $y = \sqrt{x}$ and $y = 9 - x$ and shade the area from $x = 0$ to $x = 1$.

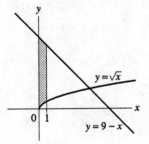

Since $y = 9 - x$ lies above $y = \sqrt{x}$ on the interval $0 \leq x \leq 1$, then

$$A = \int_0^1 \left[(9 - x) - \sqrt{x} \right] dx = \int_0^1 (9 - x - x^{1/2})\, dx$$

$$= \left[9x - \frac{x^2}{2} - \frac{2}{3}x^{3/2} \right]_0^1$$

$$= 9(1) - \frac{1^2}{2} - \frac{2}{3}(1)^{3/2} - 0$$

$$= \frac{47}{6}$$

7.   Solve $1 - x^2 = x + 4$ and sketch the graphs of $y = 1 - x^2$ and $y = x + 4$. Attempting to solve $1 - x^2 = x + 4$ yields $x^2 + x + 3 = 0$, which does not have a solution. Thus, the enclosed area lies between $y = 1 - x^2$ and $y = x + 4$ from $x = -3$ to $x = 1$.

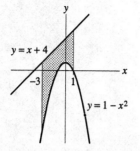

The graph of $y = x + 4$ lies above $y = 1 - x^2$ on the entire interval $-3 \leq x \leq 1$. Thus,

$$A = \int_{-3}^{1} \left[(x + 4) - (1 - x^2) \right] dx = \int_{-3}^{1} (x^2 + x + 3) \, dx$$

$$= \left[\frac{x^3}{3} + \frac{x^2}{2} + 3x \right]_{-3}^{1}$$

$$= \left(\frac{1}{3} + \frac{1}{2} + 3 \right) - \left[\frac{(-3)^3}{3} + \frac{(-3)^2}{2} + 3(-3) \right]$$

$$= \frac{1}{3} + \frac{1}{2} + 3 - \left(-9 + \frac{9}{2} - 9 \right)$$

$$= \frac{1}{3} + \frac{1}{2} + 3 + 18 - \frac{9}{2}$$

$$= \frac{52}{3}$$

9.   Since $y = x + 1$ lies above $y = \sqrt{x}$ on the interval $1 \leq x \leq 4$, then

$$A = \int_{1}^{4} (x + 1 - \sqrt{x}) \, dx = \int_{1}^{4} (x + 1 - x^{1/2}) \, dx$$

$$= \left[\frac{x^2}{2} + x - \frac{2}{3} x^{3/2} \right]_{1}^{4}$$

$$= \left[8 + 4 - \frac{2}{3} (4)^{3/2} \right] - \left(\frac{1}{2} + 1 - \frac{2}{3} \right)$$

$$= \left(12 - \frac{16}{3} \right) - \left(\frac{3}{2} - \frac{2}{3} \right)$$

$$= \frac{35}{6}$$

11.   Since $y = 3 - x$ lies above $y = 2x - x^2$ on the interval $0 \leq x \leq 2$, then

$$A = \int_{0}^{2} [3 - x - (2x - x^2)] \, dx = \int_{0}^{2} (3 - 3x + x^2) \, dx$$

$$= \left[3x - \frac{3}{2} x^2 + \frac{x^3}{3} \right]_{0}^{2}$$

$$= \left(6 - 6 + \frac{8}{3} \right) - (0 - 0 + 0)$$

$$= \frac{8}{3}$$

13. Solve $x^2 = 3x$ and sketch the graphs of $y = x^2$ and $y = 3x$. Shade the area between the points of intersection.

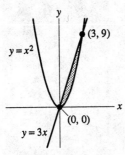

Solving $x^2 = 3x$ yields
$$x^2 - 3x = 0$$
$$x(x - 3) = 0$$
$$x = 0, x = 3$$

Since $y = 3x$ lies above $y = x^2$ on the interval $0 \leq x \leq 3$, then

$$A = \int_0^3 (3x - x^2)\, dx = \left[\frac{3x^2}{2} - \frac{x^3}{3} \right]_0^3$$
$$= \left(\frac{27}{2} - \frac{27}{3} \right) - 0$$
$$= \frac{9}{2}$$

15. Solve $x^2 + 1 = 2x + 1$ and sketch the graphs of $y = x^2 + 1$ and $y = 2x + 1$. Shade the area between the points of intersection.

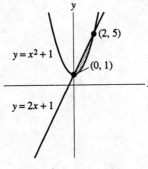

Solving $x^2 + 1 = 2x + 1$ yields
$$x^2 - 2x = 0$$
$$x(x - 2) = 0$$
$$x = 0, x = 2$$

Since $y = 2x + 1$ lies above $y = x^2 + 1$ on the interval $0 \leq x \leq 2$, then

$$A = \int_0^2 \left[(2x + 1) - (x^2 + 1) \right] dx = \int_0^2 (2x - x^2)\, dx$$
$$= \left[x^2 - \frac{x^3}{3} \right]_0^2$$
$$= \left(4 - \frac{8}{3} \right) - (0 - 0)$$
$$= \frac{4}{3}$$

17. Solve $x^3 = x^2$ and sketch the graphs of $y = x^3$ and $y = x^2$. Shade the area between the points of intersection.

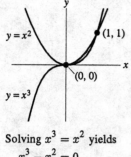

Solving $x^3 = x^2$ yields

$$x^3 - x^2 = 0$$
$$x^2(x - 1) = 0$$
$$x = 0, x = 1$$

From the graph, $y = x^2$ lies above $y = x^3$ on the interval $0 \le x \le 1$, thus

$$A = \int_0^1 (x^2 - x^3)\, dx = \left[\frac{x^3}{3} - \frac{x^4}{4} \right]_0^1$$
$$= \left(\frac{1}{3} - \frac{1}{4} \right) - (0 - 0)$$
$$= \frac{1}{12}$$

19. Solve $x^2 = \sqrt{x}$ and sketch the graphs of $y = \sqrt{x}$ and $y = x^2$. Shade the area between the points of intersection.

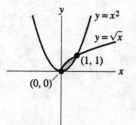

Solving $x^2 = \sqrt{x}$ yields

$$x^4 = x$$
$$x^4 - x = 0$$
$$x(x^3 - 1) = 0$$
$$x(x - 1)(x^2 + x + 1) = 0$$
$$x = 0, x = 1$$

Since $y = \sqrt{x}$ lies above $y = x^2$ on the interval $0 \le x \le 1$, then

$$A = \int_0^1 (\sqrt{x} - x^2)\, dx = \int_0^1 (x^{1/2} - x^2)\, dx = \left[\frac{2}{3} x^{3/2} - \frac{1}{3} x^3 \right]_0^1$$
$$= \left(\frac{2}{3} - \frac{1}{3} \right) - (0 - 0)$$
$$= \frac{1}{3}$$

21.   Solve $x^2 - 2x + 1 = -2x + 2$ and sketch the graphs of $y = x^2 - 2x + 1$ and $y = -2x + 2$. Shade the area between the points of intersection.

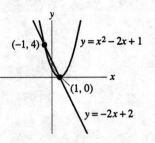

Solving $x^2 - 2x + 1 = -2x + 2$ yields
$$x^2 - 1 = 0$$
$$(x - 1)(x + 1) = 0$$
$$x = 1, x = -1$$

Since $y = -2x + 2$ lies above $y = x^2 - 2x + 1$ on the interval $-1 \le x \le 1$, then

$$A = \int_{-1}^{1} \left[(-2x + 2) - (x^2 - 2x + 1) \right] dx = \int_{-1}^{1} (1 - x^2)\, dx$$
$$= \left[x - \frac{x^3}{3} \right]_{-1}^{1}$$
$$= \left(1 - \frac{1}{3} \right) - \left(-1 + \frac{1}{3} \right)$$
$$= 2 - \frac{2}{3}$$
$$= \frac{4}{3}$$

23.   Sketch the graphs of $y = e^x$, $y = 1$, and $x = 1$ and shade the enclosed area.

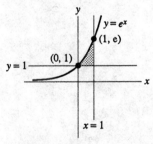

Since $y = e^x$ lies above $y = 1$ on the interval $0 \le x \le 1$, then

$$A = \int_{0}^{1} (e^x - 1)\, dx = \left[e^x - x \right]_{0}^{1}$$
$$= (e^1 - 1) - (e^0 - 0)$$
$$= e - 2$$

25. Solve $y = x^2 - 2x - 3 = 0$ and sketch the graph of $y = x^2 - 2x - 3$. Shade the area between $x = -2$ and $x = 3$.

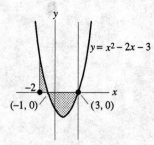

Solving $x^2 - 2x - 3 = 0$ yields
$$(x - 3)(x + 1) = 0$$
$$x = 3, x = -1$$

The function $y = f(x) = x^2 - 2x - 3$ is below the x axis on the interval $-1 \leq x \leq 2$, but $f(x)$ is above the x axis on the interval $-2 \leq x \leq -1$. Thus,

$$A = \int_{-2}^{-1} f(x)\, dx + \int_{-1}^{2} -f(x)\, dx = \int_{-2}^{-1} (x^2 - 2x - 3)\, dx + \int_{-1}^{2} (-x^2 + 2x + 3)\, dx$$

$$= \left[\frac{x^3}{3} - x^2 - 3x \right]_{-2}^{-1} + \left[-\frac{x^3}{3} + x^2 + 3x \right]_{-1}^{2}$$

$$= \left(-\frac{1}{3} - 1 + 3 \right) - \left(-\frac{8}{3} - 4 + 6 \right) + \left(-\frac{27}{3} + 9 + 9 \right) - \left(\frac{1}{3} + 1 - 3 \right)$$

$$= \left(-\frac{1}{3} + \frac{8}{3} - \frac{27}{3} - \frac{1}{3} \right) + 2 - 2 + 18 + 2$$

$$= -7 + 20$$

$$= 13$$

27. Solve $x^2 - 4 = 0$ and sketch the graph of $y = x^2 - 4$. Shade the area between $x = -1$ and $x = 4$.

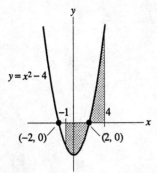

Solving $x^2 - 4 = (x - 2)(x + 2) = 0$ yields

$x = 2, x = -2$

The function $y = f(x) = x^2 - 4$ lies below the x axis on the interval $-1 \le x \le 2$, and $f(x)$ lies above the x axis on the interval $2 \le x \le 4$. Thus,

$$A = \int_{-1}^{2} -f(x)\,dx + \int_{2}^{4} f(x)\,dx$$

$$= \int_{-1}^{2} (-x^2 + 4)\,dx + \int_{2}^{4} (x^2 - 4)\,dx$$

$$= \left[-\frac{x^3}{3} + 4x \right]_{-1}^{2} + \left[\frac{x^3}{3} - 4x \right]_{2}^{4}$$

$$= \left(-\frac{8}{3} + 8 \right) - \left(\frac{1}{3} - 4 \right) + \left(\frac{64}{3} - 16 \right) - \left(\frac{8}{3} - 8 \right)$$

$$= \frac{47}{3} + 4$$

$$= \frac{59}{3}$$

29. Solve $y = x^2 - 2x = 0$ and sketch the graph of $y = x^2 - 2x$. Shade the area between $x = 1$ and $x = 3$.

Solving $x^2 - 2x = x(x - 2) = 0$ yields $x = 0$, $x = 2$

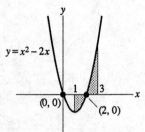

The function $y = f(x) = x^2 - 2x$ lies below the x axis on the interval $1 \le x \le 2$, and $f(x)$ lies above the x axis on the interval $2 \le x \le 3$. Thus,

$$A = \int_1^2 -f(x)\, dx + \int_2^3 f(x)\, dx$$
$$= \int_1^2 (-x^2 + 2x)\, dx + \int_2^3 (x^2 - 2x)\, dx$$
$$= \left[-\frac{x^3}{3} + x^2 \right]_1^2 + \left[\frac{x^3}{3} - x^2 \right]_2^3$$
$$= \left(-\frac{8}{3} + 4 \right) - \left(-\frac{1}{3} + 1 \right) + \left(\frac{27}{3} - 9 \right) - \left(\frac{8}{3} - 4 \right)$$
$$= -\frac{8}{3} + 4 + \frac{1}{3} - 1 + 9 - 9 - \frac{8}{3} + 4$$
$$= 2$$

31. Solve $x^3 = 4x$ and sketch the graphs of $y = x^3$ and $y = 4x$. Shade the area between the points of intersection.

Solving $x^3 = 4x$ yields
$$x^3 - 4x = 0$$
$$x(x^2 - 4) = x(x - 2)(x + 2) = 0$$
$$x = 0, x = 2, x = -2$$

On the interval $-2 \leq x \leq 0$, the function $y = x^3$ lies above $y = 4x$, but on the interval $0 \leq x \leq 2$, the function $y = 4x$ lies above $y = x^3$. Thus,

$$A = \int_{-2}^{0} (x^3 - 4x)\,dx + \int_{0}^{2} (4x - x^3)\,dx$$

$$= \left[\frac{x^4}{4} - 2x^2 \right]_{-2}^{0} + \left[2x^2 - \frac{x^4}{4} \right]_{0}^{2}$$

$$= (0 - 0) - \left[\frac{16}{4} - 2(4) \right] + \left[2(4) - \frac{16}{4} \right] - (0 - 0)$$

$$= -4 + 8 + 8 - 4$$

$$A = 8$$

33. Solve $-x^3 = -x$ and sketch the graphs of $y = -x^3$ and $y = -x$. Shade the area between the points of intersection.

Solving $-x^3 = -x$ yields

$$x^3 - x = x(x^2 - 1) = x(x - 1)(x + 1) = 0$$
$$x = 0, x = 1, x = -1$$

The function $y = -x$ lies above $y = -x^3$ on the interval $-1 \leq x \leq 0$, but on the interval $0 \leq x \leq 1, y = -x^3$ lies above $y = -x$. Thus,

$$A = \int_{-1}^{0} \left[-x - (-x^3) \right] dx + \int_{0}^{1} \left[-x^3 - (-x) \right] dx$$

$$= \int_{-1}^{0} (-x + x^3) \, dx + \int_{0}^{1} (-x^3 + x) \, dx$$

$$= \left[-\frac{x^2}{2} + \frac{x^4}{4} \right]_{-1}^{0} + \left[-\frac{x^4}{4} + \frac{x^2}{2} \right]_{0}^{1}$$

$$= (0 + 0) - \left(-\frac{1}{2} + \frac{1}{4} \right) + \left(-\frac{1}{4} + \frac{1}{2} \right) - (0 + 0)$$

$$= \frac{1}{2} - \frac{1}{4} - \frac{1}{4} + \frac{1}{2}$$

$$= \frac{1}{2}$$

35. Solve $x^3 - 4 = x - 4$ and sketch the graphs of $y = x^3 - 4$ and $y = x - y$. Shade the area between the points of intersection.

Solving $x^3 - 4 = x - 4$ yields

$$x^3 - x = x(x^2 - 1) = x(x - 1)(x + 1) = 0$$
$$x = 0, x = 1, x = -1$$

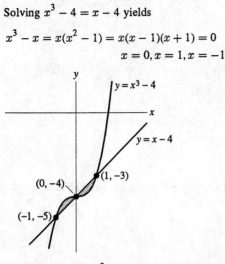

The function $y = x^3 - 4$ lies above $y = x - 4$ on the interval $-1 \le x \le 0$, but on the interval $0 \le x \le 1$, the function $y = x - 4$ lies above $y = x^3 - 4$. Thus,

$$A = \int_{-1}^{0} \left[(x^3 - 4) - (x - 4) \right] dx + \int_{0}^{1} \left[(x - 4) - (x^3 - 4) \right] dx$$

$$= \int_{-1}^{0} (x^3 - x)\, dx + \int_{0}^{1} (x - x^3)\, dx$$

$$= \left[\frac{x^4}{4} - \frac{x^2}{2} \right]_{-1}^{0} + \left[\frac{x^2}{2} - \frac{x^4}{4} \right]_{0}^{1}$$

$$= (0 - 0) - \left(\frac{1}{4} - \frac{1}{2} \right) + \left(\frac{1}{2} - \frac{1}{4} \right) - (0 + 0)$$

$$= -\frac{1}{4} + \frac{1}{2} + \frac{1}{2} - \frac{1}{4}$$

$$= \frac{1}{2}$$

Note: The area computed in Exercises 33, 34, and 35 is the same area since the graphs are simple translations or reflections of each other.

37. Solve $x^3 - 3x = 0$ and sketch the graph of $y = x^3 - 3x$. (Note: $y = 0$ is the x axis.) Shade the enclosed area.

Solving $x^3 - 3x = x(x^2 - 3) = x(x - \sqrt{3})(x + \sqrt{3})$
$$x = 0, x = \sqrt{3}, x = -\sqrt{3}$$

The function $y = f(x) = x^3 - 3x$ lies above the x axis on the interval $-\sqrt{3} \le x \le 0$, but on the interval $0 \le x \le \sqrt{3}$, the function lies below the x axis. Thus,

$$A = \int_{-\sqrt{3}}^{0} f(x)\,dx + \int_{0}^{\sqrt{3}} -f(x)\,dx$$

$$= \int_{-\sqrt{3}}^{0} (x^3 - 3x)\,dx + \int_{0}^{\sqrt{3}} (-x^3 + 3x)\,dx$$

$$= \left[\frac{x^4}{4} - \frac{3}{2}x^2\right]_{-\sqrt{3}}^{0} + \left[-\frac{x^4}{4} + \frac{3}{2}x^2\right]_{0}^{\sqrt{3}}$$

$$= (0 - 0) - \left[\frac{9}{4} - \frac{3}{2}(3)\right] + \left[-\frac{9}{4} + \frac{3}{2}(3)\right] - (0 - 0)$$

$$= -\frac{9}{4} + \frac{9}{2} - \frac{9}{4} + \frac{9}{2}$$

$$= \frac{9}{2}$$

39. Solve $x^4 = x^2$ and sketch the graphs of $y = x^4$ and $y = x^2$. Shade the area between the points of intersection.

Solving $x^4 = x^2$ yields

$$x^4 - x^2 = x^2(x^2 - 1) = x(x-1)(x+1) = 0$$
$$x = 0, x = 1, x = -1$$

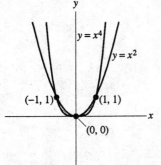

The function $y = x^2$ lies above $y = x^4$ on the entire interval $-1 \le x \le 1$. Thus,

$$\begin{aligned}
A = \int_{-1}^{1} (x^2 - x^4)\,dx &= \left[\frac{x^3}{3} - \frac{1}{5}x^5 \right]_{-1}^{1} \\
&= \left(\frac{1}{3} - \frac{1}{5} \right) - \left(-\frac{1}{3} + \frac{1}{5} \right) \\
&= \frac{1}{3} - \frac{1}{5} + \frac{1}{3} - \frac{1}{5} \\
&= \frac{4}{15}
\end{aligned}$$

41. Consider the following figure.

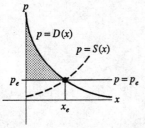

The consumer's surplus is the shaded area and is determined by the definite integral

$$\int_{0}^{x_e} (D(x) - p_e)\,dx$$

43.   Solve $x^3 - 3x + 3 = 2x^2 + 3$ and sketch the graphs of $y = x^3 - 3x + 3$ and $y = 2x^2 + 3$. Shade the area between the points of intersection.

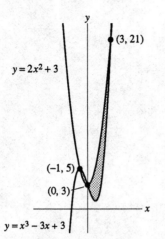

Solving $x^3 - 3x + 3 = 2x^2 + 3$ yields
$$x^3 - 2x^2 - 3x = 0$$
$$x(x^2 - 2x - 3) = x(x - 3)(x + 1) = 0$$
$$x = 0, x = 3, x = -1$$

The function $y = x^3 - 3x + 3$ lies above the function $y = 2x^2 + 3$ on the interval $-1 \leq x \leq 0$, but on the interval $0 \leq x \leq 3$, the function $y = 2x^2 + 3$ lies above $y = x^3 - 3x + 3$. Thus,

$$A = \int_{-1}^{0} \left[(x^3 - 3x + 3) - (2x^2 + 3) \right] dx + \int_{0}^{3} \left[(2x^2 + 3) - (x^3 - 3x + 3) \right] dx$$

$$= \int_{-1}^{0} (x^3 - 2x^2 - 3x) \, dx + \int_{0}^{3} (-x^3 + 2x^2 + 3x) \, dx$$

$$= \left[\frac{x^4}{4} - \frac{2}{3}x^3 - \frac{3}{2}x^2 \right]_{-1}^{0} + \left[-\frac{x^4}{4} + \frac{2}{3}x^3 + \frac{3}{2}x^2 \right]_{0}^{3}$$

$$= (0 - 0 - 0) - \left(\frac{1}{4} + \frac{2}{3} - \frac{3}{2} \right) + \left[-\frac{81}{4} + \frac{2}{3}(27) + \frac{3}{2}(9) \right] - (0 + 0 + 0)$$

$$= -\frac{1}{4} - \frac{2}{3} + \frac{3}{2} - \frac{81}{4} + 18 + \frac{27}{2}$$

$$= \frac{71}{6}$$

45.   Solve $\frac{1}{x} = \frac{1}{e}$ and sketch the graphs of $y = \frac{1}{x}$ and $y = \frac{1}{e}$. Shade the area between the points of intersection.

Solving $\dfrac{1}{x} = \dfrac{1}{e}$ yields

$$x = e$$

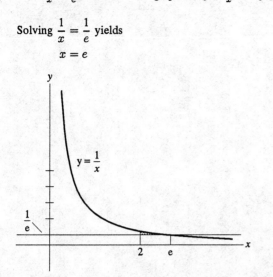

The small shaded section shows that $y = \frac{1}{x}$ lies above $y = \frac{1}{e}$ on the interval $2 \le x \le e$. Thus,

$$A = \int_2^e \left(\frac{1}{x} - \frac{1}{e} \right) dx = \left[\ln |x| - \frac{1}{e} x \right]_2^e$$

$$= \left(\ln e - \frac{e}{e} \right) - \left(\ln 2 - \frac{2}{e} \right)$$

$$= 1 - 1 - \ln 2 + \frac{2}{e}$$

$$= \frac{2}{e} - \ln 2 \approx 0.043$$

47. Solve $|x| = -x^2 + 2$ and sketch the graphs of $y = |x| = \begin{cases} x, & x \ge 0 \\ -x, & x < 0 \end{cases}$ and $y = -x^2 + 2$. Shade the area between the points of intersection.

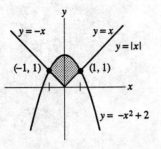

Solving $|x| = -x^2 + 2$ yields

Case 1: $x > 0$,

$$x = -x^2 + 2$$
$$x^2 + x - 2 = 0$$
$$(x - 1)(x + 2) = 0$$
$$x = 1, x = -2$$

Only $x = 1$ satisfies $x > 0$

Case 2: $x < 0$,

$$-x = -x^2 + 2$$
$$x^2 - x - 2 = 0$$
$$(x - 2)(x + 1) = 0$$
$$x = 2, x = -1$$

Only $x = -1$ satisfies $x < 0$

Because $y = |x|$, the area is computed as the sum of two definite integrals.

$$A = \int_{-1}^{0} \left[(-x^2 + 2) - (-x) \right] dx + \int_{0}^{1} \left[(-x^2 + 2) - x \right] dx$$

$$= \int_{-1}^{0} (-x^2 + x + 2) \, dx + \int_{0}^{1} (-x^2 - x + 2) \, dx$$

$$= \left[-\frac{x^3}{3} + \frac{x^2}{2} + 2x \right]_{-1}^{0} + \left[-\frac{x^3}{3} - \frac{x^2}{2} + 2x \right]_{0}^{1}$$

$$= (-0 + 0 + 0) - \left(\frac{1}{3} + \frac{1}{2} - 2 \right) + \left(-\frac{1}{3} - \frac{1}{2} + 2 \right) - (-0 - 0 + 0)$$

$$= -\frac{1}{3} - \frac{1}{2} + 2 - \frac{1}{3} - \frac{1}{2} + 2$$

$$= \frac{7}{3}$$

49. We must find the point of intersection of the lines $y = -x$ and $y = x - 6$. It is found by solving

$$-x = x - 6$$
$$6 = 2x$$
$$x = 3$$

Next, we need the point of intersection of the curves $y = x - 6$ and $y = \sqrt{x}$. It is found by solving

$$x - 6 = \sqrt{x}$$
$$x^2 - 12x + 36 = x$$
$$x^2 - 13x + 36 = 0$$
$$(x - 4)(x - 9) = 0$$
$$x = 4, \ x = 9$$

$x = 4$ is an extraneous root (it solves $x - 6 = -\sqrt{x}$). The correct value is $x = 9$. The area breaks up into two integrals:

$$A = \int_0^3 [\sqrt{x} - (-x)]\, dx + \int_3^9 [\sqrt{x} - (x - 6)]\, dx$$

$$= \int_0^3 (x^{1/2} + x)\, dx + \int_3^9 (x^{1/2} - x + 6)\, dx$$

$$= \left[\frac{2}{3}x^{3/2} + \frac{x^2}{2}\right]_0^3 + \left[\frac{2}{3}x^{3/2} - \frac{x^2}{2} + 6x\right]_3^9$$

$$= \left[\frac{2}{3}(3)^{3/2} + \frac{9}{2}\right] - (0 + 0) + \left[\frac{2}{3}(9)^{3/2} - \frac{9^2}{2} + 6(9)\right] - \left[\frac{2}{3}(3)^{3/2} - \frac{9}{2} + 6(3)\right]$$

$$= \frac{2}{3} \cdot 27 - \frac{81}{2} + 54 - 18$$

$$= \frac{27}{2}$$

51. The value of $\int_1^{10} f(x)\, dx$ is negative. This can be seen by inspection because the area between the curve and the x axis for that part of the curve beneath the x axis is larger than that for the part of the curve above the x axis.

SECTION 6.7 Technology Exercises

1. $f(x) = 2\sqrt{x + 6}$; $g(x) = 0.3x^4 + 2$

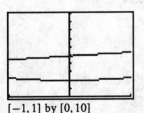

$[-1, 1]$ by $[0, 10]$

3. $f(x) = 10 - 0.5x^2$; $g(x) = x^3 + x - 5$

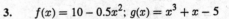
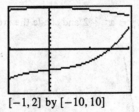

$[-1, 2]$ by $[-10, 10]$

5. $x = 2.3$ and $x = 5.9$

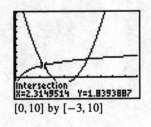

Intersection
X=2.3149514 Y=1.8393887
$[0, 10]$ by $[-3, 10]$

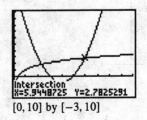

Intersection
X=5.9448725 Y=2.7825291
$[0, 10]$ by $[-3, 10]$

188 188 Chapter 6/Integration

7. $x = 0.8$ and $x = 6.2$

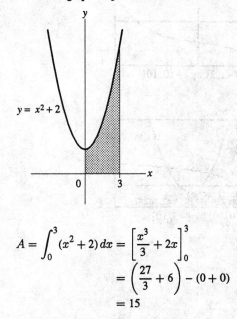

Intersection
X=.8074176 Y=-3.031099
$[0, 10]$ by $[-10, 10]$

Intersection
X=6.1925824 Y=3.4310989
$[0, 10]$ by $[-10, 10]$

$$\text{Area} = \int_{0.8}^{6.2} [(1.2x - 4) - (x^2 - 5.8x + 1)]\, dx = \left(0.6x^2 - 4x - \frac{x^3}{3} + 2.9x^2 - x\right)\Big|_{0.8}^{6.2} = 26.028$$

REVIEW EXERCISES FOR CHAPTER 6   pages 363–365

1. $\displaystyle\int (8x + 2)\, dx = 4x^2 + 2x + C$

3. $\displaystyle\int (10x^4 - x^2)\, dx = 2x^5 - \frac{x^3}{3} + C$

5. $\displaystyle\int (1 + \sqrt{x})\, dx = \int (1 + x^{1/2})\, dx = x + \frac{2}{3}x^{3/2} + C$

7. $\displaystyle\int \frac{3}{t^2}\, dt = \int 3t^{-2}\, dt = -3t^{-1} + C = -\frac{3}{t} + C$

9. $\displaystyle\int \frac{2}{x}\, dx = 2\ln|x| + C$

11. $\displaystyle\int e^{-0.02x}\, dx = -\frac{1}{0.02}e^{-0.02x} + C = -50e^{-0.02x} + C$

13. $\displaystyle\int_0^5 (2x - 3)\, dx = \left[x^2 - 3x\right]_0^5 = (25 - 15) - (0 - 0)$
$$= 10$$

15. $\displaystyle\int_1^2 (3 - t^{-2})\, dt = \left[3t + t^{-1}\right]_1^2$
$$= (6 + 2^{-1}) - (3 + 1)$$
$$= 6 + \frac{1}{2} - 4$$
$$= \frac{5}{2}$$

17. $\displaystyle\int_1^6 \frac{1}{t}\, dt = \left[\ln|t|\right]_1^6$
$$= \ln 6 - \ln 1$$
$$= \ln 6$$

19. $\displaystyle\int_1^{10} e^{0.04x}\, dx = \left[\frac{1}{0.04}e^{0.04x}\right]_1^{10}$
$$= 25\left(e^{0.4} - e^{0.04}\right)$$
$$\approx 11.28$$

21. Sketch the graph of $y = x^2 + 2$ and shade the area from $x = 0$ to $x = 3$.

$$A = \int_0^3 (x^2 + 2)\, dx = \left[\frac{x^3}{3} + 2x\right]_0^3$$
$$= \left(\frac{27}{3} + 6\right) - (0 + 0)$$
$$= 15$$

Copyright © Houghton Mifflin Company. All rights reserved.

23. Sketch the graphs of $y = 4 - x$ and $y = e^x$ and shade the area from $x = 0$ to $x = 1$.

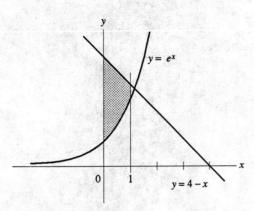

Since the function $y = 4 - x$ lies above $y = e^x$ on the interval $0 \leq x \leq 1$, then

$$A = \int_0^1 \left[(4 - x) - e^x \right] dx = \int_0^1 (4 - x - e^x) \, dx$$

$$= \left[4x - \frac{x^2}{2} - e^x \right]_0^1$$

$$= \left(4 - \frac{1}{2} - e^1 \right) - (0 - 0 - e^0)$$

$$= 4 - \frac{1}{2} - e + 1$$

$$= \frac{9}{2} - e$$

25. Solve $x^2 = 8 - x^2$, and sketch the graphs of $y = x^2$ and $y = 8 - x^2$. Shade the area between the points of intersection.

Solving $x^2 = 8 - x^2$ yields

$$2x^2 = 8$$
$$x^2 = 4$$
$$x = -2, x = 2$$

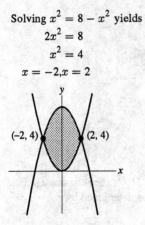

$(-2, 4)$ $(2, 4)$

The function $y = 8 - x^2$ lies above $y = x^2$ on the interval $-2 \leq x \leq 2$. Thus,

$$A = \int_{-2}^2 (8 - x^2 - x^2) \, dx$$

$$= \int_{-2}^2 (8 - 2x^2) \, dx$$

$$= \left[8x - \frac{2}{3}x^3 \right]_{-2}^2$$

$$= \left(16 - \frac{16}{3} \right) - \left(-16 + \frac{16}{3} \right)$$

$$= \frac{64}{3}$$

27. If the marginal revenue is $R'(x) = 0.65 + 0.002x$, then

$$R(x) = \int R'(x)\,dx = \int (0.65 + 0.002x)\,dx = 0.65x + 0.001x^2 + C$$

Assuming the revenue is zero when no bottles of cola are sold ($x = 0$), then

$$R(0) = 0 + 0 + C = 0$$
$$C = 0$$

$$R(x) = 0.65x + 0.001x^2$$
Thus for $x = 50$, $R(50) = 0.65(50) + 0.001(50)^2$
$$= \$35$$

29. Let v represent the velocity of the car. Then

$$\frac{dv}{dt} = 18$$

Hence $v = 18t + C$, for C constant. The car started from rest; hence $v = 0$ when $t = 0$. Therefore, $0 = 18(0) + C$, so $C = 0$.

$$v = 18t$$

The distance traveled in the first 5 seconds is given by

$$\int_0^5 18t\,dt = \left[9t^2\right]_0^5 = 9(5)^2 - 9(0)^2 = 225 \text{ feet}$$

31. If the rate at which petroleum was consumed in the United States was approximately $\frac{dc}{dt} = 0.2t + 5.7$ billion barrels per year from 1985 to 1988, where $t = 0$ corresponds to 1985, then the total amount of petroleum consumed from 1985 to 1988 is given by

$$\int_0^3 (0.2t + 5.7)\,dt = \left[0.1t^2 + 5.7t\right]_0^3$$
$$= [0.1(3^2) + 5.7(3)] - [0.1(0^2) + 5.7(0)]$$
$$= 0.9 + 17.1$$
$$= 18 \text{ billion barrels}$$

33. The total amount of water added is

$$\int_0^4 (1000 + 100t)\,dt = \left[1000t + 50t^2\right]_0^4$$
$$= (4000 + 800) - (0 + 0)$$
$$= 4800 \text{ gallons}$$

35. If the number of people who will have the flu after t days is $n(t) = 8t + 3\sqrt{t} = 8t + 3t^{1/2}$, then the average number of people who will have the flu between the ninth ($t = 9$) and the sixteenth ($t = 16$) days is determined by

$$\frac{1}{16 - 9} \int_9^{16} (8t + 3t^{1/2})\,dt = \frac{1}{7}\left[4t^2 + 2t^{3/2}\right]_9^{16}$$
$$= \frac{1}{7}\left\{\left[4(16)^2 + 2(16)^{3/2}\right] - \left[4(9)^2 + 2(9)^{3/2}\right]\right\}$$
$$= \frac{1}{7}(774)$$
$$\approx 111 \text{ people}$$

37.   Average value $= \dfrac{1}{27-8} \displaystyle\int_8^{27} x^{2/3}\, dx = \dfrac{1}{19}\left[\dfrac{3}{5}x^{5/3}\right]_8^{27}$

$$= \dfrac{3}{95}\left(27^{5/3} - 8^{5/3}\right)$$

$$= \dfrac{3}{95}(243 - 32)$$

$$= \dfrac{633}{95}$$

39.   Sketch the graph of $y = 2e^x$ and $y = 0$ and shade the volume of revolution between $x = -1$ and $x = 0$.

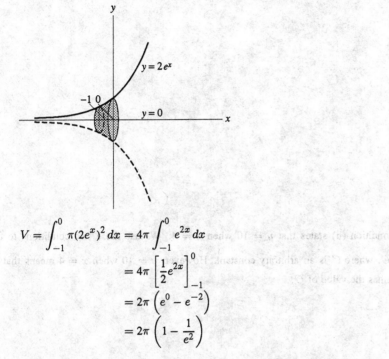

$$V = \int_{-1}^{0} \pi(2e^x)^2\, dx = 4\pi \int_{-1}^{0} e^{2x}\, dx$$

$$= 4\pi\left[\dfrac{1}{2}e^{2x}\right]_{-1}^{0}$$

$$= 2\pi\left(e^0 - e^{-2}\right)$$

$$= 2\pi\left(1 - \dfrac{1}{e^2}\right)$$

41.   Given $S(x) = 0.4x + 3$ and $D(x) = 15 - 0.2x$, then the equilibrium point is determined by solving $S(x) = D(x)$.

Solving $S(x) = D(x)$ yields $0.4x + 3 = 15 - 0.2x$

$$0.6x = 12$$
$$x = 20$$
$$S(20) = 0.4(20) + 3 = 11$$

Equilibrium point: $(20, 11)$

Consumer's surplus $= \displaystyle\int_0^{20} (15 - 0.2x)\, dx - 20(11)$

$$= \left[15x - 0.1x^2\right]_0^{20} - 20(11)$$

$$= [15(20) - 0.1(20)^2] - (0 - 0) - 20(11)$$

$$= \$40$$

Producer's surplus $= 20(11) - \displaystyle\int_0^{20} (0.4x + 3)\, dx$

$$= 20(11) - \left[0.2x^2 + 3x\right]_0^{20}$$

$$= 20(11) - \left[0.2(20)^2 + 3(20) - (0 + 0)\right]$$

$$= \$80$$

43.   Using summation notation,

$$x_1 f(x_1) + x_2 f(x_2) + \cdots + x_n f(x_n) = \sum_{i=1}^{n} x_i f(x_i)$$

45.   **a.**   Area $= \int_0^1 x^2 \, dx = \left[\dfrac{x^3}{3} \right]_0^1 = \dfrac{1}{3} - 0 = \dfrac{1}{3}$

    b.   Area $= \int_0^1 (\sqrt{x} - x^2) \, dx$

$$= \left[\frac{2}{3} x^{3/2} - \frac{x^3}{3} \right]_0^1$$

$$= \left(\frac{2}{3} - \frac{1}{3} \right) - (0 - 0)$$

$$= \frac{1}{3}$$

    c.   Area $= \int_0^1 (1 - \sqrt{x}) \, dx$

$$= \left[x - \frac{2}{3} x^{3/2} \right]_0^1$$

$$= \left(1 - \frac{2}{3} \right) - (0 - 0)$$

$$= \frac{1}{3}$$

    d.   All three areas are the same.

47.   Condition (i) states that $\frac{dy}{dx} = 2x$. Condition (ii) states that $y = 10$ when $x = 4$. We use these two conditions to find $y = f(x)$. $\frac{dy}{dx} = 2x$ gives $y = x^2 + C$, where C is an arbitrary constant. However, $y = 10$ when $x = 4$ means that we must have $10 = 4^2 + C$, which determines the value of C.
$C = -6$
Thus the equation of the curve is $y = x^2 - 6$.

49. Recall that

$$|x| = \begin{cases} x & \text{if } x \geq 0 \\ -x & \text{if } x < 0 \end{cases}$$

Then

a. $\displaystyle\int_3^4 |x|\, dx = \int_3^4 x\, dx$ (since for x values between 3 and 4, $|x| = x$)

$$= \left[\frac{x^2}{2}\right]_3^4$$

$$= \frac{16}{2} - \frac{9}{2}$$

$$= \frac{7}{2}$$

b. $\displaystyle\int_{-2}^{-1} |x|\, dx = \int_{-2}^{-1} (-x)\, dx$ (since for x values between -2 and -1, $|x| = -x$)

$$= \left[-\frac{x^2}{2}\right]_{-2}^{-1}$$

$$= \frac{-(-1)^2}{2} - \frac{-(-2)^2}{2}$$

$$= -\frac{1}{2} + \frac{4}{2}$$

$$= \frac{3}{2}$$

c. $\displaystyle\int_{-5}^{2} |x|\, dx = \int_{-5}^{0} |x|\, dx + \int_{0}^{2} |x|\, dx$

$$= \int_{-5}^{0} (-x)\, dx + \int_{0}^{2} x\, dx \quad \text{(since for } -5 < x < 0, |x| = -x \text{ and for } 0 < x < 2, |x| = x)$$

$$= \left[-\frac{x^2}{2}\right]_{-5}^{0} + \left[\frac{x^2}{2}\right]_{0}^{2}$$

$$= \left[\frac{-0^2}{2} - \frac{-(-5)^2}{2}\right] + \left(\frac{2^2}{2} - \frac{0^2}{2}\right)$$

$$= \frac{25}{2} + \frac{4}{2}$$

$$= \frac{29}{2}$$

SECTION 7.1 pages 375–377

1. $\int (x^2 + 3)^5 \, 2x \, dx = \int u^5 \, du = \frac{1}{6} u^6 + C = \frac{1}{6} \left(x^2 + 3 \right)^6 + C$

Let $u = x^2 + 3$
$\dfrac{du}{dx} = 2x$
$du = 2x \, dx$

3. $\int 2x \sqrt{x^2 - 6} \, dx = \int \left(x^2 - 6 \right)^{1/2} 2x \, dx = \int u^{1/2} \, du = \frac{2}{3} u^{3/2} + C = \frac{2}{3} \left(x^2 - 6 \right)^{3/2} + C$

Let $u = x^2 - 6$
$\dfrac{du}{dx} = 2x$
$du = 2x \, dx$

5. $\displaystyle \int (3x - 2)^6 \, dx = \frac{1}{3} \int (3x - 2)^6 \, 3 \, dx = \frac{1}{3} \int u^6 \, du = \frac{1}{3} \cdot \frac{1}{7} u^7 + C$

$\qquad\qquad\qquad\qquad\qquad = \dfrac{1}{21} (3x - 2)^7 + C$

Let $u = 3x - 2$
$\dfrac{du}{dx} = 3$
$du = 3 \, dx$

7. $\displaystyle \int x \sqrt{x^2 - 3} \, dx = \int \left(x^2 - 3 \right)^{1/2} x \, dx = \frac{1}{2} \int \left(x^2 - 3 \right)^{1/2} 2x \, dx = \frac{1}{2} \int u^{1/2} \, du$

$\qquad\qquad\qquad\qquad\qquad\qquad = \dfrac{1}{3} u^{3/2} + C$

$\qquad\qquad\qquad\qquad\qquad\qquad = \dfrac{1}{3} \left(x^2 - 3 \right)^{3/2} + C$

Let $u = x^2 - 3$
$\dfrac{du}{dx} = 2x$
$du = 2x \, dx$

9. $\displaystyle \int \left(5x^3 + 1 \right)^4 x^2 \, dx = \frac{1}{15} \int (5x^3 + 1)^4 \, 15x^2 \, dx = \frac{1}{15} \int u^4 \, du$

$\qquad\qquad\qquad\qquad\qquad\qquad = \dfrac{1}{75} u^5 + C$

$\qquad\qquad\qquad\qquad\qquad\qquad = \dfrac{1}{75} \left(5x^3 + 1 \right)^5 + C$

Let $u = 5x^3 + 1$
$\dfrac{du}{dx} = 15x^2$
$du = 15x^2 \, dx$

11. $\displaystyle\int \frac{1}{(7x+2)^3}\,dx = \int (7x+2)^{-3}\,dx = \frac{1}{7}\int (7x+2)^{-3}\,7\,dx = \frac{1}{7}\int u^{-3}\,du$

$$= -\frac{1}{14}u^{-2} + C$$

$$= -\frac{1}{14}(7x+2)^{-2} + C$$

Let $u = 7x + 2$

$\dfrac{du}{dx} = 7$

$du = 7\,dx$

13. $\displaystyle\int \frac{dx}{\sqrt{3x+2}} = \int (3x+2)^{-1/2}\,dx = \frac{1}{3}\int (3x+2)^{-1/2}\,3\,dx = \frac{1}{3}\int u^{-1/2}\,du$

$$= \frac{2}{3}u^{1/2} + C$$

$$= \frac{2}{3}(3x+2)^{1/2} + C$$

Let $u = 3x + 2$

$\dfrac{du}{dx} = 3$

$du = 3\,dx$

15. $\displaystyle\int 3(x+2)^7\,dx = 3\int (x+2)^7\,dx = 3\int u^7\,du = \frac{3}{8}u^8 + C$

$$= \frac{3}{8}(x+2)^8 + C$$

Let $u = x + 2$

$\dfrac{du}{dx} = 1$

$du = dx$

17. $\displaystyle\int (x^2 - 4x + 1)^5(x-2)\,dx = \frac{1}{2}\int (x^2 - 4x + 1)^5\,2(x-2)\,dx$

$$= \frac{1}{2}\int u^5\,du$$

$$= \frac{1}{12}u^6 + C$$

$$= \frac{1}{12}(x^2 - 4x + 1)^6 + C$$

Let $u = x^2 - 4x + 1$

$\dfrac{du}{dx} = 2x - 4$

$du = 2(x-2)\,dx$

19. $\int \left(x^{1/2}+1\right)^4 \frac{1}{x^{1/2}}\,dx = \int \left(x^{1/2}+1\right)^4 x^{-1/2}\,dx = 2\int \left(x^{1/2}+1\right)^4 \left(\frac{1}{2}x^{-1/2}\,dx\right)$

$$= 2\int u^4\,du$$

$$= \frac{2}{5}u^5 + C$$

$$= \frac{2}{5}\left(x^{1/2}+1\right)^5 + C$$

Let $u = x^{1/2}+1$

$\dfrac{du}{dx} = \dfrac{1}{2}x^{-1/2}$

$du = \dfrac{1}{2}x^{-1/2}\,dx$

21. $\displaystyle\int_0^1 (x+1)^5\,dx = \left[\frac{1}{6}(x+1)^6\right]_0^1 = \frac{1}{6}\left[(1+1)^6 - (0+1)^6\right]$

$$= \frac{1}{6}\left(2^6 - 1\right)$$

$$= \frac{32}{3}$$

Let $u = x+1$

$\dfrac{du}{dx} = 1$

$du = dx$

23. $\displaystyle\int_1^2 (4x-3)^3\,dx = \frac{1}{4}\int_1^2 (4x-3)^3\,4\,dx = \left[\frac{1}{16}(4x-3)^4\right]_1^2$

$$= \frac{1}{16}\left\{[4(2)-3]^4 - [4(1)-3]^4\right\}$$

$$= \frac{1}{16}\left(5^4 - 1^4\right)$$

$$= 39$$

Let $u = 4x-3$

$\dfrac{du}{dx} = 4$

$du = 4\,dx$

25. $\displaystyle\int_2^3 \frac{dx}{(2x-3)^2} = \int_2^3 (2x-3)^{-2}\,dx = \frac{1}{2}\int_2^3 (2x-3)^{-2}\,2\,dx = \left[-\frac{1}{2}(2x-3)^{-1}\right]_2^3$

$$= -\frac{1}{2}\left[(6-3)^{-1} - (4-3)^{-1}\right]$$

$$= -\frac{1}{2}\left(\frac{1}{3} - 1\right)$$

$$= \frac{1}{3}$$

Let $u = 2x-3$

$\dfrac{du}{dx} = 2$

$du = 2\,dx$

27. $\displaystyle\int_0^4 x\sqrt{2x^2+4}\,dx = \int_0^4 x(2x^2+4)^{1/2}\,dx = \frac{1}{4}\int_0^4 (2x^2+4)^{1/2}\,4x\,dx$

$$= \left[\frac{1}{6}\left(2x^2+4\right)^{3/2}\right]_0^4$$

$$= \frac{1}{6}\left\{\left[2(4)^2+4\right]^{3/2} - (0+4)^{3/2}\right\}$$

$$= \frac{1}{6}\left(36^{3/2} - 4^{3/2}\right)$$

$$= \frac{104}{3}$$

Let $u = 2x^2 + 4$

$\dfrac{du}{dx} = 4x$

$du = 4x\,dx$

29. $\displaystyle\int_0^4 \frac{x}{\sqrt{1+3x^2}}\,dx = \int_0^4 \left(1+3x^2\right)^{-1/2} x\,dx = \frac{1}{6}\int_0^4 \left(1+3x^2\right)^{-1/2} 6x\,dx$

$$= \left[\frac{1}{3}\left(1+3x^2\right)^{1/2}\right]_0^4$$

$$= \frac{1}{3}\left\{\left[1+3(4)^2\right]^{1/2} - (1+0)^{1/2}\right\}$$

$$= \frac{1}{3}\left[(49)^{1/2} - 1\right]$$

$$= 2$$

Let $u = 1 + 3x^2$

$\dfrac{du}{dx} = 6x$

$du = 6x\,dx$

31. $\displaystyle\int_1^4 \frac{(1+\sqrt{x})^2}{\sqrt{x}}\,dx = \int_1^4 \left(1+x^{1/2}\right)^2 x^{-1/2}\,dx = 2\int_1^4 \left(1+x^{1/2}\right)^2 \left(\frac{1}{2}x^{-1/2}\,dx\right)$

$$= \left[\frac{2}{3}\left(1+x^{1/2}\right)^3\right]_1^4$$

$$= \frac{2}{3}\left[\left(1+4^{1/2}\right)^3 - (1+1)^3\right]$$

$$= \frac{2}{3}(27-8)$$

$$= \frac{38}{3}$$

Let $u = 1 + x^{1/2}$

$\dfrac{du}{dx} = \dfrac{1}{2}x^{-1/2}$

$du = \dfrac{1}{2}x^{-1/2}\,dx$

33. $\displaystyle\int 3x^2 e^{x^3}\,dx = \int e^u\,du = e^u + C = e^{x^3} + C$

Let $u = x^3$

$\dfrac{du}{dx} = 3x^2$

$du = 3x^2\,dx$

35. $\int e^{x+1}\,dx = \int e^u\,du = e^u + C = \;\; e^{x+1} + C$

Let $u = x + 1$

$\quad \dfrac{du}{dx} = 1$

$\quad du = dx$

37. $\int e^{-x}\,dx = -\int e^{-x}\,(-dx) = -\int e^u\,du = -e^u + C = \;\; -e^{-x} + C$

Let $u = -x$

$\quad \dfrac{du}{dx} = -1$

$\quad du = -dx$

39. $\int te^{3t^2}\,dt = \frac{1}{6}\int e^{3t^2}\,6t\,dt = \frac{1}{6}\int e^u\,du = \frac{1}{6}e^u + C = \;\; \frac{1}{6}e^{3t^2} + C$

Let $u = 3t^2$

$\quad \dfrac{du}{dt} = 6t$

$\quad du = 6t\,dt$

41. $\displaystyle\int \left(e^x + e^{-x}\right)\,dx = \int e^x\,dx + \int e^{-x}\,dx$

$\qquad\qquad\qquad\quad = e^x - e^{-x} + C$

43. $\displaystyle\int \frac{1}{x+1}\,dx = \int \frac{1}{u}\,du = \ln|u| + C = \;\; \ln|x+1| + C$

Let $u = x + 1$

$\quad \dfrac{du}{dx} = 1$

$\quad du = dx$

45. $\displaystyle\int \frac{dx}{5x+2} = \frac{1}{5}\int \frac{1}{5x+2}(5\,dx) = \frac{1}{5}\int \frac{1}{u}\,du = \frac{1}{5}\ln|u| + C$

$\qquad\qquad\qquad\qquad\qquad\qquad\qquad = \frac{1}{5}\ln|5x+2| + C$

Let $u = 5x + 2$

$\quad \dfrac{du}{dx} = 5$

$\quad du = 5\,dx$

47. $\displaystyle\int \frac{3x^2}{1+x^3}\,dx = \int \frac{1}{u}\,du = \ln|u| + C = \;\; \ln|1+x^3| + C$

Let $u = 1 + x^3$

$\quad \dfrac{du}{dx} = 3x^2$

$\quad du = 3x^2\,dx$

49. $\displaystyle\int \frac{x^{1/2}}{1+x^{3/2}}\,dx = \frac{2}{3}\int \frac{1}{1+x^{3/2}}\left(\frac{3}{2}x^{1/2}\,dx\right) = \frac{2}{3}\int \frac{1}{u}\,du$

$$= \frac{2}{3}\ln|u| + C$$

$$= \frac{2}{3}\ln|1+x^{3/2}| + C$$

Let $u = 1 + x^{3/2}$

$\quad\displaystyle\frac{du}{dx} = \frac{3}{2}x^{1/2}$

$\quad\displaystyle du = \frac{3}{2}x^{1/2}\,dx$

51. $\displaystyle\int \frac{x^2+4x}{x^3+6x^2-15}\,dx = \frac{1}{3}\int \frac{1}{x^3+6x^2-15}\left[3\left(x^2+4x\right)dx\right]$

$$= \frac{1}{3}\int \frac{1}{u}\,du$$

$$= \frac{1}{3}\ln|u| + C$$

$$= \frac{1}{3}\ln|x^3+6x^2-15| + C$$

Let $u = x^3 + 6x^2 - 15$

$\quad\displaystyle\frac{du}{dx} = 3x^2 + 12x$

$\quad du = 3(x^2+4x)\,dx$

53. $\displaystyle\int \frac{x}{1+x^2}\,dx = \frac{1}{2}\int \frac{2x\,dx}{1+x^2} = \frac{1}{2}\int \frac{1}{u}\,du = \frac{1}{2}\ln|u| + C$

$$= \frac{1}{2}\ln|1+x^2| + C$$

Let $u = 1 + x^2$

$\quad\displaystyle\frac{du}{dx} = 2x$

$\quad du = 2x\,dx$

55. $\displaystyle\int \left(1+e^{3t}\right)dt = \int dt + \int e^{3t}\,dt$

$$= t + \frac{1}{3}e^{3t} + C$$

57. $\displaystyle\int \left(\frac{1}{x}+1\right)dx = \int \frac{1}{x}\,dx + \int dx$

$$= \ln|x| + x + C$$

59. $\displaystyle\int \frac{e^{2x}}{1-e^{2x}}\,dx = -\frac{1}{2}\int \frac{-2e^{2x}\,dx}{1-e^{2x}} = -\frac{1}{2}\int \frac{1}{u}\,du$

$$= -\frac{1}{2}\ln|u| + C$$

$$= -\frac{1}{2}\ln|1-e^{2x}| + C$$

Let $u = 1 - e^{2x}$

$\quad\displaystyle\frac{du}{dx} = -2e^{2x}$

$\quad du = -2e^{2x}\,dx$

61. $\displaystyle\int (\ln x)^4 \cdot \frac{1}{x}\, dx = \int u^4\, du = \frac{1}{5}u^5 + C$

$$= \frac{1}{5}(\ln x)^5 + C$$

Let $u = \ln x$

$\dfrac{du}{dx} = \dfrac{1}{x}$

$dn = \dfrac{1}{x}\, dx$

63. $\displaystyle\int \frac{1}{x(\ln x)^2}\, dx = \int \frac{1}{(\ln x)^2}\left(\frac{1}{x}\, dx\right) = \int \frac{1}{u^2}\, du$

$$= \int u^{-2}\, du$$

$$= -u^{-1} + C$$

$$= -\frac{1}{u} + C$$

$$= -\frac{1}{\ln x} + C$$

Let $u = \ln x$

$\dfrac{du}{dx} = \dfrac{1}{x}$

$du = \dfrac{1}{x}\, dx$

65. $\displaystyle\int \left(1 - \frac{1}{e^x}\right)\, dx = \int \left(1 - e^{-x}\right)\, dx$

$$= \int dx - \int e^{-x}\, dx$$

$$= x - \left(-e^{-x}\right) + C$$

$$= x + e^{-x} + C$$

67. $\displaystyle\int \frac{\ln x^2}{x}\, dx = \int \frac{2\ln x}{x}\, dx = 2\int \ln x \left(\frac{1}{x}\, dx\right)$

$$= 2\int u\, du$$

$$= u^2 + C$$

$$= (\ln x)^2 + C$$

Let $u = \ln x$

$\dfrac{du}{dx} = \dfrac{1}{x}$

$du = \dfrac{1}{x}\, dx$

69. $\displaystyle\int \frac{(\ln x)^2}{x}\, dx = \int u^2\, du = \frac{1}{3}u^3 + C$

$$= \frac{1}{3}(\ln x)^3 + C$$

Let $u = \ln x$

$\dfrac{du}{dx} = \dfrac{1}{x}$

$du = \dfrac{1}{x}\, dx$

71. $\displaystyle\int_0^1 \frac{2x\,dx}{1+x^2} = \int_1^2 \frac{1}{u}\,du = \Big[\ln |u|\Big]_1^2$

$$= \ln 2 - \ln 1$$
$$= \ln 2$$

Let $u = 1 + x^2$ $u(0) = 1$

$\dfrac{du}{dx} = 2x$ $u(1) = 2$

$du = 2x\,dx$

73. $\displaystyle\int_0^1 \frac{e^x}{1+e^x}\,dx = \int_2^{1+e} \frac{1}{u}\,du = \Big[\ln |u|\Big]_2^{1+e} = \ln(1+e) - \ln 2$

Let $u = 1 + e^x$ $u(0) = 1 + e^0 = 2$

$\dfrac{du}{dx} = e^x$ $u(1) = 1 + e$

$du = e^x\,dx$

75. $\displaystyle\int_0^1 xe^{-x^2}\,dx = -\frac{1}{2}\int_0^1 e^{-x^2}(-2x\,dx) = -\frac{1}{2}\int_0^{-1} e^u\,du$

$$= -\frac{1}{2}\Big[e^u\Big]_0^{-1}$$
$$= -\frac{1}{2}\left(e^{-1} - e^0\right)$$
$$= \frac{1}{2}\left(1 - \frac{1}{e}\right)$$

Let $u = -x^2$ $u(0) = 0$

$\dfrac{du}{dx} = -2x$ $u(1) = -1$

$du = -2x\,dx$

77. $\displaystyle\int_0^{e-1} \frac{1}{x+1}\,dx = \int_1^e \frac{1}{u}\,du = \Big[\ln |u|\Big]_1^e$

$$= \ln e - \ln 1$$
$$= 1$$

Let $u = x + 1$ $u(0) = 1$

$\dfrac{du}{dx} = 1$ $u(e-1) = e$

$du = dx$

79. $\displaystyle\int_1^e \frac{\ln x}{x}\,dx = \int_0^1 u\,du = \left[\frac{u^2}{2}\right]_0^1 = \frac{1}{2} - 0$

$$= \frac{1}{2}$$

Let $u = \ln x$ $u(1) = 0$

$\dfrac{du}{dx} = \dfrac{1}{x}$ $u(e) = 1$

$du = \dfrac{1}{x}\,dx$

81.
$$\int_0^{\sqrt{2}} \frac{x\,dx}{3-x^2} = -\frac{1}{2}\int_0^{\sqrt{2}} \frac{-2x\,dx}{3-x^2} = -\frac{1}{2}\int_3^1 \frac{1}{u}\,du$$
$$= -\frac{1}{2}\Big[\ln|u|\Big]_3^1$$
$$= -\frac{1}{2}(\ln 1 - \ln 3)$$
$$= \frac{1}{2}\ln 3$$

Let $u = 3 - x^2$ $u(0) = 3$

$\dfrac{du}{dx} = -2x$ $u(\sqrt{2}) = 3 - 2 = 1$

$du = -2x\,dx$

83.
$$\int e^2\,dx = e^2 x + C$$

Note: e^2 is a constant.

85.
$$\int \frac{\ln\sqrt{x}}{x}\,dx = \int \frac{\ln x^{1/2}}{x}\,dx = \frac{1}{2}\int \frac{\ln x}{x}\,dx = \frac{1}{2}\int u\,du$$
$$= \frac{1}{4}u^2 + C$$
$$= \frac{1}{4}(\ln x)^2 + C$$

Let $u = \ln x$

$\dfrac{du}{dx} = \dfrac{1}{x}$

$du = \dfrac{1}{x}\,dx$

87. Using long division on $\frac{x^2+2x+4}{x+1}$ yields

$$
\begin{array}{r}
x + 1 \\
x+1\,\overline{)\,x^2 + 2x + 4} \\
\underline{x^2 + x} \\
x + 4 \\
\underline{x + 1} \\
3
\end{array}
$$

thus $\dfrac{x^2 + 2x + 4}{x + 1} = x + 1 + \dfrac{3}{x+1}$

and $\displaystyle\int \frac{x^2 + 2x + 4}{x + 1}\,dx = \int \left(x + 1 + \frac{3}{x+1}\right)dx = \int (x+1)\,dx + 3\int \frac{1}{x+1}\,dx$
$$= x^2 + 2x + 3\ln|x+1| + C$$

89. Using long division on $\frac{3x}{x-1}$ yields

$$
\begin{array}{r}
3 \\
x-1\,\overline{)\,3x} \\
\underline{3x - 3} \\
3
\end{array}
$$

Thus $\dfrac{3x}{x-1} = 3 + \dfrac{3}{x-1}$

and $\displaystyle\int \frac{3x}{x-1}\,dx = \int \left(3 + \frac{3}{x-1}\right)dx = 3\int dx + 3\int \frac{1}{x-1}\,dx$
$$= 3x + 3\ln|x-1| + C$$

91. Assume the equation of the curve in question is $y = f(x)$. If the slope of the curve is $4xe^{x^2}$, then $f'(x) = 4xe^{x^2}$. Evaluate the indefinite integral $\int 4xe^{x^2}\,dx$ and use the condition $f(0) = 5$ to determine $f(x)$.

$$f(x) = \int 4xe^{x^2}\,dx = 2\int e^{x^2}\, 2x\,dx = 2e^{x^2} + C$$

Let $u = x^2$

$$\frac{du}{dx} = 2x$$

$$du = 2x\,dx$$

$$f(0) = 2e^0 + C = 5$$
$$C = 3$$

Thus, $f(x) = 2e^{x^2} + 3$

93. Average value of $f(x) = \dfrac{1}{12 - 4}\displaystyle\int_4^{12} \sqrt{2x+1}\,dx$

$$= \frac{1}{8}\int_4^{12} (2x+1)^{1/2}\,dx = \frac{1}{8}\int_4^{12} (2x+1)^{1/2}\, 2\,dx$$

$$= \frac{2}{8}\int_9^{25} u^{1/2}\,dn$$

$$= \frac{1}{4}\left[\frac{2}{3}u^{3/2}\right]_9^{25}$$

$$= \frac{1}{6}\left(25^{3/2} - 9^{3/2}\right)$$

$$= \frac{1}{6}(125 - 27)$$

$$= \frac{49}{3}$$

Let $u = 2x + 1$ $\qquad u(4) = 9$

$$\frac{du}{dx} = 2 \qquad u(12) = 25$$

$$du = 2\,dx$$

95. Consider the graph of $y = (7x + 1)^{1/3}$ and the area shaded between $x = 0$ and $x = 1$.

$$A = \int_0^1 (7x+1)^{1/3}\,dx = \frac{1}{7}\int_1^8 u^{1/3}\,du = \frac{3}{28}\left[u^{4/3}\right]_1^8$$

$$= \frac{3}{28}\left(8^{4/3} - 1\right)$$

$$= \frac{45}{28}$$

Let $u = 7x + 1$ $\qquad u(0) = 1$

$$\frac{du}{dx} = 7 \qquad u(1) = 8$$

$$du = 7\,dx$$

97. Sketch the graph of the region bounded by $y = \frac{1}{2x+3}$, the x axis, $x = 2$, and $x = 4$. Shade the volume generated by revolving it about the x axis.

$$V = \int_2^4 \pi \left(\frac{1}{2x+3} \right)^2 dx = \pi \int_2^4 \frac{1}{(2x+3)^2} dx = \frac{\pi}{2} \int_7^{11} \frac{1}{u^2} du$$

$$= \frac{\pi}{2} \int_7^{11} u^{-2} du$$

$$= -\frac{\pi}{2} \left[\frac{1}{u} \right]_7^{11}$$

$$= -\frac{\pi}{2} \left(\frac{1}{11} - \frac{1}{7} \right)$$

$$= \frac{2\pi}{77}$$

Let $u = 2x + 3$ $u(2) = 7$

$\quad \dfrac{du}{dx} = 2$ $u(4) = 11$

$\quad du = 2x$

99. If the rate of change of the height of the tree is $\frac{dh}{dt} = 3 + \frac{1}{2\sqrt{t+1}} = 3 + \frac{1}{2}(t+1)^{-1/2}$, then the amount the tree will grow in the first three years is determined by the definite integral $\int_0^3 \left[3 + \frac{1}{2}(t+1)^{-1/2} \right] dt$.

$$\int_0^3 \left[3 + \frac{1}{2}(t+1)^{-1/2} \right] dt = \int_0^3 3\, dt + \frac{1}{2} \int_0^3 (t+1)^{-1/2} dt$$

$$= [3t]_0^3 + \left[(t+1)^{1/2} \right]_0^3$$

$$= 9 - 0 + 4^{1/2} - 1$$

$$= 10 \text{ feet}$$

Let $u = t + 1$

$\quad \dfrac{du}{dt} = 1$

$\quad du = dt$

101. If the rate at which oil is being piped is $\frac{dO}{dt} = 15\sqrt{10t + 9}$ gallons per minute, then the number of gallons piped in the first four minutes is

$$\int_0^4 (15\sqrt{10t + 9})\, dt = \int_0^4 15(10t + 9)^{1/2}\, dt$$

$$= \left[15\frac{2}{3}(10t + 9)^{3/2} \cdot \frac{1}{10} \right]_0^4$$

$$= \left[(10t + 9)^{3/2} \right]_0^4$$

$$= (49)^{3/2} - (9)^{3/2}$$

$$= 343 - 27$$

$$= 316$$

103. Consider the two integrals $\int (x^2 + 1)^{18}\, 2\, dx$ and $\int (2x + 1)^{18}\, dx$.

a. $\int (2x + 1)^{18}\, dx$ can be evaluated by substitution. If $u = 2x + 1$, then $du = 2\, dx$ and the missing constant factor of 2 can be inserted by multiplying by $1 = \frac{2}{2}$. Thus,

$$\int (2x + 1)^{18}\, dx = \int (2x + 1)^{18}\frac{2}{2}\, dx$$

$$= \int \frac{1}{2}(2x + 1)^{18}\, 2\, dx$$

$$= \frac{1}{2}\int (2x + 1)^{18}\, 2\, dx$$

$$= \frac{1}{2}\int u^{18}\, du$$

$$= \frac{1}{38}u^{19} + C$$

$$= \frac{1}{38}(2x + 1)^{19} + C$$

b. $\int (x^2 + 1)^{18}\, dx$ cannot be evaluated by substitution. If one attempts to generate the form $\int u^{18}\, du$, then $u = x^2 + 1$ would be the substitution. This creates a problem, since $du = 2x\, dx$ and there is a missing x factor that cannot be inserted in the same fashion as the constant factor 2. The factor x cannot pass through the integral sign like the constant 2.

Note: one could, using the binomial theorem, expand $(x^2 + 1)^{18}$ into a polynomial, but it would be extremely tedious!

SECTION 7.1 Technology Exercises

1. $x = 0$ and $x = 3$

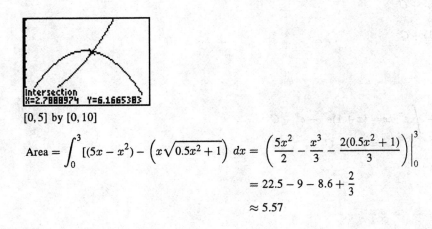

[0, 5] by [0, 10]

$$\text{Area} = \int_0^3 \left[(5x - x^2) - \left(x\sqrt{0.5x^2 + 1} \right) \right]\, dx = \left(\frac{5x^2}{2} - \frac{x^3}{3} - \frac{2(0.5x^2 + 1)}{3} \right)\Big|_0^3$$

$$= 22.5 - 9 - 8.6 + \frac{2}{3}$$

$$\approx 5.57$$

3. a.

n	Area
10	53.01801801
50	50.93662997
100	50.66915656

b. Area $= \displaystyle\int_0^3 6\sqrt{5x+1}\,dx = \dfrac{4(5x+1)^{3/2}}{5}\Big|_0^3 = 51.2 - 0.8 = 50.4$

SECTION 7.2 pages 383–385

1. Let $u = x \rightarrow du = dx$

$\quad dv = e^{2x}\,dx \rightarrow v = \dfrac{1}{2}e^{2x}$

$\displaystyle\int xe^{2x}\,dx = \dfrac{1}{2}xe^{2x} - \dfrac{1}{2}\int e^{2x}\,dx = \dfrac{1}{2}xe^{2x} - \dfrac{1}{4}e^{2x} + C$

$\qquad\qquad\qquad = \dfrac{1}{4}(x-1)e^{2x} + C$

3. Let $u = \ln x \rightarrow du = \dfrac{1}{x}\,dx$

$\quad dv = x\,dx \rightarrow v = \dfrac{1}{2}x^2$

$\displaystyle\int x\ln x\,dx = \dfrac{1}{2}x^2\ln x - \int \dfrac{1}{2}x^2\left(\dfrac{1}{x}\right)dx = \dfrac{1}{2}x^2\ln x - \dfrac{1}{2}\int x\,dx$

$\qquad\qquad\qquad = \dfrac{1}{2}x^2\ln x - \dfrac{1}{4}x^2 + C$

$\qquad\qquad\qquad = \dfrac{1}{4}x^2(2\ln x - 1) + C$

5. Let $u = \ln x \rightarrow du = \dfrac{1}{x}\,dx$

$\quad dv = x^2\,dx \rightarrow v = \dfrac{1}{3}x^3$

$\displaystyle\int x^2\ln x\,dx = \dfrac{1}{3}x^3\ln x - \int \dfrac{1}{3}x^3\left(\dfrac{1}{x}\right)dx$

$\qquad\qquad\qquad = \dfrac{1}{3}x^3\ln x - \dfrac{1}{3}\int x^2\,dx$

$\qquad\qquad\qquad = \dfrac{1}{3}x^3\ln x - \dfrac{1}{9}x^3 + C$

$\qquad\qquad\qquad = \dfrac{1}{9}x^3(3\ln x - 1) + C$

7. Let $u = x + 1 \rightarrow du = dx$

$\quad dv = e^x\,dx \rightarrow v = e^x$

$\displaystyle\int (x+1)e^x\,dx = (x+1)e^x - \int e^x\,dx = (x+1)e^x - e^x + C$

$\qquad\qquad\qquad = xe^x + C$

9. Let $u = \ln x \rightarrow du = \dfrac{1}{x} dx$

$$dv = \frac{1}{x^2} dx = x^{-2} dx \rightarrow v = -\frac{1}{x}$$

$$\int \frac{\ln x}{x^2} dx = -\frac{1}{x} \ln x - \int -\frac{1}{x} \left(\frac{1}{x} dx \right)$$

$$= -\frac{1}{x} \ln x + \int \frac{1}{x^2} dx$$

$$= -\frac{1}{x} \ln x - \frac{1}{x} + C$$

$$= -\frac{1}{x} (\ln x + 1) + C$$

11. Let $u = x \rightarrow du = dx$

$$dv = (x+3)^4 dx \rightarrow v = \frac{1}{5}(x+3)^5$$

$$\int x(x+3)^4 dx = \frac{1}{5} x(x+3)^5 - \int \frac{1}{5}(x+3)^5 dx$$

$$= \frac{x}{5}(x+3)^5 - \frac{1}{30}(x+3)^6 + C$$

$$= \frac{1}{30}(x+3)^5 [6x - (x+3)] + C$$

$$= \frac{1}{30}(x+3)^5 (5x - 3) + C$$

13. Let $u = x \rightarrow du = dx$

$$dv = (x+7)^{-3} dx \rightarrow v = -\frac{1}{2}(x+7)^{-2}$$

$$\int \frac{x}{(x+7)^3} dx = \int x(x+7)^{-3} dx$$

$$= -\frac{x}{2}(x+7)^{-2} + \frac{1}{2} \int (x+7)^{-2} dx$$

$$= -\frac{x}{2}(x+7)^{-2} - \frac{1}{2}(x+7)^{-1} + C$$

$$= -\frac{1}{2}(x+7)^{-2}(x + x + 7) + C$$

$$= -\frac{2x + 7}{2(x+7)^2} + C$$

15. Let $u = \ln x \rightarrow du = \dfrac{1}{x} dx$

$$dv = x^{-1/2} dx \rightarrow v = 2x^{1/2}$$

$$\int \frac{\ln x}{\sqrt{x}} dx = \int x^{-1/2} \ln x \, dx$$

$$= 2x^{1/2} \ln x - 2 \int x^{1/2} \left(\frac{1}{x} dx \right)$$

$$= 2x^{1/2} \ln x - 2 \int x^{-1/2} dx$$

$$= 2x^{1/2} \ln x - 4x^{1/2} + C$$

$$= 2x^{1/2} (\ln x - 2) + C$$

17. The integration of $\int x^3 e^x \, dx$ requires several applications of integration by parts.

Let $u = x^3 \rightarrow du = 3x^2 \, dx$
$dv = e^x \, dx \rightarrow v = e^x$

$$\int x^3 e^x \, dx = x^3 e^x - 3 \int x^2 e^x \, dx$$

Let $u = x^2 \rightarrow du = 2x \, dx$
$dv = e^x \, dx \rightarrow v = e^x$

$$= x^3 e^x - 3 \left(x^2 e^x - 2 \int x e^x \, dx \right)$$

$$= x^3 e^x - 3x^2 e^x + 6 \int x e^x \, dx$$

Let $u = x \rightarrow du = dx$
$dv = e^x \, dx \rightarrow v = e^x$

$$= x^3 e^x - 3x^2 e^x + 6 \left(x e^x - \int e^x \, dx \right)$$

$$= x^3 e^x - 3x^2 e^x + 6x e^x - 6e^x + C$$

$$= \left(x^3 - 3x^2 + 6x - 6 \right) e^x + C$$

19. Let $u = x \rightarrow du = dx$

$$dv = (x + 2)^{-3} \, dx \rightarrow v = -\frac{1}{2}(x + 2)^{-2}$$

$$\int x(x + 2)^{-3} \, dx = -\frac{x}{2}(x + 2)^{-2} + \frac{1}{2} \int (x + 2)^{-2} \, dx$$

$$= -\frac{x}{2}(x + 2)^{-2} - \frac{1}{2}(x + 2)^{-1} + C$$

$$= -\frac{1}{2}(x + 2)^{-2} [x + (x + 2)] + C$$

$$= -\frac{x + 1}{(x + 2)^2} + C$$

21. Let $u = x \rightarrow du = dx$
$dv = e^x \, dx \rightarrow v = e^x$

$$\int_1^2 x e^x \, dx = \left[x e^x \right]_1^2 - \int_1^2 e^x \, dx = \left[x e^x \right]_1^2 - \left[e^x \right]_1^2$$

$$= 2e^2 - e^1 - \left(e^2 - e^1 \right)$$

$$= e^2$$

23. Let $u = \ln x \rightarrow du = \frac{1}{x} \, dx$

$$dv = dx \rightarrow v = x$$

$$\int_1^e \ln x \, dx = [x \ln x]_1^e - \int_1^3 dx = [x \ln x]_1^e - [x]_1^e$$

$$= e \ln e - 1 \ln 1 - (e - 1)$$

$$= e - e + 1$$

$$= 1$$

25. Let $u = x \rightarrow du = dx$

$dv = \left(1 + e^x\right) dx \rightarrow v = x + e^x$

$$\int_0^1 x\left(1 + e^x\right) dx = \left[x\left(x + e^x\right)\right]_0^1 - \int_0^1 \left(x + e^x\right) dx$$

$$= \left[x\left(x + e^x\right)\right]_0^1 - \left[\frac{x^2}{2} + e^x\right]_0^1$$

$$= \left[1\left(1 + e^1\right) - 0\left(0 + e^0\right)\right] - \left[\left(\frac{1}{2} + e^1\right) - \left(0 + e^0\right)\right]$$

$$= (1 + e + 0) - \left(\frac{1}{2} + e - 1\right)$$

$$= \frac{3}{2}$$

27. Let $u = x \rightarrow du = dx$

$dv = e^{-x} dx \rightarrow v = -e^{-x}$

$$\int_{-1}^0 \frac{x}{e^x} dx = \int_{-1}^0 xe^{-x} dx = \left[-xe^{-x}\right]_{-1}^0 + \int_{-1}^0 e^{-x} dx$$

$$= \left[-xe^{-x}\right]_{-1}^0 - \left[e^{-x}\right]_{-1}^0$$

$$= -\left[0 - (-e^1)\right] - \left(e^0 - e^1\right)$$

$$= -e - e^0 + e$$

$$= -1$$

29. First evaluate $\int 30x(x + 1)^4 \, dx$ and then compute the definite integral.

Let $u = x \rightarrow du = dx$

$dv = (x + 1)^4 \, dx \rightarrow v = \frac{1}{5}(x + 1)^5$

$$\int 30x(x + 1)^4 \, dx = 30\left[\frac{x}{5}(x + 1)^5 - \frac{1}{5}\int (x + 1)^5 \, dx\right]$$

$$= 30\left[\frac{x}{5}(x + 1)^5 - \frac{1}{30}(x + 1)^6\right]$$

$$= \frac{30}{30}(x + 1)^5\left[6x - (x + 1)\right]$$

$$= (x + 1)^5(5x - 1)$$

Therefore,

$$\int_2^3 30x(x + 1)^4 \, dx = \left[(x + 1)^5(5x - 1)\right]_2^3$$

$$= 4^5(14) - (3)^5(9)$$

$$= 12{,}149$$

31. Let $u = x^2$

$du = 2x \, dx$

$$\int xe^{x^2} \, dx = \frac{1}{2}\int e^{x^2} (2x \, dx)$$

$$= \frac{1}{2}e^{x^2} + C$$

33. Let $u = \ln x$

$$du = \frac{1}{x} dx$$

$$\int \frac{\ln x}{x} dx = \int u \, du = \frac{u^2}{2} + C = \frac{(\ln x)^2}{2} + C$$

35. Let $u = \ln 2x \rightarrow du = \frac{1}{2x}(2) \, dx$

$$dv = dx \rightarrow v = x$$

$$\int \ln 2x \, dx = x \ln 2x - \int dx = x \ln 2x - x + C$$

$$= x(\ln 2x - 1) + C$$

37. Let $u = x \rightarrow du = dx$

$$dv = (1 + x)^{1/2} \, dx \rightarrow v = \frac{2}{3}(1 + x)^{3/2}$$

$$\int x\sqrt{1 + x} \, dx = \int x(1 + x)^{1/2} \, dx$$

$$= \frac{2x}{3}(1 + x)^{3/2} - \frac{2}{3}\int (1 + x)^{3/2} \, dx$$

$$= \frac{2x}{3}(1 + x)^{3/2} - \frac{4}{15}(1 + x)^{5/2} + C$$

$$= \frac{2}{3}(1 + x)^{3/2}\left[x - \frac{2}{5}(1 + x)\right] + C$$

$$= \frac{2}{15}(1 + x)^{3/2}(3x - 2) + C$$

39. Let $u = 1 + x^2$

$$du = 2x \, dx$$

$$\int x\sqrt{1 + x^2} \, dx = \frac{1}{2}\int (1 + x^2)^{1/2}(2x \, dx) = \frac{1}{3}(1 + x^2)^{3/2} + C$$

41. Let $u = x \rightarrow du = dx$

$$dv = e^{-0.04x} \, dx \rightarrow v = -\frac{1}{0.04}e^{-0.04x}$$

$$= -25e^{-0.04x}$$

$$\int xe^{-0.04x} \, dx = -25xe^{-0.04x} + 25\int e^{-0.04x} \, dx$$

$$= -25xe^{-0.04x} - \frac{25}{0.04}e^{-0.04x} + C$$

$$= -25(x + 25)e^{-0.04x} + C$$

43. Let $u = x \rightarrow du = dx$

$$dv = e^{-0.08x} \, dx \rightarrow v = -\frac{1}{0.08}e^{-0.08x}$$

$$= -12.5e^{-0.08x}$$

$$\int 12xe^{-0.08x} \, dx = 12\left(-12.5xe^{-0.08x} + 12.5\int e^{-0.08x} \, dx\right)$$

$$= 12\left(-12.5xe^{-0.08x} - \frac{12.5}{0.08}e^{-0.08x}\right) + C$$

$$= -150(x + 12.5)e^{-0.08x} + C$$

45. $\int xe^{-0.05x}\,dx = -20(x+20)e^{-0.05x} + C$

(See answer to Exercise 42.)

47. The present value of the income stream is given by

$$P = \int_0^T f(t)e^{-rt}\,dt \qquad \text{where } f(t) = 20{,}000 + 3000t$$

$$r = 0.05$$
$$T = 4$$

Thus, $P = \int_0^4 (20{,}000 + 3000t)e^{0.05t}\,dt$

$$= 20{,}000 \int_0^4 e^{-0.05t} + 3000 \int_0^4 te^{-0.05t}\,dt$$

$$= \left[\frac{20{,}000}{-0.05}e^{-0.05t}\right]_0^4 + 3000\left(\left[-20te^{-0.05t}\right]_0^4 + 20\int_0^4 e^{-0.05t}\,dt\right)$$

$$= \left[-400{,}000e^{-0.05t}\right]_0^4 + 3000\left(\left[-20te^{-0.05t}\right]_0^4 - \left[400e^{-0.05t}\right]_0^4\right)$$

$$= -400{,}000\left(e^{-0.2} - e^0\right) + 3000\left\{\left[-20(4)e^{-0.2} - 0\right] - 400\left(e^{-0.2} - e^0\right)\right\}$$

$$= -400{,}000(-0.18127) - 240{,}000e^{-0.2} - 1{,}200{,}000(-0.18127)$$

$$\approx \$93{,}535$$

Let $u = t \rightarrow du = dt$

$$dv = e^{-0.05t}\,dt \rightarrow v = -\frac{1}{0.05}e^{-0.05t}$$

$$= -20e^{-0.05t}$$

49. The present value of the income stream is given by $P = \int_0^T f(t)e^{-rt}\,dt$

where $f(t) = 7000 - 300t$
$$r = 0.08$$
$$T = 6$$

Thus, $P = \int_0^6 (7000 - 300t)e^{-0.08t}\,dt$. First find the antiderivative and then evaluate the definite integral.

Let $u = t \rightarrow du = dt$
$$dv = e^{-0.08t}\,dt \rightarrow v = -\frac{1}{0.08}e^{-0.08t}$$

$$\int (7000 - 300t)e^{-0.08t}\,dt = 7000\int e^{-0.08t}\,dt - 300\int te^{0.08t}\,dt$$

$$= \frac{7000}{-0.08}e^{-0.08t} - 300\left(-12.5te^{-0.08t} + 12.5\int e^{-0.08t}\,dt\right)$$

$$= -87{,}500e^{-0.08t} - 300\left(-12.5te^{-0.08t} - \frac{12.5}{0.08}e^{-0.08t}\right)$$

$$= -87{,}500e^{-0.08t} + 3750te^{-0.08t} + 46{,}875e^{-0.08t}$$

$$= (3750t - 40{,}625)e^{-0.08t}$$

Therefore, $P = \int_0^6 (7000 - 300t)e^{-0.08t}\,dt = \left[(3750t - 40{,}625)e^{-0.08t}\right]_0^6$

$$= [3750(6) - 40{,}625]\,e^{-0.48} - (-40{,}625)e^0$$

$$\approx \$29{,}410$$

51.   Given that $\frac{dP}{dt} = 1 + \ln t$, $t \geq 1$, then

$$P = \int (1 + \ln t)\,dt$$

$$= t + \frac{1}{|t|} + C \qquad \text{for } C \text{ an arbitrary constant}$$

$$= t + \frac{1}{t} + C \qquad \text{since } t \geq 1, \text{ then } |t| = t$$

Since $P = 60$ when $t = 1$, then $60 = 1 + \frac{1}{1} + C$

$$C = 58$$

Hence the population at any time t is

$$P(t) = t + \frac{1}{t} + 58$$

53.   The amount of medicine absorbed into the bloodstream in the first 20 minutes is

$$\int_0^{20} te^{-0.1t}\,dt$$

First, we evaluate $\int te^{-0.1t}\,dt$.

$$\int te^{-0.1t}\,dt = t\frac{e^{-0.1t}}{(-0.1)} - \int \frac{e^{-0.1t}}{(-0.1)}\,dt$$
$$= -10te^{-0.1t} - 100e^{-0.1t} + C$$

Then $\int_0^{20} te^{-0.1t}\,dt = \left[-10te^{-0.1t} - 100e^{-0.1t} + C\right]_0^{20}$

$$= [-10(20)e^{-0.1(20)} - 100e^{-0.1(20)}] - [-10(0)(1) - 100(1)]$$
$$= 100 - 200e^{-2} - 100e^{-2}$$
$$= 100 - 300e^{-2}$$
$$\approx 59.4 \text{ milligrams}$$

55.   Average value of $f(x) = \frac{1}{1-0}\int_0^1 xe^x\,dx$

$$= \int_0^1 xe^x\,dx$$

$$= \left[xe^x\right]_0^1 - \int_0^1 e^x\,dx$$

$$= \left[xe^x\right]_0^1 - \left[e^x\right]_0^1$$

$$= (e - 0) - (e - e^0)$$

$$= 1$$

Let $u = x \rightarrow dv = dx$
    $dv = e^x\,dx \rightarrow v = e^x$

57. Let $y = f(x)$ represent the equation of the curve. Then $f'(x) = \ln x$ and $f(1) = -1$. Evaluate the indefinite integral $\int f'(x)\,dx = \int \ln x\,dx$ to find $f(x)$.

$$f(x) = \int \ln x\,dx = x\ln x - \int dx = x\ln x - x + C$$

Let $u = \ln x \rightarrow du = \dfrac{1}{x}\,dx$

$\quad dv = dx \rightarrow v = x$

Using $f(1) = -1$, then $f(1) = 1\ln 1 - 1 + C = -1$

$$C = 0$$

Thus, $f(x) = x\ln x - x$

$\qquad\qquad = x(\ln x - 1)$

59. Sketch the graph of $y = xe^{-x}$ and shade the area between $x = 1$ and $x = 3$.

$$A = \int_1^3 xe^{-x}\,dx = -\left[xe^{-x}\right]_1^3 + \int_1^3 e^{-x}\,dx$$

$$= -\left[xe^{-x}\right]_1^3 - \left[e^{-x}\right]_1^3$$

$$= -\left(3e^{-3} - e^{-1}\right) - \left(e^{-3} - e^{-1}\right)$$

$$= -4e^{-3} + 2e^{-1}$$

$$= 2\left(\frac{1}{e} - \frac{2}{e^3}\right)$$

Let $u = x \rightarrow du = dx$

$\quad dv = e^{-x}\,dx \rightarrow v = -e^{-x}$

61. Sketch the graph of $y = xe^x$ and shade the region bounded by $y = xe^x$, the x axis, $x = 0$, and $x = 1$.

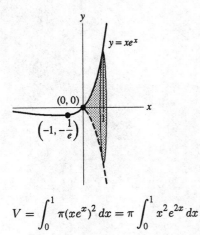

$$V = \int_0^1 \pi(xe^x)^2\,dx = \pi \int_0^1 x^2 e^{2x}\,dx$$

Find the indefinite integral using two applications of integration by parts and then evaluate the definite integral.

$$\int x^2 e^{2x}\,dx = \frac{1}{2}x^2 e^{2x} - \int xe^{2x}\,dx = \frac{1}{2}x^2 e^{2x} - \left[\frac{1}{2}xe^{2x} - \frac{1}{2}\int e^{2x}\,dx\right]$$

$$= \frac{1}{2}x^2 e^{2x} - \frac{1}{2}xe^{2x} + \frac{1}{4}e^{2x} = \frac{1}{4}\left(2x^2 - 2x + 1\right)e^{2x}$$

Let $u = x^2 \rightarrow du = 2x\,dx$ Let $u = x \rightarrow du = dx$

$\quad dv = e^{2x}\,dx \rightarrow v = \frac{1}{2}e^{2x}$ $\qquad dv = e^{2x}\,dx \rightarrow v = \frac{1}{2}e^{2x}$

Thus,

$$V = \pi \int_0^1 x^2 e^{2x}\,dx = \frac{\pi}{4}\left[\left(2x^2 - 2x + 1\right)e^{2x}\right]_0^1 = \frac{\pi}{4}\left[(2 - 2 + 1)e^2 - (0 - 0 + 1)e^0\right]$$

$$V = \frac{\pi}{4}\left(e^2 - 1\right)$$

63. It is not possible to use $u = 1$ and $dv = \ln x\,dx$ to perform integration by parts on $\int \ln x\,dx$ because $du = 0$ and $v = \int \ln x\,dx$, which would result in the formal identity

$$\int \ln x\,dx = uv - \int v\,du$$

$$= 1 \cdot \int \ln x\,dx - 0$$

$$= \int \ln x\,dx$$

SECTION 7.2 Technology Exercises

1.

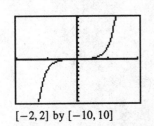

$[-2, 2]$ by $[-10, 10]$

The average value over $[-2, 2]$ is 0. Since $f(-x) = -f(x)$, the graph is symmetric with respect to the origin. Thus the average value $f(x)$ on any closed interval of the form $[-a, a]$, where a is a positive real number, must be zero.

SECTION 7.3 pages 388–389

1. Using formula 8 in Table 5 with $u = x$ and $a = 4$ yields

$$\int \sqrt{x^2 + 16}\,dx = \frac{x}{2}\sqrt{x^2 + 16} + 8\ln\left|x + \sqrt{x^2 + 16}\right| + C$$

3. Using formula 8 in Table 5 with $u = 3x$ and $a = \sqrt{5}$ yields $du = 3\,dx$ and

$$\int \sqrt{9x^2 + 5}\,dx = \frac{1}{3}\int \sqrt{(3x)^2 + (\sqrt{5})^2}\,3\,dx$$

$$= \frac{1}{3}\int \sqrt{u^2 + a^2}\,du$$

$$= \frac{1}{3}\left[\frac{u}{2}\sqrt{u^2 + a^2}\right] + \frac{a^2}{2}\ln\left|u + \sqrt{u^2 + a^2}\right| + C$$

$$= \frac{1}{3}\left[3x\sqrt{9x^2 + 5}\right] + \frac{5}{2}\ln\left|3x + \sqrt{9x^2 + 5}\right| + C$$

$$= x\sqrt{9x^2 + 5} + \frac{5}{6}\ln\left|3x + \sqrt{9x^2 + 5}\right| + C$$

5. Using formula 16 in Table 5 with $u = x$ and $a = 7$ yields

$$\int \frac{dx}{x^2 - 7^2} = \frac{1}{14}\ln\left|\frac{x-7}{x+7}\right| + C$$

7. Using formula 16 in Table 5 with $u = 5x$ and $a = 9$ yields $du = 5\,dx$ and

$$\int \frac{dx}{25x^2 - 81} = \frac{1}{5}\int \frac{5\,dx}{(5x)^2 - 9^2}$$

$$= \frac{1}{5}\left(\frac{1}{18}\ln\left|\frac{5x-9}{5x+9}\right|\right) + C$$

$$= \frac{1}{90}\ln\left|\frac{5x-9}{5x+9}\right| + C$$

9. Using formula 18 in Table 5 with $u = 7x$ yields $du = 7\,dx$ and

$$\int \frac{dx}{1 + e^{7x}} = \frac{1}{7}\int \frac{7\,dx}{1 + e^{7x}}$$

$$= \frac{1}{7}\left[7x - \ln\left(1 + e^{7x}\right)\right] + C$$

$$= x - \frac{1}{7}\ln\left(1 + e^{7x}\right) + C$$

11. Using formula 18 in Table 5 with $u = -4x$ yields $du = -4\,dx$ and

$$\int \frac{dx}{1 + e^{-4x}} = -\frac{1}{4}\int \frac{-4\,dx}{1 + e^{-4x}}$$

$$= -\frac{1}{4}\left[-4x - \ln\left(1 + e^{-4x}\right)\right] + C$$

$$= x + \frac{1}{4}\ln\left(1 + e^{-4x}\right) + C$$

13. Using formula 9 in Table 5 with $u = x$ and $a = 5$ yields

$$\int \frac{dx}{\sqrt{x^2 + 5^2}} = \ln\left|x + \sqrt{x^2 + 25}\right| + C$$

15. Using formula 9 in Table 5 with $u = 3x$ and $a = 4$ yields $du = 3\,dx$ and

$$\int \frac{dx}{\sqrt{9x^2 + 16}} = \frac{1}{3} \int \frac{3\,dx}{\sqrt{3x^2 + 4^2}}$$
$$= \frac{1}{3} \ln \left| 3x + \sqrt{9x^2 + 16} \right| + C$$

17. Using formula 13 in Table 5 with $u = x$ and $a = 1$ yields

$$\int \frac{dx}{x^2 \sqrt{x^2 + 1}} = -\frac{\sqrt{x^2 + 1}}{x} + C$$

19. Using formula 13 in Table 5 with $u = 2x$ and $a = \sqrt{3}$ yields $du = 2\,dx$ and

$$\int \frac{dx}{4x^2 \sqrt{4x^2 + 3}} = \frac{1}{2} \int \frac{2\,dx}{(2x)^2 \sqrt{(2x)^2 + (\sqrt{3})^2}}$$
$$= \frac{1}{2} \left[-\frac{\sqrt{4x^2 + 3}}{3(2x)} \right] + C$$
$$= -\frac{\sqrt{4x^2 + 3}}{12x} + C$$

21. Using formula 13 in Table 5 with $u = 2x$ and $a = \sqrt{3}$ yields $du = 2\,dx$ and

$$\int \frac{dx}{x^2 \sqrt{4x^2 + 3}} = \int \frac{4\,dx}{4x^2 \sqrt{4x^2 + 3}}$$
$$= \frac{4}{2} \int \frac{2\,dx}{(2x)^2 \sqrt{(2x)^2 + (\sqrt{3})^2}}$$
$$= 2 \left[-\frac{\sqrt{4x^2 + 3}}{3(2x)} \right] + C$$
$$= -\frac{\sqrt{4x^2 + 3}}{3x} + C$$

23. Using formula 16 in Table 5 with $u = x$ and $a = 3$ yields

$$\int \frac{dx}{x^2 - 9} = \frac{1}{6} \ln \left| \frac{x - 3}{x + 3} \right| + C$$

25. Using formula 16 in Table 5 with $u = 3x$ and $a = 1$ yields $du = 3\,dx$ and

$$\int \frac{dx}{9x^2 - 1} = \frac{1}{3} \int \frac{3\,dx}{(3x)^2 - 1}$$
$$= \frac{1}{3} \left(\frac{1}{2} \ln \left| \frac{3x - 1}{3x + 1} \right| \right) + C$$
$$= \frac{1}{6} \ln \left| \frac{3x - 1}{3x + 1} \right| + C$$

27. Using formula 17 in Table 5 with $u = x$ and $n = 2$ yields

$$\int x^2 \ln x\,dx = \frac{x^3}{3} \ln x - \frac{x^3}{9} + C$$

29. Using formula 17 in Table 5 with $u = x$ and $n = 5$ yields

$$\int x^5 \ln x\,dx = \frac{x^6}{6} \ln x - \frac{x^6}{36} + C$$

31. Using formula 11 in Table 5 with $u = x$ and $n = 1$ yields

$$\int \frac{dx}{x\sqrt{x^2+1}} = -\ln \left| \frac{1+\sqrt{x^2+1}}{x} \right| + C$$

33. Using formula 11 in Table 5 with $u = 2x$ and $a = 5$ yields $du = 2\,dx$ and

$$\int \frac{dx}{2x\sqrt{4x^2+25}} = \frac{1}{2} \int \frac{2\,dx}{2x\sqrt{(2x)^2+5^2}}$$

$$= \frac{1}{2} \left(-\frac{1}{5} \ln \left| \frac{5+\sqrt{4x^2+25}}{2x} \right| \right) + C$$

$$= -\frac{1}{10} \ln \left| \frac{5+\sqrt{4x^2+25}}{2x} \right| + C$$

35. Using formula 11 in Table 5 with $u = 3x$ and $a = 2$ yields $du = 3\,dx$ and

$$\int \frac{dx}{x\sqrt{9x^2+4}} = \int \frac{3\,dx}{3x\sqrt{(3x)^2+2^2}}$$

$$= -\frac{1}{2} \ln \left| \frac{2+\sqrt{9x^2+4}}{3x} \right| + C$$

37. Using reduction formula 19 in Table 5, repeatedly, yields

$$\int (\ln x)^3\,dx = x(\ln x)^3 - 3 \int (\ln x)^2\,dx$$

$$= x(\ln x)^3 - 3 \left[x(\ln x)^2 - 2 \int (\ln x)\,dx \right]$$

$$= x(\ln x)^3 - 3x(\ln x)^2 + 6 \int \ln x\,dx$$

$$= x(\ln x)^3 - 3x(\ln x)^2 + 6[x\ln x - \int dx]$$

$$= x(\ln x)^3 - 3x(\ln x)^2 + 6x\ln x - 6x + C$$

$$= x \left[(\ln x)^3 - 3(\ln x)^2 + 6\ln x - 6 \right] + C$$

39. Using reduction formula 19 in Table 5 with $n = 1$ yields

$$\int \ln x\,dx = x\ln x - \int dx$$

$$= x\ln x - x + C$$

41. Using reduction formula 20 in Table 5 yields

$$\int xe^x\,dx = xe^x - \int e^x\,dx$$

$$= xe^x - e^x + C$$

43. Using reduction formula 20 in Table 5, repeatedly, yields

$$\int x^2 e^x\,dx = x^2 e^x - 2 \int xe^x\,dx$$

$$= x^2 e^x - 2 \left(xe^x - \int e^x\,dx \right)$$

$$= x^2 e^x - 2xe^x + 2e^x + C$$

$$= \left(x^2 - 2x + 2 \right) e^x + C$$

45. The right-hand side of formula 18 in Table 5 is written $u - \ln(1+e^u) + C = \ln e^u - \ln(1+e^u) + C$ since $\ln e^u = u \ln e = u$, thus, using $\ln\left(\frac{P}{Q}\right) = \ln P - \ln Q$, one can write

$$u - \ln\left(1 + e^u\right) = \ln e^u - \ln(1 + e^u) = \ln\frac{e^u}{1 + e^u}$$

where $P = e^u$
$\qquad Q = 1 + e^u$

47. The average value of $f(x) = x^3 \ln x$ over the interval $[1,3]$ is given by the definite integral

$$\frac{1}{3-1}\int_1^3 x^3 \ln x \, dx = \frac{1}{2}\int_1^3 x^3 \ln x \, dx$$

Using formula 17 in Table 5 with $n = 3$ yields

$$
\begin{aligned}
\text{Average value} &= \frac{1}{2}\int_1^3 x^3 \ln x \, dx = \frac{1}{2}\left[\frac{x^4}{4}\ln x - \frac{x^4}{16}\right]_1^3 \\
&= \frac{1}{2}\left[\left(\frac{3^4}{4}\ln 3 - \frac{3^4}{16}\right) - \left(\frac{1}{4}\ln 1 - \frac{1}{16}\right)\right] \\
&= \frac{1}{2}\left(\frac{81}{4}\ln 3 - \frac{81}{16} + \frac{1}{16}\right) \\
&= \frac{1}{2}\left(\frac{81}{4}\ln 3 - 5\right)
\end{aligned}
$$

49. Sketch the graph of $y = \dfrac{3}{\sqrt{x^2-9}}$ and shade the area between $x = 5$ and $x = 7$ (see the figure). Use formula 10 in Table 5 to evaluate the integral.

$$
\begin{aligned}
A = \int_5^7 \frac{3\,dx}{\sqrt{x^2-9}} &= 3\left[\ln\left|x + \sqrt{x^2-9}\right|\right]_5^7 \\
&= 3\left[\ln(7 + \sqrt{40}) - \ln(5 + \sqrt{16})\right] \\
&= 3\left[\ln(7 + 2\sqrt{10}) - \ln 9\right] \\
&\approx 1.18
\end{aligned}
$$

SECTION 7.4 pages 395–397

1. For interval $[0,4]$ and $n = 4$,

$$\Delta x = \frac{4-0}{4} = 1$$

and $x_0 = 0$, $x_1 = 1$, $x_2 = 2$, $x_3 = 3$, $x_4 = 4$

3. For interval $[1,7]$ and $n = 6$,

$$\Delta x = \frac{7-1}{6} = 1$$

and $x_0 = 1, x_1 = 2, x_2 = 3, x_3 = 4, x_4 = 5, x_5 = 6, x_6 = 7$

5. For interval $[2, 5]$ and $n = 6$,

$$\Delta x = \frac{5 - 2}{6} = \frac{3}{6} = 0.5$$

and $x_0 = 2, x_1 = 2.5, x_2 = 3.0, x_3 = 3.5, x_4 = 4.0, x_5 = 4.5, x_6 = 5.0$

7. For interval $[2, 6]$ and $n = 8$,

$$\Delta x = \frac{6 - 2}{8} = \frac{4}{8} = 0.5$$

and $x_0 = 2, x_1 = 2.5, x_2 = 3.0, x_3 = 3.5, x_4 = 4.0, x_5 = 4.5, x_6 = 5.0, x_7 = 5.5, x_8 = 6.0$

9. For interval $[3, 5]$ and $n = 8$,

$$\Delta x = \frac{5 - 3}{8} = \frac{2}{8} = 0.25$$

and $x_0 = 3, x_1 = 3.25, x_2 = 3.50, x_3 = 3.75, x_4 = 4.00, x_5 = 4.25, x_6 = 4.50, x_7 = 4.75, x_8 = 5.0$

11. To use the trapezoidal rule on $\int_0^2 x^2 \, dx, n = 4$, let $f(x) = x^2, \Delta x = \frac{2-0}{4} = 0.5$, and $x_0 = 0, x_1 = 0.5, x_2 = 1.0, x_3 = 1.5$, and $x_4 = 2.0$.

Thus, $\displaystyle \int_0^2 x^2 \, dx = \frac{0.5}{2} \left[0^2 + 2(0.5)^2 + 2(1.0)^2 + 2(1.5)^2 + (2.0)^2 \right]$

$$= 2.75$$

13. To use the trapezoidal rule on $\int_0^3 \sqrt{x^2 + 1} \, dx, n = 6$, let $f(x) = \sqrt{x^2 + 1}, \Delta x = \frac{3-0}{6} = 0.5$, and $x_0 = 0, x_1 = 0.5, x_2 = 1.0, x_3 = 1.5, x_4 = 2.0, x_5 = 2.5$, and $x_6 = 3.0$.

Thus,

$$\int_0^3 \sqrt{x^2 + 1} \, dx = \frac{0.5}{2} \left[\sqrt{0^2 + 1} + 2\sqrt{(0.5)^2 + 1} + 2\sqrt{(1.0)^2 + 1} + 2\sqrt{(1.5)^2 + 1} + 2\sqrt{(2.0)^2 + 1} \right.$$
$$\left. + 2\sqrt{(2.5)^2 + 1} + \sqrt{(3.0)^2 + 1} \right]$$
$$= 5.6724$$

15. To use the trapezoidal rule on $\int_{-1}^5 \frac{1}{x+2} \, dx, n = 6$, let $f(x) = \frac{1}{x+2}, \Delta x = \frac{5-(-1)}{6} = 1$, and $x_0 = -1, x_1 = 0, x_2 = 1, x_3 = 2, x_4 = 3, x_5 = 4$, and $x_6 = 5$.

Thus,

$$\int_{-1}^5 \frac{1}{x+2} \, dx = \frac{1}{2} \left[\frac{1}{-1+2} + 2\left(\frac{1}{0+2}\right) + 2\left(\frac{1}{1+2}\right) + 2\left(\frac{1}{2+2}\right) + 2\left(\frac{1}{3+2}\right) + 2\left(\frac{1}{4+2}\right) + \frac{1}{5+2} \right]$$
$$= 2.0214$$

17. To use the trapezoidal rule on $\int_0^8 x\sqrt{x+1} \, dx, n = 4$, let $f(x) = x\sqrt{x+1}, \Delta x = \frac{8-0}{4} = 2$, and $x_0 = 0, x_1 = 2, x_2 = 4, x_3 = 6$, and $x_4 = 8$.

Thus $\displaystyle \int_0^8 x\sqrt{x+1} \, dx = \frac{2}{2} \left[0\sqrt{0+1} + 2(2\sqrt{2+1}) + 2(4\sqrt{4+1}) + 2(6\sqrt{6+1}) + 8\sqrt{8+1} \right]$

$$= 80.5658$$

19. To use the trapezoidal rule on $\int_1^5 \ln x \, dx, n = 4$, let $f(x) = \ln x, \Delta x = \frac{5-1}{4} = 1$, and $x_0 = 1, x_1 = 2, x_2 = 3, x_3 = 4$, and $x_4 = 5$.

Thus,

$$\int_1^5 \ln x \, dx = \frac{1}{2} \left(\ln 1 + 2\ln 2 + 2\ln 3 + 2\ln 4 + \ln 5 \right)$$
$$= 39,828$$

21. To use Simpson's rule on $\int_1^5 (x^2 + 3)\,dx, n = 4$, let $f(x) = x^2 + 3$, $\Delta x = \frac{5-1}{4} = 1$, and $x_0 = 1, x_1 = 2, x_2 = 3, x_3 = 4$, and $x_4 = 5$.

Thus,

$$\int_1^5 \left(x^2 + 3\right) dx = \frac{1}{3}\left[\left(1^2 + 3\right) + 4\left(2^2 + 3\right) + 2\left(3^2 + 3\right) + 4\left(4^2 + 3\right) + \left(5^2 + 3\right)\right]$$
$$= 53.3333$$

23. To use Simpson's rule on $\int_0^4 \sqrt{x^2 + 1}\,dx, n = 4$, let $f(x) = \sqrt{x^2 + 1}$, $\Delta x = \frac{4-0}{4} = 1$, and $x_0 = 0, x_1 = 1, x_2 = 2, x_3 = 3$, and $x_4 = 4$.

Thus,

$$\int_0^4 \sqrt{x^2 + 1}\,dx = \frac{1}{3}\left(\sqrt{0^2 + 1} + 4\sqrt{1^2 + 1} + 2\sqrt{2^2 + 1} + 4\sqrt{3^2 + 1} + \sqrt{4^2 + 1}\right)$$
$$= 9.3004$$

25. To use Simpson's rule on $\int_{-1}^2 \sqrt{x^3 + 1}\,dx, n = 6$, let $f(x) = \sqrt{x^3 + 1}$, $\Delta x = \frac{2-(-1)}{6} = 0.5$, and $x_0 = -1, x_1 = -0.5, x_2 = 0, x_3 = 0.5, x_4 = 1.0, x_5 = 1.5$, and $x_6 = 2.0$.

Thus,

$$\int_{-1}^2 \sqrt{x^3 + 1}\,dx = \frac{0.5}{3}\left(\sqrt{-1^3 + 1} + 4\sqrt{-0.5^3 + 1} + 2\sqrt{0^3 + 1} + 4\sqrt{0.5^3 + 1} + 2\sqrt{1^3 + 1} + 4\sqrt{1.5^3 + 1} + \sqrt{2^3 + 1}\right)$$
$$= 4.0299$$

27. To use Simpson's rule on $\int_0^2 \frac{1}{x+1}\,dx, n = 8$, let $f(x) = \frac{1}{x+1}$, $\Delta x = \frac{2-0}{8} = 0.25$, and $x_0 = 0, x_1 = 0.25, x_2 = 0.50, x_3 = 0.75, x_4 = 1.00, x_5 = 1.25, x_6 = 1.50, x_7 = 1.75$, and $x_8 = 2.00$.

Thus,

$$\int_0^2 \frac{1}{x+1}\,dx = \frac{0.25}{3}\left[\frac{1}{0+1} + 4\left(\frac{1}{0.25+1}\right) + 2\left(\frac{1}{0.5+1}\right) + 4\left(\frac{1}{0.75+1}\right) + 2\left(\frac{1}{1.00+1}\right) + 4\left(\frac{1}{1.25+1}\right)\right.$$
$$\left. + 2\left(\frac{1}{1.50+1}\right) + 4\left(\frac{1}{1.75+1}\right) + \left(\frac{1}{2.0+1}\right)\right]$$
$$= 1.0987$$

29. To use Simpson's rule on $\int_0^3 \frac{1}{1+e^x}\,dx, n = 6$, let $f(x) = \frac{1}{1+e^x}$, $\Delta x = \frac{3-0}{6} = 0.5$, and $x_0 = 0, x_1 = 0.5, x_2 = 1.0, x_3 = 1.5, x_4 = 2.0, x_5 = 2.5$, and $x_6 = 3.0$.

Thus,

$$\int_0^3 \frac{1}{1+e^x}\,dx = \frac{0.5}{3}\left[\frac{1}{1+e^0} + 4\left(\frac{1}{1+e^{0.5}}\right) + 2\left(\frac{1}{1+e^{1.0}}\right) + 4\left(\frac{1}{1+e^{1.5}}\right) + 2\left(\frac{1}{1+e^{2.0}}\right)\right.$$
$$\left. + 4\left(\frac{1}{1+e^{2.5}}\right) + \frac{1}{1+e^{3.0}}\right]$$
$$= 0.6445$$

31. To evaluate $\int_0^4 x^2\, dx, n = 4$, let $f(x) = x^2\, \Delta x = \frac{4-0}{4} = 1$, and $x_0 = 0, x_1 = 1, x_2 = 2, x_3 = 3$, and $x_4 = 4$.

   a. Trapezoidal rule:

$$\int_0^4 x^2\, dx = \frac{1}{2}\left[0^2 + 2(1)^2 + 2(2)^2 + 2(3)^2 + 4^2\right]$$
$$= 22$$

   b. Simpson's rule:

$$\int_0^4 x^2\, dx = \frac{1}{3}\left[0^2 + 4(1)^2 + 2(2)^2 + 4(3)^2 + 4^2\right]$$
$$= 21.3333$$

   c. Exact value: $\int_0^4 x^2\, dx = \left[\frac{x^3}{3}\right]_0^4 = \frac{64}{3}$

Simpson's rule gives the exact value in this case.

33. To evaluate $\int_1^4 x^3\, dx, n = 6$, let $f(x) = x^3, \Delta x = \frac{4-1}{6} = 0.5$, and $x_0 = 1, x_1 = 1.5, x_2 = 2.0, x_3 = 2.5, x_4 = 3.0, x_5 = 3.5$, and $x_6 = 4.0$.

   a. Trapezoidal rule:

$$\int_1^4 x^3\, dx = \frac{0.5}{2}\left[1^3 + 2(1.5)^3 + 2(2.0)^3 + 2(2.5)^3 + 2(3.0)^3 + 2(3.5)^3 + 4^3\right]$$
$$= 64.6875$$

   b. Simpson's rule:

$$\int_1^4 x^3\, dx = \frac{0.5}{3}\left[1^3 + 4(1.5)^3 + 2(2.0)^3 + 4(2.5)^3 + 2(3.0)^3 + 4(3.5)^3 + 4^3\right]$$
$$= 63.75$$

   c. Exact value:

$$\int_1^4 x^3\, dx = \left[\frac{x^4}{4}\right]_1^4 = \frac{1}{4}\left(4^4 - 1\right) = 63.75$$

Simpson's rule gives the exact value.

35. To evaluate $\int_1^4 \sqrt{x}\,dx, n = 6$, let $f(x) = \sqrt{x}, \Delta x = \frac{4-1}{6} = 0.5$, and $x_0 = 1, x_1 = 1.5, x_2 = 2.0, x_3 = 2.5, x_4 = 3.0, x_5 = 3.5$, and $x_6 = 4.0$.

   a. Trapezoidal rule:

$$\int_1^4 \sqrt{x}\,dx = \frac{0.5}{2}\left[\sqrt{1} + 2\sqrt{1.5} + 2\sqrt{2.0} + 2\sqrt{2.5} + 2\sqrt{3.0} + 2\sqrt{3.5} + \sqrt{4.0}\right]$$
$$= 4.6615$$

   b. Simpson's rule:

$$\int_1^4 \sqrt{x}\,dx = \frac{0.5}{3}\left[\sqrt{1} + 4\sqrt{1.5} + 2\sqrt{2.0} + 4\sqrt{2.5} + 2\sqrt{3.0} + 4\sqrt{3.5} + \sqrt{4.0}\right]$$
$$= 4.6666$$

   c. Exact value:

$$\int_1^4 \sqrt{x}\,dx = \int_1^4 x^{1/2}\,dx = \left[\frac{2}{3}x^{3/2}\right]_1^4$$
$$= \frac{2}{3}\left(4^{3/2} - 1^{3/2}\right)$$
$$= \frac{2}{3}(8 - 1)$$
$$= \frac{14}{3}$$

Simpson's rule is *almost* the exact value.

37. To evaluate $\int_0^1 xe^{x^2}\,dx, n = 4$, let $f(x) = xe^{x^2}, \Delta x = \frac{1-0}{4} = 0.25$, and $x_0 = 0, x_1 = 0.25, x_2 = 0.50, x_3 = 0.75$, and $x_4 = 1.0$.

   a. Trapezoidal rule:

$$\int_0^1 xe^{x^2}\,dx = \frac{0.25}{2}\left[0e^0 + 2\left(0.25e^{0.25^2}\right) + 2\left(0.5e^{0.5^2}\right) + 2\left(0.75e^{0.75^2}\right) + 1e^{1^2}\right]$$
$$= 0.8959$$

   b. Simpson's rule:

$$\int_0^1 xe^{x^2}\,dx = \frac{0.25}{3}\left[0e^0 + 4\left(0.25e^{0.25^2}\right) + 2\left(0.5e^{0.5^2}\right) + 4\left(0.75e^{0.75^2}\right) + 1e^{1^2}\right]$$
$$= 0.8610$$

   c. Exact value:

$$\int_0^1 xe^{x^2}\,dx = \frac{1}{2}\int_0^1 e^{x^2}2x\,dx = \frac{1}{2}\int_0^1 e^u\,du = \frac{1}{2}\left[e^u\right]_0^1$$
$$= \frac{1}{2}\left(e - e^0\right)$$
$$= \frac{1}{2}(e - 1)$$
$$\approx 0.8591$$

Let $u = x^2$ $u(0) = 0$
$du = 2x\,dx$ $u(1) = 1$

39. To evaluate $\int_0^2 x\sqrt{4-x^2}\,dx, n = 8$, let $f(x) = x\sqrt{4-x^2}, \Delta x = \frac{2-0}{8} = 0.25$, and $x_0 = 0, x_1 = 0.25, x_2 = 0.50, x_3 = 0.75, x_4 = 1.0, x_5 = 1.25, x_6 = 1.50, x_7 = 1.75$, and $x_8 = 2.0$.

a. Trapezoidal rule:

$$\int_0^2 x\sqrt{4-x^2}\,dx = \frac{0.25}{2}\left[0\sqrt{4-0^2} + 2(0.25\sqrt{4-0.25^2}) + 2(0.5\sqrt{4-0.5^2})\right.$$
$$+ 2(0.75\sqrt{4-0.75^2}) + 2(1.0\sqrt{4-1.0^2}) + 2(1.25\sqrt{4-1.25^2})$$
$$\left.+ 2(1.5\sqrt{4-15^2}) + 2(1.75\sqrt{4-1.75^2}) + 2\sqrt{4-2^2}\right]$$
$$= 2.5543$$

b. Simpson's rule:

$$\int_0^2 x\sqrt{4-x^2}\,dx = \frac{0.25}{3}\left[0\sqrt{4-0^2} + 4(0.25\sqrt{4-0.25^2}) + 2(0.5\sqrt{4-0.5^2})\right.$$
$$+ 4(0.75\sqrt{4-0.75^2}) + 2(1.0\sqrt{4-1.0^2}) + 4(1.25\sqrt{4-1.25^2}) + 2(1.5\sqrt{4-1.5^2})$$
$$\left.+ 4(1.75\sqrt{4-1.75^2}) + 2\sqrt{4-2^2}\right]$$
$$= 2.6250$$

c. Exact value:

$$\int_0^2 x\sqrt{4-x^2} = \frac{1}{2}\int_0^2 \sqrt{4-x^2}(2x\,dx) = \frac{1}{2}\int_0^4 u^{1/2}\,du = \frac{1}{3}\left[u^{3/2}\right]_0^4$$
$$= \frac{1}{3}\left(4^{3/2} - 0\right)$$
$$= \frac{8}{3} \approx 2.6667$$

Let $u = x^2$ $u(0) = 0$
$du = 2x\,dx$ $u(2) = 4$

41. The shaded area is determined by the definite integral $\int_0^2 \sqrt{4-x^2}\,dx$.

a. For the trapezoidal rule with $n = 4$, let $f(x) = \sqrt{4-x^2}, \Delta x = \frac{2-0}{4} = 0.5$, and $x_0 = 0, x_1 = 0.5, x_2 = 1.0, x_3 = 1.5$, and $x_4 = 2.0$.

$$\int_0^2 \sqrt{4-x^2}\,dx = \frac{0.5}{2}\left[\sqrt{4-0^2} + 2\sqrt{4-0.5^2} + 2\sqrt{4-1^2} + 2\sqrt{4-1.5^2} + \sqrt{4-2^2}\right]$$
$$= 2.9957$$

b. Simpson's rule with same conditions as in a.

$$\int_0^2 \sqrt{4-x^2}\,dx = \frac{0.5}{3}\left[\sqrt{4-0^2} + 4\sqrt{4-0.5^2} + 2\sqrt{4-1^2} + 4\sqrt{4-1.5^2} + \sqrt{4-2^2}\right]$$
$$= 3.0836$$

c. Using $A = \frac{\pi r^2}{4}$ with $r = 2$ and $\pi = 3.1416$,
$$A = 3.1416$$

43. Using the trapezoidal rule to approximate the area of the property shown, we have

$n = 4$, $x_0 = 0$, $x_1 = 50$, $x_2 = 100$, $x_3 = 150$, $x_4 = 200$, and $\Delta x = 50$

Then

$$\text{Area} \approx \frac{50}{2}[f(0) + 2f(50) + 2f(100) + 2f(150) + f(200)]$$

where we use $f(0) = 210$, $f(50) = 200$, $f(100) = 160$, $f(150) = 120$, and $f(200) = 90$ (i.e., the function f gives the width of the property at the point x along the base of the property). Hence

$\text{Area} \approx 25[210 + 2(200) + 2(160) + 2(120) + 90]$

$\qquad = 31{,}500$ square feet

45. Given $\int_0^2 x^4\,dx$, $n = 4$, then $f(x) = x^4$ and $f'(x) = 4x^3$, $f''(x) = 12x^2$, $f'''(x) = 24x$, and $f^{(4)}(x) = 24$.

a. Using the trapezoidal rule, the error estimate is $E \leq \frac{(2-0)^3}{12 \cdot 4^2} \cdot M$ where M is the maximum value of $\left|f''(x)\right|$ on the interval $[0, 2]$. Since $f''(x) = 12x^2$ is a parabola with minimum value at $x = 0$ and increasing for $x > 0$, the maximum value occurs at the endpoint $x = 2$. Thus, $M = \left|f''(2)\right| = |48|$ and $E \leq \frac{8}{12 \cdot 16}(48) = 2$. The maximum error is 2.0.

b. Using Simpson's rule, the error estimate is $E \leq \frac{(2-0)^5}{180 \cdot 4^4} \cdot M$ where M is the maximum value of $\left|f^{(4)}(x)\right|$ on the interval $[0, 2]$. Since $f^{(4)}(x) = 24$ is a constant, $M = 24$ and $E \leq \frac{32}{18 \cdot 4^4} \cdot 24 = \frac{1}{60} = 0.0167$

The maximum error is 0.0167.

47. Given $\int_1^2 \frac{1}{x}\,dx$, $n = 8$, then $f(x) = \frac{1}{x}$, $f'(x) = -\frac{1}{x^2}$, $f''(x) = \frac{2}{x^3}$, $f'''(x) = -\frac{6}{x^4}$, and $f^{(4)}(x) = \frac{24}{x^5}$.

a. Using the trapezoidal rule, the error estimate is $E \leq \frac{(2-1)^3}{12 \cdot 8^2} \cdot M$ where M is the maximum value of $\left|f''(x)\right|$ on the interval $[1, 2]$. Since $f''(x) = \frac{2}{x^3} > 0$ and is decreasing on the interval $[1, 2]$, the maximum value of $\left|f''(x)\right|$ occurs at the interval endpoint $x = 1$. Thus, $M = \left|f''(1)\right| = 2$ and $E \leq \frac{1}{12 \cdot 8^2} \cdot 2 = 0.0026$. The maximum error is 0.0026.

b. Using Simpson's rule, the error estimate is $E \leq \frac{(2-1)^5}{180 \cdot 8^4} \cdot M$ where M is the maximum value of $\left|f^{(4)}(x)\right|$ on the interval $[1, 2]$. Similar to the argument in part a, $\left|f^{(4)}(x)\right|$ has a maximum value at the interval endpoint $x = 1$. Thus, $M = \left|f^{(4)}(1)\right| = 24$ and $E \leq \frac{1}{180 \cdot 8^4} \cdot 24 = 0.00003$. The maximum error is 0.00003.

49. Given $\int_0^1 e^{-x}\,dx$, $n = 4$, then $f(x) = e^{-x}$, $f'(x) = -e^{-x}$, $f''(x) = e^{-x}$, $f'''(x) = -e^{-x}$ and $f^{(4)}(x) = e^{-x}$.

a. Using the trapezoidal rule, the error estimate is $E \leq \frac{(1-0)^3}{12 \cdot 4^2} \cdot M$ where M is the maximum value of $\left|f''(x)\right|$ on the interval $[0, 1]$. Since $f''(x) = e^{-x} > 0$ and is decreasing on the interval $[0, 1]$, the maximum value of $\left|f''(x)\right|$ occurs at the interval endpoint $x = 0$. Thus, $M = \left|f''(0)\right| = 2$ and $E \leq \frac{1}{12 \cdot 4^2} \cdot 1 = 0.0052$. The maximum error is 0.0052.

b. Using Simpson's rule, the error estimate is $E \leq \frac{(1-0)^5}{180 \cdot 4^4} \cdot M$ where M is the maximum value of $\left|f^{(4)}(x)\right|$ on the interval $[0, 1]$. Identical to the argument in part a, $M = 1$. Thus, $E \leq \frac{1}{180 \cdot 4^4} \cdot 1 = 0.00002$. The maximum error is 0.00002.

51. To determine how large n must be so that the trapezoidal approximation of $\int_1^3 \frac{1}{x^2}\,dx$ generates an error $E \leq 0.001$, first find M. Since $f(x) = \frac{1}{x^2}$, then $f''(x) = \frac{6}{x^4}$ and on the interval $[1, 3]$, $M = \left|f''(1)\right| = 6$. It follows that $E = \frac{(3-1)^3}{12 \cdot n^2} \cdot 6 = 0.001$ and solving for n^2 yields $n^2 = \frac{8 \cdot 6}{12(0.001)}$

$$n \geq 64$$

53. To determine how large n must be so that the trapezoidal approximation of $\int_0^2 x^4\,dx$ generates an error $E \leq 0.0001$, first find M. Since $f(x) = x^4$, then $f''(x) = 12x^2$, and on the interval $[0, 2]$, $M = \left|f''(2)\right| = 48$. It follows that $E = \frac{(2-0)^3}{12 \cdot n^2} \cdot 48 = 0.0001$ and solving for n^2 yields $n^2 = \frac{8 \cdot 48}{12(0.0001)}$

$$n \geq 566$$

55. The function, $f(x) = x^2$, in Exercise 37 is a parabola. Since Simpson's rule approximates the definite integral by using parabolic segments, it yielded the exact value.

SECTION 7.4 Technology Exercises

1. **a.** For $n = 4$, area $= 3.9828$, which is the same result as Exercise 19.

   b.

n	Area
12	4.039815165
20	4.044527255
50	4.046763008
100	4.047082903

   For $n = 100$, the answer is correct to 3 decimal places.

3. **a.** For $n = 8$, area $= 1.0987$, which is the same result as in Exercise 27.

   b.

n	Area
12	1.098636168
20	1.098615505
50	1.098612373

   Note that for $n = 5$, the answer is correct to 6 decimal places.

5. Exact answer is $\dfrac{\tan^{-1}\left(\frac{1}{2}\right)}{4} \approx 0.11591190225$.

   b.

n	Area
4	0.1157032557
10	0.1158785609
20	0.1159035684
50	0.1159105689
60	0.1159109763
70	0.115911222
80	0.1159113814
170	0.1159117869
190	0.1159118099
200	0.1159118189
300	0.1159118652
400	0.1159118814
550	0.1159118912
980	0.1159118988
1000	0.1159118989
1500	0.1159119008

7. Exact answer is $\dfrac{\ln\left(\frac{3}{2}\right)}{2} \approx 0.202732554054$.

n	Area
4	0.2098214286
1000	0.202732671
1200	0.2027326352
1300	0.2027326232
1400	0.2027326137
1450	0.2027326097
1470	0.2027326082
1490	0.2027326067
1500	0.202732606
1600	0.2027325997

9. Exact answer $= \ln(2\sqrt{10} + 7) - 2\ln(3) \approx 0.392384020327$.

n	Area
4	0.3934297415
1000	0.3923840371

SECTION 7.5 pages 404–406

1. $\displaystyle\lim_{b \to \infty} \frac{1}{b^2} = 0$

3. $\displaystyle\lim_{a \to -\infty} \frac{2}{a} = 0$

5. $\displaystyle\lim_{b \to \infty} \sqrt{b+1} = \infty$

7. $\displaystyle\lim_{b \to \infty} \frac{1}{\sqrt{2b}} = 0$

9. $\displaystyle\lim_{b \to \infty} (b^{1/2} + 1) = \infty$

11. $\displaystyle\lim_{b \to \infty} \ln b = \infty$

13. $\displaystyle\lim_{b \to \infty} e^b = \infty$

15. $\displaystyle\lim_{a \to -\infty} (e^a + 3) = \lim_{a \to -\infty} e^a + 3 = 0 + 3 = 3$

17. $\displaystyle\lim_{b\to\infty} b^3 = \infty$

19. $\displaystyle\lim_{a\to-\infty} \frac{1}{e^a} = \infty$

21. $\displaystyle\lim_{b\to\infty}\left(2 - \frac{1}{\sqrt{b}}\right) = 2 - \lim_{b\to\infty}\frac{1}{\sqrt{b}} = 2 - 0 = 2$

23. $\displaystyle\int_1^\infty \frac{1}{x^3}\,dx = \lim_{b\to\infty}\left(\int_1^b x^{-3}\,dx\right)$

$\displaystyle\qquad\qquad = \lim_{b\to\infty}\left[-\frac{1}{2}x^{-2}\right]_1^b$

$\displaystyle\qquad\qquad = \lim_{b\to\infty}\left(-\frac{1}{2b^2} + \frac{1}{2}\right)$

$\displaystyle\qquad\qquad = 0 + \frac{1}{2}$

$\displaystyle\qquad\qquad = \frac{1}{2}$

25. $\displaystyle\int_1^\infty x^{-4}\,dx = \lim_{b\to\infty}\left(\int_1^b x^{-4}\,dx\right)$

$\displaystyle\qquad\qquad = \lim_{b\to\infty}\left[-\frac{1}{3}x^{-3}\right]_1^b$

$\displaystyle\qquad\qquad = \lim_{b\to\infty}\left[-\frac{1}{3}\cdot\frac{1}{b^3} + \frac{1}{3}(1)\right]$

$\displaystyle\qquad\qquad = 0 + \frac{1}{3}$

$\displaystyle\qquad\qquad = \frac{1}{3}$

27. $\displaystyle\int_1^\infty \frac{1}{2x}\,dx = \frac{1}{2}\lim_{b\to\infty}\left(\int_1^b \frac{1}{x}\,dx\right)$

$\displaystyle\qquad\qquad = \frac{1}{2}\lim_{b\to\infty}[\ln x]_1^b$

$\displaystyle\qquad\qquad = \frac{1}{2}\lim_{b\to\infty}(\ln b - \ln 1)$

$\displaystyle\qquad\qquad = \infty \qquad \text{divergent}$

29. $\displaystyle\int_1^\infty \frac{1}{\sqrt{x}}\,dx = \lim_{b\to\infty}\left(\int_1^b x^{-1/2}\,dx\right)$

$\displaystyle\qquad\qquad = \lim_{b\to\infty}\left[2x^{1/2}\right]_1^b$

$\displaystyle\qquad\qquad = \lim_{b\to\infty}\left(2b^{1/2} - 2\right)$

$\displaystyle\qquad\qquad = \infty \qquad \text{divergent}$

31. $\displaystyle\int_0^\infty e^x\,dx = \lim_{b\to\infty}\left(\int_0^b e^x\,dx\right)$

$\displaystyle\qquad\qquad = \lim_{b\to\infty}\left[e^x\right]_0^b$

$\displaystyle\qquad\qquad = \lim_{b\to\infty}\left(e^b - 1\right)$

$\displaystyle\qquad\qquad = \infty \qquad \text{divergent}$

33. $\displaystyle\int_1^\infty e^{-x}\,dx = \lim_{b\to\infty}\left(\int_1^b e^{-x}\,dx\right)$

$\displaystyle\qquad\qquad = \lim_{b\to\infty}\left[-e^{-x}\right]_1^b$

$\displaystyle\qquad\qquad = \lim_{b\to\infty}\left(-e^{-b} + e^{-1}\right)$

$\displaystyle\qquad\qquad = 0 + \frac{1}{e}$

$\displaystyle\qquad\qquad = \frac{1}{e}$

35. $\displaystyle\int_0^\infty \frac{dx}{x+1} = \lim_{b\to\infty}\left(\int_0^b \frac{1}{x+1}\,dx\right)$

$\displaystyle\qquad\qquad = \lim_{b\to\infty}\left[\ln|x+1|\right]_0^b$

$\displaystyle\qquad\qquad = \lim_{b\to\infty}\left[\ln(b+1) - \ln 1\right]$

$\displaystyle\qquad\qquad = \infty \qquad \text{divergent}$

37. $\displaystyle\int_0^\infty \sqrt{2x+9}\,dx = \lim_{b\to\infty}\left[\int_0^b (2x+9)^{1/2}\,dx\right]$

Let $u = 2x + 9$

$du = 2\,dx$

$\displaystyle = \lim_{b\to\infty}\left[\frac{1}{2}\int_0^b (2x+9)^{1/2}2\,dx\right]$

$\displaystyle = \lim_{b\to\infty}\left[\left(\frac{1}{2}\right)\left(\frac{2}{3}\right)(2x+9)^{3/2}\right]_0^b$

$\displaystyle = \lim_{b\to\infty}\left[\frac{1}{3}(2b+9)^{3/2} - \frac{1}{3}(9)^{3/2}\right]$

$= \infty \quad$ divergent

39. $\displaystyle\int_0^\infty \frac{x}{1+x^2}\,dx = \lim_{b\to\infty}\left(\int_0^b \frac{x}{1+x^2}\,dx\right)$

Let $u = 1 + x^2$

$du = 2x\,dx$

$\displaystyle = \lim_{b\to\infty}\left(\frac{1}{2}\int_0^b \frac{1}{1+x^2}2x\,dx\right)$

$\displaystyle = \lim_{b\to\infty}\left[\frac{1}{2}\ln(1+x^2)\right]_0^b$

$\displaystyle = \lim_{b\to\infty}\left[\frac{1}{2}\ln(1+b^2) - \ln 1\right]$

$\displaystyle = \lim_{b\to\infty}\frac{1}{2}\ln(1+b^2)$

$= \infty \quad$ divergent

41. $\displaystyle\int_1^\infty \frac{\ln x}{x}\,dx = \lim_{b\to\infty}\left(\int_1^b \frac{\ln x}{x}\,dx\right)$

Let $u = \ln x$

$du = \frac{1}{x}\,dx$

$\displaystyle = \lim_{b\to\infty}\left[\int_1^b \ln x\left(\frac{1}{x}\,dx\right)\right]$

$\displaystyle = \lim_{b\to\infty}\left[\frac{(\ln x)^2}{2}\right]_1^b$

$\displaystyle = \lim_{b\to\infty}\left[\frac{(\ln b)^2}{2} - \frac{(\ln 1)^2}{2}\right]$

$\displaystyle = \lim_{b\to\infty}\frac{(\ln b)^2}{2}$

$= \infty \quad$ divergent

43. $\displaystyle\int_0^\infty e^{-x/2}\,dx = \lim_{b\to\infty}\left(\int_0^b e^{-x/2}\,dx\right)$

$\displaystyle = \lim_{b\to\infty}\left[-2e^{-x/2}\right]_0^b$

$\displaystyle = \lim_{b\to\infty}\left(-2e^{-b/2} + 2e^0\right)$

$= 0 + 2$

$= 2$

45.   Sketch the graph of $y = e^{-x}$ and shade the indicated area.

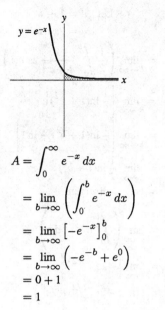

$$A = \int_0^\infty e^{-x}\, dx$$

$$= \lim_{b \to \infty} \left(\int_0^b e^{-x}\, dx \right)$$

$$= \lim_{b \to \infty} \left[-e^{-x} \right]_0^b$$

$$= \lim_{b \to \infty} \left(-e^{-b} + e^0 \right)$$

$$= 0 + 1$$

$$= 1$$

47.   Sketch the graph of $y = x^{-3}$ and shade the indicated area.

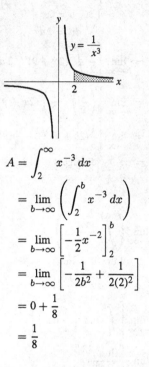

$$A = \int_2^\infty x^{-3}\, dx$$

$$= \lim_{b \to \infty} \left(\int_2^b x^{-3}\, dx \right)$$

$$= \lim_{b \to \infty} \left[-\frac{1}{2} x^{-2} \right]_2^b$$

$$= \lim_{b \to \infty} \left[-\frac{1}{2b^2} + \frac{1}{2(2)^2} \right]$$

$$= 0 + \frac{1}{8}$$

$$= \frac{1}{8}$$

49.   Sketch the graph of $y = \frac{1}{(x-1)^2}$ and shade the indicated area.

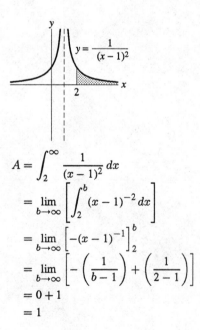

$$A = \int_2^\infty \frac{1}{(x-1)^2}\, dx$$

$$= \lim_{b \to \infty} \left[\int_2^b (x-1)^{-2}\, dx \right]$$

$$= \lim_{b \to \infty} \left[-(x-1)^{-1} \right]_2^b$$

$$= \lim_{b \to \infty} \left[-\left(\frac{1}{b-1} \right) + \left(\frac{1}{2-1} \right) \right]$$

$$= 0 + 1$$

$$= 1$$

51.   The total amount of waste that will be dumped into the lake is given by the improper integral

$$\int_0^\infty 5e^{-0.1t} = \lim_{b \to \infty} \left(5 \int_0^b e^{-0.1t}\, dt \right)$$

$$= 5 \lim_{b \to \infty} \left[-\frac{1}{0.1} e^{-0.1t} \right]_0^b$$

$$= 5 \lim_{b \to \infty} \left(-10e^{-0.1b} + 10e^0 \right)$$

$$= 5(0 + 10)$$

$$= 50 \text{ pounds}$$

53. The total amount received by the investor is given by the improper integral

$$\int_0^\infty 4000 e^{-0.08t}\, dt = \lim_{b\to\infty} \left(4000 \int_0^b e^{-0.08t}\, dt \right)$$

$$= 4000 \lim_{b\to\infty} \left[-\frac{1}{0.08} e^{-0.08t} \right]_0^b$$

$$= 4000 \lim_{b\to\infty} \left(-12.5 e^{-0.08b} + 12.5 e^0 \right)$$

$$= 4000(0 + 12.5)$$

$$= \$50,000$$

55. Given the annual rent of \$6390 and the annual interest rate of 9%, the capital value is given by the improper integral.

$$\int_0^\infty 6390 e^{-0.09t}\, dt = \lim_{b\to\infty} \left(6390 \int_0^b e^{-0.09t}\, dt \right)$$

$$= 6390 \lim_{b\to\infty} \left[-\frac{1}{0.09} e^{-0.09t} \right]_0^b$$

$$= \frac{6390}{-0.09} \lim_{b\to\infty} \left(e^{-0.09b} - e^0 \right)$$

$$= -71,000(0 - 1)$$

$$= \$71,000$$

The capital value is \$71,000.

57.

$$\int_{-\infty}^{-1} \frac{1}{x^3}\, dx = \lim_{a\to-\infty} \left(\int_a^{-1} x^{-3}\, dx \right)$$

$$= \lim_{a\to-\infty} \left[-\frac{1}{2} x^{-2} \right]_a^{-1}$$

$$= \lim_{a\to-\infty} \left(-\frac{1}{2} + \frac{1}{2} \cdot \frac{1}{a^2} \right)$$

$$= -\frac{1}{2} + 0$$

$$= -\frac{1}{2}$$

59.

$$\int_{-\infty}^{0} e^{3x}\, dx = \lim_{a\to-\infty} \left(\int_a^0 e^{3x}\, dx \right)$$

$$= \lim_{a\to-\infty} \left[\frac{1}{3} e^{3x} \right]_a^0$$

$$= \frac{1}{3} \lim_{a\to-\infty} \left(e^0 - e^{3a} \right)$$

$$= \frac{1}{3}(1 - 0)$$

$$= \frac{1}{3}$$

61.

$$\int_{-\infty}^{0} e^{-2x}\, dx = \lim_{a\to-\infty} \left(\int_a^0 e^{-2x}\, dx \right)$$

$$= \lim_{a\to-\infty} \left[-\frac{1}{2} e^{-2x} \right]_a^0$$

$$= -\frac{1}{2} \lim_{a\to-\infty} \left(e^0 - e^{-2a} \right)$$

$$= \infty \quad \text{divergent}$$

63.

$$\int_{-\infty}^{0} \frac{x}{1+x^2}\, dx = \lim_{a\to-\infty} \left(\int_a^0 \frac{x}{1+x^2}\, dx \right)$$

$$\text{Let} \quad u = 1 + x^2$$

$$du = 2x\, dx$$

$$= \lim_{a\to-\infty} \left[\frac{1}{2} \int_a^0 \frac{1}{1+x^2}(2x\, dx) \right]$$

$$= \frac{1}{2} \lim_{a\to-\infty} \left[\ln(1+x^2) \right]_a^0$$

$$= \frac{1}{2} \lim_{a\to-\infty} \ln(1) - \ln(1 + a^2)$$

$$= \frac{1}{2} \lim_{a\to-\infty} \ln(1 + a^2)$$

$$= -\infty \quad \text{divergent}$$

65. $\displaystyle\int_{-\infty}^{0} \frac{dx}{(x-2)^3} = \lim_{a\to-\infty}\left[\int_{a}^{0}(x-2)^{-3}\,dx\right]$

$\displaystyle = \lim_{a\to-\infty}\left[-\frac{1}{2}(x-2)^{-2}\right]_{a}^{0}$

$\displaystyle = -\frac{1}{2}\lim_{a\to-\infty}\left[(0-2)^{-2}-(a-2)^{-2}\right]$

$\displaystyle = -\frac{1}{2}\lim_{a\to-\infty}\left[\frac{1}{4}-\frac{1}{(a-2)^2}\right]$

$\displaystyle = -\frac{1}{2}\left(\frac{1}{4}-0\right)$

$\displaystyle = -\frac{1}{8}$

67. $\displaystyle\int_{-\infty}^{-2} \frac{dx}{(4-x)^2} = \lim_{a\to-\infty}\left[\int_{a}^{-2}(4-x)^{-2}\,dx\right]$

Let $u = 4-x$

$\qquad du = -dx$

$\displaystyle = \lim_{a\to-\infty}\left[-\int_{a}^{-2}(4-x)^{-2}(-dx)\right]$

$\displaystyle = -\lim_{a\to-\infty}\left[\frac{1}{-1}(4-x)^{-1}\right]_{a}^{-2}$

$\displaystyle = \lim_{a\to-\infty}\left[\frac{1}{4-x}\right]_{a}^{-2}$

$\displaystyle = \lim_{a\to-\infty}\left(\frac{1}{4+2}-\frac{1}{4-a}\right)$

$\displaystyle = \frac{1}{6}-0$

$\displaystyle = \frac{1}{6}$

69. Sketch the graph of $y = e^x$ and shade the indicated area.

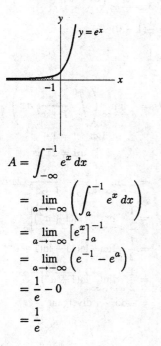

$\displaystyle A = \int_{-\infty}^{-1} e^x\,dx$

$\displaystyle = \lim_{a\to-\infty}\left(\int_{a}^{-1} e^x\,dx\right)$

$\displaystyle = \lim_{a\to-\infty}\left[e^x\right]_{a}^{-1}$

$\displaystyle = \lim_{a\to-\infty}\left(e^{-1}-e^a\right)$

$\displaystyle = \frac{1}{e}-0$

$\displaystyle = \frac{1}{e}$

71. Sketch the graph of $y = \frac{1}{(x-1)^2}$ and shade the indicated area.

$y = \dfrac{1}{(x-1)^2}$

$x = 1$

$\displaystyle A = \int_{-\infty}^{-2} \frac{1}{(x-1)^2}\,dx$

$\displaystyle = \lim_{a\to-\infty}\left[\int_{a}^{-2}(x-1)^{-2}\,dx\right]$

$\displaystyle = \lim_{a\to-\infty}\left[-(x-1)^{-1}\right]_{a}^{-2}$

$\displaystyle = \lim_{a\to-\infty}\left[-(-3)^{-1}+(a-1)^{-1}\right]$

$\displaystyle = \lim_{a\to-\infty}\left(\frac{1}{3}+\frac{1}{a-1}\right)$

$\displaystyle = \frac{1}{3}+0$

$\displaystyle = \frac{1}{3}$

73. Sketch the graph of $y = \frac{1}{x^3}$ and shade the indicated area.

Since the area lies below the x axis, the function $y = -\frac{1}{x^3}$ must be used to compute the area.

$$A = \int_{-\infty}^{-4} -\frac{1}{x^3}\, dx$$

$$= \lim_{a \to -\infty} \left(\int_{a}^{-4} -\frac{1}{x^3}\, dx \right)$$

$$= -\lim_{a \to -\infty} \left(\int_{a}^{-4} x^{-3}\, dx \right)$$

$$= -\lim_{a \to -\infty} \left[-\frac{1}{2}x^{-2} \right]_{a}^{-4}$$

$$= \frac{1}{2} \lim_{a \to -\infty} \left[(-4)^{-2} - a^{-2} \right]$$

$$= \frac{1}{2} \lim_{a \to -\infty} \left(\frac{1}{16} - \frac{1}{a^2} \right)$$

$$= \frac{1}{2} \left(\frac{1}{16} - 0 \right)$$

$$= \frac{1}{32}$$

75.
$$\int_{-\infty}^{\infty} x\, dx = \int_{-\infty}^{0} x\, dx + \int_{0}^{\infty} x\, dx$$

$$= \lim_{a \to -\infty} \left(\int_{a}^{0} x\, dx \right) + \lim_{b \to \infty} \left(\int_{0}^{b} x\, dx \right)$$

$$= \lim_{a \to -\infty} \left[\frac{1}{2}x^2 \right]_{a}^{0} + \lim_{b \to \infty} \left[\frac{1}{2}x^2 \right]_{0}^{b}$$

$$= \lim_{a \to -\infty} \left(0 - \frac{1}{2}a^2 \right) + \lim_{b \to \infty} \left(\frac{1}{2}b^2 - 0 \right)$$

$$= \infty \quad \text{divergent}$$

77.
$$\int_{-\infty}^{\infty} e^{-x}\, dx = \int_{-\infty}^{0} e^{-x}\, dx + \int_{0}^{\infty} e^{-x}\, dx$$

$$= \lim_{a \to -\infty} \left(\int_{a}^{0} e^{-x}\, dx \right) + \lim_{b \to \infty} \left(\int_{0}^{b} e^{-x}\, dx \right)$$

$$= \lim_{a \to -\infty} \left[-e^{-x} \right]_{a}^{0} + \lim_{b \to \infty} \left[-e^{-x} \right]_{0}^{b}$$

$$= \lim_{a \to -\infty} \left(-e^{0} + e^{-a} \right) + \lim_{b \to \infty} \left(-e^{-b} + e^{0} \right)$$

$$= \infty + (0 + 1)$$

$$= \infty \qquad \text{divergent}$$

Note: Although $\int_{0}^{\infty} e^{-x}\, dx$ converges, the other integral, $\int_{-\infty}^{0} e^{-x}\, dx$, diverges.

79.

$$\int_{-\infty}^{\infty} x^2 e^{-x^3}\, dx = \int_{-\infty}^{0} x^2 e^{-x^3}\, dx + \int_{0}^{\infty} x^2 e^{-x^3}\, dx$$

$$= \lim_{a \to -\infty} \left(\int_{a}^{0} x^2 e^{-x^3}\, dx \right) + \lim_{b \to \infty} \left(\int_{0}^{b} x^2 e^{-x^3}\, dx \right)$$

$$\text{Let } u = -x^3$$
$$du = -3x^2\, dx$$

$$= \lim_{a \to -\infty} \left[-\frac{1}{3} \int_{a}^{0} e^{-x^3} (-3x^2\, dx) \right] + \lim_{b \to \infty} \left[-\frac{1}{3} \int_{0}^{b} e^{-x^3} \left(-3x^2\, dx \right) \right]$$

$$= -\frac{1}{3} \lim_{a \to -\infty} \left[e^{-x^3} \right]_{a}^{0} - \frac{1}{3} \lim_{b \to \infty} \left[e^{-x^3} \right]_{0}^{b}$$

$$= -\frac{1}{3} \lim_{a \to -\infty} \left(e^0 - e^{-a^3} \right) - \frac{1}{3} \lim_{b \to \infty} \left(e^{-b^3} - e^0 \right)$$

$$= -\frac{1}{3}(1 - \infty) - \frac{1}{3}(0 - 1)$$

$$= \infty \qquad \text{divergent}$$

81.

$$\int_{-\infty}^{\infty} \frac{x}{\left(1 + x^2\right)^2}\, dx = \int_{-\infty}^{0} \frac{x}{\left(1 + x^2\right)^2}\, dx + \int_{0}^{\infty} \frac{x}{\left(1 + x^2\right)^2}\, dx$$

$$= \lim_{a \to -\infty} \left[\int_{a}^{0} \frac{x}{\left(1 + x^2\right)^2}\, dx \right] + \lim_{b \to \infty} \left[\int_{0}^{b} \frac{x}{\left(1 + x^2\right)^2}\, dx \right]$$

$$\text{Let } u = 1 + x^2$$
$$du = 2x\, dx$$

$$= \lim_{a \to -\infty} \left[\frac{1}{2} \int_{a}^{0} \left(1 + x^2\right)^{-2} (2x\, dx) \right] + \lim_{b \to \infty} \left[\frac{1}{2} \int_{0}^{b} \left(1 + x^2\right)^{-2} (2x\, dx) \right]$$

$$= \frac{1}{2} \lim_{a \to -\infty} \left[-\left(1 + x^2\right)^{-1} \right]_{a}^{0} + \frac{1}{2} \lim_{b \to \infty} \left[-\left(1 + x^2\right)^{-1} \right]_{0}^{b}$$

$$= \frac{1}{2} \lim_{a \to -\infty} \left(-\frac{1}{1} + \frac{1}{1 + a^2} \right) + \frac{1}{2} \lim_{b \to \infty} \left(-\frac{1}{1 + b^2} + \frac{1}{1} \right)$$

$$= \frac{1}{2}(-1 + 0) + \frac{1}{2}(0 + 1)$$

$$= -\frac{1}{2} + \frac{1}{2}$$

$$= 0$$

83.

$$\int_{-\infty}^{\infty} x e^{-2x^2}\, dx = \int_{-\infty}^{0} x e^{-2x^2}\, dx + \int_{0}^{\infty} x e^{-2x^2}\, dx$$

$$= \lim_{a \to -\infty} \left(\int_{a}^{0} x e^{-2x^2}\, dx \right) + \lim_{b \to \infty} \left(\int_{0}^{b} x e^{-2x^2}\, dx \right)$$

$$\text{Let } u = -2x^2$$
$$du = -4x\, dx$$

$$= \lim_{a \to -\infty} \left[-\frac{1}{4} \int_{a}^{0} e^{-2x^2} (-4x\, dx) \right] + \lim_{b \to \infty} \left[-\frac{1}{4} \int_{0}^{b} e^{-2x^2} (-4x\, dx) \right]$$

$$= -\frac{1}{4} \lim_{a \to -\infty} \left[e^{-2x^2} \right]_{a}^{0} - \frac{1}{4} \lim_{b \to \infty} \left[e^{-2x^2} \right]_{0}^{b}$$

$$= -\frac{1}{4} \lim_{a \to -\infty} \left(e^0 - e^{-2a^2} \right) - \frac{1}{4} \lim_{b \to \infty} \left(e^{-2b^2} - e^0 \right)$$

$$= -\frac{1}{4}(1 - 0) - \frac{1}{4}(0 - 1)$$

$$= -\frac{1}{4} + \frac{1}{4}$$

$$= 0$$

85. $\displaystyle\int_{-\infty}^{\infty} \frac{x}{\sqrt{x^2+1}}\,dx = \int_{-\infty}^{0} \frac{x}{\sqrt{x^2+1}}\,dx + \left(\int_{0}^{\infty} \frac{x}{\sqrt{x^2+1}}\,dx \right)$

$\displaystyle = \lim_{a \to -\infty} \left(\int_{a}^{0} \frac{x}{\sqrt{x^2+1}}\,dx \right) + \lim_{b \to \infty} \left(\int_{0}^{b} \frac{x}{\sqrt{x^2+1}}\,dx \right)$

Let $u = x^2 + 1$

$du = 2x\,dx$

$\displaystyle = \lim_{a \to -\infty} \left[\frac{1}{2} \int_{a}^{0} \left(x^2+1 \right)^{-1/2} (2x\,dx) \right] + \lim_{b \to \infty} \left[\frac{1}{2} \int_{0}^{b} \left(x^2+1 \right)^{-1/2} (2x\,dx) \right]$

$\displaystyle = \frac{1}{2} \lim_{a \to -\infty} \left[2 \left(x^2+1 \right)^{1/2} \right]_{a}^{0} + \frac{1}{2} \lim_{b \to \infty} \left[2 \left(x^2+1 \right)^{1/2} \right]_{0}^{b}$

$\displaystyle = \frac{2}{2} \lim_{a \to -\infty} \left[1 - \left(a^2+1 \right)^{1/2} \right] + \frac{2}{2} \lim_{b \to \infty} \left[\left(b^2+1 \right)^{1/2} - 1 \right]$

$= (1 - \infty) + (\infty - 1)$

$\displaystyle\int_{-\infty}^{\infty} \frac{x}{\sqrt{x^2+1}}\,dx$ is divergent

Note: Both improper integrals are divergent, but $\infty - \infty \neq 0$.

87. Since $\int_{1}^{\infty} \frac{1}{x^2}\,dx = 1$, the area is one square unit.

89. Gabriel's horn has volume given by

$\displaystyle\int_{1}^{\infty} \pi \left(\frac{1}{x} \right)^2 dx = \pi \int_{1}^{\infty} x^{-2}\,dx$

$\displaystyle = \pi \lim_{b \to \infty} \int_{1}^{b} x^{-2}\,dx$

$\displaystyle = \pi \lim_{b \to \infty} \left[\frac{-1}{x} \right]_{1}^{b}$

$\displaystyle = \pi \lim_{b \to \infty} \left[\frac{-1}{b} - \frac{(-1)}{1} \right]$

$= \pi (0 + 1)$

$= \pi$

SECTION 7.5 Technology Exercises

1.

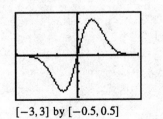

$[-3, 3]$ by $[-0.5, 0.5]$

The graph is clearly symmetric with respect to the origin $[f(-x) = -f(x)]$, so the integral can be written as

$\displaystyle\int_{-\infty}^{\infty} xe^{-x^2}\,dx = \int_{-\infty}^{0} xe^{-x^2}\,dx + \int_{0}^{\infty} xe^{-x^2}\,dx$

$\displaystyle = -\int_{0}^{\infty} xe^{-x^2}\,dx + \int_{0}^{\infty} xe^{-x^2}\,dx$

$= 0$

REVIEW EXERCISES FOR CHAPTER 7 pages 407–408

1.
$$\int x\sqrt{1+x^2}\,dx = \frac{1}{2}\int\left(1+x^2\right)^{1/2}2x\,dx$$
$$= \frac{1}{2}\left(\frac{2}{3}\right)\left(1+x^2\right)^{3/2}+C$$
$$= \frac{1}{3}\left(1+x^2\right)^{3/2}+C$$

Let $u = 1+x^2$
$du = 2x\,dx$

3.   Use formula 7 in Table 5 with $u = x, a = 1,$ and $b = 2.$

$$\int\frac{x\,dx}{\sqrt{1+2x}} = \frac{2(2x-2)}{3\cdot2^2}\sqrt{1+2x}+C$$
$$= \frac{x-1}{3}\sqrt{1+2x}+C$$

5. $\displaystyle\int(x-2)^3\,dx = \frac{1}{4}(x-2)^4+C$

$u = x-2$
$du = dx$

7.   Use integration by parts.

Let $u = x \rightarrow du = dx$

$$dv = (x-2)^3\,dx \rightarrow v = \frac{1}{4}(x-2)^4$$

$$\int x(x-2)^3\,dx = \frac{x}{4}(x-2)^4 - \frac{1}{4}\int(x-2)^4\,dx$$
$$= \frac{x}{4}(x-2)^4 - \frac{1}{20}(x-2)^5+C$$
$$= \frac{1}{20}(x-2)^4\left[5x-(x-2)\right]+C$$
$$= \frac{1}{20}(x-2)^4(4x+2)+C$$
$$= \frac{1}{10}(x-2)^4(2x+1)+C$$

9. $\displaystyle\int xe^{x^2}\,dx = \frac{1}{2}\int e^{x^2}(2x\,dx) = \frac{1}{2}e^{x^2}+C$

Let $u = x^2$
$du = 2x\,dx$

11.   Use reduction formula 20 in Table 5 (or use integration by parts) with $u = 3x, n = 1$
$du = 3\,dx$

$$\int xe^{3x}\,dx = \frac{1}{9}\int 3xe^{3x}\,3\,dx = \frac{1}{9}\int ue^u\,du$$
$$= \frac{1}{9}\left(ue^u - \int e^u\,du\right)$$
$$= \frac{1}{9}\left(ue^u - e^u\right)+C$$
$$= \frac{1}{9}(u-1)e^u+C$$
$$= \frac{1}{9}(3x-1)e^{3x}+C$$

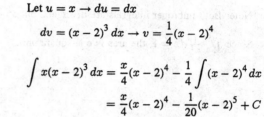

13. $\displaystyle\int \frac{x}{\sqrt{x^2+1}}\,dx = \frac{1}{2}\int \left(x^2+1\right)^{-1/2}(2x\,dx) = \frac{1}{2}(2)\left(x^2+1\right)^{1/2}+C$

$$= \left(x^2+1\right)^{1/2}+C$$

Let $u = x^2+1$
$du = 2x\,dx$

15. Use formula 9 in Table 5 with $u = x$ and $a = 1$.

$$\int \frac{1}{\sqrt{x^2+1}}\,dx = \ln\left|x+\sqrt{x^2+1}\right|+C$$

17. Use formula 17 in Table 5 with $u = 2x$ and $n = 0$.
$$du = 2\,dx$$

$$\int \ln 2x\,dx = \frac{1}{2}\int (\ln 2x)(2\,dx) = \frac{1}{2}\int \ln|u|\,du$$

$$= \frac{1}{2}\left(u\ln|u| - \frac{u}{1^2}\right)+C$$

$$= \frac{1}{2}u\ln|u| - \frac{u}{2}+C$$

$$= \frac{1}{2}(2x)\ln|2x| - \frac{2x}{2}+C$$

$$= x\ln|2x| - x+C$$

19. $\displaystyle\int \frac{\ln 2x}{x}\,dx = \int (\ln 2x)\left(\frac{1}{x}\,dx\right) = \frac{1}{2}(\ln 2x)^2+C$

Let $u = \ln 2x$

$du = \dfrac{1}{2x}(2)\,dx$

$\quad = \dfrac{1}{x}\,dx$

21. $\displaystyle\int \frac{e^{2x}}{1+e^{2x}}\,dx = \frac{1}{2}\int \frac{1}{1+e^{2x}}\left(2e^{2x}\,dx\right)$

$$= \frac{1}{2}\ln\left(1+e^{2x}\right)+C$$

Let $u = 1+e^{2x}$
$du = 2e^{2x}\,dx$

23. $\displaystyle\int \frac{1}{1+e^{2x}}\,dx = \int \left(1 - \frac{e^{2x}}{1+e^{2x}}\right)dx$

$$= \int dx - \int \frac{e^{2x}}{1+e^{2x}}\,dx$$

Let $u = 1+e^{2x}$

$du = 2e^{2x}\,dx$

$$= \int dx - \frac{1}{2}\int \frac{1}{1+e^{2x}}\left(2e^{2x}\,dx\right)$$

$$= x - \frac{1}{2}\ln\left(1+e^{2x}\right)+C$$

Note: By long division,

$1+e^{2x}\overline{)1}^{\;\frac{1}{1}}$

$\quad\dfrac{1+e^{2x}}{-e^{2x}}$

from which it follows that $\frac{1}{1+e^{2x}} = 1 - \frac{e^{2x}}{1+e^{2x}}$

25. Given $\int_0^2 \sqrt{9 - x^2}\, dx, n = 4$, then $f(x) = \sqrt{9 - x^2}, \Delta x = \frac{2-0}{4} = 0.5$, and $x_0 = 0, x_1 = 0.5, x_2 = 1.0, x_3 = 1.5$, and $x_4 = 2.0$.

   a. Trapezoidal rule:

$$\int_0^2 \sqrt{9 - x^2}\, dx = \frac{0.5}{2}\left(\sqrt{9 - 0^2} + 2\sqrt{9 - 0.5^2} + 2\sqrt{9 - 1.0^2} + 2\sqrt{9 - 1.5^2} + \sqrt{9 - 2.0^2}\right)$$
$$= 5.5013$$

   b. Simpson's rule:

$$\int_0^2 \sqrt{9 - x^2}\, dx = \frac{0.5}{3}\left(\sqrt{9 - 0^2} + 4\sqrt{9 - 0.5^2} + 2\sqrt{9 - 1.0^2} + 4\sqrt{9 - 1.5^2} + \sqrt{9 - 2.0^2}\right)$$
$$= 5.5196$$

27. Given $\int_1^4 \frac{1}{x^2+4}\, dx, n = 6$, then $f(x) = \frac{1}{x^2+4}, \Delta x = \frac{4-1}{6} = 0.5$, and $x_0 = 1, x_1 = 1.5, x_2 = 2.0, x_3 = 2.5, x_4 = 3.0, x_5 = 3.5$, and $x_6 = 4.0$.

   a. Trapezoidal rule:

$$\int_1^4 \frac{1}{x^2 + 4}\, dx = \frac{0.5}{2}\left[\frac{1}{1^2 + 4} + 2\left(\frac{1}{1.5^2 + 4}\right) + 2\left(\frac{1}{2^2 + 4}\right) + 2\left(\frac{1}{2.5^2 + 4}\right) + 2\left(\frac{1}{3^2 + 4}\right)\right.$$
$$\left. + 2\left(\frac{1}{3.5^2 + 4}\right) + \frac{1}{4^2 + 4}\right]$$
$$= 0.3230$$

   b. Simpson's rule:

$$\int_1^4 \frac{1}{x^2 + 4}\, dx = \frac{0.5}{3}\left[\frac{1}{1^2 + 4} + 4\left(\frac{1}{1.5^2 + 4}\right) + 2\left(\frac{1}{2^2 + 4}\right) + 4\left(\frac{1}{2.5^2 + 4}\right) + 2\left(\frac{1}{3^2 + 4}\right)\right.$$
$$\left. + 4\left(\frac{1}{3.5^2 + 4}\right) + \frac{1}{4^2 + 4}\right]$$
$$= 0.3217$$

29.
$$\int_1^\infty \frac{1}{x^4}\, dx = \lim_{b \to \infty}\left(\int_1^b x^{-4}\, dx\right)$$
$$= \lim_{b \to \infty}\left[-\frac{1}{3}x^{-3}\right]_1^b$$
$$= -\frac{1}{3}\lim_{b \to \infty}\left(\frac{1}{b^3} - \frac{1}{1}\right)$$
$$= -\frac{1}{3}(0 - 1)$$
$$= \frac{1}{3}$$

31.
$$\int_{-\infty}^0 e^{-0.5x}\, dx = \lim_{a \to -\infty}\left(\int_a^0 e^{-0.5x}\, dx\right)$$
$$= \lim_{a \to -\infty}\left[-\frac{1}{0.5}e^{-0.5x}\right]_a^0$$
$$= -2\lim_{a \to -\infty}\left(e^0 - e^{-0.5a}\right)$$
$$= \infty \qquad \text{divergent}$$

33.
$$\int_2^\infty x^{-2/3}\, dx = \lim_{b \to \infty}\left(\int_2^b x^{-2/3}\, dx\right)$$
$$= \lim_{b \to \infty}\left[3x^{1/3}\right]_2^b$$
$$= 3\lim_{b \to \infty}\left(b^{1/3} - 2^{1/3}\right)$$
$$= \infty \qquad \text{divergent}$$

35. $\displaystyle\int_{-\infty}^{\infty} \frac{x}{x^2+2}\,dx = \int_{-\infty}^{0} \frac{x}{x^2+2}\,dx + \int_{0}^{\infty} \frac{x}{x^2+2}\,dx$

$$= \lim_{a\to-\infty}\left(\int_a^0 \frac{x}{x^2+2}\,dx\right) + \lim_{b\to\infty}\left(\int_0^b \frac{x}{x^2+2}\,dx\right)$$

Let $u = x^2 + 2$
$du = 2x\,dx$

$$= \lim_{a\to-\infty}\left[\frac{1}{2}\int_a^0 \frac{1}{x^2+2}(2x\,dx)\right] + \lim_{b\to\infty}\left[\frac{1}{2}\int_0^b \frac{1}{x^2+2}(2x\,dx)\right]$$

$$= \frac{1}{2}\lim_{a\to-\infty}\left[\ln\left(x^2+2\right)\right]_a^0 + \frac{1}{2}\lim_{b\to\infty}\left[\ln(x^2+2)\right]_0^b$$

$$= \frac{1}{2}\lim_{a\to-\infty}\left[\ln(2) - \ln\left(a^2+2\right)\right] + \frac{1}{2}\lim_{b\to\infty}\left[\ln(b^2+2) - \ln 2\right]$$

$$= \frac{1}{2}(\ln 2 - \infty) + \frac{1}{2}(\infty - \ln 2)$$

$\displaystyle\int_{-\infty}^{\infty} \frac{x}{x^2+2}\,dx$ is divergent

37. The profit function $P(x)$ is given by

$$P(x) = \int \ln(x+1)\,dx$$

$$= x\ln(x+1) - \int \frac{x}{x+1}\,dx \qquad \text{using } u = \ln(x+1) \to du = \frac{1}{x+1}\,dx$$

$$dv = dx \to v = x$$

$$= x\ln(x+1) - \int \left(1 - \frac{1}{x+1}\right)dx \qquad \text{using } \frac{x}{x+1} = 1 - \frac{1}{x+1}$$

$$= x\ln(x+1) - x + \ln(x+1) + C \qquad \text{where } C \text{ is an arbitrary constant}$$

$P(0) = -120$ implies that
$-120 = 0\ln(1) - 0 + \ln(1) + C$
$C = -120$

The profit function is $P(x) = x\ln(x+1) - x + \ln(x+1) - 120$.

39. The present value of the income stream is P, given by

$$P = \int_0^I f(t)e^{-rt}\,dt$$

where $f(t)$ is the rate at which income is generated, t is the time in years, r is the prevailing annual interest rate, and T is the time period. We have

$$P = \int_0^4 (30{,}000 + 6000t)e^{-0.05t}\,dt$$

We shall evaluate in turn the integrals:

$$\int_0^4 30{,}000e^{-0.05t}\,dt \quad\text{and}\quad \int_0^4 6000te^{-0.05t}\,dt$$

$$\int_0^4 30{,}000e^{-0.05t}\,dt = \left[\frac{30{,}000}{-0.05}e^{-0.05t}\right]_0^4$$

$$= -600{,}000(e^{-0.2} - e^0)$$

$$= 108{,}761.55$$

To evaluate $\int_0^4 6000te^{-0.05t}\,dt$, we first evaluate $\int 6000te^{-0.05t}\,dt$.

$$\int 6000te^{-0.05t}\,dt = 6000t\left(\frac{1}{-0.05}\right)e^{-0.05t} - \int 6000\left(\frac{1}{-0.05}\right)e^{-0.05t}\,dt$$

$$= -120{,}000te^{-0.05t} + 120{,}000\int e^{-0.05t}\,dt$$

$$= -120{,}000te^{-0.05t} - 2{,}400{,}000e^{-0.05t}$$

Then $\displaystyle\int_0^4 6000te^{-0.05t}\,dt = \left[-120{,}000te^{-0.05t} - 2{,}400{,}000e^{-0.05t}\right]_0^4$

$$= -120{,}000(4)e^{-0.2} - 2{,}400{,}000e^{-0.2} + 2{,}400{,}000$$

$$\approx 42{,}055.43$$

Thus $P = 108{,}761.55 + 42{,}055.43$

$$= 150{,}816.98 \text{ dollars}$$

41. The required area is given by

$$\int_1^4 \ln x\,dx$$

First, $\int \ln x\,dx = x\ln x - \int \frac{1}{x}x\,dx = x\ln x - x$ using $u = \ln x \to du = \frac{1}{x}\,dx$ and $dv = dx \to v = x$. Then

$$\int_1^4 \ln x\,dx = [x\ln x - x]_1^4 = 4\ln 4 - 4 - 1\ln 1 + 1$$

$$= 4\ln 4 - 3$$

$$\approx 2.55$$

43. Since $y = 25 - x^2$ lies above $y = \sqrt{2x+1}$ for $0 \le x \le 4$, the required area is given by

$$\int_0^4 (25 - x^2 - \sqrt{2x+1})\, dx = \left[25x - \frac{x^3}{3} - \frac{2}{3}\frac{1}{2}(2x+1)^{3/2} \right]_0^4$$

$$= \left[100 - \frac{64}{3} - \frac{1}{3}(9)^{3/2} \right] - \left[0 - 0 - \frac{1}{3}(1)^{3/2} \right]$$

$$= \frac{236}{3} - 9 + \frac{1}{3}$$

$$= \frac{210}{3}$$

$$= 70$$

45. The average value of $f(x) = x\sqrt{x^2+9}$ over the interval $[0, 4]$ is

$$\frac{1}{4}\int_0^4 x\sqrt{x^2+9}\, dx = \frac{1}{4}\int_0^4 x(x^2+9)^{1/2}\, dx$$

$$= \left[\frac{1}{4} \cdot \frac{1}{2} \cdot \frac{2}{3}(x^2+9)^{3/2} \right]_0^4$$

$$= \frac{1}{12}[(25^{3/2} - (9)^{3/2}]$$

$$= \frac{1}{12}(125 - 27)$$

$$= \frac{98}{12}$$

$$= \frac{49}{6}$$

$$= 8\frac{1}{6}$$

$$\approx 8.167$$

47. We try to determine $y = f(x)$, where $\frac{dy}{dx} = xe^x$ and $y = 7$ when $x = 1$. Now $\frac{dy}{dx} = xe^x$ means that

$$y = \int xe^x\, dx = xe^x - \int e^x\, dx = xe^x - e^x + C$$

(using integration by parts with $u = x \to du = dx$ and $dv = e^x\, dx \to v = e^x$). So

$$y = xe^x - e^x + C$$

$y = 7$ when $x = 1$ means that $7 = 1e^1 - e^1 + C$

$$C = 7$$

Hence $y = xe^x - e^x + 7$.

SECTION 8.1 pages 416–418

1.   **a.** $P(5 \le x \le 6) = (0.3)(1) = 0.3$

    b. $P(6 \le x \le 8) = (0.2)(2) = 0.4$

    c. $P(6 \le x \le 9) = P(6 \le x \le 8) + P(8 \le x \le 9)$
$$= (0.2)(2) + (0.3)(1)$$
$$= 0.4 + 0.3$$
$$= 0.7$$

    d. $P(5 \le x \le 9) = P(5 \le x \le 6) + P(6 \le x \le 8) + P(8 \le x \le 9)$
$$= (0.3)(1) + (0.2)(2) + (0.3)(1)$$
$$= 0.3 + 0.4 + 0.3$$
$$= 1.0$$

3.   **a.** $P(7 \le x \le 8) = (0.4)(1) = 0.4$

    b. $P(5 \le x \le 7) = P(5 \le x \le 6) + P(6 \le x \le 7)$
$$= (0.2)(1) + (0.3)(1)$$
$$= 0.5$$

    c. $P(4 \le x \le 8) = P(4 \le x \le 5) + P(5 \le x \le 7) + P(7 \le x \le 8)$
$$= (0.1)(1) + 0.5 + 0.4 \quad \text{from a and b}$$
$$= 1.0$$

    d. $P(4 \le x \le 7) = P(4 \le x \le 5) + P(5 \le x \le 7)$
$$= (0.1)(1) + 0.5 \quad \text{from b}$$
$$= 0.6$$

5.   Show $f(x) = \dfrac{1}{30}x \ge 0$ on [2, 8] and $\displaystyle\int_2^8 \dfrac{1}{30}x \, dx = 1$.

Clearly, $f(x) = \dfrac{1}{30}x \ge 0$ since $x \ge 2 > 0$.

Also, $\displaystyle\int_2^8 \dfrac{1}{30}x \, dx = \dfrac{1}{30}\left[\dfrac{x^2}{2}\right]_2^8 = \dfrac{1}{30}\left[\dfrac{64}{2} - \dfrac{4}{2}\right] = 1$

Thus, $f(x) = \dfrac{1}{30}x$ is a probability density function on [2, 8].

7.   Show $f(x) = \dfrac{1}{12}(3x^2 + 2x) \ge 0$ on the interval [0, 2] and $\displaystyle\int_0^2 \dfrac{1}{12}(3x^2 + 2x) \, dx = 1$.

Computing the derivative $f'(x) = \dfrac{1}{6}(3x + 1)$, it follows that $f'(x) > 0$ for $x > -\dfrac{1}{3}$. Hence, $f(x)$ is increasing for $x > -\dfrac{1}{3}$. Since $f(0) = 0$, it follows that $f(x) \ge 0$ on $0 \le x \le 2$.

Also,

$$\int_0^2 \dfrac{1}{12}(3x^2 + 2x) \, dx = \dfrac{1}{12}\left[x^3 + x^2\right]_0^2 = \dfrac{1}{12}[(8 + 4) - 0] = 1$$

Thus, $f(x) = \dfrac{1}{12}(3x^2 + 2x)$ is a probability density function on [0, 2].

9. Show $f(x) = \dfrac{3}{38}\sqrt{x} \geq 0$ on the interval [4, 9] and $\displaystyle\int_4^9 \dfrac{3}{38}\sqrt{x}\, dx = 1$.

The square root function $\sqrt{x} \geq 0$ for all $x \geq 0$; hence $f(x) = \dfrac{3}{38}\sqrt{x} \geq 0$ on [4, 9].

Also,

$$\int_4^9 \dfrac{3}{38}x^{1/2}\, dx = \dfrac{3}{38}\left[\dfrac{2}{3}x^{3/2}\right]_4^9 = \dfrac{1}{19}\left(9^{3/2} - 4^{3/2}\right)$$
$$= \dfrac{1}{19}[27 - 8]$$
$$= 1$$

Thus, $f(x) = \dfrac{3}{38}\sqrt{x}$ is a probability density function on [4, 9].

11. Show $f(x) = \dfrac{10}{9x^2} \geq 0$ on the interval [1, 10] and $\displaystyle\int_1^{10} \dfrac{10}{9x^2}\, dx = 1$

If $1 \leq x \leq 10$, then $1 \leq x^2 \leq 100$ and $\dfrac{1}{100} \leq \dfrac{1}{x^2} \leq 1$.

Therefore, $f(x) = \dfrac{10}{9x^2} \geq \dfrac{1}{90} > 0$ for $1 \leq x \leq 10$.

Also,

$$\int_1^{10} \dfrac{10}{9x^2}\, dx = \dfrac{10}{9}\int_1^{10} x^{-2}\, dx = \dfrac{10}{9}\left[-x^{-1}\right]_1^{10}$$
$$= \dfrac{10}{9}\left(-\dfrac{1}{10} + 1\right)$$
$$= \dfrac{10}{9}\left[\dfrac{9}{10}\right]$$
$$= 1$$

Thus, $f(x) = \dfrac{10}{9x^2}$ is a probability density function on [1, 10].

13. Given the probability density function $f(x) = \dfrac{3}{64}x^2$ on [0, 4], then

a. $P(1 \leq x \leq 4) = \displaystyle\int_1^4 \dfrac{3}{64}x^2\, dx = \dfrac{3}{64}\left[\dfrac{x^3}{3}\right]_1^4 = \dfrac{1}{64}\left(4^3 - 1^3\right)$
$$= \dfrac{63}{64} \approx 0.9844$$

b. $P(0 \leq x \leq 2) = \displaystyle\int_0^2 \dfrac{3}{64}x^2\, dx = \dfrac{3}{64}\left[\dfrac{x^3}{3}\right]_0^2 = \dfrac{1}{64}(8 - 0)$
$$= \dfrac{1}{8} = 0.125$$

15. Given the probability density function $f(x) = \dfrac{1}{10}$ on [0, 10], then

a. $P(1 \leq x \leq 6) = \displaystyle\int_1^6 \dfrac{1}{10}\, dx = \dfrac{1}{10}[x]_1^6 = \dfrac{1}{10}(6 - 1) = \dfrac{1}{2} = 0.5$

b. $P(7 \leq x \leq 10) = \displaystyle\int_7^{10} \dfrac{1}{10}\, dx = \dfrac{1}{10}[x]_7^{10} = \dfrac{1}{10}(10 - 7) = \dfrac{3}{10} = 0.3$

17. Given the probability density function $f(x) = \dfrac{1}{x}$ on $[1, e]$, then

a. $P(1 \le x \le 2) = \displaystyle\int_1^2 \frac{1}{x}\, dx = [\ln\, x]_1^2 = \ln\, 2 - \ln\, 1$

$$= \ln\, 2$$
$$\approx 0.6931$$

b. $P(2 \le x \le e) = \displaystyle\int_2^e \frac{1}{x}\, dx = [\ln\, x]_2^e = \ln\, e - \ln\, 2$

$$= 1 - \ln\, 2$$
$$\approx 0.3069$$

19. Given $f(x) = 2x$ on $[1, 8]$, then

$$\int_1^8 2x\, dx = [x^2]_1^8 = 8^2 - 1^2 = 63$$

Thus, $g(x) = \dfrac{2}{63}x$ is a probability density function on $[1, 8]$.

21. Given $f(x) = x^3$ on $[0, 1]$, then

$$\int_0^1 x^3\, dx = \left[\frac{x^4}{4}\right]_0^1 = \frac{1}{4} - 0 = \frac{1}{4}$$

Thus, $g(x) = 4x^3$ is a probability density function on $[0, 1]$.

23. Given $f(x) = x - 5$ on $[6, 10]$, then

$$\int_6^{10} (x - 5)\, dx = \left[\frac{x^2}{2} - 5x\right]_6^{10} = \left(\frac{100}{2} - 50\right) - \left(\frac{36}{2} - 30\right)$$

$$= 0 - (18 - 30)$$
$$= 12$$

Thus, $g(x) = \dfrac{1}{12}(x - 5)$ is a probability density function on $[6, 10]$.

25. The probability that the store will sell at least 40 newspapers tomorrow is determined by $P(40 \le x \le 50)$ where $f(x) = 0.0008x$ is the probability density function.

$$P(40 \le x \le 50) = \int_{40}^{50} 0.0008x\, dx = 0.0008\left[\frac{x^2}{2}\right]_{40}^{50}$$

$$= 0.0004\left(50^2 - 40^2\right)$$
$$= 0.36$$

27. Given the probability density function $f(x) = \dfrac{1}{30}$ on $0 \le x \le 30$, then the probability that you will see a flash within 6 seconds is

$$P(0 \le x \le 6) = \int_0^6 \frac{1}{30}\, dx = \frac{1}{30}[x]_0^6 = \frac{1}{30}(6 - 0)$$

$$= \frac{1}{5} = 0.2$$

29. Given the probability density function

$$f(x) = 0.25e^{-0.25x} \quad \text{on} \quad x \geq 0, \text{ then}$$

a. The probability that a phone call will last no more than 4 minutes is

$$P(0 \leq x \leq 4) = \int_0^4 0.25e^{-0.25x}\, dx$$

$$= 0.25\left[-\frac{1}{0.25}e^{-0.25x}\right]_0^4$$

$$= -\left(e^{-1.0} - e^0\right)$$

$$= 1 - e^{-1.0}$$

$$= 0.6321$$

b. The probability that a phone call will last between 4 and 10 minutes is

$$P(4 \leq x \leq 10) = \int_4^{10} 0.25e^{-0.25x}\, dx = 0.25\left[-\frac{1}{0.25}e^{-0.25x}\right]_4^{10}$$

$$= -\left(e^{-2.5} - e^{-1.0}\right)$$

$$= 0.2858$$

31. Given the probability density function

$$f(x) = \frac{30}{13x^2} \quad \text{on} \quad 2 \leq x \leq 15, \text{ then}$$

a. The probability that a subject chosen at random would learn the task in 5 minutes or less is

$$P(2 \leq x \leq 5) = \int_2^5 \frac{30}{13x^2}\, dx = \frac{30}{13}\int_2^5 x^{-2}\, dx$$

$$= \frac{30}{13}\left[-x^{-1}\right]_2^5 = -\frac{30}{13}\left(\frac{1}{5} - \frac{1}{2}\right)$$

$$= \frac{9}{13} = 0.6923$$

b. The probability that a subject chosen at random would take at least 10 minutes to learn the task is

$$P(10 \leq x \leq 15) = \int_{10}^{15} \frac{30}{13x^2}\, dx = \frac{30}{13}\int_{10}^{15} x^{-2}\, dx$$

$$= \frac{30}{13}\left[-x^{-1}\right]_{10}^{15} = -\frac{30}{13}\left(\frac{1}{15} - \frac{1}{10}\right)$$

$$= \frac{1}{13} \approx 0.0769$$

33. It is *not* possible for $f(x)$ to be a probability density function. Using the properties of the definite integral,

$$\int_0^{10} f(x)\, dx = \int_0^1 f(x)\, dx + \int_1^4 f(x)\, dx + \int_4^{10} f(x)\, dx.$$

Since $f(x) \geq 0$, then $\int_0^1 f(x)\, dx \geq 0$ and $\int_4^{10} f(x)\, dx \geq 0$.

Thus, $\int_0^{10} f(x)\, dx = \int_0^1 f(x)\, dx + 2.5 + \int_4^{10} f(x)\, dx \geq 2.5 > 1$, which does not satisfy $\int_1^{10} f(x)\, dx = 1$.

35. The candle will take between 3 and 5 hours to burn out.

SECTION 8.1 Technology Exercises

1.

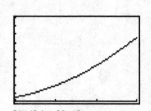

[1, 4] by [0, 1]

$P(2.5 \leq x \leq 4)$ is greater because there is more area under the curve between 2.5 and 4 than there is between 1 and 2.5.

SECTION 8.2 pages 425–426

1.
$$E(x) = \int_a^b x f(x)\, dx = \int_6^8 x \left(\frac{1}{2}\right) dx = \frac{1}{2} \int_6^8 x\, dx$$
$$= \frac{1}{2} \left[\frac{x^2}{2}\right]_6^8$$
$$= \frac{1}{4} \left(8^2 - 6^2\right)$$
$$= 7$$

3.
$$E(x) = \int_a^b x f(x)\, dx = \int_0^6 x \left(\frac{1}{18}x\right) dx = \frac{1}{18} \int_0^6 x^2\, dx = \frac{1}{54} \left[x^3\right]_0^6$$
$$= \frac{1}{54} \left(6^3 - 0\right)$$
$$= 4$$

5.
$$E(x) = \int_a^b x f(x)\, dx = \int_1^4 x \left(\frac{1}{21}x^2\right) dx = \frac{1}{21} \int_1^4 x^3\, dx = \frac{1}{84} \left[x^4\right]_1^4$$
$$= \frac{1}{84} \left(4^4 - 1^4\right)$$
$$= 3.04$$

7.
$$E(x) = \int_a^b x f(x)\, dx = \int_1^{16} x \left(\frac{1}{6\sqrt{x}}\right) dx = \frac{1}{6} \int_1^{16} x^{1/2}\, dx$$
$$= \frac{1}{6} \left[\frac{2}{3}x^{3/2}\right]_1^{16}$$
$$= \frac{1}{9} \left(16^{3/2} - 1\right)$$
$$= \frac{1}{9}(64 - 1)$$
$$= 7$$

9.
$$E(x) = \int_a^b x f(x)\, dx = \int_0^4 x \left(\frac{6 - 3\sqrt{x}}{8}\right) dx = \frac{1}{8} \int_0^4 (6x - 3x^{3/2})\, dx$$
$$= \frac{1}{8} \left[3x^2 - \frac{6}{5}x^{5/2}\right]_0^4$$
$$= \frac{1}{8} \left[\left(3 \cdot 4^2 - \frac{6}{5} \cdot 4^{5/2}\right) - 0\right]$$
$$= 1.2$$

11. μ is located at e.   **13.** μ is located at f.

15. μ is located at d.

17. Given probability density function $f(x) = \frac{1}{6}$ on $4 \leq x \leq 10$, then the expected value is

$$\mu = E(x) = \int_4^{10} x \left(\frac{1}{6}\right) \, dx = \frac{1}{6} \int_4^{10} x \, dx = \frac{1}{6}\left[\frac{x^2}{2}\right]_4^{10} = \frac{1}{12}(10^2 - 4^2)$$
$$= 7$$

The variance is

$$\text{var}(x) = \int_4^{10} x^2 \left(\frac{1}{6}\right) \, dx - \mu^2$$
$$= \frac{1}{6} \int_4^{10} x^2 \, dx - 7^2$$
$$= \frac{1}{6}\left[\frac{1}{3}x^3\right]_4^{10} - 7^2$$
$$= \frac{1}{18}(10^3 - 4^3) - 49$$
$$= 3$$

The standard deviation is

$$\sigma = \sqrt{3}$$
$$= 1.73$$

19. Given the probability density function $f(x) = \frac{2x}{15}$ on $1 \leq x \leq 4$, then the expected value is

$$\mu = E(x) = \int_1^4 x \left(\frac{2x}{15}\right) \, dx = \frac{2}{15} \int_1^4 x^2 \, dx = \frac{2}{15}\left[\frac{1}{3}x^3\right]_1^4$$
$$= \frac{2}{45}\left(4^3 - 1\right)$$
$$= 2.8$$

The variance is

$$\text{var}(x) = \int_1^4 x^2 \left(\frac{2x}{15}\right) \, dx - \mu^2 = \frac{2}{15} \int_1^4 x^3 \, dx - (2.8)^2$$
$$= \frac{2}{15}\left[\frac{1}{4}x^4\right]_1^4 - (2.8)^2$$
$$= \frac{1}{30}\left(4^4 - 1\right) - (2.8)^2$$
$$= 0.66$$

The standard deviation is $\sigma = \sqrt{\text{var}(x)}$
$$= \sqrt{0.66}$$
$$= 0.81$$

21. Given the probability density function $f(x) = \frac{1}{8}(4 - x)$ on $0 \leq x \leq 4$, then the expected value is

$$\mu = E(x) = \int_0^4 x \left[\frac{1}{8}(4 - x) \right] \, dx = \frac{1}{8} \int_0^4 (4x - x^2) \, dx$$

$$= \frac{1}{8} \left[2x^2 - \frac{x^3}{3} \right]_0^4$$

$$= \frac{1}{8} \left[2(4)^2 - \frac{4^3}{3} - 0 \right]$$

$$= \frac{4}{3} \approx 1.33$$

The variance is

$$\text{var}(x) = \int_0^4 x^2 \left[\frac{1}{8}(4 - x) \right] \, dx - \mu^2 = \frac{1}{8} \int_0^4 (4x^2 - x^3) \, dx - \left(\frac{4}{3} \right)^2$$

$$= \frac{1}{8} \left[\frac{4}{3}x^3 - \frac{1}{4}x^4 \right]_0^4 - \left(\frac{4}{3} \right)^2$$

$$= \frac{1}{8} \left[x^3 \left(\frac{4}{3} - \frac{1}{4}x \right) \right]_0^4 - \left(\frac{4}{3} \right)^2$$

$$= \frac{1}{8} \left[4^3 \left(\frac{4}{3} - 1 \right) - 0 \right] - \left(\frac{4}{3} \right)^2$$

$$= \frac{8}{3} - \frac{16}{9}$$

$$\text{var}(x) = 0.89$$

The standard deviation is

$$\sigma = \sqrt{\text{var}(x)}$$
$$= \sqrt{0.89}$$
$$= 0.94$$

23. Given the probability density function $f(x) = \frac{1}{2\sqrt{x}}$ on $9 \leq x \leq 16$, then the expected value is

$$\mu = E(x) = \int_9^{16} x \left(\frac{1}{2\sqrt{x}} \right) \, dx = \frac{1}{2} \int_9^{16} x^{1/2} \, dx = \frac{1}{2} \left[\frac{2}{3}x^{3/2} \right]_9^{16}$$

$$= \frac{1}{3} \left(16^{3/2} - 9^{3/2} \right)$$

$$= \frac{1}{3}(64 - 27)$$

$$\approx 12.33$$

The variance is

$$\text{var}(x) = \int_9^{16} x^2 \left(\frac{1}{2\sqrt{x}} \right) \, dx - \mu^2 = \frac{1}{2} \int_9^{16} x^{3/2} \, dx - (12.33)^2$$

$$= \frac{1}{2} \left[\frac{2}{5}x^{5/2} \right]_9^{16} - (12.33)^2$$

$$= \frac{1}{5} \left(16^{5/2} - 9^{5/2} \right) - (12.33)^2$$

$$\approx 4.17$$

The standard deviation is

$$\sigma = \sqrt{\text{var}(x)}$$
$$= \sqrt{4.17}$$
$$\approx 2.04$$

25. Given the probability density function $f(x) = 0.005x$ on the interval $0 \le x \le 20$, where x is in minutes, then the length of the average wait is the expected value

$$E(x) = \int_0^{20} x(0.005x)\, dx = 0.005 \int_0^{20} x^2\, dx = 0.005 \left[\frac{x^3}{3}\right]_0^{20}$$

$$= 0.005 \left(\frac{20^3}{3} - 0\right)$$

$$\approx 13.33 \text{ minutes}$$

27. Given the probability density function $f(x) = 0.2 - 0.02x$ on the interval $0 \le x \le 10$, where x is in years, then

a. The average life expectancy $= \int_0^{10} x(0.2 - 0.02x)\, dx$

$$= \int_0^{10} (0.2x - 0.02x^2)\, dx$$

$$= \left[0.1x^2 - \frac{0.02}{3}x^3\right]_0^{10}$$

$$= 0.1(10)^2 - \frac{0.02}{3}(10)^3 - 0$$

$$\approx 3.33 \text{ years}$$

b. The variance is

$$\text{var}(x) = \int_0^{10} x^2(0.2 - 0.02x)\, dx - (3.33)^2$$

$$= \int_0^{10} (0.2x^2 - 0.02x^3)\, dx - (3.33)^2$$

$$= \left[\frac{0.2x^3}{3} - 0.005x^4\right]_0^{10} - (3.33)^2$$

$$= \left[\frac{0.2}{3}(10^3) - 0.005(10^4) - 0\right] - (3.33)^2$$

$$\approx 5.58 \text{ years}$$

29. Given the probability density function $f(x) = 0.125 - 0.00075x^2$ on the interval $0 \le x \le 10$, where x is the number of years the tree will live, then

   a. The expected value is

$$E(x) = \int_0^{10} x(0.125 - 0.00075x^2)\,dx = \int_0^{10} (0.125x - 0.00075x^3)\,dx$$

$$= \left[\frac{0.125x^2}{2} - \frac{0.00075x^4}{4} \right]_0^{10}$$

$$= \left[\frac{0.125(10)^2}{2} - \frac{0.00075(10)^4}{4} \right] - (0 - 0)$$

$$\approx 4.375 \text{ years}$$

   b. The average life expectancy of a tree is 4.375 years.

   c. The variance is

$$\text{var}(x) = \int_0^{10} x^2(0.125 - 0.00075x^2)\,dx - (4.375)^2$$

$$= \int_0^{10} (0.125x^2 - 0.00075x^4)\,dx - (4.375)^2$$

$$= \left[\frac{0.125x^3}{3} - \frac{0.00075x^5}{5} \right]_0^{10} - (4.375)^2$$

$$= \left[\frac{0.125(10)^3}{3} - \frac{0.00075(10)^5}{5} \right] - (0 - 0) - (4.375)^2$$

$$\approx 7.53 \text{ years}$$

The standard deviation is $\sigma = \sqrt{7.53} \approx 2.74$ years

SECTION 8.2 Technology Exercises

1. 2

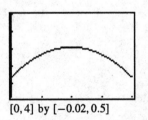

[0, 4] by [−0.02, 0.5]

3. 3

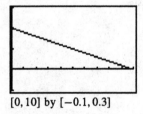

[0, 10] by [−0.1, 0.3]

SECTION 8.3 pages 429–431

1. Given the uniform distribution function $f(x) = \frac{1}{20}$ on $0 \le x \le 20$, then the probability that you will see a flash within 5 seconds is

$$P(0 \le x \le 5) = \int_0^5 \frac{1}{20}\,dx = \left[\frac{1}{20}x \right]_0^5 = \frac{1}{20}(5 - 0) = \frac{1}{4} = 0.25$$

3. Given the probability density function $f(x) = \dfrac{1}{3}$ on $5 \le x \le 8$, then

a. Clearly $f(x) = \dfrac{1}{3} \ge 0$ for all x and $\displaystyle\int_5^8 \dfrac{1}{3}\, dx = \left[\dfrac{1}{3}x\right]_5^8 = \dfrac{1}{3}(8-5) = 1$. Thus, $f(x)$ is indeed a probability density function.

b. $P(5 \le x \le 6) = \displaystyle\int_5^6 \dfrac{1}{3}\, dx = \left[\dfrac{1}{3}x\right]_5^6 = \dfrac{1}{3}(6-5) = \dfrac{1}{3} \approx 0.333$

c. The random variable x is uniformly distributed, because $f(x) = \dfrac{1}{8-5} = \dfrac{1}{3}$ over the interval $5 \le x \le 8$.

5. If the interval for the random variable x in Exercise 1 is changed to $0 \le x \le 25$, then the uniform distribution function is

$$f(x) = \frac{1}{25-0} = \frac{1}{25}$$

7. If the interval for the random variable x in Exercise 3 is changed to $4 \le x \le 10$, then the uniform distribution function is

$$f(x) = \frac{1}{10-4} = \frac{1}{6}$$

9. Given the exponential probability density function $f(x) = 0.0015e^{-0.0015x}$ for $x \ge 0$, then

a. $P(0 \le x \le 400) = \displaystyle\int_0^{400} 0.0015e^{-0.0015x}\, dx = \left[-e^{-0.0015x}\right]_0^{400}$

$$= -\left[e^{-400(0.0015)} - e^0\right]$$

$$\approx 0.451$$

b. $P(100 \le x \le 600) = \displaystyle\int_{100}^{600} 0.0015e^{-0.0015x}\, dx = \left[-e^{-0.0015x}\right]_{100}^{600}$

$$= -\left[e^{-0.0015(600)} - e^{-0.0015(100)}\right]$$

$$\approx 0.454$$

11. Given the exponential probability density function $f(x) = 0.025e^{-0.025x}$ for $x \ge 0$, then

a. $P(0 \le x \le 20) = \displaystyle\int_0^{20} 0.025e^{-0.025x}\, dx = \left[-e^{-0.025x}\right]_0^{20}$

$$= -\left[e^{-0.025(20)} - 1\right]$$

$$\approx 0.393$$

b. $P(30 \le x \le 60) = \displaystyle\int_{30}^{60} 0.025e^{-0.025x}\, dx = \left[-e^{-0.025x}\right]_{30}^{60}$

$$= -\left[e^{-0.025(60)} - e^{-0.025(30)}\right]$$

$$\approx 0.249$$

c. $P(x \ge 80) = \displaystyle\int_{80}^{\infty} 0.025e^{-0.025x}\, dx = \lim_{b\to\infty} \left(\int_{80}^{b} 0.025e^{-0.025x}\, dx\right)$

$$= \lim_{b\to\infty} \left[-e^{-0.025x}\right]_{80}^{b}$$

$$= -\lim_{b\to\infty} \left[e^{-0.025b} - e^{-0.025(80)}\right]$$

$$= -\left(0 - e^{-2}\right)$$

$$\approx 0.135$$

13.   Given the exponential probability density function $f(x) = 0.04e^{-0.04x}$ for $x \geq 0$, then the desired probability is

$$P(0 \leq x \leq 100) = \int_0^{100} 0.04e^{-0.04x}\, dx = \left[-e^{-0.04x}\right]_0^{100}$$
$$= -\left[e^{-0.04(100)} - 1\right]$$
$$\approx 0.982$$

15.   Given the exponential probability density function $0.2e^{-0.2x}$, then $a = 0.2$ and

   a.   The average length of a phone call is $\mu = \dfrac{1}{a} = 5$ minutes

   b.   If the mean length of a phone call is to be 8 minutes, then $\mu = \dfrac{1}{a} = 8$, which yields $a = \dfrac{1}{8} = 0.125$. The exponential probability density function becomes $f(x) = 0.125e^{-0.125x}$ for $x \geq 0$

17.   If the mean life expectancy in Exercise 12 is to be 4 years, then $\mu = \dfrac{1}{a} = 4$ and $a = \dfrac{1}{4} = 0.25$. Thus, the exponential probability density function becomes $f(x) = 0.25e^{-0.25x}$ for $x \geq 0$

19.   The mean of the uniform probability density function, $f(x) = \dfrac{1}{b - a}$ is given by

$$\mu = \int_a^b x\left(\frac{1}{b-a}\right)\, dx = \frac{1}{b-a}\int_a^b x\, dx$$
$$= \frac{1}{b-a}\left[\frac{x^2}{2}\right]_a^b$$
$$= \frac{1}{2(b-a)}\left(b^2 - a^2\right)$$
$$= \frac{1}{2(b-a)}(b-a)(b+a)$$
$$= \frac{b+a}{2}$$
$$= \frac{1}{2}(a+b)$$

SECTION 8.4 pages 438–439

1. $P(0 \leq z \leq 1.1) = 0.3643$

3. $P(0 \leq z \leq 0.73) = 0.2673$

5. $\begin{aligned} P(z \leq 0.42) &= P(z \leq 0) + P(0 \leq z \leq 0.42) \\ &= 0.5 + 0.1628 \\ &= 0.6628 \end{aligned}$

7. $\begin{aligned} P(z \leq 1.45) &= P(z \leq 0) + P(0 \leq z \leq 1.45) \\ &= 0.5 + 0.4265 \\ &= 0.9265 \end{aligned}$

9. $\begin{aligned} P(-1.6 \leq z \leq 0) &= P(0 \leq z \leq 1.6) \qquad \text{by symmetry} \\ &= 0.4452 \end{aligned}$

11. $\begin{aligned} P(-2.1 \leq z \leq 0) &= P(0 \leq z \leq 2.1) \qquad \text{by symmetry} \\ &= 0.4821 \end{aligned}$

13. $\begin{aligned} P(z \geq 0.84) &= 1 - P(z \leq 0.84) \\ &= 1 - [P(z \leq 0) + P(0 \leq z \leq 0.84)] \\ &= 1 - (0.5 + 0.2995) \\ &= 1 - 0.7995 \\ &= 0.2005 \end{aligned}$

15. $P(z \geq 1.72) = 1 - P(z \leq 1.72)$
$$= 1 - [P(z \leq 0) + P(0 \leq z \leq 1.72)]$$
$$= 1 - (0.5 + 0.4573)$$
$$= 1 - 0.9573$$
$$= 0.0427$$

17. $P(-0.95 \leq z \leq 1.3) = P(-0.95 \leq z \leq 0) + P(0 \leq z \leq 1.3)$
$$= P(0 \leq z \leq 0.95) + P(0 \leq z \leq 1.3)$$
$$= 0.3289 + 0.4032$$
$$= 0.7321$$

19. $P(-0.8 \leq z \leq 2.15) = P(-0.8 \leq z \leq 0) + P(0 \leq z \leq 2.15)$
$$= P(0 \leq z \leq 0.8) + P(0 \leq z \leq 2.15)$$
$$= 0.2881 + 0.4842$$
$$= 0.7723$$

21. $P(0.25 \leq z \leq 1) = P(0 \leq z \leq 1) - P(0 \leq z \leq 0.25)$
$$= 0.3413 - 0.0987$$
$$= 0.2426$$

23. $P(1.3 \leq z \leq 2.45) = P(0 \leq z \leq 2.45) - P(0 \leq z \leq 1.3)$
$$= 0.4929 - 0.4032$$
$$= 0.0897$$

25. $P(z \leq -0.82) = P(z \geq 0.82) \quad$ by symmetry
$$= 1 - P(z \leq 0.82)$$
$$= 1 - [P(z \leq 0) + P(0 \leq z \leq 0.82)]$$
$$= 1 - (0.5 + 0.2939)$$
$$= 1 - 0.7939$$
$$= 0.2061$$

27. $P(z \leq -1.2) = P(z \geq 1.2) \quad$ by symmetry
$$= 1 - P(z \leq 1.2)$$
$$= 1 - [P(z \leq 0) + P(0 \leq z \leq 1.2)]$$
$$= 1 - (0.5 + 0.3849)$$
$$= 1 - 0.8849$$
$$= 0.1151$$

29. First convert the normal random variable x to the standard normal random variable z using $z = \dfrac{x - \mu}{\sigma}$, where $\mu = 14$ and

$\sigma = 2$. If $x = 17$, then $z = \dfrac{17 - 14}{2} = \dfrac{3}{2} = 1.5$ and

$$P(x \leq 17) = P(z \leq 1.5) = P(z \leq 0) + P(0 \leq z \leq 1.5)$$
$$= 0.5 + 0.4332$$
$$= 0.9332$$

31. First convert the normal random variable x to the standard normal random variable z using $z = \dfrac{x - \mu}{\sigma}$, where $\mu = 20$ and

$\sigma = 4$. If $x = 14$, then $z = \dfrac{14 - 20}{4} = \dfrac{-6}{4} = -1.5$ and

$$
\begin{aligned}
P(x \geq 14) &= P(z \geq -1.5) \\
&= P(-1.5 \leq z \leq 0) + P(z \geq 0) \\
&= P(0 \leq z \leq 1.5) + P(z \geq 0) \\
&= 0.4332 + 0.5 \\
&= 0.9332
\end{aligned}
$$

33. First convert the normal random variable x to the standard normal random variable z using $z = \dfrac{x - \mu}{\sigma}$, where $\mu = 10$ and

$\sigma = 5$. If $x = 11$, then $z = \dfrac{11 - 10}{5} = \dfrac{1}{5} = 0.2$; if $x = 14$, then $z = \dfrac{14 - 10}{5} = \dfrac{4}{5} = 0.8$. Thus,

$$
\begin{aligned}
P(11 \leq x \leq 14) &= P(0.2 \leq z \leq 0.8) \\
&= P(0 \leq z \leq 0.8) - P(0 \leq z \leq 0.2) \\
&= 0.2881 - 0.0793 \\
&= 0.2088
\end{aligned}
$$

35. First convert the normal random variable x to the standard normal random variable z using $z = \dfrac{x - \mu}{\sigma}$, where $\mu = 20$ and

$\sigma = 4$. If $x = 18$, then $z = \dfrac{18 - 20}{4} = -\dfrac{2}{4} = -0.5$; if $x = 25$, then $z = \dfrac{25 - 20}{4} = \dfrac{5}{4} = 1.25$.

Thus, $\begin{aligned}[t] P(18 \leq x \leq 25) &= P(-0.5 \leq z \leq 1.25) \\
&= P(-0.5 \leq z \leq 0) + P(0 \leq z \leq 1.25) \\
&= P(0 \leq z \leq 0.5) + P(0 \leq z \leq 1.25) \\
&= 0.1915 + 0.3944 \\
&= 0.5859 \end{aligned}$

37. The desired probability is $P(100 \leq x \leq 130)$. Using $z = \frac{x - 100}{15}$, this becomes $P(0 \leq z \leq 2) = 0.4772$

39. The desired probability is $P(x \geq 115)$. Using $z = \frac{x - 100}{15}$, this becomes $P(z \geq 1)$

Thus,

$$
\begin{aligned}
P(z \geq 1) &= 1 - P(z \leq 1) \\
&= 1 - [P(z \leq 0) + P(0 \leq z \leq 1)] \\
&= 1 - (0.5 + 0.3413) \\
&= 1 - 0.8413 \\
&= 0.1587
\end{aligned}
$$

41. The desired probability is $P(x \leq 100)$. Using $z = \frac{x - 100}{15}$, this becomes $P(z \leq 0) = 0.5$

43. The desired probability is $P(90 \leq x \leq 100)$. Using $z = \frac{x - 100}{15}$, this becomes $P(-0.67 \leq z \leq 0)$. Thus,

$$
\begin{aligned}
P(-0.67 \leq z \leq 0) &= P(0 \leq z \leq 0.67) \\
&= 0.2486
\end{aligned}
$$

45. Given that the lengths of the leaves are normally distributed, then the desired probability is $P(x \geq 3.5)$, where $\mu = 4$ and $\sigma = 0.5$. Using $z = \dfrac{x - 4}{0.5} = \dfrac{3.5 - 4}{0.5} = -1.0$, then $P(x \geq 3.5) = P(z \geq -1.0)$

Thus,

$$
\begin{aligned}
P(z \geq -1.0) &= P(-1.0 \leq z \leq 0) + P(z \geq 0) \\
&= P(0 \leq z \leq 1.0) + P(z \geq 0) \\
&= 0.3413 + 0.5 \\
&= 0.8413
\end{aligned}
$$

The percentage of leaves at least 3.5 inches long is 84.13%.

47. Assume the annual snowfall is normally distributed with $\mu = 24$ and $\sigma = 4$.

a. The desired probability is $P(x \geq 30)$. Using $z = \frac{x-24}{4}$, this becomes $P(z \geq 1.5)$.

Thus,

$$
\begin{aligned}
P(z \geq 1.5) &= 1 - P(z \leq 1.5) \\
&= 1 - [P(z \leq 0) + P(0 \leq z \leq 1.5)] \\
&= 1 - (0.5 + 0.4332) \\
&= 1 - 0.9332 \\
&= 0.0668
\end{aligned}
$$

b. The desired probability is $P(x \leq 20)$. Using $z = \frac{x-24}{4}$, this becomes $P(z \leq -1)$.

Thus,

$$
\begin{aligned}
P(z \leq -1) &= P(z \geq 1) = 1 - P(z \leq 1) \\
&= 1 - [P(z \leq 0) + P(0 \leq z \leq 1)] \\
&= 1 - (0.5 + 0.3413) \\
&= 1 - 0.8413 \\
&= 0.1587
\end{aligned}
$$

49. Given that the SAT scores are normally distributed, then the desired probability is $P(x \geq 680)$, where $\mu = 500$ and $\sigma = 100$. Using

$$
z = \frac{x - 500}{100} = \frac{680 - 500}{100} = 1.8
$$

Then

$$
\begin{aligned}
P(x \geq 680 &= P(z \geq 1.8) = 1 - P(z \leq 1.8) \\
&= 1 - [P(z \leq 0) + P(0 \leq z \leq 1.8)] \\
&= 1 - (0.5 + 0.4641) \\
&= 1 - 0.9641 \\
&= 0.0359
\end{aligned}
$$

The percentage of those meeting the SAT-math requirement is 3.59%.

51. Given that systolic blood pressure is normally distributed, then the desired probability is $P(118 \leq x \leq 144)$, where $\mu = 130$ and $\sigma = 20$. Using $z = \frac{x-130}{20}$, then for $x = 118$, $z = \frac{118-130}{20} = -0.6$ and for $x = 144$, $z = \frac{144-130}{20} = 0.7$.

Thus,

$$
\begin{aligned}
P(118 \leq x \leq 144) &= P(-0.6 \leq z \leq 0.7) \\
&= P(-0.6 \leq z \leq 0) + P(0 \leq z \leq 0.7) \\
&= P(0 \leq z \leq 0.6) + P(0 \leq z \leq 0.7) \\
&= 0.2257 + 0.2580 \\
&= 0.4837
\end{aligned}
$$

53. Given the normal distribution function $f(x) = \dfrac{1}{\sigma\sqrt{2\pi}} e^{-(x-\mu)^2/(2\sigma^2)}$, let $\mu = 0$ and $\sigma = 1$.

Then, $f(x) = \dfrac{1}{(1)\sqrt{2\pi}} e^{-(x-0)^2/(2 \cdot 1^2)} = \dfrac{1}{\sqrt{2\pi}} e^{-x^2/2}$

55. If z is the standard normal random variable, then $P(-\infty < z < \infty) = 1$ because it is the total area under the standard normal probability density function.

57. The standard normal probability density function is given by

$$f(x) = \frac{1}{\sqrt{2\pi}} e^{-x^2/2} \qquad -\infty < x < \infty$$

a. $\int_{-\infty}^{\infty} \frac{1}{\sqrt{2\pi}} e^{-x^2/2}\, dx = 1$

The value of the integral is required to be 1 if $f(x)$, as given, is a probability density function. The reason for this is that $\int_{-\infty}^{\infty} \frac{1}{\sqrt{2\pi}} e^{-x^2/2}\, dx = P(-\infty < x < \infty)$, the probability that the random variable x takes on a value between $-\infty$ and ∞, and this happens with certainty (i.e., probability 1).

b. Since $\int_{-\infty}^{\infty} e^{-x^2/2}\, dx = \sqrt{2\pi}$, then the function $e^{-x^2/2}$ must be "normalized" so that we have a function $f(x) = \frac{1}{\sqrt{2\pi}} e^{-x^2/2}$ such that $\int_{-\infty}^{\infty} f(x)\, dx = 1$, one of the requirements of a probability density function. (That is, the probability that an outcome is one of all possible outcomes is certainty, i.e., 1.)

SECTION 8.4 Technology Exercises

1. **a.** 0.24   **b.** 0.05

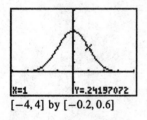

X=1   Y=.24197072
$[-4, 4]$ by $[-0.2, 0.6]$

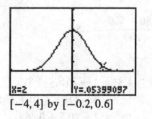

X=2   Y=.05399097
$[-4, 4]$ by $[-0.2, 0.6]$

REVIEW EXERCISES FOR CHAPTER 8 pages 440–441

1. Given $f(x) = \frac{1}{42}x$ on $[4, 10]$, then clearly $f(x) = \frac{1}{42}x \geq 0$ since $0 < 4 \leq x \leq 10$.

Also, $\displaystyle\int_4^{10} \frac{1}{42}x\, dx = \frac{1}{42}\left[\frac{x^2}{2}\right]_4^{10} = \frac{1}{84}\left(10^2 - 4^2\right) = \frac{84}{84} = 1.$

Thus, $f(x) = \frac{1}{42}x$ on $[4, 10]$ is a probability density function.

3. Given the probability density function $f(x) = \frac{x^3}{4}$ on $[0, 2]$, then

$$P(1 \le x \le 2) = \int_1^2 \frac{x^3}{4}\, dx = \frac{1}{16}\left[x^4\right]_1^2$$
$$= \frac{1}{16}\left(2^4 - 1\right)$$
$$= \frac{15}{16} = 0.9375$$

5. Given the probability density function $f(x) = 0.00005x$ on $0 \le x \le 200$, then

a. $P(0 \le x \le 30) = \int_0^{30} 0.00005x\, dx = 0.00005\left[\frac{x^2}{2}\right]_0^{30}$
$$= \frac{0.00005}{2}(30^2 - 0)$$
$$= 0.0225$$

b. $P(x \ge 60) = \int_{60}^{200} 0.00005x\, dx = 0.00005\left[\frac{x^2}{2}\right]_{60}^{200}$
$$= \frac{0.00005}{2}\left(200^2 - 60^2\right)$$
$$= 0.91$$

7. $P(x \ge 70) = \int_{70}^{100} f(x)\, dx$
$$= \int_{70}^{100} 0.0002x\, dx$$
$$= 0.0002\left[\frac{x^2}{2}\right]_{70}^{100}$$
$$= 0.0002\left(\frac{100^2}{2} - \frac{70^2}{2}\right)$$
$$= 0.0002(5000 - 2450)$$
$$= 0.51$$

9. Given the probability density function $f(x) = 0.1x$ on $[4, 6]$, then the expected value is

$$E(x) = \int_4^6 x(0.1x)\, dx = 0.1\int_4^6 x^2\, dx$$
$$= \frac{0.1}{3}\left[x^3\right]_4^6$$
$$= 5.07$$

11. Given the probability density function $f(x) = \frac{1}{9}x^2$ on [0, 3], then the expected value is

$$E(x) = \int_0^3 x\left(\frac{1}{9}x^2\right) dx = \frac{1}{9}\int_0^3 x^3 dx$$
$$= \frac{1}{9}\left[\frac{1}{4}x^4\right]_0^3$$
$$= \frac{1}{36}(3^4 - 0)$$
$$= 2.25$$

The variance is

$$\text{var}(x) = \int_0^3 x^2\left(\frac{1}{9}x^2\right) dx - \mu^2$$
$$= \frac{1}{9}\int_0^3 x^4 dx - (2.25)^2$$
$$= \frac{1}{9}\left[\frac{1}{5}x^5\right]_0^3 - (2.25)^2$$
$$= \frac{1}{45}(3^5 - 0) - (2.25)^2$$
$$\text{Var}(x) = 0.3375$$

The standard deviation is

$$\sigma = \sqrt{\text{var}(x)}$$
$$= \sqrt{0.3375}$$
$$= 0.5809$$

13. Given the probability density function $f(x) = \frac{1}{10}$ on $0 \le x \le 10$, then the average wait is

$$E(x) = \int_0^{10} x\left(\frac{1}{10}\right) dx = \frac{1}{10}\int_0^{10} x\, dx$$
$$= \frac{1}{10}\left[\frac{x^2}{2}\right]_0^{10}$$
$$= \frac{1}{20}(10^2 - 0)$$
$$= \frac{1}{20}(100)$$
$$= 5$$

The average wait for the bus is 5 minutes.

15. Given the probability density function $f(x) = 0.3e^{-0.3x}$, $x \geq 0$, then

a. $P(0 \leq x \leq 5) = \displaystyle\int_0^5 0.3e^{-0.3x}\, dx$

$$= \left[-e^{-0.3x}\right]_0^5$$

$$= -\left[e^{-0.3(5)} - e^0\right]$$

$$= 0.7769$$

The probability that a phone call will last no more than 5 minutes is 0.7769.

b. $P(x \geq 10) = \displaystyle\int_{10}^\infty 0.3e^{-0.3x}\, dx = \lim_{b \to \infty}\left(\int_{10}^b 0.3e^{-0.3x}\, dx\right)$

$$= \lim_{b \to \infty}\left[-e^{-0.3x}\right]_{10}^b$$

$$= -\lim_{b \to \infty}\left(e^{-0.3b} - e^{-3.0}\right)$$

$$= -[0 - 0.0498]$$

$$= 0.0498$$

The probability that a phone call will last at least 10 minutes is 0.0498.

17. $P(0 \leq z \leq 0.57) = 0.2157$

19. $P(-1.8 \leq z \leq 2.14) = P(-1.8 \leq z \leq 0) + P(0 \leq z \leq 2.14)$

$$= P(0 \leq z \leq 1.8) + P(0 \leq z \leq 2.14)$$

$$= 0.4641 + 0.4838$$

$$= 0.9479$$

21. $P(0.72 \leq z \leq 2.83) = P(0 \leq z \leq 2.83) - P(0 \leq z \leq 0.72)$

$$= 0.4977 - 0.2642$$

$$= 0.2335$$

23. First convert the normal random variable x to the standard normal random variable z using $z = \frac{x-\mu}{\sigma}$, where $\mu = 12$ and $\sigma = 5$. If $x = 19$, then $z = \frac{19-12}{5} = \frac{7}{5} = 1.4$ and

$$P(x \geq 19) = P(z \geq 1.4) = 1 - P(z \leq 1.4)$$

$$= 1 - [P(z \leq 0) + P(0 \leq z \leq 1.4)]$$

$$= 1 - (0.5 + 0.4192)$$

$$= 1 - 0.9192$$

$$= 0.0808$$

25. First convert the normal random variable x to the standard normal random variable z using $z = \frac{x-\mu}{\sigma}$, where $\mu = 50$ and $\sigma = 4$. If $x = 51$, then $z = \frac{51-50}{4} = \frac{1}{4} = 0.25$; if $x = 59$, then $z = \frac{59-50}{4} = \frac{9}{4} = 2.25$.

Thus,

$$P(51 \leq x \leq 59) = P(0.25 \leq z \leq 2.25)$$

$$= P(0 \leq z \leq 2.25) - P(0 \leq z \leq 0.25)$$

$$= 0.4878 - 0.0987$$

$$= 0.3891$$

27. Given that the amount poured into the can is normally distributed, then the desired probability is $P(x \geq 12)$, where $\mu = 12.15$ and $\sigma = 0.05$. Convert the normal random variable x to the standard normal random variable z using

$$z = \frac{x - \mu}{\sigma} = \frac{12 - 12.15}{0.05} = -3$$

Thus,

$$
\begin{aligned}
P(x \geq 12) = P(z \geq -3) &= P(z \leq 3) \\
&= P(z \leq 0) + P(0 \leq z \leq 3) \\
&= 0.5 + 0.4987 \\
&= 0.9987
\end{aligned}
$$

29. f is probability density function defined on the interval $[0, 8]$. It follows that $\int_0^8 f(x)\, dx = 1$. Now, given that $\int_3^8 f(x)\, dx = 0.75$, we may write

$$1 = \int_0^8 f(x)\, dx = \int_0^3 f(x)\, dx + \int_3^8 f(x)\, dx = \int_0^3 f(x)\, dx + 0.75$$

Hence,

$$\int_0^3 f(x)\, dx = 1 - 0.75 = 0.25$$

SECTION 9.1 page 447

1. If $y = 5x^2$, then $y' = 10x$. Substituting y and y' into the differential equation $xy' = 2y$, one gets

$$x(10x) \stackrel{?}{=} 2(5x^2)$$
$$10x^2 = 10x^2 \qquad \text{which is an identity}$$

3. If $y = e^{4x}$, then $y' = 4e^{4x}$. Substituting y and y' into the differential equation $y' - 4y = 0$, one gets

$$4e^{4x} - 4(e^{4x}) = 4e^{4x} - 4e^{4x} = 0$$

5. If $y = 4x^{3/2} - 2$, then $y' = 6x^{1/2}$. Substituting y and y' into the differential equation $xy' - 1.5y = 3$ yields

$$x\left(6x^{1/2}\right) - 1.5\left(4x^{3/2} - 2\right) = 6x^{3/2} - 6x^{3/2} + 3 = 0 + 3 = 3$$

7. If $y = x^2 + 6x + 16$, then $y' = 2x + 6$ and $y'' = 2$.

Substituting y, y', and y'' into the differential equation $y'' - 3y' + y = x^2$ yields

$$2 - 3(2x + 6) + x^2 + 6x + 16 = 2 - 6x - 18 + x^2 + 6x + 16$$
$$= -6x - 16 + x^2 + 6x + 16$$
$$= x^2$$

9. If $y = 1 - 2x$, then $y' = -2$. Substituting y and y' into the differential equation $(y')^2 - 4y - 8x = 0$ yields

$$(-2)^2 - 4(1 - 2x) - 8x = 4 - 4 + 8x - 8x = 0$$

11. Given $y' = 6x + 19$, then integrating both sides yields

$$y = \int (6x + 19)\, dx = 3x^2 + 19x + C$$

The general solution is $y = 3x^2 + 19x + C$.

13. Given $y' = e^x + 1$, then integrating both sides yields

$$y = \int (e^x + 1)\, dx = e^x + x + C$$

The general solution is $y = e^x + x + C$.

15. Given $f'(x) = 2 + \sqrt{x} = 2 + x^{1/2}$, then integrating both sides yields

$$f(x) = \int (2 + x^{1/2})\, dx = 2x + \frac{2}{3}x^{3/2} + C$$

The general solution is $f(x) = 2x + \frac{2}{3}x^{3/2} + C$.

17. Given $\frac{dy}{dt} = e^{-2t}$, then integrating both sides yields

$$y = \int e^{-2t}\, dt = -\frac{1}{2}e^{-2t} + C$$

The general solution is $y = -\frac{1}{2}e^{-2t} + C$.

19.   Given $f'(t) = 1 + \dfrac{3}{t}$, then integrating both sides yields

$$f(t) = \int \left(1 + \frac{3}{t}\right) \, dt = t + 3 \, \ln \, |t| + C$$

The general solution is $f(t) = t + 3 \, \ln \, |t| + C$.

21.   Given $y' = 6x^2 - 2x$, $y(0) = 5$, then integrating both sides yields

$$y = \int (6x^2 - 2x) \, dx = 2x^3 - x^2 + C$$

Using the given condition,

$$y(0) = 0 - 0 + C = 5$$
$$C = 5$$

The particular solution is $y = 2x^3 - x^2 + 5$.

23.   Given $f'(x) = x^7 + 3$, $f(0) = 14$, then integrating both sides yields

$$f(x) = \int (x^7 + 3) \, dx = \frac{1}{8}x^8 + 3x + C$$

Using the given condition,

$$f(0) = 0 + 0 + C = 14$$
$$C = 14$$

The particular solution is $f(x) = \frac{1}{8}x^8 + 3x + 14$.

25.   Given $\dfrac{dy}{dx} = 10x - e^x$, $y(0) = 0$, then integrating both sides yields

$$y = \int (10x - e^x) \, dx = 5x^2 - e^x + C$$

Using the given condition,

$$y(0) = 0 - e^0 + C = 0$$
$$-1 + C = 0$$
$$C = 1$$

The particular solution is $y = 5x^2 - e^x + 1$.

27.   Given $\dfrac{dy}{dx} = 3\sqrt{x}$, $y(4) = 11$, then integrating both sides yields

$$y = \int 3n\sqrt{x} \, dx = 3 \int x^{1/2} \, dx = 3 \left(\frac{2}{3}\right) x^{3/2} + C = 2x^{3/2} + C$$

Using the given condition,

$$y(4) = 2(4)^{3/2} + C = 16 + C = 11$$
$$C = -5$$

The particular solution is $y = 2x^{3/2} - 5$.

29.   Given $\frac{dy}{dt} = \frac{8}{t}$, $y(1) = 3$, then integrating both sides yields

$$y = \int \frac{8}{t}\, dt = 8 \ \ln |t| + C$$

Using the given condition,

$$y(1) = 8 \ \ln (1) + C = 8(0) + C = 3$$
$$C = 3$$

The particular solution is $y = 8 \ \ln |t| + 3$.

31.   Given $C'(x) = 50 - 0.06x$, $C(0) = 150$, then integrating both sides yields
$$C(x) = \int (50 - 0.06x)\, dx$$
$$= 50x - 0.03x^2 + k$$
where k is an arbitrary constant. $C(0) = 150$ implies that
$$150 = 50(0) - 0.03(0)^2 + k$$
$$k = 150$$
Hence,
$$C(x) = 50x - 0.03x^2 + 150$$

33.   Given $R'(x) = 5 + 0.0002x$, $R(0) = 0$, then integrating both sides yields
$$R(x) = \int (5 + 0.0002x)\, dx$$
$$= 5x + 0.0001x^2 + C$$
$R(0) = 0$ implies that $0 = C$. Hence, $R(x) = 5x + 0.0001x^2$.

35.   Given $P'(x) = 80 - 0.3\sqrt{x}$, $P(0) = -50$, then integrating both sides of the equation yields
$$P(x) = \int (80 - 0.3\sqrt{x})\, dx$$
$$= \int (80 - 0.3x^{1/2})\, dx$$
$$= 80x - 0.3\left(\frac{2}{3}\right)x^{3/2} + C$$
$$= 80x - \frac{1}{5}x^{3/2} + C$$

$P(0) = -50$ implies that $-50 = C$. Hence, $P(x) = 80x - \frac{1}{5}x^{3/2} - 50$.

37.   Yes, $y = 3$ is the solution of the differential equation $y' + y^2 = 9$.

39.   Let $y = f(x)$ denote the required curve.

    a.   The curve has slope $3x^2$ means that $\frac{dy}{dx} = 3x^2$. The statement that the curve passes through the point $(2, 11)$ means that $y = 11$ when $x = 2$, or equivalently in function notation writing $y = y(x)$, we have $y(2) = 11$. Thus, the differential equation together with initial condition is
$$\frac{dy}{dx} = 3x^2$$
$$y(2) = 11$$

    b. $\frac{dy}{dx} = 3x^2$
$$\int dy = \int 3x^2\, dx$$
$$y = x^3 + C$$
$y(2) = 11$ implies that $11 = 2^3 + C$, so $C = 3$. Hence, the solution is $y(x) = x^3 + 3$.

41. a. $y^2 - x^2 = C$

Use implicit differentiation to obtain

$$2y\frac{dy}{dx} - 2x = 0$$

$$2y\frac{dy}{dx} = 2x$$

$$\frac{dy}{dx} = \frac{x}{y}$$

Thus, the differential equation $\frac{dy}{dx} = \frac{x}{y}$ has the general solution $y^2 - x^2 = C$, where C is a constant.

b. The specific differentiation process used is implicit differentiation, where y is treated as an implicit function of x, i.e., $y = y(x)$.

SECTION 9.1 Technology Exercises

1. a. $y = x^2 + C$
   b.

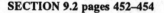

[−5, 5] by [−5, 10]

When $C = 0$, we get the graph of $y = x^2$; when $C = 3$, the graph is moved up 3 units; when $C = -2$, the graph is moved down 2 units.

3. a. $y = x^3 + C$
   b.

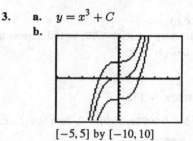

[−5, 5] by [−10, 10]

When $C = 0$, we get the graph of $y = x^3$; when $C = 4$, the graph is moved up 4 units; when $C = -5$, the graph is moved down 5 units.

SECTION 9.2 pages 452–454

1. Given $\frac{dy}{dx} = 2x$, then separating the variables yields

$$dy = 2x\,dx$$

Integrating both sides gives

$$\int dy = \int 2x\,dx$$
$$y = x^2 + C$$

3. Given $\frac{dy}{dx} = xy$, then separating the variables yields

$$\frac{dy}{y} = x\,dx$$

Integrating both sides gives

$$\int \frac{dy}{y} = \int x\,dx$$
$$\ln|y| = \frac{x^2}{2} + C_1$$

Using the exponential form results in

$$y = e^{x^2/2 + C_1} = e^{x^2/2}e^{C_1}$$
$$= Ce^{x^2/2}$$

5.   Given $\dfrac{dy}{dt} = te^{-y}$, then separating the variables yields

$\dfrac{dy}{e^{-y}} = t\,dt$ or $e^{y}\,dy = t\,dt$

Integrating both sides gives

$$\int e^{y}\,dy = \int t\,dt$$
$$e^{y} = \dfrac{t^2}{2} + C$$

Taking the natural log of both sides results in

$$y = \ln\left(\dfrac{t^2}{2} + C\right)$$

7.   Given $y' = 6xy^2 + 5y^2 = (6x+5)y^2$, then separating the variables, where $y' = \dfrac{dy}{dx}$, yields

$$\dfrac{dy}{y^2} = (6x+5)\,dx$$
$$y^{-2}\,dy = (6x+5)\,dx$$

Integrating both sides gives

$$\int y^{-2}\,dy = \int (6x+5)\,dx$$
$$-y^{-1} = 3x^2 + 5x + C$$

Solving for y results in $y = -\dfrac{1}{3x^2 + 5x + C}$

9.   Given $x\,dy + y\,dx = 0$, then rewriting as $x\,dy = -y\,dx$ and separating the variables yields

$$\dfrac{dy}{y} = -\dfrac{dx}{x}$$

Integrating both sides gives

$$\int \dfrac{dy}{y} = -\int \dfrac{dx}{x}$$
$$\ln|y| = -\ln|x| + C_1$$

Let $C = e^{C_1}$ which means $\ln C = C_1$ and use the log properties to obtain

$$\ln|y| = -\ln|x| + \ln C$$
$$\ln|y| = \ln\left|\dfrac{C}{x}\right| \qquad \text{difference of logs is the log of a quotient}$$
$$y = \dfrac{C}{x}$$

11. Given $\dfrac{dy}{e^x} = \dfrac{dx}{e^y}$, then separating the variables yields

$$e^y \, dy = e^x \, dx$$

Integrating both sides gives

$$\int e^y \, dy = \int e^x \, dx$$
$$e^y = e^x + C$$

Using the natural log to solve for y results in

$$y = \ln\left(e^x + C\right)$$

13. Given $x^2 \dfrac{dy}{dx} - 1 = 0$, then rewriting as $x^2 \, dy - dx = 0$ and separating the variables yields

$$dy = \dfrac{dx}{x^2} = x^{-2} \, dx$$

Integrating both sides gives

$$\int dy = \int x^{-2} \, dx$$
$$y = -x^{-1} + C$$
$$= -\dfrac{1}{x} + C$$

15. Given $2t \, dy - y^3 \, dt = 0$, then separating the variables yields

$$\dfrac{1}{y^3} \, dy = \dfrac{1}{2t} \, dt$$

Integrating both sides gives

$$\int y^{-3} \, dy = \dfrac{1}{2} \int \dfrac{dt}{t}$$
$$-\dfrac{1}{2} y^{-2} = \dfrac{1}{2} \ln|t| + C_1$$
$$-\dfrac{1}{y^2} = \ln|t| + 2C_1$$

Solving for y^2 yields $\quad y^2 = -\dfrac{1}{\ln|t| + C}$

17. Given $x^2 \, dx = (1 + x^3)y^4 \, dy$, then separating the variables yields

$$\dfrac{x^2}{1 + x^3} \, dx = y^4 \, dy$$

Integrating both sides by letting $u = 1 + x^3$, $du = 3x^2 \, dx$ gives

$$\dfrac{1}{3} \int \dfrac{3x^2 \, dx}{1 + x^3} = \int y^4 \, dy$$
$$\dfrac{1}{3} \ln|1 + x^3| = \dfrac{1}{5} y^5 + C_1$$

Multiplying by 15 and solving for y^5 gives

$$3y^5 = 5 \ln|1 + x^3| + C$$

19. Given $y' - 2xy = 0$ $(y > 0)$, then rewriting as $\dfrac{dy}{dx} - 2xy = 0$ and separating the variables yields

$$\frac{dy}{y} = 2x\, dx$$

Integrating both sides gives

$$\int \frac{dy}{y} = 2\int x\, dx$$
$$\ln\, y = x^2 + C_1$$

Using the exponential form, $y = e^{x^2 + C_1} = e^{x^2} e^{C_1} = Ce^{x^2}$

$$y = Ce^{x^2}$$

21. Given $y' = \frac{x}{y}$, $y(0) = 4$, then rewriting as $\dfrac{dy}{dx} = \dfrac{x}{y}$ and separating the variables yields

$$y\, dy = x\, dx$$

Integrating both sides gives

$$\int y\, dy = \int x\, dx$$
$$\frac{y^2}{2} = \frac{x^2}{2} + C$$

Using the given condition that $y = 4$ when $x = 0$ results in

$$\frac{4^2}{2} = \frac{0^2}{2} + C$$
$$C = 8$$

The particular solution is $\dfrac{y^2}{2} = \dfrac{x^2}{2} + 8$
$$y^2 = x^2 + 16$$

23. Given $y' = 2xy$, $y(0) = 2$, then rewriting as $\dfrac{dy}{dx} = 2xy$ and separating the variables yields

$$\frac{dy}{y} = 2x\, dx$$

Integrating both sides gives

$$\int \frac{dy}{y} = \int 2x\, dx$$
$$\ln |y| = x^2 + C_1$$
$$\text{or} \quad y = Ce^{x^2}$$

Using the condition that $y = 2$ when $x = 0$ results in

$$2 = Ce^0 = C$$

The particular solution is $y = 2e^{x^2}$.

25. Given $\dfrac{dy}{dx} = 4xe^{-y}$, $y(0) = 0$, then separating the variables yields

$$\frac{dy}{e^{-y}} = 4x \, dx$$

Integrating both sides gives

$$\int e^y \, dy = 4 \int x \, dx$$
$$e^y = 2x^2 + C$$

Using the condition that $y = 0$ when $x = 0$ results in

$$e^0 = 2(0) + C$$
$$1 = C$$

The particular solution is $e^y = 2x^2 + 1$

$$\text{or} \quad y = \ln(2x^2 + 1)$$

27. Given $\dfrac{dy}{dx} = \dfrac{y}{x}$, $y(1) = e$, then separating the variables yields

$$\frac{dy}{y} = \frac{dx}{x}$$

Integrating both sides gives

$$\int \frac{dy}{y} = \int \frac{dx}{x}$$
$$\ln|y| = \ln|x| + C$$

Using the condition that $y = e$ when $x = 1$ results in

$$\ln e = \ln 1 + C$$
$$\ln e = C$$

The particular solution is $\ln|y| = \ln|x| + \ln e$

$$\ln|y| = \ln|ex|$$
$$y = ex$$

29. Given $3\dfrac{dy}{dx} = 4x$, $y(0) = 1$, then separating the variables yields

$$3 \, dy = 4x \, dx$$

Integrating both sides gives

$$\int 3 \, dy = \int 4x \, dx$$
$$3y = 2x^2 + C$$

Using the condition that $y = 1$ when $x = 0$ results in

$$3(1) = 0 + C$$
$$C = 3$$

The particular solution is $3y = 2x^2 + 3$.

31. $\dfrac{dy}{dx} = x - 3$

33. $\dfrac{dB}{dt} = 0.05B$

35. $\dfrac{dM}{dt} = -0.02M$ *Note*: It is $-0.02M$ because the amount M is decreasing.

37. a. $\dfrac{dA}{dt} = 0.09A$

  b. Separating the variables and integrating both sides yields

$$\frac{dA}{A} = 0.09\ dt$$

$$\int \frac{dA}{A} = \int 0.09\ dt$$

$$\ln |A| = 0.09t + C$$

Converting to the exponential form gives

$$A = e^{0.09t + C_1} = e^{C_1} e^{0.09t}$$
$$= Ce^{0.09t}$$

  c. If $A = 3000$ when $t = 0$, then $A = Ce^0 = C = 3000$

$$A = 3000e^{0.09t}$$

39. a. $\dfrac{dA}{dt} = 0.03A, \ \ A(0) = 100{,}000{,}000$

  b. Separating the variables and integrating both sides yields

$$\frac{dA}{A} = 0.03\ dt$$

$$\int \frac{dA}{A} = \int 0.03\ dt$$

$$\ln A = 0.03t + C_1$$

Converting to the exponential form,

$$A = e^{0.03t + C_1} = e^{C_1} e^{0.03t}$$
$$= Ce^{0.03t}$$

Using $A(0) = 100{,}000{,}000$, then $A(0) = Ce^0 = C = 100{,}000{,}000$

$$A = 100{,}000{,}000e^{0.03t}$$

41. a. $\dfrac{dA}{dt} = -0.08A, \ \ A(0) = 10$

Note: The initial condition is the amount of the injection, and the minus sign is used because the amount decreases.

  b. Separating the variables and integrating both sides yields

$$\frac{dA}{A} = -0.08\ dt$$

$$\int \frac{dA}{A} = \int -0.08\ dt$$

$$\ln A = -0.08t + C_1$$

Converting to the exponential form gives

$$A = e^{-0.08t + C_1} = e^{C_1} e^{-0.08t}$$
$$A = Ce^{-0.08t}$$

Using $A(0) = 10$, then $A(0) = Ce^0 = C = 10$

$$A = 10e^{-0.08t}$$

43. The differential equation for the decline in the value of money is $\dfrac{dA}{dt} = -0.05A$, $A(0) = 1$.

Separating the variables and integrating both sides yields

$$\frac{dA}{A} = -0.05 \, dt$$

$$\int \frac{dA}{A} = -0.05 \int dt$$

$$\ln A = -0.05t + C_1$$

Converting to the exponential form results in

$$A = e^{-0.05t + C_1} = e^{C_1}e^{-0.05t}$$

$$= Ce^{-0.05t}$$

Using $A(0) = 1$ gives

$$A(0) = Ce^0 = 1$$

$$C = 1$$

$$A = e^{-0.05t}$$

For $t = 10$, $A(10) = e^{-0.05(10)} \approx 0.61$

The value of a dollar will be worth 0.61 (61 cents) in 10 years.

45. a. The differential equation to model the rate of decay is $\dfrac{dA}{dt} = -0.081A$

b. Separating the variables and integrating both sides yields

$$\frac{dA}{A} = -0.081 \, dt$$

$$\int \frac{dA}{A} = -0.081 \int dt$$

$$\ln A = -0.081t + C_1$$

Converting to the exponential form results in

$$A = e^{-0.081t + C_1} = e^{C_1}e^{-0.081t} = Ce^{-0.081t}$$

$$A = Ce^{-0.081t}$$

c. If A_0 is the initial amount, then $\frac{1}{2}A_0 = A_0e^{-0.081t}$ is the equation that represents half the initial amount. Dividing by A_0 and using the natural log yields

$$-0.081t = \ln \frac{1}{2}$$

$$t = \frac{\ln 0.5}{-0.081} \approx 8.6 \text{ days}$$

Half-life is 8.6 days.

47. Given a first-order differential equation that contains the derivative $\dfrac{dy}{dx}$ and has initial condition $y(a) = b$, then, if the solution is an equation involving x, y, and C, the values of x and y can be replaced by a and b, which leaves only the value of C to determine.

49. We require the equation of a curve for which the slope of the tangent line at (x, y) is $\frac{-4x}{9y}$, so $\frac{dy}{dx} = \frac{-4x}{9y}$, and which passes through the point $(0, 2)$. Thus, we must solve

$$\frac{dy}{dx} = \frac{-4x}{9y}$$
$$y(0) = 2$$

Separating variables and integrating the differential equation yields

$$\int 9y \, dy = \int -4x \, dx$$
$$\frac{9y^2}{2} = -2x^2 + C$$

To determine C, use $y = 2$ when $x = 0$:

$$\frac{9(2)^2}{2} = -2(0)^2 + C$$
$$C = 18$$

Hence, $\frac{9y^2}{2} = -2x^2 + 18$ (solution)

$$9y^2 = -4x^2 + 36$$
$$9y^2 + 4x^2 = 36$$
$$\frac{y^2}{4} + \frac{x^2}{9} = 1$$ (alternate form)

SECTION 9.2 Technology Exercises

1. **a.** $e^y = 2x^2 + 1$
$$\ln e^y = \ln(2x^2 + 1)$$
$$y = \ln(2x^2 + 1)$$

b.

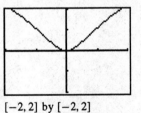

$[-2, 2]$ by $[-2, 2]$

Yes, since $2x^2 + 1 > 0$.

c.   Yes; $\left.\dfrac{dy}{dx}\right|_{x=0} = 0$

3. **a.** $\dfrac{dy}{dx} = -0.04y$

b. $y(0) = 1$

c. $y = e^{-0.04x}$

d.   in about $6\frac{1}{2}$ years

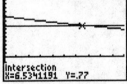

$[0, 10]$ by $[-0.5, 1.5]$

SECTION 9.3 pages 464–465

1.   a.   The differential equation to model this savings plan is $\dfrac{dA}{dt} = 0.08A + 500$ $A(0) = 3000$

Separating the variables and integrating both sides yields

$$\frac{dA}{0.08A + 500} = dt$$

$$\int \frac{dA}{0.08A + 500} = \int dt$$

Let $u = 0.08A + 500$

$\quad du = 0.08 \, dA$

$$\frac{1}{0.08} \ln (0.08A + 500) = t + C_1$$

$$\ln (0.08A + 500) = 0.08t + 0.08C_1$$

Converting to the exponential form results in

$$0.08A + 500 = e^{0.08t + 0.08C_1} = e^{0.08C_1} e^{0.08t}$$

Solving for A, $A = \dfrac{1}{0.08} e^{0.08C_1} e^{0.08t} - \dfrac{500}{0.08}$

$$A = Ce^{0.08t} - 6250$$

Using the condition $A(0) = 3000$,

$$A(0) = Ce^0 - 6250 = 3000$$

$$C = 9250$$

$$A = 9250e^{0.08t} - 6250$$

b.   For $t = 9$, $A = 9250e^{(0.08)(9)} - 6250$

$$\approx \$12{,}754$$

3. **a.** The differential equation that models the rate of debt payment is

$$\frac{dA}{dt} = 0.05A - 200,000 \qquad A(0) = 10,000,000$$

Note: The debt is increasing at 5% per year, but the $-200,000$ represents a payment to reduce the debt.

b. Separating the variables and integrating both sides yields

$$\frac{dA}{0.05A - 200,000} = dt \qquad \text{and} \qquad \int \frac{dA}{0.05A - 200,000} = \int dt$$

$$\frac{1}{0.05} \ln(0.05A - 200,000) = t + C_1$$

$$\ln(0.05A - 200,000) = 0.05t + 0.05C_1$$

Converting to the exponential form and solving for A results in

$$0.05A - 200,000 = e^{0.05t + 0.05C_1} = e^{0.05C_1} e^{0.05t}$$

$$A = \left(\frac{1}{0.05} e^{0.05C_1} \right) e^{0.05t} + \frac{200,000}{0.05}$$

$$= Ce^{0.05t} + 4,000,000$$

Using $A(0) = 10,000,000$, then

$$A(0) = Ce^0 + 4,000,000 = 10,000,000$$

$$C = 6,000,000$$

$$A = 6,000,000e^{0.05t} + 4,000,000$$

c. For $t = 4$, $A = 6,000,000e^{0.05(4)} + 4,000,000$

$$= \$11,328,416$$

d. The country is continuing to go further into debt, since the debt after 4 years is greater than the original debt. The country is not covering the interest payment.

5. **a.** The differential equation to model the increase in debt is

$$\frac{dA}{dt} = 0.05A + 200,000 \qquad A(0) = 10,000,000$$

b. Using the result of Exercise 3 above,

$$A = Ce^{0.05t} - 4,000,000$$

and the condition $A(0) = 10,000,000$ gives

$$A(0) = Ce^0 - 4,000,000 = 10,000,000$$

$$C = 14,000,000$$

$$A = 14,000,000e^{0.05t} - 4,000,000$$

c. For $t = 4$, $A = 14,000,000e^{0.05(4)} - 4,000,000$

$$A \approx \$13,099,639$$

7.   Given $E = -\dfrac{p}{x}\dfrac{dx}{dp} = 0.1p$ and $p = 20$ when $x = 1$, then separating the variables and integrating both sides yields

$$-\frac{p}{x}\,dx = 0.1p\,dp$$

$$-\frac{dx}{x} = 0.1\,dp$$

$$-\int \frac{dx}{x} = 0.1\int dp$$

$$-\ln\,x = 0.1p + C$$

Using the condition that $p = 20$ when $x = 1$ and solving for p gives

$$-\ln\,1 = 0.1(20) + C$$

$$0 = 2 + C$$

$$C = -2$$

$$-\ln\,x = 0.1p - 2$$

$$p = \frac{2}{0.1} - \frac{1}{0.1}\,\ln\,x$$

$$= 20 - 10\,\ln\,x$$

9.   **a.**   According to Newton's law of cooling, the rate of change of temperature is given by the differential equation

$$\frac{dT}{dt} = k(T - 70) \qquad T(0) = 20$$

b.   Given the addition condition that $T(10) = 40$, then separating the variables and integrating both sides yields

$$\frac{dT}{T - 70} = k\,dt$$

$$\int \frac{dT}{T - 70} = k\int dt$$

$$\ln\,(T - 70) = kt + C_1$$

or $\quad T - 70 = e^{kt + C_1} = e^{C_1}e^{kt}$

$$T = Ce^{kt} + 70$$

Using $T(0) = 20$, then

$$T(0) = Ce^0 + 70 = 20$$

$$T = -50e^{kt} + 70 \qquad C = -50$$

Using $T(10) = 40$ and solving for k gives

$$T(10) = -50e^{10k} + 70 = 40$$

$$e^{10k} = 0.6$$

$$10k = \ln\,0.6$$

$$k \approx -0.051$$

Thus, $T = -50e^{-0.051t} + 70$

11. The differential equation that models the temperature change of the glass beaker is

$$\frac{dT}{dt} = k(T - 70) \qquad \begin{aligned} T(0) &= 400 \\ T(1) &= 300 \end{aligned}$$

Separating the variables and integrating both sides yields

$$\frac{dT}{T - 70} = k \, dt$$

$$\int \frac{dT}{T - 70} = k \int dt$$

$$\ln (T - 70) = kt + C_1$$

or $T - 70 = e^{kt + C_1} = e^{C_1} e^{kt}$

$$T = Ce^{kt} + 70$$

Using $T(0) = 400$, then

$$T(0) = Ce^0 + 70 = 400$$

$$C = 330$$

$$T = 330e^{kt} + 70$$

Using $T(1) = 300$, then $T(1) = 330e^k + 70 = 300$, and solving for k results in

$$e^k = \frac{23}{33} \quad \text{or} \quad k = \ln \frac{23}{33} \approx -0.361$$

$$T = 330e^{-0.361t} + 70$$

Let $T = 100 = 330e^{-0.361t} + 70$ and solve for t.

$$330e^{-0.361t} = 30$$

$$-0.361t = \ln \frac{3}{33}$$

$$t = \frac{\ln \frac{1}{11}}{-0.361} \approx 6.64$$

It will take about 6.64 minutes for the beaker to cool down to $100°$.

13. **a.** The statement of the problem about the spread of the flu indicates that it is a logistic growth problem; hence the function y becomes $y = \dfrac{N}{1 + Ce^{-Nkt}}$, where t is measured in days and $N = 40,000$. When $t = 0$, $y = 200$, and when $t = 5$, $y = 400$.

Therefore, $y = \dfrac{40,000}{1 + Ce^{-40,000kt}}$

and

$$200 = \frac{40,000}{1 + Ce^0}$$
$$200 + 200C = 40,000$$
$$200C = 39,800$$
$$C = 199$$

Thus, $y = \dfrac{40,000}{1 + 199e^{-40,000kt}}$

Using $y = 400$ when $t = 5$, $\quad 400 = \dfrac{40,000}{1 + 199e^{-40,000k(5)}} = \dfrac{40,000}{1 + 199e^{-200,000k}}$

$$400 + 79,600e^{-200,000k} = 40,000$$
$$e^{-200,000k} = 0.4975$$
$$k \approx \frac{\ln 0.4975}{-200,000} = 0.0000035$$

Finally, $y = \dfrac{40,000}{1 + 199e^{-0.14t}}$

b. Find the value of t such that
$$5000 = \frac{40,000}{1 + 199e^{-0.14t}}$$
$$5000 + 995,000e^{-0.14t} = 40,000$$
$$e^{-0.14t} = 0.0352$$
$$t \approx \frac{\ln 0.0352}{-0.14} \approx 23.9$$

It will take approximately 23.9 days to infect 5000 people.

15. The statement of the spread of the rumor indicates that this is a logistic growth problem; hence the function y becomes $y = \frac{N}{1 + Ce^{-Nkt}}$, where t is measured in days and $N = 2000$.

When $t = 0$, $y = 4$, and when $t = 2$, $y = 30$.

Therefore, $y = \dfrac{2000}{1 + Ce^{-2000kt}}$

and $4 = \dfrac{2000}{1 + Ce^0}$

$4 + 4C = 2000$

$4C = 1996$

$C = 499$

Thus, $y = \dfrac{2000}{1 + 499e^{-2000kt}}$

Using $y = 30$ when $t = 2$,

$$30 = \frac{2000}{1 + 499e^{-4000k}}$$

$$30 + 14{,}970e^{-4000k} = 2000$$

$$e^{-4000k} = \frac{1970}{14{,}970}$$

$$k = \frac{\ln \frac{197}{1497}}{-4000} \approx 0.00051$$

Finally, $y = \dfrac{2000}{1 + 499e^{-1.02t}}$

Let $y = 1000 = \dfrac{2000}{1 + 499e^{-1.02t}}$ and solve for t.

$1 + 499e^{-1.02t} = 2$

$e^{-1.02t} = \dfrac{1}{499}$

$t = \dfrac{\ln \frac{1}{499}}{-1.02} \approx 6.1$

Half the school will hear the rumor in about 6 days.

SECTION 9.3 Technology Exercises

1.

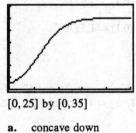

[0, 25] by [0, 35]

a. concave down
b. false

3.

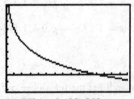

[1, 75] by [−20, 90]

a. No, if $x > 54$, the price becomes negative.
b. increases
c. decreases

5.   **a.**   about 1445 fish

b.   about 27 months

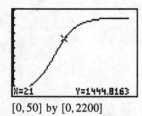

[0, 50] by [0, 2200]

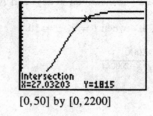

[0, 50] by [0, 2200]

SECTION 9.4 pages 472–473

1.   Given $y' = 4xy$, then it fits the form $y' = g(x, y) = 4xy$.

Using $y_{i+1} = y_i + g(x_i, y_i)\,\Delta x$ with $\Delta x = 0.1$, $x_0 = 1$, and $y_0 = 2$, then one gets the following sequence of values: $x_0 = 1$, $x_1 = 1.1$, $x_2 = 1.2$, and $x_3 = 1.3$.

$y_1 = y_0 + g(x_0, y_0)\,\Delta x = 2 + g(1, 2)(0.1) = 2 + 4(1)(2)(0.1) = 2.8$

$y_2 = y_1 + g(x_1, y_1)\,\Delta x = 2.8 + g(1.1, 2.8)(0.1) = 2.8 + 4(1.1)(2.8)(0.1) = 4.032$

$y_3 = y_2 + g(x_2, y_2)\,\Delta x = 4.032 + g(1.2, 4.032)(0.1) = 4.032 + 4(1.1)(4.032)(0.1) = 5.8061$

$y(1.3) \approx 5.8061$

3.   Given $y' = x + y$, then it fits the form $y' = g(x, y) = x + y$.

Using $y_{i+1} = y_i + g(x_i, y_i)\,\Delta x$ with $\Delta x = 0.1$, $x_0 = 0$, and $y_0 = 1$, then one gets the following sequence of values: $x_0 = 0$, $x_1 = 0.1$, $x_2 = 0.2$, $x_3 = 0.3$, and $x_4 = 0.4$.

$y_1 = y_0 + g(x_0, y_0)\,\Delta x = 1 + g(0 > 1)(0.1) = 1 + (0 + 1)(0.1) = 1.1$

$y_2 = y_1 + g(x_1, y_1)\,\Delta x = 1.1 + g(0.1, 1.1)(0.1) = 1.1 + (0.1 + 1.1)(0.1) = 1.22$

$y_3 = y_2 + g(x_2, y_2)\,\Delta x = 1.22 + g(0.2, 1.22)(0.1) = 1.22 + (0.2 + 1.22)(0.1) = 1.362$

$y_4 = y_3 + g(x_3, y_3)\,\Delta x = 1.362 + g(0.3, 1.362)(0.1) = 1.362 + (0.3 + 1.362)(0.1) = 1.5282$

$y(0.4) \approx 1.5282$

5.   Given $y' = x^2 + y^2$, then it fits the form $y' = g(x, y) = x^2 + y^2$. Using $y_{i+1} = y_i + g(x_i, y_i)\,\Delta x$ with $\Delta x = 0.1$, $x_0 = 0$, and $y_0 = 1$, then one gets the following sequence of values: $x_0 = 0$, $x_1 = 0.1$, $x_2 = 0.2$, $x_3 = 0.3$, $x_4 = 0.4$, and $x_5 = 0.5$.

$y_1 = y_0 + g(x_0, y_0)\,\Delta x = 1 + g(0 > 1)(0.1) = 1 + (0 + 1)(0.1) = 1.1$

$y_2 = y_1 + g(x_1, y_1)\,\Delta x = 1.1 + g(0.1, 1.1)(0.1) = 1.1 + \left[(0.1)^2 + (1.1)^2\right](0.1) = 1.222$

$y_3 = y_2 + g(x_2, y_2)\,\Delta x = 1.222 + g(0.2, 1.222)(0.1) = 1.222 + \left[(0.2)^2 + (1.222)^2\right](0.1) \approx 1.3753$

$y_4 = y_3 + g(x_3, y_3)\,\Delta x = 1.3753 + g(0.3, 1.3753)(0.1) = 1.3753 + \left[(0.3)^2 + (1.3753)^2\right](0.1) \approx 1.5734$

$y_5 = y_4 + g(x_4, y_4)\,\Delta x = 1.5734 + g(0.4, 1.5734)(0.1) = 1.5734 + \left[(0.4)^2 + (1.5734)^2\right](0.1) \approx 1.8370$

$y(0.5) \approx 1.8370$

7.   Given $y' = 2xy - y$, then it fits the form $y' = g(x, y) = 2xy - y$. Using $y_{i+1} = y_i + g(x_i, y_i)\,\Delta x$ with $\Delta x = 0.05$, $x_0 = 1$, and $y_0 = 2$, then one gets the following sequence of values: $x_0 = 1$, $x_1 = 1.05$, $x_2 = 1.1$, $x_3 = 1.15$, and $x_4 = 1.2$.

$y_1 = y_0 + g(x_0, y_0)\,\Delta x = 2 + g(1, 2)(0.05) = 2 + [2(1)(2) - 2](0.05) = 2.1$

$y_2 = y_1 + g(x_1, y_1)\,\Delta x = 2.1 + g(1.05, 2.1)(0.05) = 2.1 + [2(1.05)(2.1) - 2.1](0.05) = 2.2155$

$y_3 = y_2 + g(x_2, y_2)\,\Delta x = 2.2155 + g(1.1, 2.2155)(0.05) = 2.2155 + [2(1.1)(2.2155) - 2.2155](0.05) = 2.3484$

$y_4 = y_3 + g(x_3, y_3)\,\Delta x = 2.3484 + g(1.15, 2.3484)(0.05) = 2.3484 + [2(1.15)(2.3484) - 2.3484](0.05) = 2.5010$

$y(1.2) \approx 2.5010$

9.   Given $y' = 1 + e^x$, then it fits the form $y = g(x, y) = 1 + e^x$. Using $y_{i+1} = y_i + g(x_i, y_i)\,\Delta x$ with $\Delta x = 0.05$, $x_0 = 0$, and $y_0 = 1$, then one gets the following sequence of values: $x_0 = 0$, $x_1 = 0.05$, $x_2 = 0.10$, $x_3 = 0.15$, $x_4 = 0.20$, $x_5 = 0.25$, and $x_6 = 0.30$.

$$y_1 = y_0 + g(x_0, y_0)\,\Delta x = 1 + g(0, 1)(0.05) = 1 + (1 + e^0)(0.05) = 1.1$$
$$y_2 = y_1 + g(x_1, y_1)\,\Delta x = 1.1 + g(0.05, 1.1)(0.05) = 1.1 + (1 + e^{0.05})(0.05) = 1.2026$$
$$y_3 = y_2 + g(x_2, y_2)\,\Delta x = 1.2026 + g(0.1, 1.2026)(0.05) = 1.2026 + (1 + e^{0.1})(0.05) = 1.3079$$
$$y_4 = y_3 + g(x_3, y_3)\,\Delta x = 1.3079 + g(0.15, 1.3079)(0.05) = 1.3079 + (1 + e^{0.15})(0.05) = 1.4160$$
$$y_5 = y_4 + g(x_4, y_4)\,\Delta x = 1.4160 + g(0.20, 1.4160)(0.05) = 1.4160 + (1 + e^{0.20})(0.05) = 1.5271$$
$$y_6 = y_5 + g(x_5, y_5)\,\Delta x = 1.5271 + g(0.25, 1.5271)(0.05) = 1.5271 + (1 + e^{0.25})(0.05) = 1.6413$$

$$y(0.3) \approx 1.6413$$

11.   Solving $y' = 1 + e^x$ by exact methods yields

$$\frac{dy}{dx} = 1 + e^x$$
$$dy = (1 + e^x)\,dx$$
$$y = \int (1 + e^x)\,dx = x + e^x + C$$
$$y = x + e^x + C$$

Using the condition $y(0) = 1$, then

$$y(0) = 0 + e^0 + C = 1$$
$$C = 0$$

$$y = f(x) = x + e^x$$

For $x = 0.3$, $f(0.3) = 0.3 + e^{0.3} \approx 1.6499$; the approximate solution is $y(0.3) \approx 1.6413$.

13.   Solving $y' = 2xy - y$ by exact methods yields

$$\frac{dy}{dx} = 2xy - y = (2x - 1)y$$
$$\frac{dy}{y} = (2x - 1)\,dx$$
$$\int \frac{dy}{y} = \int (2x - 1)\,dx$$
$$\ln|y| = x^2 - x + C$$

Using the condition that $y = 2$ when $x = 1$, then

$$\ln 2 = 1^2 - 1 + C$$
$$C = \ln 2$$

Thus, $\ln|y| = x^2 - x + \ln 2$
$$\ln|y| - \ln 2 = x^2 - x$$
$$\ln\left|\frac{y}{2}\right| = x^2 - x \quad \text{or} \qquad \frac{y}{2} = e^{x^2 - x}$$
$$y = f(x) = 2e^{x^2 - x}$$

For $x = 1.2$, $f(1.2) = 2e^{(1.2)^2 - 1.2} \approx 2.5425$; the approximate solution is $y(1.2) \approx 2.5010$.

15.   Given $y' = xy + x$, then it fits the form $y' = g(x, y) = x(y + 1)$.

Using $y_{i+1} = y_i + g(x_i, y_i) \Delta x$ with $\Delta x = 0.1$, $x_0 = 0$, and $y_0 = 1$, then, for the interval $[0, 0.5]$, one gets the following sequence of values: $x_0 = 0$, $x_1 = 0.1$, $x_2 = 0.2$, $x_3 = 0.3$, $x_4 = 0.4$, and $x_5 = 0.5$.

$y_1 = y_0 + g(x_0, y_0) \Delta x = 1 + g(0, 1)(0.1) = 1 + 0(1 + 1)(0.1) = 1$
$y_2 = y_1 + g(x_1, y_1) \Delta x = 1 + g(0.1, 1)(0.1) = 1 + 0.1(1 + 1)(0.1) = 1.02$
$y_3 = y_2 + g(x_2, y_2) \Delta x = 1.02 + g(0.2, 1.02)(0.1) = 1.02 + 0.2(1.02 + 1)(0.1) = 1.0604$
$y_4 = y_3 + g(x_3, y_3) \Delta x = 1.0604 + g(0.3, 1.0604)(0.1) = 1.0604 + 0.3(1.0604 + 1)(0.1) = 1.1222$
$y_5 = y_4 + g(x_4, y_4) \Delta x = 1.1222 + g(0.4, 1.1222)(0.1) = 1.1222 + 0.4(1.1222 + 1)(0.1) = 1.2071$

Thus, $y(0) = 1$
$y(0.1) = 1$
$y(0.2) = 1.02$
$y(0.3) = 1.0604$
$y(0.4) = 1.1222$
$y(0.5) = 1.2071$

17.   Given $y' = x - y$, then it fits the form $y' = g(x, y) = x - y$. Using $y_{i+1} = y_i + g(x_i, y_i) \Delta x$ with $\Delta x = 0.05$, $x_0 = 0$, and $y_0 = 3$, then, for the interval $[0, 0.3]$, one gets the following sequence of values: $x_0 = 0$, $x_1 = 0.05$, $x_2 = 0.10$, $x_3 = 0.15$, $x_4 = 0.20$, $x_5 = 0.25$, and $x_6 = 0.30$.

$y_1 = y_0 + g(x_0, y_0) \Delta x = 3 + g(0, 3)(0.05) = 3 + (0 - 3)(0.05) = 2.85$
$y_2 = y_1 + g(x_1, y_1) \Delta x = 2.85 + g(0.05, 2.85)(0.05) = 2.85 + (0.05 - 2.85)(0.05) = 2.71$
$y_3 = y_2 + g(x_2, y_2) \Delta x = 2.71 + g(0.10, 2.71)(0.05) = 2.71 + (0.10 - 2.71)(0.05) = 2.5795$
$y_4 = y_3 + g(x_3, y_3) \Delta x = 2.5795 + g(0.15, 2.5795)(0.05) = 2.5795 + (0.15 - 2.5795)(0.05) = 2.4580$
$y_5 = y_4 + g(x_4, y_4) \Delta x = 2.4580 + g(0.20, 2.4580)(0.05) = 2.4580 + (0.20 - 2.4580)(0.05) = 2.3451$
$y_6 = y_5 + g(x_5, y_5) \Delta x = 2.3451 + g(0.25, 2.3451)(0.05) = 2.3451 + (0.25 - 2.3451)(0.05) = 2.2403$

Thus, $y(0) = 3$
$y(0.05) = 2.85$
$y(0.10) = 2.71$
$y(0.15) = 2.5795$
$y(0.20) = 2.4580$
$y(0.25) = 2.3451$
$y(0.30) = 2.2403$

19.   Given $y' = 6 - 2y$, then it fits the form $y' = g(x, y) = 6 - 2y$. Using $y_{i+1} = y_i + g(x_i, y_i) \Delta x$ with $\Delta x = 0.1$, $x_0 = 0$, and $y_0 = 2$, then, for the interval $[0, 0.6]$, one gets the following sequence of values: $x_0 = 0$, $x_1 = 0.1$, $x_2 = 0.2$, $x_3 = 0.3$, $x_4 = 0.4$, $x_5 = 0.5$, and $x_6 = 0.6$.

$y_1 = y_0 + g(x_0, y_0) \Delta x = 2 + g(0, 2)(0.1) = 2 + [6 - 2(2)](0.1) = 2.2$
$y_2 = y_1 + g(x_1, y_1) \Delta x = 2.2 + g(0.1, 2.2)(0.1) = 2.2 + [6 - 2(2.2)](0.1) = 2.36$
$y_3 = y_2 + g(x_2, y_2) \Delta x = 2.36 + g(0.2, 2.36)(0.1) = 2.36 + [6 - 2(2.36)](0.1) = 2.488$
$y_4 = y_3 + g(x_3, y_3) \Delta x = 2.488 + g(0.3, 2.488)(0.1) = 2.448 + [6 - 2(2.488)](0.1) = 2.5904$
$y_5 = y_4 + g(x_4, y_4) \Delta x = 2.5904 + g(0.4, 2.5904)(0.1) = 2.5904 + [6 - 2(2.5904)](0.1) = 2.6723$
$y_6 = y_5 + g(x_5, y_5) \Delta x = 2.6723 + g(0.5, 2.6723)(0.1) = 2.6723 + [6 - 2(2.6723)](0.1) = 2.7378$

Thus, $y(0) = 2$
$y(0.1) = 2.2$
$y(0.2) = 2.36$
$y(0.3) = 2.488$
$y(0.4) = 2.5904$
$y(0.5) = 2.6723$
$y(0.6) = 2.7378$

21. Given $y' = 2xy - y$, then it fits the form $y = g(x, y) = 2xy - y = (2x - 1)y$. Using $y_{i+1} = y_i + g(x_i, y_i) \Delta x$ with $\Delta x = 0.1$, $x_0 = 1$, and $y_0 = 1$, then, for the interval $[1, 1.5]$, one gets the following sequence of values: $x_0 = 1$, $x_1 = 1.1$, $x_2 = 1.2$, $x_3 = 1.3$, $x_4 = 1.5$, and $x_5 = 1.5$.

$y_1 = y_0 + g(x_0, y_0) \Delta x = 1 + g(1, 1)(0.1) = 1 + [2(1) - 1](1)(0.1) = 1.1$

$y_2 = y_1 + g(x_1, y_1) \Delta x = 1 + g(1.1, 1.1)(0.1) = 1.1 + [2(1.1) - 1](1.1)(0.1) = 1.232$

$y_3 = y_2 + g(x_2, y_2) \Delta x = 1.232 + g(1.2, 1.232)(0.1) = 1.232 + [2(1.2) - 1](1.232)(0.1) = 1.4045$

$y_4 = y_3 + g(x_3, y_3) \Delta x = 1.4045 + g(1.3, 1.4045)(0.1) = 1.4045 + [2(1, 3) - 1](1.4045)(0.1) = 1.6292$

$y_5 = y_4 + g(x_4, y_4) \Delta x = 1.6292 + g(1.4, 1.6292)(0.1) = 1.6292 + [2(1.4) - 1](1.6292)(0.1) = 1.9225$

Thus, $y(1) = 1$

$\quad y(1.1) = 1.1$

$\quad y(1.2) = 1.232$

$\quad y(1.3) = 1.4045$

$\quad y(1.4) = 1.6292$

$\quad y(1.5) = 1.9225$

23. Let $n(t)$ represent the number of animals at time t in months. If the initial number of animals was 357, then the initial condition is $n(0) = 357$.

25. The condition $y(3) = 40$ means that there are 40 milligrams of mold after 3 hours.

27. Given $n' = \dfrac{dn}{dt} = 0.1(1000 - n)\sqrt{n}$ then $g(t, n) = 0.1(1000 - n)\sqrt{n}$, where $\Delta t = 0.25$ and $n(0) = 10$; that is, $t_0 = 0$ and $n_0 = 10$.

Using $n_{i+1} = n_i + g(t_i, n_i) \Delta t_i$, then, for the interval $[0, 1]$, one gets the following sequence of values: $t_0 = 0$, $t_1 = 0.25$, $t_2 = 0.50$, $t_3 = 0.75$, and $t_4 = 1.0$.

$n_1 = n_0 + g(t_0, n_0) \Delta t = 10 + g(0, 10)(0.25)$

$\qquad = 10 + (0.1)(1000 - 10)(\sqrt{10})(0.25)$

$\qquad = 88.27$

$n_2 = n_1 + g(t_1, n_1) \Delta t = 88.27 + g(0.25, 88.27)(0.25)$

$\qquad = 88.27 + 0.1(1000 - 88.27)(\sqrt{88.27})(0.25)$

$\qquad = 302.42$

$n_3 = n_2 + g(t_2, n_2) \Delta t = 302.42 + g(0.50, 302.42)(0.25)$

$\qquad = 302.42 + 0.1(1000 - 302.42)(\sqrt{302.42})(0.25)$

$\qquad = 605.70$

$n_4 = n_3 + g(t_3, n_3) \Delta t = 605.70 + g(0.75, 605.70)(0.25)$

$\qquad = 605.70 + 0.1(1000 - 605.70)(\sqrt{605.70})(0.25)$

$\qquad = 848.30$

The approximate number of students who have heard the rumor after an hour is 848 students.

29.   For Example 1, $y' = \dfrac{dy}{dx} = 2xy$, $y(0) = 1$.

Separating the variables and integrating both sides yields

$$\frac{dy}{y} = 2x\,dx$$

$$\int \frac{dy}{y} = \int 2x\,dx$$

$$\ln|y| = x^2 + C$$

Using the condition that $y = 1$ when $x = 0$ results in

$$\ln 1 = 0^2 + C$$
$$0 = C$$

Thus, $\ln|y| = x^2$ or $y = f(x) = e^{x^2}$

For $x = 0.6$, $f(0.6) = e^{(0.6)^2} = 1.4333$

SECTION 9.4 Technology Exercises

1. $y_1 = 1$
$y_2 = 1.02$
$y_3 = 1.0608$
$y_4 = 1.124448$
$y_5 = 1.21440384$
$y_6 = 1.335844224$
$y_7 = 1.496145531$

3. $y_1 = 1$
$y_2 = 1.02$
$y_3 = 1.0604$
$y_4 = 1.122212$
$y_5 = 1.20710048$

5. $y_1 = 2.2$
$y_2 = 2.36$
$y_3 = 2.488$
$y_4 = 2.5904$
$y_5 = 2.67232$
$y_6 = 2.737856$

REVIEW EXERCISES FOR CHAPTER 9 pages 474–475

1.   To show that $y = 1 - 6x^2$ is a solution of the differential equation $xy' = 2y - 2$, find the derivative y' and substitute. Differentiating yields $y' = -12x$ and

$$xy' = x(-12x) = -12x^2$$

$$2y - 2 = 2(1 - 6x^2) - 2 = 2 - 12x^2 - 2 = -12x^2$$

Thus, $xy' = -12x^2 = 2y - 2$.

3.   Given $y' = 1 - x^3$, then integrate both sides to get

$$y = \int (1 - x^3)\,dx$$
$$= x - \frac{x^4}{4} + C$$

5. Given $x^3\, dy = dx$, then separate the variables and integrate both sides to get

$$dy = \frac{1}{x^3}\, dx$$

$$\int dy = \int x^{-3}\, dx$$

$$y = -\frac{1}{2}x^{-2} + C$$

$$= -\frac{1}{2x^2} + C$$

7. Given $y\, dx - x\, dy = 0$, then separate the variables and integrate both sides to get

$$x\, dy = y\, dx$$

$$\frac{dy}{y} = \frac{dx}{x}$$

$$\int \frac{dy}{y} = \int \frac{dx}{x}$$

$$\ln |y| = \ln |x| + C_1$$

$$y = e^{\ln |x| + C_1} = e^{C_1}e^{\ln |x|} = Cx$$

$$y = Cx$$

9. Given $\frac{dy}{t} - \frac{dt}{y} = 0$, then separate the variables and integrate both sides to get

$$\frac{dy}{t} = \frac{dt}{y}$$

$$y\, dy = t\, dt$$

$$\int y\, dy = \int t\, dt$$

$$\frac{y^2}{2} = \frac{t^2}{2} + C_1$$

$$y^2 = t^2 + C \qquad (C = 2C_1)$$

11. Given $y' = \frac{2}{\sqrt{x}} = 2x^{-1/2}$, $y(1) = 5$, then integrate to get

$$y = \int 2x^{-1/2}\, dx = 4x^{1/2} + C$$

Using the condition $y(1) = 5$ yields

$$y(1) = 4(1)^{1/2} + C = 5$$

$$C = 1$$

Thus, $y = 4\sqrt{x} + 1$

13.   Given $dy = x\sqrt{y}\, dx$, $y(0) = 9$, then separate the variables and integrate to get

$$\frac{dy}{\sqrt{y}} = x\, dx$$

$$\int y^{-1/2}\, dy = \int x\, dx$$

$$2y^{1/2} = \frac{x^2}{2} + C$$

Using the condition $y(0) = 9$, yields

$$2(9)^{1/2} = 0 + C$$

$$C = 6$$

Thus, $2y^{1/2} = \frac{x^2}{2} + 6$

$$y^{1/2} = \frac{x^2}{4} + 3$$

15.   **a.**   The differential equation that models the growth of bacteria is $\dfrac{dA}{dt} = 0.08A$.

b.   Separate the variables and integrate both sides to get

$$\frac{dA}{A} = 0.08\, dt$$

$$\int \frac{dA}{A} = \int 0.08\, dt$$

$$\ln|A| = 0.08t + C_1$$

$$A = e^{0.08t + C_1} = e^{C_1} e^{0.08t}$$

$$= Ce^{0.08t}$$

c.   If the initial condition is $A(0) = 2000$, then

$$A(0) = Ce^0 = 2000$$

$$C = 2000$$

$$A = 2000e^{0.08t}$$

17. $R'(x) = 12 + 0.04x$, $R(0) = 0$. So $R(x) = 12x + 0.02x^2 + C$. $R(0) = 0$ implies that $C = 0$. Hence, $R(x) = 12x + 0.02x^2$.

19.   The elasticity equation is

$$E = \frac{-p}{x}\frac{dx}{dp}$$

We have $E = 0.02p$ and $p = 50$ when $x = 1$. Hence, we must solve

$$0.02p = \frac{-p}{x}\frac{dx}{dp}; \qquad p(1) = 50$$

Separating variables and integrating yields

$$\int 0.02\, dp = -\int \frac{dx}{x}$$

$$0.02p = -\ln|x| + C = -\ln x + C$$

since demand $x > 0$, $p = 50$ when $x = 1$ implies that $0.02(50) = 0 + C$

$$C = 1$$

So, $0.02p = -\ln x + 1$

$$p = 50(1 - \ln x)$$

21.   Given $y' = 4xy^2$, then it fits the form $y' = g(x,y) = 4xy^2$. Using $y_{i+1} = y_i + g(x_i, y_i) \Delta x$ with $\Delta x = 0.1$, $x_0 = 0$, and $y_0 = 1$, then, for the interval $[0, 0.5]$, one gets the following sequence of values: $x_0 = 0$, $x_1 = 0.1$, $x_2 = 0.2$, $x_3 = 0.3$, $x_4 = 0.4$, and $x_5 = 0.5$.

$$y_1 = y_0 + g(x_0, y_0) \Delta x = 1 + g(0, 1)(0.1) = 1 + 4(0)(1)^2(0.1) = 1$$
$$y_2 = y_1 + g(x_1, y_1) \Delta x = 1 + g(0.1, 1)(0.1) = 1 + 4(0.1)(1)^2(0.1) = 1.04$$
$$y_3 = y_2 + g(x_2, y_2) \Delta x = 1.04 + g(0.2, 1.04)(0.1) = 1.04 + 4(0.2)(1.04)^2(0.1) = 1.1265$$
$$y_4 = y_3 + g(x_3, y_3) \Delta x = 1.1265 + g(0.3, 1.1265)(0.1) = 1.1265 + 4(0.3)(1.1265)^2(0.1) = 1.2788$$
$$y_5 = y_4 + g(x_4, y_4) \Delta x = 1.2788 + g(0.4, 1.2788)(0.1) = 1.2788 + 4(0.4)(1.2788)^2(0.1) = 1.5405$$

Thus, $y(0) = 1$
$$y(0.1) = 1$$
$$y(0.2) = 1.04$$
$$y(0.3) = 1.1265$$
$$y(0.4) = 1.2788$$
$$y(0.5) = 1.5405$$

23. $\frac{dN}{dt} = bN - dN$, where N is the number of animals in the population at time t and b and d are the constant birth and death rates, respectively.

a.   The differential equation says that the rate of change of the animal population $\frac{dN}{dt}$ is the difference between the number of births and the number of deaths.

b. $$\frac{dN}{dt} = (b - d)N$$
Separating variables and integrating yields
$$\int \frac{dN}{N} = \int (b - d)\, dt$$
$$ln\,|N| = (b - d)t + C_1$$
$$ln\,N = (b - d)t + C_1$$
$$N = e^{(b-d)t + C_1} = e^{C_1} e^{(b-d)t} = C e^{(b-d)t}$$

When $t = 0$, $N = N_0$ implies that
$$N_0 = C e^{(b-d)0} = C$$

Thus, $N = N_0 e^{(b-d)t}$

c.   If $b < d$, then the birth rate is less than the death rate and so the animal population goes to zero; i.e., the animals die out. This can be seen since $N = N_0 e^{(b-d)t}$, where $b - d < 0$ if $b < d$ so that $\lim_{t \to \infty} N = 0$.

d.   If $b > d$, then the birth rate is greater than the death rate and so the animal population grows without bound. In fact, since $N = N_0 e^{(b-d)t}$, where $b - d > 0$ since $b > d$, then
$$\lim_{t \to \infty} N = \lim_{t \to \infty} N_0 e^{(b-d)t} = \infty.$$

i.e., we have exponential population growth.

SECTION 10.1 pages 485–487

1. Given $f(x,y) = x^2 + y^2$, then

$$f(4,2) = 4^2 + 2^2 = 20$$
$$f(-1,6) = (-1)^2 + 6^2 = 37$$
$$f(0,2) = 0^2 + 2^2 = 4$$
$$f(1,0) = 1^2 + 0^2 = 1$$
$$f(0,1) = 0^2 + 1^2 = 1$$

3. Given $f(x,y) = \dfrac{x}{x+y}$, then

$$f(4,2) = \frac{4}{4+2} = \frac{2}{3}$$
$$f(-1,6) = \frac{-1}{-1+6} = -\frac{1}{5}$$
$$f(0,2) = \frac{0}{0+2} = 0$$
$$f(1,0) = \frac{1}{1+0} = 1$$
$$f(0,1) = \frac{0}{0+1} = 0$$

5. Given $f(x,y) = 1 - x - y$, then

$$f(4,2) = 1 - 4 - 2 = -5$$
$$f(-1,6) = 1 + 1 - 6 = -4$$
$$f(0,2) = 1 - 0 - 2 = -1$$
$$f(1,0) = 1 - 1 - 0 = 0$$
$$f(0,1) = 1 - 0 - 1 = 0$$

7. Given $f(x,y) = 3x^2 - 7y$, then

$$f(4,2) = 3(4)^2 - 7(2) = 34$$
$$f(-1,6) = 3(-1)^2 - 7(6) = -39$$
$$f(0,2) = 3(0)^2 - 7(2) = -14$$
$$f(1,0) = 3(1)^2 - 7(0) = 3$$
$$f(0,1) = 3(0)^2 - 7(1) = -7$$

9. Given $f(x,y) = \sqrt{5 + x^2 + y^2}$, then

$$f(4,2) = \sqrt{5 + 4^2 + 2^2} = \sqrt{25} = 5$$
$$f(-1,6) = \sqrt{5 + (-1)^2 + 6^2} = \sqrt{42}$$
$$f(0,2) = \sqrt{5 + 0^2 + 2^2} = \sqrt{9} = 3$$
$$f(1,0) = \sqrt{5 + 1^2 + 0^2} = \sqrt{6}$$
$$f(0,1) = \sqrt{5 + 0^2 + 1^2} = \sqrt{6}$$

11. Given $g(x,y) = y \ln x$, then

$$g(1,4) = 4 \ln 1 = 0$$
$$g(e,0) = 0 \ln e = 0$$

13. Given $g(x,y) = y + x \ln x$, then

$$g(1,4) = 4 + 1 \ln 1 = 4$$
$$g(e,0) = 0 + e \ln e = e$$

15. Given $f(x,y.z) = x^2 + y^2 - z^2 + 7$, then

$$f(0,1,2) = 0^2 + 1^2 - 2^2 + 7 = 4$$

17. Given $f(x,y,z) = \frac{x+y}{2y}$, then $f(0,1,2) = \frac{0+1}{2(1)} = \frac{1}{2}$

19. Given $f(p,r,t) = pe^{0.01rt}$, then

a. $f(1000,8,2) = 1000e^{0.01(8)(2)} = \$1173.51$

b. The given conditions indicate that $p = 3000$, $r = 10$, and $t = 7$; thus, $f(3000,10,7) = 3000e^{0.01(10)(7)} = \$6041.26$

21. Given $f(x,y) = 20x^{0.4}y^{0.6}$ with $x = 2400$ and $y = 4000$, then

$$f(2400,4000) = 20(2400)^{0.4}(4000)^{0.6} \approx 65,215.45$$

23.   Given $f(a,m) = 100 \cdot \frac{m}{a}$, then

   a. $f(10,13) = 100 \cdot \frac{13}{10} = 130$

   $IQ = 130$

   b. $f(10,8) = 100 \cdot \frac{8}{10} = 80$

   $IQ = 80$

   c.   An IQ of 100 means that a person's mental age is equal to the person's actual age.

25.   Let $x =$ the number of free throws, worth 1 point each
   $y =$ the number of regular field goals, worth 2 points each
   $z =$ the number of "long" field goals, worth 3 points each

   The total number of points scored by a basketball player would be $P(x,y,z) = x + 2y + 3z$.

27.   **a.**   Given $R(l,r) = k \cdot \frac{l}{r^4}$, where k is a constant, l is the length of the capillary, and r is the radius of the capillary, then

   $R(64,2) = k \cdot \frac{64}{2^4} = 4k$

   $R(64,1) = k \cdot \frac{64}{1^2} = 64k$

   b.   From part a, it would appear that when the radius of the capillary is reduced to half its original size, then the resistance within the capillary is 16 times as great.

29.   Let $x =$ the number of large flags produced, which sell for $6.50 each
   $6.5x =$ the revenue from the sale of large flags
   $y =$ the number of small flags produced, which sell for $5 each
   $5y =$ the revenue from the sale of small flags

   a.   The revenue function is $R(x,y) = 6.5x + 5y$

   b.   Using the result from Exercise 28, the profit function is $P(x,y) = R(x,y) - C(x,y)$
   $$= 6.5x + 5y - (4x + 3y)$$
   $$= 2.5x + 2y$$

31.   **a.**   For a rectangular box, let $x =$ length
   $y =$ width
   $z =$ height

   Then the volume is $V(x,y,z) = xyz$

   b.   If $z = 2y$, then $V(x,y,z) = V(x,y,2y) = xy(2y)$
   $$= 2xy^2$$

33.   Let $f(x,y) = x + y$. Since there is no division by zero or even root of a negative number, the domain is all ordered pairs of real numbers.

35.   Let $f(x,y) = x^2 + y^2 - 9$. Since there is no division by zero or even root of a negative number, the domain is all ordered pairs of real numbers.

37.   Let $z = \sqrt{y - x}$. Since there is a square root, the (x,y) pairs must be chosen such that $y - x \geq 0$. The domain is all pairs of real numbers (x,y) such that $y \geq x$.

39.   Let $z = \dfrac{x}{1 - y}$. Since $1 - y$ is the denominator, one must have $1 - y \neq 0$. The domain is all ordered pairs of real numbers (x,y) such that $y \neq 1$.

41. Let $g(x,y) = \dfrac{x^2 + y^2}{x - y}$. Since $x - y$ is the denominator, one must have $x - y \neq 0$. The domain is the set of all ordered pairs of real numbers (x,y) such that $y \neq x$.

43. Let $f(x,y) = \dfrac{\sqrt{5x}}{2y + 3}$. There is both a square root of $5x$ and division by $2y+3$. Thus, one must have $5x \geq 0$ and $2y+3 \neq 0$.

The domain is all ordered pairs of real numbers (x,y) such that $x \geq 0$ and $y \neq -\frac{3}{2}$.

45. Let $z = 5xe^y$. Since there is no division by zero or even root of a negative number, the domain is the set of all ordered pairs of real numbers.

Note: The exponential function is defined for all real numbers.

47. Let $z = y \ln(x - 1)$. There is no division by zero or even root of a negative number, but the natural log function requires that $x - 1 > 0$. The domain is the set of all ordered pairs of real numbers (x,y) such that $x > 1$.

49. Let $f(x,y) = 9 - x^2 - y^2$.

c	Intermediate result	Level curve
1	$9 - x^2 - y^2 = 1$	$x^2 + y^2 = 8$
3	$9 - x^2 - y^2 = 3$	$x^2 + y^2 = 6$
5	$9 - x^2 - y^2 = 5$	$x^2 + y^2 = 4$
7	$9 - x^2 - y^2 = 7$	$x^2 + y^2 = 2$

51. Let $f(x,y) = 16 - x^2 - y^2$.

c	Intermediate result	Level curve
0	$16 - x^2 - y^2 = 0$	$x^2 + y^2 = 16$
7	$16 - x^2 - y^2 = 7$	$x^2 + y^2 = 9$
12	$16 - x^2 - y^2 = 12$	$x^2 + y^2 = 4$
15	$16 - x^2 - y^2 = 15$	$x^2 + y^2 = 1$

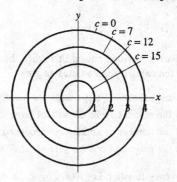

53. Let $f(x,y) = x^2 - y + 1$.

c	Intermediate result	Level curve
0	$x^2 - y + 1 = 0$	$y = x^2 + 1$
1	$x^2 - y + 1 = 1$	$y = x^2$
2	$x^2 - y + 1 = 2$	$y = x^2 - 1$

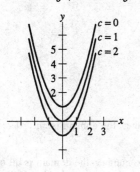

55. Let $f(x,y) = x - y + 2$

c	Intermediate result	Level curve
0	$x - y + 2 = 0$	$y = x + 2$
2	$x - y + 2 = 2$	$y = x$
4	$x - y + 2 = 4$	$y = x - 2$
6	$x - y + 2 = 6$	$y = x - 4$

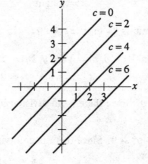

57. Let $f(x, y) = 1 - x - y$.

c	Intermediate result	Level curve
1	$1 - x - y = 1$	$y = -x$
3	$1 - x - y = 3$	$y = -x - 2$
5	$1 - x - y = 5$	$y = -x - 4$
7	$1 - x - y = 7$	$y = -x - 6$

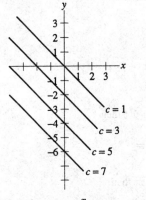

59. Let $f(x, y) = \frac{y}{x}$.

c	Intermediate result	Level curve
1	$\frac{y}{x} = 1$	$y = x$
2	$\frac{y}{x} = 2$	$y = 2x$
3	$\frac{y}{x} = 3$	$y = 3x$
4	$\frac{y}{x} = 4$	$y = 4x$

61. Let $f(x, y) = e^x - y$.

c	Intermediate result	Level curve
-3	$e^x - y = -3$	$y = e^x + 3$
-2	$e^x - y = -2$	$y = e^x + 2$
-1	$e^x - y = -1$	$y = e^x + 1$
0	$e^x - y = 0$	$y = e^x$

63. Let $f(x, y) = \ln x - y$.

c	Intermediate result	Level curve
-2	$\ln x - y = -2$	$y = \ln x + 2$
-1	$\ln x - y = -1$	$y = \ln x + 1$
0	$\ln x - y = 0$	$y = \ln x$
1	$\ln x - y = 1$	$y = \ln x - 1$

65. $f(P, E) = \frac{P}{E}$

a. $P = \$42$, $f(P, E) = 15$

$$15 = \frac{42}{E}$$

$$E = \frac{42}{15} = \$2.80$$

b. If P increases while E remains unchanged, then $\frac{P}{E}$ increases.

67. The limit as x approaches 0 and y approaches 1 of the function $f(x, y)$ is 2.5.

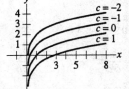

SECTION 10.1 Technology Exercises

1. $y = x^2 + 2$ is a level curve.

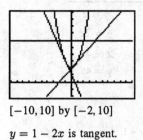

[−10, 10] by [−2, 10]

$y = 1 - 2x$ is tangent.

3.

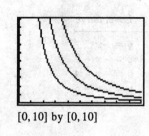

[0, 10] by [0, 10]

a. y_1

b. y_3

SECTION 10.2 pages 494–496

1.   Let $f(x, y) = 2x + 5y$; then

$$\frac{\partial f}{\partial x} = 2 \qquad \frac{\partial f}{\partial y} = 5$$

3.   Let $f(x, y) = x^3 - 4y^2$; then

$$\frac{\partial f}{\partial x} = 3x^2 \qquad \frac{\partial f}{\partial y} = -8y$$

5.   Let $f(x, y) = \frac{x}{y} = xy^{-1}$; then

$$\frac{\partial f}{\partial x} = \frac{1}{y} \qquad \frac{\partial f}{\partial y} = -\frac{x}{y^2}$$

7.   Let $f(x, y) = y \ln x$; then

$$\frac{\partial f}{\partial x} = \frac{y}{x} \qquad \frac{\partial f}{\partial y} = \ln x$$

9.   Let $f(x, y) = e^{3xy}$; then

$$\frac{\partial f}{\partial x} = e^{3xy} \frac{\partial f}{\partial x}(3xy) \qquad \frac{\partial f}{\partial y} = e^{3xy} \frac{\partial f}{\partial y}(3xy)$$
$$= 3ye^{3xy} \qquad\qquad = 3xe^{3xy}$$

11.   Let $f(x, y) = x\sqrt{y} = xy^{1/2}$; then

$$\frac{\partial f}{\partial x} = y^{1/2} \qquad \frac{\partial f}{\partial y} = \frac{1}{2}xy^{-1/2}$$
$$\qquad\qquad\qquad \frac{\partial f}{\partial y} = \frac{x}{2\sqrt{y}}$$

13.   Let $f(x, y) = \sqrt{x^2 + y^2} = (x^2 + y^2)^{1/2}$; then

$$\frac{\partial f}{\partial x} = \frac{1}{2}(x^2 + y^2)^{-1/2} \frac{\partial}{\partial x}(x^2 + y^2) \qquad \frac{\partial f}{\partial y} = (x^2 + y^2)^{-1/2} \frac{\partial}{\partial y}(x^2 + y^2)$$
$$= \frac{1}{2}(x^2 + y^2)^{-1/2}(2x) \qquad\qquad = \frac{1}{2}(x^2 + y^2)^{-1/2}(2y)$$
$$= \frac{x}{\sqrt{x^2 + y^2}} \qquad\qquad\qquad = \frac{y}{\sqrt{x^2 + y^2}}$$

15.   Let $f(x, y) = \frac{x}{x+y} = x(x + y)^{-1}$; then

$$\frac{\partial f}{\partial x} = \frac{(x + y)(1) - x(1)}{(x + y)^2} \qquad \frac{\partial f}{\partial y} = x\left[-1(x + y)^{-2}(1)\right]$$
$$= \frac{y}{(x + y)^2} \qquad\qquad = -\frac{x}{(x + y)^2}$$

17.   Let $f(x, y) = x^3 y^5$; then

$$f_x(x, y) = 3x^2 y^5 \qquad f_y(x, y) = 5x^3 y^4$$

19.   Let $f(x, y) = \ln (x^2 + y^2)$; then

$$f_x(x, y) = \frac{1}{x^2 + y^2} \frac{\partial}{\partial x}(x^2 + y^2) \qquad f_y(x, y) = \frac{1}{x^2 + y^2} \frac{\partial}{\partial y}(x^2 + y^2)$$
$$= \frac{2x}{x^2 + y^2} \qquad\qquad\qquad = \frac{2y}{x^2 + y^2}$$

21. Let $f(x,y) = xe^{-y}$; then

$$f_x(x,y) = e^{-y} \qquad f_y(x,y) = -xe^{-y}$$

23. Let $f(x,y) = xy$; then

$$\begin{aligned}
\frac{\partial f}{\partial x} &= \lim_{\Delta x \to 0} \frac{f(x + \Delta x, y) - f(x,y)}{\Delta x} \\
&= \lim_{\Delta x \to 0} \frac{(x + \Delta x)y - xy}{\Delta x} \\
&= \lim_{\Delta x \to 0} \frac{xy + (\Delta x)y - xy}{\Delta x} \\
&= \lim_{\Delta x \to 0} y \\
&= y
\end{aligned}$$

25. Let $f(x,y) = x^2$; then

$$\begin{aligned}
\frac{\partial f}{\partial x} &= \lim_{\Delta x \to 0} \frac{f(x + \Delta xy,) - (f(x,y)}{\Delta x} \\
&= \lim_{\Delta x \to 0} \frac{(x + \Delta x)^2 - x^2}{\Delta x} \\
&= \lim_{\Delta x \to 0} \frac{x^2 + 2x(\Delta x) + (\Delta x)^2 - x^2}{\Delta x} \\
&= \lim_{\Delta x \to 0} \frac{\Delta x(2x + \Delta x)}{\Delta x} \\
&= \lim_{\Delta x \to 0} 2x + \Delta x \\
&= 2x + 0 \\
&= 2x
\end{aligned}$$

27. Let $f(x,y) = 3y$; then

$$\begin{aligned}
\frac{\partial f}{\partial x} &= \lim_{\Delta x \to 0} \frac{(f + \Delta x, y) - f(x,y)}{\Delta x} \\
&= \lim_{\Delta x \to 0} \frac{3y - 3y}{\Delta x} \\
&= \lim_{\Delta x \to 0} \frac{0}{\Delta x} \\
&= \lim_{\Delta x \to 0} 0 \\
&= 0
\end{aligned}$$

29. Let $f(x,y) = x^2y^2$; then

$$\begin{aligned}
\frac{\delta f}{\delta x} &= \lim_{\Delta x \to 0} \frac{f(x + \Delta x, y) - f(x,y)}{\Delta x} \\
&= \lim_{\Delta x \to 0} \frac{(x + \Delta x)^2 y^2 - x^2 y^2}{\Delta x} \\
&= \lim_{\Delta x \to 0} \frac{\left[x^2 + 2x(\Delta x) + (\Delta x)^2 \right] y^2 - x^2 y^2}{\Delta x} \\
&= \lim_{\Delta x \to 0} \frac{x^2 y^2 + [2x(\Delta x)] y^2 + (\Delta x)^2 y^2 - x^2 y^2}{\Delta x} \\
&= \lim_{\Delta x \to 0} \frac{\Delta x(2xy^2 + \Delta xy^2)}{\Delta x} \\
&= \lim_{\Delta x \to 0} 2xy^2 + \Delta xy^2 \\
&= 2xy^2 + 0 \\
&= 2xy^2
\end{aligned}$$

31. Let $f(x,y) = xy$; then

$$\begin{aligned}
\frac{\delta f}{\delta y} &= \lim_{\Delta y \to 0} \frac{f(x, y + \Delta y) - f(x,y)}{\Delta y} \\
&= \lim_{\Delta y \to 0} \frac{x(y + \Delta y) - xy}{\Delta y} \\
&= \lim_{\Delta y \to 0} x \\
&= x
\end{aligned}$$

33. Let $f(x,y) = x^2$; then

$$\begin{aligned}
\frac{\delta f}{\delta y} &= \lim_{\Delta y \to 0} \frac{f(x, y + \Delta y) - f(x,y)}{\Delta y} \\
&= \lim_{\Delta y \to 0} \frac{x^2 - x^2}{\Delta y} \\
&= \lim_{\Delta y \to 0} 0 \\
&= 0
\end{aligned}$$

35. Let $f(x,y) = 3y$; then

$$\begin{aligned}
\frac{\partial f}{\partial y} &= \lim_{\Delta y \to 0} \frac{f(x, y + \Delta y) - f(x,y)}{\Delta y} \\
&= \lim_{\Delta y \to 0} \frac{3(y + \Delta y) - 3y}{\Delta y} \\
&= \lim_{\Delta y \to 0} 3 \\
&= 3
\end{aligned}$$

37. Let $f(x,y) = x^2 y^2$; then

$$\frac{\delta f}{\delta y} = \lim_{\Delta y \to 0} \frac{f(x, y + \Delta y) - f(x,y)}{\Delta y}$$

$$= \lim_{\Delta y \to 0} \frac{x^2 (y + \Delta y)^2 - x^2 y^2}{\Delta y}$$

$$= \lim_{\Delta y \to 0} \frac{x^2 \left[y^2 + 2y(\Delta y) + (\Delta y)^2 \right] - x^2 y^2}{\Delta y}$$

$$= \lim_{\Delta y \to 0} \frac{x^2 y^2 + 2x^2 y(\Delta y) + x^2 (\Delta y)^2 - x^2 y^2}{\Delta y}$$

$$= \lim_{\Delta y \to 0} \frac{\Delta y \left[2x^2 y + x^2 (\Delta y) \right]}{\Delta y}$$

$$= \lim_{\Delta y \to 0} 2x^2 y + x^2 (\Delta y)$$

$$= 2x^2 y + 0$$

$$= 2x^2 y$$

39. Given $f(x,y) = x^2 y^2 - 3x + 2y$, then

$$\frac{\partial f}{\partial x} = f_x(x,y) = 2xy^2 - 3 \quad \text{and} \quad \frac{\partial f}{\partial y} = f_y(x,y) = 2x^2 y + 2$$

a. $f_x(5,4) = 2(5)(4)^2 - 3$
    $= 157$

b. $f_y(-1,8) = 2(-1)^2(8) + 2$
    $= 18$

c. $\frac{\partial f}{\partial x}(1,-5) = 2(1)(-5)^2 - 3$
    $= 47$

d. $\frac{\partial f}{\partial y}(0,9) = 2(0)^2(9) + 2$
    $= 2$

41. Given $g(x,y) = x \ln y + xy$, then

$$\frac{\partial g}{\partial x} = g_x(x,y) = \ln y + y \quad \text{and} \quad \frac{\partial g}{\partial y} = g_y(x,y) = \frac{x}{y} + x$$

a. $g_y(8,2) = \frac{8}{2} + 8$
    $= 12$

b. $g_x(3,1) = \ln 1 + 1$
    $= 1$

c. $\frac{\partial g}{\partial x}(4,e) = \ln e + e$
    $= 1 + e$

d. $\frac{\partial g}{\partial y}(2e,e) = \frac{2e}{e} + 2e$
    $= 2 + 2e$
    $= 2(1 + e)$

43. Let $f(x,y,z) = x^2 + y^2 + z^2$; then

$f_x = 2x \qquad f_y = 2y \qquad f_z = 2z$

45. Let $f(x,y,z) = xyz - x + y$; then

$f_x = yz - 1 \qquad f_y = xz + 1 \qquad f_z = xy$

47. Let $f(x, y, z) = xye^z$; then

$$f_x = ye^z \qquad f_y = xe^z \qquad f_z = xye^z$$

49. Let $f(x, y, z) = \frac{x}{y+z} = x(y + z)^{-1}$; then

$$f_x = \frac{1}{y+z} \qquad f_y = -x(y+z)^{-2}(1) \qquad f_z = -x(y+z)^{-2}(1)$$
$$= -\frac{x}{(y+z)^2} \qquad\qquad = -\frac{x}{(y+z)^2}$$

51. Let $f(x, y) = x^2 + xy + y^2$; then

$$f_x = 2x + y \qquad f_y = x + 2y$$
and
$$f_{xx} = 2 \qquad f_{yy} = 2$$
$$f_{xy} = 1 \qquad f_{yx} = 1$$

53. Let $f(x, y) = y \ln x$; then

$$f_x = \frac{y}{x} = yx^{-1} \qquad f_y = \ln x$$
and
$$f_{xx} = -\frac{y}{x^2} \qquad f_{yy} = 0$$
$$f_{xy} = \frac{1}{x} \qquad f_{yx} = \frac{1}{x}$$

55. Let $g(x, y) = 3xe^y$; then

$$g_x = 3e^y \qquad g_y = 3xe^y$$
and
$$g_{xx} = 0 \qquad g_{yy} = 3xe^y$$
$$g_{xy} = 3e^y \qquad g_{yx} = 3e^y$$

57. Let $h(x, y) = x^2 \ln y$; then

$$h_x = 2x \ln y \qquad h_y = \frac{x^2}{y} = x^2 y^{-1}$$
and
$$h_{xx} = 2 \ln y \qquad h_{yy} = -\frac{x^2}{y^2}$$
$$h_{xy} = \frac{2x}{y} \qquad h_{yx} = \frac{2x}{y}$$

59. Let $f(x, y) = \ln(x + y^2)$

$$f_x = \frac{1}{x+y^2}(1) \qquad\qquad f_y = \frac{1}{x+y^2}(2y)$$
$$= \frac{1}{x+y^2} = (x+y^2)^{-1} \qquad = \frac{2y}{x+y^2} = 2y(x+y^2)^{-1}$$

$$f_{xx} = -(x+y^2)^{-2}(1) \qquad f_{yy} = \frac{(x+y^2)(2) - 2y(2y)}{(x+y^2)^2}$$
$$= -\frac{1}{(x+y^2)^2} \qquad\qquad = \frac{2x + 2y^2 - 4y^2}{(x+y^2)^2}$$
$$= \frac{2(x-y^2)}{(x+y^2)^2}$$

$$f_{xy} = -(x+y^2)^{-2}(2y) \qquad f_{yx} = -2y(x+y^2)^{-2}(1)$$
$$= -\frac{2y}{(x+y^2)^2} \qquad\qquad = -\frac{2y}{(x+y^2)^2}$$

61.   From Example 7, the revenue function is

$R(x, y) = 100x + 150y - 0.03x^2 - 0.02y^2$

a.   The desired rate of change for the stated conditions is

$\dfrac{\partial R}{\partial y}(50, 40)$. It follows that $\dfrac{\partial r}{\partial y} = 150 - 0.04y$ and

$\dfrac{\partial R}{\partial y}(50, 40) = 150 - 0.04(40) = 148.40$

The approximate additional revenue is \$148.40.

b.   The desired rate of change for the new conditions is

$\dfrac{\partial R}{\partial x}(60, 38)$. It follows that

$\dfrac{\partial R}{\partial x} = 100 - 0.06x$ and

$\dfrac{\partial R}{\partial x}(60, 38) = 100 - 0.06(60) = 96.40$

The approximate additional revenue is \$96.40.

63.   Given $f(x, y) = 2x^{0.4}y^{0.6}$, then

a.   The marginal productivity of labor is $\dfrac{\partial f}{\partial x} = 0.8x^{-0.6}y^{0.6}$

b.   The marginal productivity of capital is $\dfrac{\partial f}{\partial y} = 1.2x^{0.4}y^{-0.4}$

65.   Given $f(x, y) = 20x^{1/4}y^{3/4}$ at $x = 256$ units of labor and $y = 81$ units of capital, then the marginal productivity of labor is $\dfrac{\partial f}{\partial x}(256, 81)$ (see Exercise 73). Computing $\dfrac{\partial f}{\partial x} = \dfrac{20}{4}x^{-3/4}y^{3/4}$ yields

$\dfrac{\partial f}{\partial x}(256, 81) = 5(256)^{-3/4}(81)^{3/4}$

$\qquad = \dfrac{5(27)}{64}$

$\qquad = \dfrac{135}{64} \approx 2.11$

The marginal productivity of labor is $\frac{135}{64} \approx 2.11$.

67. The temperature on the surface of the heated plate is given by $T(x, y) = 350 - x^2 - y^2$.

   a. At the origin, $T(0,0) = 350$

   b. The temperature at the origin is the greatest since the terms $-x^2$ and $-y^2$ would be negative for any other choice of (x, y) and, when added to 350, would make the value of T less than 350. *Note:* $T(x, y) = 350 - (x^2 + y^2) \le 350$.

   c. $\dfrac{\partial T}{\partial x} = -2x$; thus, $\dfrac{\partial T}{\partial x}(10, 6) = -20$

   The rate of change of temperature with respect to distance x at the point (10, 6) is decreasing at $20°$ per centimeter.

   d. $\dfrac{\partial T}{\partial y} = -2y$, thus, $\dfrac{\partial T}{\partial y}(10, 6) = -12$

   The rate of change of temperature with respect to distance y at the point (10, 6) is decreasing at $12°$ per centimeter.

   e. The rates in parts c and d are negative because the plate is hottest at the origin and must get cooler as one moves away from the origin in either the x or the y direction. That is, $T(x, y)$ is a decreasing function when x varies and y is held fixed or when y varies and x is held fixed.

69. Given $V(r, h) = \pi r^2 h$, then $\dfrac{\partial V}{\partial h} = \pi r^2$

71. Given $P(T, V) = k \cdot \dfrac{T}{V}$, where k is a constant, then

   a. $\dfrac{\partial P}{\partial T} = \dfrac{k}{V}$

   b. $\dfrac{\partial P}{\partial V} = -\dfrac{kT}{V^2}$

   c. $\dfrac{\partial P}{\partial V}$ is the rate of change of pressure with respect to volume, assuming the temperature is kept constant.

73. The surface area function is given by $S(w, h) = 0.0072 w^{0.425} h^{0.725}$ square meters, where w is in kilograms and h is in centimeters.

   a. $S(80, 178) = 1.9847$ square meters

   b. $S_w(w, h) = 0.00306 w^{-0.575} h^{0.725}$

   $S_h(w, h) = 0.00522 w^{0.425} h^{-0.275}$

   c. $S_w(80, 178) = 0.0105$

   $S_h(80, 178) = 0.0081$

   d. S_w is the rate of change of surface area with respect to the change in weight when the height remains fixed.

   S_h is the rate of change of surface area with respect to the change in height when the weight remains fixed.

75. When two resistors R_1 and R_2 are connected in parallel, the total resistance R that results is given by

$$\frac{1}{R} = \frac{1}{R_1} + \frac{1}{R_2}$$

$$\frac{1}{R} = \frac{R_2 + R_1}{R_1 R_2}$$

$$R = \frac{R_1 R_2}{R_1 + R_2}$$

$$\frac{\partial R}{\partial R_1} = \frac{(R_1 + R_2)R_2 - R_1 R_2(1)}{(R_1 + R_2)^2}$$

$$= \frac{R_1 R_2 + R_2^2 - R_1 R_2}{(R_1 + R_2)^2}$$

$$= \frac{R_2^2}{(R_1 + R_2)^2}$$

When $R_1 = 10$ ohms and $R_2 = 15$ ohms,

$$\frac{\partial R}{\partial R_1} = \frac{15^2}{(10 + 15)^2} = \frac{9}{25}$$

SECTION 10.3 pages 503–505

1. Given $f(x, y) = x^2 + y^2 - 6x + 2y$, then find the first partial derivatives $f_x = 2x - 6$ and $f_y = 2y + 2$.

   Solving $f_x = 2x - 6 = 0$ yields $x = 3$

             $f_y = 2y + 2 = 0$ $y = -1$

   The critical point is $(3, -1)$.

3. Given $f(x, y) = 3x^3 + y^2 - 36x - 10y + 7$, then find the first partial derivatives $f_x = 9x^2 - 36 = 9(x^2 - 4) = 9(x - 2)(x + 2)$
   $$f_y = 2y - 10 = 2(y - 5)$$

   Solving $f_x = 9(x - 2)(x + 2) = 0$ yields $x = 2,\ x = -2$

             $f_y = 2(y - 5) = 0$ $y = 5$

   There are two critical points, $(2, 5)$ and $(-2, 5)$.

5. Given $g(x, y) = 2x^3 + 3x^2 + y^2 - 8y + 5$, then find the first partial derivatives $g_x = 6x^2 + 6x = 6x(x + 1)$
   $$g_y = 2y - 8 = 2(y - 4)$$

   Solving $g_x = 6x(x + 1) = 0$ yields $x = 0,\ x = -1$

             $g_y = 2(y - 4) = 0$ $y = 4$

   There are two critical points, $(0, 4)$ and $(-1, 4)$.

7. Given $f(x, y) = x^3 + y^3 - 3x - 27y + 4$, then find the first partial derivatives $f_x = 3x^2 - 3 = 3(x^2 - 1) = 3(x - 1)(x + 1)$
   $$f_y = 3y^2 - 27 = 3(y^2 - 9) = 3(y - 3)(y + 3)$$

   Solving $f_x = 3(x - 1)(x + 1) = 0$ yields $x = 1,\ x = -1$

             $f_y = 3(y - 3)(y + 3) = 0$ $y = 3,\ y = -3$

   Since the equations are independently equal to zero, there are four combinations.

   The critical points are $(1, 3)$, $(1, -3)$, $(-1, 3)$, $(-1, -3)$.

9.   Given $h(x,y) = x^2 + 6xy + 2y^2 - 6x + 10y + 1$, then find the first partial derivatives

$h_x = 2x + 6y - 6$
$h_y = 6x + 4y + 10$

Solving

$h_x = 2x + 6y - 6 = 0$
$h_y = 6x + 4y + 10 = 0$

requires the simultaneous solution of the system of equations

$x + 3y = 3$
$3x + 2y = -5$

Solve the first equation for x and substitute into the second equation.

$$x = 3 - 3y$$
$$3x + 2y = 3(3 - 3y) + 2y = -5$$
$$9 - 9y + 2y = -5$$
$$-7y = -14$$
$$y = 2$$

Using $y = 2$ in the equation $x = 3 - 3y$ yields

$x = 3 - 3(2)$
$x = -3$

There is one critical point, $(-3, \ 2)$.

11.   Given $f(x,y) = x^3 + y^3 - 3x^2 - 3y^2 - 9x + 3$, then find the first partial derivatives

$f_x = 3x^2 - 6x - 9 = 3(x^2 - 2x - 3) = 3(x - 3)(x + 1)$
$f_y = 3y^2 - 6y = 3y(y - 2)$

Solving $f_x = 3(x - 3)(x + 1) = 0$ yields $x = -1, 3$
           $f_y = 3y(y - 2) = 0$ $y = 0, 2$

Since the equations are independently equal to zero, there are four combinations.

The four critical points are $(-1, 0)$, $(-1, 2)$, $(3, 0)$, $(3, 2)$.

13.   Given $f(x, y) = \frac{1}{3}x^3 - xy + \frac{1}{2}y^2 - 3$, then find the first partial derivatives

$$f_x = x^2 - y$$
$$f_y = -x + y$$

To solve the system of equations

$$f_x = x^2 - y = 0$$
$$f_y = -x + y = 0$$

first solve the second equation to obtain

$$-x + y = 0$$
$$y = x$$

then substitute $y = x$ into the first equation to get

$$x^2 - y = x^2 - x = 0$$
$$x(x - 1) = 0$$
$$x = 0, \ x = 1$$

Thus, for $x = 0$, then $y = 0$.

For $x = 1$, then $y = 1$.

There are two critical points, $(0, 0)$ and $(1, 1)$.

15.   Given $f(x, y) = x^2 + y^2 + 8x - 2y + 5$, then find the first and second partial derivatives:

$$f_x = 2x + 8 = 2(x + 4) \qquad f_y = 2y - 2 = 2(y - 1)$$
$$f_{xx} = 2 \qquad\qquad\qquad f_{yy} = 2$$
$$f_{xy} = 0$$

Solving the system of equations

$$f_x = 2(x + 4) = 0 \qquad \text{yields} \qquad x = -4$$
$$f_y = 2(y - 1) = 0 \qquad\qquad\qquad y = 1$$

Using the critical point $(-4, 1)$, compute the value of

$$D(-4, 1) = f_{xx}(-4, 1)f_{yy}(-4, 1) - \left[f_{xy}(-4, 1)\right]^2$$
$$= 2 \cdot 2 - 0^2$$
$$= 4$$

$$f(-4, 1) = (-4)^2 + (1)^2 + 8(-4) - 2(1) + 5 = -12$$

Since $D = 4 > 0$ and $f_{xx} > 0$, then $f(-4, 1) = -12$ is a relative minimum.

17. Given $f(x, y) = 1 + 4x - 6y - x^2 - y^2$, then find the first and second partial derivatives:

$$f_x = 4 - 2x \qquad f_y = -6 - 2y$$
$$f_{xx} = -2 \qquad f_{yy} = -2$$
$$f_{xy} = 0$$

Solving the system of equations

$$f_x = 4 - 2x = 0 \qquad \text{yields} \qquad x = 2$$
$$f_y = -6 - 2y = 0 \qquad\qquad y = -3$$

Using the critical point $(2, -3)$, compute the value of

$$D(2, -3) = f_{xx}(2, -3)f_{yy}(2, -3) - \left[f_{xy}(2, -3)\right]^2$$
$$= (-2)(-2) - 0^2$$
$$= 4 > 0$$

$$f(2, -3) = 1 + 4(2) - 6(-3) - (2)^2 - (-3)^2 = 14$$

Since $D > 0$ and $f_{xx} < 0$, then $f(2, -3) = 14$ is a relative maximum.

19. Given $f(x, y) = -x^2 + xy - y^2 - 2x - 2y + 3$, then find the first and second partial derivatives:

$$f_x = -2x + y - 2 \qquad f_y = x - 2y - 2$$
$$f_{xx} = -2 \qquad f_{yy} = -2$$
$$f_{xy} = 1$$

To solve the system of equations

$$f_x = -2x + y - 2 = 0$$
$$f_y = x - 2y - 2 = 0$$

first solve the equation $-2x + y - 2 = 0$ for y to obtain $y = 2x + 2$ and then substitute y into the equation $x - 2y - 2 = 0$ to get

$$x - 2y - 2 = x - 2(2x + 2) - 2 = 0$$
$$x - 4x - 4 - 2 = 0$$
$$-3x = 6$$
$$x = -2$$

Substituting $x = -2$ in $y = 2x + 2$ yields

$$y = 2(-2) + 2$$
$$= -2$$

Using the critical point $(-2, -2)$, compute the value of

$$D(-2, -2) = f_{xx}(-2, -2)f_{yy}(-2, -2) - \left[f_{xy}(-2, -2)\right]^2$$
$$= (-2)(-2) - 1^2$$
$$= 3$$

$$f(-2, -2) = -(-2)^2 + (-2)(-2) - (-2)^2 - 2(-2) - 2(-2) + 3 = 7$$

Since $D = 3 > 0$ and $f_{xx} = -2 < 0$, then $f(-2, -2) = 7$ is a relative maximum.

21.   Given $f(x,y) = x^2 - 4xy + y^3 + 4y - 7$, then find the first and second partial derivatives:

$$f_x = 2x - 4y \qquad f_y = -4x + 3y^2 + 4$$
$$f_{xx} = 2 \qquad\qquad f_{yy} = 6y$$
$$f_{xy} = -4$$

To solve the system of equations

$$f_x = 2x - 4y = 0$$
$$f_y = -4x + 3y^2 + 4 = 0$$

first solve the equation $2x - 4y = 0$ for x to obtain

$$2x = 4y$$
$$x = 2y$$

and then substitute x into $-4x + 3y^2 + 4 = 0$ to get

$$-4x + 3y^2 + 4 = -4(2y) + 3y^2 + 4 = 0$$
$$3y^2 - 8y + 4 = 0$$
$$(3y - 2)(y - 2) = 0$$
$$y = \frac{2}{3}, \ y = 2$$

Since $x = 2y$, then $x = \dfrac{4}{3}$

$$x = 4$$

There are two critical points, $(\frac{4}{3}, \frac{2}{3})$ and $(4, 2)$, and one must compute D for each one.

$$D\left(\frac{4}{3}, \frac{2}{3}\right) = f_{xx}\left(\frac{4}{3}, \frac{2}{3}\right) f_{yy}\left(\frac{4}{3}, \frac{2}{3}\right) - \left[f_{xy}\left(\frac{4}{3}, \frac{2}{3}\right)\right]^2 = 2(4) - (-4)^2 = -8$$

$$f\left(\frac{4}{3}, \frac{2}{3}\right) = \left(\frac{4}{3}\right)^2 - 4\left(\frac{4}{3}\right)\left(\frac{2}{3}\right) + \left(\frac{2}{3}\right)^3 + 4\left(\frac{2}{3}\right) - 7 = -\frac{157}{27}$$

Since $D\left(\frac{4}{3}, \frac{2}{3}\right) = -8 < 0$, then $f\left(\frac{4}{3}, \frac{2}{3}\right) = -\frac{157}{27}$ is a saddle point.

$$D(4, 2) = f_{xx}(4, 2) f_{yy}(4, 2) - \left[f_{xy}(4, 2)\right]^2 = 2(12) - (-4)^2 = 8$$

$$f(4, 2) = (4)^2 - 4(4)(2) + (2)^3 + 4(2) - 7 = -7$$

Since $D(4, 2) = 8 > 0$ and $f_{xx} = 2 > 0$, then $f(4, 2) = -7$ is a relative minimum.

23. Given $f(x, y) = x^3 + y^3 - 3x^2 - 3y^2 - 9x + 4$, then find the first and second partial derivatives:

$$f_x = 3x^2 - 6x - 9 \qquad = 3(x^2 - 2x - 3) \qquad f_y = 3y^2 - 6y = 3y(y - 2)$$
$$f_{xx} = 6x - 6 \qquad = 3(x - 3)(x + 1) \qquad f_{yy} = 6y - 6$$
$$f_{xy} = 0$$

Solving the system of equations

$$f_x = 3(x - 3)(x + 1) = 0$$
$$f_y = 3y(y - 2) = 0$$

yields

$$x = 3, \ x = -1$$
$$y = 0 \ y = 2$$

Since these are independent solutions, there are four combinations. The critical points are $(3, 0)$, $(3, 2)$, $(-1, 0)$, and $(-1, 2)$, and one must compute D for all four.

$$D(3, 0) = f_{xx}(3, 0)f_{yy}(3, 0) - \left[f_{xy}(3, 0)\right]^2 = (12)(-6) - 0^2 = -72 < 0$$
$$f(3, 0) = (3)^3 + (0)^3 - 3(3)^2 - 3(0)^2 - 9(3) + 4 = -23$$

Since $D(3, 0) = -72 < 0$, then $f(3, 0) = -23$ is a saddle point.

$$D(3, 2) = f_{xx}(3, 2)f_{yy}(3, 2) - \left[f_{xy}(3, 2)\right]^2 = (12)(6) - 0^2 = 72 > 0$$
$$f(3, 2) = (3)^3 + (2)^3 - 3(3)^2 - 3(2)^2 - 9(3) + 4 = -27$$

Since $D(3, 2) = 72 > 0$ and $f_{xx}(3, 2) = 12 > 0$, then $f(3, 2) = -27$ is a relative minimum.

$$D(-1, 0) = f_{xx}(-1, 0)f_{yy}(-1, 0) - \left[f_{xy}(-1, 0)\right]^2 = (-12)(-6) - 0^2 = 72 > 0$$
$$f(-1, 0) = (-1)^3 + (0)^3 - 3(-1)^2 - 3(0)^2 - 9(-1) + 4 = 9$$

Since $D(-1, 0) = 72 > 0$ and $f_{xx}(-1, 0) = -12 < 0$, then $f(-1, 0) = 9$ is a relative maximum.

$$D(-1, 2) = f_{xx}(-1, 2)f_{yy}(-1, 2) - \left[f_{xy}(-1, 2)\right]^2 = (-12)(6) - 0^2 = -72 < 0$$
$$f(-1, 2) = (-1)^3 + (2)^3 - 3(-1)^2 - 3(2)^2 - 9(-1) + 4 = 5$$

Since $D(-1, 2) = -72 < 0$, then $f(-1, 2) = 5$ is a saddle point.

25.   Given $f(x, y) = x^2 + 3xy - y^2 + 4y - 6x + 1$, then find the first and second partial derivatives:

$f_x = 2x + 3y - 6$ $f_y = 3x - 2y + 4$

$f_{xx} = 2$ $f_{yy} = -2$

$f_{xy} = 3$

To solve the system of equations

$f_x = 2x + 3y - 6 = 0$

$f_y = 3x - 2y + 4 = 0$

first solve the equation $2x + 3y - 6 = 0$ for y to obtain $y = -\frac{2}{3}x + 2$, then substitute y into the equation $3x - 2y + 4 = 0$ to get

$$3x - 2y + 4 = 3x - 2\left(-\frac{2}{3}x + 2\right) + 4 = 0$$

$$3x + \frac{4}{3}x - 4 + 4 = 0$$

$$\frac{13}{3}x = 0$$

$$x = 0$$

Using $y = -\frac{2}{3}x + 2$, then

$y = 0 + 2$

$\quad = 2$

Using the critical point $(0, 2)$, compute the value of

$D(0, 2) = f_{xx}(0, 2)f_{yy}(0, 2) - \left[f_{xy}(0, 2)\right]^2$

$\qquad = (2)(-2) - (3)^2$

$\qquad = -13$

$f(0, 2) = (0)^2 + 3(0)(2) - (2)^2 + 4(2) - 6(0) + 1 = 5$

Since $D(0, 2) = -13 < 0$, then $f(0, 2) = 5$ is a saddle point.

27.   In order to maximize the profit function $P(x, y) = -2x^2 - xy - y^2 + 8x + 9y + 10$, find the first and second partial derivatives, determine the critical points, and use the value of D to test for a maximum.

$P_x = -4x - y + 8$ $P_y = -x - 2y + 9$

$P_{xx} = -4$ $P_{yy} = -2$

$P_{xy} = -1$

Solving the system of equations

$P_x = -4x - y + 8 = 0$

$P_y = -x - 2y + 9 = 0$

yields $y = -4x + 8$ and

$-x - 2(-4x + 8) + 9 = 0$

$\qquad\qquad 7x - 7 = 0$

$\qquad\qquad\quad x = 1$

$y = -4(1) + 8$

$\quad = 4$

Since $D - P_{xx}P_{yy} - (P_{xy})^2 = (-4)(-2) - (-1)^2 = 7 > 0$ and $P_{xx} = -4 < 0$, then $P(1, 4)$ is a maximum.

The company should spend $1000 on radio and $4000 on newspaper advertising.

29. Given the revenue function $R(x,y) = 12x + 15y$ and the cost function $C(x,y) = x^2 + y^2 - xy$, then the profit function is

$$P(x,y) = R(x,y) - C(x,y) = 12x + 15y - x^2 - y^2 + xy$$

To maximize the profit function, compute the first and second partial derivatives and determine the critical points.

$$P_x = 12 - 2x + y \qquad P_y = 15 - 2y + x$$
$$P_{xx} = -2 \qquad\qquad P_{yy} = -2$$
$$P_{xy} = 1$$

Solving the system of equations

$$P_x = 12 - 2x + y = 0$$
$$P_y = 15 - 2y + x = 0$$

yields $y = 2x - 12$ and

$$15 - 2(2x - 12) + x = 0$$
$$39 - 3x = 0$$
$$x = 13$$

$$y = 2(13) - 12$$
$$= 14$$

$D = P_{xx}P_{yy} - (P_{xy})^2 = (-2)(-2) - 1^2 = 3 > 0$ and $P_{xx} = -2 < 0$; thus $P(13, 14)$ is a maximum.

The company should produce 1300 and 1400 computers of the respective types to maximize the profit.

31. Let x, y, and z represent the three numbers. The given conditions require that one minimize $S(x, y, z) = x^2 + y^2 + z^2$ using the constraint that $x + y + z = 27$.

Solving $x + y + z = 27$ for z to obtain $z = 27 - x - y$ and substituting z into $x^2 + y^2 + z^2$ yields $S(x, y) = x^2 + y^2 + (27 - x - y)^2$, which is the function to be minimized.

Computing the first and second partial derivatives yields

$$S_x = 2x + 2(27 - x - y)(-1) \qquad S_y = 2y + 2(27 - x - y)(-1)$$
$$= 4x + 2y - 54 \qquad\qquad\qquad = 4y + 2x - 54$$
$$S_{xx} = 4 \qquad\qquad\qquad\qquad\quad S_{yy} = 4$$
$$S_{xy} = 2$$

Solving the system of equations

$$S_x = 4x + 2y - 54 = 0$$
$$S_y = 2x + 4y - 54 = 0$$

yields $y = -2x + 27$ and

$$2x + 4(-2x + 27) - 54 = 0$$
$$-6x + 54 = 0$$
$$x = 9$$

$$y = -2(9) + 27$$
$$= 9$$

Since $D = S_{xx}S_{yy} - (S_{xy})^2 = (4)(4) - 2^2 = 12 > 0$ and $S_{xx} = 4 > 0$, then $S(9, 9)$ is a minimum.

Using $z = 27 - x - y$, then $z = 9$.

The three numbers are $x = 9$, $y = 9$, and $z = 9$.

33. Using the figure

the volume of the package is xyz. The condition imposed by USPS is defined by $y + 2x + 2z \leq 84$. Assuming the largest volume will occur when $y + 2x + 2z = 84$, then solve for z to obtain $z = 42 - x - \frac{y}{2}$. Substituting z into the expression for the volume produces the function

$$V(x, y) = xy\left(42 - x - \frac{y}{2}\right) = 42xy - x^2y - \frac{xy^2}{2}$$

which is to be maximized.

To maximize $V(x, y)$, compute the first and second partial derivatives, determine the critical points, and test for a maximum.

$$V_x = 42y - 2xy - \frac{y^2}{2} \qquad V_y = 42x - x^2 - xy$$

$$V_{xx} = -2y \qquad\qquad\qquad V_{yy} = -x$$

$$V_{xy} = 42 - 2x - y$$

Consider the system of equations

$$V_x = 42y - 2xy - \frac{y^2}{2} = 0$$

$$V_y = 42x - x^2 - xy = 0$$

and solve the second equation for y to obtain $y = 42 - x$. (*Note*: Dividing by x is acceptable, since $x = 0$ is not a possible solution.) Substitute y into the first equation after dividing by y to produce

$$42 - 2x - \frac{y}{2} = 42 - 2x - \frac{(42 - x)}{2} = 42 - 2x - 21 + \frac{x}{2} = 0$$

$$21 + \frac{3x}{2} = 0$$

$$x = 14$$

Using $y = 42 - x$, then $y = 28$ and

$$z = 42 - x - \frac{y}{2} = 42 - 14 - 14 = 14$$

Computing D produces

$$\begin{aligned}
D(14, 28) &= V_{xx}(14, 28)V_{yy}(14, 28) - \left[V_{xy}(14, 28)\right]^2 \\
&= (-56)(-14) - (-14)^2 \\
&= 588 > 0
\end{aligned}$$

Also, $V_{xx}(14, 28) = -56 < 0$.

Thus, the dimensions for a maximum volume are $x = 14$, $y = 28$, $z = 14$.

35. We are required to make a closed rectangular box of volume 128 cubic feet. Let the width, length, and height of the box be denoted by x, y, and z, respectively. The sides have surface area $2xz + 2yz$. The top and bottom of the box have surface area $2xy$. The material for the top and bottom costs 20¢ per square foot, and the material for the sides costs 10¢ per square foot. Then, the cost function $C(x)$ for the cost of constructing the box is

$$C(x, y, z) = 0.4xy + 0.2xz + 0.2yz$$

Since the volume is 128 cubic feet, then $xyz = 128$, and we may use $z = \frac{128}{xy}$ to write C as a function of only x and y. In fact,

$$C(x, y) = 0.4xy + 0.2x\left(\frac{128}{xy}\right) + 0.2y\left(\frac{128}{xy}\right)$$
$$= 0.4xy + 25.6y^{-1} + 25.6x^{-1}$$

We have

$$C_x = 0.4y - 25.6x^{-2}$$
$$C_y = 0.4x - 25.6y^{-2}$$
$$C_{xy} = 0.4$$
$$C_{xx} = 51.2x^{-3}$$
$$C_{yy} = 51.2y^{-3}$$

Consider the system of equations

$$0 = C_x = 0.4y - 25.6x^{-2}$$
$$0 = C_y = 0.4x - 25.6y^{-2}$$

From the first equation we have that $4y = 256x^{-2}$ so that $y = 64x^{-2}$. Substitute this into the second equation to obtain

$$0 = 0.4x - 25.6\left(\frac{x^2}{64}\right)^2 = 0.4x - 0.00625x^4$$
$$= 0.00625x(64 - x^3)$$
$$x = 0 \quad \text{or} \quad x^3 = 64$$
$$x = 4$$

Then $y = \frac{64}{4^2} = 4$.

Using $z = \frac{128}{xy}$, we have $z = \frac{128}{16} = 8$. At $x = 4$, $y = 4$ we have

$$D = (C_{xx})^2(C_{yy})^2 - (C_{xy})^2$$
$$= \left(\frac{51.2}{4^3}\right)^2\left(\frac{51.2}{4^3}\right)^2 - (0.4)^2$$
$$= 0.4096 - 0.16$$
$$= 0.2496$$

and $C_{xx}(4, 4) = \frac{51.2}{4^3} > 0$. Then, using the second partials test, $x = 4$, $y = 4$ minimizes $C(x, y)$. Hence, length and width of 4 feet and height of 8 feet minimize the cost of materials.

37. Although the minimum cost of the aquarium occurs when all three dimensions equal 4 feet, the shape of a cube may not be pleasing to the eye or provide an easy shape to clean. An aquarium that is 4 feet high and sits on a stand that is $2\frac{1}{2}$ feet high would be $6\frac{1}{2}$ feet off the floor! It would be easier to reach into an aquarium which was only 2 feet high, that is, only $4\frac{1}{2}$ feet off the floor.

SECTION 10.4 pages 509–510

1.   Given $f(x, y) = xy$ subject to $x + y = 10$, then the constraint function is $g(x, y) = x + y - 10$ and the new function is

$$F(x, y, \lambda) = xy + \lambda(x + y - 10)$$
$$= xy + \lambda x + \lambda y - 10\lambda$$

The three partial derivatives and resulting system of equations become

$$F_x = y + \lambda = 0$$
$$F_y = x + \lambda = 0$$
$$F_\lambda = x + y - 10 = 0$$

Solving the first two equations for λ yields $\lambda = -y$ and $\lambda = -x$. Thus, $y = x$, and using the third equation produces

$$x + y - 10 = x + x - 10 = 0$$
$$2x = 10$$
$$x = 5$$

$$y = x = 5$$

The maximum value of $f(x, y)$ occurs at $(5, 5)$, and $f(5, 5) = 25$.

3.   Given $f(x, y) = x^2 + y^2 + 3$ subject to $2x + y = 5$, then the constraint function is $g(x, y) = 2x + y - 5$ and the new function is

$$F(x, y, \lambda) = x^2 + y^2 + 3 + \lambda(2x + y - 5)$$
$$= x^2 + y^2 + 3 + 2\lambda x + \lambda y - 5\lambda$$

The three partial derivatives and resulting system of equations become

$$F_x = 2x + 2\lambda = 0$$
$$F_y = 2y + \lambda = 0$$
$$F_\lambda = 2x + y - 5 = 0$$

Solving the first two equations for λ yields $\lambda = -x$ and $\lambda = -2y$. Thus, $-2y = -x$ or $y = \frac{1}{2}x$. Using the third equation

produces $2x + y - 5 = 2x + \frac{1}{2}x - 5 = 0$

$$\frac{5}{2}x = 5$$
$$x = 2$$

$$y = \frac{1}{2}x = \frac{1}{2}(2)$$
$$= 1$$

The minimum value of $f(x, y)$ occurs at $(2, 1)$, and $f(2, 1) = 8$.

5.   Given $f(x,y) = 4 - x^2 - y^2$ subject to $2x + y = 10$, then the constraint function is $g(x,y) = 2x + y - 10 = 0$ and the new function is

$$F(x,y,\lambda) = 4 - x^2 - y^2 + \lambda(2x + y - 10)$$
$$= 4 - x^2 - y^2 + 2\lambda x + \lambda y - 10\lambda$$

The three partial derivatives and resulting system of equations become

$$F_x = -2x + 2\lambda = 0$$
$$F_y = -2y + \lambda = 0$$
$$F_\lambda = 2x + y - 10 = 0$$

Solving the first two equations for λ yields $\lambda = x$ and $\lambda = 2y$. Thus, $2y = x$ or $y = \frac{1}{2}x$. Using the third equation produces

$$2x + y - 10 = 2x + \frac{1}{2}x - 10 = 0$$
$$\frac{5x}{2} = 10$$
$$x = 4$$

$$y = \frac{1}{2}x = \frac{1}{2}(4)$$
$$= 2$$

The maximum value of $f(x,y)$ occurs at $(4, 2)$, and $f(4,2) = -16$.

7.   Given $f(x,y) = x^2 + 2y^2 - xy$ subject to $2x - y = 4$, then the constraint function is $g(x,y) = 2x - y - 4$ and the new function is

$$F(x,y,\lambda) = x^2 + 2y^2 - xy + \lambda(2x - y - 4)$$
$$= x^2 + 2y^2 - xy + 2\lambda x - \lambda y - 4\lambda$$

The three partial derivatives and resulting system of equations become

$$F_x = 2x - y + 2\lambda = 0$$
$$F_y = 4y - x - \lambda = 0$$
$$F_\lambda = 2x - y - 4 = 0$$

Solving the first two equations for λ yields $\lambda = -x + \frac{1}{2}y$ and $\lambda = -x + 4y$. Thus, $-x + \frac{1}{2}y = -x + 4y$ or $y = 0$. Using the third equation produces

$$2x - y - 4 = 2x - 0 - 4 = 0$$
$$x = 2$$

The minimum value of $f(x,y)$ occurs at $(2, 0)$, and $f(2,0) = 4$.

9. Given $f(x, y) = 2xy - 4x$ subject to $x + y = 12$, then the constraint function is $g(x, y) = x + y - 12 = 0$ and the new function is

$$F(x, y, \lambda) = 2xy - 4x + \lambda(x + y - 12)$$
$$= 2xy - 4x + \lambda x + \lambda y - 12\lambda$$

The three partial derivatives and resulting system of equations become

$$F_x = 2y - 4 + \lambda = 0$$
$$F_y = 2x + \lambda = 0$$
$$F_\lambda = x + y - 12 = 0$$

Solving the first two equations for λ yields $\lambda = 4 - 2y$ and $\lambda = -2x$. Thus, $4 - 2y = -2x$ or $y = x + 2$. Using the third equation produces

$$x + y - 12 = x + (x + 2) - 12 = 0$$
$$2x - 10 = 0$$
$$x = 5$$

$$y = x + 2 = 5 + 2$$
$$= 7$$

The maximum value of $f(x, y)$ occurs at $(5, 7)$, and $f(5, 7) = 50$.

11. Given $f(x, y) = x^2 + xy + y^2$ subject to $x + y = 20$, then the constraint function is $g(x, y) = x + y - 20$ and the new function is

$$F(x, y, \lambda) = x^2 + xy + y^2 + \lambda(x + y - 20)$$
$$= x^2 + xy + y^2 + \lambda x + \lambda y - 20\lambda$$

The three partial derivatives and resulting system of equations become

$$F_x = 2x + y + \lambda = 0$$
$$F_y = x + 2y + \lambda = 0$$
$$F_\lambda = x + y - 20 = 0$$

Solving the first two equations for λ yields $\lambda = -2x - y$ and $\lambda = -x - 2y$. Thus, $-2x - y = -x - 2y$ or $y = x$. Using the third equation produces

$$x + y - 20 = x + x - 20 = 0$$
$$2x = 20$$
$$x = 10$$

and $y = x = 10$

The minimum value of $f(x, y)$ occurs at $(10, 10)$, and $f(10, 10) = 300$.

13. Let x and y represent the two numbers. The statement of the problem requires one to maximize the product $P(x, y) = xy$ subject to $x + y = 1000$.

Construct the new function

$$F(x, y, \lambda) = xy + \lambda(x + y - 1000)$$
$$= xy + \lambda x + \lambda y - 1000\lambda$$

The three partial derivatives and resulting system of equations become

$$F_x = y + \lambda = 0$$
$$F_y = x + \lambda = 0$$
$$F_\lambda = x + y - 1000 = 0$$

Solving the first two equations for λ and using the third equation produces $y = x$ and $2x - 1000 = 0$. Thus, $x = 500$ and $y = 500$.

 The two numbers are $x = 500$, $y = 500$.

15. Consider the figure.

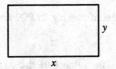

The problem is to maximize the area $A(x, y) = xy$ subject to $2x + 2y = 200$ or $x + y = 100$. Construct the new function

$$F(x, y, \lambda) = xy + \lambda(x + y - 100)$$
$$= xy + \lambda x + \lambda y - 100\lambda$$

The three partial derivatives and resulting system of equations become

$$F_x = y + \lambda = 0$$
$$F_y = x + \lambda = 0$$
$$F_\lambda = x + y - 100 = 0$$

Solving the first two equations for λ and using the third equation produces $y = x$ and $2x - 100 = 0$. Thus, $x = 50$ and $y = 50$.

 The largest area is $A(50, 50) = 2500$ square feet.

17. Referring to Example 2, the problem is now to minimize $C(x, y) = 200x + 100y$ subject to $g(x, y) = 300x^{2/3}y^{1/3} - 21,000 = 0$. The new function is

$$F(x, y, \lambda) = 200x + 100y + \lambda(300x^{2/3}y^{1/3} - 21,000)$$
$$= 200x + 100y + 300\lambda x^{2/3}y^{1/3} - 21,000\lambda$$

The three partial derivatives and resulting system of equations become

$$F_x = 200 + 200\lambda x^{-1/3}y^{1/3} = 0$$
$$F_y = 100 + 100\lambda x^{2/3}y^{-2/3} = 0$$
$$F_\lambda = 300x^{2/3}y^{1/3} - 21,000 = 0$$

Solving the first two equations for λ yields $\lambda = -x^{1/3}y^{-1/3}$ and $\lambda = -x^{2/3}y^{2/3}$. Thus, $-x^{1/3}y^{-1/3} = -x^{-2/3}y^{2/3}$ or $y = x$. Using the third equation produces

$$300x^{2/3}y^{1/3} - 21,000 = 300x^{2/3}x^{1/3} - 21,000 = 0$$
$$300x = 21,000$$
$$x = 70$$

$$y = x = 70$$

The producer should use 70 units of labor and 70 units of capital in order to minimize the cost of making 21,000 units.

The minimum cost is $C(70, 70) = \$21,000$ to produce 21,000 units.

19. Use the method of Lagrange multipliers to minimize the cost function $C(x, y) = 20x + 80y$ subject to the constraint $g(x, y) = 200x^{1/2}y^{1/2} - 24,000 = 0$. Construct the new function

$$F(x, y, \lambda) = 20x + 80y + \lambda(200x^{1/2}y^{1/2} - 24000)$$
$$= 20x + 80y + 200\lambda x^{1/2}y^{1/2} - 24000\lambda$$

The three partial derivatives and resulting system of equations become

$$F_x = 20 + 100\lambda x^{-1/2}y^{1/2} = 0$$
$$F_y = 80 + 100\lambda x^{1/2}y^{-1/2} = 0$$
$$F_\lambda = 200x^{1/2}y^{1/2} - 24,000 = 0$$

Solving the first two equations for λ yields $\lambda = -\frac{1}{5}x^{1/2}y^{-1/2}$ and $\lambda = -\frac{4}{5}x^{-1/2}y^{1/2}$. Thus, $-\frac{1}{5}x^{1/2}y^{-1/2} = -\frac{4}{5}x^{-1/2}y^{1/2}$ or $x = 4y$.

Using the third equation produces

$$200x^{1/2}y^{1/2} - 24,000 = 200(44)^{1/2}y^{1/2} - 24,000 = 0$$
$$400y = 24,000$$
$$y = 60$$

Therefore,

$$x = 4y = 4(60) = 240$$

The minimum cost of producing 24000 units is $C(240, 60) = \$9600$

21. Use the method of Lagrange multipliers to maximize the production function $f(x, y) = 600x^{2/3}y^{1/3}$ subject to the cost constraint $g(x, y) = 400x + 200y - 30{,}000 = 0$.

Construct the new function

$$F(x, y, \lambda) = 600x^{2/3}y^{1/3} + \lambda(400x + 200y - 30{,}000)$$
$$= 600x^{2/3}y^{1/3} + 400\lambda x + 200\lambda y - 30{,}000\lambda$$

The three partial derivatives and resulting system of equations become

$$F_x = 400x^{-1/3}y^{1/3} + 400\lambda = 0$$
$$F_y = 200x^{2/3}y^{-2/3} + 200\lambda = 0$$
$$F_\lambda = 400x + 200y - 30{,}000 = 0$$

Solving the first two equations for λ yields $\lambda = -x^{-1/3}y^{1/3}$ and $\lambda = -x^{2/3}y^{-2/3}$. Thus, $-x^{-1/3}y^{1/3} = -x^{2/3}y^{-2/3}$ or $y = x$. Using the third equation produces

$$400x + 200y - 30{,}000 = 400x + 200x - 30{,}000 = 0$$
$$600x = 30{,}000$$
$$x = 50$$

Therefore,

$$y = x = 50$$

In order to maximize the production at a cost of \$30,000, the producer should use 50 units of labor and 50 units of capital.

23. The volume of a cylindrical can is $\pi x^2 y$. Thus, use the method of Lagrange multipliers to minimize the surface area $S(x, y) = 2\pi xy + 2\pi x^2$ subject to the volume constraint $g(x, y) = \pi x^2 y - 200 = 0$.

Construct the new function

$$
\begin{aligned}
F(x, y, \lambda) &= 2\pi xy + 2\pi x^2 + \lambda(\pi x^2 y - 200) \\
&= 2\pi xy + 2\pi x^2 + \pi\lambda x^2 y - 200\lambda
\end{aligned}
$$

The three partial derivatives and resulting system of equations become

$$
\begin{aligned}
F_x &= 2\pi y + 4\pi x + 2\pi\lambda xy = 0 \\
F_y &= 2\pi x + \pi\lambda x^2 = 0 \\
F_\lambda &= \pi x^2 y - 200 = 0
\end{aligned}
$$

Solving the first two equations for λ yields

$$
\lambda = \frac{-4\pi x - 2\pi y}{2\pi xy} = \frac{-2x - y}{xy}
$$

and $\lambda = \dfrac{-2\pi x}{\pi x^2} = -\dfrac{2}{x}$

Thus, $-\dfrac{2}{x} = -\dfrac{2x - y}{xy}$

$$
\begin{aligned}
-2y &= -2x - y \\
y &= 2x
\end{aligned}
$$

Using the third equation produces

$$
\begin{aligned}
\pi x^2 y - 200 = \pi x^2 (2x) - 200 &= 0 \\
2\pi x^3 &= 200 \\
x^3 &= \frac{100}{\pi} \\
x &= \sqrt[3]{\frac{100}{\pi}}
\end{aligned}
$$

Therefore, $y = 2x = 2\sqrt[3]{\dfrac{100}{\pi}}$

Thus, the radius ≈ 3.17 inches and the height ≈ 6.34 inches for the least amount of material.

SECTION 10.5 pages 514–516

1. Use $n = 3$ and the listed data to determine the values of the various sums in the formulas for m and b.

$$\sum x_i = 3 + 5 + 6 = 14$$
$$\sum y_i = 8 + 11 + 12 = 31$$
$$\sum x_i y_i = 3 \cdot 8 + 5 \cdot 11 + 6 \cdot 12 = 151$$
$$\sum x_i^2 = 3^2 + 5^2 + 6^2 = 70$$
$$\left(\sum x_i\right)^2 = (14)^2 = 196$$

Substituting these numbers into the formulas yields

$$m = \frac{3 \cdot 151 - 14 \cdot 31}{3 \cdot 70 - 196} = \frac{19}{14}$$
$$b = \frac{31 - \frac{19}{14}(14)}{3} = 4$$

The least squares line for these data is

$$y = \frac{19}{14}x + 4$$

3. Use $n = 4$ and the listed data to determine the values of the various sums in the formulas for m and b.

$$\sum x_i = 8 + 9 + 10 + 12 = 39$$
$$\sum y_i = 0 + 3 + 5 + 6 = 14$$
$$\sum x_i y_i = 8 \cdot 0 + 9 \cdot 3 + 10 \cdot 5 + 12 \cdot 6 = 149$$
$$\sum x_i^2 = 8^2 + 9^2 + 10^2 + 12^2 = 389$$
$$\left(\sum x_i\right)^2 = 39^2 = 1521$$

Substituting these numbers into the formulas yields

$$m = \frac{4 \cdot 149 - 39 \cdot 14}{4 \cdot 389 - 1521} = \frac{10}{7}$$
$$b = \frac{14 - \frac{10}{7}(39)}{4} = -\frac{73}{7}$$

The least squares line for these data is

$$y = \frac{10}{7}x - \frac{73}{7}$$

5. Use $n = 5$ and the listed data to determine the values of the various sums in the formulas for m and b.

$$\sum x_i = 0 + 1 + 2 + 3 + 4 = 10$$
$$\sum y_i = 3 + 4 + 6 + 6 + 8 = 27$$
$$\sum x_i y_i = 0 \cdot 3 + 1 \cdot 4 + 2 \cdot 6 + 3 \cdot 6 + 4 \cdot 8 = 66$$
$$\sum x_i^2 = 0^2 + 1^2 + 2^2 + 3^2 + 4^2 = 30$$
$$\left(\sum x_i\right)^2 = 10^2 = 100$$

Substituting these numbers into the formulas yields

$$m = \frac{5 \cdot 66 - 10 \cdot 27}{5 \cdot 30 - 100} = \frac{6}{5}$$

$$b = \frac{27 - \frac{6}{5}(10)}{5} = 3$$

The least squares line for these data is

$$y = \frac{6}{5}x + 3$$

7. Use $n = 3$ and the listed data to determine the values of the various sums in the formulas for m and b.

$$\sum x_i = 1 + 2 + 3 = 6$$
$$\sum y_i = 4 + 5 + 8 = 17$$
$$\sum x_i y_i = 1 \cdot 4 + 2 \cdot 5 + 3 \cdot 8 = 38$$
$$\sum x_i^2 = 1^2 + 2^2 + 3^2 = 14$$
$$\left(\sum x_i\right)^2 = 6^2 = 36$$

Substituting these numbers into the formulas yields

$$m = \frac{3 \cdot 38 - 6 \cdot 17}{3 \cdot 14 - 36} = 2$$

$$b = \frac{17 - 2(6)}{3} = \frac{5}{3}$$

The least squares line for these data is

$$y = 2x + \frac{5}{3}$$

9. Use $n = 4$ and the listed data to determine the values of the various sums in the formulas for m and b.

$$\sum x_i = 0 + 1 + 2 + 4 = 7$$
$$\sum y_i = 4 + 5 + 6 + 10 = 25$$
$$\sum x_i y_i = 0 \cdot 4 + 1 \cdot 5 + 2 \cdot 6 + 4 \cdot 10 = 57$$
$$\sum x_i^2 = 0^2 + 1^2 + 2^2 + 4^2 = 21$$
$$\left(\sum x_i\right)^2 = 7^2 = 49$$

Substituting these numbers into the formulas yields

$$m = \frac{4 \cdot 57 - 7 \cdot 25}{4 \cdot 21 - 49} = \frac{53}{35}$$

$$b = \frac{25 - \frac{53}{35}(7)}{4} = \frac{18}{5}$$

The least squares line for these data is

$$y = \frac{53}{35}x + \frac{18}{5}$$

11. Use $n = 5$ and the listed data to determine the values of the various sums in the formulas for m and b.

$$\sum x_i = 1 + 2 + 3 + 4 + 5 = 15$$
$$\sum y_i = 5 + 6 + 3 + 1 + 0 = 15$$
$$\sum x_i y_i = 1 \cdot 5 + 2 \cdot 6 + 3 \cdot 3 + 4 \cdot 1 + 5 \cdot 0 = 30$$
$$\sum x_i^2 = 1^2 + 2^2 + 3^2 + 4^2 + 5^2 = 55$$
$$\left(\sum x_i\right)^2 = 15^2 = 225$$

Substituting these numbers into the formulas yields

$$m = \frac{5 \cdot 30 - 15 \cdot 15}{5 \cdot 55 - 225} = -\frac{3}{2}$$

$$b = \frac{15 - \left(-\frac{3}{2}\right)(15)}{5} = \frac{15}{2}$$

The least squares line for these data is

$$y = -\frac{3}{2}x + \frac{15}{2}$$

13.   a.   Use $n = 4$ and the listed data to determine the values of the various sums in the formulas for m and b.

$$\sum x_i = 2 + 3 + 4 + 6 = 15$$

$$\sum y_i = 7 + 6 + 6 + 2 = 21$$

$$\sum x_i y_i = 2 \cdot 7 + 3 \cdot 6 + 4 \cdot 6 + 6 \cdot 2 = 68$$

$$\sum x_i^2 = 2^2 + 3^2 + 4^2 + 6^2 = 65$$

$$\left(\sum x_i\right)^2 = 15^2 = 225$$

Substituting these numbers into the formulas yields

$$m = \frac{4 \cdot 68 - 15 \cdot 21}{4 \cdot 65 - 225} = -\frac{43}{35}$$

$$b = \frac{21 - \left(-\frac{43}{35}\right)(15)}{4} = \frac{69}{7}$$

The least squares line for these data is $y = -\frac{43}{35}x + \frac{69}{7}$

b.   For $x = 5$, $y = -\frac{43}{35}(5) + \frac{69}{7}$

$$= -\frac{26}{7}$$

c.   For $y = 4$, $4 = -\frac{43}{35}(x) + \frac{69}{7}$

$$x = \frac{4 - \frac{69}{7}}{-\frac{43}{35}}$$

$$= \frac{205}{43}$$

15.   a.   Use $n = 5$ and the listed data to determine the values of the various sums in the formulas for m and b. Assume the ACT scores are the x values and the GPA are the y values.

$$\sum x_i = 15 + 18 + 20 + 21 + 24 = 98$$

$$\sum y_i = 2.0 + 2.4 + 2.6 + 2.8 + 3.2 = 13$$

$$\sum x_i y_i = 15(2.0) + 18(2.4) + 20(2.6) + 21(2.8) + 24(3.2) = 260.8$$

$$\sum x_i^2 = 15^2 + 18^2 + 20^2 + 21^2 + 24^2 = 1966$$

$$\left(\sum x_i\right)^2 = 98^2 = 9604$$

Substituting these numbers into the formulas yields

$$m = \frac{5(260.8) - (98)(13)}{5(1966) - 9604} = \frac{15}{113}$$

$$b = \frac{13 - \frac{15}{113}(98)}{5} = -\frac{1}{565}$$

The least squares line for these data is $y = \frac{15}{113}x - \frac{1}{565}$

b.   For an ACT score of $23(x = 23)$, then $y = \frac{15}{113}(23) - \frac{1}{565} = 3.05$

For an ACT score of 23, the expected GPA is 3.05.

17. **a.** Use $n = 6$ and the listed data to determine the values of the various sums in the formulas for m and b. Assume the given temperatures are the x values and the number of grams are the y values.

$$\sum x_i = 10 + 20 + 30 + 40 + 50 + 60 = 210$$

$$\sum y_i = 61 + 65 + 72 + 77 + 85 + 90 = 450$$

$$\sum x_i y_i = 10 \cdot 61 + 20 \cdot 65 + 30 \cdot 72 + 40 \cdot 77 + 50 \cdot 85 + 60 \cdot 90 = 16{,}800$$

$$\sum x_i^2 = 10^2 + 20^2 + 30^2 + 40^2 + 50^2 + 60^2 = 9100$$

$$\left(\sum x_i\right)^2 = 210^2 = 44{,}100$$

Substituting these numbers into the formulas yields

$$m = \frac{6 \cdot 16{,}800 - 210 \cdot 450}{6 \cdot 9100 - 44{,}100} = \frac{3}{5}$$

$$b = \frac{450 - \frac{3}{5}(210)}{6} = 54$$

The least squares line for these data is $y = \frac{3}{5}x + 54$

b. If $x = 35$, then $y = \frac{3}{5}(35) + 54 = 75$

Approximately 75 grams will dissolve at $35°C$.

c. If $y = 80$, then $80 = \frac{3}{5}x + 54$

$$x = \frac{80 - 54}{\frac{3}{5}} = \frac{130}{3} \approx 43.3$$

An approximate temperature of $43.3°C$ is needed to dissolve 80 grams.

19. Starting with the least squares formula for b, write each term of the numerator over the denominator n.

$$b = \frac{\sum y_i - m \cdot \sum x_i}{n} = \frac{\sum y_i}{n} - m \cdot \frac{\sum x_i}{n}$$

The term $\dfrac{\sum y_i}{n} = \dfrac{\sum_{i=1}^{n} y_i}{n} = \overline{y}$, where $\overline{y}$ is the average value of all the y values.

The term $\dfrac{\sum x_i}{n} = \dfrac{\sum_{i=1}^{n} x_i}{n} = \overline{x}$, where $\overline{x}$ is the average value of all the x values.

Thus, $b = \overline{y} - m\overline{x}$.

21. A least squares line using the data reported by waiters and waitresses on the amount of tips left by customers as compared with the amount of their bills would probably yield $y = 0.15x$, where y is the tip and x is the amount of the bill, since it is well known to tip 15% on a restaurant bill.

SECTION 10.5 Technology Exercises

1.

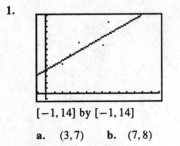

$[-1, 14]$ by $[-1, 14]$

a. $(3, 7)$ **b.** $(7, 8)$

3. $y = 0.8284x + 4.2239$

5. $y = 0.1327x - 0.0018$

SECTION 10.6 pages 519–520

1.   Given $z = f(x, y) = x^2 + y^2 + 10$, then $f_x = 2x$ and $f_y = 2y$.

Thus, $dz = f_x\, dx + f_y\, dy$
$$= 2x\, dx + 2y\, dy$$

3.   Given $z = f(x, y) = xy^2 + 3x^2 - 2y^2$, then $f_x = y^2 + 6x$ and $f_y = 2xy - 4y$.

Thus, $dz = f_x\, dx + f_y\, dy$
$$= (y^2 + 6x)\, dx + (2xy - 4y)\, dy$$

5.   Given $z = f(x, y) = xe^y + ye^x + 1$, then $f_x = e^y + ye^x$ and $f_y = xe^y + e^x$.

Thus, $dz = f_x\, dx + f_y\, dy$
$$= (e^y + ye^x)\, dx + (xe^y + e^x)\, dy$$

7.   Given $z = f(x, y) = \frac{y}{x} - 8x + 3y$, then $f_x = -\frac{y}{x^2} - 8$ and $f_y = \frac{1}{x} + 3$

Thus, $dz = f_x\, dx + f_y\, dy$
$$= \left(-\frac{y}{x^2} - 8\right)\, dx + \left(\frac{1}{x} + 3\right)\, dy$$

9.   Given $z = f(x, y) = x \ln y - x^2$, then $f_x = \ln y - 2x$ and $f_y = \frac{x}{y}$.

Thus, $dz = f_x\, dx + f_y\, dy$
$$= (\ln y - 2x)\, dx + \frac{x}{y}\, dy$$

11.   If $z = f(x, y) = 4x^2y^3$, then $dz = 8xy^3\, dx + 12x^2y^2\, dy$

For $x = 5$, $dx = 0.01$, $y = 9$, $dy = 0.02$, then
$$dz = 8(5)(9)^3(0.01) + 12(5)^2(9)^2(0.02)$$
$$= 777.6$$

13.   If $z = f(x, y) = 6x^{1/3}y^{2/3}$, then $dz = 2x^{-2/3}y^{2/3}\, dx + 4x^{1/3}y^{-1/3}\, dy$

For $x = 1$, $dx = 0.02$, $y = 8$, $dy = 0.03$,
$$dz = 2(1)^{-2/3}(8)^{2/3}(0.02) + 4(1)^{1/3}(8)^{-1/3}(0.03)$$
$$= 2(4)(0.02) + 4\left(\frac{1}{2}\right)(0.03)$$
$$= 0.16 + 0.06$$
$$= 0.22$$

15.   If $z = f(x, y) = x\sqrt{y} = xy^{1/2}$, then $dz = y^{1/2}\, dx + \frac{1}{2}xy^{-1/2}\, dy$

For $x = 12$, $dx = 0.015$, $y = 64$, $dy = 0.01$, then
$$dz = (64)^{1/2}(0.015) + \frac{1}{2}(12)(64)^{-1/2}(0.01)$$
$$= (8)(0.015) + 6\left(\frac{1}{8}\right)(0.01)$$
$$= 0.1275$$

17. If $z = f(x,y) = 5x^3y^2 + y$, then

$dz = 15x^2y^2\, dx + (10x^3y + 1)\, dy$

$dx = 4.01 - 4.00 = 0.01$
$dy = 6.02 - 6.00 = 0.02$

Using $x = 4$, $y = 6$, $dx = 0.01$, $dy = 0.02$,

$dz = 15(4)^2(6)^2(0.01) + \left[10(4)^3(6) + 1\right](0.02)$

$ = 163.22$

19. If $z = f(x,y) = x \ln y$, then

$dz = \ln y\, dx + \dfrac{x}{y}\, dy$

$dx = 10.1 - 10.0 = 0.1$
$dy = 1.2 - 1.0 = 0.2$

Using $x = 10$, $y = 1$, $dx = 0.1$, $dy = 0.2$,

$dz = (\ln 1)(0.1) + \dfrac{10}{1}(0.2)$

$ = 2$

21. If $z = f(x,y) = 12x^{2/3}y^{1/3}$, then

$dz = 8x^{-1/3}y^{1/3}\, dx + 4x^{2/3}y^{-2/3}\, dy$

$dx = 9 - 8 = 1$
$dy = 29 - 27 = 2$

Using $x = 8$, $y = 27$, $dx = 1$, $dy = 2$,

$dz = 8(8)^{-1/3}(27)^{1/3}(1) + 4(8)^{2/3}(27)^{-2/3}(2)$

$ = 8\left(\dfrac{1}{2}\right)(3) + 4(4)\left(\dfrac{1}{9}\right)(2)$

$ = 15.56$

23. Referring to Example 3, $R(x,y) = -0.25x^2 + 22x - 0.5y^2 + 18y + 300$ and $dR = (-0.50x + 22)\, dx + (-1.0y + 18)\, dy$

If x increases from 18 to 20, then $dx = 20 - 18 = 2$

If y increases from 14 to 15, then $dy = 15 - 14 = 1$

Using $x = 18$, $dx = 2$, $y = 14$, $dy = 1$,

$dz = [-0.50(18) + 22](2) + [-1.0(14) + 18](1)$

$ = 30$

The approximate increase in revenue associated with a \$200 increase in radio advertising and a \$100 increase in newspaper advertising is \$30,000.

25. The exact increase in revenue in Example 3 is given by $R(21.5, 13) - R(20, 12)$.

Computing $R(21.5, 13)$ yields

$R(21.5, 13) = -0.25(21.5)^2 + 22(21.5) - 0.5(13)^2 + 18(13) + 300$

$ = 806.9375$

Computing $R(20, 12)$ yields

$R(20, 12) = -0.25(20)^2 + 22(20) - 0.5(12)^2 + 18(12) + 300$

$ = 784$

Thus, $R(21.5, 13) - R(20, 12) = 806.9375 - 784$

$ = 22.9375$

The actual change in revenue is \$22,937.50.

27. Given the volume $V(r, h) = \pi r^2 h$, then the approximate reduction in volume is determined by $dV = 2\pi rh\, dr + \pi r^2\, dh$

If the radius r is reduced from 2 inches to 1.9 inches and if the height is reduced from 9 inches to 8.8 inches, then $dr = 1.9 - 2.0 = -0.1$ and $dh = 8.8 - 9.0 = -0.2$. Using $r = 2$, $dr = -0.1$, $h = 9$, and $dh = -0.2$,

$$dV = 2\pi(2)(9)(-0.1) + \pi(2)^2(-0.2)$$
$$= -4.4\pi$$
$$\approx -13.82$$

The approximate reduction in volume is 13.82 cubic inches.

29. Given the cost function $C(x, y) = 900 + 80x + 45y - 0.02xy$, then the approximate change in cost is determined by $dC = (80 - 0.02y)\, dx + (45 - 0.02x)\, dy$.

If x changes from 120 to 121 and y changes from 200 to 201, then $dx = 121 - 120 = 1$ and $dy = 201 - 200 = 1$.

Using $x = 120$, $dx = 1$, $y = 200$, and $dy = 1$,

$$dv = [80 - 0.02(200)]\,(1) + [45 - 0.02(120)]\,(1)$$
$$= 118.6$$

The approximate change in the cost of raising the production levels one unit each is $118.60.

31. Given the Cobb-Douglas production function $f(x, y) = 24x^{1/2}y^{1/2}$, then the approximate change in production is determined by $df = 12x^{-1/2}y^{1/2}\, dx + 12x^{1/2}y^{-1/2}\, dy$. If x changes from 25 to 26 units and y changes from 36 to 39 units, then $dx = 26 - 25 = 1$ and $dy = 39 - 36 = 3$.

Using $x = 25$, $dx = 1$, $y = 36$, and $dy = 3$,

$$df = 12(25)^{-1/2}(36)^{1/2}(1) + 12(25)^{1/2}(36)^{-1/2}(3)$$
$$= 12\left(\frac{1}{5}\right)(6) + 12(5)\left(\frac{1}{6}\right)(3)$$
$$= 44.4$$

The approximate change in production is 44.4 units.

33. No. The exact change Δz can be determined; however, dz offers a quick and good approximation. For instance, see Example 1 from this section.

SECTION 10.7 pages 528–530

1. $\displaystyle\int_1^3 12x^2y\, dx = \left[4x^3y\right]_1^3 = 4(3)^3y - 4(1)^3y$
$$= 104y$$

3. $\displaystyle\int_0^3 8xy\, dy = \left[4xy^2\right]_0^3 = 4x(3^2 - 0) = 36x$

5. $\displaystyle\int_4^7 (1 + 3x)\, dy = [y + 3xy]_4^7 = [7 + 3x(7)] - [4 + 3x(4)]$
$$= 7 + 21x - 4 - 12x$$
$$= 9x + 3$$

7. $\displaystyle\int_2^5 (2x + 2y)\, dx = \left[x^2 + 2xy\right]_2^5 = \left[5^2 + 2(5)(y)\right] - \left[2^2 + 2(2)(y)\right]$
$$= 25 + 10y - 4 - 4y$$
$$= 6y + 21$$

9. $\displaystyle\int_2^4 (x^2 + y)\, dy = \left[x^2y + \frac{y^2}{2}\right]_2^4 = \left[x^2(4) + \frac{4^2}{2}\right] - \left[x^2(2) + \frac{2^2}{2}\right]$
$$= 4x^2 + 8 - 2x^2 - 2$$
$$= 2x^2 + 6$$

11. $\displaystyle\int_1^3 \int_0^2 (2x + 6y)\, dx\, dy = \int_1^3 \left[x^2 + 6xy\right]_0^2 dy$

$$= \int_1^3 (4 + 12y)\, dy$$

$$= \left[4y + 6y^2\right]_1^3$$

$$= (12 + 54) - (4 + 6)$$

$$= 56$$

13. $\displaystyle\int_0^2 \int_1^4 8xy\, dy\, dx = \int_0^2 \left[4xy^2\right]_1^4 dx = \int_0^2 (64x - 4x)\, dx$

$$= \int_0^2 60x\, dx$$

$$= \left[30x^2\right]_0^2$$

$$= 120$$

15. $\displaystyle\int_1^4 \int_0^1 6xy^2\, dx\, dy = \int_1^4 \left[3x^2y^2\right]_0^1 dy$

$$= \int_1^4 3y^2\, dy$$

$$= \left[y^3\right]_1^4$$

$$= 63$$

17. $\displaystyle\int_0^1 \int_0^2 (x^2 + y^2)\, dy\, dx = \int_0^1 \left[x^2 y + \frac{y^3}{3}\right]_0^2 dx$

$$= \int_0^1 \left(2x^2 + \frac{8}{3}\right) dx$$

$$= \left[\frac{2}{3}x^3 + \frac{8}{3}x\right]_0^1$$

$$= \frac{2}{3} + \frac{8}{3} - 0$$

$$= \frac{10}{3}$$

19. $\displaystyle\int_3^8 \int_0^6 \sqrt{1 + x}\, dy\, dx = \int_3^8 \left[y(1 + x)^{1/2}\right]_0^6 dx$

$$= \int_3^8 6(1 + x)^{1/2}\, dx$$

$$= \left[6\left(\frac{2}{3}\right)(1 + x)^{3/2}\right]_3^8$$

$$= 4\left[(1 + 8)^{3/2} - (1 + 3)^{3/2}\right]$$

$$= 4(27 - 8)$$

$$= 76$$

21. $\displaystyle\int_0^2 \int_0^1 e^{x+y}\, dx\, dy = \int_0^2 \int_0^1 e^x e^y\, dx\, dy$

$$= \int_0^2 \left[e^x e^y\right]_0^1 dy$$

$$= \int_0^2 (e \cdot e^y - e^y)\, dy$$

$$= \left[e \cdot e^y - e^y\right]_0^2$$

$$= (e \cdot e^2 - e^2) - (e \cdot e^0 - e^0)$$

$$= e^3 - e^2 - e + 1$$

23. $\displaystyle\int_0^8 \int_1^e \frac{y}{x}\, dx\, dy = \int_0^8 \left[y \ln |x|\right]_1^e dy$

$$= \int_0^8 y(\ln\, e - \ln\, 1)\, dy$$

$$= \int_0^8 y\, dy$$

$$= \left[\frac{y^2}{2}\right]_0^8$$

$$= 32$$

25.   Reversing the order of integration in Exercise 11 yields

$$\int_0^2 \int_1^3 (2x + 6y)\, dy\, dx = \int_0^2 \left[2xy + 3y^2\right]_1^3 \, dx$$

$$= \int_0^2 [(6x + 27) - (2x + 3)]\ dx$$

$$= \int_0^2 (4x + 24)\ dx$$

$$= \left[2x^2 + 24x\right]_0^2$$

$$= 8 + 48$$

$$= 56$$

This answer agrees with that of Exercise 11.

27.   If R is the rectangular region with vertices (2,1), (4,1), (2,3) and (4,3), then $2 \le x \le 4$ and $1 \le y \le 3$. See the figure below.

Thus, $\displaystyle \int_R \int (x + 2y)\, dx\, dy = \int_1^3 \int_2^4 (x + 2y)\, dx\, dy$

$$= \int_1^3 \left[\frac{x^2}{2} + 2xy\right]_2^4 \, dy$$

$$= \int_1^3 [(8 + 8y) - (2 + 4y)]\ dy$$

$$= \int_1^3 (6 + 4y)\ dy$$

$$= \left[6y + 2y^2\right]_1^3$$

$$= (18 + 18) - (6 + 2)$$

$$= 28$$

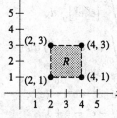

29.   Given $f(x,y)$ and region $R: 0 \le x \le 2,\ 1 \le y \le 3$, then the volume is

$$V = \int_0^2 \int_1^3 (x + y)\, dy\, dx = \int_0^2 \left[xy + \frac{y^2}{2}\right]_1^3 \, dx$$

$$= \int_0^2 \left[\left(3x + \frac{9}{2}\right) - \left(x + \frac{1}{2}\right)\right]\ dx$$

$$= \int_0^2 (2x + 4)\ dx$$

$$= \left[x^2 + 4x\right]_0^2$$

$$= 4 + 8$$

$$= 12$$

31. Given $f(x, y) = x^2 + y^2$ and the region $R: 0 \leq x \leq 2$, $1 \leq y \leq 2$, then the volume is

$$V = \int_0^2 \int_1^2 (x^2 + y^2) \, dy \, dx = \int_0^2 \left[x^2 y + \frac{y^3}{3} \right]_1^2 \, dx$$

$$= \int_0^2 \left[\left(2x^2 + \frac{8}{3} \right) - \left(x^2 + \frac{1}{3} \right) \right] \, dx$$

$$= \int_0^2 \left(x^2 + \frac{7}{3} \right) \, dx$$

$$= \left[\frac{x^3}{3} + \frac{7}{3} x \right]_0^2$$

$$= \left(\frac{8}{3} + \frac{14}{3} \right) - 0$$

$$= \frac{22}{3}$$

33. Given $f(x, y) = 1 + x^2$ and the region $R: 1 \leq x \leq 2$, $0 \leq y \leq 4$, then the volume is

$$V = \int_1^2 \int_0^4 (1 + x^2) \, dy \, dx = \int_1^2 \left[(1 + x^2) y \right]_0^4 \, dx$$

$$= \int_1^2 4(1 + x^2) \, dx$$

$$= 4 \left[x \frac{x^3}{3} \right]_1^2$$

$$= 4 \left[\left(2 + \frac{8}{3} \right) - \left(1 + \frac{1}{3} \right) \right]$$

$$= \frac{40}{3}$$

35. Given $f(x, y) = \frac{1}{y}$ and the region $R: 1 \leq x \leq 10$, $1 \leq y \leq e$, then the volume is

$$V = \int_1^{10} \int_1^e \frac{1}{y} \, dy \, dx = \int_1^{10} [\ln y]_1^e \, dx$$

$$= \int_1^{10} (\ln e - \ln 1) \, dx$$

$$= \int_1^{10} dx$$

$$= [x]_1^{10}$$

$$= 10 - 1$$

$$= 9$$

37. The area of the given region is $(5 - 2)(4 - 0) = 12$. The average value is then

$$\frac{1}{12} \int_2^5 \int_0^4 (4x + 3y) \, dy \, dx = \frac{1}{12} \int_2^5 \left[4xy + \frac{3y^2}{2} \right]_0^4 \, dx$$

$$= \frac{1}{12} \int_2^5 (16x + 24) \, dx$$

$$= \frac{1}{12} \left[8x^2 + 24x \right]_2^5$$

$$= \frac{1}{12} \{ [8(25) + 24(5)] - [8(4) + 24(4)] \}$$

Average value $= 16$

39.   The area of the given region is $(5-2)(4-1) = 9$. The average value is then

$$
\frac{1}{9} \int_2^5 \int_1^4 3x^2 y \, dy \, dx = \frac{1}{9} \int_2^5 \left[\frac{3}{2} x^2 y^2 \right]_1^4 dx
$$

$$
= \frac{1}{6} \int_2^5 (16x^2 - x^2) \, dx
$$

$$
= \frac{1}{6} \int_2^5 15x^2 \, dx
$$

$$
= \frac{1}{6} \left[5x^3 \right]_2^5
$$

$$
= \frac{5}{6} \left(5^3 - 2^3 \right)
$$

Average value $= \dfrac{195}{2}$

41.   The area of the given region is $(2-0)(3-1) = 4$. The average value is then

$$
\frac{1}{4} \int_0^2 \int_1^3 (x^2 + y^2) \, dy \, dx = \frac{1}{4} \int_0^2 \left[x^2 y + \frac{y^3}{3} \right]_1^3 dx
$$

$$
= \frac{1}{4} \int_0^2 \left[\left(3x^2 + \frac{27}{3} \right) - \left(x^2 + \frac{1}{3} \right) \right] dx
$$

$$
= \frac{1}{4} \int_0^2 \left(2x^2 + \frac{26}{3} \right) dx
$$

$$
= \frac{1}{4} \left[\frac{2x^3}{3} + \frac{26}{3} x \right]_0^2
$$

$$
= \frac{1}{4} \left(\frac{16}{3} + \frac{52}{3} - 0 \right)
$$

Average value $= \dfrac{17}{3}$

43.   The region of integration R is $2 \leq x \leq 6$ and $3 \leq y \leq 5$. Then,

$$
\int_R \int f(x, y) \, dx \, dy = \int_3^5 \int_2^6 3xy \, dx \, dy
$$

45.   The region of integration R is $1 \leq x \leq 2$ and $\frac{x}{2} \leq y \leq 2x + 1$. Then,

$$
\int_R \int f(x, y) \, dx \, dy = \int_1^2 \int_{x/2}^{2x+1} 3xy \, dy \, dx
$$

47.
$$
\int_0^1 \int_0^y e^x \, dx \, dy = \int_0^1 \left[e^x \right]_0^y dy
$$

$$
= \int_0^1 (e^y - e^0) \, dy
$$

$$
= \int_0^1 (e^y - 1) \, dy
$$

$$
= \left[e^y - y \right]_0^1
$$

$$
= (e - 1) - (e^0 - 0)
$$

$$
= e - 2
$$

49.
$$
\int_2^3 \int_1^{x^2} 4x \, dy \, dx = \int_2^3 \left[4xy \right]_1^{x^2} dx
$$

$$
= \int_2^3 \left[4x(x^2) - 4x(1) \right] dx
$$

$$
= \int_2^3 (4x^3 - 4x) \, dx
$$

$$
= \left[x^4 - 2x^2 \right]_2^3
$$

$$
= (81 - 18) - (16 - 8)
$$

$$
= 55
$$

51. $\displaystyle\int_0^2 \int_x^{x^2+1} xy \, dy \, dx = \int_0^2 \left[\frac{xy^2}{2}\right]_x^{x^2+1} dx$

$\displaystyle = \frac{1}{2}\int_0^2 \left[x(x^2+1)^2 - x(x^2)\right] dx$

$\displaystyle = \frac{1}{2}\int_0^2 (x^5 + 2x^3 + x - x^3)\, dx$

$\displaystyle = \frac{1}{2}\int_0^2 (x^5 + x^3 + x)\, dx$

$\displaystyle = \frac{1}{2}\left[\frac{x^6}{6} + \frac{x^4}{4} + \frac{x^2}{2}\right]_0^2$

$\displaystyle = \frac{1}{2}\left(\frac{64}{6} + 4 + 2\right)$

$\displaystyle = \frac{25}{3}$

53. $\displaystyle\int_0^2 \int_0^{2x} e^{x^2}\, dy \, dx = \int_0^2 \left[ye^{x^2}\right]_0^{2x} dx$

$\displaystyle = \int_0^2 2xe^{x^2}\, dx$ Let $u = x^2$

$\displaystyle = \left[e^{x^2}\right]_0^2$ $du = 2x \, dx$

$= e^4 - 1$

55. $\displaystyle\int_1^2 \int_{-y}^{2y} 3x^2 y \, dx \, dy = \int_1^2 \left[x^3 y\right]_{-y}^{2y} dy$

$\displaystyle = \int_1^2 \left[8y^3 y - (-y)^3 y\right] dy$

$\displaystyle = \int_1^2 (8y^4 + y^4)\, dy$

$\displaystyle = \int_1^2 9y^4\, dy$

$\displaystyle = \left[\frac{9}{5}y^5\right]_1^2$

$\displaystyle = \frac{9}{5}(2^5 - 1)$

$\displaystyle = \frac{279}{5}$

57. $\displaystyle\int_0^1 \int_y^{\sqrt{y}} 2xy \, dx \, dy = \int_0^1 \left[x^2 y\right]_y^{\sqrt{y}} dy$

$\displaystyle = \int_0^1 \left[(\sqrt{y})^2 y - y^2 y\right] dy$

$\displaystyle = \int_0^1 (y^2 - y^3)\, dy$

$\displaystyle = \left[\frac{y^3}{3} - \frac{y^4}{4}\right]_0^1$

$\displaystyle = \frac{1}{3} - \frac{1}{4} - 0$

$\displaystyle = \frac{1}{12}$

59. $\displaystyle\int_0^1 \int_x^{x^3} 2y \, dy \, dx = \int_0^1 \left[y^2\right]_x^{x^3} dx$

$\displaystyle = \int_0^1 \left[(x^3)^2 - x^2\right] dx$

$\displaystyle = \int_0^1 (x^6 - x^2)\, dx$

$\displaystyle = \left[\frac{x^7}{7} - \frac{x^3}{3}\right]_0^1$

$\displaystyle = \frac{1}{7} - \frac{1}{3}$

$\displaystyle = -\frac{4}{21}$

61.

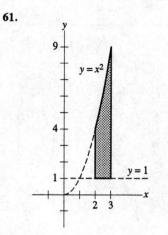

63.

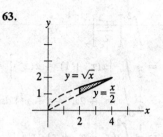

65.

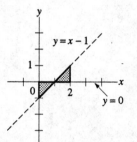

67. The temperature T at point (x, y) on the surface of the plate is given by

$$T(x, y) = 350 - x^2 - y^2$$

The average temperature of the surface of the plate is

$$
\begin{aligned}
\frac{1}{24} \int_{-2}^{2} \int_{-3}^{3} T(x, y) \, dx \, dy &= \frac{1}{24} \int_{-2}^{2} \int_{-3}^{3} (350 - x^2 - y^2) \, dx \, dy \\
&= \frac{1}{24} \int_{-2}^{2} \left[350x - \frac{x^3}{3} - xy^2 \right]_{x=-3}^{3} dy \\
&= \frac{1}{24} \int_{-2}^{2} \left\{ \left[350(3) - \frac{3^3}{3} - 3y^2 \right] - \left[350(-3) - \frac{(-3)^3}{3} - (-3)y^2 \right] \right\} dy \\
&= \frac{1}{24} \int_{-2}^{2} (2100 - 18 - 6y^2) \, dy \\
&= \frac{1}{24} \int_{-2}^{2} (2082 - 6y^2) \, dy \\
&= \frac{1}{24} \left[2082y - 2y^3 \right]_{y=-2}^{2} \\
&= \frac{1}{24} \{ [2082(2) - 2(2)^3] - [2082(-2) - 2(-2)^3] \} \\
&= \frac{1}{24} (8328 - 32) = \frac{8296}{24} = 345\frac{2}{3} \approx 345.67
\end{aligned}
$$

SECTION 10.7 Technology Exercises

1.

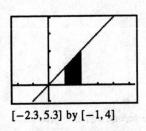

$[-2.3, 5.3]$ by $[-1, 4]$

3.

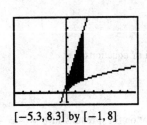

$[-5.3, 8.3]$ by $[-1, 8]$

REVIEW EXERCISES FOR CHAPTER 10 pages 531–533

1. Given $f(x, y) = \dfrac{x^2 + y^2}{2x}$, then

$$f(4, 8) = \frac{4^2 + 8^2}{2(4)} = 10$$

$$f(-6, 0) = \frac{(-6)^2 + 0^2}{2(-6)} = -3$$

3. Given $f(x, y) = \dfrac{y - 3}{x - 1}$, then division by zero must be avoided. Thus, $x - 1 \neq 0$ and the domain is all ordered pairs of real numbers (x, y) such that $x \neq 0$.

5. Given $f(x, y) = x^2 - y + 2$, then

c	Intermediate result	Level curve
-2	$x^2 - y + 2 = -2$	$y = x^2 + 4$
0	$x^2 - y + 2 = 0$	$y = x^2 + 2$
1	$x^2 - y + 2 = 1$	$y = x^2 + 1$

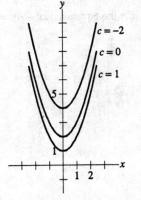

7. Given $f(x, y) = 2x - y$, then

c	Intermediate result	Level curve
1	$2x - y = 1$	$y = 2x - 1$
3	$2x - y = 3$	$y = 2x - 3$
5	$2x - y = 5$	$y = 2x - 5$

9. Given $f(x, y) = x^4 + x^2y^2 - y^4$, then

$$f_x = 4x^3 + 2xy^2$$
$$f_y = 2x^2y - 4y^3$$

11. Given $f(x, y) = e^{3x} + x \ln y$, then

$$f_x = 3e^{3x} + \ln y$$
$$f_y = \frac{x}{y}$$

13. Given $f(x, y, z) = xe^y + 3z^5$, then

$$f_x = e^y$$
$$f_y = xe^y$$
$$f_z = 15x^4$$

15. Given $f(x, y) = 5x^2 - xy + y^3$, then

$f_x = 10x - y$	$f_y = -x + 3y^2$
$f_{xx} = 10$	$f_{yy} = 6y$
$f_{xy} = -1$	$f_{yx} = -1$

17.   Given $f(x, y) = x^2 + 2xy - y^2 + 8x - 16y$ and computing the first partial derivatives yields

$$f_x = 2x + 2y + 8$$
$$f_y = 2x - 2y - 16$$

The resulting system of equations is

$$2x + 2y + 8 = 0$$
$$2x - 2y - 16 = 0$$

Solving the first equation for y results in $y = -x - 4$, and substituting the value into the second equation produces

$$2x - 2y - 16 = 2x - 2(-x - 4) - 16 = 0$$
$$4x - 8 = 0$$
$$x = 2$$

$$y = -x - 4$$
$$= -2 - 4$$
$$= -6$$

The critical point is $(2, -6)$.

19.   Given the function $f(x, y) = 2x^2 + 12xy - 2y^2 - 11$ and computing the first and second partial derivatives yields

$$f_x = 4x + 12y \qquad f_y = 12x - 4y$$
$$f_{xx} = 4 \qquad\qquad f_{yy} = -4$$
$$f_{xy} = 0$$

To solve the system of equations

$$f_x = 4x + 12y = 0$$
$$f_y = 12x - 4y = 0$$

first solve the equation $4x + 12y = 0$ for y to obtain $y = -\frac{1}{3}x$ and substitute this value into the equation $12x - 4y = 0$ to get

$$12x - 4y = 12x + \frac{4}{3}x = 0$$
$$\frac{40}{3}x = 0$$
$$x = 0$$

Therefore,

$$y = \frac{1}{3}x = 0$$

Using the only critical point $(0,0)$, calculate the value of

$$D(0, 0) = f_{xx}(0, 0)f_{yy}(0, 0) - \left[f_{xy}(0, 0)\right]^2 = 4(-4) - 0^2 = -16 < 0$$

Since $D < 0$, then $f(0, 0)$ is a saddle point.

21. The given function for a pitcher's ERA is $E(r, i) = \frac{9r}{i}$ where r is the number of earned runs scored during the number of innings i.

    a. If $r = 1$ and $i = 4$, then $E(1, 4) = \dfrac{9(1)}{4} = 2.25$

        Matt's ERA = 2.25

    b. If $r = 0$ and $i = 12$, then $E(0, 12) = \dfrac{9(0)}{12} = 0.00$

        Tanya's ERA = 0.00

23. Given the revenue function $R(x, y) = xy - x^2 - 2y^2 - x + 25y$, compute the first and second partial derivatives to get

$$R_x = y - 2x - 1 \qquad R_y = x - 4y + 25$$
$$R_{xx} = -2 \qquad\qquad R_{yy} = -4$$
$$R_{xy} = 1$$

To solve the system of equations

$$R_x = -2x + y - 1 = 0$$
$$R_y = x - 4y + 25 = 0$$

to obtain the critical point, first solve the equation $-2x + y - 1 = 0$ for y to obtain $y = 2x + 1$. Use the value in the equation $x - 4y + 25 = 0$ to get

$$x - 4y + 25 = x - 4(2x + 1) + 25 = 0$$
$$-7x + 21 = 0$$
$$x = 3$$

Thus, $y = 2x + 1 = 2(3) + 1$
$$= 7$$

Using the only critical point (3,7), compute the value of

$$D(3, 7) = f_{xx}(3, 7)f_{yy}(3, 7) - \left[f_{xy}(3, 7)\right]^2 = (-2)(-4) - 1^2 = 7 > 0$$

Since $D(3, 7) = 7 > 0$ and $f_{xx}(3, 4) = -2 < 0$, then $fR(3, 7)$ is a relative maximum.

The producer should make 300 regular models and 700 deluxe models to maximize revenue.

25.   Given the function $f(x, y) = x^2 + 2y^2 - 2x + 5$ subject to $x + 2y = 10$, then the constraint function is $g(x, y) = x + 2y - 10$.

Construct the new function

$$F(x, y, \lambda) = x^2 + 2y^2 - 2x + 5 + \lambda(x + 2y - 10)$$
$$= x^2 + 2y^2 - 2x + 5 + \lambda x + 2\lambda y - 10\lambda$$

Find the three first partial derivatives and solve the resulting system of equations

$$F_x = 2x - 2 + \lambda = 0$$
$$F_y = 4y + 2\lambda = 0$$
$$F_\lambda = x + 2y - 10 = 0$$

Solving the first two equations for λ yields $\lambda = -2x + 2$ and $\lambda = -2y$. Thus,

$$-2x + 2 = -2y$$
$$y = x - 1$$

Using this value of y in the third equation produces

$$x + 2y - 10 = x + 2(x - 1) - 10 = 0$$
$$3x - 12 = 0$$
$$x = 4$$

$$y = x - 1$$
$$= 4 - 1$$
$$= 3$$

Thus, $f(x, y)$ has a minimum value at $(4, 3)$; the minimum value is $f(4, 3) = 31$.

27.   Use $n = 8$ and the listed data to determine the values of the various sums in the formulas for m and b. Assume x represents the assessment scores and y the calculus exam.

$$\sum x_i = 20 + 21 + 23 + 25 + 26 + 27 + 28 + 30 = 200$$
$$\sum y_i = 72 + 90 + 76 + 87 + 80 + 98 + 85 + 92 = 680$$
$$\sum x_i y_i = 20 \cdot 72 + 21 \cdot 90 + 23 \cdot 76 + 25 \cdot 87 + 26 \cdot 80 + 27 \cdot 98 + 28 \cdot 85 + 30 \cdot 92 = 17{,}119$$
$$\sum x_i^2 = 20^2 + 21^2 + 23^2 + 25^2 + 26^2 + 27^2 + 28^2 + 30^2 = 5084$$
$$\left(\sum x_i \right)^2 = 40{,}000$$

Substituting these numbers into the formulas yields

$$m = \frac{8 \cdot 17119 - 200 \cdot 680}{8 \cdot 5084 - 40{,}000} = \frac{17}{12}$$

$$b = \frac{680 - \frac{17}{12}(200)}{8} = \frac{595}{12}$$

The least squares line for these data is

$$y = \tfrac{17}{12}x + \tfrac{595}{12}$$

29.   Given the volume function $V(x, y) = x^2 y$, then $dV = 2xy\, dx + x^2\, dy$ is the approximate change in volume. If the length x increases from 120 to 124 and the height y increases from 70 to 73, then $dx = 124 - 120 = 4$ and $dy = 73 - 70 = 3$. Using $x = 120$, $dx = 4$, $y = 70$, and $dy = 3$,

$$dV = 2(120)(70)(4) + (120)^2(3) = 110{,}400$$

The volume increases approximately 110,400 cubic centimeters.

31.   The center of the carpet should be at the origin of the coordinate system. Then the area $A(x, y)$ is given as

$$A(x, y) = (2x)(2y) = 4xy$$

We must maximize this subject to the constraint that $x^2 + y^2 = 4$. Thus, we wish to maximize $A(x, y) = 4xy$ subject to the constraint that $g(x, y) = 0$, where $g(x, y) = x^2 + y^2 - 4$. Then,

$$
\begin{aligned}
F(x, y, \lambda) &= A(x, y) + \lambda g(x, y) \\
&= 4xy + \lambda x^2 + \lambda y^2 - 4\lambda \\
F_x &= 4y + 2\lambda x \\
F_y &= 4x + 2\lambda y \\
F_\lambda &= x^2 + y^2 - 4
\end{aligned}
$$

We must solve $4y + 2\lambda x = 0$
$$4x + 2\lambda y = 0$$
$$x^2 + y^2 - 4 = 0$$

From the first two equations, $\lambda = \dfrac{-2y}{x}$ and $\lambda = \dfrac{-2x}{y}$. Consequently, $\dfrac{2y}{x} = \dfrac{2x}{y}$
$$y^2 = x^2$$

Substitute $y^2 = x^2$ into the third equation to obtain

$$
\begin{aligned}
2x^2 - 4 &= 0 \\
x^2 &= 2 \\
x &= \pm\sqrt{2}
\end{aligned}
$$

Then $y = \pm\sqrt{2}$. Hence, the dimensions of the carpet that maximize the area are $2\sqrt{2}$ by $2\sqrt{2}$.

33.
$$
\begin{aligned}
\int_2^8 \int_1^3 (4x - 3y)\, dx\, dy &= \int_2^8 \left[2x^2 - 3xy\right]_1^3 dy \\
&= \int_2^8 [(18 - 9y) - (2 - 3y)]\, dy \\
&= \int_2^8 (16 - 6y)\, dy \\
&= \left[16y - 3y^2\right]_2^8 \\
&= [16(8) - 3(64)] - (32 - 12) \\
&= -84
\end{aligned}
$$

35.
$$
\begin{aligned}
\int_0^5 \int_0^{1/2} 4e^{2x}\, dx\, dy &= \int_0^5 \left[2e^{2x}\right]_0^{1/2} dy \\
&= 2\int_0^5 (e^1 - e^0)\, dy \\
&= 2\int_0^5 (e - 1)\, dy \\
&= 2\left[(e - 1)y\right]_0^5 \\
&= 2(e - 1)(5) - 0 \\
&= 10(e - 1)
\end{aligned}
$$

37.
$$
\begin{aligned}
\int_{-2}^1 \int_1^4 8\, dy\, dx &= \int_{-2}^1 [8y]_1^4\, dx \\
&= \int_{-2}^1 (32 - 8)\, dx \\
&= \int_{-2}^1 24\, dx \\
&= [24x]_{-2}^1 \\
&= 24[1 - (-2)] \\
&= 72
\end{aligned}
$$

39.
$$\int_0^6 \int_0^{\sqrt{y}} (2x + 4x^3)\, dx\, dy = \int_0^6 \left[x^2 + x^4 \right]_0^{\sqrt{y}} dy$$
$$= \int_0^6 \left[(\sqrt{y})^2 + (\sqrt{y})^4 - 0 \right] dy$$
$$= \int_0^6 (y + y^2)\, dy$$
$$= \left[\frac{y^2}{2} + \frac{y^3}{3} \right]_0^6$$
$$= \frac{36}{2} + \frac{216}{3} - 0$$
$$= 90$$

41.
$$\int_0^1 \int_x^{x^2} 4y\, dy\, dx = \int_0^1 \left[2y^2 \right]_x^{x^2} dx$$
$$= \int_0^1 (2x^4 - 2x^2)\, dx$$
$$= \left[\frac{2}{5}x^5 - \frac{2}{3}x^3 \right]_0^1$$
$$= \left(\frac{2}{5} - \frac{2}{3} \right) - 0$$
$$= -\frac{4}{15}$$

SECTION 11.1 pages 539–540

1. $\sin 24° = 0.4067$

3. $\cos 37° = 0.7986$

5. $\tan 62° = 1.8807$

7. $\sin 17° = 0.2924$

9. $\cos 33° = 0.8387$

11. $\tan 41° = 0.8693$

13.   Referring to the figure below, the sine function is the appropriate trigonometric function to use to solve for x.

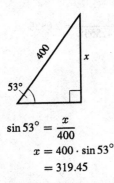

$$\sin 53° = \frac{x}{400}$$
$$x = 400 \cdot \sin 53°$$
$$= 319.45$$

The kite is 319 feet high.

15.   Referring to the figure below, the tangent function is the appropriate trigonometric function to use to solve for x.

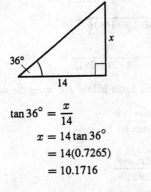

$$\tan 36° = \frac{x}{14}$$
$$x = 14 \tan 36°$$
$$= 14(0.7265)$$
$$= 10.1716$$

The streetlight is 10 feet high.

17.   Referring to the figure in the exercise, the following right triangle can be constructed and the tangent function can be used to solve for x.

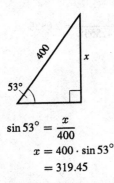

$$\tan 41° = \frac{x}{250}$$
$$x = 250 \tan 41°$$
$$= 250(0.8693)$$
$$= 217.32$$

The clouds are 217 feet high.

SECTION 11.2 pages 549–551

1. $\dfrac{\pi}{6} = \dfrac{\not\pi}{6} \cdot \dfrac{180°}{\not\pi} = 30°$

3. $\dfrac{\pi}{2} = \dfrac{\not\pi}{2} \cdot \dfrac{180°}{\not\pi} = 90°$

5. $\dfrac{5\pi}{4} = \dfrac{5\not\pi}{4} \cdot \dfrac{180°}{\not\pi} = 225°$

7. $\dfrac{4\pi}{3} = \dfrac{4\not\pi}{3} \cdot \dfrac{180°}{\not\pi} = 240°$

9. $90° = 90° \cdot \dfrac{\pi}{180°} = \dfrac{\pi}{2}$

11. $45° = 45° \cdot \dfrac{\pi}{180°} = \dfrac{\pi}{4}$

13. $120° = 120° \cdot \dfrac{\pi}{180°} = \dfrac{2\pi}{3}$

15. $210° = 210° \cdot \dfrac{\pi}{180°} = \dfrac{7\pi}{6}$

17. $\tan \dfrac{\pi}{3} = \dfrac{\sin \frac{\pi}{3}}{\cos \frac{\pi}{3}} = \dfrac{\frac{\sqrt{3}}{2}}{\frac{1}{2}} = \sqrt{3}$

19. $\tan \dfrac{7\pi}{4} = \dfrac{\sin \frac{7\pi}{4}}{\cos \frac{7\pi}{4}} = \dfrac{-\frac{\sqrt{2}}{2}}{\frac{\sqrt{2}}{2}}$
$= -1$

21. $\cot \dfrac{\pi}{2} = \dfrac{\cos \frac{\pi}{2}}{\sin \frac{\pi}{2}} = \dfrac{0}{1} = 0$

23. $\sec \pi = \dfrac{1}{\cos \pi} = \dfrac{1}{-1} = -1$

25. $\csc \dfrac{\pi}{6} = \dfrac{1}{\sin \frac{\pi}{6}} = \dfrac{1}{\frac{1}{2}} = 2$

For each of Exercises 27–38, be sure your calculator is set in the radian (R or Rad) mode. Round your answers to four decimal places.

27. $\sin 1.1 = 0.8912$

29. $\cos 0.8 = 0.6967$

31. $\tan 1.73 = -6.2281$

33. $\sec 2 = \dfrac{1}{\cos 2} = \dfrac{1}{-0.416146836} = -2.4030$

35. $\csc 0.5 = \dfrac{1}{\sin 0.5} = \dfrac{1}{0.479425538} = 2.0858$

37. $\cot 1.9 = \dfrac{1}{\tan 1.9} = \dfrac{1}{-2.927097515} = -0.3416$

39. **a.** Referring to the figure below and using the definitions

$$\sin \theta = \frac{\text{opposite side}}{\text{hypotenuse}}$$
and
$$\cos \theta = \frac{\text{adjacent side}}{\text{hypotenuse}}$$

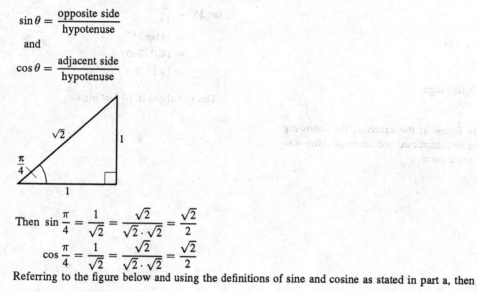

Then $\sin \dfrac{\pi}{4} = \dfrac{1}{\sqrt{2}} = \dfrac{\sqrt{2}}{\sqrt{2} \cdot \sqrt{2}} = \dfrac{\sqrt{2}}{2}$

$\cos \dfrac{\pi}{4} = \dfrac{1}{\sqrt{2}} = \dfrac{\sqrt{2}}{\sqrt{2} \cdot \sqrt{2}} = \dfrac{\sqrt{2}}{2}$

b. Referring to the figure below and using the definitions of sine and cosine as stated in part a, then

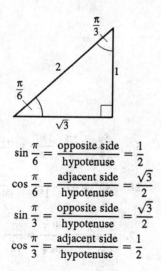

$\sin \dfrac{\pi}{6} = \dfrac{\text{opposite side}}{\text{hypotenuse}} = \dfrac{1}{2}$

$\cos \dfrac{\pi}{6} = \dfrac{\text{adjacent side}}{\text{hypotenuse}} = \dfrac{\sqrt{3}}{2}$

$\sin \dfrac{\pi}{3} = \dfrac{\text{opposite side}}{\text{hypotenuse}} = \dfrac{\sqrt{3}}{2}$

$\cos \dfrac{\pi}{3} = \dfrac{\text{adjacent side}}{\text{hypotenuse}} = \dfrac{1}{2}$

41. Let $P(t) = 105 + 25\cos 6t$ be Hamid's blood pressure function.
   a. Hamid's systolic (maximum) pressure occurs when $\cos 6t = 1$; thus, the systolic pressure is $105 + 25 = 130$.
   b. Hamid's diastolic (minimum) pressure occurs when $\cos 6t = -1$; thus, the diastolic pressure is $105 - 25 = 80$.
   c. At $t = 0$, the beginning of the test, Hamid's blood pressure is

$$P(0) = 105 + 25\cos 0 = 105 + 25 = 130$$

   d. At $t = 1$, Hamid's blood pressure is

$$P(1) = 105 + 25\cos 6$$
$$= 105 + 25(0.9602)$$
$$\approx 105 + 24$$
$$\approx 129$$

43. Given that lawn mower sales are cyclical and are determined by $S(t) = 3000 + 2000\cos\frac{\pi t}{6}$, t in months where 1 is July, 2 is August, $\ldots$, 12 is June, then

   a. For August, $t = 2$, $S(2) = 3000 + 2000\cos\frac{2\pi}{6}$

$$= 3000 + 2000\cos\frac{\pi}{3}$$
$$= 3000 + 2000\left(\frac{1}{2}\right)$$
$$= 4000$$

   b. For December, $t = 6$, $S(6) = 3000 + 2000\cos\frac{6\pi}{6}$

$$= 3000 + 2000\cos\pi$$
$$= 3000 + 2000(-1)$$
$$= 1000$$

   c. The greatest number of lawn mowers will be sold when

$$\cos\frac{\pi t}{6} = 1; \text{ thus, } S = 3000 + 2000(1)$$
$$= 5000$$

   Note: This occurs when $t = 12$, i.e., in June.
   d. The fewest number of lawn mowers will be sold when

$$\cos\frac{\pi t}{6} = -1; \text{ thus, } S = 3000 + 2000(-1)$$
$$= 1000$$

   Note: This occurs when $t = 6$, i.e., in December.

45. Given that the height of a person above the ground is given by

$$y = 41 - 39\cos\left(\frac{\pi}{20}t\right)$$

then,
   a. When $t = 0$, the height of the person above the ground is
   $y = 41 - 39\cos 0$
   $= 41 - 39$
   $= 2$
   b. The highest a person can be off the ground occurs when $\cos\left(\frac{\pi}{20}t\right) = -1$, and so this maximum height is $41 - 39(-1) = 41 + 39 = 80$.
   c. The highest point is first reached when $\frac{\pi}{20}t = \pi$ (since $x = \pi$ is the smallest positive value for which $\cos x = -1$), so $t = \frac{20\pi}{\pi} = 20$. Thus, it takes from $t = 0$ to $t = 10$ to move from the lowest to the highest point initially. Hence, it takes 20 seconds to move from the lowest to the highest point.

47. The number of daylight hours is given by

$$H(t) = 12 + 3 \sin \frac{2\pi}{365}(t - 80)$$

where $t = 1$ corresponds to January 1 and t is measured in days. Then,

a. On the 80th day of the year ($t = 80$), there are

$$H(80) = 12 + 3 \sin \frac{2\pi}{365}(80 - 80) = 12 + 3\sin 0 = 12 \text{ hours of daylight}$$

b. The longest day of the year is when H is a maximum. This occurs when $\frac{2\pi}{365}(t - 80) = \frac{\pi}{2}$

$$t - 80 = \frac{365}{4}$$

$$t = 91\frac{1}{4} + 80 = 171.25$$

The 171st day of the year is June 20, and this is the longest day, when the number of daylight hours is 15.

c. The shortest day of the year occurs when H is a minimum. This occurs when $\sin \frac{2\pi}{365}(t - 80) = -1$, and then $H = 12 - 3 = 9$.

49. Refer to Figures 14 and 15 on pages 547 and 548, respectively.

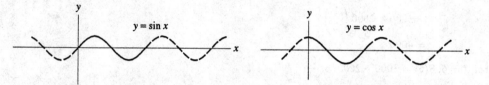

a. The limit $\lim\limits_{x \to \infty} \sin x$ does not exist because the function $\sin x$ does not approach any fixed value. It will oscillate between -1 and 1 forever.

b. Similarly, the limit $\lim\limits_{x \to \infty} \cos x$ does not exist because $\cos x$ also oscillates between -1 and 1 as $x \to \infty$.

51. The equation for the unit circle is $x^2 + y^2 = 1$. If the x value were chosen less than $-1, x < -1$, then, by the properties of inequalities, $x^2 > 1$ and $y^2 = 1 - x^2 < 0$. This is impossible, since $y^2 \geq 0$ for any y. Therefore, $-1 \leq x$.

(*Note:* $-1 \leq x \leq 1$, since $x > 1$ means $x^2 > 1$ also. See the answer to Exercise 50.)

SECTION 11.2 Technology Exercises

1.

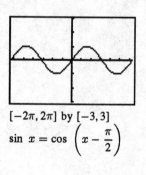

$[-2\pi, 2\pi]$ by $[-3, 3]$

$$\sin x = \cos\left(x - \frac{\pi}{2}\right)$$

3.

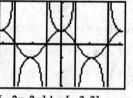

$[-2\pi, 2\pi]$ by $[-3, 3]$

a. When $\cos x = 0$, there is a vertical asymptote for $y = \sec x$. The sign of $\sec x$ is always the same as the sign of $\cos x$.

b. $x = \pm\frac{\pi}{2}$

5.   **a.**

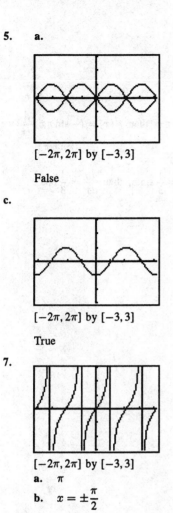

$[-2\pi, 2\pi]$ by $[-3, 3]$

False

b.

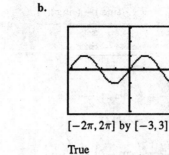

$[-2\pi, 2\pi]$ by $[-3, 3]$

True

c.

$[-2\pi, 2\pi]$ by $[-3, 3]$

True

d.

$[-2\pi, 2\pi]$ by $[-3, 3]$

False

7.

$[-2\pi, 2\pi]$ by $[-3, 3]$

   a. π

   b. $x = \pm\dfrac{\pi}{2}$

c.

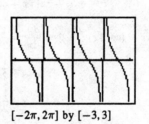

$[-2\pi, 2\pi]$ by $[-3, 3]$

False

9.   3.3

11.   3.2

SECTION 11.3 pages 558–562

1.   Given $y = \sin 2x$, then

$$\frac{dy}{dx} = (\cos 2x)\frac{d}{dx}(2x)$$
$$= 2\cos 2x$$

3.   Given $y = 7\sin x$, $\frac{dy}{dx} = 7\cos x$

5.   Given $y = \sin x^2$, then $\dfrac{dy}{dx} = (\cos x^2)\dfrac{d}{dx}(x^2)$
$$= 2x\cos x^2$$

7.   Given $y = \sin^2 x$, then $\dfrac{dy}{dx} = 2(\sin x)\dfrac{d}{dx}(\sin x)$
$$= 2\sin x \cos x$$

Note: $\sin^2 x = (\sin x)^2$

9.   Given $f(x) = x\sin 4x$, then $f'(x) = x\dfrac{d}{dx}(\sin 4x) + (\sin 4x)(1)$ product rule

$$= x(\cos 4x)\frac{d}{dx}(4x) + \sin 4x$$
$$= 4x\cos 4x + \sin 4x$$

11. Given $y = \dfrac{\sin x}{x}$, then $\dfrac{dy}{dx} = \dfrac{x\frac{d}{dx}(\sin x) - (\sin x)(1)}{x^2}$ quotient rule

$$= \dfrac{x\cos x - \sin x}{x^2}$$

13. Given $y = \cos 2x$, then $\dfrac{dy}{dx} = (-\sin 2x)\dfrac{d}{dx}(2x)$

$$= -2\sin 2x$$

15. Given $f(x) = \cos \pi x$, then $f'(x) = (-\sin \pi x)\dfrac{d}{dx}(\pi x)$

$$= -\pi \sin \pi x$$

17. Given $y = \sin \dfrac{\pi t}{3}$, then $\dfrac{dy}{dt} = \left(\cos \dfrac{\pi t}{3}\right)\dfrac{d}{dt}\left(\dfrac{\pi t}{3}\right)$

$$= \dfrac{\pi}{3}\cos \dfrac{\pi t}{3}$$

19. Given $y = \dfrac{\sin x}{3} = \dfrac{1}{3}\sin x$, then $\dfrac{dy}{dx} = \dfrac{1}{3}\cos x$

21. Given $y = 1 + \cos^2 2x$, then $\dfrac{dy}{dx} = 0 + 2(\cos 2x)\dfrac{d}{dx}(\cos 2x)$

$$= 2(\cos 2x)(-2\sin 2x)$$

$$= -4\cos 2x \sin 2x$$

23. Given $g(x) = x\cos x$, then $g'(x) = x\dfrac{d}{dx}(\cos x) + (\cos x)(1)$ product rule

$$= -x\sin x + \cos x$$

25. Given $y = \sqrt{\cos 4x} = (\cos 4x)^{1/2}$, then $\dfrac{dy}{dx} = \dfrac{1}{2}(\cos 4x)^{-1/2}\dfrac{d}{dx}(\cos 4x)$

$$= \dfrac{1}{2}(\cos 4x)^{-1/2}\left[(-\sin 4x)\dfrac{d}{dx}(4x)\right]$$

$$= \dfrac{1}{2}(\cos 4x)^{-1/2}(-4\sin 4x)$$

$$= -\dfrac{2\sin 4x}{\sqrt{\cos 4x}}$$

Using trigonometric identities, this answer has other forms.

For example, $\dfrac{dy}{dx} = \dfrac{-2\sin 4x\sqrt{\cos 4x}}{\sqrt{\cos 4x}\sqrt{\cos 4x}} = \dfrac{-2\sin 4x}{\cos 4x}\sqrt{\cos 4x} = -2\tan 4x\sqrt{\cos 4x}$

27. Given $f(x) = e^x \sin x$, then $f'(x) = e^x\dfrac{d}{dx}(\sin x) + (\sin x)\dfrac{d}{dx}(e^x)$ product rule

$$= e^x \cos x + e^x \sin x$$

$$= e^x(\cos x + \sin x)$$

29. Given $y = \dfrac{\cos x}{x}$, then $\dfrac{dy}{dx} = \dfrac{x\frac{d}{dx}(\cos x) - (\cos x)(1)}{x^2}$ quotient rule

$$= \dfrac{-x\sin x - \cos x}{x^2}$$

$$= -\dfrac{x\sin x + \cos x}{x^2}$$

31. Given $y = \tan 4x$, then $\dfrac{dy}{dx} = (\sec^2 4x)\dfrac{d}{dx}(4x)$

$$= 4\sec^2 4x$$

33. Given $y = 8\csc 2t$, then $\dfrac{dy}{dt} = 8(-\csc 2t \cot 2t)\dfrac{d}{dt}(2t)$

$$= -16\csc 2t \cot 2t$$

35. Given $y = 1 + \sec \pi t$, then $\dfrac{dy}{dt} = 0 + (\sec \pi t \tan \pi t)\dfrac{d}{dt}(\pi t)$

$$= \pi \sec \pi t \tan \pi t$$

37. Given $y = 2 \csc x^3$, then $\dfrac{dy}{dx} = 2\left[(-\csc x^3 \cot x^3)\dfrac{d}{dx}(x^3)\right]$

$$= 2(-\csc x^3 \cot x^3)(3x^2)$$
$$= -6x^2 \csc x^3 \cot x^3$$

39. Given $f(x) = \sqrt{\cot x} = (\cot x)^{1/2}$, then $f'(x) = \dfrac{1}{2}(\cot x)^{-1/2}\dfrac{d}{dx}(\cot x)$

$$= \dfrac{1}{2}(\cot x)^{-1/2}(-\csc^2 x)$$
$$= \dfrac{-\csc^2 x}{2\sqrt{\cot x}}$$

41. Given $y = -5 \cot 2\pi x$, then $\dfrac{dy}{dx} = -5\left[(-\csc^2 2\pi x)\dfrac{d}{dx}(2\pi x)\right]$

$$= -10\pi \csc^2 2\pi x$$

43. Given $y = \tan^2 3x$, then $\dfrac{dy}{dx} = 2(\tan 3x)\dfrac{d}{dx}(\tan 3x)$

$$= 2(\tan 3x)\left[(\sec^2 3x)\dfrac{d}{dx}(3x)\right]$$
$$= 6 \tan 3x \sec^2 3x$$

45. Given $y = e^x \sec x$, then $\dfrac{dy}{dx} = e^x \dfrac{d}{dx}(\sec x) + (\sec x)\dfrac{d}{dx}(e^x)$

$$= e^x \sec x \tan x + e^x \sec x$$
$$= e^x \sec x(1 + \tan x)$$

47. Given $f(x) = 2x \tan x$, then $f'(x) = 2x\dfrac{d}{dx}(\tan x) + (\tan x)\dfrac{d}{dx}(2x)$

$$= 2x \sec^2 x + 2 \tan x$$

49. If the number of snow shovels sold each month is given by $S(t) = 10{,}000 + 9000 \cos \frac{\pi t}{6}$, where t is the time in months ($t = 1$ is January, etc.), then

    a. For June, $t = 6$, and $S(6) = 10{,}000 + 9000 \cos \pi$

$$= 10{,}000 + 9000(-1)$$
$$= 1000$$

    Only 1000 shovels are sold in June.

    b. For December, $t = 12$, and $S(12) = 10{,}000 + 9000 \cos 2\pi$

$$= 10{,}000 + 9000(1)$$
$$= 19{,}000$$

    In December, 19,000 shovels are sold.

    c. $\dfrac{dS}{dt} = 0 + 9000\left[\left(-\sin \dfrac{\pi t}{6}\right)\left(\dfrac{\pi}{6}\right)\right] = -1500\pi \sin \dfrac{\pi t}{6}$

    d. For September, $t = 9$, $\dfrac{dS}{dt}(9) = -1500\pi \sin \dfrac{3\pi}{2} = -1500\pi(-1)$

$$= 1500\pi$$

    The sales in September are increasing at a rate of 1500π (≈ 4712) shovels per month.

    e. For March, $t = 3$, $\dfrac{dS}{dt}(3) = -1500\pi \sin \dfrac{\pi}{2} = -1500\pi(1) = -1500\pi$

    The sales in March are decreasing at a rate of 1500π (≈ 4712) shovels per month.

51. If the height of the tide at any time of the day is given by $H(t) = 6 + 4 \sin \frac{\pi t}{6}$, where t is measured in hours after midnight on a 24-hour clock, $t = 0$ is midnight, then

a. For $t = 3$, 3 A.M.,

$$H(3) = 6 + 4 \sin \frac{\pi}{2} = 6 + 4(1) = \boxed{10} \quad \text{and for } t = 15, \text{ 3 P.M.}$$

$$H(15) = 6 + 4 \sin \frac{5\pi}{2} = 6 + 4(1) = \boxed{10}$$

b. For $t = 9$, 9 A.M.

$$H(9) = 6 + 4 \sin \frac{3\pi}{2} = 6 + 4(-1) = \boxed{2} \quad \text{and for } t = 21, \text{ 9 P.M.}$$

$$H(21) = 6 + 4 \sin \frac{7\pi}{2} = 6 + 4(-1) = \boxed{2}$$

c.
$$\frac{dH}{dt} = 0 + 4 \left(\cos \frac{\pi t}{6} \right) \left(\frac{\pi}{6} \right)$$
$$= \frac{2\pi}{3} \cos \frac{\pi t}{6}$$

d. For $t = 3$, $\frac{dH}{dt} = \frac{2\pi}{3} \cos \frac{\pi}{2} = \frac{2\pi}{3}(0) = \boxed{0}$

For $t = 15$, $\frac{dH}{dt} = \frac{2\pi}{3} \cos \frac{5\pi}{2} = \frac{2\pi}{3}(0) = \boxed{0}$

For $t = 9$, $\frac{dH}{dt} = \frac{2\pi}{3} \cos \frac{3\pi}{2} = \frac{2\pi}{3}(0) = \boxed{0}$

For $t = 21$, $\frac{dH}{dt} = \frac{2\pi}{3} \cos \frac{7\pi}{2} = \frac{2\pi}{3}(0) = \boxed{0}$

e. If $H(t)$ measures the height of the tide, then high tide and low tide represent the maximum and minimum values of $H(t)$, which occur at the critical points where $\frac{dH}{dt} = 0$.

53. If the predator-prey functions are given by

Predator: $D(t) = 1000 + 500 \sin \dfrac{\pi t}{12}$

Prey : $Y(t) = 4000 + 2000 \cos \dfrac{\pi t}{12}$

where t is time in months, then

a. For $t = 12$, $D(12) = 1000 + 500 \sin \pi$

$$= 1000 + 500(0)$$
$$= 1000$$

b. For $t = 12$, $Y(12) = 4000 + 2000 \cos \pi$

$$= 4000 + 2000(-1)$$
$$= 2000$$

c. Computing $D'(t)$ yields $D'(t) = 0 + 500 \left(\cos \dfrac{\pi t}{12} \right) \left(\dfrac{\pi}{12} \right)$

$$= \dfrac{125\pi}{3} \cos \dfrac{\pi t}{12}$$

For $t = 12$, $D'(12) = \dfrac{125\pi}{3} \cos \pi$

$$= \dfrac{125\pi}{3}(-1)$$
$$= -\dfrac{125\pi}{3} \approx -131$$

The predator population, at $t = 12$, is decreasing at a rate of approximately 131 predators per month.

d. Computing $Y'(t)$ yields $Y'(t) = 2000 \left(-\sin \dfrac{\pi t}{12} \right) \left(\dfrac{\pi}{12} \right)$

$$= -\dfrac{500\pi}{3} \sin \dfrac{\pi t}{12}$$

For $t = 12$, $Y'(12) = -\dfrac{500\pi}{3} \sin \pi$

$$= -\dfrac{500\pi}{3}(0)$$
$$= 0$$

At $t = 12$, the derivative of $Y(t)$, $Y'(t) = 0$, which implies that $t = 12$ is a critical number of $Y(t)$ and may yield a relative minimum value. This is consistent with the statement that the prey population has reached its lowest level at $t = 12$.

55. From the diagram we see that $\cos \theta = \frac{x}{8}$.
a. Differentiate both sides of the equation with respect to angle θ to obtain

$$-\sin \theta = \frac{1}{8} \frac{dx}{d\theta}$$

Hence, $\dfrac{dx}{d\theta} = -8 \sin \theta$

b. As θ increases, the length of shadow shortens; i.e., x decreases. This is consistent with part a in that as θ increases (for 0 to $\frac{\pi}{2}$), $-8 \sin \theta$ is negative; thus dx is negative, and so x decreases.

57. From the diagram, we see that $\tan \theta = \frac{y}{100}$. Both θ and y are functions of time t. Differentiate both sides of the equation with respect to time t to obtain

$$\sec^2 \theta \, \frac{d\theta}{dt} = \frac{1}{100} \, \frac{dy}{dt}$$

Then,

$$\frac{dy}{dt} = 100 \, \sec^2 \theta \, \frac{d\theta}{dt}$$

When $\theta = 0.9$ radian, $\frac{d\theta}{dt} = 0.1$ radian per minute, and $\frac{dy}{dt} = 100(\sec 0.9)^2 (0.1)$

$$\approx 25.88 \text{ meters per minute}$$

59.

t	$\sin t$	$\frac{\sin t}{t}$
0.1	0.099833416	0.998334166
0.01	0.009999833	0.999983333
0.001	0.000999999	0.999999833
0.0001	0.000099999	0.999999998
−0.1	−0.099833416	0.998334166
−0.01	−0.009999833	0.999983333
−0.001	−0.000999999	0.999999833
−0.0001	−0.000099999	0.999999998

It seems clear from the table of values that

$$\lim_{x \to 0} \frac{\sin t}{t} = 1$$

61.

x	$\frac{\pi}{2} - x$	$\sin\left(\frac{\pi}{2} - x\right)$	$\cos x$
0.3	1.2708	0.9553	0.9553
0.7	0.8708	0.7648	0.7648
1.2	0.3708	0.3624	0.3624
2.3	−0.7292	−0.6663	−0.6663
3.5	−1.9292	−0.9365	−0.9365
4.1	−2.5292	−0.5748	−0.5748

Rounded to four decimal places
It seems clear from the table of values that

$$\sin\left(\frac{\pi}{2} - x\right) = \cos x$$

63. Using the quotient rule on $\cot x = \dfrac{\cos x}{\sin x}$ yields

$$\frac{d}{dx}(\cot\ x) = \frac{d}{dx}\left(\frac{\cos\ x}{\sin\ x}\right) = \frac{(\sin\ x)(-\sin\ x) - (\cos\ x)(\cos\ x)}{\sin^2\ x}$$

$$= \frac{-\sin^2\ x - \cos^2\ x}{\sin^2\ x}$$

$$= \frac{-(\sin^2\ x + \cos^2\ x)}{\sin^2\ x}$$

Using the identities $\sin^2\ x + \cos^2\ x = 1$ and $\dfrac{1}{\sin^2\ x} = \csc^2\ x$ produces

$$\frac{d}{dx}(\cot\ x) = -\frac{1}{\sin^2\ x}$$

$$= -\csc^2\ x$$

65. Using the identity $\csc\ x = \dfrac{1}{\sin\ x} = (\sin\ x)^{-1}$ yields

$$\frac{d}{dx}(\csc\ x) = -(\sin\ x)^{-2}(\cos\ x) = -\frac{\cos\ x}{\sin^2\ x}$$

$$= \frac{1}{\sin\ x} \cdot -\frac{\cos\ x}{\sin\ x}$$

Using the identities $\cot\ x = \dfrac{\cos\ x}{\sin\ x}$ and $\csc\ x = \dfrac{1}{\sin\ x}$ produces

$$\frac{d}{dx}(\csc\ x) = -\csc\ x\ \cot\ x$$

67. Given $y = \sin\ 2x$, then $\dfrac{dy}{dx} = 2\ \cos\ 2x$ and $\dfrac{d^2y}{dx^2} = -4\ \sin\ 2x$.

At $x = \dfrac{\pi}{3}$, $\dfrac{d^2y}{dx^2} = -4\sin 2\left(\dfrac{\pi}{3}\right) = -2\sqrt{3} < 0$

The graph of $y = \sin\ 2x$ is concave downward at $x = \dfrac{\pi}{3}$.

69. To find the slope of the line tangent to the graph of $y = 3 + 8\ \cos\ 2x$ at the point $\left(\dfrac{\pi}{4}, 3\right)$, find the value of $\dfrac{dy}{dx}$ at $x = \dfrac{\pi}{4}$.

Differentiating $y = 3 + 8\ \cos\ 2x$ yields $\dfrac{dy}{dx} = -16\ \sin\ 2x$ and $\dfrac{dy}{dx}\left(\dfrac{\pi}{4}\right) = -16\ \sin\ 2\left(\dfrac{\pi}{4}\right)$

$$= -16\ \sin\ \frac{\pi}{2}$$

$$= -16$$

The slope is -16.

71. Using implicit differentiation on $2x = \sin\ y$ yields

$$2 = (\cos\ y)\frac{dy}{dx}$$

Solving for $\dfrac{dy}{dx}$ produces $\dfrac{dy}{dx} = \dfrac{2}{\cos\ y}$

$$= 2\ \sec\ y$$

73. Using implicit differentiation on $x = e^y \cos x$ yields

$$1 = e^y(-\sin x) + (\cos x)\left(e^y \frac{dy}{dx}\right)$$

Solving for $\frac{dy}{dx}$ produces $e^y \cos x \frac{dy}{dx} = 1 + e^y \sin x$

$$\frac{dy}{dx} = \frac{1 + e^y \sin x}{e^y \cos x}$$

75. Using implicit differentiation on $x = \tan xy$ yields

$$1 = \frac{d}{dx}(\tan xy)$$

$$= (\sec^2 xy)\frac{d}{dx}(xy)$$

$$= (\sec^2 xy)\left[x\frac{dy}{dx} + y(1)\right]$$

Solving for $\frac{dy}{dx}$ produces

$$1 = x \sec^2 xy \frac{dy}{dx} + y \sec^2 xy$$

$$x \sec^2 xy \frac{dy}{dx} = 1 - y \sec^2 xy$$

$$\frac{dy}{dx} = \frac{1}{x \sec^2 xy} - \frac{y \sec^2 xy}{x \sec^2 xy}$$

$$= \frac{\cos^2 xy}{x} - \frac{y}{x}$$

$$= \frac{\cos^2 xy - y}{x}$$

77. From the graph we see that $y = \sin x$ has a relative minimum at $x = \frac{3\pi}{2}$. Hence, the value of $\frac{dy}{dx}$ at $x = \frac{3\pi}{2}$ is zero.

SECTION 11.3 Technology Exercises

1.
  a. concave down
  b. concave up
  c. concave up
  d. concave down
  e. concave up
  f. concave down

3.
  a. negative
  b. positive
  c. positive
  d. negative
  e. negative
  f. negative

5.

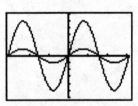

$[-2\pi, 2\pi]$ by $[-6, 6]$

The slope of $y = 5 \sin x$ is always 5 times the slope of $y = \sin x$. Concavity is the same for both graphs, and relative extrema occur at the same x values for both graphs.

7. 12.6

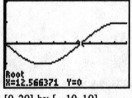

$[0, 20]$ by $[-10, 10]$

9.   2.4

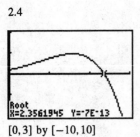

[0, 3] by [−10, 10]

11.   0

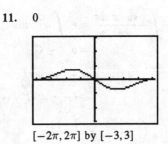

[−2π, 2π] by [−3, 3]

13.   0.5

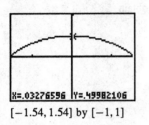

X=.03276596 Y=.49982106

[−1.54, 1.54] by [−1, 1]

15.   0.8

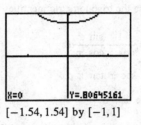

X=0   Y=.80645161

[−1.54, 1.54] by [−1, 1]

SECTION 11.4 pages 568–570

1. $\displaystyle\int \sin\ 2x\ dx = \frac{1}{2}\int (\sin\ 2x)(2\ dx) = -\frac{1}{2}\ \cos\ 2x + C$

Let $u = 2x$
$\quad du = 2\ dx$

3. $\displaystyle\int \cos\ 5x\ dx = \frac{1}{5}\int (\cos\ 5x)(5\ dx) = \frac{1}{5}\ \sin\ 5x + C$

Let $u = 5x$
$\quad du = 5\ dx$

5. $\displaystyle\int x\ \cos\ x^2\ dx = \frac{1}{2}\int (\cos\ x^2)(2x\ dx) = \frac{1}{2}\ \sin\ x^2 + C$

Let $u = x^2$
$\quad du = 2x\ dx$

7. $\displaystyle\int \sin\ (x+1)\ dx = -\cos\ (x+1) + C$

Let $u = x + 1$
$\quad du = dx$

9. $\displaystyle\int \sin^2\ x\ \cos\ x\ dx = \int u^2\ du = \frac{1}{3}u^3 + C$
$$= \frac{1}{3}\ \sin^3\ x + C$$

Let $u = \sin\ x$
$\quad du = \cos\ x\ dx$

11. $\displaystyle\int \cos\ x\ \sin\ x\ dx = \int u\ du = \frac{u^2}{2} + C$
$$= \frac{1}{2}\ \sin^2\ x + C$$

Let $u = \sin\ x$
$\quad du = \cos\ x\ dx$

13. $\displaystyle\int \frac{\sin x}{\cos^2 x}\, dx = -\int -\frac{\sin x\, dx}{\cos^2 x} = -\int u^{-2}\, du$

$$= u^{-1} + C$$

$$= \frac{1}{\cos x} + C$$

$$= \sec x + C$$

Let $u = \cos x$

$du = -\sin x\, dx$

Note: One could use the trigonometric identities $\frac{1}{\cos x} = \sec x$ and $\frac{\sin x}{\cos x} = \tan x$ to obtain

$$\int \frac{\sin x}{\cos^2 x}\, dx = \int \frac{1}{\cos x}\frac{\sin x}{\cos x}\, dx$$

$$= \int \sec x \tan x\, dx$$

$$= \sec x + C$$

15. $\displaystyle\int \sqrt{1 + \cos x}\, \sin x\, dx = -\int (1 + \cos x)^{1/2}(-\sin x\, dx)$

$$= -\int u^{1/2}\, du$$

$$= -\frac{2}{3}u^{3/2} + C$$

$$= -\frac{2}{3}(1 + \cos x)^{3/2} + C$$

Let $u = 1 + \cos x$

$du = -\sin x\, dx$

17. $\displaystyle\int \frac{\sin x}{1 + \cos x}\, dx = -\int \frac{-\sin x\, dx}{1 + \cos x} = -\int \frac{du}{u}$

$$= -\ln |u| + C$$

$$= -\ln |1 + \cos x| + C$$

Let $u = 1 + \cos x$

$du = -\sin x\, dx$

19. $\displaystyle\int_0^{\pi/4} \cos 2x\, dx = \frac{1}{2}\int_0^{\pi/4} (\cos 2x)(2\, dx) = \frac{1}{2}\left[\sin 2x\right]_0^{\pi/4}$

$$= \frac{1}{2}\left[\sin 2\left(\frac{\pi}{4}\right) - \sin 0\right]$$

$$= \frac{1}{2}(1 - 0)$$

$$= \frac{1}{2}$$

Let $u = 2x$

$du = 2\, dx$

21. $\displaystyle\int_{\pi/4}^{\pi/2} \sin\ 4x\ dx = \frac{1}{4}\int_{\pi/4}^{\pi/2}(\sin\ 4x)(4\ dx) = -\frac{1}{4}\left[\cos\ 4x\right]_{\pi/4}^{\pi/2}$

$$= -\frac{1}{4}\left[\cos\ 4\left(\frac{\pi}{2}\right) - \cos\ 4\left(\frac{\pi}{4}\right)\right]$$

$$= -\frac{1}{4}(\cos\ 2\pi - \cos\ \pi)$$

$$= -\frac{1}{4}[1 - (-1)]$$

$$= -\frac{1}{2}$$

Let $u = 4x$

   $du = 4\ dx$

23. $\displaystyle\int_{0}^{\pi/3}\cos^2\ x\ \sin\ x\ dx = -\int_{0}^{\pi/3}(\cos^2\ x)(-\sin\ x\ dx) = -\int_{1}^{1/2}u^2\ du$

$$= -\frac{1}{3}[u^3]_{1}^{1/2}$$

$$= -\frac{1}{3}\left[\left(\frac{1}{2}\right)^3 - 1^3\right]$$

$$= -\frac{1}{3}\left(\frac{1}{8} - 1\right)$$

$$= \frac{7}{24}$$

Let $u = \cos\ x$

   $du = -\sin\ x\ dx$

when $x = 0,\quad u = \cos\ 0 = 1$

$$x = \frac{\pi}{3},\quad u = \cos\ \frac{\pi}{3} = \frac{1}{2}$$

25. $\displaystyle\int \tan\ 4x\ dx = \frac{1}{4}\int(\tan\ 4x)(4\ dx) = -\frac{1}{4}\ \ln\ |\cos\ 4x| + C$

Let $u = 4x$

   $du = 4\ dx$

27. $\displaystyle\int x\ \tan\ x^2\ dx = \frac{1}{2}\int(\tan\ x^2)(2x\ dx) = -\frac{1}{2}\ \ln\ |\cos\ x^2| + C$

Let $u = x^2$

   $du = 2x\ dx$

29. $\displaystyle\int \sec^2\ 2x\ dx = \frac{1}{2}\int(\sec^2\ 2x)(2\ dx) = \frac{1}{2}\ \tan\ 2x + C$

Let $u = 2x$

   $du = 2\ dx$

31. $\displaystyle\int \sec\ 3x\ \tan\ 3x\ dx = \frac{1}{3}\int(\sec\ 3x\ \tan\ 3x)(3\ dx) = \frac{1}{3}\ \sec\ 3x + C$

Let $u = 3x$

   $du = 3\ dx$

33. $\displaystyle\int \frac{\sec^2 x}{1 + \tan x}\, dx = \int \frac{du}{u} = \ln |u| + C$

$\hspace{6cm} = \ln |1 + \tan x| + C$

Let $u = 1 + \tan x$

$\quad du = \sec^2 dx$

35. $\displaystyle\int \cot 2x\, dx = \frac{1}{2}\int (\cot 2x)(2\, dx) = \frac{1}{2}\ln |\sin 2x| + C$

Let $u = 2x$

$\quad du = 2\, dx$

37. $\displaystyle\int \tan^5 x\, \sec^2 x\, dx = \int u^5\, du = \frac{1}{6}u^6 + C$

$\hspace{6cm} = \frac{1}{6}\tan^6 x + C$

Let $u = \tan x$

$\quad du = \sec^2 x\, dx$

39. Sketch the graph of $y = \sin x$ and shade the area of the interval $\frac{\pi}{6} \le x \le \pi$.

$\text{Area} = \displaystyle\int_{\pi/6}^{\pi} \sin x\, dx = -[\cos x]_{\pi/6}^{\pi}$

$\hspace{2.2cm} = -\left(\cos \pi - \cos \frac{\pi}{6}\right)$

$\hspace{2.2cm} = -\left(-1 - \frac{\sqrt{3}}{2}\right)$

$\hspace{2.2cm} = 1 + \frac{\sqrt{3}}{2}$

41. Sketch the graph of $y = \cos 2x$ and shade the area on the interval $0 \le x \le \frac{\pi}{4}$.

$\text{Area} = \displaystyle\int_0^{\pi/4} \cos 2x\, dx$

$\hspace{1.4cm} = \frac{1}{2}[\sin 2x]_0^{\pi/4}$

$\hspace{1.4cm} = \frac{1}{2}\left[\sin 2\left(\frac{\pi}{4}\right) - \sin 0\right]$

$\hspace{1.4cm} = \frac{1}{2}(1 - 0)$

$\hspace{1.4cm} = \frac{1}{2}$

43.   Sketch the graph of $y = \sin 3x$ and shade the area on the interval $\frac{\pi}{6} \le x \le \frac{\pi}{3}$.

$$\text{Area} = \int_{\pi/6}^{\pi/3} \sin 3x\, dx$$

$$= -\frac{1}{3}\left[\cos 3x\right]_{\pi/6}^{\pi/3}$$

$$= -\frac{1}{3}\left[\cos 3\left(\frac{\pi}{3}\right) - \cos 3\left(\frac{\pi}{6}\right)\right]$$

$$= -\frac{1}{3}\left(\cos \pi - \cos \frac{\pi}{2}\right)$$

$$= -\frac{1}{3}(-1 - 0)$$

$$= \frac{1}{3}$$

45.   Using the formula for the average value of a function on $a \le x \le b$, $\frac{1}{b-a}\int_a^b f(x)\, dx$, yields

$$\frac{1}{\pi - 0}\int_0^\pi 12 \sin 2x\, dx = \frac{12}{\pi}\int_0^\pi \sin 2x\, dx$$

$$= \frac{12}{\pi}\left[-\frac{1}{2}\cos 2x\right]_0^\pi$$

$$= -\frac{6}{\pi}(\cos 2\pi - \cos 0)$$

$$= -\frac{6}{\pi}(1 - 1)$$

Average value $= 0$

47.   Using the formula for the average value of a function on $a \le x \le b$, $\frac{1}{b-a}\int_a^b f(x)\, dx$ yields

$$\frac{1}{18 - 0}\int_0^{18}\left(1400 + 600 \sin \frac{\pi t}{12}\right) dt$$

The integral $\int \sin \frac{\pi t}{12}\, dt$ is of the form $\int \sin u\, du$ where $u = \frac{\pi}{12}$

$$du = \frac{\pi}{12}\, dt$$

Thus, $\int \sin \frac{\pi t}{12}\, dt = -\frac{12}{\pi}\cos \frac{\pi t}{12}$

Therefore, $\dfrac{1}{18}\displaystyle\int_0^{18}\left(1400 + 600 \sin \frac{\pi t}{12}\right) dt = \frac{1}{18}\left[1400t - \frac{7200}{\pi}\cos \frac{\pi t}{12}\right]_0^{18}$

$$= \frac{1}{18}\left[\left(1400(18) - \frac{7200}{\pi}\cos \frac{3\pi}{2}\right) - \left(0 - \frac{7200}{\pi}\cos 0\right)\right]$$

$$= \frac{1}{18}\left(25{,}200 - 0 + \frac{7200}{\pi}\right)$$

$$= 1400 - \frac{400}{\pi}$$

$$\approx 1273$$

The average predator population during the first 18 months is approximately 1273.

49. The formula for the average value of a function is $\dfrac{1}{b-a}\displaystyle\int_a^b f(x)\,dx$ over the interval $a \le x \le b$.

Given the predator function $D(t) = 1000 + 500 \ \sin \frac{\pi t}{12}$ on $0 \le t \le 24$, then

$$
\begin{aligned}
\frac{1}{24}\int_0^{24}\left(1000 + 500\ \sin\frac{\pi t}{12}\right)dt &= \frac{1}{24}\left[1000t - \frac{6000}{\pi}\ \cos\frac{\pi t}{12}\right]_0^{24} \\
&= \frac{1}{24}\left\{\left[1000(24) - \frac{600}{\pi}\ \cos\ 2\pi\right] - \left(0 - \frac{6000}{\pi}\ \cos\ 0\right)\right\} \\
&= \frac{1}{24}\left[1000(24) - \frac{6000}{\pi}(1) + \frac{6000}{\pi}(1)\right] \\
&= 1000
\end{aligned}
$$

The average predator population during the first 24 months is 1000.

Given the prey function $Y(t) = 4000 + 2000\ \cos\ \frac{\pi t}{12}$ on $0 \le t \le 24$, then

$$
\begin{aligned}
\frac{1}{24}\int_0^{24}\left(4000 + 2000\ \cos\ \frac{\pi t}{12}\right)dt &= \frac{1}{24}\left[4000t + \frac{24{,}000}{\pi}\ \sin\frac{\pi t}{12}\right]_0^{24} \\
&= \frac{1}{24}\left\{\left[4000(24) + \frac{24{,}000}{\pi}\ \sin\ 2\pi\right] - \left(0 + \frac{24{,}000}{\pi}\ \sin\ 0\right)\right\} \\
&= \frac{1}{24}\left[4000(24) + 0 - 0 + 0)\right] \\
&= 4000
\end{aligned}
$$

The average prey population during the first 24 months is 4000.

51. Given the marginal revenue function $R'(x) = 200 + 15\ \cos\ \pi x$ with the initial condition $R(0) = 0$, then

$$
\begin{aligned}
R(x) = \int R'(x)\,dx &= \int (200 + 15\ \cos\ \pi x)\,dx \\
&= 200x + \frac{15}{\pi}\ \sin\ \pi x + C
\end{aligned}
$$

Using $R(0) = 0$ yields $R(0) = 0 + \dfrac{15}{\pi}\ \sin\ 0 + C = 0$

$$C = 0$$

The revenue function is $R(x) = 200x + \frac{15}{\pi}\ \sin\ \pi x$

53.   Let the rate of consumption of soft drink be $c'(t) = 90{,}000 + 14{,}000 \sin \frac{\pi t}{6}$ cans per month, where $t = 0$ is the beginning of April, $t = 1$ the end of April, $t = 2$ the end of May, etc.

    a.   The total number of cans of soft drink consumed from the beginning of April, $t = 0$, through the end of September, $t = 6$, is given by

$$\int_0^6 \left(90{,}000 + 14{,}000 \sin \frac{\pi t}{6} \right) dt = \left[90{,}000t - 14{,}000 \left(\frac{6}{\pi} \right) \cos \frac{\pi t}{6} \right]_0^6$$

$$= \left[90{,}000(6) - \frac{84{,}000}{\pi} \cos \pi \right] - \left(0 - \frac{84{,}000}{\pi} \cos 0 \right)$$

$$= 540{,}000 - \frac{84{,}000}{\pi}(-1) + \frac{84{,}000}{\pi}$$

$$= 540{,}000 + \frac{168{,}000}{\pi}$$

$$\approx 593{,}476$$

    b.   The total number of cans of soft drink consumed from the end of September, $t = 6$, through the end of March, $t = 12$, is given by

$$\int_6^{12} \left(90{,}000 + 14{,}000 \sin \frac{\pi t}{6} \right) dt = \left[90{,}000t - 14{,}000 \left(\frac{6}{\pi} \right) \cos \frac{\pi t}{6} \right]_6^{12}$$

$$= \left[90{,}000(12) - \frac{84{,}000}{\pi} \cos 2\pi \right] - \left[90{,}000(6) - \frac{84{,}000}{\pi} \cos \pi \right]$$

$$= (90{,}000)(12) - \frac{84{,}000}{\pi} - 90{,}000(6) - \frac{84{,}000}{\pi}$$

$$= 540{,}000 - \frac{168{,}000}{\pi}$$

$$\approx 486{,}524$$

55.   Given $y' = 2x - \sec^2 x$, then integrating both sides yields

$$y = \int (2x - \sec^2 x)\, dx$$

$$= x^2 - \tan x + C$$

57.   Given $\cos x \, dy = \sin x \, dx$, then separating the variables and integrating both sides yields

$$dy = \frac{\sin x}{\cos x} \, dx = \tan x \, dx$$

$$\int dy = \int \tan x \, dx$$

$$y = -\ln |\cos x| + C$$

59.   Given $\sec x \, dy = \csc y \, dx$, then separating the variables and integrating both sides yields

$$\frac{1}{\csc y} dy = \frac{1}{\sec x} dx$$

$$\sin y \, dy = \cos x \, dx$$

$$\int \sin y \, dy = \int \cos x \, dx$$

$$-\cos y = \sin x + C$$

61.   The area shaded is given by

$$\int_{\pi/4}^{5\pi/4} (\sin\ x - \cos\ x)\ dx = [-\cos\ x - \sin\ x]_{\pi/4}^{5\pi/4}$$

$$= \left(-\cos\ \frac{5\pi}{4} - \sin\ \frac{5\pi}{4}\right) - \left(-\cos\ \frac{\pi}{4} - \sin\ \frac{\pi}{4}\right)$$

$$= \frac{\sqrt{2}}{2} + \frac{\sqrt{2}}{2} - \left(-\frac{\sqrt{2}}{2} - \frac{\sqrt{2}}{2}\right)$$

$$= \sqrt{2} + \sqrt{2}$$

$$= 2\sqrt{2}$$

63.   The area shaded is

$$\int_{0}^{\pi/4} \left(\cos\ x - \frac{\sqrt{2}}{2}\right)\ dx = \left[\sin\ x - \frac{\sqrt{2}}{2}x\right]_{0}^{\pi/4}$$

$$= \left(\sin\ \frac{\pi}{4} - \frac{\sqrt{2}}{2} \cdot \frac{\pi}{4}\right) - \left[\sin\ 0 - \frac{\sqrt{2}}{2}(0)\right]$$

$$= \frac{\sqrt{2}}{2} - \frac{\sqrt{2}}{2} \cdot \frac{\pi}{4}$$

$$= \frac{\sqrt{2}}{2}\left(1 - \frac{\pi}{4}\right)$$

65.   The required volume is

$$\int_{0}^{\pi} \pi y^2\ dx = \pi \int_{0}^{\pi} \sin\ x\ dx$$

$$= \pi\ [-\cos\ x]_{0}^{\pi}$$

$$= \pi[-\cos\ \pi - (-\cos\ 0)]$$

$$= \pi[-(-1) + 1]$$

$$= 2\pi$$

67.   The answer in Example 4 is $\ln\ |2 + \sin\ x| + C$, which can be written as $\ln\ (2 + \sin\ x) + C$. The absolute value can be removed because $-1 \le \sin\ x \le 1$, and adding 2 to the inequality yields $1 \le \sin\ x + 2 \le 3$.

Thus, $\sin\ x + 2 \ge 1 > 0$ for all x.

SECTION 11.4 Technology Exercises

1.   **a.**

n	Area
4	0.4935579005
10	0.4989714932

b.

n	Area
4	0.5000672925
10	0.5000016961

Exact area $= 0.5$

SECTION 11.5 page 572

1.   Given $\int x\ \sin\ x\ dx$, let $u = x$ $dv = \sin\ x\ dx$

$du = dx$ $v = -\cos\ x$, then integration by parts yields

$$\int x\ \sin\ x\ dx = -x\ \cos\ x + \int \cos\ x\ dx$$

$$= -x\ \cos\ x + \sin\ x + C$$

3. Given $\int x \sin x^2 \, dx$, let $u = x^2$, $du = 2x \, dx$; then by substitution

$$\int x \sin x^2 \, dx = \frac{1}{2} \int (\sin x^2)(2x \, dx) = \frac{1}{2} \int \sin u \, du$$

$$= -\frac{1}{2} \cos u + C$$

$$= -\frac{1}{2} \cos x^2 + C$$

5. $\int (x + \sin x) \, dx = \dfrac{x^2}{2} - \cos x + C$

7. Given $\int x \cos 4x \, dx$, let $u = x$, $dv = \cos 4x \, dx$

$$du = dx \qquad v = \frac{1}{4} \sin 4x$$

then integration by parts yields

$$\int x \cos 4x \, dx = \frac{x}{4} \sin 4x - \frac{1}{4} \int \sin 4x \, dx$$

$$= \frac{x}{4} \sin 4x + \frac{1}{16} \cos 4x + C$$

9. Given $\int \sin x \cos x \, dx$, let $u = \sin x$, $du = \cos x \, dx$; then by substitution

$$\int \sin x \cos x \, dx = \int u \, du = \frac{u^2}{2} + C$$

$$= \frac{1}{2} \sin^2 x + C$$

11. $\int x^2 \sin x \, dx$ requires two applications of integration by parts.

Let $u = x^2 \qquad dv = \sin x \, dx$
$\quad du = 2x \, dx \qquad v = -\cos x$, then

$$\int x^2 \sin x \, dx = -x^2 \cos x + 2 \int x \cos x \, dx$$

Let $u = x \qquad dv = \cos x \, dx$
$\quad du = dx \qquad v = \sin x$, thus

$$\int x^2 \sin x \, dx = -x^2 \cos x + 2(x \sin x - \int \sin x \, dx)$$

$$= -x^2 \cos x + 2x \sin x + 2 \cos x + C$$

13. $\int (1 + \sec^2 x) \, dx = x + \tan x + C$

15. Given $\int x \sec^2 x \, dx$, let $u = x \quad dv = \sec^2 x \, dx$

$$du = dx \quad v = \tan x$$

then integration by parts yields

$$\int x \sec^2 x \, dx = x \tan x - \int \tan x \, dx$$

$$= x \tan x + \ln |\cos x| + C$$

17. Given $\int \frac{1 + \sec^2 x}{x + \tan x}\, dx$, let $u = x + \tan x$

$$du = (1 + \sec^2 x)dx, \text{ then by substitution}$$

$$\int \frac{1 + \sec^2 x}{x + \tan x}\, dx = \int \frac{du}{u} = \ln |u| + C$$

$$= \ln |x + \tan x| + C$$

19. In Example 1, we made the substitution $u = x$, and so $dv = \sin x\, dx$. This is a good choice because $du = dx$ and $v = -\cos x$, so integration by parts leaves us with the integral $\int \cos x\, dx$ to perform, and this is $\sin x + C$.

REVIEW EXERCISES FOR CHAPTER 11 pages 573–574

1. $\frac{7\pi}{6} = \frac{7\cancel{\pi}}{6} \cdot \frac{180°}{\cancel{\pi}} = 210°$

3. $225° = 225 \cdot \frac{\pi}{180} = \frac{5\pi}{4}$

5. $\tan \frac{\pi}{6} = \frac{\sin \frac{\pi}{6}}{\cos \frac{\pi}{6}} = \frac{\frac{1}{2}}{\frac{\sqrt{3}}{2}} = \frac{1}{\sqrt{3}} = \frac{\sqrt{3}}{3}$

7. $\sec \frac{\pi}{4} = \frac{1}{\cos \frac{\pi}{4}} = \frac{1}{\frac{\sqrt{2}}{2}} = \frac{2}{\sqrt{2}} = \frac{2\sqrt{2}}{\sqrt{2}\sqrt{2}} = \sqrt{2}$

9. Given $f(t) = 4 \sin \frac{\pi t}{4}$, then

    a. $f(1) = 4 \sin \frac{\pi}{4}(1) = 4 \sin \frac{\pi}{4} = \frac{4\sqrt{2}}{2}$

$$= 2\sqrt{2}$$

    b. $f(2) = 4 \sin \frac{\pi}{4}(2) = 4 \sin \frac{\pi}{2} = 4(1)$

$$= 4$$

11. We see from the diagram that $\tan 31° = \frac{h}{17}$, where h is the height to which the player must raise his hand to block the kick. Then, $h = 17 \tan 31°$

$$\approx 10.21 \text{ feet}$$

13. Given $y = \sin (2x + 1)$, then

$$\frac{dy}{dx} = \cos (2x + 1)\frac{d}{dx}(2x + 1)$$

$$= 2 \cos (2x + 1)$$

15. Given $y = \cos^2 3x$, then

$$\frac{dy}{dx} = 2(\cos 3x)\frac{d}{dx}(\cos 3x)$$

$$= 2(\cos 3x)\left[(-\sin 3x)\frac{d}{dx}(3x)\right]$$

$$= -6 \cos 3x \sin 3x$$

17. Given $f(x) = x \sec x$, then, by the product rule,

$$f'(x) = x(\sec x \tan x) + (\sec x)(1)$$

$$= (1 + x \tan x)\sec x$$

19. Given $y = \frac{\tan x}{x}$, then, using the quotient rule,

$$\frac{dy}{dx} = \frac{x(\sec^2 x) - (\tan x)(1)}{x^2}$$

$$= \frac{x \sec^2 x - \tan x}{x^2}$$

21. Given $y = (1 + \tan x)^3$, then

$$\frac{dy}{dx} = 3(1 + \tan x)^2\frac{d}{dx}(1 + \tan x)$$

$$= 3(1 + \tan x)^2 \sec^2 x$$

23. Given $f(x) = \sin e^x$, then

$$f'(x) = (\cos e^x)\frac{d}{dx}(e^x)$$

$$= e^x \cos e^x$$

25. Given $y = \ln (\sin x)$, then

$$\frac{dy}{dx} = \frac{1}{\sin x} \frac{d}{dx}(\sin x)$$

$$= \frac{1}{\sin x}(\cos x)$$

$$= \cot x$$

27. $\displaystyle\int \cos 4x \, dx = \frac{1}{4} \int (\cos 4x)(4 \, dx) = \frac{1}{4} \sin 4x + C$

Let $u = 4x$

$\quad du = 4 \, dx$

29. $\displaystyle\int e^x \sin e^x \, dx = \int (\sin e^x)(e^x \, dx) = -\cos e^x + C$

Let $u = e^x$

$\quad du = e^x \, dx$

31. $\displaystyle\int 5 \sin 3x \, dx = 5 \int \sin 3x \, dx = \frac{5}{3} \int (\sin 3x)(3 \, dx)$

$$= -\frac{5}{3} \cos 3x + C$$

Let $u = 3x$

$\quad du = 3 \, dx$

33. $\displaystyle\int \cos (x + \pi) \, dx = \sin (x + \pi) + C$

Let $u = x + \pi$

$\quad du = dx$

35. $\displaystyle\int_0^{\pi/6} \sin 2x \, dx = \frac{1}{2} \int_0^{\pi/6} (\sin 2x)(2 \, dx) = -\frac{1}{2}[\cos 2x]_0^{\pi/6}$

$$= -\frac{1}{2}\left(\cos \frac{2\pi}{6} - \cos 0 \right)$$

$$= -\frac{1}{2}\left(\frac{1}{2} - 1 \right)$$

$$= \frac{1}{4}$$

Let $u = 2x$

$\quad du = 2 \, dx$

37. $\displaystyle\int_{\pi/3}^{\pi} \sin \frac{1}{2}x \, dx = 2 \int_{\pi/3}^{\pi} \left(\sin \frac{1}{2}x \right)\left(\frac{1}{2} \, dx \right)$

$$= -2 \left[\cos \frac{1}{2}x \right]_{\pi/3}^{\pi}$$

$$= -2 \left(\cos \frac{\pi}{2} - \cos \frac{\pi}{6} \right)$$

$$= -2 \left(0 - \frac{\sqrt{3}}{2} \right)$$

$$= \sqrt{3}$$

Let $u = \frac{1}{2}x$

$\quad du = \frac{1}{2} \, dx$

39. Given $\displaystyle\int \frac{5}{\cos^2 x} \, dx = 5 \int \sec^2 x \, dx = 5 \tan x + C$

41.   Given $\displaystyle\int \frac{\cos\ x + \sin\ x}{\cos\ x}\ dx = \int \left(\frac{\cos\ x}{\cos\ x} + \frac{\sin\ x}{\cos\ x}\right)\ dx$

$$= \int \left(1 + \frac{\sin\ x}{\cos\ x}\right)\ dx$$

$$= x - \ln\ |\cos\ x| + C$$

43.   Given $\displaystyle\int (x+1)\ \sin\ x\ dx$, let $u = x + 1$ and $dv = \sin\ x\ dx$

$\qquad\qquad\qquad\qquad\qquad\qquad du = dx \qquad\qquad v = -\cos\ x$, then using integration by parts yields

$$\int (x+1)\ \sin\ x\ dx = -(x+1)\ \cos\ x + \int \cos\ x\ dx$$

$$= -(x+1)\ \cos\ x + \sin\ x + C$$

45.   Sketch the graph of $y = \cos\ x$ and shade the area on the interval $0 \le x \le \frac{\pi}{3}$.

$A = \displaystyle\int_0^{\pi/3} \cos\ x\ dx = [\sin\ x]_0^{\pi/3}$

$\qquad\qquad = \sin\ \dfrac{\pi}{3} - \sin\ 0$

$\qquad\qquad = \dfrac{\sqrt{3}}{2} - 0$

$\qquad\qquad = \dfrac{\sqrt{3}}{2}$

47.   Sketch the graph of $y = \sin\ 2x$ and shade the area on the interval $0 \le x \le \frac{\pi}{6}$.

$A = \displaystyle\int_0^{\pi/6} \sin\ 2x\ dx$

$\quad = -\dfrac{1}{2}[\cos\ 2x]_0^{\pi/6}$

$\quad = -\dfrac{1}{2}\left(\cos\ \dfrac{\pi}{3} - \cos\ 0\right)$

$\quad = -\dfrac{1}{2}\left(\dfrac{1}{2} - 1\right)$

$\quad = \dfrac{1}{4}$

49. $\sin\ x = \cos\ x$ when $x = \frac{\pi}{4}$. The required area breaks up into two integrals

$\displaystyle\int_0^{\pi/4} (\cos\ x - \sin\ x)\ dx + \int_{\pi/4}^{\pi/2} (\sin\ x - \cos\ x)\ dx$

$= [\sin\ x + \cos\ x]_0^{\pi/4} + [-\cos\ x - \sin\ x]_{\pi/4}^{\pi/2}$

$= \left(\sin\ \dfrac{\pi}{4} + \cos\ \dfrac{\pi}{4}\right) - (\sin\ 0 + \cos\ 0) + \left(-\cos\ \dfrac{\pi}{2} - \sin\ \dfrac{\pi}{2}\right) - \left(-\cos\ \dfrac{\pi}{4} - \sin\ \dfrac{\pi}{4}\right)$

$= \dfrac{\sqrt{2}}{2} + \dfrac{\sqrt{2}}{2} - 0 - 1 - 0 - 1 + \dfrac{\sqrt{2}}{2} + \dfrac{\sqrt{2}}{2}$

$= 2\sqrt{2} - 2$

51. The total revenue for the year is given by

$$\int_0^{12} \left(150{,}000 - 150{,}000 \cos \frac{\pi t}{6}\right) dt = 150{,}000 \int_0^{12} \left(1 - \cos \frac{\pi t}{6}\right) dt$$

$$= 150{,}000 \left[t - \frac{6}{\pi} \sin \frac{\pi t}{6}\right]_0^{12}$$

$$= 150{,}000 \left\{\left[12 - \frac{6}{\pi} \sin \frac{\pi}{6}(12)\right] - \left[0 - \frac{6}{\pi} \sin \frac{\pi}{6}(0)\right]\right\}$$

$$= 150{,}000 \left(12 - \frac{6}{\pi} \sin 2\pi\right)$$

$$= 150{,}000(12)$$

$$= 1{,}800{,}000 \text{ dollars}$$

53. To show that $y = 2x + \cos x$ is a solution of the differential equation

$$y'' - xy' + y = x \sin x$$

we find y' and y'' and substitute them into the differential equation to show that it is satisfied.

$$y' = 2 - \sin x$$
$$y'' = -\cos x$$

Then,

$$y'' - xy' + y = -\cos x - x(2 - \sin x) + 2x + \cos x$$
$$= x \sin x$$

Hence, $y = 2x + \cos x$ solves the differential equation.

55. A critical point of the function $f(x)$ is $x = \frac{\pi}{6}$, since this is where $f'(x)$ is shown to be zero by the graph. This is associated with a relative minimum value of $f(x)$ since $f'(x)$ is negative for values of x less than $\frac{\pi}{6}$ (so f is decreasing for x just less than $\frac{\pi}{6}$) and f' is positive for values of x greater than $\frac{\pi}{6}$ (so f is increasing for x just greater than $\frac{\pi}{6}$). Hence, a relative minimum at $x = \frac{\pi}{6}$.

SECTION 12.1 page 579

1. Consider the series $\frac{9}{10} + \frac{9}{100} + \frac{9}{1000} + \cdots + \frac{9}{10^n} + \cdots$ and construct the following table of values:

n	sum of the first n terms
1	0.9
2	0.99
3	0.999
4	0.9999
5	0.99999
6	0.999999
7	0.9999999
8	0.99999999
9	0.999999999
10	0.9999999999

    From the table, it is clear that as n gets larger, the series converges to 1.0.

3. Consider the series $\frac{6}{10} + \frac{6}{100} + \frac{6}{1000} + \frac{6}{10,000} + \cdots + \frac{6}{10^n} + \cdots$ and construct the following table of values:

n	sum of the first n terms
1	0.6
2	0.66
3	0.666
4	0.6666
5	0.66666
6	0.666666
7	0.6666666
8	0.66666666
9	0.666666666
10	0.6666666666

    From the table, it is clear that as n gets larger, the series converges to $0.66666666\ldots = \frac{2}{3}$.

5. Consider the series $\frac{1}{4} + \frac{1}{8} + \frac{1}{16} + \frac{1}{32} + \frac{1}{64} + \cdots + \frac{1}{2^{n+1}} + \cdots$ and construct the following table of values:

n	sum of the first n terms
1	0.25
2	0.375
3	04375
4	0.46875
5	0.484375
6	0.4921875
7	0.49609375
8	0.498046875
9	0.499023437
10	0.499511718

    From the table, it appears that as n gets larger, the series converges to 0.5.

7. Consider the series $1 + \frac{1}{4} + \frac{1}{16} + \frac{1}{64} + \cdots + \frac{1}{4^{n-1}} + \cdots$ and construct the following table of values:

n	sum of the first n terms
1	1
2	1.25
3	1.3125
4	1.328125
5	1.33203125
6	1.333007813
7	1.333251953
8	1.333312988
9	1.333328247
10	1.333332062

From the table, it appears that as n gets larger, the series converges to $1.33333\ldots = 1\frac{1}{3}$.

9. $7! = 1 \cdot 2 \cdot 3 \cdot 4 \cdot 5 \cdot 6 \cdot 7 = 5040$

11. $8! = 1 \cdot 2 \cdot 3 \cdot 4 \cdot 5 \cdot 6 \cdot 7 \cdot 8 = 40{,}320$

13. Consider the series in Exercises 1 and 3 and assume $a = \sum_{n=1}^{\infty} \frac{9}{10^n} = 9 \sum_{n=1}^{\infty} \frac{1}{10^n}$ and $b = \sum_{n=1}^{\infty} \frac{6}{10^n} = 6 \sum_{n=1}^{\infty} \frac{1}{10^n}$.

Since $6 = \frac{2}{3}(9)$, it is clear that $b = \frac{2}{3}a$.

Therefore, if $a = 1$, then $\sum_{n=1}^{\infty} \frac{6}{10^n} = b = \frac{2}{3}(1) = \frac{2}{3}$.

15. If one wishes to use the relationship that $n! = n(n-1)!$, then it forces one to define $0! = 1$.

Consider the following:

$$\underbrace{1 = 1! = 1(1-1)! = 1 \cdot 0! = 0!}_{1 = 0!}$$

SECTION 12.1 Technology Exercises

1. $4! = 24$ **3.** $8! = 40{,}320$ **5.** $13! = 6{,}227{,}020{,}800$

SECTION 12.2 pages 585–587

1. The series $\frac{1}{2} + \frac{1}{4} + \frac{1}{8} + \cdots$ is a geometric series with $r = \dfrac{\frac{1}{4}}{\frac{1}{2}} = \frac{1}{2}$ and $a_1 = \frac{1}{2}$.

Thus, $S_6 = \dfrac{\frac{1}{2}\left[1 - \left(\frac{1}{2}\right)^6\right]}{1 - \frac{1}{2}} = \dfrac{\frac{1}{2}}{\frac{1}{2}}\left(1 - \frac{1}{64}\right) = \dfrac{63}{64}$

3. The series $3 + 1 + \frac{1}{3} + \cdots$ is a geometric series with $r = \frac{1}{3}$ and $a_1 = 3$.

Thus, $S_6 = \dfrac{3\left[1 - \left(\frac{1}{3}\right)^6\right]}{1 - \frac{1}{3}} = \dfrac{3}{\frac{2}{3}}\left(1 - \frac{1}{729}\right) = \dfrac{9}{2}\left(\dfrac{728}{729}\right)$

$$= \dfrac{364}{81}$$

5. The series $2 - 1 + \frac{1}{2} - \frac{1}{4} + \cdots$ is a geometric series with $r_1 = -\frac{1}{2}$ and $a_1 = 2$.

Thus, $S_6 = \dfrac{2\left[1 - \left(-\frac{1}{2}\right)^6\right]}{1 - \left(-\frac{1}{2}\right)} = \dfrac{2}{\frac{3}{2}}\left(1 - \dfrac{1}{64}\right) = \dfrac{4}{3}\left(\dfrac{63}{64}\right)$

$\qquad = \dfrac{21}{16}$

7. The series $3 + 2 + \frac{4}{3} + \cdots$ is a geometric series with $r = \frac{2}{3}$ and $a_1 = 3$.

Thus, $S_6 = \dfrac{3\left[1 - \left(\frac{2}{3}\right)^6\right]}{1 - \frac{2}{3}} = \dfrac{3}{\frac{1}{3}}\left(1 - \dfrac{64}{729}\right) = 9\left(\dfrac{665}{729}\right)$

$\qquad = \dfrac{665}{81}$

9. Given the geometric series $1 + \frac{1}{3} + \frac{1}{9} + \cdots$, then $r = \dfrac{\frac{1}{3}}{1} = \dfrac{1}{3}$. Since $|r| = \dfrac{1}{3} < 1$, the series converges.

11. Given the geometric series $1 + 2 + 4 + \cdots$, then $r = \dfrac{2}{1} = 2$. Since $|r| = 2 > 1$, the series diverges.

13. Given the geometric series $6 - 3 + \frac{3}{2} - \cdots$, then $r = -\dfrac{3}{6} = -\dfrac{1}{2}$. Since $|r| = |-\frac{1}{2}| = \dfrac{1}{2} < 1$, the series converges.

15. Given the geometric series $\frac{8}{5} + \frac{12}{5} + \frac{18}{5} + \cdots$, then $r = \dfrac{\frac{12}{5}}{\frac{8}{5}} = \dfrac{12}{8} = \dfrac{3}{2}$. Since $|r| = \dfrac{3}{2} > 1$, the series diverges.

17. Given the geometric series $-\frac{16}{3} + 4 - 3 + \cdots$, then $r = \dfrac{4}{-\frac{16}{3}} = -\dfrac{3}{4}$.

Since $|r| = |-\frac{3}{4}| = \dfrac{3}{4} < 1$, the series converges.

19. Given the geometric series $\frac{5}{7} + \frac{15}{14} + \frac{45}{28} + \cdots$, then $r = \dfrac{\frac{15}{14}}{\frac{5}{7}} = \dfrac{3}{2}$. Since $|r| = \dfrac{3}{2} > 1$, the series diverges.

21. Given the convergent geometric series $1 + \frac{1}{4} + \frac{1}{16} + \cdots$, $a_1 = 1$ and $r = \frac{1}{4}$.

Thus, the series converges to

$S = \dfrac{1}{1 - \frac{1}{4}} = \dfrac{1}{\frac{3}{4}} = \dfrac{4}{3}$

23. Given the convergent geometric series $\frac{1}{2} - \frac{1}{4} + \frac{1}{8} - \cdots$, then $a_1 = \frac{1}{2}$ and $r = \dfrac{-\frac{1}{4}}{\frac{1}{2}} = -\dfrac{1}{2}$.

Thus, the series converges to

$S = \dfrac{\frac{1}{2}}{1 - \left(-\frac{1}{2}\right)} = \dfrac{\frac{1}{2}}{\frac{3}{2}} = \dfrac{1}{3}$

25. Given the convergent geometric series $14 + 4 + \dfrac{8}{7} + \cdots$, then $a_1 = 14$ and $r = \dfrac{4}{14} = \dfrac{2}{7}$.

Thus, the series converges to

$$S = \frac{14}{1 - \frac{2}{7}} = \frac{14}{\frac{5}{7}} = \frac{98}{5}$$

27. Given the convergent geometric series $\dfrac{3}{5} + \dfrac{2}{5} + \dfrac{4}{15} + \cdots$, then $a_1 = \dfrac{3}{5}$ and $r = \dfrac{\frac{2}{5}}{\frac{3}{5}} = \dfrac{2}{3}$.

Thus, the series converges to

$$S = \frac{\frac{3}{5}}{1 - \frac{2}{3}} = \frac{\frac{3}{5}}{\frac{1}{3}} = \frac{9}{5}$$

29. Given the convergent geometric series $-\dfrac{16}{5} + \dfrac{12}{5} - \dfrac{9}{5} + \cdots$, then $a_1 = -\dfrac{16}{5}$ and $r = \dfrac{\frac{12}{5}}{-\frac{16}{5}} = -\dfrac{12}{16} = -\dfrac{3}{4}$.

Thus, the series converges to

$$S = \frac{-\frac{16}{5}}{1 - \left(-\frac{3}{4}\right)} = \frac{-\frac{16}{5}}{\frac{7}{4}} = -\frac{64}{35}$$

31. Given the convergent geometric series $25 - 15 + 9 - \cdots$, then $a_1 = 25$ and $r = -\dfrac{15}{25} = -\dfrac{3}{5}$.

Thus, the series converges to

$$S = \frac{25}{1 - \left(-\frac{3}{5}\right)} = \frac{25}{\frac{8}{5}} = \frac{125}{8}$$

33. The given conditions imply a geometric series. The general term of the series is the compound interest formula $P\left(1 + \dfrac{r}{m}\right)^n$ where $P = 50$, $r = 6\% = 0.06$, and $m = 12$. The value of n varies from 24 months to 1 month.

Thus, $P\left(1 + \dfrac{r}{m}\right)^n = 50\left(1 + \dfrac{0.06}{12}\right)^n = 50(1.005)^n$ and the sum of the series is

$$S_{24} = 50(1.005) + 50(1.005)^2 + \cdots + 50(1.005)^{24}$$

where $a_1 = 50(1.005) = 50.25$ and $r = 1.005$.

$$\text{The total amount} = \frac{50.25[1 - (1.005)^{24}]}{1 - 1.005}$$
$$\approx \$1278$$

35. S_n represents the height of the nth bounce (S_1 is the initial position).

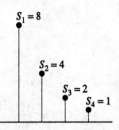

The total distance traveled by the ball is represented by $S = S_1 + S_2 + S_3 + S_4 + \cdots$
$$= 8 + 4 + 2 + 1 + \cdots$$

This sum suggests a geometric series with $a_1 = 8$ and $r = \frac{4}{8} = \frac{1}{2}$. Such a geometric series is convergent and has the limit

$$S = \frac{8}{1 - \frac{1}{2}} = \frac{8}{\frac{1}{2}} = 16$$

Thus, the total distance traveled by the ball is approximately 16 feet.

37.   Using the arguments of Example 4 and changing the percentages to 95% spent and 5% saved yields the following geometric series for the total spending:

$$S = 5(0.95) + 5(0.95)^2 + 5(0.95)^3 + \cdots$$

For this geometric series, $a_1 = 5(0.95)$ and $r = 0.95$, which produces the sum

$$S = \frac{a_1}{1 - r} = \frac{5(0.95)}{1 - 0.95} = \frac{5(0.95)}{0.05} = 95$$

Thus, the $5 billion tax cut will result in $95 billion of economic activity.

39.   For the stated conditions the sum of money is given by the first 64 terms of the geometric series

$$S = 1 + 2 + 2^2 + 2^3 + 2^4 + \cdots$$

For $n = 64$, $a_1 = 1$, and $r = 2$, this sum is

$$S_{64} = \frac{a_1(1 - r^n)}{1 - 2} = \frac{1(1 - 2^{64})}{1 - 2} = -(1 - 2^{64})$$
$$= 1.8446744 \times 10^{19} \text{ cents}$$

The dollar amount is $\dfrac{S_{64}}{100} = \$1.8446744 \times 10^{17}$
$$\approx 184 \text{ quadrillion dollars}$$

41.   **a.**   If one reads the rhyme very carefully, then it is clear that only the storyteller is going *to* Saint Ives. All the others the story teller *met going away* from Saint Ives.

Thus, the answer to the rhyme is one.

b.   The total number of wives, sacks, cats, and kits is a partial sum of the geometric series

$$S = 7 + 7^2 + 7^3 + 7^4 + \cdots$$

Since there are four items to consider, then $n = 4$, $a_1 = 7$, and $r = 7$.

Thus, $S_4 = \dfrac{a_1(1 - r^n)}{1 - r} = \dfrac{7(1 - 7^4)}{1 - 7} = 2800$

43. Let $S = a_1 + a_2 + a_3 + a_4 + \cdots$ be a series of positive constants, and assume that the magnitudes of the terms are decreasing, that is, $a_2 < a_1$, $a_3 < a_2$, etc.

a. If S is a geometric series, than it *must converge* because $r = \frac{a_2}{a_1} < 1$ since $a_2 < a_1$.

b. If S is not a geometric series, then it may *or* may not converge. Two examples will illustrate this.

$S = 1 + \frac{1}{2} + \frac{1}{3} + \frac{1}{4} + \cdots$ is divergent (see Section 12.1)

but

$S = \frac{1}{2} + \frac{1}{4} + \frac{1}{16} + \frac{1}{256} + \cdots$ is convergent. Note: It is not geometric, since there is no common ratio. The general

term is $a_n = \frac{1}{2^{2^n}}$ for $n = 0, 1, 2, \ldots$.

SECTION 12.3 page 589

1. Using $\frac{1}{1-x} = 1 + x + x^2 + x^3 + \cdots$, then

$$\frac{2}{1-x} = 2\left(\frac{1}{1-x}\right) = 2(1 + x + x^2 + x^3 + \cdots)$$
$$= 2 + 2x + 2x^2 + 2x^3 + \cdots$$

3. Using $\frac{1}{1-x} = 1 + x + x^2 + x^3 + \cdots$, then

$$\frac{3x}{1-x} = 3x\left(\frac{1}{1-x}\right) = 3x\left(1 + x + x^2 + x^3 + \cdots\right)$$
$$= 3x + 3x^2 + 3x^3 + 3x^4 + \cdots$$

5. Given $\frac{1}{1-x^3}$ and assuming $\frac{1}{1-u} = \frac{1}{1-x^3}$, then $u = x^3$. Using $\frac{1}{1-u} = 1 + u + u^2 + u^3 + u^4 + \cdots$ produces the power series

$$\frac{1}{1-x^3} = 1 + x^3 + (x^3)^2 + (x^3)^3 + (x^3)^4 + \cdots$$
$$= 1 + x^3 + x^6 + x^9 + x^{12} + \cdots$$

7. Given $\frac{1}{1+9x^2}$ and assuming $\frac{1}{1-u} = \frac{1}{1+9x^2} = \frac{1}{1-(-9x^2)}$, then $u = -9x^2$. Using $\frac{1}{1-u} = 1 + u + u^2 + u^3 + \cdots$ produces the power series

$$\frac{1}{1+9x^2} = 1 + (-9x^2) + (-9x^2)^2 + (-9x^2)^3 + \cdots$$
$$= 1 - 9x^2 + 81x^4 - 729x^6 + \cdots$$

9. Given $\frac{3}{1+x^2} = 3\left(\frac{1}{1+x^2}\right)$ and assuming $\frac{1}{1-u} = \frac{1}{1+x^2} = \frac{1}{1-(-x^2)}$, then $u = -x^2$.

Using $\frac{1}{1-u} = 1 + u + u^2 + u^3 + u^4 + \cdots$ produces the power series

$$3\left(\frac{1}{1+x^2}\right) = 3\left[1 + (-x^2) + (-x^2)^2 + (-x^2)^3 + (-x^2)^4 + \cdots\right]$$
$$= 3(1 - x^2 + x^4 - x^6 + x^8 - \cdots)$$
$$= 3 - 3x^2 + 3x^4 - 3x^6 + 3x^8 - \cdots$$

11. Given $\dfrac{1}{1+2x}$ and assuming $\dfrac{1}{1-u} = \dfrac{1}{1+2x} = \dfrac{1}{1-(-2x)}$, then $u = -2x$. Using $\dfrac{1}{1-u} = 1 + u + u^2 + u^3 + u^4 + \cdots$ produces the power series

$$\frac{1}{1+2x} = 1 + (-2x) + (-2x)^2 + (-2x)^3 + (-2x)^4 + \cdots$$
$$= 1 - 2x + 4x^2 - 8x^3 + 16x^4 - \cdots$$

13. Given $\dfrac{x}{1-3x}$ and assuming $\dfrac{1}{1-u} = \dfrac{1}{1-3x}$, then $u = 3x$. Using $\dfrac{1}{1-u} = 1 + u + u^2 + u^3 + u^4 + \cdots$ produces the power series

$$\frac{x}{1-3x} = x\left(\frac{1}{1-3x}\right) = x\left[1 + 3x + (3x)^2 + (3x)^3 + (3x)^4 + \cdots\right]$$
$$= x(1 + 3x + 9x^2 + 27x^3 + 81x^4 + \cdots)$$
$$= x + 3x^2 + 9x^3 + 27x^4 + 81x^5 + \cdots$$

15. Given $\dfrac{1}{x-1} = -\dfrac{1}{1-x}$, then $-\dfrac{1}{1-x} = -\left(\dfrac{1}{1-x}\right)$

$$= -(1 + x + x^2 + x^3 + x^4 + \cdots)$$
$$\frac{1}{x-1} = -1 - x - x^2 - x^3 - x^4 - \cdots$$

17. The series

$$1 + u + u^2 + u^3 + \cdots$$

is considered to be a geometric series because each term is u times the preceding term

19. $1 + 2x + 4x^2 + 8x^3 + \cdots = 1 + 2x + (2x)^2 + (2x)^3 + \cdots$
$$= \frac{1}{1-2x}$$

21. $3 - 3x + 3x^2 - 3x^3 + \cdots = 3(1 - x + x^2 - x^3 + \cdots)$
$$= 3[1 + (-x) + (-x)^2 + (-x)^3 + \cdots]$$
$$= 3\frac{1}{1-(-x)}$$
$$= \frac{3}{1+x}$$

SECTION 12.4 pages 595–597

1. To obtain the first four nonzero terms of the Taylor series about zero for $f(x) = \sin x$, then begin by computing the first few derivatives and evaluating them at zero.

Thus,
$$
\begin{aligned}
f(x) &= \sin x & f(0) &= 0 \\
f'(x) &= \cos x & f'(0) &= 1 \\
f''(x) &= -\sin x & f''(0) &= 0 \\
f'''(x) &= -\cos x & f'''(0) &= -1 \\
f^{(4)}(x) &= \sin x & f^{(4)}(0) &= 0 \\
f^{(5)}(x) &= \cos x & f^{(5)}(0) &= 1 \\
f^{(6)}(x) &= -\sin x & f^{(6)}(0) &= 0 \\
f^{(7)}(x) &= -\cos x & f^{(7)}(0) &= -1
\end{aligned}
$$

and $f(x) = \sin x = f(0) + f'(0) \cdot x + f''(0)\dfrac{x^2}{2!} + f'''(0)\dfrac{x^3}{3!} + \cdots + f^{(7)}(0)\dfrac{x^7}{7!}$

$$\sin x = x - \frac{x^3}{3!} + \frac{x^5}{5!} - \frac{x^7}{7!} + \cdots$$

3. To obtain the first four nonzero terms of the Taylor series about zero for $f(x) = e^{2x}$, then begin by computing the first few derivatives and evaluating them at zero.

Thus,
$$f(x) = e^{2x} \qquad f(0) = 1$$
$$f'(x) = 2e^{2x} \qquad f'(0) = 2$$
$$f''(x) = 4e^{2x} \qquad f''(0) = 4$$
$$f'''(x) = 8e^{2x} \qquad f'''(0) = 8$$

and
$$f(x) = e^{2x} = f(0) + f'(0) \cdot x + \frac{f''(0)x^2}{2!} + \frac{f'''(0)x^3}{3!} + \cdots$$
$$= 1 + 2x + \frac{4x^2}{2!} + \frac{8x^3}{3!} + \cdots$$
$$= 1 + 2x + \frac{(2x)^2}{2!} + \frac{(2x)^3}{3!} + \cdots$$

5. To obtain the first four nonzero terms of the Taylor series about zero for $f(x) = \ln(1-x)$, then begin by computing the first few derivatives and evaluating them at zero.

Thus,
$$f(x) = \ln(1-x) \qquad f(0) = 0$$
$$f'(x) = \frac{-1}{1-x} = -(1-x)^{-1} \qquad f'(0) = -1$$
$$f''(x) = -(1-x)^{-2} = -\frac{1}{(1-x)^2} \qquad f''(0) = -1$$
$$f'''(x) = -2(1-x)^{-3} = -\frac{2}{(1-x)^3} \qquad f'''(0) = -2 = -2!$$
$$f^{(4)}(x) = -6(1-x)^{-4} = -\frac{-6}{(1-x)^4} \qquad f^{(4)}(0) = -6 = -3!$$

and
$$f(x) = \ln(1-x) = f(0) + f'(0) \cdot x + \frac{f''(0)x^2}{2!} + \frac{f'''(0)x^3}{3!} + \frac{f^4(0)x^4}{4!} + \cdots$$
$$= -x - \frac{x^2}{2!} - \frac{2!x^3}{3!} - \frac{3!x^4}{4!} + \cdots$$
$$= -x - \frac{x^2}{2} - \frac{x^3}{3} - \frac{x^4}{4} + \cdots$$

or
$$\ln(1-x) = -\left(x + \frac{x^2}{2} + \frac{x^3}{3} + \frac{x^4}{4} + \cdots\right)$$

7. To obtain the first two nonzero terms of the Taylor series about zero for $f(x) = \tan x$, then begin by computing the first few derivatives and evaluating them at zero.

Thus,
$$f(x) = \tan x \qquad f(0) = 0$$
$$f'(x) = \sec^2 x \qquad f'(0) = 1$$
$$f''(x) = (2\sec x)(\sec x \tan x) \qquad f''(0) = 0$$
$$= 2\sec^2 x \tan x$$
$$f'''(x) = (2\sec^2 x)(\sec^2 x) + 2(\tan x)(2\sec x)(\sec x \tan x)$$
$$= 2\sec^4 x + 4\sec^2 x \tan^2 x \qquad f'''(0) = 2$$

and
$$f(x) = \tan x = f(0) + f'(0) \cdot x + \frac{f''(0)x^2}{2!} + \frac{f'''(0)x^3}{3!} + \cdots$$
$$= x + \frac{2x^3}{3!} + \cdots$$
$$\tan x = x + \frac{x^3}{3} + \cdots$$

9. To obtain the first two nonzero terms of the Taylor series about zero for $f(x) = e^{\sin x}$, then begin by computing the first few derivatives and evaluating them at zero.

Thus,
$$f(x) = e^{\sin x} \qquad f(0) = e^0 = 1$$
$$f'(x) = e^{\sin x}(\cos x) \qquad f(0) = e^0(1) = 1$$

and $f(x) = e^{\sin x} = f(0) + f'(0) \cdot x + \cdots$
$$e^{\sin x} = 1 + x + \cdots$$

11. Using the first four terms, $e^x = 1 + x + \dfrac{x^2}{2!} + \dfrac{x^3}{3!}$, then

$$e^{0.2} = 1 + 0.2 + \frac{(0.2)^2}{2} + \frac{(0.2)^3}{6}$$
$$\approx 1.2213$$

13. Using the first five terms, $e^x = 1 + x + \dfrac{x^2}{2!} + \dfrac{x^3}{3!} + \dfrac{x^4}{4!}$, then

$$e = e^1 = 1 + 1 + \frac{1}{2!} + \frac{1}{3!} + \frac{1}{4!}$$
$$\approx 2.7083$$

15. Using $\sin x = x - \dfrac{x^3}{3!} + \dfrac{x^5}{5!} - \dfrac{x^7}{7!} + \cdots$, then it is clear that $\sin 0 = 0 - \dfrac{0}{3!} + \dfrac{0}{5!} + \dfrac{0}{7!} + \cdots$
$$= 0$$

17. Using the first three terms, $\cos x = 1 - \dfrac{x^2}{2!} + \dfrac{x^4}{4!}$, then

$$\cos 1.2 = 1 - \frac{(1.2)^2}{2} + \frac{(1.2)^4}{24}$$
$$\approx 0.3664$$

19. a. Using the first four terms,
$$e^x = 1 + x + \frac{x^2}{2!} + \frac{x^3}{3!}, \text{ then}$$

$$e^{0.5} = 1 + 0.5 + \frac{(0.5)^2}{2} + \frac{(0.5)^3}{6}$$
$$\approx 1.6458$$

b. Since the polynomial
$$e^x = 1 + x + \frac{x^2}{2} + \frac{x^3}{6} \text{ is a polynomial of degree 3, then the maximum error in the approximation is } M \cdot \frac{|0.5|^{3+1}}{(3+1)!}$$
where M is the largest value of $\left|f^{(3+1)}(x)\right|$ on the interval $0 \le x \le 0.5$. Since $f^{(4)}(x) = e^x$ is an increasing function, then $M = e^{0.5} < 2$.

Thus, the maximum error is less than $\frac{2(0.5)^4}{24} = 0.0052$

21. a.   Using the first five terms,

$$e^{-x} = 1 - x + \frac{x^2}{2!} - \frac{x^3}{3!} + \frac{x^4}{4!}, \text{ then}$$

$$e^{-0.4} = 1 - 0.4 + \frac{(0.4)^2}{2} - \frac{(0.4)^3}{6} + \frac{(0.4)^4}{24}$$

$$\approx 0.67040$$

b.   The maximum error in the approximation is $M \cdot \frac{|a|^{n+1}}{(n+1)!}$ where $a = 0.4$, $n = 4$, and M is the largest value of $\left|f^{(n+1)}(x)\right| = \left|f^{(5)}(x)\right| = \left|-e^{-x}\right| = e^{-x}$ on the interval $0 \le x \le 0.4$. Since $\left|f^{(5)}(x)\right| = e^{-x}$ is decreasing, then $M = e^0 = 1$.

Thus, the maximum error is less than $\frac{1(0.4)^5}{5!} = 0.000085$

23.   Given $f(x) = e^{x^2}$ and using $e^u = 1 + u + \frac{u^2}{2!} + \frac{u^3}{3!} + \frac{u^4}{4!} + \cdots$, then letting $u = x^2$ produces

$$e^{x^2} = 1 + x^2 + \frac{(x^2)^2}{2!} + \frac{(x^2)^3}{3!} + \frac{(x^2)^4}{4!} + \cdots$$

$$= 1 + x^2 + \frac{x^4}{2!} + \frac{x^6}{3!} + \frac{x^8}{4!} + \cdots$$

25.   Given $f(x) = e^{3x}$ and using $e^u = 1 + u + \frac{u^2}{2!} + \frac{u^3}{3!} + \frac{u^4}{4!} + \cdots$, then letting $u = 3x$ produces

$$e^{3x} = 1 + 3x + \frac{(3x)^2}{2!} + \frac{(3x)^3}{3!} + \frac{(3x)^4}{4!} \cdots$$

$$= 1 + 3x + \frac{9x^2}{2!} + \frac{27x^3}{3!} + \frac{81x^4}{4!} + \cdots$$

27.   Given $f(x) = xe^{x^2}$ and using $e^u = 1 + u + \frac{u^2}{2!} + \frac{u^3}{3!} + \frac{u^4}{4!} + \cdots$, then letting $u = x^2$ produces

$$e^{x^2} = 1 + x^2 + \frac{(x^2)^2}{2!} + \frac{(x^2)^3}{3!} + \frac{(x^2)^4}{4!} + \cdots$$

$$= 1 + x^2 + \frac{x^4}{2!} + \frac{x^6}{3!} + \frac{x^8}{4!} + \cdots$$

and $xe^{x^2} = x\left(1 + x^2 + \frac{x^4}{2!} + \frac{x^6}{3!} + \frac{x^8}{4!} + \cdots\right)$

$$= x + x^3 + \frac{x^5}{2!} + \frac{x^7}{3!} + \frac{x^9}{4!} + \cdots$$

29.   Given $f(x) = \sin x^2$ and using $\sin u = u - \frac{u^3}{3!} + \frac{u^5}{5!} - \frac{u^7}{7!} + \cdots$, then letting $u = x^2$ produces

$$\sin x^2 = x^2 - \frac{(x^2)^3}{3!} + \frac{(x^2)^5}{5!} - \frac{(x^2)^7}{7!} + \cdots$$

$$= x^2 - \frac{x^6}{3!} + \frac{x^{10}}{5!} - \frac{x^{14}}{7!} + \cdots$$

31.   Given $f(x) = \cos 2x$ and using $\cos u = 1 - \frac{u^2}{2!} + \frac{u^4}{4!} - \frac{u^6}{6!} + \cdots$, then letting $u = 2x$ produces

$$\cos 2x = 1 - \frac{(2x)^2}{2!} + \frac{(2x)^4}{4!} - \frac{(2x)^6}{6!} + \cdots$$

$$= 1 - \frac{4x^2}{2!} + \frac{16x^4}{4!} - \frac{64x^6}{6!} + \cdots$$

33. Given $f(x) = \sin \frac{1}{2}x$ and using $\sin u = u - \dfrac{u^3}{3!} + \dfrac{u^5}{5!} - \dfrac{u^7}{7!} + \cdots$, then letting $u = \frac{1}{2}x$ produces

$$\sin \frac{1}{2}x = \frac{x}{2} - \frac{\left(\frac{x}{2}\right)^3}{3!} + \frac{\left(\frac{x}{2}\right)^5}{5!} - \frac{\left(\frac{x}{2}\right)^7}{7!} + \cdots$$

$$= \frac{x}{2} - \frac{x^3}{2^3 \cdot 3!} + \frac{x^5}{2^5 \cdot 5!} - \frac{x^7}{2^7 \cdot 7!} + \cdots$$

35. Given $f(x) = x \cos x$ and using $\cos x = 1 - \dfrac{x^2}{2!} + \dfrac{x^4}{4!} - \dfrac{x^6}{6!} + \cdots$, then

$$x \cos x = x\left(1 - \frac{x^2}{2!} + \frac{x^4}{4!} - \frac{x^6}{6!} + \cdots\right)$$

$$= x - \frac{x^3}{2!} + \frac{x^5}{4!} - \frac{x^7}{6!} + \cdots$$

37. Given $f(x) = \dfrac{1 - \cos x}{x}$ and using $\cos x = 1 - \dfrac{x^2}{2!} + \dfrac{x^4}{4!} - \dfrac{x^6}{6!} + \dfrac{x^8}{8!} - \dfrac{x^{10}}{10!}$

Then $1 - \cos x = 1 - \left(1 - \dfrac{x^2}{2!} + \dfrac{x^4}{4!} - \dfrac{x^6}{6!} + \dfrac{x^8}{8!} - \dfrac{x^{10}}{10!} + \cdots\right)$

$$= \cancel{1} - \cancel{1} + \frac{x^2}{2!} - \frac{x^4}{4!} + \frac{x^6}{6!} - \frac{x^8}{8!} + \frac{x^{10}}{10!} - \cdots$$

$$= \frac{x^2}{2!} - \frac{x^4}{4!} + \frac{x^6}{6!} - \frac{x^8}{8!} + \frac{x^{10}}{10!} \cdots$$

and $\dfrac{1 - \cos x}{x} = \dfrac{1}{x}\left(\dfrac{x^2}{2!} - \dfrac{x^4}{4!} + \dfrac{x^6}{6!} - \dfrac{x^8}{8!} + \dfrac{x^{10}}{10!} - \cdots\right)$

$$= \frac{x}{2!} - \frac{x^3}{4!} + \frac{x^5}{6!} - \frac{x^7}{8!} + \frac{x^9}{10!} - \cdots$$

39. Given $f(x) = \cos x + \sin x$ and using the two series

$$\cos x = 1 - \frac{x^2}{2!} + \frac{x^4}{4!} - \frac{x^6}{6!} + \frac{x^8}{8!} - \cdots \qquad \text{and}$$

$$\sin x = x - \frac{x^3}{3!} + \frac{x^5}{5!} - \frac{x^7}{7!} + \frac{x^9}{9!} - \cdots, \qquad \text{then}$$

$$\cos x + \sin x = \left(1 - \frac{x^2}{2!} + \frac{x^4}{4!} - \frac{x^6}{6!} + \frac{x^8}{8!} - \cdots\right) + \left(x - \frac{x^3}{3!} + \frac{x^5}{5!} - \frac{x^7}{7!} + \frac{x^9}{9!} - \cdots\right)$$

$$= 1 + x - \frac{x^2}{2!} - \frac{x^3}{3!} + \frac{x^4}{4!} + \cdots$$

41. If $\sinh x = \frac{1}{2}(e^x - e^{-x})$, then using the two series

$$e^x = 1 + x + \frac{x^2}{2!} + \frac{x^3}{3!} + \frac{x^4}{4!} + \frac{x^5}{5!} + \frac{x^6}{6!} + \frac{x^7}{7!} + \cdots \quad \text{and}$$

$$e^{-x} = 1 - x + \frac{x^2}{2!} - \frac{x^3}{3!} + \frac{x^4}{4!} - \frac{x^5}{5!} + \frac{x^6}{6!} - \frac{x^7}{7!} + \cdots \quad \text{produces}$$

$$\frac{1}{2}(e^x - e^{-x}) = \frac{1}{2}\left[\left(1 + x + \frac{x^2}{2!} + \frac{x^3}{3!} + \frac{x^4}{4!} + \frac{x^5}{5!} + \frac{x^6}{6!} + \frac{x^7}{7!} + \cdots\right)\right.$$

$$\left. - \left(1 - x + \frac{x^2}{2!} - \frac{x^3}{3!} + \frac{x^4}{4!} - \frac{x^5}{5!} + \frac{x^6}{6!} - \frac{x^7}{7!} + \cdots\right)\right]$$

$$= \frac{1}{2}\left[\cancel{1} + x + \cancel{\frac{x^2}{2!}} + \frac{x^3}{3!} + \cancel{\frac{x^4}{4!}} + \frac{x^5}{5!} + \cancel{\frac{x^6}{6!}} + \frac{x^7}{7!} + \cdots - \cancel{1} + x - \cancel{\frac{x^2}{2!}} + \frac{x^3}{3!} - \cancel{\frac{x^4}{4!}} + \frac{x^5}{5!} - \cancel{\frac{x^6}{6!}} + \frac{x^7}{7!} + \cdots\right]$$

$$= \frac{1}{2}\left(2x + \frac{2x^3}{3!} + \frac{2x^5}{5!} + \frac{2x^7}{7!} + \cdots\right)$$

Thus, $\sinh x = x + \frac{x^3}{3!} + \frac{x^5}{5!} + \frac{x^7}{7!} + \cdots$

43. For Example 7, the series for $\ln(1+x)$ is

$$\ln(1+x) = x - \frac{x^2}{2} + \frac{x^3}{3} - \frac{x^4}{4} + \cdots.$$

To obtain an approximation of $\ln(1.08)$, let $x = 0.08$ and use

$$\ln(1+0.08) = \ln(1.08) = 0.08 - \frac{(0.08)^2}{2} + \frac{(0.08)^3}{3} - \frac{(0.08)^4}{4} + \cdots$$

Thus, $\ln(1.08) \approx 0.07696$

45. The Taylor series for $\ln(1+x)$ has an interval of convergence given by $(-1, 1]$. The value $x = -1$ is excluded because $\ln[1 + (-1)] = \ln 0$ is not defined.

47. No. The series representation of $\sin x$ includes only odd powers of x, so there is a $P_3(x)$ and $P_5(x)$ but no polynomial $P_4(x)$ where the degree of the highest-power term is 4. Specifically,

$P_0 = 0$
$P_1 = x$
$P_2 = 0$
$P_3 = x - \frac{x^3}{3!}$
$P_4 = 0$
$P_5 = x - \frac{x^3}{3!} + \frac{x^5}{5!}$

SECTION 12.4 Technology Exercises

1. **a.** Approximation is good.   **b.** Approximation is poor.   **c.** Approximation is good.

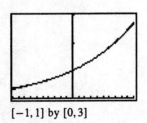

$[-1, 1]$ by $[0, 3]$

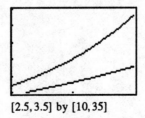

$[2.5, 3.5]$ by $[10, 35]$

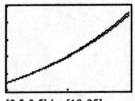

$[2.5, 3.5]$ by $[10, 35]$

3.

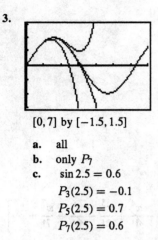

$[0, 7]$ by $[-1.5, 1.5]$

a. all

b. only P_7

c. $\sin 2.5 = 0.6$

$P_3(2.5) = -0.1$

$P_5(2.5) = 0.7$

$P_7(2.5) = 0.6$

SECTION 12.5 pages 600–601

1. The Taylor series for $\cos x^2$ can be determined by using $\cos x = 1 - \dfrac{x^2}{2!} + \dfrac{x^4}{4!} - \dfrac{x^6}{6!} + \cdots$ and replacing x with x^2.

Thus, $\cos x^2 = 1 - \dfrac{(x^2)^2}{2!} + \dfrac{(x^2)^4}{4!} - \cdots$

$\qquad\quad = 1 - \dfrac{x^4}{2} + \dfrac{x^8}{24} - \cdots$

and $\displaystyle\int_0^1 \cos x^2 \, dx \approx \int_0^1 \left(1 - \dfrac{x^4}{2} + \dfrac{x^8}{24}\right)/\,dx$

$\qquad\qquad\qquad\quad \approx \left[x - \dfrac{x^5}{10} + \dfrac{x^9}{216}\right]_0^1$

$\qquad\qquad\qquad\quad \approx \left(1 - \dfrac{1}{10} + \dfrac{1}{216}\right) - (0 - 0 + 0)$

$\qquad\qquad\qquad\quad \approx 0.9046$

3. The Taylor series for $\dfrac{\sin x}{x}$ can be determined by using $\sin x = x - \dfrac{x^3}{3!} + \dfrac{x^5}{5!} - \cdots$ and dividing by x.

Thus, $\dfrac{\sin x}{x} = 1 - \dfrac{x^2}{3!} + \dfrac{x^4}{5!} - \cdots$

and $\displaystyle\int_0^{0.1} \dfrac{\sin x}{x} \, dx \approx \int_0^{0.1} \left(1 - \dfrac{x^2}{6}\right) dx$

$\qquad\qquad\qquad\qquad \approx \left[x - \dfrac{x^3}{18}\right]_0^{0.1}$

$\qquad\qquad\qquad\qquad \approx \left[0.1 - \dfrac{(0.1)^3}{18}\right] - (0 - 0)$

$\qquad\qquad\qquad\qquad \approx \dfrac{17}{18} \approx 0.944444 \approx 0.0999$

5. The Taylor series for $\cos \sqrt{x}$ can be determined by using $\cos x = 1 - \dfrac{x^2}{2!} + \dfrac{x^4}{4!} - \cdots$ and replacing x with $\sqrt{x}$.

Thus, $\cos \sqrt{x} = 1 - \dfrac{(\sqrt{x})^2}{2!} + \dfrac{(\sqrt{x})^4}{4!} - \cdots$

$\qquad\qquad = 1 - \dfrac{x}{2!} + \dfrac{x^2}{4!} - \cdots$

and $\displaystyle\int_0^{0.5} \cos \sqrt{x}\, dx \approx \int_0^{0.5} \left(1 - \dfrac{x}{2} + \dfrac{x^2}{24} \right) dx$

$\qquad\qquad\qquad \approx \left[x - \dfrac{x^2}{4} + \dfrac{x^3}{72} \right]_0^{0.5}$

$\qquad\qquad\qquad \approx \left[0.5 - \dfrac{(0.5)^2}{4} + \dfrac{(0.5)^3}{72} \right] - (0 - 0 + 0)$

$\qquad\qquad\qquad \approx 0.4392$

7. The Taylor series for $\dfrac{1 - \cos x}{x}$ can be determined by using $\cos x = 1 - \dfrac{x^2}{2!} + \dfrac{x^4}{4!} - \dfrac{x^6}{6!} + \cdots$ and changing the signs, adding 1, and dividing the resulting series by x.

Thus, $\dfrac{1 - \cos x}{x} = \dfrac{\cancel{1} - \cancel{1} + \dfrac{x^2}{2!} - \dfrac{x^4}{4!} + \dfrac{x^6}{6!} - \cdots}{x}$

$\qquad\qquad\quad = \dfrac{x}{2!} - \dfrac{x^3}{4!} + \dfrac{x^5}{6!} - \cdots$

and $\displaystyle\int_0^1 \dfrac{1 - \cos x}{x}\, dx \approx \int_0^1 \left(\dfrac{x}{2} - \dfrac{x^3}{24} + \dfrac{x^5}{720} \right) dx$

$\qquad\qquad\qquad \approx \left[\dfrac{x^2}{4} - \dfrac{x^4}{96} + \dfrac{x^6}{4320} \right]_0^1$

$\qquad\qquad\qquad \approx \left(\dfrac{1}{4} - \dfrac{1}{96} + \dfrac{1}{4320} \right) - (0 - 0 + 0)$

$\qquad\qquad\qquad \approx 0.2398$

9. The Taylor series for $\dfrac{1}{1 + x^3}$ can be determined by using $\dfrac{1}{1 - x} = 1 + x + x^2 + x^3 + \cdots$ and replacing x by $-x^3$.

Thus, $\dfrac{1}{1 + x^3} = \dfrac{1}{1 - (-x^3)} = 1 + (-x^3) + (-x^3)^2 + \cdots$

$\qquad\qquad\quad = 1 - x^3 + x^6 - \cdots$

and $\displaystyle\int_0^{0.4} \left(\dfrac{1}{1 + x^3} \right) dx \approx \int_0^{0.4} (1 - x^3 + x^6)\, dx$

$\qquad\qquad\qquad \approx \left[x - \dfrac{x^4}{4} + \dfrac{x^7}{7} \right]_0^{0.4}$

$\qquad\qquad\qquad \approx \left[0.4 - \dfrac{(0.4)^4}{4} + \dfrac{(0.4)^7}{7} \right] - (0 - 0 + 0)$

$\qquad\qquad\qquad \approx 0.3938$

11. The Taylor series for $\dfrac{1}{1+x^2}$ can be determined by using $\dfrac{1}{1-x} = 1 + x + x^2 + x^3 + \cdots$ and replacing x with $-x^2$.

Thus, $\dfrac{1}{1+x^2} = \dfrac{1}{1-(-x^2)} = 1 + (-x^2) + (-x^2)^2 + \cdots$

$$= 1 - x^2 + x^4 - \cdots$$

and $\displaystyle\int_0^{0.3} \dfrac{1}{1+x^2}\,dx \approx \int_0^{0.3} (1 - x^2 + x^4)\,dx$

$$\approx \left[x - \dfrac{x^3}{3} + \dfrac{x^5}{5} \right]_0^{0.3}$$

$$\approx \left[0.3 - \dfrac{(0.3)^3}{3} + \dfrac{(0.3)^5}{5} \right] - (0 - 0 + 0)$$

$$\approx 0.2915$$

13. The area under the graph of $y = e^{-x^2}$ from $x = 0$ to $x = 1$ is given by $\displaystyle\int_0^1 e^{-x^2}\,dx$.

Using the results of Example 3,

$$\int_0^1 e^{-x^2}\,dx \approx \left[x - \dfrac{x^3}{3} + \dfrac{x^5}{5 \cdot 2!} - \dfrac{x^7}{7 \cdot 3!} \right]_0^1$$

$$\approx \left(1 - \dfrac{1}{3} + \dfrac{1}{10} - \dfrac{1}{42} \right) - (0 - 0 + 0 - 0)$$

$$\approx 0.7429$$

15. The area under the curve $f(x) = e^{x^2}$ from $x = 0$ to $x = 1$ is given by $\displaystyle\int_0^1 e^{x^2}\,dx$.

To approximate this area, use the Taylor series expansion $e^{x^2} = 1 + x^2 + \dfrac{(x^2)^2}{2!} + \dfrac{(x^2)^3}{3!} + \cdots$

$$= 1 + x^2 + \dfrac{x^4}{2} + \dfrac{x^6}{6} + \cdots$$

and integrate the series

$$\int_0^1 e^{x^2}\,dx \approx \int_0^1 \left(1 + x^2 + \dfrac{x^4}{2} + \dfrac{x^6}{6} \right) dx$$

$$\approx \left[x + \dfrac{x^3}{3} + \dfrac{x^5}{10} + \dfrac{x^7}{42} \right]_0^1$$

$$\approx \left(1 + \dfrac{1}{3} + \dfrac{1}{10} + \dfrac{1}{42} \right) - (0 + 0 + 0 + 0)$$

Area ≈ 1.4571

17. The area under the curve $f(x) = e^{\sqrt{x}} = e^{x^{1/2}}$ from $x = 0$ to $x = 1$ is given by $\int_0^1 e^{x^{1/2}} \, dx$.

To approximate this area, use the Taylor series expansion

$$e^{x^{1/2}} = 1 + x^{1/2} + \frac{(x^{1/2})^2}{2!} + \frac{(x^{1/2})^3}{3!} + \cdots$$
$$= 1 + x^{1/2} + \frac{x}{2} + \frac{x^{3/2}}{6} + \cdots$$

and integrate the series.

$$\int_0^1 e^{x^{1/2}} \, dx \approx \left(1 + x^{1/2} + \frac{x}{2} + \frac{x^{3/2}}{6} \right) dx$$
$$\approx \left[x + \frac{2}{3} x^{3/2} + \frac{x^2}{4} + \frac{1}{15} x^{5/2} \right]_0^1$$
$$\approx \left(1 + \frac{2}{3} + \frac{1}{4} + \frac{1}{15} \right) - (0 + 0 + 0 + 0)$$

Area ≈ 1.9833

19. The area under the curve $f(x) = \cos x^2$ from $x = 0$ to $x = 1$ is given by $\int_0^1 \cos x^2 \, dx$.

To approximate this area, use the Taylor series for

$$\cos x = 1 - \frac{x^2}{2!} + \frac{x^4}{4!} - \frac{x^6}{6!} + \cdots \text{ and replace } x \text{ with } x^2 \text{ to get } \cos x^2 = 1 - \frac{(x^2)^2}{2!} + \frac{(x^2)^4}{4!} - \frac{(x^2)^6}{6!} + \cdots$$
$$= 1 - \frac{x^4}{2!} + \frac{x^8}{4!} - \frac{x^{12}}{6!} + \cdots$$

then integrate the series.

$$\int_0^1 \cos x^2 \, dx \approx \int_0^1 \left(1 - \frac{x^4}{2} + \frac{x^8}{24} - \frac{x^{12}}{720} \right) dx$$
$$\approx \left[x - \frac{x^5}{10} + \frac{x^9}{9 \cdot 24} - \frac{x^{13}}{13 \cdot 720} \right]_0^1$$
$$\approx \left(1 - \frac{1}{10} + \frac{1}{216} - \frac{1}{9360} \right) - (0 - 0 + 0 - 0)$$

Area ≈ 0.9045

21. The average value of $f(x) = e^{x^2}$ over the interval [0, 1] is determined by $\dfrac{1}{1-0}\displaystyle\int_0^1 e^{x^2}\,dx = \displaystyle\int_0^1 e^{x^2}\,dx$.

To approximate the average value, use the Taylor series expansion

$$e^{x^2} = 1 + x^2 + \frac{(x^2)^2}{2!} + \frac{(x^2)^3}{3!} + \cdots$$

$$= 1 + x^2 + \frac{x^4}{2!} + \frac{x^6}{3!} + \cdots$$

and integrate the series.

$$\int_0^1 e^{x^2}\,dx \approx \int_0^1 \left(1 + x^2 + \frac{x^4}{2} + \frac{x^6}{6}\right)dx$$

$$\approx \left[x + \frac{x^3}{3} + \frac{x^5}{10} + \frac{x^7}{42}\right]_0^1$$

$$\approx 1 + \frac{1}{3} + \frac{1}{10} + \frac{1}{42}$$

Average value ≈ 1.4571

23. The average value of $f(x) = e^{\sqrt{x}} = e^{x^{1/2}}$ over the interval [1, 2] is determined by

$$\frac{1}{2-1}\int_1^2 e^{x^{1/2}}\,dx = \int_1^2 e^{x^{1/2}}\,dx$$

To approximate the average value, use the Taylor series expansion

$$e^{x^{1/2}} = 1 + x^{1/2} + \frac{(x^{1/2})^2}{2!} + \frac{(x^{1/2})^3}{3!} + \cdots$$

$$= 1 + x^{1/2} + \frac{x}{2!} + \frac{x^{3/2}}{3!} + \cdots$$

and integrate the series.

$$\int_1^2 e^{x^{1/2}}\,dx \approx \int_1^2 \left(1 + x^{1/2} + \frac{x}{2} + \frac{x^{3/2}}{6}\right)dx$$

$$\approx \left[x + \frac{2}{3}x^{3/2} + \frac{x^2}{4} + \frac{1}{15}x^{5/2}\right]_1^2$$

$$\approx \left[2 + \frac{2}{3}(2)^{3/2} + \frac{2^2}{4} + \frac{1}{15}(2)^{5/2}\right] - \left[1 + \frac{2}{3} + \frac{1}{4} + \frac{1}{15}\right]$$

Average value ≈ 3.2794

SECTION 12.6 pages 608–609

In Exercises 1–10, there is no unique first choice for x. The chosen values "seem" to be good values with which to begin.

1. Given $f(x) = 5x^2 - x - 48$, choose $x = 2$ and construct the table of values.

x	$f(x)$
2	-30
3	-6
4	28

Since $f(3)$ is negative and $f(4)$ is positive, there is a zero between $x = 3$ and $x = 4$.

3. Given $f(x) = x^3 + 6x^2 + 3x - 17$, choose $x = 0$ and construct the table of values.

x	$f(x)$
0	-17
1	-7
2	21

Since $f(1)$ is negative and $f(2)$ is positive, there is a zero between $x = 1$ and $x = 2$.

5. Given $f(x) = 2x^3 - 4x^2 - 3x - 2$, choose $x = 0$ and construct the table of values.

x	$f(x)$
0	-2
1	-7
2	-8
3	7

Since $f(2)$ is negative and $f(3)$ is positive, there is a zero between $x = 2$ and $x = 3$.

9. Given $f(x) = 3 - \ln x$, choose $x = 18$ and construct the table of values.

x	$f(x)$ (approximately)
18	0.1
19	0.05
20	0.004
21	-0.04

Since $f(20)$ is positive and $f(21)$ is negative, there is a zero between $x = 20$ and $x = 21$.

Note: $x = 18$ is chosen because $e^3 \approx 2.6^3 \approx 18$ and $\ln e^3 = 3$.

13. Given $f(x) = x^3 - e^x$, then $f'(x) = 3x^2 - e^x$ and Newton's iteration formula is

$$x_{n+1} = x_n - \frac{(x_n^3 - e^{x_n})}{3x_n^2 - e^{x_n}}$$

Beginning with $x_1 = 2$ yields

$$x_2 = 2 - \frac{(2^3 - e^2)}{3(4) - e^2} \approx 1.868$$

$$x_3 = 1.868 - \frac{(1.868^3 - e^{1.868})}{3(1.868)^2 - e^{1.868}}$$

$$\approx 1.857$$

7. Given $f(x) = 2e^x - 101$, choose $x = 2$ and construct the table of values.

x	$f(x)$ (approximately)
2	-86.2
3	-60.8
4	8.2

Since $f(3)$ is negative and $f(4)$ is positive, there is a zero between $x = 3$ and $x = 4$.

11. Given $f(x) = x^3 - x - 1$, then $f'(x) = 3x^2 - 1$ and Newton's iteration formula is

$$x_{n+1} = x_n - \frac{(x_n^3 - x_n - 1)}{3x_n^2 - 1}.$$

Beginning with $x_1 = 1$ yields

$$x_2 = 1 - \frac{(1^3 - 1 - 1)}{3 \cdot 1^2 - 1} = 1 + \frac{1}{2} = \frac{3}{2} = 1.5$$

$$x_3 = 1.5 - \frac{(1.5^3 - 1.5 - 1)}{3(1.5)^2 - 1}$$

$$\approx 1.348$$

In Exercises 15–20, the answers will vary slightly depending on the choice of x_1.

15.   Given $f(x) = x^3 + x^2 - 4$, then begin by determining the interval that contains a positive zero. Choose $x = 0$ and construct the table of values.

x	$f(x)$
0	-4
1	-2
2	8

Since $f(1)$ is negative and $f(2)$ is positive, then there is a zero between $x = 1$ and $x = 2$.

Computing $f'(x) = 3x^2 + 2x$ produces Newton's iteration formula

$$x_{n+1} = x_n - \frac{\left(x_n^3 + x_n^2 - 4\right)}{3x_n^2 + 2x_n}.$$

Beginning with $x_1 = 1$ yields

$$x_2 = 1 - \frac{\left(1^3 + 1^2 - 4\right)}{3(1)^2 + 2(1)} = 1 + \frac{2}{5} = 1.4$$

$$x_3 = 1.4 - \frac{\left[(1.4)^3 + (1.4)^2 - 4\right]}{3(1.4)^2 + 2(1.4)} \approx 1.3189$$

$$x_4 = 1.3189 - \frac{\left[(1.3189)^3 + (1.3189)^2 - 4\right]}{3(1.3189)^2 + 2(1.3189)}$$

$$x_4 \approx 1.3146$$

17.   Given $f(x) = x^3 + 3x - 2$, then begin by determining the interval that contains a positive zero. Choose $x = 0$ and construct the table of values.

x	$f(x)$
0	-2
1	2

Since $f(0)$ is negative and $f(1)$ is positive, there is a zero between $x = 0$ and $x = 2$.

Computing $f'(x) = 3x^2 + 3$ produces Newton's iteration formula

$$x_{n+1} = x_n - \frac{x_n^3 + 3x_n - 2}{3x_n^2 + 3}$$

Beginning with $x_1 = 0$ yields

$$x_2 = 0 - \frac{(0 + 0 - 2)}{0 + 3} = \frac{2}{3} \approx 0.6667$$

$$x_3 = 0.6667 - \frac{(0.6667)^3 + 3(0.6667) - 2}{3(0.6667)^2 + 3} \approx 0.5983$$

$$x_4 = 0.5983 - \frac{(0.5983)^3 + 3(0.5983) - 2}{3(0.5983)^2 + 3}$$

$$\approx 0.5961$$

19. Given $f(x) = 2x - e^{-x^2}$, then begin by determining the interval that contains a positive zero. Choose $x = 0$ and construct the table of values.

x	$f(x)$ (approx.)
0	-1
1	1.6

Since $f(0)$ is negative and $f(1)$ is positive, there is a zero between $x = 0$ and $x = 1$.

Computing $f'(x) = 2 + 2xe^{-x^2}$ produces Newton's iteration formula

$$x_{n+1} = x_n - \frac{2x_n - e^{-x_n^2}}{2 + 2x_n e^{-x_n^2}}$$

Beginning with $x_1 = 0$ yields

$$x_2 = 0 - \frac{0 - 1}{2 + 0} = \frac{1}{2} = 0.5$$

$$x_3 = 0.5 - \frac{2(0.5) - e^{-(0.5)^2}}{2 + 2(0.5)(e^{-(0.5)^2})} \approx 0.4204$$

$$x_4 = (0.4204) - \frac{2(0.4204) - e^{-(0.4204)^2}}{2 + 2(0.4204)(e^{-(0.4204)^2})}$$

$$x_4 \approx 0.4194$$

21. Given $f(x) = x^3 - 3x^2 + 1$, then $f'(x) = 3x^2 - 6x$ and Newton's iteration formula is

$$x_{n+1} = x_n - \frac{x_n^3 - 3x_n^2 + 1}{3x_n^2 - 6x_n}$$

Beginning with $x_1 = 2$ yields

$$x_2 = 2 - \frac{2^3 - 3(2)^2 + 1}{3(2)^2 - 6(2)} = 2 + \frac{3}{0}$$

Since division by zero is not defined, the first iteration fails.

Geometrically, this means that the tangent line to the curve at $x = 2$ is horizontal (slope $= 0$), and hence the tangent line *does not* intersect the x axis to produce a new estimate x_2.

23. To solve $e^x - x^3 = 0$ is equivalent to finding the zeros of $f(x) = e^x - x^3$. Although there are two zeros for this function, the exercise requires the solution near $x_1 = 2$.

Compute $f'(x) = e^x - 3x^2$ and form Newton's iteration formula

$$x_{n+1} = x_n - \frac{e^x - x_n^3}{e^x - 3x_n^2}$$

Beginning with $x_1 = 2$ yields

$$x_2 = 2 - \frac{e^2 - 2^3}{e^2 - 3(2)^2} \approx 1.87$$

$$x_3 = 1.87 - \frac{e^{1.87} - 1.87^3}{e^{1.87} - 3(1.87)^2} \approx 1.86$$

$$x_4 = 1.86 - \frac{e^{1.86} - 1.86^3}{e^{1.86} - 3(1.86)^2} \approx 1.86$$

The desired solution to two decimal places is $x = 1.86$.

Note: There is another solution between $x = 4$ and $x = 5$.

25. To solve $x + \ln x = 0$ is equivalent to finding the zeros of $f(x) = x + \ln x$. Rewriting $x + \ln x = 0$ as $\ln x = -x$ and sketching the graph of $y = \ln x$ and $y = -x$ reveals that there is only one solution and it appears to be between $x = 0$ and $x = 1$.

Compute $f'(x) = 1 + \frac{1}{x}$ and form Newton's iteration formula

$$x_{n+1} = x_n - \frac{x_n + \ln x_n}{1 + \frac{1}{x_n}}$$

Beginning with $x_1 = 1$ yields

$$x_2 = 1 - \frac{1 + \ln 1}{1 + \frac{1}{1}} = 1 - \frac{1}{2} = 0.50$$

$$x_3 = 0.5 - \frac{0.5 + \ln 0.5}{1 + \frac{1}{0.5}} \approx 0.56$$

$$x_4 = 0.56 - \frac{0.56 + \ln 0.56}{1 + \frac{1}{0.56}} \approx 0.57$$

$$x_5 = 0.57 - \frac{0.57 + \ln 0.57}{1 + \frac{1}{0.57}} \approx 0.57$$

The desired solution to two decimal places is $x = 0.57$.

27. To solve $e^x + x^2 - 5 = 0$ for the positive solution is equivalent to finding the positive zero of $f(x) = e^x + x^2 - 5$. Rewriting $e^x + x^2 - 5 = 0$ as $e^x = 5 - x^2$ and sketching the graph of $y = e^x$ and $y = 5 - x^2$ reveals that there are two solutions: one positive, one negative. The positive solution appears to be near $x = 1$.

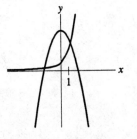

Constructing the table of values yields

x	$f(x)$ (approximately)
1	-1.3
2	6.4

Since $f(1)$ is negative and $f(2)$ is positive, there is a zero between $x = 1$ and $x = 2$.

Compute $f'(x) = e^x + 2x$ and form Newton's iteration formula

$$x_{n+1} = x_n - \frac{e^{x_n} + x_n^2 - 5}{e^{x_n} + 2x_n}$$

Beginning with $x_1 = 1$ yields

$$x_2 = 1 - \frac{e^1 + 1^2 - 5}{e^1 + 2(1)} \approx 1.27$$

$$x_3 = 1.27 - \frac{e^{1.27} + 1.27^2 - 5}{e^{1.27} + 2(1.27)} \approx 1.24$$

$$x_4 = 1.24 - \frac{e^{1.24} + 1.24^2 - 5}{e^{1.24} + 2(1.24)} \approx 1.24$$

The desired positive solution to two decimal places is $x = 1.24$.

29. To find the x coordinate of the point of intersection of $y = x^3 - 3x^2 + x - 3$ and $y = x + 1$ is equivalent to solving $x^3 - 3x^2 + x - 3 = x + 1$ or finding the zero of $f(x) = x^3 - 3x^2 - 4$. Beginning with $x = 2$ and constructing the table of values yields

x	$f(x)$
2	-8
3	-4
4	12

Since $f(3)$ is negative and $f(4)$ is positive, there is a zero between $x = 3$ and $x = 4$.

Compute $f'(x) = 3x^2 - 6x$ and form Newton's iteration formula

$$x_{n+1} = x_n - \frac{x_n^3 - 3x_n^2 - 4}{3x_n^2 - 6x_n}$$

Beginning with $x_1 = 3$ yields

$$x_2 = 3 - \frac{3^3 - 3(3)^2 - 4}{3(3)^2 - 6(3)} \approx 3.44$$

$$x_3 = 3.44 - \frac{3.44^3 - 3(3.44)^2 - 4}{3(3.44)^2 - 6(3.44)} \approx 3.36$$

$$x_4 = 3.36 - \frac{3.36^3 - 3(3.36)^2 - 4}{3(3.36)^2 - 6(3.36)} \approx 3.36$$

The x coordinate of the point of intersection is approximately $x = 3.36$.

31. To find the x coordinate of the point of intersection of $y = \ln x$ and $y = -3x$ is equivalent to solving $\ln x = -3x$ or finding the zero of $f(x) = \ln x + 3x$. Sketching the graph of $y = \ln x$ and $y = -3x$ reveals that there is only one point of intersection and it is near $x = 1$.

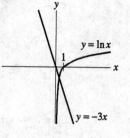

Compute $f'(x) = \frac{1}{x} + 3$ and form Newton's iteration formula

$$x_{n+1} = x_n - \frac{\ln x_n + 3x_n}{\frac{1}{x_n} + 3}$$

Beginning with $x_1 = 1$ yields

$$x_2 = 1 - \frac{\ln 1 + 3(1)}{\frac{1}{1} + 3} = 1 - \frac{3}{4} = 0.25$$

$$x_3 = 0.25 - \frac{\ln 0.25 + 3(0.25)}{\frac{1}{0.25} + 3} \approx 0.34$$

$$x_4 = 0.34 - \frac{\ln 0.34 + 3(0.34)}{\frac{1}{0.34} + 3} \approx 0.35$$

$$x_5 = 0.35 - \frac{\ln 0.35 + 3(0.35)}{\frac{1}{0.35} + 3} \approx 0.35$$

The x coordinate of the point of intersection is approximately $x = 0.35$.

33. To find the x coordinate $(x > 1)$ of the point of intersection of $y = 0.5e^x$ and $y = x+1$ is equivalent to solving $0.5e^x = x+1$
     or finding the zero of $f(x) = 0.5e^x - x - 1$. Sketching the graph of $y = 0.5e^x$ and $y = x+1$ reveals that there is only one
     point of intersection, $x > 1$, and it is near $x = 1$.

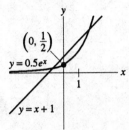

Compute $f'(x) = 0.5e^x - 1$ and form Newton's iteration formula

$$x_{n+1} = x_n - \frac{0.5e^{x_n} - x_n - 1}{0.5e^{x_n}}$$

Beginning with $x_1 = 1$ yields

$$x_2 = 1 - \frac{0.5e^1 - 1 - 1}{0.5e^1} \approx 1.47$$

$$x_3 = 1.47 - \frac{0.5e^{1.47} - 1.47 - 1}{0.5e^{1.47}} \approx 1.61$$

$$x_4 = 1.61 - \frac{0.5e^{1.61} - 1.61 - 1}{0.5e^{1.61}} \approx 1.65$$

$$x_5 = 1.65 - \frac{0.5e^{1.65} - 1.65 - 1}{0.5e^{1.65}} \approx 1.67$$

$$x_6 = 1.67 - \frac{0.5e^{1.67} - 1.67 - 1}{0.5e^{1.67}} \approx 1.68$$

$$x_7 = 1.68 - \frac{0.5e^{1.68} - 1.68 - 1}{0.5e^{1.68}} \approx 1.68$$

The x coordinate of the point of intersection, $x > 1$, is approximately $x = 1.68$.

35. To find the x coordinate ($x > 1$) of the point of intersection of $y = \ln x$ and $y = x - 2$ is equivalent to solving $\ln x = x - 2$ or finding the zero of $f(x) = \ln x - x + 2$. Sketching the graph of $y = \ln x$ and $y = x - 2$ reveals that there is only one point of intersection, $x > 1$, and it is near $x = 3$.

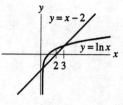

Compute $f'(x) = \frac{1}{x} - 1$ and form Newton's iteration formula

$$x_{n+1} = x_n - \frac{\ln x_n - x_n + 2}{\frac{1}{x_n} - 1}$$

Beginning with $x_1 = 3$ yields

$$x_2 = 3 - \frac{\ln 3 - 3 + 2}{\frac{1}{3} - 1} \approx 3.15$$

$$x_3 = 3.15 - \frac{\ln 3.15 - 3.15 + 2}{\frac{1}{3.15} - 1} \approx 3.15$$

The x coordinate of the point of intersection, $x > 1$, is approximately $x = 3.15$.

37. From the figure associated with the given example, it appears that $y = e^x$ and $y = x + 3$ intersect at a point whose x coordinate is between $x = -3$ and $x = -2$. To find the solution is equivalent to finding the zero of $f(x) = e^x - x - 3$ near $x = -3$. Newton's iteration formula is

$$x_{n+1} = x_n - \frac{e^{x_n} - x_n - 3}{e^{x_n} - 1}.$$

Beginning with $x_1 = -3$ yields

$$x_2 = -3 - \frac{e^{-3} - (-3) - 3}{e^{-3} - 1} \approx -2.95$$

$$x_3 = -2.95 - \frac{e^{-2.95} - (-2.95) - 3}{e^{-2.95} - 1} \approx -2.95$$

The x coordinate of the point of intersection is approximately $x = -2.95$.

39. a. Given $f(x) = x^{1/3}$, then clearly $f(0) = 0$. Also, $f'(x) = \frac{1}{3}x^{-2/3} = \frac{1}{3x^{2/3}}$ is always positive except at $x = 0$, where it is undefined. Thus, $f(x)$ is always increasing except at $x = 0$, where it has a vertical tangent line. The graph of $f(x)$ is given below.

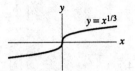

b. Newton's iteration formula becomes

$$x_{n+1} = x_n - \frac{x_n^{1/3}}{\frac{1}{3}x_n^{-2/3}}$$

$$x_{n+1} = -2x_n$$

Beginning with $x_1 = 1$ yields

$$x_2 = -2(1) = -2$$
$$x_3 = -2(-2) = 4$$
$$x_4 = -2(4) = -8$$

The successive iterations *do not* appear to be getting close to $x = 0$.

c. Beginning with $x_1 = -0.5$ yields

$$x_2 = -2(-0.5) = 1$$
$$x_3 = -2(1) = -2$$
$$x_4 = -2(-2) = 4$$

Again, the successive iterations *do not* appear to be getting close to $x = 0$.

41. The function $f(x) = \frac{1}{4}x^4 - x^3 + \frac{1}{2}x^2 + 9$ has a horizontal tangent line when $f'(x) = x^3 - 3x^2 + x = 0$. Clearly $f'(0) = 0$. To find the zero for $x > 1$, use Newton's method. Computing $f''(x) = 3x^2 - 6x + 1$ yields the iteration formula

$$x_{n+1} = x_n - \frac{x_n^3 - 3x_n^2 + x_n}{3x_n^2 - 6x_n + 1}$$

Since $f'(2) = -2$ and $f'(3) = 3$, there is a zero between $x = 2$ and $x = 3$.

Beginning with $x_1 = 2$ yields

$$x_2 = 2 - \frac{2^3 - 3(2)^2 + 2}{3(2)^2 - 6(2) + 1} = 4$$

$$x_3 = 4 - \frac{4^3 - 3(4)^2 + 4}{3(4)^2 - 6(4) + 1} \approx 3.2$$

$$x_4 = 3.2 - \frac{3.2^3 - 3(3.2)^2 + 3.2}{3(3.2)^2 - 6(3.2) + 1}$$

$$\approx 2.7808$$

43. The function $f(x) = x^5 - 16x^3 - x - 11$ has a critical number for a value of x such that $f'(x) = 5x^4 - 48x^2 - 1 = 0$. Use Newton's method to estimate a positive zero of $f'(x) = 5x^4 - 48x^2 - 1$. Construct the table of values beginning with $x = 1$.

x	$f'(x)$
1	-44
2	-113
3	-28
4	511

Since $f'(3)$ is negative and $f'(4)$ is positive, there is a zero between $x = 3$ and $x = 4$.

Computing $f''(x) = 20x^3 - 96x$ produces the iteration formula

$$x_{n+1} = x_n - \frac{5x_n^4 - 48x_n^2 - 1}{20x_n^3 - 96x_n}$$

Beginning with $x_1 = 3$ yields

$$x_2 = 3 - \frac{5(3)^4 - 48(3)^2 - 1}{20(3)^3 - 96(3)} \approx 3.1111$$

$$x_3 = 3.1111 - \frac{5(3.1111)^4 - 48(3.1111)^2 - 1}{20(3.1111)^3 - 96(3.1111)} \approx 3.1018$$

$$x_4 = 3.1018 - \frac{5(3.1018)^4 - 48(3.1018)^2 - 1}{20(3.1018)^3 - 96(3.1018)}$$

$$\approx 3.1017$$

45. If revenue is $R(x) = 0.2x^3$ and cost is $C(x) = 12 - 0.6x^2$, then the company will break even when $R(x) = C(x)$. Solving $0.2x^3 = 12 - 0.6x^2$ is equivalent to finding the positive zero of $f(x) = 0.2x^3 + 0.6x^2 - 12$.

Since $f(3) = -1.2$ and $f(4) = 10.4$, then there is a positive zero between $x = 3$ and $x = 4$.

Computing $f'(x) = 0.6x^2 + 1.2x$ produces Newton's iteration formula

$$x_{n+1} = x_n - \frac{0.2x_n^3 + 0.6x_n^2 - 12}{0.6x_n^2 + 1.2x_n}$$

Beginning with $x_1 = 3$ yields

$$x_2 = 3 - \frac{0.2(3)^3 + 0.6(3)^2 - 12}{0.6(3)^2 + 1.2(3)} \approx 3.1333$$

$$x_3 = 3.1333 - \frac{0.2(3.1333)^3 + 0.6(3.1333)^2 - 12}{0.6(3.1333)^2 + 1.2(3.1333)} \approx 3.1289$$

$$x_4 = 3.1289 - \frac{0.2(3.1289)^3 + 0.6(3.1289)^2 - 12}{0.6(3.1289)^2 + 1.2(3.1289)}$$

$$\approx 3.1289$$

The company will break even when approximately 313 units are sold.

47. **a.** Since x_1 is a relative minimum, then $f'(x_1) = 0$. Hence, we will have the problem of division by zero in the algorithm to give the next approximation x_2.

  b. Analyzing the development of the algorithm for Newton's method, we see that the next approximation to the root is given by the point of intersection of the x axis with the tangent line to the curve at the present approximation. Since x_1 is a relative minimum, the tangent line to the curve at this point is horizontal, i.e., parallel to the x axis. So there is no point of intersection of this tangent with the x axis. Hence, no value for x_2 is generated.

SECTION 12.6 Technology Exercises

1. **a.** between 2, 3 and 26, 27   **b.** between 5 and 6   **c.** between 3 and 4

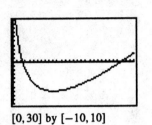

[0, 30] by [−10, 10]

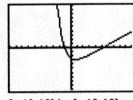

[−10, 10] by [−10, 10]

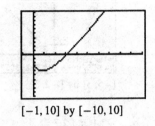

[−1, 10] by [−10, 10]

3. **a.** 2.7

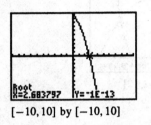

[−10, 10] by [−10, 10]

b. −1.8 and 8.4

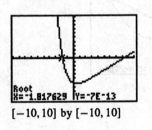

[−10, 10] by [−10, 10]

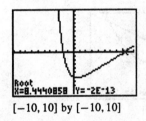

[−10, 10] by [−10, 10]

c. −1.3 and 1.3

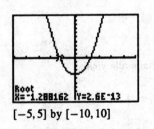

[−5, 5] by [−10, 10]

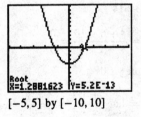

[−5, 5] by [−10, 10]

5. **a.** 1.0

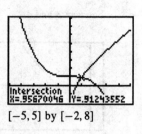

[−5, 5] by [−2, 8]

b. −2.4 and 2.7

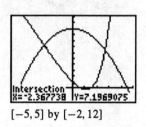

[−5, 5] by [−2, 12]

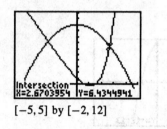

[−5, 5] by [−2, 12]

c. 0.8 and 2.6

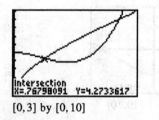

[0, 3] by [0, 10]

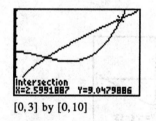

[0, 3] by [0, 10]

9. 1.85718

11. 1.35914

SECTION 12.7 pages 613–614

1. $\lim\limits_{x \to 2} \dfrac{x^2 + 3x - 10}{x^2 - x - 2} = \dfrac{4 + 6 - 10}{4 - 2 - 2} = \dfrac{0}{0}$

Using L'Hôpital's rule yields

$\lim\limits_{x \to 2} \dfrac{x^2 + 3x - 10}{x^2 - x - 2} = \lim\limits_{x \to 2} \dfrac{2x + 3}{2x - 1} = \dfrac{4 + 3}{4 - 1} = \dfrac{7}{3}$

5. $\lim\limits_{x \to 1} \dfrac{9x - 9}{x^2 - 1} = \dfrac{9 - 9}{1 - 1} = \dfrac{0}{0}$

Using L'Hôpital's rule yields

$\lim\limits_{x \to 1} \dfrac{9x - 9}{x^2 - 1} = \lim\limits_{x \to 1} \dfrac{9}{2x} = \dfrac{9}{2}$

9. $\lim\limits_{x \to -1} \dfrac{x + 1}{x^3 + 8} = \dfrac{-1 + 1}{(-1)^3 + 8} = \dfrac{0}{7} = 0$

3. $\lim\limits_{t \to 0} \dfrac{7t}{t} = \dfrac{0}{0}$

Using L'Hôpital's rule yields

$\lim\limits_{t \to 0} \dfrac{7t}{t} = \lim\limits_{t \to 0} \dfrac{7}{1} = 7$

7. $\lim\limits_{x \to 1} \dfrac{x^2 + 6x + 1}{x^2 + 3x} = \dfrac{1 + 6 + 1}{1 + 3} = \dfrac{8}{4} = 2$

11. $\lim\limits_{x \to 0} \dfrac{2x}{e^x - 1} = \dfrac{0}{e^0 - 1} = \dfrac{0}{0}$

Using L'Hôpital's rule yields

$\lim\limits_{x \to 0} \dfrac{2x}{e^x - 1} = \lim\limits_{x \to 0} \dfrac{2}{e^x} = \dfrac{2}{e^0} = 2$

13. $\lim\limits_{x\to 0}\dfrac{3x}{5x+1}=\dfrac{0}{0+1}=0$

15. $\lim\limits_{x\to 0}\dfrac{x}{e^x}=\dfrac{0}{e^0}=\dfrac{0}{1}=0$

17. $\lim\limits_{x\to 1}\dfrac{\ln x}{x-1}=\dfrac{\ln 1}{1-1}=\dfrac{0}{0}$

Using L'Hôpital's rule yields

$\lim\limits_{x\to 1}\dfrac{\ln x}{x-1}=\lim\limits_{x\to 1}\dfrac{\frac{1}{x}}{1}=\dfrac{1}{1}=1$

19. $\lim\limits_{t\to 1}\dfrac{\ln t}{t}=\dfrac{\ln 1}{1}=\dfrac{0}{1}=0$

21. $\lim\limits_{x\to 0}\dfrac{2x}{\ln(1+3x)}=\dfrac{0}{\ln(1+0)}=\dfrac{0}{\ln 1}=\dfrac{0}{0}$

Using L'Hôpital's rule yields

$\lim\limits_{x\to 0}\dfrac{2x}{\ln(1+3x)}=\lim\limits_{x\to 0}\dfrac{2}{\left(\frac{1}{1+3x}\right)(3)}=\dfrac{2}{\frac{3}{1+0}}=\dfrac{2}{3}$

23. $\lim\limits_{x\to 0}\dfrac{x}{e^{2x}-1}=\dfrac{0}{e^0-1}=\dfrac{0}{1-1}=\dfrac{0}{0}$

Using L'Hôpital's rule yields

$\lim\limits_{x\to 0}\dfrac{x}{e^{2x}-1}=\lim\limits_{x\to 0}\dfrac{1}{2e^{2x}}=\dfrac{1}{2e^0}=\dfrac{1}{2}$

25. $\lim\limits_{x\to 2}\dfrac{x^2-4}{\ln(x^2-3)}=\dfrac{4-4}{\ln(4-3)}=\dfrac{0}{\ln 1}=\dfrac{0}{0}$

Using L'Hôpital's rule yields

$\lim\limits_{x\to 2}\dfrac{x^2-4}{\ln(x^2-3)}=\lim\limits_{x\to 2}\dfrac{2x}{\frac{1}{x^2-3}(2x)}=\lim\limits_{x\to 2}x^2-3=4-3=1$

27. $\lim\limits_{x\to 0}\dfrac{\cos x-1}{x}=\dfrac{\cos 0-1}{0}=\dfrac{1-1}{0}=\dfrac{0}{0}$

Using L'Hôpital's rule yields

$\lim\limits_{x\to 0}\dfrac{\cos x-1}{x}=\lim\limits_{x\to 0}-\dfrac{\sin x}{1}=\dfrac{-\sin 0}{1}=0$

29. $\lim\limits_{t\to 0}\dfrac{1-\cos t}{t^2}=\dfrac{1-\cos 0}{0}=\dfrac{1-1}{0}=\dfrac{0}{0}$

Using L'Hôpital's rule yields

$\lim\limits_{t\to 0}\dfrac{1-\cos t}{t^2}=\lim\limits_{t\to 0}\dfrac{\sin t}{2t}=\dfrac{\sin 0}{0}=\dfrac{0}{0}$

Applying L'Hôpital's rule again yields

$\lim\limits_{t\to 0}\dfrac{\sin t}{2t}=\lim\limits_{t\to 0}\dfrac{\cos t}{2}=\dfrac{\cos 0}{2}=\dfrac{1}{2}$

31. $\lim\limits_{x\to 0}\dfrac{x^2}{\sin x}=\dfrac{0}{\sin 0}=\dfrac{0}{0}$

Using L'Hôpital's rule yields

$\lim\limits_{x\to 0}\dfrac{x^2}{\sin x}=\lim\limits_{x\to 0}\dfrac{2x}{\cos x}=\dfrac{0}{\cos 0}=0$

33. $\lim\limits_{x\to 0}\dfrac{\sin x}{1-e^x}=\dfrac{\sin 0}{1-e^0}=\dfrac{0}{1-1}=\dfrac{0}{0}$

Using L'Hôpital's rule yields

$\lim\limits_{x\to 0}\dfrac{\sin x}{1-e^x}=\lim\limits_{x\to 0}\dfrac{\cos x}{-e^x}=\dfrac{\cos 0}{-e^0}=\dfrac{1}{-1}=-1$

35. $\lim\limits_{x\to 0}\dfrac{\ln(x+1)}{\sin x}=\dfrac{\ln(0+1)}{\sin 0}=\dfrac{\ln 1}{0}=\dfrac{0}{0}$

Using L'Hôpital's rule yields

$\lim\limits_{x\to 0}\dfrac{\ln(x+1)}{\sin x}=\lim\limits_{x\to 0}\dfrac{\frac{1}{x+1}}{\cos x}=\dfrac{\frac{1}{0+1}}{\cos 0}=\dfrac{1}{1}=1$

37. $\displaystyle\lim_{x \to 0} \frac{1 - \cos x}{e^x + e^{-x} - 2} = \frac{1 - \cos 0}{e^0 + e^0 - 2} = \frac{1 - 1}{1 + 1 - 2} = \frac{0}{0}$

Using L'Hôpital's rule yields

$$\lim_{x \to 0} \frac{1 - \cos x}{e^x + e^{-x} - 2} = \lim_{x \to 0} \frac{\sin x}{e^x - e^{-x}} = \frac{\sin 0}{e^0 - e^0} = \frac{0}{1 - 1} = \frac{0}{0}$$

Applying L'Hôpital's rule again yields

$$\lim_{x \to 0} \frac{\sin x}{e^x - e^{-x}} = \lim_{x \to 0} \frac{\cos x}{e^x + e^{-x}} = \frac{\cos 0}{e^0 + e^0} = \frac{1}{1 + 1} = \frac{1}{2}$$

39. $\displaystyle\lim_{x \to 0} \frac{\sin^2 x}{3x^2} = \frac{\sin^2 0}{3(0)^2} = \frac{0}{0}$

Using L'Hôpital's rule yields

$$\lim_{x \to 0} \frac{\sin^2 x}{3x^2} = \lim_{x \to 0} \frac{2 \sin x \cos x}{6x} = \frac{2 \sin 0 \cos 0}{6(0)} = \frac{0}{0}$$

Applying L'Hôpital's rule again yields

$$\begin{aligned}
\lim_{x \to 0} \frac{\sin x \cos x}{3x} &= \lim_{x \to 0} \frac{(\sin x)(-\sin x) + (\cos x)(\cos x)}{3} \\
&= \frac{\sin^2 0 + \cos^2 0}{3} \\
&= \frac{1}{3}
\end{aligned}$$

41. **a.** $\displaystyle\lim_{x \to 0} \frac{x^2 + x}{1 + e^x}$ cannot be evaluated using L'Hôpital's rule because it is not an indeterminate form $\frac{0}{0}$. In fact,

$$\lim_{x \to 0} \frac{x^2 + x}{1 + e^x} = \frac{0}{2} = 0$$

b. $\displaystyle\lim_{x \to 0} \frac{e^x}{x^2}$ cannot be evaluated using L'Hôpital's rule because it is not an indeterminate form $\frac{0}{0}$. This limit, in fact, does not exist as a real value.

SECTION 12.7 Technology Exercises

1. 2

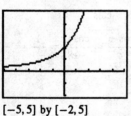

[−5, 5] by [−2, 5]

3. 0

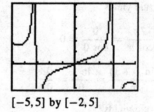

[−5, 5] by [−2, 5]

REVIEW EXERCISES FOR CHAPTER 12 pages 615–616

1. Given the geometric series $8 + 2 + \frac{1}{2} + \cdots$, then $a_1 = 8$ and $r = \frac{2}{8} = \frac{1}{4}$.

For $n = 5$,

$$\begin{aligned}
S_5 = \frac{a_1\left(1 - r^5\right)}{1 - r} = \frac{8\left[1 - \left(\frac{1}{4}\right)^5\right]}{1 - \frac{1}{4}} = \frac{8\left(\frac{1023}{1024}\right)}{\frac{3}{4}} = \frac{32(1023)}{3(1024)} \\
= \frac{341}{32}
\end{aligned}$$

3. Given the geometric series $\dfrac{9}{4} + \dfrac{3}{2} + 1 + \cdots$, then

$$r = \frac{\frac{3}{2}}{\frac{9}{4}} = \frac{2}{3}$$

5. Given the geometric series $10 - 4 + \dfrac{8}{5} - \cdots$, then $a_1 = 10$ and $r = -\dfrac{4}{10} = -\dfrac{2}{5}$. Since $|r| = \dfrac{2}{5} < 1$, then the series converges.

$$S = \frac{a_1}{1-r} = \frac{10}{1-(-\frac{2}{5})} = \frac{10}{1+\frac{2}{5}}$$

$$= \frac{50}{7}$$

7. $0.4444\overline{4} = \dfrac{4}{10} + \dfrac{4}{100} + \dfrac{4}{1000} + \dfrac{4}{10000} + \dfrac{4}{100000} + \cdots$

$$= \frac{\frac{4}{10}}{1 - \frac{1}{10}}$$

$$= \frac{\frac{4}{10}}{\frac{9}{10}}$$

$$= \frac{4}{10} \cdot \frac{10}{9}$$

$$= \frac{4}{9}$$

9. Using the given conditions, if the pattern of revolutions is geometric, then the number of revolutions is the sum of the geometric series $36 + 24 + 16 + \dfrac{32}{3} + \cdots$

For this geometric series, $a_1 = 36$ and $r = \dfrac{24}{36} = \dfrac{2}{3}$.

Thus, $S = \dfrac{a_1}{1-r} = \dfrac{36}{1 - \frac{2}{3}} = \dfrac{36}{\frac{1}{3}} = 108$

The top makes 108 revolutions.

11. Given $\dfrac{4}{1-x^2}$, then use the power series $\dfrac{1}{1-u} = 1 + u + u^2 + u^3 + \cdots$, with $u = x^2$ to get

$$\frac{1}{1-x^2} = 1 + x^2 + \left(x^2\right)^2 + \left(x^2\right)^3 + \cdots$$

$$= 1 + x^2 + x^4 + x^6 + \cdots$$

$$\frac{4}{1-x^2} = 4\left[1 + x^2 + x^4 + x^6 + \cdots\right]$$

$$= 4 + 4x^2 + 4x^4 + 4x^6 + \cdots$$

13. Given $f(x) = e^{3x}$, then compute the appropriate derivatives and evaluate them at $x = 0$ to obtain

$$f(x) = f(0) + f'(0)x + f''(0)\frac{x^2}{2!} + f'''(0)\frac{x^3}{3!} + \cdots$$

$$\begin{array}{ll} f(x) = e^{3x} & f(0) = e^0 = 1 \\ f'(x) = 3e^{3x} & f'(0) = 3e^0 = 3 \\ f''(x) = 9e^{3x} & f''(0) = 9e^0 = 9 \\ f'''(x) = 27e^{3x} & f'''(0) = 27e^0 = 27 \end{array}$$

Thus,

$$f(x) = e^{3x} = 1 + 3x + \frac{9x^2}{2!} + \frac{27x^3}{3!}$$

15. Using $\sin x = x - \dfrac{x^3}{3!} + \dfrac{x^5}{5!} - \dfrac{x^7}{7!} + \cdots$ with x replaced by $3x$ yields

$$f(x) = \sin 3x = 3x - \frac{(3x)^3}{3!} + \frac{(3x)^5}{5!} - \cdots$$

$$= 3x - \frac{27x^3}{3!} + \frac{243x^5}{5!}$$

17. Using $\cos x = 1 - \dfrac{x^2}{2!} + \dfrac{x^4}{4!} + \cdots$, then, for $x = 1$,

$$\cos 1 \approx 1 - \frac{1}{2!} + \frac{1}{4!}$$

$$\approx 1 - \frac{1}{2} + \frac{1}{24}$$

$$\approx \frac{13}{24} \approx 0.5417$$

19. Using $\sin x = x - \dfrac{x^3}{3!} + \dfrac{x^5}{5!} + \cdots$ with x replaced by $\sqrt{x} = x^{1/2}$ yields

$$\sin \sqrt{x} = x^{1/2} - \frac{\left(x^{1/2}\right)^3}{3!} + \frac{\left(x^{1/2}\right)^5}{5!} - \cdots$$

$$= x^{1/2} - \frac{x^{3/2}}{6} + \frac{x^{5/2}}{120} - \cdots$$

Thus, $\displaystyle\int_0^1 \sin\sqrt{x}\,dx \approx \int_0^1 \left(x^{1/2} - \frac{x^{3/2}}{6} + \frac{x^{5/2}}{120}\right) dx$

$$\approx \left[\frac{2}{3}x^{3/2} - \frac{1}{15}x^{5/2} + \frac{1}{420}x^{7/2}\right]_0^1$$

$$\approx \left(\frac{2}{3} - \frac{1}{15} + \frac{1}{420}\right) - (0 - 0 + 0)$$

$$\approx 0.6024$$

21. Given $f(x) = x^3 - 4x^2 + 6$, construct the following table of values beginning with $x = 0$.

x	$f(x)$
0	6
1	3
2	-2

Since $f(1)$ is positive and $f(2)$ is negative, there is a zero between $x = 1$ and $x = 2$.

23. Let $f(x) = x^3 + 7x^2 + 9x - 2$. Determine the interval that contains a positive zero by constructing the following table of values beginning with $x = 0$.

x	$f(x)$
0	-2
1	15

Since $f(0)$ is negative and $f(1)$ is positive, there is a zero between $x = 0$ and $x = 1$.

Computing $f'(x) = 3x^2 + 14x + 9$ produces Newton's iteration formula

$$x_{n+1} = x_n - \frac{x_n^3 + 7x_n^2 + 9x_n - 2}{3x_n^2 + 14x_n + 9}$$

Beginning with $x_1 = 0$ yields

$$x_2 = 0 - \frac{0 + 0 + 0 - 2}{0 + 0 + 9} \approx 0.2222$$

$$x_3 = 0.2222 - \frac{0.2222^3 + 7(0.2222)^2 + 9(0.2222) - 2}{3(0.2222)^2 + 14(0.2222) + 9}$$

$$\approx 0.1931$$

$$x_4 = 0.1931 - \frac{0.1931^3 + 7(0.1931)^2 + 9(0.1931) - 2}{3(0.1931)^2 + 14(0.1931) + 9}$$

$$\approx 0.1926$$

25. To find the approximate solution of $e^x + 3x - 12 = 0$ is equivalent to finding the zero of $f(x) = e^x + 3x - 12$.

Rewriting $e^x + 3x - 12 = 0$ as $e^x = 12 - 3x$ and graphing $y = e^x$ and $y = 12 - 3x$ reveals that there is only one solution and it is near $x = 2$.

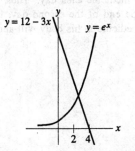

Computing $f'(x) = e^x + 3$ produces Newton's iteration formula

$$x_{n+1} = x_n - \left(\frac{e^{x_n} + 3x_n - 12}{e^{x_n} + 3} \right)$$

Beginning with $x_1 = 2$ yields

$$x_2 = 2 - \frac{e^2 + 3(2) - 12}{e^2 + 3} \approx 1.8663$$

$$x_3 = 1.8663 - \frac{e^{1.8663} + 3(1.8663) - 12}{e^{1.8663} + 3} \approx 1.8596$$

$$x_4 = 1.8596 - \frac{e^{1.8596} + 3(1.8596) - 12}{e^{1.8596} + 3}$$

$$\approx 1.8596$$

27. $\displaystyle \lim_{x \to 1} \frac{x^3 - 1}{x - 1} = \frac{1 - 1}{1 - 1} = \frac{0}{0}$

Using L'Hôpital's rule yields

$$\lim_{x \to 1} \frac{x^3 - 1}{x - 1} = \lim_{x \to 1} \frac{3x^2}{1} = \frac{3(1)^2}{1} = 3$$

29. $\lim\limits_{x \to 0} \dfrac{1 - e^{2x}}{5x} = \dfrac{1 - e^0}{0} = \dfrac{1 - 1}{0} = \dfrac{0}{0}$

Using L'Hôpital's rule yields

$\lim\limits_{x \to 0} \dfrac{1 - e^{2x}}{5x} = \lim\limits_{x \to 0} \dfrac{-2e^{2x}}{5} = \dfrac{-2e^0}{5} = -\dfrac{2}{5}$

31. $\lim\limits_{x \to 0} \dfrac{1 - \cos x}{x} = \dfrac{1 - \cos 0}{0} = \dfrac{1 - 1}{0} = \dfrac{0}{0}$

Using L'Hôpital's rule yields

$\lim\limits_{x \to 0} \dfrac{1 - \cos x}{x} = \lim\limits_{x \to 0} \dfrac{\sin x}{1} = \dfrac{\sin 0}{1} = \dfrac{0}{1} = 0$

33. We evaluate $\dfrac{2x}{e^x}$ for large values of x to investigate the value of $\lim\limits_{x \to \infty} \dfrac{2x}{e^x}$.

x	$\dfrac{2x}{e^x}$
10	9.08×10^{-4}
50	1.9287×10^{-20}
100	7.4402×10^{-42}
150	2.1525×10^{-63}
210	2.6388×10^{-89}

The values in the table suggest that $\lim\limits_{x \to \infty} \dfrac{2x}{e^x} = 0$.

35. A man takes 300 milligrams of medication each day. His body eliminates 90% of the medicine each day. Thus, at the end of the first day, he has $0.1(300) = 30$ milligrams of medicine in his body. At the end of the second day, he has $0.1(300) + (0.1)^2(300)$ milligrams of medicine in his body. Eventually, the amount of medicine in his body will approach the sum of the geometric series

$(0.1)(300) + (0.1)^2(300) + (0.1)^3(300) + \cdots$

The sum of this geometric series is given by

$\dfrac{0.1(300)}{1 - 0.1} = \dfrac{0.1(300)}{0.9} = \dfrac{300}{9} = 33\dfrac{1}{3}$ milligrams

The amount of medicine in his body will approach $33\dfrac{1}{3}$ milligrams if he continues to take this dose of medicine daily.